# CRIMINOLOGY

## A SOCIOLOGICAL APPROACH

### FIFTH EDITION

*Piers Beirne*
UNIVERSITY OF SOUTHERN MAINE

*James W. Messerschmidt*
UNIVERSITY OF SOUTHERN MAINE

NEW YORK    OXFORD
OXFORD UNIVERSITY PRESS
2011

Oxford University Press, Inc., publishes works that further Oxford University's
objective of excellence in research, scholarship, and education.

Oxford   New York
Auckland   Cape Town   Dar es Salaam   Hong Kong   Karachi
Kuala Lumpur   Madrid   Melbourne   Mexico City   Nairobi
New Delhi   Shanghai   Taipei   Toronto

With offices in
Argentina   Austria   Brazil   Chile   Czech Republic   France   Greece
Guatemala   Hungary   Italy   Japan   Poland   Portugal   Singapore
South Korea   Switzerland   Thailand   Turkey   Ukraine   Vietnam

Published by Oxford University Press, Inc.
198 Madison Avenue, New York, New York 10016
www.oup.com

Oxford is a registered trademark of Oxford University Press

**Library of Congress Cataloging-in-Publication Data**
Beirne, Piers.
   Criminology : a sociological approach / Piers Beirne, James W. Messerschmidt.—5th ed.
      p. cm.
Includes bibliographical references and index.
ISBN 978-0-19-539476-4 (pbk. : alk. paper)
1. Criminology. I. Messerschmidt, James W. II. Title.
HV6025.B43   2010
364—dc22        2009026620

Printing number:   9  8  7  6  5  4  3  2  1

Printed in the United States of America
on acid-free paper

# BRIEF CONTENTS

# CONTENTS

# LIST OF BOXES, FIGURES, AND TABLES

## TABLES

# PREFACE

This fifth edition of *Criminology: A Sociological Approach* reorganizes the order and presentation of the chapters in the fourth edition so that the structure of the book has a greater coherence. In making these changes we have carefully considered the generous comments made by the several reviewers commissioned by Oxford University Press. As a result of their suggestions we have decided to reverse the order of the chapters so that in the current edition the chapters in Part II, on "Criminological Theory" (Chapters 4–9), now precede those in Part III, on "Inequalities and Crime" (Chapters 10–14). As it did to a majority of the reviewers, this order also now makes more obvious sense to us. We hope that the learning process for students will be significantly enhanced by this change.

Also, the chapters that deal specifically with theory are organized in this edition somewhat less with a view to how they fit into the historical development of criminology and more with whether they are relatively self-contained and internally coherent. We hope that this order will bring the greatest happiness to the greatest number of students and faculty.

Where necessary, of course, we have revised many sections of the book, adding material in some cases and subtracting it in others. New and up-to-date empirical data are presented throughout the book, and we discuss new departures not addressed before (for instance, cultural criminology and green criminology) as well as new types of crime not addressed in previous editions (such as whiteness and crime, the rape–war connection, Ponzi schemes, domestic right-wing terrorism, and state-sanctioned torture).

The aim of *Criminology: A Sociological Approach* remains constant: to introduce the basic aspects of modern criminology to undergraduate students. This is no easy task in such a diverse discipline. All textbook authors have to make a number of hard choices. This book very much reflects our teaching experience in the undergraduate criminology program at the University of Southern Maine, where our introductory course in criminology both surveys the major areas of the discipline and provides an introduction to more specialized, upper-level courses in criminology. We have attempted not only to strike a balance between depth of analysis and breadth of coverage but also to make the book comprehensive in its presentation of the *sociological* aspects of criminology. Although we aim to survey all the major aspects of the field, we especially emphasize the importance of historical, feminist, nonspeciesist, and comparative perspectives on crime.

## FEATURES OF THE FIFTH EDITION

This book is divided into three parts. Part I (Chapters 1–3) focuses on three areas of questions: First, what is crime? How are perceptions of it influenced by the mass media and by fear of crime? Second, how can we measure how much crime there is in the United States? Relatedly, how often does crime occur and with what degrees of seriousness? Third, how can we compare rates of crime (and other forms of harm) in different societies, and how is the task of making such comparisons made harder by complicating factors such as globalization? Part II (Chapters 4–9) is a systematic guide to modern criminological theory and its historical development. Part III (Chapters 10–14) examines specific types of crime, including property crime, interpersonal violence, white-collar crime, and political crime. It begins by examining how patterns of crime and victimization are structured by the sociological variables of social class, gender, race, and age.

*Part I* serves as an introduction to some of the major themes of criminology. Chapter 1 outlines the major ways in which popular discourse about crime is articulated—through the mass media, through fear of crime, and through the pronouncements of the moral entrepreneurs of social problems. The chapter briefly summarizes the key elements of crime as a legal category before stressing the importance of sociological definitions of crime. Chapter 2 outlines the major empirical sources of crime data. We stress here that data do not speak for themselves! How crime data are explained, therefore, depends both on our concepts of crime and on the assumptions underlying our theories of crime. The importance of this point will become clearer as the contents of the book unfold. Chapter 3 raises some basic cross-cultural questions about crime, including why some countries have low crime rates and whether a criminological theory developed in one society can explain patterns of crime in other societies. The chapter also takes very seriously some of the many problems associated with engaging in comparative study, especially those involving cultural relativism and globalization.

*Part II* (Chapters 4–9) introduces students to criminological theory. The theories that we outline are included either because they are chiefly sociological—and not, therefore, ones based on the study of individual actors (e.g., in psychology and psychiatry)—or else because they contribute to a sociological understanding of the development of criminology (e.g., the presociological discourses of eighteenth-century classical criminology and of nineteenth-century positivist analyses of crime). With respects to its contents, each of the six chapters in Part II tends to unfold chronologically. In describing each theory, we try to show why it arose when it did, what theories it supplanted or modified, how it was understood and criticized by its competitors, and how it contributes to our understanding of crime today.

*Part III* (Chapters 10–14) provides an introduction to the relationship between social inequalities and various types of crime. Chapter 10 offers the rudiments of a critical sociological perspective on the relationship between crime and structured social inequality. Here, we examine the influence of four major forms of social inequality—social class, gender, race, and age—on patterns of crime and victimization in the United States. Chapters 11–14 serve as an introduction to various types of crime. Typologies of crime can be constructed in an infinite variety of ways. We have chosen a sociological typology that combines (1) those crimes usually defined in the legal codes and (2) those crimes and social harms outside the criminal law that have received much attention in the sociological and criminological literature. Because crime is found in every social institution, the chapters in Part III offer a comprehensive understanding of the nature, extent, types, and costs of crime found not only in the street but also in the family, the workplace, and the state. In these chapters, we rely heavily on research done in the United States, but we also include material from other countries, such as Canada, Australia, and Britain.

We have avoided altogether the common division in criminology textbooks between crime and criminal justice by omitting the usual lengthy descriptions of the criminal justice system. Our focus in this book is not criminal justice but crime, and we have tried to discuss the complexity of the latter in the depth we believe it warrants. However, various aspects of social control (criminalization, labeling, police practices, comparative penal policies, and so on) naturally press their claims for attention, and we explore them here, especially when they affect the links between crime and structured social inequality.

## HOW TO USE THIS BOOK

Students should make use of a number of aids in each chapter, including a chapter preview, a list of key terms, a chapter review, questions for class discussion, and suggestions for further study, which include a list of additional readings and recommended websites.

## CHAPTER PREVIEWS AND CHAPTER REVIEWS

Each chapter begins with a chapter preview of the main themes that follow. Included in the preview is a list of key terms that you should be especially aware of as you read the chapter. These terms are highlighted in bold in the text and then followed immediately by a definition to help you understand them more easily. At the end of each chapter, a chapter review outlines the major points that have been discussed.

## QUESTIONS FOR CLASS DISCUSSION AND SUGGESTIONS FOR FURTHER STUDY

Each chapter review is followed by several questions for classroom discussion. These questions are followed by a list of suggested readings that will be helpful for essays or term papers. Each of these suggested readings is then followed by a list of several websites that offer additional information on specific crimes and theories.

## WEBSITES

Because the Internet is an important source of information for criminology, we recommend that students start their virtual journeys by exploring the websites we have listed at the end of each chapter. Use of these websites will allow students to expand and update their horizons somewhat beyond the information and analysis presented in any given chapter.

For instance, if you are curious about recent data on workplace deaths and injuries, you can point your web browser to the site provided at the end of the chapter, search for the federal and state legislation governing workplace safety, and thereby begin to compile a report on the topic. Indeed, most government agencies maintain websites, and many activist organizations devote resources to their own websites.

## REFERENCES AND GLOSSARY

Following the main text is a comprehensive, alphabetical list of references cited in the book. In the body of the text, you will find the references cited in the following way: (Smith, 2011:21). This example begins with the last name of the author (Smith), then gives the year the material was published or written (2011), and ends with the page number of the citation (21). In the glossary, students will find brief definitions of all of the key terms used in the book.

## A NOTE ON THE UNWELCOMING LANGUAGE OF STRUCTURED SOCIAL INEQUALITY

In writing this textbook we have been especially sensitive to the language of structured social inequality. This sort of self-interested language tends to create the impression that one particular group—gender, race, country, species, and so on—is superior to another. For example, we have tried to avoid the use of *he, his* or *him* when referring to people in general because these terms effectively exclude women (it is another matter altogether, though this difficulty does not arise anywhere in this book, that the use of *he, his,* or *him* tends wrongly to be reserved for humans, and *it* for an animal other than a human).

Similarly, with the exception of the specific meaning attached to the somewhat archaic term *American exceptionalism,* we do not refer to the United States as *America* because the latter term should properly be reserved for the entirety of North, Central, and South America.

## ACKNOWLEDGMENTS

A book such as this inevitably incurs many debts. First and foremost, we thank our many students, who often forced us to clarify our ideas and who provided us with critical comments during our classroom presentations of the material. In particular, with good humor, accuracy, and enviable energy, Mallory Huskins, Mary Sohl, and Jacqui White provided us with excellent research assistance.

Our colleagues in the Department of Criminology at the University of Southern Maine have contributed to various editions of the text, as has Rosemary Miller, our wonderful department administrative assistant.

Many colleagues at other institutions were kind enough to read portions of the manuscript. Their comments have undoubtedly turned it into a far better book than it otherwise would have been. In this regard, we would like to express our thanks to:

Valerie J. Callanan, University of Akron
Lynn S. Chancer, Hunter College
Kimberly J. Cook, University of North Carolina—Wilmington
Dusten Hollist, University of Montana—Missoula
P.J. McGann, University of Michigan
Maureen Outlaw, Providence College
Karen Weiss, West Virginia University
L. Susan Williams, Kansas State University

For their editorial and other skills we wish to acknowledge the staff at Oxford University Press. In this regard we wish to thank, especially, Sherith Pankratz, Whitney Laemmli, Marianne Paul, Harriet Lewis and Elliot Simon. Finally, we wish to thank and salute each other. We have been working together on the five editions of this book for almost 25 years, always as the best of colleagues and as dear and cherished friends. It has been a wonderfully respectful, supportive, and collaboratively intellectual relationship throughout.

# ABOUT THE AUTHORS

**Piers Beirne** is Professor of Sociology and Legal Studies in the Criminology Department at the University of Southern Maine. Among his previous books are *Inventing Criminology: The Rise of 'Homo Criminalis'* (1993); *Issues in Green Criminology* (2007, edited with Nigel South); and *Confronting Animal Abuse: Law, Criminology, and Human–Animal Relationships* (2009). He is the founding coeditor of the international journal *Theoretical Criminology*,

**James W. Messerschmidt** is Professor of Sociology in the Criminology Department and the Women's and Gender Studies Program at the University of Southern Maine. In addition to numerous articles and book chapters, he is the author of *The Trial of Leonard Peltier* (1983), *Capitalism, Patriarchy, and Crime: Toward a Socialist Feminist Criminology* (1986), *Masculinities and Crime: A Critique and Reconceptualization of Theory* (1993), *Crime as Structured Action: Gender, Race, Class, and Crime in the Making* (1997), *Nine Lives: Adolescent Masculinities, the Body, and Violence* (2000), *Flesh and Blood: Adolescent Gender Diversity and Violence* (2004), and *Hegemonic Masculinities and Camouflaged Politics: Unmasking the Bush Dynasty and Its War Against Iraq* (2010).

# INTRODUCTION TO CRIMINOLOGY

# THE PROBLEM OF CRIME

**1.1 Images of Crime**
- Crime as a Social Problem
- Crime and the Culture of Fear
- Crime in the Mass Media
- Newsmaking Criminology

**1.2 Crime, Criminal Law, and Criminalization**
- Crime as a Legal Category
- Law and State
- Law and Criminalization

**1.3 Crime as a Sociological Problem**
- Crime as a Violation of Conduct Norms
- Crime as Social Harm and Analogous Social Injury
- Crime as a Violation of Rights
- Crime and Deviance
- Crime, Globalization, and Global Conduct Norms

**PREVIEW**

Chapter 1 introduces:
- The distorted images of crime projected by the mass media.
- How crime as a sociological problem differs from crime as a social problem.
- Three of the key concepts of criminology: *crime, criminal law,* and *criminalization*.
- Various sociological definitions of crime, including crime as a violation of conduct norms, crime as social harm, crime as a form of deviance, crime as a violation of human rights, and crime as a violation of global conduct norms.

**KEY TERMS**

analogous social injury
animal rights
conduct norms
crime
criminal justice system
criminal law

criminalization
deviance
fear of crime
globalization
global conduct norms
human rights

newsmaking criminology
social control
social harm

social problem
sociological problem
the state

## 1.1 IMAGES OF CRIME

Our focus in this book is crime. What is crime? How much crime is there? How can we explain it? Even before reading this book, you probably have strong opinions about the causes of crime, its harmful effects, and how best to tackle it. Let's start our journey into the study of crime with a brief discussion of how and why crime is viewed as a social problem.

## CRIME AS A SOCIAL PROBLEM

Some of us have been directly affected by crime. Many others, because we are fearful of it, have been indirectly victimized by crime. Each of us already has a great store of knowledge about crime. We know, for example, that some areas of cities are not safe to walk in at night. We therefore avoid them. We go elsewhere. Or we stay at home. We know that it is dangerous to leave infants unattended, front doors unbolted, cars unlocked, and bicycles unchained. We routinely process such knowledge, and we take defensive action accordingly. We know, or at least we think we know, what sorts of people are likely to commit crime. Each of us has an image of the typical criminal—perhaps a sick, degenerate, violent person who preys on the innocent and the vulnerable.

Crime exacts a high price on federal, state, and household budgets. According to economist David Anderson (1999), the annual cost of crime in the United States is an astounding $1.7 trillion. This estimate includes crime-induced production, the opportunity costs of crime, the value of risks to life and health, and economic transfers. To put this figure in perspective, it is about four times higher than the annual budget of the U.S. Defense Department and represents a cost of roughly $5,100 per person per year.

Partly because of its huge expense and partly because of the fear that it produces, crime is regarded by the public as one of the leading social problems today. But what is a social problem? How is some social condition constructed as a social problem, by whom, and for what reasons? How and why is crime widely seen as a **social problem**?

We must stress that there is no objective set of social conditions whose harmful effects necessarily make them social problems. Something is a social problem only if it is perceived as such. What is regarded as a social problem thus varies over time. Child abuse, for example, has been seen as a full-blown problem only since the early 1960s. In some places and times marijuana use, prostitution, and gambling have been seen as social problems, even ones worthy of criminalization, yet in others the same social practices have been seen as private vices best regulated by individual morality rather than criminal law. To give one further example of this social selectivity, not all events that have the potential for being labeled "terrorism" are in fact so labeled. Sometimes this is because public bureaucracies (e.g., the FBI) don't consider an event or events as acts of terror; sometimes it is the particular moral view of an administration that determines this. This was clearly the case with the hundreds of violent acts against abortion centers during the 1980s and early 1990s. These were not condemned as acts of terror until 1993, when President Clinton, a Democrat, entered the White House (see Jenkins, 2009:43–44).

The perception of something as a social problem also varies from person to person and from one social group to another. For example, some people regard social inequality as a social problem; others see it as a virtue that encourages competition and economic responsibility. Some people regard the use of animals in laboratory experiments as a necessary step in the elimination of human diseases; others see it as unjustified abuse of our fellow creatures. And so on. Some social problems quickly capture public attention and remain as objects of national concern for a long time.

Several factors determine how a social problem is constructed and whether it is defined as a social problem in a particular society (Best, 2007). These factors include (1) the arguments, rhetoric, and power of claims makers and moral entrepreneurs, who may be as diverse as the U.S. Department of Justice, the Pope, Pearl Jam, Rush Limbaugh, and U2's Bono; (2) the pressure tactics of powerful private interest groups, such as the American Medical Association, the National Rifle Association, and Mothers Against Drunk Driving; and (3) the professional utterances of public officials, such as politicians, judges, right-wing fundamentalists, police and correctional officers, and, on occasion, those engaged in teaching, writing, and research in the social sciences, including criminology.

At least two additional factors are decisive in determining the meaning and seriousness of any given social problem. The first is the mass media. Successful claims makers are those who are able to use the mass media to broadcast their message that a certain problem needs attention and amelioration. We will have much more to say about the images of crime in the mass media in the next few pages. The second factor is fear. Many of us fear crime. In our conversations with family and friends, on TV, and in our worst nightmares, our images of crime as a serious social problem are constantly fueled by our **fear of crime**. Given that our fear of it is seldom based on careful

reflection, crime is a difficult phenomenon to explain. Let us therefore delve into the origins of the culture of fear that surrounds crime.

## CRIME AND THE CULTURE OF FEAR

Four decades ago, the National Commission on the Causes and Prevention of Violence made the following bleak predictions about the quality of life in large cities in the near future (1970:38–39):

> High-rise apartment buildings and residential compounds protected by private guards and security devices will be fortified cells for upper-middle- and high-income populations living at prime locations in the city.
>
> Suburban neighborhoods, geographically far removed from the central city, will be protected mainly by economic homogeneity and by distance from population groups with the highest propensities to commit crimes.
>
> Lacking a sharp change in federal and state policies, ownership of guns will be almost universal in the suburbs, homes will be fortified by an array of devices from window grills to electronic surveillance equipment, armed citizen volunteers in cars will supplement inadequate police patrols in neighborhoods closer to the central city, and extreme left-wing and right-wing groups will have tremendous armories of weapons that could be brought into play without any provocation.
>
> High-speed, patrolled expressways will be sanitized corridors connecting safe areas, and private automobiles, taxicabs, and commercial vehicles will be equipped routinely with unbreakable glass, light armor, and other security features. Inside garages or valet parking will be available at safe buildings in or near the central city. Armed guards will ride shotgun on all forms of public transportation.
>
> Streets and residential neighborhoods in the central city will be unsafe in differing degrees, and the ghetto slum neighborhoods will be places

of terror with widespread crime, perhaps entirely out of police control during nighttime hours. Armed guards will protect all public facilities such as schools, libraries, and playgrounds in these areas.

Between the unsafe, deteriorating central city on the one hand and the network of safe, prosperous areas and sanitized corridors on the other, there will be, not unnaturally, intensifying hatred and deepening division. Violence will increase further, and the defensive response of the affluent will become still more elaborate.

Because of our great fear of crime, the commission warned, we are in danger of closeting ourselves in anticrime fortresses. To a certain extent the commission's terrifying images of life in large cities have not been contradicted, at least not in the minds of a fearful public. Both before and after September 11, 2001, the United States seems to have become a society whose increasing fears about crime, including its cost, reach into almost every corner of public and private life. Nowadays the government fights "wars" on crime—the war on drugs, for example, and wars on gangs, pornography, illegal immigrants, and terrorism. Candidates for political office routinely campaign on the promise of restoring law and order to the nation's streets and of waging war against terrorism worldwide. Woe betide the politician who is perceived as soft on crime!

Get-tough-on-crime rhetoric on the campaign trail and in Congress has led to a mass of new federal and state anticrime legislation, prominent examples of which include "three strikes" laws and minimum-sentence legislation. The new "homeland security" legislation enacted after September 11, such as the U.S.A. Patriot Act and the Port and Maritime Security Act, has extended government surveillance to public transport and the approaches to many public buildings, including government offices and courts, airports, bus and train stations, ports, and ferry terminals.

The outsourcing of jobs, economic insecurity, anger, and fear of crime all contribute to widespread public support for harsh punishment for criminals (J. Simon, 2007; Costelloe, Chiricos, and Gertz, 2009; Johnson, 2009). Community crime watch programs, police-citizen action committees, and groups like the Guardian Angels have prospered across the United States. Private video surveillance systems (CCTV), which were created in the 1970s to assist in road traffic management, have been rapidly extended to the workplace, city streets, stores, sports stadiums, and residential areas. Whether these systems deter crime or, instead, increase fear of crime is a matter of some debate (e.g., Ditton, 2000; Gill, Bryan, and Allen, 2007).

Some evidence suggests that in Britain, where there are 4.2 million CCTVs, or one security camera for every 15 citizens, and where the average Londoner is filmed 300 times per day (Goering, 2008), CCTV has failed to make a significant impact in deterring or solving street robberies. No more than 3 percent of London street robberies were solved with the use of CCTV images (Bowcott, 2008).

In the United States, according to opinion polls and victimization surveys, such as those of the nonpartisan Pew Research Center, after September 11, 2001, members of the public transferred their highest level of fear from the violence of street crime to the violence of terrorism (Revkin, 2009:A13; Lee, 2007:201–204).

Thereafter, these two fears have been closely followed by concerns about unemployment, war, and health care. The list of crimes and criminals that the public fears is a lengthy one indeed. To this list must be added another—namely, the deep-seated, daily anxieties about environmental risks and hazards, nuclear proliferation, the spread of viruses such as SARS and swine flu, and the dangers posed by technology's destructive effects on planet Earth, on humans, and on other animals.

Public fear of violent criminal acts is quite wide ranging and conjures up numerous images. Among these are terrorism, serial murder, gang violence, stranger rapes, carjackings, random muggings, road rage, "going postal," razor blades in Halloween cookies, drive-by shootings, child kidnappings, police brutality, and plane crashes. These acts are committed by killer kids, black males, Internet predators, pedophile priests, child pornographers, gun-toting madmen, crazed druggies, and serial murderers. Moreover, opinion polls today regularly show that about half of the public believes that crime rates continue to rise in the United States. (Ironically, as we will see later in this book, government-produced crime data show that they have been falling for the past two decades.)

What is the source of fear of crime? This is a complicated question, not least because research has not devoted enough attention to exactly what "fear" of crime is and how often and how intensely it is felt. Much debate has raged among criminologists about the definition of fear of crime, its causes, how to measure it, and how social and penal policies can remedy it (Lee, 2007:5; Gray, Jackson, and Farrall, 2008). Is this "fear" fear for oneself or fear that others may be victimized? How can we distinguish fear of crime from general anxieties about modern life and from worry and risk evaluation?

As an unwelcome fact of modern life, fear of crime has numerous sources. Although criminologists may debate whether fear of crime accurately reflects the likelihood of victimization, it must be said that in the United States fear of crime stems partly from "American exceptionalism." This exceptionalism is the simple fact that crimes of violence, especially homicide, occur at a much higher rate in the United States than they do in other technologically developed societies.

Besides its problematic relationship with crime itself, including the cost of crime, fear of crime also derives from numerous other factors, both sociological and psychological. Research consistently shows that the relatively powerless sections of the community experience the greatest fear of crime and suffer the greatest psychological trauma from its effects (e.g., E. Stanko, 2000). These relatively powerless groups are those with the least economic, political, and cultural assets. They include the elderly, females, and racial minorities. The elderly and youth are generally more fearful of crime than the middle-aged. Minorities are generally more fearful of crime than whites. Both males and females especially fear physical violence (J. Lane and Meeker, 2003b).

Fear of crime is therefore associated with one's position in society—with one's gender, for example, and with one's age, race, social class, education, and so on. It also derives from people's lived experiences gained from where they reside and where they work, from their conversations with their family and their friends, and from the mass media.

Above all, it is through the self-interested and often distorted lenses of the mass media that most of us, most of the time, acquire our dominant images of crime. Mass media include TV and newspapers, in particular, but also the Internet, radio, movies, and videos. The mass media provide us with certain information about crime, and, as they do so, they generate fear of crime.

Clearly, different social groups are affected differently by the everyday images of crime that they view in the mass media. Three studies have examined the link between audience characteristics and fear of crime:

- Eschholz's (2002) study of TV content and TV audiences in a southern state found that, overall, individuals who watched more TV were more fearful of crime. But when the audience was analyzed by race, this relationship was found to apply mostly to minorities, including African Americans, Hispanics, and Asians. Whites' levels of fear of crime rose, moreover, in proportion to the presence of minority offenders depicted on TV.

- Eschholz, Chiricos, and Gertz's (2003) research on TV viewers in Leon County, Florida, found that the strongest relationships between local news programs and tabloid TV programs on the one hand and fear of crime on the other are found among those who perceive themselves to be living in a neighborhood with 25 percent or more black residents in it.

- In a study of residents in Orange County, California, J. Lane and Meeker (2003a) found that whites, who rely more on newspapers for their crime news, have less fear of crime than Latinos, who rely more on TV for their crime news. They suggest that people probably fear crime more if the news story is about crime in their neighborhood, because their perceived risk of crime increases.

There is a triangular relationship among fear of crime, crime itself, and the images of crime constructed by the media (and for a spectacular parody, see Figure 1.1). One of criminology's most important tasks is to examine the relationships in this triangle. If we experience heightened fear of crime, the quality of our lives is significantly reduced. If much of our fear of crime comes from the mass media's images of crime, we need to explore those images and try to determine whether they reflect or, rather, distort the nature and seriousness of crime in our lives. In short, fear of crime may be as costly as crime itself. Understanding the dimensions of a problem is of course a key first step in trying to solve it in an informed way.

## CRIME IN THE MASS MEDIA

We need now to focus on the stereotypical images of crime routinely presented by the mass media. How much crime is portrayed in the media? How accurately do media portrayals of crime reflect the incidence of crime in real life?

**FIGURE 1.1**   La Société du Spectacle
*Source*: Guy Debord (1967), front cover.

We should not be too surprised to learn that the mass media's images of crime are almost never objective. After all, the mass media depend for their financial existence on reporting—or creating—the apparently unusual. When social life is routine and orderly, there is little news. Media executives know full well that nothing sells to advertisers quite so well as violence. To maximize their audience, the media feature unusual events rather than representative events. They emphasize the sensational rather than the mundane. The media's portrayal of violence feeds directly into viewers' fear of crime

Neither the amount of crime nor the distribution of different types of crime depicted in news on TV and in newspapers bears much resemblance to what is reported in official crime data such as the FBI's Uniform Crime Reports (see Section 2.2). Yet it is chiefly from TV and print media that we acquire knowledge of what is newsworthy. In fact, as we will now see, victimization rates of persons in the media have less to do with the public's actual victimization risk than with fear of crime (Surette, 2007:61).

The mass media create the image of a society with an enormous amount of violent crime—especially of murder but also of assault, rape, and armed robbery. Indeed, from the 1940s to the present, the percentage of total TV program time devoted to crime-related shows has persistently increased; however, according to official crime data, the violent crime rate has fallen sharply, beginning in about 1990 and continuing until today. Although in real life murders are only a tiny fraction of all serious crimes, media researcher Doris Graber (1980; Heath and Gilbert, 1996) has found that it consumes 26.2 percent of all crime news reported in the *Chicago Tribune*. Moreover, whereas nonviolent crimes such as theft compose 47 percent of all crimes reported to the police, such crimes constitute only 4 percent of all crime items in newspapers (Graber, 1980; and see Section 2.1).

When media researchers have examined bias in what the media considers newsworthy, most of their attention has been directed to TV. According to the Project for Excellence in Journalism (2008), local TV stations consistently practice "hook and hold"—they try to hook and hold an audience by leaning heavily on stories about "public safety" at the beginning of newscasts, perhaps for the first three to four items, and only then proceed to offer items of soft news.

It has also been documented that about one-third of total TV program time in the United States is devoted to crime or law-enforcement shows, with a concentration at prime time. Among the numerous popular TV programs are:

- Crime reality shows: *Cops, The First 48, Forensic Files, America's Most Wanted,* and *Homeland Security*

- Documentary shows: *Unsolved Mysteries, 48 Hours, 60 Minutes,* and *Dateline.*
- Prime-time shows: *The Shield, CSI, CSI Miami, CSI New York, Cold Case, Law & Order, NCIS, Bones, Damages, Dexter, Criminal Minds, The Mentalist, Numb3rs,* and *Without a Trace.*
- The "Crime and Investigation Network" (part of A&E) is devoted entirely to documenting "actual" case crimes, criminals, and investigations and features documentary shows such as *48 Hours Mystery, Anatomy of Crime, The First 48, Cold Case Files, Born to Kill, Crimes of Passion, Crime and Punishment, Women Behind Bars, Final Justice,* and *Mafia Empire.*

Nearly all this TV programming has violent crime as its chief subject matter. According to a violence index used by researcher George Gerbner from 1967 to 1987, approximately 80 percent of all TV programs contain violence (Liebert and Sprafkin, 1988). In addition, at least 90 percent of children's cartoon shows contain violence. Although Gerbner's definition of violence may seem overly broad (it includes violence in humorous situations, for example), the fact remains that violence, however defined, is the staple of the crime-related TV diet. It has even been calculated that by the time they are 18 years old, children will have seen 200,000 acts of violence on TV, including 40,000 murders (Huston, Fairchild, and Donnerstein, 1992).

Second, some types of violence are more likely to be reported in the mass media than others, often depending on the identity of offenders or victims. For example, in Chicago's two daily newspapers the homicides most likely to be reported are those occurring in middle-class neighborhoods; the least likely to be reported are those with African-American victims (Johnstone, Hawkins, and Michener, 1994; and see Beckett and Sasson, 2004). Another study examined the newspaper coverage of homicide between 1986 and 1994 in Houston, Texas, and found that black and Hispanic victims were the least likely to be mentioned (Paulsen, 2003). Similarly, of the homicides that were reported in national newspapers in England and Wales from 1993 to 1996, newspapers were quite selective about which murders they chose to cover (Peelo, Francis, Soothill, Pearson, and Ackerley, 2004). Those most likely to be reported were sexual homicides, homicides involving a clear motive for monetary gain or revenge, motiveless homicides, and those involving young children, though not infanticides. The homicides least likely to be reported were those involving marginalized groups, such as those of persons of color.

We should also mention three other studies of how racist ideologies easily masquerade as objective news. One study has shown that *Time* and *Newsweek* misrepresent crime as primarily a problem of urban African Americans (Barlow, 1998). Another documents that in the coverage of the 2005 Hurricane Katrina disaster in Florida, African Americans were overwhelmingly portrayed as victims and whites almost solely as saviors—despite the fact that both races were much in evidence in both categories (C. Lee and Gandy, 2006). The third has looked at the representation on TV of Asian/Pacific Islander Americans (APIAs) (Deo, Chin, Lee, Milman, and Yuen, 2009). The authors found that APIAs are stereotyped on prime-time TV shows as scholastic overachievers, math geniuses, or geeky science/computer nerds. This representation, the authors argue, reinforces the misperception that "APIAs have overcome all racial barriers to achieving the American Dream (p. 154). Nothing could be further from the truth.

Besides bias in the actual content of media coverage of newsworthy events, bias is also seen in important news events that are not reported by the media. In general, white-collar crimes are the crimes least likely to be reported on TV. In a study of 878 chemical spills reported to the Environmental Protection Agency in Hillsborough County, Florida, between 1987 and 1997, M. Lynch, Stretesky, and Hammond (2000) found that only nine (or 1.5 percent) were newsworthy enough to gain coverage in the county's largest newspaper, the *Tampa Tribune*. It was also found that this low frequency reflected the public's own low concern with environmental and corporate crimes such as environmental pollution and the dumping of hazardous waste (which can, of course, be every bit as deadly as street crime).

Sometimes, when the media accurately depict the volume of violent crime, they distort its seriousness. For example, one study has found that 84 percent of prime-time TV shows contain at least one episode of sexual harassment, which perhaps accurately reflects the commonplace nature of this violent crime (Grauerholz and King, 1997). But the depiction of sexual harassment in the media tends to reflect several myths, including the view that it is not a serious offense and that its victims can often remedy the situation themselves (pp. 142–143).

In a study of media coverage of the Enron and WorldCom corporate scandals of 2001–2002, J. Williams (2008) analyzed the reportage of more than 300 articles in the prestigious newspapers the *New York Times*, the *Washington Post*, the *Los Angeles Times*, the *Globe and Mail*, and *The Economist*. His findings are rather different in nature from those we have mentioned so far: The media did not so much underrepresent the crimes of the powerful or distort them as put them in a different context. The type and focuses of corporate illegalities varied considerably, Williams reported. The causes of the scandals ranged from individual misconduct ("bad apples") to systemic problems to too much government regulation or too little. However, although the causes and solutions put forward by the media were quite various, their distortion was not so much one of omission as of commission: At root, the media showed themselves to be business-friendly and, even, allies of corporate interests. As such, there was much common ground shared by the newspapers' reportage of the corporate scandals, including their assertions that "(1) market-based capitalism is the preferred mode of economic organization; (2) laws are exogenous to markets and distort market efficiencies; [and] (3) investor confidence is a natural barometer of the health of the market and an essential benchmark for all policy moves" (p. 487).

Occasionally, the mass media will channel viewer attention toward particular sorts of immoral or criminal behavior. These episodic processes are known by criminologists, to use the term coined by Stanley Cohen (1972), as *moral panics*. Well-documented examples of moral panics that are fueled and fanned by the media include the white slavers of the Progressive Era (c. 1890–1910), sex fiends in the 1940s, communists in the 1950s, serial murderers during the 1980s, youth crime and juvenile gangs in the 1990s, pedophile priests and illegal immigrants in the new millennium, and the ever-present druggie. It is unclear why moral panics arise when and as they do. But it is nevertheless true that every so often a society becomes engrossed in a process of public frenzy directed to certain forms of crime and deviance.

Jenkins (2009) identifies a number of features that need to be present for the emergence of the ideal type of moral panic (see Box 1.1). Jenkins (2009; and see Mawby and Gisby, 2009) also examines the interesting question of why it is, when some social problems have all the features needed to generate a frenzy, sometimes no moral panic emerges. He gives a number of examples of such "failures to launch," including the social problem that is the online child-pornography trade. Jenkins refers in particular to the so-called prized "KG and KX series" photos. These photos were bought and sold on the Internet in the 1990s and from 2000 onwards and included 4- and 5-year old girls performing oral sex and masturbation on adult men (p. 37). Numerous children were visibly subjected to serious abuse of various forms. The business included a considerable number of sinister men: 50,000–100,000 individual viewers and demon figures in the form of serial child molesters and powerful international dealers.

In short, the Internet child pornography scene had all the classic features of a potential moral panic. It had vulnerable victims, folk devils, and a potential army of enraged feminists and conservative moral-majority types. But no frenzy happened. There were no outraged bishops. The U.S. media, Jenkins documents, have paid little attention to child pornography. Congressional hearings come and go, and little is done.

Jenkins explains this "failure to launch" in a number of ways. Child porn is an unusual legal area in the United States—journalistic access to original child pornography is entirely forbidden. Control of child pornography is entirely within the domain of federal law-enforcement agencies. These agencies are under no pressure to tackle the core of the problem, and their efforts are not subject to public scrutiny. On the rare occasion that a user of child porn is caught, he or she is almost always a faceless, lone, and uninfluential novice. But the major reason is technological. Electronic interception of child pornography by police is very uncommon.

Most law-enforcement agencies work at a technological level that is simply too low to comprehend the trade as it existed a decade ago and still less today. They have little idea of the nature of the trade and its complex world of concealment and deception through proxies and anonymizers, to say nothing of the more recent shift into P2P networks (Jenkins, 2009:38).

Knowing that the mass media construct their images of crime in self-interested and distorted ways is an important discovery. But this revelation does not, of course, teach us much about the nature of crime. Some criminologists

---

**BOX 1.1   CONDITIONS CONDUCIVE TO A MORAL PANIC**

- A diversity of agencies and interest groups must exist, from which the media can draw and which can make rival claims. Ideally, each should have some degree of public prestige and media access. Panics are most likely to flourish and escalate when their subject matter is contested between competing forces.
- The story must be comprehensible to agencies and journalists themselves before it can be repackaged for the general public.
- The issue must be sufficiently overt and accessible that ordinary consumers will have some chance of encountering what they believe to be its manifestations.

- The panic should offer a narrative, with characters who are easily understood: Heroes and villains must have identifiable faces.
- The story should lend itself to visual portrayal. There should be some standard faces or settings that can be used as stereotypical points of reference. Examples might include the scene of gang fights, drug supermarkets, and the faces of serial killers.
- The narrative must also have an outcome, in that solutions, plausible or otherwise, must be identified.
- For consumers, the narrative will have maximum impact if it meshes with previous expectations and knowledge, often because earlier movements and controversies have laid the foundations for later explosions.

Source: Jenkins (2009:45).

---

have therefore tried to counter mass media images of crime with alternative discourses of their own.

### NEWSMAKING CRIMINOLOGY

The mass media's distorted and self-interested offerings on crime can be countered if criminologists attempt to make their own analyses more available to the public (Currie, 2007). Instead of, or perhaps at the same time as, academics and graduate students of criminology are forced to "publish or perish" by placing their work in a handful of little-read academic journals, Currie urges that criminologists should enter the public arena and try to have their scholarly research influence social policies toward crime. Social justice surely demands this.

One approach that criminologists have used to replace media discourses of crime with more thoughtful, in-depth analysis is **newsmaking criminology**. This has been defined as "the conscious efforts and activities of criminologists to interpret, influence, or shape the representation of 'newsworthy' items about crime and justice…[and] to locat[e] the mass-media

portrayals of incidences of 'serious' crimes in the context of all illegal and harmful activities" (Barak, 2007:191–192; and see Cottle, 2006; Ferrell, Hayward, and Young, 2008:125–137).

While we will have more to say about the importance of "harmful activities" later in this chapter, it is very worthwhile to point out that only rarely do the mass media pay intention to what criminologists have to say about crime. Typically, media sound bites are uttered by people who work as state officials in the justice system (judges, lawyers, police officers) or else by talk show hosts and others in the entertainment business. Short sound bites do not lend themselves to reasoned analysis. With this goal in mind, Kramer (2004, cited in G. Barak, 2007:196–197) and G. Barak (1996, 2007), for example, have hosted radio shows that have allowed them on air to address and bring more clarity to the O.J. Simpson trial, violence against women, solid-waste management, corporate crime, and the Palestinian–Israeli conflict.

This call to action gets us a little ahead of ourselves, however. We need to begin by exploring some of criminology's basic concepts.

## 1.2 CRIME, CRIMINAL LAW, AND CRIMINALIZATION

In order to have a clear idea of what crime actually is, we need a working definition of **crime**. Yet the question "What is crime?" is a surprisingly difficult one to answer. Consider two illustrations of this difficulty.

Think, first, about the unfortunate pirate William Kidd. During the 1690s the soon-to-be-infamous Captain William Kidd was an obscure naval pirate who was based in New York and operated in the Caribbean. In 1695 he obtained a commission as a privateer, which allowed him to engage essentially in the same piratical activities, but this time with the economic support and moral blessings of the king and of some of the most powerful families in England. Kidd's commission directed him to sail to the Indian Ocean and to end the practices of pirates from the North American colonies who were plundering British East India Company ships. For attacking and capturing one or more pirate ships and bringing some pirates to trial, Kidd, as well as the king and all the backers of the scheme, would earn a handsome profit (Ritchie, 1986).

But for doing roughly what he had been commissioned to do, Kidd did not earn the fame and fortune to which he believed he was legally entitled. In 1701, in London, Kidd was tried on charges of murder and multiple conspiracies, convicted, sentenced to death by hanging, and executed.

Kidd had been caught in the complicated and rapidly changing web of maritime trade of seventeenth-century British imperialism. Although there was little evidence that he had engaged in (illegal) piracy rather than (legal) privateering, Kidd's Red Sea against the French and against the Dutch East India Company ensnared him in a larger movement that would find him a convenient symbol for a much broader problem, even though Kidd was never very successful either as a pirate or as a privateer.

Kidd was squeezed by the coincidence of two forces. On the one hand were thriving British companies such as the East India Company that needed order and regularity on the high seas for the profitable expansion of their commerce. On the other hand were the administrative and military apparatuses of the British state that, after tremendous expansion as a result of various European wars, could not tolerate maverick and unpredictable challenges to its power. Privateering, or legalized piracy, was therefore doomed. Kidd's activities as a privateer commissioned by royalty and by the rich were suddenly renamed piracy.

Kidd's story is a good example of how difficult it is to pinpoint the precise nature of crime. Clearly, his actions were defined as piracy rather than national heroics largely because of the changing fortunes of British imperialism. It is also clear that nothing in the nature of Kidd's actions was inherently criminal.

Consider, second, a very different example that also illustrates the difficulty in trying to determine exactly what crime might be: the origins of the criminalization of marijuana use in the United States. Before 1937 there were no legal penalties involved in the "proper" use or sale of marijuana. However, in 1937, according to the provisions of the Marihuana Tax Act, a federal tax was mandated for anyone who dealt commercially in cannabis, hemp, or marijuana (Galliher and Walker, 1977). It is not really relevant to our point here either that the origins of the act were wrapped up with anti-Hispanic prejudice in California and in Congress or that the act was intended to be only a symbolic piece of legislation administered and enforced by the federal Bureau of Narcotics. What matters is that beforehand marijuana possession was not considered a crime and then, simply by legislative fiat in 1937, it was regarded as a violation of criminal law. What, then, does this mean? One obvious answer: Whether marijuana use is a crime or not depends only on whether it is stated as such by criminal law.

In other words, sometimes—in some places, times, and cultures—marijuana use is defined as a crime. In others, it is not. Moreover, suppose that in any given jurisdiction rules of criminal law state that marijuana use is criminal behavior. What, then, does criminalization mean if local police decide that they have more important things to prosecute than marijuana possession? Suppose, further, that juries are unwilling to convict those prosecuted under antimarijuana provisions?

What, then, is crime? As a historical phenomenon, the concept of crime is of fairly recent origin. Prior to the eighteenth century, both in western Europe and in colonial North America, most offenses—when not handled privately—were typically the domain of either canon law (religious law) or civil law (especially the law of torts). Criminal law did not yet exist. Moreover, what constitutes crime varies from one culture to another. Thus, anthropologists have been unable to find any behavior that is universally defined as crime (see Section 3.3). For example, although all known societies have a concept of murder, societies differ in how they define the act of murder. Given such variation, it is nearly impossible for criminologists to agree either on a precise definition of crime or even on the definition of an act as seemingly simple to define as murder. Many sociologists and historians suggest that there is nothing in the nature of any behavior that makes it inherently criminal, because even what counts as crime changes over time within the same culture.

How, then, should crime be defined? Serious debate among criminologists about the proper definition of crime can be traced to a 1933 report by New York's oddly—named Bureau of Social Hygiene (Michael and Adler, 1971). Written by lawyer Jerome Michael and philosopher Mortimer Adler, this report stressed that great confusion will arise unless criminologists agree on a precise definition of crime. Only if crime is defined clearly and precisely can we distinguish criminal behavior from noncriminal behavior:

> The most precise and least ambiguous definition of crime is that which defines it as behavior which is prohibited by the criminal code. It follows that a criminal is a person who has behaved in some way prohibited by the criminal law. (pp. 2–3)

Agreeing with Michael and Adler's argument, Paul Tappan (1947) claimed that crime is an intentional act in violation of the criminal law (statutory and case law), committed without defense or excuse, and penalized by the state as a felony or misdemeanor. In this view, therefore, crime is simply a legalistic category of behavior. Let us examine some of the major aspects of the legalistic definition of crime.

## CRIME AS A LEGAL CATEGORY

The preceding legalistic definition of crime contains several elements whose formal origins can be traced to the English common law (customary law) of the twelfth century. First and foremost, a crime must be forbidden by criminal law. So, too, criminal law must provide punishment for a crime—a basic principle expressed in the English common law doctrine *nullum crimen sine lege, nulla poena sine lege* (no crime without law, no punishment without law). The formal purpose of **criminal law** is to protect members of the public from the wrongdoing of others. Rules of criminal law can be found either in statutory law (enacted by legislatures) or in common law (judge-made decisions and opinions based on the principle known as *stare decisis*). Criminal law is distinguished from civil law—such as tort law and contract law—which deals with private wrongs. Whereas a violation of civil law leaves a defendant open to civil suit, a violation of criminal law potentially places a defendant at the point of entry into the **criminal justice system.**

Criminal law categorizes crime in two ways. First, crimes are either *mala in se* or *mala prohibita.* This old and somewhat artificial distinction refers to the apparent differences between "acts that are evil in themselves" (*mala in se*) and "acts that are merely prohibited" (*mala prohibita*). Lawyers take this distinction to mean that crimes *mala in se* are acts so inherently wrong that they are universally considered evil, whereas crimes *mala prohibita,* the list of which changes over time, are acts prohibited by statute. Second, the criminal law distinguishes between felonies and misdemeanors. Although these two categories of crime are often separated by procedural differences, the most important difference is that felonies are punishable either by death or by imprisonment in a state penitentiary for a term of not less than one year, whereas misdemeanors are punishable either by fine or by a term in a local jail of less than one year.

A second element of a crime is that it must be a voluntary illegal act or omission (an *actus reus,* some examples of which are given in Figure 2.1. This means that no one can be prosecuted for bad or evil thoughts—although words (such as incitement to riot) can sometimes constitute a criminal act—and that failure to act (omission) can be criminal in situations where there is a legal duty to act. Leaving the scene of a traffic accident and failing to file an annual tax return with the Internal Revenue Service are examples of crimes by omission.

Culpability for a crime depends on a defendant's mental state, variously known as criminal intent or *mens rea,* and its coincidence with the *actus reus.* According to the American Law Institute's Model Penal Code (§2.02), someone is not guilty of an offense unless he or she acted with purpose to do the forbidden act, or with knowledge of the nature of the act, or with recklessness or negligence. In some cases intent can

be transferred, as, for example, when A intends to shoot B but misses and kills C.

To legal scholars, the precise meaning of the term *intent* is often quite elusive. For example, certain categories of individuals are judged legally incapable of forming intent: juveniles under the age of 14 and those certified as insane or severely retarded. Moreover, in cases of strict liability, intent is not a necessary requirement of guilt. Examples of strict liability offenses include felony murder (a murder committed during a serious felony, such as rape or arson) and statutory rape (sexual intercourse with a juvenile, which usually means under age 16).

An act or omission is not a crime if a defendant has a socially legitimate justification for doing it or if the person lacks the criminal responsibility required by the element of *mens rea.* The defense of justification can be raised in three instances: duress, necessity, and duty. The defense of *duress* is typically limited to homicides. Thus, a killing may be justified if an individual reasonably believes that he or she is about to be killed or seriously harmed by another. The defense of *necessity* is available to defendants who are somehow threatened by natural circumstances over which they have no control, but this defense can be used only when there was no other reasonable course of action available. For example, one would not be guilty of vandalism if, trapped inside a burning department store, one smashed a window in order to escape. The defense of *duty* is typically raised by public authorities such as police officers. Many killings by police officers in the line of duty are therefore termed *justifiable homicides.*

Finally, an act or omission may not be a crime if one lacks the necessary criminal responsibility, a condition that negates *mens rea* in several ways and that includes the controversial pleas of entrapment and insanity. The defense of *entrapment* is intended to discourage the state from creating a crime where none would otherwise have existed. According to the Model Penal Code (§2.13), entrapment occurs when police methods entice an average law-abiding citizen to commit a crime. The defense of *insanity* differs from all other defenses in that, if the plea is successful, in most jurisdictions the defendant is neither acquitted nor released but found "not guilty by reason of insanity." In some states defendants may be found "guilty but mentally ill," in which case they are confined to mental institutions until "cured," at which point they must finish their sentences in prison. This verdict almost always results in the commitment of defendants to mental institutions, often for a longer period than if they had been found guilty of the crime and sentenced to prison. In the United States the majority of states base the legal criteria of insanity on the definition contained in the Model Penal Code (§4.01):

1. A person is not responsible for criminal conduct if at the time of such conduct, as a result of mental disease or defect, he lacks substantial capacity to appreciate the criminality (wrongfulness) of his conduct, or to conform his conduct to the requirements of law.
2. The terms *mental disease* and *defect* do not include an abnormality manifested only by repeated criminal or otherwise antisocial conduct.

A key element of the legalistic definition of crime—*mens rea*—is based on the assumption that crime is behavior engaged in by individuals who are capable of exercising free will. As we progress through this book, it will become clear that such an assumption cannot be used to explain crime. Rather, we will suggest that the actions of individuals are, in varying degrees, influenced by their position in society.

At this point we would do well to ask why it is that for most nonsociological purposes crime is usually defined as behavior that violates criminal law. To put this another way: Why is it that criminal law usually defines criminal behavior? As soon as we ask (dangerously circular) questions such as these, we should realize that criminology cannot be confined to the study of criminal behavior because the concept of criminal behavior depends for its meaning on the concept of criminal law.

A few introductory words about the role of law, state, and criminal law in the process of criminalization are now appropriate.

## LAW AND STATE

Sociologically, the ideas and institutions of law vary greatly from one culture to another. Negatively, this means that law is not necessarily what some lawmakers or zealots claim it to be. Law is not an earthly expression of the will of God. It may not represent the interests of "the people." It has no necessary connection with justice. Law is above all else a social phenomenon created by members of society under specific historical conditions. Law has not always existed in the past. It might not exist in the future.

The great bulk of research in sociology and anthropology reveals that law originated with the emergence of social inequality and, specifically, that it accompanies the transition from stateless societies to state societies. Law has not always existed because not all human societies have been characterized by social inequality. Indeed, until approximately 10,000 years ago, hunting-and-gathering societies were the dominant form of social organization, and these societies had egalitarian social, economic, and political relations. In these small-scale societies (about 50 members), property was communally owned, there were no social classes, and there was no organized state or societal ruler. Even in horticultural societies, which emerged after hunting-and-gathering societies, social relations were highly egalitarian, significant differences in wealth and power did not occur, and leaders typically had no coercive powers over others. Neither in hunting-and-gathering societies nor in horticultural societies did states exist, and a common morality was maintained by the authority of custom rather than by the rule of law (Diamond, 1973). Within these stateless societies, offenses and conflicts were managed informally in a variety of nonlegal ways, such as self-help, avoidance, negotiation, settlement by a third party, and tolerance (D. Black, 1989; and see Durkheim's analysis in Section 5.1).

Not until the development of agricultural societies—in which economic productivity was expanded by new techniques such as the plow, fertilization, and irrigation—did class inequalities become prevalent. Increased productivity permitted new lifestyles that were not devoted solely to economic survival and subsistence. In some agricultural societies—such as in classical Greece—class relations developed in which slaves did most of the productive labor and slave owners dominated and appropriated the economic surplus. In other agricultural societies—such as those of medieval Europe—peasants made up most of the population, but the monarch, the nobles, and the church owned most of the land, which they obtained through military might and conquest. In both slave and feudal agricultural societies, a particular class controlled and appropriated the economic surplus, creating significant social inequalities.

An important feature of agricultural societies was the rise of states and legal systems. The **state** may be defined as the central political institution of a given society. Its major apparatuses are the government (legislative and executive), the legal system, the military, and a variety of public bureaucracies for the collection of taxes, the management of public health, the maintenance of law and order, and so on. The legal system is both a state apparatus and, through its constitutional and administrative branches, the chief mechanism for defining the sphere of state activities.

Rules of law have a variety of sources, such as superstition, divine oracles, religion, prophecy, charismatic leadership, court cases, and legislatures. Law differs from other rules of behavior—habit, convention, tradition, and custom—by its coercive nature and by the professional enforcement of its codes. Law's coercive nature can be expressed in shame, ridicule, censure, ostracism, imprisonment, torture, terror, and death. Law's professional interpreters and enforcers can comprise witches and wizards, kings and queens, popes and rabbis, village elders, chiefs, prophets, military warlords, federal judges, and state legislators, among others.

As a social phenomenon, law is a state form of **social control.** As such, its object is to manufacture conformity and to suppress what the state defines as deviance. In his classic book *The Behavior of Law,* Donald Black (1976:2) defined law as governmental social control and suggested that there are four basic styles of law, each corresponding to a broader style of social control: penal, compensatory, therapeutic, and conciliatory (p. 46). Each style defines deviant behavior in its own way, with its own logic, methods, and language.

In the penal style of social control, for example, the problem is to establish guilt when an offender has violated a prohibition, and the solution is punishment. Black argues that both the quantity and the style of law in a given society vary inversely with certain factors, such as the power of other forms of social control and the levels of social inequality. When other forms of social control—family ties, religion, and so on—are weak, for example, the power and the extent of law will be relatively strong (D. Black, 1976). Moreover, following the lengthy conflict tradition in the sociology and anthropology of law (see Chapter 8), Black argues that law varies directly with social inequality. That is, the societies with the most law are those with the most social inequality and simple tribes, chiefdoms and societies with developed state institutions (pp. 13–16).

Many criminologists argue that the relationship between social inequality and crime is especially evident in the process of criminalization. We turn now to this important concept.

## LAW AND CRIMINALIZATION

The term **criminalization** refers to the process whereby criminal law is selectively applied to social behavior. This threefold process involves (1) the enactment of legislation that outlaws certain types of behavior; (2) the surveillance and policing of that behavior; and (3), if detected, the punishment of that behavior. The study of criminalization is therefore an indispensable part of the study of crime, and in this book we offer frequent examples of this process.

The nature and contours of the criminalization process in Western industrialized societies are heatedly debated by criminologists. Argument rages over three wide-ranging questions. First, how did the criminalization process contribute to the rise of Western industrialized societies when they first emerged during the seventeenth century? Second, is criminalization today a neutral process, or does it generally serve the interests of the powerful? Third, does criminalization contribute to the maintenance of specific forms of social inequality today?

The answers to these questions fall at or between two extremes. One extreme claims that since its inception on a large scale (during the eighteenth century), the criminalization process has on the whole contributed to the rise of modern society in rational and humane ways. The other extreme suggests that criminalization has operated, in more or less subtle ways, as an instrument to defend the interests of powerful new social classes (for example, the capitalist class) and to undermine the interests of the powerless.

Our general view of criminalization, and thus also of criminal law itself, is that it tends to reflect the interests of the powerful. We will therefore often look at the ways in which the criminalization process tends to maintain unequal social relationships between the powerful and the powerless—especially in the areas of class, gender, race, and age. Sometimes, criminalization is a direct product of power struggles and inevitably reflects the political strengths of specific power groups. At other times, however, it is connected to power struggles only marginally. At still other times, it appears to transcend power struggles altogether.

## 1.3   CRIME AS A SOCIOLOGICAL PROBLEM

Neither the misleading images of crime manufactured by the mass media nor the definition of crime as a legal category can depict the complex social realities of crime. The purpose of criminology is to chip away at stereotypical or value-laden images of crime and then to try to explain what remains.

The academic discipline of criminology has a lengthy intellectual history. As we outline in Chapter 4 here, the origins of criminology can be traced to the rise of the classical (1760–1820) and the positivist (1820–1890) schools of thought, both of which, in certain key respects, flourish today. The term *criminology* derives from the Latin word *crimen*, meaning "judgment," "accusation," or "offense." Though the word *criminologist* appeared in Britain in the 1850s, the term *criminology* itself was first used to define the academic study of crime by the Italian sociologist Raffaele Garofalo in 1885.

Establishing itself as a respectable academic discipline in the United States around 1900, criminology has since become an interdisciplinary field. Although most criminologists today are drawn from sociology, other academic disciplines

**BOX 1.2** THE RISE OF SOCIOLOGY IN
THE UNITED STATES, 1890–1910

Three major factors fostered the intellectual and institutional rise of sociology in the United States

1. The Progressive Era (1890–1910)—a combination of secular and Christian (especially Protestant) reform movements inspired by the professional middle classes (lawyers, doctors, teachers, and so on) and designed to improve the lot of the poor in the wake of the problems associated with the ill effects of industrialization and urbanization.
2. The rapid expansion of the university system in the United States and the institutionalization of the social sciences and of statistics at elite universities (Colum-

bia, Johns Hopkins, Yale, Harvard, and, especially, the University of Chicago) between the mid-1870s and 1915. The first course in sociology was probably offered in 1876 by Sumner; the first book on sociology was Lester Ward's *Dynamic Sociology* (1883). The first book on criminology to use sociology specifically as one of its multifactorial perspectives was probably Kellor's *Experimental Sociology* (1901).
3. The government's recognition, between 1865 and 1905, of new academic associations—including the American Social Science Association, the American Economic Association, the American Historical Association, and the American Sociological Society—for the professional security and advancement of the social science community.

are also well represented, including political science, law, economics, history, anthropology, psychology, biology, and geography.

We now explore four definitions of crime that are favored by sociologists:

1. Crime as a violation of conduct norms.
2. Crime as a social harm and analogous social injury.
3. Crime as a violation of rights.
4. Crime as a form of deviance
5. Crime as a violation of global conduct norms.

## CRIME AS A VIOLATION OF CONDUCT NORMS

In his influential book *Culture Conflict and Crime* (1938), Thorsten Sellin complained that "criminology as traditionally conceived is a bastard science grown out of public preoccupation with a plague" (p. 3). Sellin believed that it is unscientific for criminologists to study simply what the public happens to regard as a plague or as a social problem. Scientists should study objective facts as they occur in their natural states rather than as they are seen by the subjective concerns of the public, the government,

powerful social groups, and the criminal law. As Sellin stated:

> The unqualified acceptance of the legal definitions of the basic units or elements of criminological inquiry violates a fundamental criterion of science. The scientist must have freedom to define his own terms, based on the intrinsic character of his material and designating properties in that material which are assumed to be universal. (p. 23)

Sellin urged that the basic units of criminological research be **conduct norms.** For every person there are normal (right) and abnormal (wrong) forms of conduct—and the norm depends on the social values of the group that formulates it. Such norms are the rules that govern appropriate behavior. Sellin insisted that there are different types of conduct norms, including custom, tradition, ethics, religion, and rules of criminal law. Conduct norms are found wherever social groups are found. They are not created by any one normative group, they are not confined within political boundaries, and they are not necessarily embodied in law. Sellin concluded therefore that a scientific criminology should focus on the violation of all forms of conduct norms and on the study of abnormal conduct in general. Crime is but one form of conduct norm, distinguished from others in that it violates the conduct norms specifically defined by the criminal law.

Sellin's rejection of the legalistic definition of crime and his advice about the proper subject matter of criminology are quite attractive. Clearly, criminologists would be foolish to limit their studies simply to what the criminal law happens to forbid. Imagine, for example, how hard it would be to study trends in the crime of marijuana use in a state where marijuana was constantly criminalized and decriminalized according to the changing whims of legislative and public opinion!

Sellin's advice has yet to exert much influence among criminologists, partly because they would be overwhelmed if they studied violations of all forms of conduct norms. However, Sellin's recommendation moves us to ask a question of much relevance to criminological research: Why are violations of one particular form of conduct regarded as crime and not others?

## CRIME AS SOCIAL HARM AND ANALOGOUS SOCIAL INJURY

A direct outgrowth of this debate about an appropriate definition of crime is Edwin Sutherland's position, voiced in his book *White Collar Crime* (1949). Sutherland was angry that many white-collar offenses were processed as civil violations rather than as crimes. He argued:

> The essential characteristic of crime is that it is behavior which is prohibited by the State as an injury to the State and against which the State may react, at least as a last resort, by punishment. The two abstract criteria generally regarded by legal scholars as necessary elements in a definition of crime are legal description of an act as socially harmful and legal provision of a penalty for the act. (1983:46)

To Sutherland it is unfair that white-collar offenders—for example, those found in civil suits to have violated regulatory laws such as the Sherman Antitrust Act or to have engaged in deceptive advertising—are not stigmatized as criminals. The behavior of white-collar offenders meets the two characteristics of his definition of crime: Their behavior is socially harmful, and they are punished for it (by fines). Because white-collar "offenses" are in fact crimes (however such behavior is defined by the state), they should be studied by criminologists. Although Sutherland's perspective on white-collar offenses has had great influence in criminology (see Chapter 7), his perspective is not opposed to the legalistic definition of crime. Rather, he suggests the use of an expanded definition of crime based on behavior prohibited by either criminal law or regulatory law.

Whereas Sutherland argues that any illegalities that cause **social harm** should be criminalized, others urge that any behavior should be criminalized if it causes social harm or analogous social injury. This extension of Sutherland's position has far-reaching implications. Under this view, crimes might include any violent or untimely death; illness or disease; deprivation of adequate food, clothing, shelter, or medical care; and the reduction or elimination of the opportunity for individuals to participate effectively in the political decision-making processes that affect their lives.

Thus, Ray Michalowski (2007:63; and see Friedrichs, 2007; Wonders, 2007) defines **analogous social injury** as legally permissible acts or social conditions that result in "(1) bodily harms such as violent or untimely death, injury, illness or disease, (2) significant deprivations of food, clothing, shelter, medical care, or education, and/or (3) intentional or structural limitations on political and/or social participation." Such acts and conditions, he insists, are the sociological equivalents of crime and should therefore be studied as such. Michalowski thus rightly condemns as transnational social injury and therefore as wrongful the U.S. government's Operation Gatekeeper—the expanded high-tech militarization of the U.S./Mexico border from 1994 up to today. Directly because of this intentionally violent U.S. policy, several thousand migrants have died from starvation, thirst, and exposure in the desert and from bites from scorpions, snakes, and centipedes. These injuries happened, Michalowski observes about the war against migrants that he personally witnessed along the Arizona/Mexico border, despite the perverse contradiction that Border Patrol agents routinely help migrants in distress, often saving lives in the process (p. 66). Moreover, tens of thousands of would-be migrants have been injured and numerous more have suffered humiliation and dehumanization, and, after a successful border crossing, "illegals" suffer exploitative work conditions, anti-immigrant violence, grossly inadequate health care, and constant fear of arrest and deportation.

Consider some other examples of injurious events that are not generally regarded as crimes by any legal system but that would be crimes if analogous social injury were the criterion of wrongful behavior:

- According to the Centers for Disease Control and Prevention (2008:1), 438,000 deaths are caused each year in the United States by tobacco use.
- Each year in the United States more than 200,000 citizens are injured or killed because of negligence by doctors (Jesilow, Pontell, and Geis, 1993).
- Each year nearly 6,000 workers are killed in job-related accidents in the United (U.S. Department of Labor Statistics, 2008).

Expanded definitions of crime that include both social harm and analogous social injury are

therefore fitting correctives to the biased values underlying the legalistic definition of crime. Of course, these expanded definitions leave themselves open to the objection that what counts as social harm or as analogous social injury is as value-laden a category as criminal law.

### CRIME AS A VIOLATION OF RIGHTS

To some criminologists, crime is any behavior that violates **human rights**. In this view, simply because we are human beings we all have certain natural and inalienable rights. These include the rights to life, liberty, happiness, and so on. Violations of these rights, the argument continues, provide criminology with a more objective unit of analysis than does the legalistic definition of crime.

The case that crime be defined in terms of human rights was first made by Herman Schwendinger and Julia Schwendinger (1975). For the Schwendingers there are two sorts of human rights: those personal rights that are absolutely essential to life (such as the right to good health) and those rights essential to a dignified human existence (freedom of movement, free speech, a good education, employment, the right to unionize, a certain standard of housing, and so on). The Schwendingers also argue that anything that causes a social injury should be considered a crime. Examples of social injury include imperialism, sexism, racism, and poverty. They suggest, too, that a government should be considered criminal if it does nothing to alleviate poverty.

To take this a step further, former President George W. Bush said that the United States has never handed people over to countries that practice torture ("extraordinary rendition"), yet the cases of rendition that have come to light starkly contradict that claim. Persons suspected of terrorist activity have been transferred by the United States to countries where torture is common, such as Syria, Egypt, and Jordan. The exact number of people that the United States has subjected to rendition abroad is not known. CIA Director Michael Hayden suggested in a September 7, 2007, speech before the Council on Foreign Relations that far fewer than 100 people—"midrange two figures"—had been rendered abroad since the attacks of September 11, 2001 (Human Rights Watch, 2008; see also Hamm, 2007). Yet, in respect of torture, Article 17 of the Third Geneva Convention states: "No physical or mental torture, nor any other form of coercion, may be inflicted on prisoners of war to secure from them information of any kind whatever."

Philippe Sands (2008), professor of international law at University College London, has documented in his book on Guantanamo interrogation techniques that approval for abuse tantamount to torture was pushed for by lawyers at the highest levels of George W. Bush's administration (see Figure 1.2). In 2009, classified U.S. intelligence memos were released by the Obama administration—these showed that during their interrogations of detainees at Guantanamo the CIA employed a form of near-drowning torture known as *water-boarding* (see Figure 1.3) and that this was used on two captured Al Qaeda operatives a total of 266 times (Baker and Shane, 2009:A1).

To the importance of human rights in the definition of crime must be added the fact that humans frequently violate the rights of nonhuman animals to a natural and peaceable existence. Since the middle of the nineteenth century, some **animal rights** have been recognized and secured both in state anticruelty laws and in federal legislation. Quite apart from the legal or illegal abuses routinely committed against them in factory farms, rodeos, circuses, zoos, and laboratories, animals are sometimes abused by humans in domestic households or in their wild or natural habitats. Violations of animal rights are also harms that merit attention from criminologists.

The suggestion that violations of rights should be the basis of criminology seems to offer criminology a less subjective definition of crime than the legalistic concept of crime. Moreover, the concept of rights opens up for analysis the obvious fact that legal categories themselves might sometimes be criminal—laws that detain people unjustly, that authorize torture, that forbid freedom of speech, that limit opposition to political parties, and so on.

Let us point out, too, that a potential major difficulty for the human rights approach in

**FIGURE 1.2**   Guantanamo Bay Detention Facility
*Source*: John Riley / Corbis

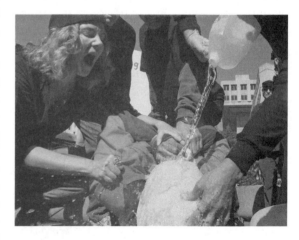

**FIGURE 1.3**   Waterboarding at Guantanamo Bay: In this reconstruction, the subject is strapped down and waterboarded: The technique simulates drowning
*Source*: Mark Wilson / Getty Images

criminology is that, as with the content of criminal law, the content of rights is culturally quite variable. In some societies human rights tend to be defined in individualistic terms—i.e., the rights of individuals to do certain things. In other societies human rights are defined in more social terms: the right to employment and to minimum standards of housing, health, and education. Given these differences of definition, it is hard to agree on which violations of what rights should constitute crime.

Conflict between China and the United States illustrates how allegations of human rights abuses can be used as political weapons and how concepts of rights vary from one society to another: The United States, on the one hand, frequently criticizes China's human rights record as "poor," as evidenced by its persecution of ethnic minorities and dissidents; on the other hand, China was sharply critical of a mess of social ills in the United States, including a high rate of violent crime and the gap between rich and poor and, in its foreign policy, its overseas arms sales, and its "trampling" of the sovereignty of other countries, including Iraq (Wines, 2009).

Moreover, though the last fifty years has seen a tremendous growth in human rights legislation (associated with the United Nations and the European Union, for example), many societies in the world reject the idea that human rights can or should be universal. In parts of Africa, the Middle East, South Asia, and elsewhere, the attempt by outsiders to impose human rights is sometimes branded as just another form of imperialism. "Human rights imperialism!" is thus the angry chant of many members of Islamic countries against aid workers and foreign armies of occupation bent on implanting Western notions of democracy, governance, and the like.

## CRIME AND DEVIANCE

Sociological theories of deviance have greatly influenced criminology. **Deviance** is any social behavior or social characteristic that departs from a society's conventional norms and standards and for which the deviant is sanctioned. Examples of deviant social behavior include witchcraft, bank robbery, picking one's nose in public, mental illness, and stuttering. Examples of deviant social characteristics are extremes of height and weight, aggressiveness, laziness, and beauty.

Several aspects of deviance shed light on the study of crime. Even from the few examples just given, it is clear, first, that enormous variation exists in the practices and social characteristics regarded as deviant. What constitutes deviance varies from era to era and from society to society. What we call homosexuality, for example, was often regarded in classical Greece not as deviance but as a conforming social practice. Moreover, within the same society perceptions of deviance often vary by class, gender, race, and age. Second, deviance is commonplace. Each of us has committed a deviant act at one time or another. Some of us commit many deviant acts in the course of a single day! Third, all deviance is potentially subject to sanction. Deviant behavior can be subject to positive sanctions (such as winning a Nobel prize for promoting peace) or to negative sanctions (e.g., imprisonment for theft). Fourth, the norms and standards violated by deviant acts are quite diverse. They can originate in religion, custom, political belief, etiquette, fashion, and criminal law. Of course, not all deviant acts are criminal acts (and vice versa).

The deviance perspective implies that there is nothing in the nature of any act that makes it as deviant. Rather, deviance is in the eye of the beholder. This implication raises several important sociological questions for the study of crime. Although we explore these questions in greater depth later, some should be mentioned now.

1. Who defines behavior as deviant? How? Why?
2. Why are some deviant practices defined as criminal but not others?

3. What are the consequences for an individual whose deviant behavior is subject to sanction?

## CRIME, GLOBALIZATION, AND GLOBAL CONDUCT NORMS

In several of the chapters that follow, we will discuss the extraordinary influence of globalization on crime, whose general importance to criminology has only recently begun to be understood (e.g., Findlay, 2008; Wotipka and Tsutsui, 2008; Loader and Sparks, 2002). **Globalization** refers to the worldwide process whereby individuals, peoples, economies, and nation-states are becoming increasingly interconnected and interdependent. The driving engine of globalization is the movement of capital, credit, and cash that occurs as multinational corporations search for profit in the ever-expanding and seemingly infinite global economic market.

The rise of globalization has been facilitated by numerous factors—some large, some small, some arising from above, some from below. Perhaps the most important geopolitical factor in the rise of globalization is the end of the Cold War, which was marked around 1990 by both the collapse of communism in eastern Europe and the political, economic, military and cultural dominance of the United States and its allies.

An essential part of globalization's redrafting of political and geographical space is that the world seems much smaller. The sense that a global village is in the making has been greatly encouraged by new methods of communication, including CNN and other live-TV coverage of international events and crises, the Internet, and e-mail. Because of the growth of these mass media, it is much easier to see that what goes on in one part of the world often has ripple effects around the globe.

One obvious consequence of the globalizing process is crime. Crime is an integral part of the new global network because globalization promotes a host of new opportunities for crime. We will discuss the influence of globalization on crime, and vice versa, later in the book in our discussions of comparative criminology; the commerce in illicit drugs; the traffic in women, children, and endangered species; the exploitation of cheap labor; the destruction of the environment; syndicated crime; white-collar crimes, including crimes involving electronic transfers of capital and credit; and political crimes, such as corruption and terrorism.

Consider September 11, 2001, as an example of how globalization affects crime. People of numerous nationalities were killed by the planes that were deliberately crashed into the World Trade Center, the Pentagon, and a field in Pennsylvania. They were killed on U.S. soil by terrorists of several nationalities, who were praised by their supporters as "Jihadists" or "liberation fighters" and who believed that this sort of action was their only effective recourse to U.S. foreign policies toward the Arab world, especially its interventions in the Israeli–Palestinian conflict. Thus, the catastrophic events of September 11 can only be fully understood by understanding events halfway around the world from the United States. So, too, the war on terror is a global phenomenon fraught with difficulties of international cooperation, blurring of national boundaries, and ambiguities in the detection, detention, and prosecution of terrorists. Its battlefields are in the United States, western Europe, the Middle East, Africa, and South Asia and Southeast Asia.

Globalization has also been accompanied by the emergence of **global conduct norms** about certain sorts of serious crime. These are rules of conduct, apparently agreed on by the international community, that allow for prosecution of certain coercive relationships between a state and its citizenry and between one state and another.

While these conduct norms are not yet truly global in their acceptance, with the growth of international criminal law since the end of World War II they are certainly moving in that direction. In 2009 the United Nations had peacemaking missions in 18 countries, involving 113,000 soldiers, police officers, and civilians. Their areas of peacekeeping include such explosive situations as along the Israeli–Syrian border, Haiti, Darfur, Chad, the eastern Congo, and Somalia.

This movement toward greater international criminal justice and enforcement began in 1945–46 with the trial of leading Nazis in the Nuremberg war trials and the creation of the United Nations, and it was consolidated when nearly 100 nations ratified the powers of the International Criminal Court (ICC) as enacted in the Treaty of Rome of 2002. The ICC has jurisdiction over very serious international crimes, such as genocide, crimes against humanity, and war crimes. Those who are responsible for such crimes are now more likely to be held accountable for them. ICC activity can be seen in the following cases.

- The fugitive and former Bosnian Serb President Radovan Karadvic was arrested in July, 2008, by Serbian authorities and then indicted by the ICC and charged on fifteen counts of war crimes, including genocide, committed during the 1992–1995 Bosnian civil war. Among Karadvic's alleged crimes were the 1995 murder, torture, imprisonment, and expulsion of non-Serbs from parts of Bosnia and, in the same year, the murder of 8,000 Muslim men and boys in Srebrenica. The latter act has been described by the U.N. as "scenes from hell written on the darkest pages of human history" (Sebastian, 1999, p.1). It was the worst massacre in Europe since the end of the 1939–1945 war.
- For their roles in the Kosovan war of 1999, five leading Serbs, including politicians and generals, were given lengthy prison sentences by the ICC for their contributions to genocide, including deportation, forcible transfer of ethnic populations, murder, and persecution (Simons, 2009).
- In January, 2009, Thomas Lubanga was arrested and brought before the ICC on six charges of war crimes he committed in the Democratic Republic of Congo (DRC). Specifically, Lubanga was charged with recruiting, training, and using male and female child soldiers in the DRC's civil war in 2001–2003 (Associated Press).
- An arrest warrant was issued in February, 2009, by judges at the International Criminal Court for President Zomar Hassan al-Bashir, then the sitting head of state of Sudan. The charges against him are likely to include war crimes, genocide and crimes against humanity (Simons and MacFarquhar, 2009).
- In 2009 a hybrid trial of Cambodian and foreign judges and prosecutors supported by the United Nations put on trial a senior Khmer Rouge cadre. Kaing Guek Eav, 66, alias "Duch," was accused of war crimes committed in the years between 1975 and 1979 while he was commandant of the Tuol Sleng prison and torture house in Phnom Penh and sent at least 14,000 Cambodians to die in the notorious killing fields. Duch has admitted his guilt and asked to be forgiven. It is unclear how influential the U.N. will be in this judicial format and whether the court will be independent of the current Cambodian government (Mydans, 2009).

Violations of global conduct norms will undoubtedly be embraced by criminology, and they will be written into its agenda. Perhaps the development of global conduct norms will provide a counterweight to the rise of ethnic politics and to atrocities committed in the name of racial, ethnic, and religious purity. But in a world where political borders and territorial integrity become ever more blurred and where international organizations are still in such a rudimentary stage, it is unclear how global and normal global conduct norms will become. Will they be stamped "Made in the U.S.A."? Will they be genuinely democratic?

### ASSESSMENT

This book views crime as a **sociological problem**. To focus on crime as a sociological problem is to explain how patterns of crime arise from the interplay of political, economic, social, and cultural forces. We do not therefore look at those explanations of crime that reduce its causes to the level of the individual. In pure form, examples of such reductionism are found, for example, in biological explanations of crime that emphasize the links between criminality and the physical constitution of the individual, as well as in psychological explanations that focus on the links between crime and such factors as defective character and loose morals.

We hold to no fixed or dogmatic position concerning the definition of crime. Sometimes we agree with the way in which criminal law defines crime; at other times we simply question its adequacy. Occasionally we prefer and use other definitions of crime. For example, because we believe that animals other than humans also have the right to be considered "beings" or "persons," we consider animal abuse to be among the crimes of interpersonal violence (Chapter 12). In Sections 12.1–12.2 we also point out that many women are victimized every year by the act of forcible rape, as it is defined by criminal law; but we also acknowledge that the traditional criminal law definition of rape—sexual intercourse obtained through the threat or actual use of physical violence—ignores other acts that could be defined as rape, such as forms of nonphysical sexual coercion (for example, the male who informs his economically dependent mate: "If you don't put out, I'll leave you!").

In Section 13.2 we go considerably beyond the legalistic definition of crime (including both criminal and regulatory law), arguing that *corporate crime* is any illegal or socially injurious act of intent or indifference that occurs for the purpose of furthering corporate goals and that physically or economically abuses individuals in the United States or abroad. Finally, our definition of *political crime* (see Chapter 14) is somewhat broader than the legalistic definition, in that it includes not only crimes committed against the state but also crimes committed by the state. In the latter we include both domestic political crimes (unlawful or unethical acts committed by state officials and state agencies inside the United States) and international political crimes (violations of domestic and international law by state officials and agencies outside the United States).

### REVIEW

This chapter introduced the different images of crime found in the discourses of social problem movements, the culture of fear, the mass media, and sociology. The major task of the chapter was to introduce key sociological concepts of criminology.

## IMAGES OF CRIME

1. Crime has become one of the leading social problems in the United States. But there is no objective set of social conditions whose perceived harmful effects necessarily make them social problems. What is regarded as a social problem varies over time and across cultures. What is defined as a social problem depends on numerous factors, including the activities of moral entrepreneurs.
2. There is a widespread culture of fear in the United States, and mass media undoubtedly contribute to fear of crime.
3. Mass media have become the most influential mechanisms for organizing public sentiment so that a certain social condition is perceived as a social problem.
4. Mass media routinely provide distorted information about the amount of crime, the most common types of crime, and who typically commits crimes.

## CRIME, CRIMINAL LAW, AND CRIMINALIZATION

1. The term *criminalization* refers to the process whereby criminal law is selectively applied to social behavior. The sociological study of criminal law is therefore an integral part of criminology. Specifically, the criminalization process involves the enactment of legislation that outlaws certain types of behavior. It also provides for the surveillance, policing, and, if detected, punishment of that behavior.
2. Criminal law distinguishes between crimes *mala in se* and *mala prohibita* and between felonies and misdemeanors. To constitute a crime, behavior must be prohibited by law, must be voluntary, and must coincide with a defendant's mental state. An act or omission is not a crime if a defendant is justified in doing (or not doing) it or if the person lacks the criminal responsibility required by *mens rea*.
3. Not all societies have had law. Law originated with the emergence of social inequality and accompanied the transition from stateless to state societies. The distinguishing features of law are its coercive nature, its reliance on a professional staff, and its use as a state form of social control.
4. In this book, the general view of the criminalization process, and thus also of criminal law, is that it tends to reflect the interests of the relatively powerful (in terms of class, gender, race, and age).

## CRIME AS A SOCIOLOGICAL PROBLEM

1. This book views crime as a sociological problem. It surveys the various sociological approaches to crime found in the discipline of criminology. To focus on crime as a sociological problem is to explain how patterns of crime arise from the interplay of political, economic, social, and cultural forces in society.
2. The question "What is crime?" is difficult to answer because there is little agreement about the defining sociological characteristics of crime. Criminologists use a variety of sociological definitions of crime, including crime as a violation of conduct norms,

crime as a social harm, crime as a violation of rights (both human and animal), crime as a form of deviance, and crime as a violation of global conduct norms.

## QUESTIONS FOR CLASS DISCUSSION

1. Consider the facts in the following short story about cannibalism among a group of cave (speluncean) explorers caught in a life-threatening situation in the Commonwealth of "Newgarth." The story is adapted from a fictitious law case created by legal philosopher Lon Fuller (1949, excerpted in Schur, 1968:19–20). Although "The Case of the Speluncean Explorers" is fictitious, it is probably based on an actual case of cannibalism at sea in 1884 and on the bizarre trial that resulted from it in England.

### THE CASE OF THE SPELUNCEAN EXPLORERS

Five members of an amateur cave-exploring society were trapped inside a deep and isolated cave following a landslide. After some time, through the efforts of relatives and the cave-exploring society, rescuers located the cave only to encounter repeated obstacles to removing the trapped men. At great monetary expense and the cost of ten rescuers' lives (in a subsequent landslide), the rescue operation finally succeeded thirty-two days after the men entered the cave. On the twentieth day, communication between the rescuers and the trapped explorers had been established, when it was discovered that the latter had with them in the cave a radio transmitter-receiver. At that time, the trapped men asked for medical advice as to whether they could live without food (there was none in the cave) for the time engineers had determined would be required to rescue them. A physicians' committee at the rescue site stated that they could not. When the trapped men later inquired if they could survive by consuming the flesh of one of their number, the reply (reluctant) was in the affirmative. But the explorers could get no guidance at all (from the physicians or from any clergyman or judge) when they went on to ask about the advisability of casting lots to determine who should be killed and eaten.

When the men were finally released, the rescuers learned that on the twenty-third day one of them, Whetmore, had been killed and eaten by the other four. Although originally it had been Whetmore's idea (at first resisted by his companions) that such an act might be necessary for survival and also that a casting of lots would be the fairest means of selection, just before the dice were cast, Whetmore changed his mind. His companions disallowed this sudden switch, however, and cast the dice for him, after obtaining his agreement that this procedure was fair; he lost and was put to death and eaten by the others.

After they had recuperated, the four survivors were charged with Whetmore's murder.

Having read the facts in "The Case of the Speluncean Explorers," you should also know that Newgarth law commands, "Whoever shall willfully take the life of another shall be punished by death." In this case the defendants were charged with the crime of murder, convicted, and sentenced to death.

Assume that the defendants appealed the verdict and the sentence in "The Case of the Speluncean Explorers" and that you are a member of the appeals court. How would you decide the appeal? Are the defendants guilty of murder? What defense is available to them, if any? If their conviction in the lower court is upheld, would you recommend executive clemency (a pardon)?

2. In the late 1920s, lawyer Jerome Michael and philosopher Mortimer Adler were commissioned by Columbia University Law School and by the Bureau of Social Hygiene in New York City to write a report on the desirability of establishing an institute of criminology in the United States. In their lengthy final report, Michael and Adler scrutinized the scientific status of existing criminology and concluded that "the work of criminologists has not resulted in scientific knowledge of the phenomena of crime" (1971:54). Do you agree with this claim?

3. According to the Centers for Disease Control and Prevention (2008:1), 438,000 deaths are caused each year in the United States by tobacco use. According to the World Health Organization, rising tobacco use in developing countries, such as China and Russia, will contribute greatly to a doubling of global cancer deaths by 2030 (*Associated Press*, December 10, 2008). Do you think tobacco manufacturers and distributors should be held legally liable for these deaths? Should relatives of the deceased be allowed to sue them for damages? Should cigarette producers be prosecuted for murder or manslaughter?

4. Summarizing many recent studies, criminologist Ray Surette (2007:61) says that victims in the news tend to be portrayed as female, very young or old, or of high status like celebrities. Female victims, in particular, tend to be portrayed as helpless fodder: There are fewer female villains, more female assistant heroes, and many more female victims. How would you interpret Surette's findings?

5. In the preface to a 2008 report by Physicians for Human Rights on the "medical evidence of torture by the United States," former Abu Ghraib investigator and retired Army Major General Antonio Taguba writes that President George W. Bush "authorized a systematic regime of torture" that has stained "our national honor" (cited at http://brokenlives.info/). The report found that medical examinations of eleven former detainees revealed "scars and other injuries consistent with their accounts of beatings, electric shocks, shackling and, in at least one case, sodomy." Taguba accused the Bush administration of committing war crimes. Should the administration be so charged and brought before the International Criminal Court?

6. Three criminologists have termed the U.S. war in Iraq "the supreme international crime" (Kramer, Michalowski, and Rothe, 2005). Do you agree with their assessment?

## FOR FURTHER STUDY

### READINGS

Barak, Greg. 2007. Doing Newsmaking Criminology from Within the Academy. *Theoretical Criminology* 11 (2): 191–207.

Rafter, Nicole. 2000. *Shots in the Mirror: Crime Films and Society.* New York: Oxford University Press.

Roversi, Antonio. 2008. *Hate on the Net: Extremist Sites, Neo-Fascism On-Line, Electronic Jihad.* Williston, VT: Ashgate.

Simon, Jonathan. 2007. *Governing Through Crime: How the War on Crime Transformed American Democracy and Created a Culture of Fear.* New York: Oxford University Press.

Surette, Ray. 2007. *Media, Crime, and Criminal Justice: Images, Realities, and Policies.* Belmont, CA: Thomson Wadsworth.

### WEBSITES

1. <http://www.journalism.org/>: This is the website of the Pew Research Center's Project for Excellence in Journalism, whose goal is to raise journalists' standards of objectivity. Reports numerous analyses of news content for national and local TV, biases, and news profitability.

2. <http://www.law.cornell.edu/states/listing.html>: This useful site provides links to each state's laws, including criminal codes and procedures and rules of evidence.

3. <http://www.amnesty.org>: This site for Amnesty International includes a general statement about the organization: its history, mission, and current activities. You may want to click on some of Amnesty's campaigns, including:
   - Stop violence against women.
   - Control arms.
   - Abolish the death penalty.
   - Counter terror with justice.

4. <http://www.iccnow.org>: This is the website of the Coalition for the International Criminal Court, a network of over 2,000 nongovernmental organizations advocating for a fair, effective, and independent International Criminal Court (ICC).

5. <http://www.hg.org/practiceareas.html>: This website hosts a comprehensive guide to local and international laws and regulations organized into seventy areas, including animals/wildlife, food and drugs, and white-collar crime. The directory provides links to treaties, organizations, and regulatory agencies related to each area and also contains links to law resources for 142 countries.

# THE MEASUREMENT OF CRIME

**2.1 Caution: Data Do Not Speak for Themselves!**

**2.2 Official Crime Data**
- Police-Based Data: Uniform Crime Reports (UCR)
- Police-Based Data: National Incident-Based Reporting System (NIBRS)
- Evaluation of the UCR
- Victimization Data: National Crime Victimization Surveys (NCVS)
- Evaluation of the NCVS
- Federal Data on White-Collar Crime, Corporate Crime, and Internet Crime

**2.3 Unofficial Crime Data**
- Self-Report Data
- Life-Course Data
- Life-History Data
- Criminal Biographies
- Observation Research and Participant Observation Research
- Comparative and Historical Research

**PREVIEW**

Chapter 2 introduces:
- The major sources of official crime data.
- The major sources of unofficial crime data.
- The idea that crime data do not have a factual, objective existence independent of concepts about crime.

**KEY TERMS**

comparative criminology
crime rate
criminal biographies
historical data
life-course data
life-history studies

methodology
official crime data
participant observation
positivist criminology
self-reports
victimization surveys

Chapter 2 outlines the major sources of crime data; precisely what such data tell us about specific types of crime is outlined in later chapters. Criminologists often distinguish between official crime data and unofficial crime data. **Official crime data** are those collected by the government and by government agencies, such as the Federal Bureau of Investigation (FBI) and the Department of Justice. **Unofficial crime data** are the nongovernmental data usually collected by private or independent agencies and researchers. Thus, the sources and types of unofficial crime data are quite varied. In distinguishing between official and unofficial sources of crime data, we do not imply that one data source is in principle better than another—although in practice this is often the case. Rather, official and unofficial crime data typically construct crime differently.

The majority of crime data are presented in the form of statistics. The term *statistics* derives from the mid-seventeenth-century English term *state-istics*, which referred to state data about births, marriages, and deaths. Because contemporary statistical data are so extensively used for social purposes, we tend to be lulled into thinking that they represent objective facts. However, neither statistics nor data nor facts can ever be entirely free of the biases inherent in how they are constructed. The implications of this crucial point will soon become clear.

## 2.1 CAUTION: DATA DO NOT SPEAK FOR THEMSELVES!

In the following pages we describe the major sources of data for studying crime today. But before we describe these types of data we must discuss how they are influenced by concepts and theories.

In the early nineteenth century, when official crime data were first systematically recorded, positivist criminologists such as Adolphe Quetelet believed that crime could be observed directly by using the procedures of the natural sciences (see Section 4.2). In this view, crime—like rocks, plants, and insects—exists in a natural state, independent of the concepts and the theories of the criminologist. **Positivist criminology** is based on the idea that the collection of data about human beings follows the same scientific procedures as the collection of data in the natural sciences. This view, however, greatly distorts the process of scientific investigation. Why this is so can be understood by an analogy with astronomy.

Suppose that two astronomers are examining the surface of the moon through a telescope. Suppose also that one of the astronomers is peering into her telescope in the year 1500 (pre-Copernicus) and the other in the year 1900 (post-Copernicus). Would the two astronomers see the same thing? It can be argued that both astronomers would see the same image projected by the moon: a roundish, bright, yellowish object in the sky.

But beyond the optico-chemical level of sensory perception, would our two astronomers really "see" the same image? The answer is probably "no." The astronomers would see lunar data in terms of (1) their respective concepts of "the moon," of "optics," and so on, and (2) their theories of planetary motion. The early-sixteenth-century astronomer would see a roundish, bright, yellowish object that moves in orbit around the Earth. The twentieth-century astronomer, relying on modern theories of astronomy, would see a roundish, bright, yellowish object that not only moves in orbit around the Earth but has a certain alignment with the Earth and the sun. The astronomers' perceptions of lunar images, in other words, would be structured by their respective astronomical concepts and theories.

This example demonstrates that data are not objective facts that exist independent of the concepts and theories of those who observe them. Data do not speak for themselves!

Let us apply this heavenly insight to the world of crime. When studying crime, it would be wrong to believe that we can simply observe, measure, and collect the facts and nothing but the facts about crime. We do not—indeed cannot—collect facts about crime through direct observation. What constitutes a fact about crime depends on our concepts and theories of crime. Crime data, like all other data, are structured by concepts and theories. What count as crime data are therefore very much open to debate.

In Section 1.2 we noted that the recognition of certain behavioral data (such as killing someone) as crime depends on whichever concept of crime is accepted as authoritative. According to the legalistic concept of crime, for example, murder is limited to those killings that are contrary to rules of criminal law. Thus, if a police officer kills someone, the killing is not murder, according to criminal law, if it is reasonable under the circumstances and if it occurs in the lawful execution of police duties. Another concept of crime, such as human rights (a concept that is itself quite culturally variable), yields very different crime data. Thus, to some proponents of human rights, murder might also include negligent surgery, workers' deaths caused by an employer's neglect of safety conditions, smoking-related deaths resulting from the commercial activities of tobacco companies, and the like.

## 2.2 OFFICIAL CRIME DATA

The publication of national crime statistics was pioneered in France in 1827 (see Section 4.2). A century later, in 1927, a committee on Uniform Crime Records was set up in the United States. In 1930, after some bureaucratic wrangling between the FBI and the Bureau of the Census, 400 cities representing 20 million inhabitants in 43 states began to participate in the FBI's Uniform Crime Reports (or UCR) program.

The UCR, which has been published under congressional mandate each year since 1930, is popularly regarded as the most reliable set of crime data in the United States. Our task now is to examine what the UCR measures and then to assess its reliability.

### POLICE-BASED DATA: UNIFORM CRIME REPORTS (UCR)

The UCR is compiled each year in Washington, D.C., by FBI statisticians. In 2007 the FBI received data from crime reports submitted voluntarily by nearly 17,000 city, county, state, tribal, and federal law-enforcement agencies. These agencies had jurisdiction over more than 285 million U.S. inhabitants, or 94.6 percent of the total population. The coverage is 95.7 percent in large cities and 90 percent in rural areas. (FBI, 2008).

The meaning of much UCR data hinges on a distinction drawn by the FBI between Part I and Part II crimes. The UCR provides diverse statistical information about eight Part I crimes, which the FBI regards as the most serious: murder and nonnegligent manslaughter, forcible rape, robbery, aggravated assault, burglary, larceny-theft, motor vehicle theft, and arson (see Figure 2.1 for definitions of these offenses). It provides much less information about the 21 Part II crimes, which include simple assault; forgery and counterfeiting; fraud; embezzlement; buying, receiving, and possessing stolen property; carrying and possessing weapons; prostitution and commercialized vice; sex offenses (except forcible rape and prostitution); drug abuse violations; gambling; offenses against family and children; driving under the influence; liquor law offenses; drunkenness; disorderly conduct; vagrancy; all other offenses (except traffic); suspicion; curfew and loitering law violations; and runaway persons under age 18. The UCR also presents data on hate crimes, including the number of hate crime offenses and their motivation.

In addition to the FBI's view that Part I crimes are more serious than Part II crimes (a subject to

- **Murder and Nonnegligent Manslaughter:** The willful (nonnegligent) killing of one human being by another.
- **Forcible Rape:** The carnal knowledge of a female forcibly and against her will. (Attempts are included, but statutory rape [without force] and other sex offenses are not.)
- **Robbery:** The taking of or attempting to take anything of value from the care, custody, or control of a person or persons by force or by threat of force or violence and/or by putting the victim in fear.
- **Aggravated Assault:** The unlawful attack by one person upon another for the purpose of inflicting severe or aggravated bodily injury. (This type of assault is usually accompanied by the use of a weapon, and it includes attempts.)
- **Burglary:** The unlawful entry of a structure to commit a felony or theft. (Three subdivisions include forcible entry, unlawful entry where no force is used, and attempted forcible entry.)
- **Larceny-theft:** The unlawful taking, carrying, leading, or riding away of property from the possession or constructive possession of another. (Included are shoplifting, pocket-picking, purse-snatching, thefts from motor vehicles, thefts or motor vehicle parts and accessories, bicycle thefts, and so forth, in which no force. violence, or fraud occurs.)
- **Motor Vehicle Theft:** The theft or attempted theft of a motor vehicle. (Included are the stealing of automobiles, trucks, buses, motorcycles, motor scooters, and snowmobiles.)
- **Arson:** Any willful burning or malicious burning or attempt to burn, with or without intent to defraud, a dwelling house, public building, motor vehicle or aircraft, personal property of another....(Excluded are fires of suspicious or unknown origin.)

**FIGURE 2.1** Uniform Crime Reports—Part I Crime Definitions
*Source*: Federal Bureau of Investigation, 2008, adapted from pp. 15–64.

which we return in a moment), UCR crime data are distinguished by their source. Data about Part I crimes derive from information that comes to the attention of police departments provided by victims of crime and other members of the public. Part II crime data are limited to cases involving actual police arrests.

The UCR focuses primarily on trends of the Part I crimes. In this regard the UCR tabulates:

1. The number of offenses.
2. The offense rate per 100,000 population.
3. The percentage change from the previous year.
4. The offense rate by region (for example, South, North, Northeast, Midwest).
5. The nature of the offense (age, gender, and race of offenders and victims).
6. The arrest (or clearance) rates for the offense.

The UCR displays the following data: relative frequency of Part I crimes; changes in the number and in the rate of violent crime, including

murder (see Figure 2.2); the number and the rate of property crime (see Figure 2.3); and the respective crime rates of the four regions—Northeast,

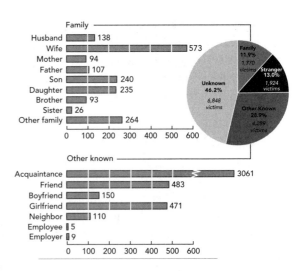

**FIGURE 2.2** Murder (percent distribution), by Relationship of Victim to Offender, 2007
*Source*: FBI. 2008. Uniform Crime Reports, 2007. Available at: http://www.fbi.gov/ucr/cius2007/offenses/expanded_information/homicide.html.

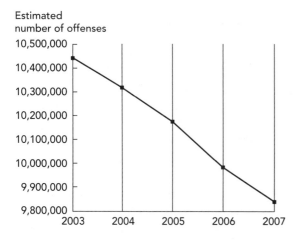

Estimated
number of offenses

**FIGURE 2.3**  Property Crime Trend, 2003–2007
*Source*: FBI. 2008. Uniform Crime Reports, 2007. Available
at: http://www.fbi.gov/ucr/cius2007/about/table_title.html.

Midwest, South, and West—and of individual states and of cities and towns of varying size. In addition, the UCR provides data about arrest trends by state, city, and suburban and rural areas, as well as about police employment by region, state, cities, suburban and rural counties, and universities and colleges.

Before examining the actual reliability of the crime data provided by the UCR, we emphasize how important the UCR program is in certain quarters as a source of crime data. In the words of the FBI itself:

It is important for users of UCR data to remember that the FBI's primary objective is to generate a reliable set of crime statistics for use in law enforcement administration, operation, and management. The FBI does not provide a ranking of agencies but merely alphabetical tabulations of states, metropolitan statistical areas, cities with over 10,000 inhabitants, suburban and rural counties, and colleges and universities. Law enforcement officials use these data for their designed purposes. Additionally, the American public relies on these data for information on the fluctuations

in the level of crime from year to year, and criminologists, sociologists, legislators, city planners, the media, and other students of criminal justice use them for a variety of research and planning purposes. Since crime is a sociological phenomenon influenced by a variety of factors, the FBI discourages data users from ranking agencies and using the data as a measurement of law enforcement effectiveness. (FBI, 2009)

## POLICE-BASED DATA: NATIONAL INCIDENT-BASED REPORTING SYSTEM (NIBRS)

Working with state and local law enforcement agencies, the FBI has developed a new supplementary reporting system, which it terms the National Incident-Based Reporting System (NIBRS); it is a modified and far more detailed version of the traditional UCR. Not quite fully operational, NIBRS is a computerized system whereby local agencies report data to the national UCR program on each single incident and arrest within twenty-two offense categories comprising forty-six crimes (the eight index offenses and thirty-six other crimes). These are known as Group A offenses (see Table 2.1). The NIBRS collects details about the time, date, place, and circumstances of the crime; information about offenders' and victims' age, gender, race, and relationship to each other; the presence of guns or drugs; details of property loss; and whether hate/bias motivation was involved.

## EVALUATION OF THE UCR

Criminologists often debate the question of how well the UCR measures the crime rate. Answers to this question tend to be twofold. First, some critics claim that although the UCR does commendable job of measuring the crime rate, it could do even better with more sophisticated or more sensitive methodological techniques Second, other critics claim that because

**TABLE 2.1 NIBRS: GROUP A OFFENSE CATEGORIES**

| | |
|---|---|
| Arson | Homicide offenses |
| Assault offenses | Kidnapping/abduction |
| Bribery | Larceny/theft offenses |
| Burglary/breaking and entering | Motor vehicle theft |
| Counterfeiting/forgery | Pornography/obscene material |
| Destruction/damage/ vandalism of property | Prostitution offenses |
| Drug offenses | Robbery |
| Embezzlement | Sex offenses, forcible |
| Extortion/blackmail | Sex offenses, nonforcible |
| Fraud offenses | Stolen property offenses |
| Gambling offenses | Weapon law violation |

Source: FBI. 2008. Uniform Crime Reports, 2007. http://www.fbi.gov/hq/cjisd/nibrsfaq.

of various inherent conceptual biases, the UCR does not and cannot measure "the crime rate" very accurately.

Here are some of the most important criticisms of the UCR.

1.  **The dark figure of crime.** An unknown, but probably massive, amount of crime goes unreported to the police and therefore never shows up in the UCR. This unknown component is often termed *the dark figure* of crime. Methodologically, as we shall see, the size of the dark figure of crime can to a certain extent be estimated with the use of victimization surveys and self-report studies.

2.  **Police participation in the UCR is voluntary.** Because participation in the UCR program is voluntary, not all police departments send crime reports to the FBI. Consequently, the FBI attempts to estimate crime rates in such jurisdictions. It is, of course, difficult to assess the accuracy of their estimates.

3.  **No federal crimes in the UCR.** The UCR does not include federal crimes (such as blackmail), an omission that tends to underestimate the crime rate.

4.  **The hierarchy rule.** In any single criminal event, only the most serious crime reported to the police is included in the UCR. This is known as the *hierarchy rule*. For example, if an armed man breaks into a person's home (burglary or criminal trespass), forces a woman inside to engage in sexual intercourse with him (rape), kills her (murder), and escapes with some of her belongings (robbery), only the murder is reflected in the UCR. Arguably, this practice understates the volume of crime.

5.  **Criminal law rules.** The UCR records only legally defined categories of crime (see Section 1.2). It must be stressed that UCR categories are not scientific or objective categories—they reflect the biases enshrined in the rules of criminal law and in the values of legislatures and the judicial system. Given one's personal viewpoints, UCR's biases may be seen as good, bad, or neutral, but biases they undoubtedly are. For example, there is little or no space for crimes committed by the government, against the environment, or against animals.

6.  **Measurements of seriousness.** The composition of Part I crimes gives a distorted image of the seriousness of crime. Recall that the Part I crimes include murder, rape, robbery, aggravated assault, burglary, larceny, motor vehicle theft, and arson. The FBI apparently counts these as Part I crimes because they occur in large numbers and because the public regards them as the most serious crimes. But these two reasons are rather flimsy. There

is considerable agreement that murder, rape, robbery, aggravated assault, and arson are very serious crimes and that they should be recorded as such. But are all burglaries, larcenies, and motor vehicle thefts sufficiently serious to warrant inclusion in Part I? How is it that the theft of a bicycle (a larceny) is recorded as a serious crime but child abuse is not? Moreover, with the exception of larceny, the crimes recorded in the greatest numbers (for instance, fraud, drug abuse violations, driving under the influence) are actually Part II crimes.

The FBI is also often accused of omitting a variety of serious crimes from Part I. With the exception of arson, all Part I crimes are typically committed by members of relatively powerless sections of society. White-collar, corporate, and political crimes—which the public increasingly views as serious crimes—committed by members of the more powerful sections of society are given relatively little attention by the FBI. Why the FBI omits these latter crimes from the index is a matter of broad speculation, including: the FBI recognizes the fact that crimes typically or exclusively committed by the powerful are difficult to detect, are often covered up, and are seldom reported to the police; the FBI is insensitive to the plight of the powerless; and the FBI is politically biased in favor of the powerful.

7. **UCR: Measuring crime or police activity?** Ultimately, it is next to impossible to know whether the UCR actually measures criminal behavior (whether defined in terms of legal categories or human rights) or, instead, the bureaucratic activities of official agencies such as the police and the FBI.

Countless factors influence how official crime data are socially constructed. Consider for a moment the situation of the police. Quite apart from a change in actual criminal behavior, official crime statistics can be altered by changes in police reporting procedures; improved or faster technological assistance, changes in relations between the police and the citizenry, crusades against particular crimes, an increase in the ratio of police officers to population, and even by simple manipulation of crime reports. On this last point, we must stress that all police agencies are faced with two contradictory pressures in the representation of their activities to the FBI, to the media, and to the public:

1. It is in the best interests of police departments to ensure that officially recorded crime rates are low, thereby suggesting that the police are successfully doing their job of fighting crime.
2. It is in the best interests of police departments to ensure that officially recorded crime rates are high, thereby allowing the police to ask for larger budgets and more personnel.

All police departments operate at some point at or between these two pressures. The precise situation of any given police department depends on many factors, including levels of criminal activity; the honesty of police chiefs; local and national politics; media crusades, and pressure from the public.

Some time ago, sociologists John Kitsuse and Aaron Cicourel (1963) suggested that criminologists should be concerned chiefly with how crime rates are constructed by official agencies. Rather than searching for some mythical crime rate independent of how it is socially constructed, criminologists should examine the bureaucratic practices of agencies that record crime. The starting point of criminology, their argument implies, is understanding the behavior of those who define, classify, and record certain behavior as crime.

If we apply this method to the process by which criminal behavior enters the UCR, we find that for a crime report to enter the UCR, at least five things must happen:

1. Someone must perceive an event or behavior as a crime.
2. The crime must somehow come to the attention of the police, either through police observation, which is rare, or through a report from a victim, a confession, or detective work.
3. The police must agree that a crime has occurred.
4. The police must code the crime on the proper UCR form and submit it to the FBI.
5. The FBI must include the crime in the UCR.

Each of these events is subject to enormous social interpretation and negotiation. The facts in these events, in other words, do not speak for themselves; each event is socially constructed.

An excellent example of how crime rates may reflect official activity more than they reflect criminal behavior is provided by Philip Jenkins' controversial research on serial murder (1988, 1994; and see Wadsworth and Roberts, 2008). Jenkins was initially puzzled by the substantial and well-publicized increase in the serial murder rate that apparently occurred between 1983 and 1985. According to Jenkins, it was the mass media that first presented the volume of serial murders in the United States as an "epidemic" unknown in other societies. This epidemic was often tied to the growth of the pornography industry, whose sexually explicit materials allegedly tended to arouse the aggressive nature of certain individuals who had been abused as children. Harrowing TV interviews with convicted serial killers— Ted Bundy, Edmund Kemper, and Henry Lee Lucas—added fuel to media fires. Jenkins quoted

a Justice Department claim that as many as 4,000 Americans a year, half of them under the age of 18, are murdered by serial killers.

Jenkins suggests that although serial murder may well represent a growing and heinous menace to society, the mass media and Justice Department officials grossly inflated their estimates of the annual total of serial murders. According to Jenkins' analysis, serial killers accounted for no more than 350–400 murders each year during the 1980s.

How, then, is it possible to distort and exaggerate UCR homicide data? What motives prompt such distortions? Jenkins describes the bureaucratic process that makes homicide data especially susceptible to manipulation. Whenever a murder is detected, the police department of jurisdiction is required to complete a lengthy UCR report and submit it to the FBI. But the police must also

submit a supplementary homicide report, addressing topics like characteristics of the victim and offender; weapon; relationship of victim to offender; circumstances surrounding death; and so on. "Offenders" can be single, multiple, or unknown. At this early stage, the police might well know neither the offender, a motive, nor the exact circumstances of the death. All these would thus be recorded as unknown. Weeks or months later, the situation might well change, and the correct procedure would be for the department to submit a new report to amend the first. Here, though, there is enormous room for cutting corners. The Justice Department has already been notified of the death, and whether a further form is submitted depends on many factors. A conscientious officer in a professionally oriented department with an efficient recording system probably would notify the reporting center that the murder was no longer unsolved or lacking known circumstances, especially in an area where murder was a rare crime. Other officers in other departments might well feel that they have more important things to do than to submit a revised version of a form they have already completed. This would in fact represent a third recension on a single case.

The chance of follow-up information being supplied will depend on a number of factors: the frequency of murder in the community; the importance accorded to record-keeping by a particular chief or supervisor; the organizational structure of the department; and the professional standards of the department. The vast majority of departments are likely to record the fact of a murder being committed, but only some will provide the result of any subsequent investigation. (Jenkins, 1994:61–62)

The result of this bureaucratic process is that for many cases of homicide, even though an offender and a motive were subsequently discovered, the FBI will have only a "motiveless/offender unknown" entry in its records. In 1966 the UCR recorded 11,000 murders in the United States; of these, 644 (5.9 percent) were "motiveless." In 1982 there were 23,000 murders, with 4,118 (17.8 percent) "motiveless." By 1984 the motiveless category had risen to 22 percent. As Jenkins described it, there was an alarming tendency on the part of the media and the Department of Justice to assume that all or most motiveless murders were the work of serial killers.

Why would the Justice Department continue with this fabrication? Jenkins opposes the idea of a conspiracy, with the Justice Department seen as responsible for creating the illusion of an epidemic of serial murders. Nevertheless, he claims, the serial murder "epidemic" served certain organizational goals of the Justice Department. Although some FBI officials placed the number of serial murders at several hundred rather than several thousand, the latter figure was never formally contradicted by the FBI. Why not? According to Jenkins (1994:68), the serial murder "epidemic" was used as a justification for a new Violent Criminal Apprehension Program

(VICAP) at a new proposed National Center for the Analysis of Violent Crime at the FBI Academy in Quantico, Virginia.

Jenkins' account of this transformation of "unsolved" homicide data into data about serial murders is one specific example of the way in which crime data are socially constructed. Of equal interest, and perhaps even more compelling, are the ways in which crime data are routinely constructed by the public and the police.

In this respect, consider the findings of Donald Black's (1970) classic study of members of the public who report crimes to the police. Whether or not police agree that a crime has occurred and, if so, whether they formally record it as a crime are outcomes preceded by complicated processes of social interpretation and negotiation. Black investigated these processes in his study of routine police work in predominantly working-class residential areas of Boston, Chicago, and Washington, D.C. He noted that after a victim or an observer of a crime (a complainant) has reported the crime to the police, five conditions influence whether a crime is actually accepted and formally recorded as a crime by the police:

1. **The legal seriousness of the crime.** The police are more likely to write a crime report if the crime is a felony rather than a misdemeanor. In Black's study, 72 percent of felonies but only 53 percent of misdemeanors were written up as reports. "It remains noteworthy," wrote Black, "that the police officially disregard one-fourth of the felonies they handle in encounters with complainants" (p. 738).

2. **The complainant's preferences.** When called to the scene of a crime the police are extremely dependent on a complainant's definition of the situation. Does the complainant want the police to take official action? Does the complainant want

the matter settled informally and outside official channels? Is the complainant indifferent as to further action? Black found that the police almost always agree with a complainant's preference for informal action. In situations where a complainant wished official police action, the police complied in 84 percent of felony situations and 64 percent of misdemeanor situations.

3. **The relational distance.** How seriously the police regard a complainant depends partly on the relational distance between the victim and the alleged offender. The social relationship between a crime victim and an offender can be of three types: (1) fellow family members; (2) friends, neighbors, or acquaintances; and (3) strangers. Black found that when a complainant expresses a preference for official action, the police are least likely to comply in type 1, more likely in type 2, and most likely in type 3. Black also found that relational distance is often more important than the legal seriousness of the crime: "The police are more likely to give official recognition to a misdemeanor involving strangers…than to a felony involving friends, neighbors, or acquaintances" (p. 740).

4. **The complainant's deference.** Not surprisingly, Black found that the more deference or respect shown police by a complainant, in both felony and misdemeanor situations, the more likely police are to file an official crime report. As Black puts it: "Official crime rates and the justice done through police detection of criminal offenders, therefore, reflect the politeness of victims" (p. 744).

5. **The complainant's status.** Do the police discriminate in favor of complainants of high social status? In trying to answer this question, Black considered both social class and race as aspects of status. For class, Black found that the police tend to discriminate in favor of white-collar complainants in felony situations. Thus, the higher a complainant's social status, the more likely it is that police will respond to a complaint that a crime has been committed. For race, however, Black found it almost impossible to reach a solid conclusion about discrimination, because most crime is intraracial (for instance, whites tend to commit crimes against whites, blacks against blacks, Hispanics against Hispanics, and so on). Suppose, for example, that the police tend to respond more often to a white complainant than to a black complainant. It is hard to know whether this response is discriminatory because, given that whites tend to commit crimes against whites more often than against minorities, in favoring a white complainant the police would also be more likely to be pursuing a white offender. Similarly, if the police are less likely to respond to a black complainant, they are more likely to be discriminating in favor of a black offender.

## VICTIMIZATION DATA: NATIONAL CRIME VICTIMIZATION SURVEYS (NCVS)

We have seen that the size and content of the unreported "dark figure" of crime shed an interesting light on the statistical data present in the UCR. We have implied that the actual size of the dark figure is unknowable and that there is no good reason to suppose either that it is constant from year to year or that it has a fixed ratio with reported crime. Moreover, because the volume of crime reported in the UCR depends as much on police activity as it does on the actual amount of criminal activity, the size of the dark figure of crime is, in principle, infinite. Simply put, there is as much officially recorded crime as the criminal law defines, as the public reports, and as the police acknowledge.

Criminologists have increasingly turned to **victimization surveys** to understand more about the volume and the rate of crime. Victimization surveys examine representative samples of a general population in an attempt to discern what crimes have been experienced in a given period. In the United States a victimization survey of a large national sample has been conducted by the Bureau of Justice Statistics each year since 1972. This is the National Crime Victimization Survey (NCVS).

The NCVS is based on a representative sample of the U.S. population (which in 2007 included 76,000 households and 135,300 persons aged 12 and over). The entire sample is interviewed by rotation twice each year for three and a half years. In person and by way of computer-assisted telephones, interviewers ask the household residents about their victimization histories during the previous year. One of the NCVS's intended advantages over the UCR is its ability to discover information about crimes not reported to the police—or, in other words, about the "dark figure" of crime. The crimes examined by the NCVS include rape, robbery, aggravated and simple assault, robbery or assault resulting in personal injury, personal theft, burglary, household larceny, and motor vehicle theft.

The NCVS is designed more as a substitute for the UCR program than as a complement. Indeed, direct comparisons of NCVS and UCR data are of dubious value, because the sources from which they derive are quite different. Whereas crime rates in the UCR derive from reports of incidents of crime to the police, the rates in the NCVS derive from reports of victimizations to survey interviewers. In other words, NCVS data are based on individuals actually victimized; UCR data are based on reported criminal acts. Because their sources of data differ, the UCR and the NCVS tend to diverge in what they tell us about crime (J. Lynch and Addington, 2007).

Here are some of the main findings of the NCVS (Bureau of Justice Statistics, 2008; and see Figures 2.4 and 2.5) for 2007.

- Less than half of all victimizations are reported to the police.
- Persons aged 12 or older experienced approximately 23 million crimes; 76 percent (17.5 million) were property crimes and 23 percent (5.2 million) were crimes of violence.

**Violent crime rates**
Adjusted victimization rate
per 1,000 persons age 12 and over

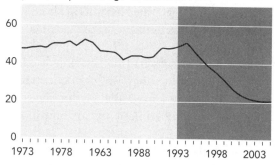

**FIGURE 2.4** Trend in Violent Victimizations, 1973–2006
*Source*: Bureau of Justice Statistics. 2008. *Crime and Victims Statistics*. Available at: http://www.ojp.usdoj.gov/bjs/cvict.htm.

**Property crime rates**
Adjusted victimization rate
per 1,000 households

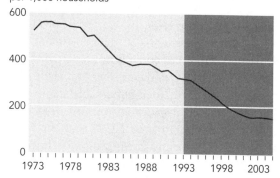

**FIGURE 2.5** Trend in Property Crime Victimizations, 1973–2006
*Source*: Bureau of Justice Statistics. 2008. *Crime and Victims Statistics*. Available at: http://www.ojp.usdoj.gov/bjs/cvict.htm.

- Violent victimizations were at or near the lowest levels ever recorded.
- For every 1,000 persons aged 12 or older, there occurred one rape or sexual assault; one assault with injury; and two robberies.
- Teens and young adults experience the highest rates of violent crime.
- Property victimizations continued a more than 25-year decline.
- Between 1973 and 2002, males had significantly higher victimization rates than females for all violent crimes except rape/sexual assault. Males were twice as likely to experience robbery and aggravated assault. In about half of all violent victimizations, the victim knew the offender.
- African Americans had higher violent crime victimization rates than whites or other races, and they experienced the highest rates of overall property crime, burglary, and motor vehicle theft.
- In general, younger persons were more likely to suffer violent victimizations. Those aged 65 or older were more likely to experience property victimizations.

## EVALUATION OF THE NCVS

The NCVS was originally devised to provide a better idea of the size of the dark figure of crime unreported in the UCR. In this task it has been reasonably successful: NCVS data document that a massive amount of crime is not reported to the police. Indeed, NCVS data reveal that victimization rates have remained remarkably stable during the past two decades. In the first decade of the new millennium, the NCVS and the UCR showed that crime and victimization declined to almost all-time measured lows.

But the NCVS has its limitations. There are three problems in particular: underreporting to interviewers; response bias; and time-in-sample bias (Sparks, 1981; Cantor and Lynch, 2000).

1. Although victimization surveys always reveal more crime than that recorded in police-based documents such as the UCR, the NCVS also understates the crime rate. For example, because many crimes are often somewhat insignificant to their victims, they tend to be forgotten. This tendency to forget increases as the time between the crime and an NCVS interview increases. Reflect, too, on how reluctant a female interviewee will be to report her domestic victimization to a telephone interviewer if her abuser is within earshot or if her telephone line is shared with another party—as sometimes happens, especially in rural areas.
2. The rate of underreporting is distributed unevenly throughout the class structure. Irrespective of actual victimization, whites are more likely than blacks to report having been victimized, as are college graduates compared to those with less formal education.
3. NCVS respondents are supposed to be interviewed every six months for a total of seven interviews. As interviewee participation in the NCVS increases, reported victimization rates decrease consistently. This decrease may arise because respondents, having been made more aware of victimization simply by exposure to interviewers' questions, take greater precautions against victimization. The reported victimization rates of often-interviewed participants also might fall because respondents are less cooperative and less candid in later interviews.

In light of these problems, the Bureau of Justice Statistics has made several important changes to the NCVS. The redesigned NCVS now has better strategies for improving the accuracy of victimization-incident recall; for easing respondents' fears about anonymity, with the use of computer-assisted interviewing, for example; and for expanding the scope of crimes covered, including vandalism. The redesigned NCVS also includes a strategy for dealing with changing victimization rates over a longer period of time (a longitudinal design), so as to permit analysis of such issues as:

- Whether crime victimization is a factor in the geographic mobility of respondents.
- Long-term health and economic consequences of victimization.
- Victim contacts with the criminal justice system over an extended period of time.
- The characteristics of victims, including victims who experience one-time, periodic, or relatively continuous victimization, together with such factors as the type of crime and victim (or offender characteristics), which vary across these different temporal patterns.
- The degree to which respondents in one year also account for victimizations in other years.

## FEDERAL DATA ON WHITE-COLLAR CRIME, CORPORATE CRIME, AND INTERNET CRIME

Neither the UCR nor the NCVS contain data about corporate crime. Though we discuss corporate crime at some length in Section 13.2, it is worth mentioning here that important sources of official data about corporate crime are the deliberations of various federal agencies and regulatory bodies, such as the Environmental Protection Agency and the Occupational Safety and Health Administration. Corporate violations become known to these agencies in many ways, including consumer complaints, government investigations, congressional committees, and complaints made by corporate competitors. However, it is important to realize that the amount of corporate misconduct not reported in the documents of federal agencies is enormous. Such data thus suffer from some of the same problems encountered by police-based data.

Data on Internet fraud have been collected since 2001 by the Internet Crime Complaint Center (ICCC), which is a joint venture of the FBI and the National White-Collar Crime Center. The stated goal of the ICCC is to act as a repository for Internet crime and to provide strategies for consumers to avoid Internet scams. According to its *Internet Crime Report* (2009), the ICCC received 275,284 complaints in 2008 (a 33 percent increase over 2007). These complaints, amounting to a total of $54 million defrauded, or $264 per complaint, included nondelivery of merchandise and payment fraud (32.9 percent of

---

**BOX 2.1  SOURCES OF CORPORATE CRIME DATA**

Among the federal agencies from which information about corporate crime can be gathered are:

- For financial violations, the Securities and Exchange Commission.
- For environmental violations, the Environmental Protection Agency.
- For labor violations, the Equal Employment Opportunity Commission and the Occupational Wage and Hour Division of the Department of Labor.

- For manufacturing violations, the Consumer Product Safety Commission, the National Highway Traffic Safety Administration, and the Food and Drug Administration.
- For unfair trade practices, the Federal Commission.
- For contaminated-food violations, the Food and Drug Administration.
- For administrative violations, U.S. federal courts.

In addition, some data about transnational corporate crime are contained in the reports, as are activities of a variety of international agencies, such as the World Health Organization.

referred complaints), auction fraud (25.5 percent), credit/debit card fraud (9 percent), and about 2 percent each for investment fraud, business fraud, confidence fraud, and identity theft. The ICCC also publishes information on patterns of fraud, including the age, gender, and geographical location of victims and offenders.

## 2.3 UNOFFICIAL CRIME DATA

In addition to the official crime data just described, there are several unofficial (i.e., non-governmental) sources of crime data: self-reports; life-course data; life-history data; biographies; participant observation; and comparative and historical research. We shall refer often to these data sources in this book.

### SELF-REPORT DATA

Given that the volume of crime is always underestimated by official crime statistics such as the police-based UCR and the victim-based NCVS, criminologists have long felt that a more complete picture of criminal activity can be had by using information provided by offenders themselves. Offender-based data typically derive either from analysis of offenders' responses (**self-reports**) to anonymous questionnaires or from personal interviews with offenders.

In many self-report studies, researchers distribute questionnaires to respondents and ask them to admit anonymously whether they have committed certain offenses and, if so, how often. In his study of delinquency among male and female Texas college students, Austin Porterfield (1946) was probably the first researcher to use a self-report questionnaire. Porterfield found no significant difference between the delinquent involvement of the students and that of a group of youths who had been processed by the juvenile court. But he also found a significant difference in court appearances between the two groups and that this difference grew out of both the

powerlessness of the court children—who were overwhelmingly of low socioeconomic status—and the social disruption of their families.

Self-report studies have shown that police-based data seriously underestimate the criminal activity of certain segments of the population (Wiesner, Capaldi, and Kim, 2007; and see Piquero, Farrington, and Blumstein, 2007:92–95). Thus, whereas police-based data show that those who commit crimes are disproportionately young, male, and black, self-report studies have typically found far fewer differences among offenders, especially in terms of their social class.

For example, from a self-report study of middle-class delinquency Weis (1976) found that "the often-cited 1:6 ratio of male to female arrestees is twice as large as the mean ratio of 1:2.56 self-reported participants in delinquent behavior" (p. 23). However, Weis also discovered large gender differences in the prevalence (the proportion of a given population that commits crime), incidence (the rate at which a given criminal population commits crime), and seriousness of delinquent involvement: Young males are more often involved than young females in the most serious offenses. A large-scale, international self-report study has also found that in thirteen Western countries boys commit more offenses than girls (Junger-Tas, 1994:374–375).

Moreover, using self-report data between 1976 and 2000, numerous National Youth Survey studies (e.g., Paternoster and Brame, 1997; A. Piquero, Farrington, and Blumstein, 2007:211) have found that for adolescents between the ages of 11 and 17, middle-class youths (both males and females) are less likely to be involved in serious offenses than working- or lower-class youths. Even when they are involved in serious crimes, middle-class youths commit fewer offenses than working- and lower-class youths. There are substantial class differences in both the prevalence and incidence of serious crime.

When the focus is shifted from serious offenses to delinquent acts in general, few significant class differences occur in the proportions of youth reporting one or more delinquent acts. The frequency at which delinquent acts are committed does vary by class for males, however. Middle-class males commit substantially fewer delinquent acts each year than working- and lower-class males. Females of all classes have relatively low rates of offending compared to working- and lower-class males, but there is no consistent pattern of class differences in female incidence rates.

Critics point out that self-report studies have several methodological defects. First, young males, especially, often exaggerate the extent of their delinquency, even on anonymous questionnaires. Second, some respondents forget their delinquent acts, especially the more trivial ones. Third, until quite recently most of the items on self-report questionnaires concern relatively minor offenses. They have tended to ignore the more serious offenses involving violence. Fourth, the respondents in many self-report studies are sometimes drawn not from a representative sample of the population but from a group easily accessible to researchers, such as prisoners and high school or college students.

Each of these problems casts doubt on the findings of self-report studies, especially about serious crime. We should stress, too, that the interpretation of self-report findings is open to considerable debate. It is one thing to show empirically that males, African Americans, and members of the lower class tend to commit serious crimes more often than females, whites, and members of the middle and upper classes do. But it is another matter altogether to explain why this might be so.

## LIFE-COURSE DATA

The last decade has seen great interest in the collection and interpretation of data about patterns of crime over the course of offenders' lives. These **life-course data** include official crime data; self-reports; psychological evaluations; IQ tests; criminal histories; court records; incarceration records; and coroners' reports.

Life-course data are typically collected and then integrated through large-scale longitudinal studies that look backwards over offenders' lives. They are used to try to explain why some adolescents commit crimes and others don't and then subsequently to examine the factors that lead to the onset of criminality; the differing social characteristics of those who commit trivial and serious offenses, respectively; the continuance, persistence, and escalation of crime; desistance from crime; and the consequences for offenders and their families of a career in crime (e.g., Loeber, Slot, and Stouthamer-Loeber, 2006; A. Piquero, Farrington, and Blumstein, 2007). Ongoing longitudinal life-course research includes the Cambridge Study in Delinquent Development, the Denver Youth Survey, the Pittsburgh Youth Study, and the Rochester Youth Development Study.

A major question posed by life-course researchers is whether there is a small group of chronic offenders who continue to offend during and even after middle age. Finding an answer to this question has been bedeviled by a number of problems, including relatively small offender samples and the inability to track a large number of offenders over their entire life course, both backwards and forward. Research by Robert Sampson and John Laub (2003) has managed largely to overcome these obstacles. They have been able to do follow-up studies on a group of 500 men who were committed to Massachusetts reform schools in their adolescence in the 1940s. Among their findings is that, even for chronic offenders, crime does indeed decline with age in aggregate, though property offenses, violence, and alcohol/drug offenses peak at somewhat different ages. Crime declines, of course, not only

---

**BOX 2.2  ON THE DEVELOPMENT OF OFFENDING**

1. The age of onset of offending is typically between ages 8 and 14, earlier with self-report data and later with official records, while the age of desistance from offending is typically between 20 and 29.
2. The prevalence of offending peaks in the late teen-age years.
3. An early age of onset predicts a relatively long criminal career duration and the commission of relatively more offenses.
4. There is marked continuity in offending and antisocial behavior from childhood to the teenage years and adulthood. In other words, people who commit relatively many offenses during one age range have

a high probability of also committing relatively many offenses during a later range.

5. A small fraction of the population ("chronic offenders") commitS a large fraction of all crimes.
6. Offending is more versatile than specialized; violent offenders in particular appear to offend frequently in other kinds of offenses.
7. The reasons given for offending up to the late teen-age years are quite variable, including excitement/enjoyment, boredom, and/or utilitarian reasons. From age 30 onward, utilitarian motives become increasingly dominant.

Source: Adapted from Piquero, Farrington, and Blumstein (2007, p. 3).

---

because offenders age but also because, as they age, offenders achieve greater stability and more responsibilities, jobs, children, and mortgages (but see Gadd and Farrall, 2004).

### LIFE-HISTORY DATA

Another way of looking at crime over the life course is with the gathering of information in the life history. The goal of **life-history studies** is to craft a rich document of offenders' changing personal choices and life experiences over time. Some life histories (or *life stories* or *pathways*) are mainly sociological, while others, like Jefferson's (1996; and see Gadd and Jefferson, 2007; Brown, 2007) work on the boxer Mike Tyson's life history ("From 'Little Fairy Boy' to the 'Compleat Destroyer'") are more psychosocial in their perspective. But all life histories try to uncover the continuous "lived experiences" of individuals. They involve a close evaluation of the meanings and contradictions of social life for those who enact it—revealing their choices, experiences, practices, and social world.

Messerschmidt (2000, 2004; and see Flavin, 2003; Chesney-Lind and Shelden, 2004), for example, has investigated adolescent perpetrators

of sexual and assaultive violence in the context of their entire lives, from their earliest memories to the point at which he encountered them. Such life-history accounts lead to an understanding of the stages and critical periods in the processes of violent and nonviolent development and of how particular individuals are both enabled and constrained by their position in society. As an example, consider a segment of Messerschmidt's (2004) dialogue on gendered power and inequality in a street gang with "Kelly" (age 15), a female gang member and on probation for assault. The dialogue explores Kelly's experiences of sexism in the gang and how the boys limited what she could and could not do in gang activities (pp. 101–102).

Q. *What was your relationship like with the boys in the gang?*

A. The guys would always tell me what to do 'cause I'm a girl, you know. They'd say I don't know shit, and stuff like that, you know. A lot of guys are sexist and didn't want me around a lot.

Q. *How were they sexist?*

A. You know. They'd think that 'cause they're guys they are tougher and better. But I can beat the shit out of a lot of the guys. But they got to do things I didn't.

Q. *Can you give me an example?*

A. Ah, you know. Like they always got to go on robberies and burglaries, you know, and stompin' [beating up people found in their "hood"], just 'cause they're guys.

Q. *You didn't always participate when the boys were involved in those crimes?*

A. No, 'cause sometime they thought I'd get hurt, and then they'd have to deal with me. I'd get in the way and stuff like that, you know, when they gonna use knives, guns, and baseball bats.

## CRIMINAL BIOGRAPHIES

**Criminal biographies** are another source of life-course data. Criminal biographies document criminals' own personal accounts of their activities, usually as recorded by ethnographers with offenders themselves.

Although one must be cautious in generalizing from the subjective experiences of a few criminals to an entire segment of society, biographies of criminals can be a fertile source for further investigation. Each of the studies shown in Box 2.3 adds relevant information to our stock of knowledge about the social world of the professional criminal.

## OBSERVATION RESEARCH AND PARTICIPANT OBSERVATION RESEARCH

Observation research is a type of field study whereby researchers focus on observing people in their natural settings. Sometimes, the people they are studying fully know they are being observed. For instance, Jill McCorkle (2003) spent considerable time as a researcher—known as such to all—inside a women's medium-security prison, examining the effects of gender-neutral policies and initiatives on inmates' daily lives there.

At other times, however, to gain authentic or natural data, observation researchers go "underground" and try to blend into or with their subjects as unobtrusively as is possible. This type of observation research—**participant observation**—is especially useful for observing the behavior of people who, for one reason or another, usually resist the participation of

---

**BOX 2.3**  **BIOGRAPHIES OF CRIME**

Prominent biographies in the literature of criminology include the following:

- Edwin Sutherland, *The Professional Thief* (1937), based on the recollections of Broadway Jones, alias Chic Conwell, a professional thief, ex-drug addict, and ex-convict from Philadelphia who worked for twenty years as a pimp, pickpocket, shoplifter, and confidence man.
- Darrell Steffensmeier and Jeffrey Ulmer, *Confessions of a Dying Thief* (2004), based on Sam Goodman's life as a fence; Goodman used his antique shop as a front to deal in stolen merchandise. In the book, Goodman discusses the relationships among fences, thieves, customers, and criminal justice personnel, and the skills required to perform fencing activities.

- Stuart Hills, *Tragic Magic* (Hills and Santiago, 1992), records the escapades of recovering addict Ron Santiago, a 42-year-old black male of Cuban ancestry. Set in New York, this is a harrowing and engrossing story of robberies, burglaries, drugs, and prison.
- Steve Hall, Simon Winlow, and Craig Ancrum, *Criminal Identities and Consumer Culture* (2008). Ethnographies of "Billy," a 21-year-old resident of a public-sector housing estate who admits to being a shoplifter, car thief, and drug dealer and who is curiously silent about his childhood but who reveals himself to be driven, most of all, by his consumerist desire to be seen as having the materialist symbols of success; and of "Tony," aged 41, a lifelong committed criminal and ex-con, who has never quite made the big time but who focuses on the external trappings of success (a BMW, good clothes, etc.).

**BOX 2.4**   PARTICIPANT OBSERVATION
STUDIES

Among the many participation studies in criminology and
the sociology of deviance are the following:

- Laud Humphreys, *Tearoom Trade* (1970).
  Humphreys' account of impersonal homosexual
  encounters in public facilities was the result of
  field research, during the course of which he
  gained entry into the subculture by posing as a
  lookout.
- Jason Ditton, *Part-Time Crime* (1977a). The English
  criminologist Ditton went undercover as a dispatch
  operative, observing the routine swindles ("fiddles')
  to which sales operatives in Wellbread's Bakery were
  prone.

- Jack Douglas and Paul Rasmussen, *The Nude Beach*
  (1977). Douglas and Rasmussen observed the complicated interaction among bathers on a nude beach
  in La Jolla, California.
- Marc Reisner, *Game Wars* (1991). Reisner takes us
  inside the underworld of Cajun alligator poachers
  and ivory importers, focusing on the dangerous
  investigations of undercover U.S. Fish and Wildlife
  game warden Dave Hall.
- Jeff Ferrell and Mark Hamm, *Ethnography at the
  Edge* (1998). In this edited collection twelve authors
  describe their observation and participant observation studies, including encounters with street gangs,
  the homeless, paramilitary units, sex work and
  gender work, drug subcultures, and sky divers and
  motorcyclists.

---

outsiders in their social world. Examples include
members of criminal syndicates such as the Hell's
Angels and paramilitary survivalists. Ideally, participant observation requires that the subjects of
study be unaware that the observer is in fact an
observer.

The actual practice of participant observation
is plagued with difficult questions. Some questions concern objectivity. For example, how can
one study something objectively if one is a part
of what one studies? Other questions concern
ethics. Where is the dividing line between the
appropriate gathering of data about human subjects and the invasion of their right to privacy?
Does the researcher have an ethical obligation
to report a crime when he or she witnesses one?
Both Humphreys' (1970) research on homosexual encounters and Douglas and Rasmussen's
(1977) observation of nudists have been attacked
for being unethical. Still other questions concern
danger. What happens if researchers' true identities are detected by their subjects?

Largely because of the effect of questions
such as these, neither courts of law nor university institutional review boards look with

much favor on participant observation studies.
Indeed, in a tragic example of what Patricia and
Peter Adler (1998) refer to as "the Dark Ages"
for ethnographers, Rik Scarce, a graduate sociology student at Washington State University,
served six months in prison in the early 1990s
for contempt of court for refusing to reveal
information about the activities of a group of
radical environmentalists and animal rights
activists with whom he had mixed in the course
of his research.

## COMPARATIVE AND HISTORICAL
RESEARCH

The great French sociologist Émile Durkheim
(1984:157) once remarked that comparative
sociology is not a special branch of sociology,
it is sociology itself. So it is, too, with criminology. **Comparative criminology** is an indispensable aspect of criminological inquiry and a rich
source of data for its theories.

The focus of comparative criminology is
the systematic comparison of crime in two or
more societies. Comparative studies allow us to

compare present crime rates in the United States, for example, with those in other cultures, places, and times. Does the United States have a higher homicide rate, for instance, than Japan, Canada, or England? If it does, why? Using Table 3.1, for example, you can compare the homicide rates of various industrialized countries. Comparative criminology also enables us to examine the effectiveness of social and government policies toward crime. For instance, to what extent does gun control legislation affect the number of murders in which firearms are used?

Comparative crime data, like other crime data, have both official and unofficial sources. Official comparative crime data derive from the activities and reports of national governments and government agencies. Such data can be found in the reports of international agencies such as the United Nations, the World Court, the World Health Organization, and the International Police Organization (Interpol). Some organizations, such as the United Nations, the Dutch Ministry of Justice, and the United Kingdom's Home Office, also sponsor and conduct cross-national victimization surveys. Unofficial comparative crime data can be gleaned from the reports and findings of such private organizations as Amnesty International, Doctors Without Borders, and Human Rights Watch. These data are often especially useful for documenting crimes committed by governments or by the military against their own populations.

As we will see in more depth in Chapter 3, the use of national crime data for cross-national purposes is not without difficulty. Crime data are not items that can simply be pried loose from one culture and compared with those of another. For example, societies differ in how they define crime and in the degree of seriousness with which they regard certain types of crime, making simple comparisons of crime rates hazardous.

Other types of comparative studies can be based on **historical data**, including official statistics (on crime, prison populations, health, and so on); court records; books; newspapers; journals; pamphlets; plays; and oral histories. Historical data help us examine the past in order to understand how we have arrived at the present. Ideally, they allow us to make generalizations about crime that stand outside the particularities of any given era. Historical studies of crime are therefore also implicitly comparative. Douglas Hay's (1975) study of crime and criminal law in eighteenth-century England, for example, revealed that in societies where the criminal justice system is based on terror—in this case, execution for the most petty of offenses—a national police force might be quite unnecessary. Occasionally, historical studies of crime are also cross-cultural. A classic example of a study that is both historical and cross-cultural is *The Politics of Crime and Conflict* (Gurr, Grabosky, and Hula, 1977; and see Srebnick and Lévy, 2005; and Kilday, 2007). This study revealed that the relationship between public policies and crime rates in Calcutta, London, Stockholm, and Sydney during a 150-year period was in many ways strikingly similar, despite the enormous social, economic, and political differences among these disparate cities. To give another example, in her book *Women and Violent Crime in Enlightenment Scotland*, Anne-Marie Kilday (2007) uses case studies of murder, infanticide, and assault in eighteenth-century Scotland to challenge the idea that, when they act violently, women are always first and foremost victims of men. In this analysis of crime and gender studies Kilday also draws the comparative conclusion that Scottish women were at that time considerably more violent than English women.

## ASSESSMENT

In this chapter we have described the major sources of crime data. We stress that crime data can never represent criminal behavior, however defined, in a neutral or unbiased way. Data do not speak for themselves! A particular crime rate identified and measured by official crime data, for example, depends on the legalistic concepts that guide the process of measurement. We do not, of course, mean to suggest that criminologists intentionally distort data to suit their own purposes. Rather, we mean that data are identified and defined by concepts and that criminologists naturally differ in the concepts of crime they hold appropriate for the study of crime.

This point is important. As you read this book, you will learn that how criminologists explain or interpret crime data depends both on their concepts of crime and on the assumptions underlying their theories of crime. Theories are sets of assumptions, mediated by concepts, that guide the interpretation of data. Theories try to explain both regularities and irregularities in data. In the same way that what constitutes crime data depends on any given concept of crime, so, too, how we explain crime data depends on the assumptions of our theories.

## REVIEW

This chapter has outlined the major sources of crime data. Official crime data are published by the state and by state agencies. In the United States such publications include the Uniform Crime Reports (UCR), the National Crime Victimization Survey (NCVS), and federal records of corporate crime. Unofficial crime data include self-report data, life-course and life-history data, criminal biographies, participant observation, and comparative and historical data.

In this chapter you also learned that crime data can never represent criminal behavior in a neutral or unbiased way. We now review the major points of the chapter.

### CAUTION: DATA DO NOT SPEAK FOR THEMSELVES!

1. Data are not objective facts that exist independently of the concepts and theories of those who observe them. Data can never represent criminal behavior in a neutral or unbiased way.
2. Data are identified and defined by concepts, about whose appropriateness criminologists naturally differ in their perceptions. In the same way that what constitutes crime data depends on any given concept of crime, so, too, how we explain crime data depends, to a certain extent, on the assumptions of our theories.

### OFFICIAL CRIME DATA

1. The UCR distinguishes between eight Part I and twenty-one Part II crimes. Data about Part I crimes derive from reports to the police. Data about Part II crimes derive from police arrests.
2. The UCR and NIBRS annually tabulate data about the number and rate of crimes; crime trends by year and region; the age, sex, and race of offenders and victims; and offense clearance rates.

3. There are both methodological and conceptual criticisms of the UCR. Among the latter is the limitation that the UCR cover only legally defined categories of crime. Ultimately, we cannot be sure if the UCR measure criminal behavior or, rather, the bureaucratic activities of official agencies. Whether or not police accept a crime report depends on the legal seriousness of the crime; the complainant's preferences; the relational distance between victim and offender; and the complainant's deference and social status.

4. The NCVS is based on reports of victimizations. It is designed to complement the UCR, but comparisons between the NCVS and the UCR are of dubious value because each attempts to measure different entities.

5. The NCVS indicates that only 39 percent of all crimes are reported to the police, that females and black males are among the most victimized groups in the population, and that nearly one-third of all households suffer some form of victimization annually.

6. Problems with NCVS data include underreporting to interviewers, response bias, and time-in-sample bias.

7. Neither the UCR nor the NCVS contains any data about corporate crime. However, various federal agencies and regulatory bodies are important sources of such data.

## UNOFFICIAL CRIME DATA

1. Self-report data are offender-based data obtained. These data tend to show that middle-class youth commit as much crime as working-class youth but that there are large gender differences in the prevalence, incidence, and seriousness of crime. Critics argue that self-report data suffer from exaggeration by young males; from biases due to the failure of some interviewees to recall delinquency; and from a concentration on relatively minor juvenile offenses.

2. Life-course and life-history studies collect and interpret patterns of crime over the course of offenders' entire lives.

3. Criminal biographies are accounts of personal activities given by criminals to criminologists. Biographies can be a fertile source for further investigation but are notoriously resistant to generalization.

4. Participant observation is a form of field research. Its goal is to observe people in their natural settings as unobtrusively as possible. Its actual practice is plagued with difficult questions, including the problem of where to place a dividing line between the appropriate gathering of data about human subjects and the invasion of their right to privacy.

5. Comparative and historical data are closely related. Comparative data derive chiefly from the activities and reports of national governments and such international agencies as the United Nations, the World Health Organization, and Interpol. Such data are typically used to compare crime in two or more countries at one point in time. Historical data derive from a great diversity of sources and allow us to generalize about crime free from the particularities of any given era. Occasionally, historical data are also cross-cultural.

## QUESTIONS FOR CLASS DISCUSSION

1. What does the UCR measure: activities of offenders, activities of complainants, or activities of the police?
2. Do victimization surveys help us understand the true extent of the "dark figure" of crime?
3. Can crime data ever represent objective facts?
4. The English language has more than 85 words for "killers" and "killing". How many of them can you name? (*Hint*: Go to http://phrontistery.info/kill.) Among them are *aborticide, avicide, biocide, deicide, felicide, femicide, fratricide, fungicide, genocide, herbicide, homicide, infanticide, liberticide, matricide, parricide, pesticide, regicide, sororicide, spermicide, suicide, theriociode, tyrranicide,* and *uxoricide.* Some of these are defined as killings, others not. Which? Some are illegal, others not. Why?

## WEB EXERCISES

1. This exercise asks you to compare police-based crime rates in different parts of the United States. First, find the most recent UCR on the Internet. You can do so by going to <www.fbi.gov> and clicking on "UCR" and "year." Then select one type of crime in any two cities—for instance, robbery in Boston and in San Francisco. Next, produce two printed pages with statistics from a table titled "Offenses Known to the Police [time frame], Cities over 1,000,000 in Population." Which city had more reported robbery? Did the robbery rates in either city change from one year to the next? What factors might explain differences in the two cities' robbery rates?
2. Visit the website of the Internet Crime Complaint Center (ICCC): <www.ifccfbi.gov>. Click on "Fraud Tips." Read and then discuss the adequacy of the advice on the "Nigerian letter" scam and on identity theft.

## FOR FURTHER STUDY

### READINGS

Godfrey, Barry, Clive Emsley, and Graeme Dunstall. 2003. *Comparative Histories of Crime.* Portland, OR: Willan.

Lynch, James P., and Lynn A. Addington, eds. 2007. *Understanding Crime Statistics.* Cambridge: Cambridge University Press.

Perry, Barbara. 2008. *Silent Victims: Hate crimes Against Native Americans.* Tucson: University of Arizona Press.

Pogrebin, Mark, ed. 2004. *About Criminals: A View of the Offender's World.* Thousand Oaks, CA: Sage.

### WEBSITES

1. <http://www.fbi.gov/UCR/ucr.htm>: This site provides open access to the Uniform Crime Reports, the major official data source from the U.S. government.

2.  <http://www.usdoj.gov/>: This is the home page of the U.S. Department of Justice (DOJ). It offers access to a variety of governmental reports issued by the DOJ, including the National Crime Victimization Surveys (NCVS). To see results from the NCVS, follow the link to the Bureau of Justice Statistics (BJS) site and select "Criminal Victimization" from the publications list.

3.  <http://www.ojp.usdoj.gov/bjs/nibrs.htm>: This is the website of the National Incident-Based Reporting System (NIBRS) project from the U.S. government. It is an alternative to the UCR, taking into consideration many of the UCR's weaknesses. There is a set of links to all 50 states, updating readers on each state's activities with NIBRS. Students may examine their own state's involvement with the NIBRS here.

4.  <http://www.albany.edu/sourcebook/>: This is the website for the Sourcebook of Criminal Justice Statistics supported by the Bureau of Justice Statistics. This user-friendly reference contains U.S. criminal justice statistics gathered from over 100 sources. The Sourcebook includes data about offenders, victims, prisoners, public opinion, and many other aspects of the criminal justice system.

# COMPARATIVE CRIMINOLOGY

**3.1 Approaching Comparative Criminology**
- The Goal(s) of Comparative Criminology
- Transnational Crime
- Cultural Relativism
- A Case Study of Comparative Sexual Deviance
- Toward Uniform Cross-National Crime Statistics?
- Evaluation of Comparative Criminology

**3.2 Comparative Crime and Victimization Data**
- Cross-National Crime Data
- Cross-National Victimization Data

**3.3 Cross-National Generalizations Regarding Crime**
- Countries with Low Crime Rates
- Modernization and Crime
- Globalization and Crime
- American Exceptionalism: Crime and Incarceration in Comparative Perspective

**PREVIEW**

Chapter 3 introduces:
- How comparative criminology helps us to understand crime in the United States.
- The chief sources of cross-national crime and victimization data.
- The problem of cultural relativism.
- The problem of globalization.
- Cross-national generalizations about countries with low crime rates, modernization and crime, and globalization and crime.
- American exceptionalism: high homicide rates and punitive punishment.

**KEY TERMS**

American exceptionalism
comparative criminology
cultural relativism
epistemological relativism
ethnocentrism

globalization
methodological relativism
modernization thesis
transnational crime

In many of the chapters of this book we will refer to crime in a variety of societies. In this chapter we explicitly compare crime and crime rates in the United States with those in other parts of the world.

## 3.1 APPROACHING COMPARATIVE CRIMINOLOGY

Most theories about crime have been fashioned in the sociocultural context of just a handful of Western societies—especially societies where spoken English predominates. However, few such theories have been properly tested with evidence in other societies. Nevertheless, in the same way that all would-be scientific theories must be scrutinized under conditions that are as diverse as possible, so must theories regarding the causes of crime. Undertaken in a sensitive way, comparative criminology (or *cross-cultural* criminology) can remedy **ethnocentrism**, or the view that generalizations derived from one's own society necessarily apply to crime in all other parts of the globe. As the renowned anthropologist Margaret Mead reflected in her book *Coming of Age in Samoa* (1928), "As the traveler who has once been from home is wiser than he who has never left his doorstep, so a knowledge of one other culture should sharpen our ability to scrutinize more steadily, to appreciate more lovingly, our own."

## THE GOAL(S) OF COMPARATIVE CRIMINOLOGY

**Comparative criminology** can be defined as the systematic and theoretically informed comparison of crime in two or more cultures. A comparative perspective should help us address a number of key questions about crime. How and why do some societies differ in their patterns of crime, whereas others are quite similar? Why do some countries have low crime rates? Can we generalize cross-nationally about the causes of crime? Can a criminological theory developed in one society explain patterns of crime in other societies?

In short, we need to explore how comparative criminology should proceed. The most popular procedural guidelines for constructing comparative generalizations regarding crime are essentially those offered some time ago by Clinard and Abbott (1973):

> The goal of a comparative criminology should be to develop concepts and generalizations at a level that distinguishes between universals applicable to all societies and unique characteristics representative of one or a small set of societies....Research should proceed...first in a single culture at one point in time,...second in societies generally alike,...and third in completely dissimilar societies. (p. 2)

In other words, comparative criminology should proceed in three stages. Any generalization about crime must be tested (1) in one culture at a single point in time; (2) across two cultures that share some common sociological feature—such as a similar level of technological development or a common type of political culture; and (3) across cultures that are completely dissimilar. Because this advice follows the course often used for testing generalizations in the natural sciences, it has much to recommend it. Clearly, it is easier to generalize about the United States and England, for example, than it is about the United States and Japan.

Moreover, and arguably following some long-established procedures in the natural sciences (physics, chemistry, etc.), we can point to various procedural rules to be followed in any attempt to make cross-cultural generalizations about crime. There are at least five of these procedural rules that we might apply in the search for generalizations about rising crime rates in different societies, for example:

1. Crime in different cultures can be compared only if the definition and meaning of criminal behavior in these cultures is the same.

2. An event p (e.g., urbanization) is not the cause of rising crime rates if it occurs when rising crime rates do not occur.
3. p is not the cause of rising crime rates if it does not occur when rising crime rates do occur.
4. *p* is not the cause of rising crime rates if one or more other variables (*a,* or *a, b…n*) are present in the same circumstances as *p.*
5. For the generalization "*p* causes rising crime rates" to be intelligible, it must be explained by a theory.

Suppose we wanted to explain why homicide rates might rise and fall over time. Ultimately we would want to test our theory of changing homicide rates across a range of societies. At some point, probably fairly early on, we would need to find some empirical data about the raw number and rate (per 100,000) of homicides in various societies. One attempt to do this is represented by the homicide data for 2004 in Table 3.1.

According to these cross-national data, the United States has by far the highest homicide rate of all technologically developed societies. In the United States in 2004 the chance of being murdered was about three times greater than in Canada and in England and Wales, for example, and four times greater than in Australia.

However, rather than accept such data at face value, we must examine them more closely. Given that each country's homicide data in Table 3.1 are actually constructed by each country's national police agency, how much confidence should we have in their accuracy? Given this question, moreover, how meaningful are comparisons between crime rates in the United States and those in other parts of the world? Not the least of the obstacles facing comparative criminology is that societies vary in how their crimes are defined by their respective legal systems. Societies often vary, too, in how and how often crimes are reported to the police by the public

**TABLE 3.1 HOMICIDE AND HOMICIDE RATES IN SELECTED INDUSTRIALIZED COUNTRIES, 2004**

| Country | Homicides, 2004 | Homicides per 100,000 population, 2004 |
|---|---|---|
| Australia | 256 | 1.31 |
| Belgium | 214 | 2.07 |
| Bulgaria | 240 | 3.04 |
| Canada | 622 | 1.99 |
| England/Wales | 859 | 1.63 |
| Finland | 144 | 2.77 |
| France | 990 | 1.66 |
| Germany | 809 | 0.98 |
| Hungary | 212 | 2.08 |
| Italy | 714 | 1.23 |
| Netherlands | 204 | 1.27 |
| Norway | 36 | 0.79 |
| Portugal | 187 | 1.81 |
| Scotland | 230 | 2.57 |
| Sweden | 215 | 2.41 |
| Switzerland | 213 | 2.95 |
| United States | 16,137 | 5.5 |

Source: Adapted from United Nations (2008b).

and how the police record them. In addition, if homicides rates are so much higher in one society than in another, why is this so?

As this chapter progresses we will see that some of these difficulties can, to a certain extent, be overcome. But first let us identify two other problems that raise further difficulties for comparative criminology. One concerns transnational crime; the other, cultural relativism. Each of these problems is linked to, and further complicated by, the mutual influence between globalization and crime.

## TRANSNATIONAL CRIME

Consider the following examples of crime or possible crime.

- China and the United States are the world's two largest destinations for the $20-billion-per-year international market in the trafficking of banned and endangered animal species and animal body parts. The United States–Mexico border has therefore become a busy corridor for the smuggling of many rare species from across Latin America and other parts of the world. Drug traffickers nowadays reap extra profits by sharing routes with animal traffickers, who cram humming birds into cigarette packs and baby monkeys into car air conditioning ducts to be sold to underground pet traders in the United States (Rosenburg, 2009).

- According to the New York–based Committee to Protect Journalists (CPJ), at least sixteen journalists have been murdered in countries of the former Soviet Union since 1993. The circumstances strongly suggest the involvement of Russian organized crime. The CPJ has documented what it calls an alarming pattern of violence against Russian and East European journalists who cover crime and corruption. The CPJ also recorded that 125 journalists were in prison in 2008, and that 9 journalists were killed worldwide in 2009 (CPJ, 2009).

- In Mexico City, police arrested a gang of suspected Colombian drug smugglers linked to one of Mexico's main trafficking cartels. Police reported that the traffickers, led by Colombian drug baron Teodoro Mauricio "The Dove" Fino, are accused of shipping cocaine to Mexico for the powerful Beltran Leyva brothers to sell in the United States (Reuters, March 7, 2009).

- Federal prosecutors announced charges in New York against fifty-one alleged members of two Chinese gangs who were accused of attempted murder, immigrant smuggling, and trafficking in counterfeit clothing and purses. The gangs made tens of thousands of dollars a week, coordinating some of their crimes with associates in Asia (Associated Press, November 13, 2004).

- A Yemeni man, Mohamed Alanssi, who set himself on fire in front of the White House—and survived—was the main informer for federal prosecutors in a terrorism-financing case in Brooklyn, New York. Mr. Alanssi had been employed in an FBI antiterrorist "sting" operation and was about to testify against the Yemeni sheik Mohammed Ali Hassan al-Moayad, who had apparently boasted (in Germany and elsewhere) that he had ties to Al Qaeda and Hamas and that he had personally delivered $20 million to Osama bin Laden (*New York Times*, November 17, 2004:A260).

- Born 68 years ago in Nigeria, in 1988, widowed and with two children to support, Martina Okeke agreed to come to the United States to cook, clean, and care for the children of a Nigerian couple living in Staten Island, New York. She said they promised to pay her $300 a month, a house, and school tuition for her two children. She worked for 12 years and was never paid a penny. She now lives in a dark basement in Queens, New York, doing whatever she must to survive (Gonzalez, 2007).

In none of the foregoing cases is it quite clear where the crimes originated, in how many locations they were committed, and under which and how many jurisdictions they fell. Each of these cases involves **transnational crime,** which is crime committed across borders or across national boundaries. Sometimes, transnational crimes are committed in face-to-face encounters; at other times they are committed through flights or through airborne contaminants; in, under, or on the oceans; in outer space; and in cyberspace.

Transnational crimes typically involve criminal syndicates and the trafficking of illicit drugs from one country to another. Especially under the powerful influence of globalization and the tremendous growth in the activities of transnational corporations, the numerous forms of transnational crimes—some well organized and some not (Marshall, 2008; Gros, 2008)—include terrorism, sometimes committed by individuals, sometimes by well-organized political or religious groups, and sometimes by governments themselves against the populations of other societies; trafficking in persons (slaves, women, and children, including outright kidnappings), in identities, in animals, and in human and animal organs; drug trafficking; money laundering and other financial crimes; environmental and green crime; espionage and the illegal gathering of information; and trafficking in stones, precious metals, art, and in archaeological artifacts. We should add, too, that governments sometimes commit transnational crimes: against other societies (as in the waging of unjust wars), against the populations of other countries, and against migrants and guest workers. Sometimes those responsible for patrolling borders and national boundaries themselves commit transnational crimes (Weber and Bowling, 2008). Needless to say, local and national-based agencies of criminal justice are at a considerable disadvantage in dealing with transnational crime.

What does transnational crime imply for comparative criminology? Crucially, the networks, flows, and activities associated with transnational crime tend to blur or to make obsolete the traditional unit of comparative analysis: "societies," "nations," or "cultures." Transnational crime blurs the boundaries between these units by destroying their "purity" and their distinct identities. As such, it is becoming increasingly difficult to talk about crime "in the United States"

or "in Canada" or "in Japan" without acknowledging that crimes in these countries sometimes originate in other countries, and vice versa. For good reason, therefore, the study of transnational crime is sometimes called *border-crossing criminology* or, more simply, *global criminology*.

Although some authors believe that the global criminology and comparative criminology are quite separate endeavors (e.g., Larsen and Smandych, 2008b5–7), we are not at all convinced that this is really the case. It is true that, as it is conventionally seen, the job of comparative criminology is to compare aspects of crime in one society with those in another. It is also true that both transnational crime and the processes of globalization have muddied this "pure" comparison. But, as we will suggest, precisely how transnational crime and globalization affect different societies—in the same way, differently, or at some point in between—is also a very useful avenue of comparative enquiry. We might further enquire, for example, whether societies regarded as "failed states" are more vulnerable to transnational crime than more stable societies are. We might ask, too, whether transnational crime is more likely to penetrate societies with weak national militaries, corrupt politicians, weak informal social controls, or lengthy geographical borders.

## CULTURAL RELATIVISM

Another major area of difficulty that confronts comparative criminology is **cultural relativism**. Cultural relativism has two forms: epistemological and methodological. **Epistemological relativism** involves the extraordinary claim that one can understand another culture only through the prism of one's own culturally determined system of values. It therefore implies the impossibility of meaningful comparative generalizations other than those that stem from ethnocentrism. Thus, if our concepts of crime differ from those of another culture, it is meaningless to say that an action does or does not seem criminal to the other culture in our terms. Although this conclusion has some logical and philosophical merit, it is so pessimistic—contradictory and self-refuting, even—that for practical purposes it can only be noted and then (not entirely with satisfaction) ignored.

**Methodological relativism,** on the other hand, is a strategy that operates as a sensitizing device to variation in the definition and meaning of crime in other cultures. It reminds us that, if we are about to make comparative generalizations about crime, we should first try to understand another culture's definition and construction of crime in its terms rather than in our own. "Most knowledgeable observers agree," writes James Sheptycki (2005; and see Sheptycki. 2008, and Weber and Bowling, 2008),

> that if anything, the methodological shortcomings of quantitative empirical data render sufficient grounds for caution.…In practice quantitative data can be pragmatically employed with due regard to their shortcomings, but in order to interpret such data it is necessary to place it in its social, cultural, and historical context. By such methodological pragmatism comparative criminologists have attempted to reach out for a better understanding of their object of study. (p. 15)

The difficult issues of relativism can be better understood if we examine the methods and findings of a classic case study in the literature of comparative anthropology: Julia Brown's (1952; and see Cooney and Harbin. 2008) comparative study of deviations from sexual mores.

## A CASE STUDY OF COMPARATIVE SEXUAL DEVIANCE

In her 1952 study, Julia Brown proposed that every known society has a range of approved

sexual practices and another range of practices subject to taboo. Those members of a society who faithfully follow the approved sexual customs are rewarded; those who deviate from such customs are punished. Brown focused on the following three problems: (1) the relative frequency with which specific types of sexual practices are considered deviant by different societies, where frequency is defined as the percentage of societies that forbids such practices; (2) the relative severity with which various deviant sexual practices are punished; and (3) the degree of correlation between the frequency and the severity of punishments.

Addressing the first two problems, Brown analyzed data in Yale University's Human Relations Area File, gleaning information about the sexual practices punished by 110 "simple" societies in Africa, North America, South America, Eurasia, and Oceania. (We note, in passing, that we do not agree with Brown's characterization of technologically undeveloped societies as "simple" because in many ways, especially in the realm of certain social relationships, such societies are actually quite "advanced.") Brown's findings are summarized in Table 3.2.

Brown next determined a punishment scale for deviant sexual practices. Her scale of ratings was based on a combination of the percentage of societies that forbade a specific practice and the intensity (mild, moderate, severe, very severe) of the punishment inflicted for each sexual deviation. The scale is summarized in Table 3.3.

Tables 3.2 and 3.3 contain at least two important findings. Examining the data in Table 3.2, we learn that the sexual practices most often forbidden in Brown's sample are incest, abduction, and rape. Those practices least often forbidden are premarital affairs and intercourse with one's fiancée. Second, from the data recorded in Table 3.3 and from a series of correlational analyses, Brown inferred that the more often a given sexual practice is forbidden, the more severely

## TABLE 3.2  PERCENTAGES OF SOCIETIES PUNISHING SPECIFIC SEXUAL PRACTICES

| Number of Societies | % Punishing | Practice and Person Punished |
| --- | --- | --- |
| 54 | 100 | Incest |
| 82 | 100 | Abduction of married woman |
| 84 | 99 | Rape of married woman |
| 55 | 95 | Rape of unmarried woman |
| 43 | 95 | Sex during postpartum period |
| 15 | 93 | Bestiality by adult |
| 73 | 92 | Sex during menstruation |
| 88 | 89 | Adultery (paramour punished) |
| 93 | 87 | Adultery (wife punished) |
| 22 | 86 | Sex during lactation period |
| 57 | 86 | Infidelity of fiancée |
| 52 | 85 | Seduction of another man's fiancée |
| 74 | 85 | Illegitimate impregnation (woman punished) |
| 62 | 84 | Illegitimate impregnation (man punished) |
| 30 | 77 | Seduction of prenubile girl (man punished) |
| 44 | 68 | Male homosexuality |
| 49 | 67 | Sex during pregnancy |
| 16 | 44 | Masturbation |
| 97 | 44 | Premarital relations (woman punished) |
| 93 | 41 | Premarital relations (man punished) |
| 12 | 33 | Female homosexuality |
| 67 | 10 | Sex with one's betrothed |

Source: J. Brown (1952:138), abridged.

## TABLE 3.3  MEAN SEVERITY VALUES OF SPECIFIC PUNISHMENTS

| Mean Severity Value | Specific Punishment |
| --- | --- |
| 1.0 | Small fine |
| 1.2 | Fistfight |
| 1.4 | Quarreling within family |
| 1.5 | Parental reproof |
| 1.8 | Beating by family member |
| 2.1 | Duel |
| 2.2 | Public ridicule and disgrace |
| 2.2 | Enforced marriage |
| 2.2 | Illness |
| 2.2 | Bad luck |
| 2.3 | Danger to near kin |
| 2.4 | Ceremonial penance |
| 2.4 | Lowered bride-price |
| 2.4 | Knifing |
| 2.5 | Temporary exile |
| 2.5 | Humiliation at wedding |
| 2.5 | Heavy fine |
| 2.5 | Enslavement of relative |
| 2.5 | Divorce, and return of bride-price |
| 2.5 | Public flogging |
| 2.6 | Difficulty in acquiring a husband |
| 2.6 | Failure of hunting or fishing |
| 2.6 | Desertion of spouse |
| 2.7 | Puniness of offspring, injury to child |
| 2.9 | Divorce with disgrace, no remarriage allowed |
| 2.9 | Facial mutilation |
| 2.9 | Multiple mutilation |

*Continued*

**TABLE 3.3**  *Continued*

| Mean Severity Value | Specific Punishment |
|---|---|
| 2.9 | Madness |
| 3.0 | Spearing of legs |
| 3.1 | Repudiation of bride by groom |
| 3.1 | Sorcery to injure or kill |
| 3.3 | Loss of virility |
| 3.4 | Public raping |
| 3.4 | Enslavement |
| 3.4 | Destruction of major property |
| 3.5 | Barrenness |
| 3.6 | Permanent exile |
| 3.7 | Life imprisonment |
| 3.7 | Torture, possibly resulting in death |
| 3.7 | Enforced suicide |
| 3.9 | Death |

Source: J. Brown (1952:137), abridged.

and the more often it is punished. Assuming that severity of punishment reflects the seriousness of an offense, as Brown did, we can infer that incest, abduction, and rape are generally viewed across cultures as the most serious offenses. However, Brown went beyond this inference: "The fact that these correlations exist is of interest since it tends to support the view that there may be generalized attitudes of permissiveness and punitiveness toward sexual activity" (Brown:139).

How justified was Brown in her finding that different cultures have common attitudes toward sexual deviation? There are at least two problems with the method Brown used to arrive at this generalization: One problem involves the definition of certain behavior as criminal; the other involves the seriousness attached to such behavior.

Brown's assumption that all 110 societies criminalize sexual practices similarly is implausible. Consider incest. It is true that anthropologists have not discovered any place, past or present, where incest is tolerated in an entire society. But there are documented cases in which some cultures regard incest—however defined—as a necessary and obligatory social practice. For example, what we regard as incest seems to have been obligatory for members of royal families in Inca Peru, in Hawaii, and in ancient Egypt, where Cleopatra was the offspring of a brother–sister union (Guttmacher, 1951). In Bali, fraternal twins of the opposite sex have been permitted to marry because they had already been completely familiar in utero. Moreover, the Gusii of southwestern Kenya will not proclaim it a sexual taboo if, during the ceremony of "taking by stealth," sexual intercourse occurs between kin as close as brother and sister (Mayer, 1953).

How do such counterexamples affect Brown's generalization about sexual practices in similar "simple" societies? As formulated—there are "generalized attitudes of permissiveness or punitiveness toward sexual activity"—Brown's generalization can be neither falsified nor confirmed by counterexamples. It cannot clearly be falsified because conditional clauses (of the sort "No society exerts incest taboos during the rainy season") could in principle account for any number of counterfactual cases. This limitation is shared by all scientific and sociological attempts to generalize.

Additionally, Brown's generalization cannot be confirmed. One of the necessary criteria for an intelligible generalization is that there be an identity between the practices within its scope. But there is no way of knowing from Brown's research or from much data lodged in the Human Relations Area File whether the sexual practices defined as incestuous are the same practices in the societies observed: Are they perhaps seen as similar only by the observer's own methodology? The sexual practices defined as incestuous by the

Western observer inclined to generalizations, by the Sambia tribe in the highlands of New Guinea, and by travelers ("gypsies") in North America may in fact all be quite different.

The problem of the identity of social practices is probably acute for comparisons between simple societies. There is good reason to suppose that the problem is even more acute for comparisons between simple and modern societies and even for comparisons between modern societies with similar legal cultures and traditions. Suppose, for example, that we wanted to compare incest rates between England and the United States. Under the Sexual Offences Act of 1956, it is an offense for a male in England to have sexual intercourse with a female whom he knows to be his granddaughter, daughter, sister, or mother. But in the United States, statutory incest refers to an additional range of behavior not prohibited by English law: sexual relations between males and their grandmothers, nieces, and aunts. Moreover, marriage between first cousins is not an uncommon practice in England; in the United States it is illegal in nearly half the states.

A second difficulty with Brown's generalization is the assumption that a rank order of punishment can be applied meaningfully across cultures. How items are entered in cross-cultural rankings in part depends on the values of those doing the ranking. How is an objective order of punishment to be devised? And by whom? Brown devised her rank order on the advice of "judges conversant with anthropological phenomena" (Brown, 1952:137). Yet consider the item "death" as the most serious punishment in her scale. There are many cases recorded (in the Homeric myths, the Icelandic sagas, and others) where banishment or permanent exile is seen as a far more serious punishment than death. Moreover, in some modern cultures (for example, among the top levels of the Japanese military), enforced suicide is not a punishment but an honorable recourse to defeat in war. And in

some cultures (for instance, in England among men of gentle birth and fashion until 1850 [Andrew, 1980]), a duel is not a punishment (as in Brown's scale) but the normal form of asserting honor or reputation following insult.

Let us return to the idea of exile to illustrate another point. Exactly how much of a punishment is exile? The effect of exile partly determines the answer to this question. Exile is culturally and subjectively variable; for example, to an Orpheus exiled to Hades (the Greek underworld), to Alexander Solzhenitsyn exiled from Russia to Vermont, and to the late Michael Jackson exiled from his native United States to middle-eastern sheikdoms, expulsion certainly has very different meanings. The seriousness of expulsion depends partly "on how easy it is to attach oneself to another community and to what extent one is a second-class citizen in that community" (Moore, 1978:124): Does the exile become a refugee, a hero, an outlaw, or a welfare immigrant? The number of such complicating items can of course be multiplied greatly. But their message is a simple one: The severity of punishment attached to practices in a given society cannot simply be wrenched from its specific cultural context and inserted artificially into a "comparative" rank order.

## TOWARD UNIFORM CROSS-NATIONAL CRIME STATISTICS?

Now let us see what we can learn from one well-known attempt to measure cross-national crime rates: Marvin Wolfgang's (1967) classic study associated with methodological relativism. The major comparative problem identified by Wolfgang is the adequacy and reliability of international crime statistics. He noted correctly that statistical data produced by agents such as Interpol are based on an unwarranted assumption: that such crimes as homicide, robbery, and the rape, for example, are regarded with the same degree of seriousness by all countries. This error is aggravated by wide cultural variation in legal definitions of crime and by differing attitudes toward the sanctity of life and property.

Wolfgang made several proposals to remedy this situation. The first relates to such official administrative policies as police efficiency, quality of criminal records, and discrepancies among countries for reported crimes, trials, and convictions. According to Wolfgang (1967; and see van Dijk, 2008:26–33), national police data must be standardized. These data could easily be made more reliable because "a team of experts from an international organization could, like the field representatives of the Department of Justice in the United States, help individual countries to set up and promote reliable reporting systems" (p. 66).

Wolfgang's (1967) second proposal is even more unconventional: the elimination of legal definitions of crime for purposes of comparative measurement of crime rates. The legal components of homicide, robbery, rape, and so forth would be replaced by requests for information about the type and extent of physical injury in violent crimes and/or the monetary value of property stolen or damaged. With this approach, Wolfgang argued, specific legal definitions of crime in national data would be eliminated but cultural integrity would be maintained.

Finally, Wolfgang (1967) proposed the use of a psychophysical weighting scale. A weighted crime for each participating country could thus be had by obtaining for each country the sum of the frequency of each measured crime, multiplying by its weight, and then dividing by a constant population unit.

Would such a scale really permit a comparativist to assess the relative seriousness of crimes in different countries? We think not. Wolfgang's (1967) strategy contains a serious problem. Wolfgang's major proposal for comparative research is the elimination of legal definitions of crime. Behind this proposal lurks what should be the central theoretical problem of criminology as a discipline: If criminological generalizations are based solely on legal definitions, then criminology depends exclusively on the values enshrined in criminal law. But no criminologist enjoys the license to study solely the practices prohibited by criminal law. (see Section 1.2)

Assume that the primary goal of criminology is the construction of sociological generalizations regarding the distribution and causes of antisocial practices. Some, but not all, of such practices will be forbidden by criminal law. If this is true, then the unqualified acceptance of legal definitions of crime makes criminology a parasitic affair at the very outset. On the other hand, if legal definitions of crime are eliminated from comparative criminology (as Wolfgang [1967] would have it), then much of what is most interesting and important about different cultures—why certain cultures define certain practices and not others as illegal, cultural variation in notions of right and justice, and different penal practices, to mention but a few—is wished away by fiat.

Wolfgang's strategy is not unlike that of students of religious practices who, in attempting to compare the extent of religious sentiments in different cultures, base their analyses exclusively on official statistics of baptisms, church attendance, and marriages. Such practices aid perhaps in understanding what people do but not necessarily in understanding why people do them or what they mean. Indeed, the replacement of legal definitions of crime by such "neutral" indicators as the assessment of bodily and monetary damages still results in a criminology based on definitions of criminal justice agencies, because these assessments are provided by national police agencies. By no stretch of sociological imagination can such indicators be termed "neutral." Additionally, if the legal definition of crime is abandoned entirely as the initial object of study, we risk describing social practices and relations not as they in fact are but only as we would like them to be.

## EVALUATION OF COMPARATIVE CRIMINOLOGY

Comparative criminology is important to the process by which monocultural theories of crime might be (dis)confirmed and falsified. It broadens our intellectual horizons. Yet, as we have seen, it is fraught with perils. For example, under the influence of globalization, one of the rapidly growing areas of crime is transnational crime—yet transnational crime blurs the pure image of a "society" or "culture," which is the traditional object of comparative criminology.

Moreover, and returning to Clinard and Abbott's (1973) third stage of comparative testing, what criteria allow us to identify cultures that are completely dissimilar? Such criteria are increasingly rare in the modern world, whose outermost reaches have been penetrated by the routine operations of transnational corporations and the processes of globalization.

Assume that what Clinard and Abbott actually meant was not "completely dissimilar societies" but societies as different as possible. What sociological properties would such societies have? No doubt these properties would include major differences in religious or scientific beliefs, economic systems, political structures, and degree of technological development. The greater the difference between any two cultures along such axes, one presumes, the more entitled we are to term them "dissimilar." But this assumption is not without difficulty. The more two cultures differ, the less likely it is that they have common items to compare and the less likely it is that verifiable generalizations can be made about them.

In the face of these difficulties we probably have little choice but to follow the practical advice of Keith Dixon (1977), who urges the criminologist to "maximize his understanding of alien cultures by honest-to-God fieldwork, moral charity, intellectual humility, and a determination of the taken-for-granted assumptions of both his own and others' cultural milieu" (p. 76).

## 3.2 COMPARATIVE CRIME AND VICTIMIZATION DATA

Let's continue our exploration of comparative criminology with an outline of cross-national crime and victimization data. Most of these data are generated by large-scale international organizations, such as the United Nations, Interpol, and the World Health Organization. Some, however, can be found in the reports of private human rights organizations, such as Amnesty International, Human Rights Watch, Oxfam, the International Red Cross, and Doctors Without Borders.

### CROSS-NATIONAL CRIME DATA

*United Nations.* The United Nations has collected and analyzed comparative statistical data on crime since 1946. Although the United Nations' original concern was limited to a rather simplistic notion of the prevention of crime and the treatment of offenders, it now adopts a much broader policy toward crime. This larger view is clearly stated in Article 55 of the United Nations Charter (United Nations, 1983):

> With a view to the creation of conditions of stability and well-being which are necessary for peaceful and friendly relations among nations based on respect for the principle of equal rights and self-determination of peoples, the United Nations shall promote:
>
> A. Higher standards of living, full employment, and conditions of economic and social progress and development.
>
> B. Solutions of international economic, social, health, and related problems; and international cultural and educational cooperation.
>
> C. Universal respect for, and observance of, human rights and fundamental freedoms

for all without distinction as to race, sex, language, or religion. (p. iii)

This extension of the scope of the United Nations to encompass human rights resulted largely from the exposure of Nazi atrocities at the end of the 1939–1945 war. The perspective was extended first to war crimes and genocide and then to the widespread use of cruel, inhumane, or degrading treatment of political dissidents. It now includes the violation of human rights, political and economic abuses of colonial and institutional terrorism, and crime resulting from abuses of economic and political power by transnational enterprises. The complex organizational machinery (based in Geneva, Vienna, and New York City) of U.N. criminal policy includes the General Assembly, the Secretariat, the International Court of Justice, the Committee on Crime Prevention and Control, the Commission for Social Development, and various specialist bodies, such as the Commission of Human Rights, the Commission on Narcotic Drugs, and the Centre for International Crime Prevention (now named the UNODC Crime Programme).

The United Nations has wrestled often with the need to provide adequate sets of international crime statistics. It has tried to collect and disseminate data in various ways. Let us mention three of these.

First, since 1955, U.N. congresses on crime prevention have been held every five years; congress reports have sometimes appeared in the U.N. Crime Prevention and Criminal Justice booklets. These booklets have included reports on human rights, capital punishment, and torture; prison labor, aftercare, parole, and recidivism; economic development, crime, and colonialism; juvenile delinquency; and ethical standards in criminal justice. However, most of the articles in these booklets have provided data on only one country. As such, they would have to be significantly reinterpreted for comparative purposes.

Second, the United Nations has undertaken five surveys on Crime Trends and Operation of Criminal Justice Systems (UNCJS). These surveys contain voluminous amounts of official data on crime, criminal justice, and punishment. Crime data from the UNCJS and elsewhere have been compiled in the U.N. book *Global Report on Crime and Justice* (1999) and updated periodically at the U.S. Bureau of Justice website: http://www.ojp.gov/bjs/ijs.htm. Data for the much shorter sixth survey, of 2000, has been supplemented by data from the International Crime Victim Survey, which we will discuss shortly.

Third, at its website, http://www.uncjin.org/, the United Nations operates a clearinghouse of statistics and links for the data that it generates itself and for other data generated by public and private bodies worldwide. These data are as meaningful—no less, no more—as the sources from which they originate.

*Interpol.* The International Police Organization ("Interpol") is based in Lyon, France, and has published crime data biennially since 1950. In 2009 Interpol had 187 member countries, the national police departments in each of which provided data on murder; sex offenses (including rape); serious assault; theft (of all sorts); fraud; counterfeiting; and drug offenses. In addition, in recent years Interpol has published occasional information on crimes against humanity; terrorism; trafficking in children and adults; the illegal drug trade; and financial and high-tech corruption.

In essence, Interpol is a clearinghouse of data collected by national criminal justice agencies. Each nation's crime data are, of course, collected in different ways. To take only the crime of murder, for example, some countries include attempted murder in their definition of murder; some fail to distinguish between murder and manslaughter; some base their homicide data on murders known to the police, others on convictions. Some countries, such as those in central Africa, do not even collect crime statistics.

Interpol's police-based data, in other words, are so plagued with national idiosyncrasies that they are of dubious value for purposes of comparative criminology.

***Comparative Crime Data File.*** The centerpiece of Dane Archer and Rosemary Gartner's book *Violence and Crime in Cross-National Perspective* (1984) is the CCDF, or Comparative Crime Data File. The CCDF lists the police-based data of 110 countries and 44 large cities up to 1982. It lists both the raw number of offenses and the offense rate (per 100,000) for murder, manslaughter, homicide, rape, assault, robbery, and theft, tabulating the data under their original legal labels.

The CCDF was an important stepping stone in the attempt to develop comparative crime data. Despite all the limitations of police-based data, the CCDF still has some value for historical research.

## CROSS-NATIONAL VICTIMIZATION DATA

As discussed in Section 2.3, victimization surveys offer a complementary and arguably more reliable indicator of crime trends in the United States than police-based statistics such as the Uniform Crime Reports. Besides the National Crime Victimization Survey in the United States, national victimization surveys have also been conducted in many other societies. At first glance, the growth of these surveys offers a good source of comparative evidence about crime trends. Common sense tells us that if victims of crime are more willing to report their victimization to survey interviewers than to police officers, then victimization surveys should reveal more about the incidence of crime than police statistics.

Consider, for example, what we can learn from the comparative findings of victimization surveys conducted in thirty countries (see Figures 3.1 and 3.2). We can see that, contrary to most popular opinion and media claims about where the United States stands in the league tables of crime,

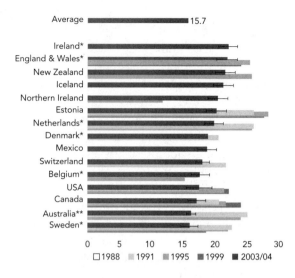

**FIGURE 3.1**  Overall Victimization Rates for 10 Crimes in the Top Fifteen Countries (percentages)
*Source*: van Dijk, van Kesteren, and Smit (2007:Figure 3, p. 43).

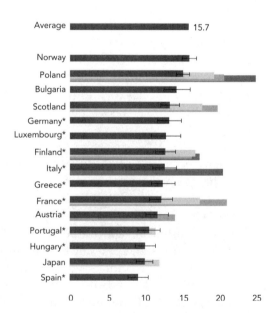

**FIGURE 3.2**  Overall Victimization Rates for 10 Crimes in the Bottom Fifteen Countries (percentages)
*Source*: van Dijk, van Kesteren, and Smit (2007:Figure 4, p. 44).

according to victimization surveys for the period 1989–2005, for ten common crimes some comparable countries had higher rates of victimization than the United States (Figure 3.1), though many had lower rates (Figure 3.2).

Yet victimization surveys have their own peculiar methodological limitations that complicate their use in comparative analysis. Most surveys outside the United States, for example, have been very small, although it is possible that these small samples are as representative of the levels of victimization of their national populations as the large samples in the U.S. National Crime Victimization Survey. Furthermore, in some countries (such as the United States), victimization rates are calculated with households as the database; in other countries (for instance, Holland), rates are based on per capita victimizations. This difference casts some doubt on the validity of some comparative studies of victimization. Because household size tends to decline with affluence, different databases tend to obscure differences in the opportunity for crime that arise from variations in population size and household composition. Further problems arise from the wording of survey questions, which reflect legal definitions of crime, which can vary from one country to another.

*International Crime Victims Surveys.* Some of these problems have been overcome in the five sweeps of the International Crime Victim Survey (ICVS; see also IVAWS, 2009; ICBS, 2009), held, respectively, in 1989, 1992, 1996, 2000, and 2004 (with the sixth survey expected in 2009–2010).

Although there is little new in the format and methodology of the survey itself, the ICVS is unique in its use of standardized questionnaires, sampling methods, and data analyses and applying them to a large number of countries. In each country, 500–2,500 subjects are selected by random-digit-dialing telephone interviews (in studies of eastern Europe and of developing societies currently under way,

the primary method of data collection is the face-to-face interview). Subjects are questioned about eleven main forms of victimization, divided into "household property crimes" and "personal crimes." Household property crimes include theft of, theft from, and vandalism to cars; theft of motorcycles; theft of bicycles; burglary with entry; attempted burglary; and break-ins to outbuildings. Personal crimes include robbery; theft of personal property, pickpocketing, and noncontact personal thefts; sexual incidents, sexual assaults, and offensive sexual behavior; and assaults/threats, assaults with force, and threats without force. If the subjects indicate that they had been victimized, more detailed questions are then asked about the event(s). Subjects are also asked a number of questions reflecting fear of crime and attitudes toward police. The data are weighted for gender, regional population distribution, age, and household composition in order to make the samples as representative as possible of actual national populations age 16 or higher.

In general, the ICVS shows that victimization levels increased between 1988 and 1991, stabilized or fell in 1995, fell further in 1999, and seemed to have stabilized somewhat by 2004. In the words of the ICVS itself:

> ICVS-based prevalence rates of 1988, 1992, 1996, 2000, and 2003/04 are available for five countries. In the USA victimisation by common crimes has peaked earlier than elsewhere. Rates of victimisation in 1992 were below those in 1988 and have continued to go down thereafter. In Canada the turning point in levels of common crime came somewhat later than in the USA, similar to what happened in most European countries and Australia.
>
> In the course of the past twenty years the levels of victimisation in the Western world seem to have converged. Differences between the USA, Canada, Australia, and Western and Central Europe have narrowed. Although trend data are available from

only two middle-income cities in the developing world, these too point at a downturn in overall victimisation since 1996 (Buenos Aires) or 2000 (Johannesburg). Crime trends across the developed and middle-income countries, then, show remarkable uniformity.

ICVS results show an increase in general crime between 1988 and 1991 and a downward trend since 1996 or 2000 across the developed world. (ICVS, 2004–2005, cited in van Dijk, van Kesteren, and Smit (2007:101–102).

One of the most revealing findings of the 2004–2005 Survey concerns the differing levels at which crimes are reported to the police (Figure 3.3). Based on the reporting of five crime types (theft from cars, burglary with entry, robbery, sexual incidents, and assaults and threats). The survey found that the highest reporting rates were in Austria (70 percent), Belgium (68 percent), Sweden (64 percent), and Switzerland (63 percent), with the United states at 49 percent. Very low rates of reporting were found

**FIGURE 3.3** Reporting of Crimes to the Police (percentages)
*Source*: van Dijk, van Kesteren, and Smit (2007:Figure 23, p. 111).

in developing countries. Brazil (Sao Paulo), Cambodia (Phnom Penh), Peru (Lima), Mexico, and Mozambique (Maputo) stand out; these had reporting rates below 20 percent. Among the many reasons for not reporting crimes to the police are the feeling that the crime was "not serious enough" or involved "no loss" or that the police could do nothing about it (van Dijk, van Kesteren, and Smit, 2007:110–113). Moreover, according to the ICVS:

> The reasons why sexual incidents and assaults and threats were reported reflected the concern of victims to stop what happened being repeated.
>
> Many victims also wanted help. For the two property offences and robbery, more than a third was reported because assistance was sought in recovering property. When a burglary or theft from a car was involved, about a third did report for insurance reasons. About four in ten victims overall referred to the obligation to notify the police, either because they felt a crime such as theirs should be reported, or because what happened had been serious. Retributive motives—the hope that offenders would be caught and punished—weighed with nearly as many victims, though this was less evident when thefts from cars were involved. Results from the 1996 and 2000 ICVS were fairly similar when the comparison is restricted to the countries participating in each sweep. (p. 113)

As interesting and suggestive as the ICVS data are, it must be stressed that their meaning is not altogether straightforward. As we already know (see Section 2.1), victimization surveys inevitably have their own methodological dilemmas. Thus, given that the rate of reporting crimes to the police varies from one country to another, as the ICVS itself shows, there is no reason to suppose that the rate of reporting to survey interviewers is the same in each country. If a society has high reported victimization rates, does that mean that more persons are victimized there? Or does it mean that the citizenry there is more sensitive to violence—that they are more intolerant of intolerance—and therefore more likely to report it?

In short, we have good reason to be cautious about the meaning and usefulness of cross-national victimization surveys in comparative criminology.

## 3.3 CROSS-NATIONAL GENERALIZATIONS REGARDING CRIME

Let us now examine three specific areas of crime about which comparative criminologists have sought to generalize:

- Countries with low crime rates.
- Modernization and crime.
- Globalization and crime.

### COUNTRIES WITH LOW CRIME RATES

Some of the most interesting questions for comparative criminology concern the nature of countries with low crime rates. Why do some countries consistently have lower crime rates than others? What, if anything, do these countries have in common? What can we learn from their experience? Let us briefly examine two countries with low crime rates: Japan and Ireland.

*Japan.* During most of the past century, according to government data, Japan had persistently low, stable, and occasionally declining crime rates. In 2007, for example, the Japanese homicide rate was 1.1 per 100,000 (or about one-fifth of the United States rate). When criminologists attempt to explain Japanese crime rates, they usually refer to the strong elements of informal social control in Japanese life, which tend to produce—from a Western perspective—a crushing conformity in social relationships. Such control, this explanation continues, is manifest in certain vital areas: the patriarchal nature of the family, the quality of formal education, the power of religion and, especially in urban areas, the surrogate family provided by economic corporations.

In such ways, Japanese life is controlled to such an extent that, to many citizens, crime and deviance are actually unthinkable. Additionally, these ordered features of Japanese life are themselves supplemented by an efficient police force that is tightly integrated with and has an excellent rapport with the Japanese public (Fenwick, 2003, 2004; Leonardsen, 2004, 2006).

Moreover, while pointing to the harsher and more certain punishment awarded criminals in Japan—which Western commentators often do not see—the Japanese criminologist Setsuo Miyazawa (1993, 2008; and see Komiya, 1999) stresses that the push to conformity begins at an early age for Japanese children. This push toward conformity is then nourished through the combined power of education, work, family, religion, and ancestor worship. Miyazawa (1993) stresses how different the routines of Japanese childhood are, compared with the daily lives of children in other parts of the world:

> The value of conformity is first taught at schools. For children, school epitomizes the conventional world. Japanese school children are among the busiest children in the world. A survey conducted by the Japanese government indicates that they do homework more than anyone else, play for a relatively short time, and sleep the least.... Japanese junior high school students spend 6 hours in the classroom each day and more than 3 hours in extracurricular activities and homework. (p. 98)

Before assessing the relevance of the Japanese experience to the possible understanding of crime in the United States, we note our disagreement with any explanation of Japan's low crime rate that begins and ends with the level of social control there. An inquiry into why Japan has relatively low rates of interpersonal crime should not be made at the expense of examining other forms of crime. It is quite possible that rates of white-collar crime, syndicated crime, and political corruption, for example, are higher in Japan than in most other industrialized societies. Thus, as some researchers have already pointed out, although the rate of individualistic forms of white-collar crime such as embezzlement may be quite low in Japan, white-collar crimes motivated for "the good of the company" may be very high there (Kerbo and Inoue, 1990).

The Japanese experience reflects the fact that high crime rates are by no means an inevitable feature of modernized societies. However, we believe that explanations of low Japanese crime rates sometimes inappropriately focus on the element of control in Japanese life. Two decades of failed get-tough conservative crime policies in the United States should tell us that control, as such, explains neither low nor high crime rates. In Japan's case the emphasis on control as an explanation of low crime rates neglects the ways in which Japanese society is more supportive of its citizenry than the United States in terms of providing social and welfare services. As many commentators on Japanese culture have pointed out, this supportive network is apparent in the relative absence in Japan of an underclass, in the fact of egalitarianism in income distribution, and in a complete absence of urban ghettos.

Time will soon tell whether the push toward lower crime rates occasioned by Japan's aging population—with relatively fewer young males—will be outweighed by recession-like economic conditions since the early 1990s (e.g., see Roberts and LaFree, 2004; David Johnson, 2008). Moreover, in trying to explain why Japan has relatively low crime rates, we need to look further afield than criminology's traditional focus on crime. Thus, it has been known at least since the time of Durkheim's (Section 5.1) analyses of homicide and suicide in France in the 1890s that any given social or personal crisis can lead to a variety of deviant responses, which themselves often vary by social class, gender, race/ethnicity, and age. If we examine in both societies the different responses over time to

rising levels of unemployment, for example, we are likely to find rising homicide rates in the United States and rising suicide rates in Japan:

> It is reasonably well established that the 50 percent increase, over a 10-year period, in the number of suicides (from approximately 21,000 in 1990 to in excess of 32,000 per annum by the end of the century)... was the product of economic stagnation and rising rates of unemployment.... Western criminologists conventionally look at how worsening economic indicators affect crime rates, but they seldom look at the act of suicide.... What is striking about the Japanese statistics is that crime rates do not seem particularly sensitive to shifts in the economic statistics (although this may also be changing). Rather, in Japan, where the cultural implications of "losing face" are more profound, and where losing one's employment amounts to a profound loss of face, the social impact of increasing numbers of men experiencing employment loss seems principally to be expressed in the dramatically rising number of suicides. (Sheptycki, 2005:14)

*Ireland.* Let us now shift our attention to the Republic of Ireland, another country with historically low crime rates. From the 1950s to the early 1970s, Ireland had exceptionally low and stable crime rates (McCullagh, 1996). However, by 1975 (approximately when Ireland became a fully industrialized society), there were five times as many recorded "shopbreakings," six times as many "housebreakings," and twenty-nine times as many robberies as had been recorded in 1951. A substantial increase was also recorded for offenses against the person, with indictable assaults rising seven times over the same 25 years (Rottman, 1980). In the 1950s the average annual number of homicides was 7.2; in the 1960s it was 10.1; and from 1970 to 1975 it was 20.8. By 2001 the annual number of homicides had risen to 59 (see Table 3.1—although compared with other industrialized countries, the rate of homicide was still very low at 1.42/100,000. Since 1995, the overall crime rate in Ireland has been declining (O'Donnell and O'Sullivan, 2003).

Such changes suggest that Ireland conforms to major strands of the modernization thesis yet also differs significantly from it. During the 1940s, the rapid decline of Irish agriculture—a decline that was not relieved but exacerbated by intensive industrialization during the early 1960s—created serious hardship among the Irish working class. Increased unemployment, in turn, led to enormous intrafamilial conflict and to other forms of dislocation, such as emigration. Rottman (1980) analyzed the changing Irish homicide patterns immediately after these great economic and social upheavals. He showed that after the early 1960s there occurred in Ireland a diminishing incidence of family homicide, an increasing proportion of homicides involving strangers, and more homicides in which females killed males. In these respects, Ireland appears to conform to the modernization thesis.

In other ways, however, Irish crime rates seem to contradict the modernization thesis. For example, after the industrialization of the 1960s, crime rates did not increase more in urban areas than in rural areas: The increase was diffuse rather than concentrated in cities (Rottman, 1980). Also, even though we are dealing with a small number of homicides, the rising percentage of men murdered by women—a 41.3 percent increase between the 1950s and the 1970s—is probably not typical of other modernized countries. Moreover, except for murder, rates of violent crime in Ireland may actually have declined between the early 1990s and the new millennium (O'Donnell and Sullivan, 2003). A recent rise in Irish homicide rates can perhaps be attributed to a great increase both in binge drinking—and therefore in street disorder—and in gangland feuding (O'Donnell, 2008).

Overall, it is therefore fair to say that Ireland is a real exception to the view that rising crime rates accompany modernization. Although there is as yet no sustained explanation of Ireland's persistently low crime rates, we note especially the powerful and longstanding (though, in the past decade, declining) influence of Roman Catholicism in government, education, and family. An additional factor is undoubtedly the relatively good relationship between the Irish citizenry and the Garda, the Irish police force. Thus, in 2007 a survey of public opinion in Ireland found that 81 percent of those surveyed were "very satisfied" or "satisfied" with the Irish police (Garda Research Unit, 2008); this probably represents a greater level of confidence in the Irish police by the Irish citizenry than in any other Irish institution.

What do Japan and Ireland have in common? It's hard to say. One attempt to find commonalities among countries with low crime rates is Freda Adler's book *Nations Not Obsessed with Crime* (1983). Adler isolated five diverse "regions" in the world (European capitalist, European socialist, Latin America, Islam, and Asia) and then selected from each region two countries (respectively: Switzerland/Ireland, Bulgaria/German Democratic Republic, Costa Rica/Peru, Algeria/Saudi Arabia, and Japan/Nepal) with the lowest or among the lowest crime rates in its region.

Adler (1983) first tried to correlate each country's arrest rates with 47 socioeconomic variables, including age, occupation, national income, education, and patterns of consumer expenditure. From this correlational analysis Adler inferred that these ten countries had no significant socioeconomic or cultural factors in common. At the same time, Adler identified some broad trends in the ten countries:

> Most low-crime countries have in common lower-than-average population densities, lower-than-average urban populations,...lower-than-average population numbers which are economically active, a lower-than-average number of radio

receivers and telephones, a higher-than-average population in agriculture,...and a higher than average crude death rate. (p. 10)

Still, there were startling sociocultural differences among these ten countries. They had a variety of state structures, including military government, parliamentary democracy, popular democracy, and absolute and constitutional monarchies. Their economies ranged from subsistence agriculture (Nepal, Peru) to extensive industrialization (GDR, Switzerland, Japan). Some had urbanized slowly (Ireland, Switzerland), others quickly (Saudi Arabia, Japan). In some (Peru), unemployment rates were high; in others (GDR, Bulgaria, Japan, Switzerland) they were low. Some of the countries contained homogeneous populations, others were heterogeneous. Adler also outlined each country's formal and informal mechanisms of social control. Each appeared to have various systems of law, politics, and criminal justice. Each had differing levels of success in solving reported crimes, ranging from high (Japan, Saudi Arabia) to low. While actual support for human rights was difficult to measure, five countries retained the use of capital punishment.

Nevertheless, Adler claimed that she had found a common aspect among countries with low crime rates: popular involvement in—or popularity of—the criminal justice system. Six of the ten countries—four highly industrialized (Japan, Switzerland, Bulgaria, and the GDR) and two underdeveloped (Nepal and Peru)—were "marked by an extraordinarily high degree of popular participation in crime control" (Frieda Adler, 1983:128). Moreover, Saudi Arabia, Algeria, and Ireland had succeeded, despite foreign intervention, in maintaining the integrity of their indigenous systems of social control. Costa Rica (which has no standing army) had fostered local self-government and was actively popularizing its criminal justice system.

Adler also found that all 10 countries had strong elements of social control outside the criminal justice system. According to Adler, these elements did not exercise control by formal constraint; rather, "they transmit and maintain values by providing for a sharing of norms and by ensuring cohesiveness" (Adler, 1983:130). First and foremost, her argument continued, was the survival of the power of the family, even during modernization. In each case the family, often patriarchal, remained a closely woven unit that exerted a powerful influence on its members. In societies where employment levels were high—with women composing a large segment of the labor force—strong efforts had been made to provide for children during work hours in day-care facilities and kindergartens. The retention of traditional family values was itself reinforced by a second system of control: religious, moral, or secular values. In all ten countries—whether Islamic, Christian, or socialist—such values exhorted the citizenry to act for the common good; they "solidify the moral obligations of the community to reaffirm in common their common sentiments" (p. 132).

Remarkably, Adler's (1983) is the only study to have specifically examined how countries with high crime rates differ from those with low ones.

But we must note three criticisms of Adler's analysis. First, her study essentially avoided all thorny methodological and relativist problems of comparative research. She paid little attention, for example, to cross-national differences in history, law, and economy. Second, when examining non-Anglophone countries, Adler relied either on statements by native government officials or on secondary English-language commentaries. But interviewing government officials about such things as the popularity of the criminal justice system, for example, is not a very reliable way to gather information about crime in other (or any) cultures. Because she relied on secondary sources, we can determine neither the accuracy of their analyses nor the range of opinions they reflected. Finally, we must note that Adler's study, unique as it remains, has been quite overtaken by recent developments—especially the power of globalization and the tremendous increase in transnational crime.

## MODERNIZATION AND CRIME

Since the early 1960s, sociologists have argued that the mere fact of technological development produces common effects that tend, irrespective of different or even antagonistic political systems, to make all societies "converge." In this scenario, technology itself is seen as an evenhanded factor that inevitably determines that all modern societies eventually converge on a common industrial model. This industrial convergence model, which in criminology is usually termed the **modernization thesis,** has eight characteristics (Lane, 1996, 2007):

1. Populations grow rapidly, family size falls, women are emancipated, and relationships between spouses become more equal.
2. Knowledge, wealth, political power, and human rights become more available to the entire population.
3. The division of labor is highly developed, and education and occupation determine individual positions in the social hierarchy.
4. Ideological differences are minimized, and a premium is placed on hard work and economic productivity.
5. Legal systems apply a more-or-less common law to individuals of all social ranks.
6. Although political ideologies can be quite different, the central government organizes all of society.
7. Human relationships tend to be specific and achievement oriented rather than diffuse and ascribed.

8. Large-scale urbanism ensures that social relationships are impersonal, superficial, and differentiated.

In criminology, industrial convergence theory suggests that, as societies modernize, their homicide rates rise quite dramatically (Beirne and Nelken, 1997). As they begin to industrialize and become more urbanized, in other words, societies of all social types often experience great social upheaval and dislocation, not the least because traditional patterns of family life are disrupted when young males in search of work move from rural areas to towns and to cities. Immense and rapid population growth in urban areas sometimes has explosive effects on infant mortality, health, sewage, food supplies, public order, and crime. It is violent crime in particular, including homicide, that escalates during the process of modernization. At the same time, this general social deterioration tends to be accompanied by the rise of the nation-state and its massive apparatuses of social control. The state tries to monopolize the use of violence through the development of formal institutions of social control, such as criminal law and police. The growth of a national network of these institutions is accompanied by the cultivation of less formal but often very effective processes of social control and moral regulation, which Elias (1978) has termed *the civilizing process.*

The diverse signs of the civilizing process are said to include respect for individual rights; conscience; proper deportment in public places; the use of polite manners; rules for games and sports and the banning of most sports involving violence against animals; and the abolition of public executions and, eventually, of capital punishment altogether.

A central aspect of the "modernization and crime" thesis has been empirically tested by LaFree and Drass (2002). Their study is based on the assumption that if modernization is indeed accompanied by high homicide rates, industrializing societies are more likely than industrialized societies to have rapid and sustained homicide booms. Using World Health Organization homicide data for thirty-four industrializing or industrialized nations from 1956 to 1998, LaFree and Drass found that 70 percent of the industrializing nations (seven of ten) but only 21 percent of the industrialized nations (five of twenty-four) had homicide booms in this period. This study therefore tends to support the modernization thesis.

Moreover, LaFree and Drass argue that several of the industrialized nations in their sample that had experienced homicide booms—such as the United States, Greece, and Spain, whose cases thus seemingly contradict the modernization thesis—were themselves suffering serious social disruption. In the 1960s and 1970, for example, the United States experienced widespread political turmoil. Rising homicide rates coincided in Greece with the fall of the military junta in 1974 and the rebirth of a democratic constitution. The rapid growth of homicide rates in Spain coincided with the death of dictator Francisco Franco in 1975. Further, unlike the persistent increase in homicide rates experienced by industrializing societies, the homicide rates of the United States, Greece, and Spain began to decline within two decades.

Social and economic inequality is one of the most plausible explanations of variation in homicide rates in industrialized societies concerns. This explanation is especially likely where inequality is accompanied by strain and a popular sense of injustice. One avenue of research has found that in thirty-four industrialized countries, high homicide rates have tended to be accompanied by high levels of income inequality and concentrated poverty (Rosenfeld and Messner, 1991; Currie, 1998); this correlation holds even when controlling for variations in gross national product, population size, population density,

and degree of urbanization. As Elliott Currie (1998) has stressed:

> The links between extreme deprivation, delinquency, and violence…are strong, consistent, and compelling. The effects are compounded by the absence of public supports to buffer economic insecurity and deprivation, and they are even more potent when racial subordination is added to the mix. And this—rather than "prosperity"—helps us begin to understand why the United States suffers more serious violent crime than other industrial democracies, and why violence has remained stubbornly high in the face of our unprecedented efforts at repressive control. (p. 131)

We must add, too, that one of the basic problems with existing modernization theory is that crime patterns in the Third World are not likely to repeat patterns of criminality in the more technologically advanced nations of the world. Criminality in the Third World is not simply a replay of the histories of more modernized nations. Indeed, many crimes committed in Third World countries actually originate in the First World and result in transnational crime.

Consider, for example, the worst industrial accident on record, which occurred when toxic gas leaked from a Union Carbide (now part of the Dow Chemical Co.) insecticide plant early on the morning of December 3, 1984, in the central Indian town of Bhopal

> Witnesses said thousands of people had been taken to hospitals gasping for breath, many frothing at the mouth, their eyes inflamed. The streets were littered with the corpses of dogs, cats, water buffalo, cows, and birds killed by the gas, methyl isocyanate, which is widely used in the preparation of insecticides. Doctors from neighboring towns and the Indian Army were rushed to the city of 900,000, where hospitals were said to be overflowing with the injured. Most of the victims were children and old people who were over whelmed by

the gas and suffocated, Indian press reports said. (*New York Times*, December 4, 1989)

The Bhopal chemical leak resulted in the immediate deaths of 8,000 residents. By 2009, the death toll in Bhopal from the chemical leak was estimated to be between 15,000 and 20,000. About 120,000 survivors continue to press their injury claims outstanding in injury compensation courts for chronic exposure-induced diseases, including breathlessness, persistent cough, early-age cataracts, loss of appetite, menstrual irregularities, recurrent fever, back and body aches, loss of sensation in limbs, fatigue, weakness, anxiety, and depression (International Campaign for Justice in Bhopal, 2009). In 2009 the Indian government was continuing to request the extradition from the United States of Union Carbide CEO Warren Anderson to stand trial for criminal liability in India, to no avail at that time.

What tragedies such as the Bhopal disaster imply is that societies "modernize" not according to some inner benevolent logic but, rather, according to the dictates of economic and political power within a global system of capitalist economies. Many patterns of crime and many large-scale acts of social harm cannot be understood if societies are viewed in isolation from each other.

## GLOBALIZATION AND CRIME

Globalization has become increasingly important in the understanding of patterns of crime in any given society. There is no society in the world whose national boundaries are insulated from the economic and cultural processes of globalization. It is a worldwide process of sameness that is modified and contextualized by varying local circumstances. As Jock Young (2007) has written in his book *The Vertigo of Late Modernity*:

Although the extent and level of economic globalization is debatable,... the impact is worldwide.

The poor are not left behind stranded in the inner cities deserted by capital, they live in intense and self-involved marketplaces and their eyes are on the outside world. The Third World peasant may not contribute much to the world economy and to the triad of the United States, Europe, and Japan, but this does not mean that they are outside the forces of economic globalization: Their coffee is sold on the world markets, they buy Coca-Cola at their local stall. (p. 38)

Not only does globalization affect how and under what conditions we work or are unemployed, but also, culturally, it affects our identities: who "we" and who our "communities" are, where we live, and what our hopes are. Although globalization, as such, is not a part of comparative criminology as it has traditionally been understood, it is nevertheless a process that profoundly affects crime in any and all societies (Young, 2007; Sheptycki and Wardak, 2005). Sometimes, not surprisingly, it is the international institutions of global governance themselves that commit crime, such as the World Bank (Friedrichs, 2007; Friedrichs and Friedrichs, 2008).

Young (2007:38–40) has made six generalizations about the complex processes by which globalization fuels discontent worldwide—and hence leads to a variety of social and intersocietal problems, including crime:

1. *Widening of income differentials.* Economically, globalization widens income differentials, both within the First World and between rich and poor countries.
2. *Cultural globalization and relative deprivation.* Culturally, through mass media images of high levels of consumption, globalization generates aspirations among the First World poor and throughout the Third World that are blocked by structural inequality and unfairness. Globalization thus fuels relative—rather than absolute—deprivation.

3. *Globalization and the crisis of identity.* This is most obvious in rising unemployment and unstable families. The poor and minority groups, above all, suffer economic and political marginalization and feel disrespected.

4. *Relative deprivation and ontological insecurity.* Perceptions of great unfairness and feelings of insecurity provide a rationalization (or "technique of neutralization") for violence, for blaming others for one's own crises, and for dehumanizing them.

5. *The narcissism of minor differences.* Given the crises of identity and of security brought about by globalization, minor differences between societies and within societies and between ethnic or racial groups are exacerbated. Some of these differences are expressed in violent passionate conflict around masculinity and heroic myths.

6. *Identity wars.* Globalization leads to identity wars. These are found in crimes of passion, rage against humiliation, expressivity, and lifestyle. They are also found at the national level, where fundamentalist Western presidents and prime ministers wage holy wars against fundamentalist terrorists.

## AMERICAN EXCEPTIONALISM: CRIME AND INCARCERATION IN COMPARATIVE PERSPECTIVE

Students often ask: "Why does the United States have one of the highest crime rates in the world?" The view that for most crimes the United States has the highest rate in the world is more or less clearly contradicted by the evidence presented in this chapter.

However, we must stress that in two important respects the United States is truly exceptional. First, among technologically developed societies, the United States continues to have by far the highest homicide rate. Second, the United States incarcerates its citizens at unprecedented rates.

One part of the explanation of the regrettable fact of the high homicide rates in the United States lies in the comparative perspective of this chapter. How does the social structure of the United States differ from that in comparable societies? Though we discuss different aspects of this in different parts of this book, it is worth stating some of these in advance.

1. The United States has had one of the highest rates of structural unemployment since 1945.

2. The United States has the largest underclass of persons economically, socially, and politically discriminated against because of race or ethnic background.

3. The United States has inferior support systems of welfare, social security, health, and education.

4. The extreme and aggressive commercialism of U.S. capitalism provides incentives and motivations to circumvent acceptable (namely, legal) means of achievement.

5. The United States has one of the highest firearm ownership rates in the world.

6. The United States has one of the most punitive criminal justice systems in the world.

Comparative evidence reveals that the United States consistently incarcerates much more of its population than other Western countries (see Table 3.4). In 2009, there were more than 2.3 million prisoners in the United States—more prisoners and at a higher rate than ever before and more than anywhere else on earth. In addition, as many as 5 million were on probation or parole in 2009. All this includes a very significant discrimination against the poor and against minorities; Latinos,

**TABLE 3.4   PRISON POPULATIONS IN SELECTED COUNTRIES, 2004–2006**

| Country | Total Prison Population | Year | Rate of Incarceration (per 100,000) |
|---|---|---|---|
| Australia | 25,353 | 2005 | 126 |
| Austria | 8,766 | 2006 | 105 |
| Belgium | 9,597 | 2006 | 91 |
| Canada | 34,096 | 2004 | 107 |
| China | 1,548,498 | 2003 | 118 |
| Colombia | 62,216 | 2006 | 134 |
| Denmark | 4,198 | 2005 | 77 |
| England/Wales | 79,861 | 2006 | 148 |
| Finland | 3,954 | 2006 | 75 |
| France | 52,009 | 2006 | 85 |
| Germany | 78,581 | 2006 | 95 |
| Greece | 9,984 | 2005 | 90 |
| Iceland | 119 | 2005 | 40 |
| India | 332,112 | 2004 | 30 |
| Ireland | 3,080 | 2006 | 72 |
| Israel | 13,909 | 2004 | 209 |
| Italy | 61,721 | 2006 | 104 |
| Japan | 79,055 | 2005 | 62 |
| Netherlands | 21,013 | 2006 | 128 |
| New Zealand | 7,620 | 2006 | 186 |
| Nigeria | 40,444 | 2005 | 30 |
| N. Ireland | 1,466 | 2006 | 84 |
| Norway | 3,048 | 2006 | 66 |
| Pakistan | 89,370 | 2005 | 57 |
| Portugal | 12,870 | 2006 | 121 |
| Saudi Arabia | 28,612 | 2002 | 132 |
| Scotland | 7,131 | 2006 | 139 |

**TABLE 3.4**   *Continued*

| Country | Total Prison Population | Year | Rate of Incarceration (per 100,000) |
|---|---|---|---|
| South Africa | 157,402 | 2005 | 335 |
| Spain | 64,215 | 2006 | 145 |
| Sweden | 7,450 | 2006 | 82 |
| Switzerland | 6,111 | 2005 | 83 |
| United States | 218,6230 | 2005 | 738 |

Source: Adapted from Roy Walmsley (2007).

for example, who comprise only 13 percent of the U.S. population, constituted 33 percent of federal prison inmates in 2008 (Pew Hispanic Center, 2009), nearly half of them convicted in the war against illegal immigration (see also Michalowski, 2007).

Similar societies have far lower incarceration rates, with most clustering around 55–120 per 100,000; some are lower still, such as Iceland at 40, Japan at 62, Ireland at 72, and Sweden at 82 per 100,000.

Moreover, and returning to a theme at the heart of Chapter 1, it is unclear whether these expanding instruments of governance in the United States—surveillance and mass incarceration—will make the public feel more secure or simply more anxious (e.g., J. Simon, 2007). Though the relationship between incarceration and crime rates has been the object of longstanding debate among criminologists, one even-handed book—*Prison State: The Challenge of Mass Incarceration*—suggests that a point has been reached where further incarceration will have no effect at all (Useem and Piehl, 2008:79–80). On the contrary: Punitive penal policies are a violent part of the very problem they are apparently designed to solve.

## REVIEW

Our chief focus in this chapter has been to supply a comparative dimension to criminology. We have examined some of the major issues involved in actually doing comparative studies and have outlined some of the most common comparative generalizations on crime.

If in Chapter 2 we saw how hard it is to measure crime rates in the United States, then in this chapter we have seen that it is just as hard—if not harder—to make intelligible comparisons between U.S. crime rates and those elsewhere in the world.

This chapter has taught the importance of testing theories under conditions as diverse as possible, and, therefore, it has explored the crucial role of comparative studies for the theoretical development of criminology in the United States. The major task of this chapter has been to outline the key concepts, data, and findings of comparative criminology. It has done so in the expanding context of transnational crime and the processes of globalization.

### APPROACHING COMPARATIVE CRIMINOLOGY

1. Comparative criminology is the systematic and theoretically informed comparison of crime in two or more cultures. It should help us answer some key questions about crime, including why some countries have low crime rates and whether a criminological theory developed in one society can explain patterns of crime in other societies.

2. Transnational crime is crime committed across borders or across national boundaries. Examples include terrorism, trafficking in persons and identities, in animals, and in human and animal organs; drug trafficking; money laundering; environmental and green crime; espionage and the illegal gathering of information; and trafficking in stones, precious metals, art, and artifacts.

3. Cultural relativism has two forms. Epistemological relativism—which we recognized and then ignored—holds that because we can never understand the beliefs of cultures different from our own, we cannot compare our culture with such cultures. Methodological relativism is a strategy for comparing different cultures that, at the same time, attempts to respect the facts of cultural diversity. The precise difficulties presented by cultural relativism were illustrated by Julia Brown's (1952) classic study of sexual deviance. We also examined Wolfgang's (1967) methodological strategy to standardize crime statistics.

### COMPARATIVE CRIME AND VICTIMIZATION DATA

1. The various sources of cross-national crime and victimization data include those of the United Nations, Interpol, and other international agencies and U.N.-sponsored victimization surveys. Other data, often on human rights violations, may be obtained from private organizations such as Amnesty International, Humans Rights Watch, Doctors Without Borders, and the International Red Cross.

2. For comparative purposes, using these sources entails the difficulty that societies define certain practices as crimes in different ways and also differ in the degree of seriousness they attach to them. Each type of cross-national crime data is subject to at least the same limitations as the crime data generated in any given society.

## CROSS-NATIONAL GENERALIZATIONS REGARDING CRIME

1. In this section several cross-national generalizations regarding crime were outlined. Each has its own merits.
2. We examined how countries with low crime rates might differ from ones with high crime rates. Little research has been completed on the sociological nature of societies with low crime rates. We outlined the available research, applied it especially to the cases of Japan and Ireland, and could offer only provisional answers. Among these are that societies with low crime rates are likely to be more egalitarian, less militaristic, and less urban.
3. We also examined the modernization thesis, which argues that generalizations can be made about the way in which industrialization and urbanization affect crime rates in all societies. The major problems with the modernization thesis are that it tends (1) to ignore relativist issues regarding differences in legal definitions of crime; (2) to be contradicted too often by empirical evidence; (3) to assume wrongly that criminality in Third World societies is a replay of the history of criminality in technologically advanced societies; and (4) to ignore the repressive colonial influence of First World countries and transnational corporations on the patterns of crime and globalization in the Third World.
4. We briefly outlined some generalizations that have been made about globalization and crime. Young's (2007) comments in this regard begin with the idea that globalization creates uncertainty and feelings of relative deprivation, which tend to lead to various forms of violence, including crime. We concluded with a brief section on American exceptionalism, namely, that, among technologically developed societies, the United States has the highest homicide rates and that it incarcerates its citizens at a much higher rate than anywhere else in the world.

## QUESTIONS FOR CLASS DISCUSSION

1. Twenty-five hundred years ago, Greek historian Herodotus (quoted in Feyerabend, 1987) recorded the following story:

    When Darius was king of Persia, he summoned the Greeks, who happened to be present at his court, and asked them what they would take to eat the dead bodies of their fathers. They replied they would not do it for any money in the world. Later, in the presence of the Greeks, and through an interpreter so that they could understand what was said, he asked some Indians, of the tribe called Callatiae, who do in fact eat their parents' dead bodies, what they would take to burn them. They uttered a cry of horror and forbade him to mention such a dreadful thing. (p. 42)

    What does this story tell us about the problem of cultural relativism?

2. Do crime rates in the Third World tend to repeat the patterns of recorded crime in countries such as the United States?
3. What lessons, if any, can U.S. policymakers derive from the incidence of crime in other countries?
4. Why are the rates of violent crime in the United States apparently so high in comparison with those of other modern industrialized countries?

## FOR FURTHER STUDY

### READINGS

Larsen, Nick, and Russell Smandych, eds. 2008a. *Global Criminology and Criminal Justice*. Peterborough, Ontario: Broadview Press.
Findlay, Mark. 2008. *Governing Through Globalised Crime*. Cullompton, Devon, UK: Willan.
Reichel, Philip, ed. 2005. *Handbook of Transnational Crime & Justice*. Thousand Oaks, CA: Sage.

### WEBSITES

1. <http://www.hrw.org>: This is the website of the humanitarian organization Human Rights Watch, which monitors human rights conditions, including prison conditions, prison abuses, and torture in some eighty countries worldwide.
2. <http://www.uncjin>: This is the home page of the United Nations Crime and Justice Information Network. The site provides a mass of information regarding crime and justice on the national and international levels.
3. <http://www.unicri.it/wwd/analysis/icvs/index.php>: This website provides data and publications from the International Crime Victimization Survey (ICVS) and the European Crime and Safety Survey (ECSS).
4. <http://www.who.int/whosis/database/mort/table1.cfm>: At this website of the World Health Organization, coroner-based homicide and suicide data are available by country.
5. <http://policy-traccc.gmu.edu/>: This is the website for the Terrorism, Transnational Crime and Corruption Center (TraCCC), a research unit within the School of Public Policy at George Mason University. Topics investigated include human smuggling and trafficking; nuclear proliferation issues; links between crime and terrorism; money laundering and other financial crimes; the impact of organized crime and terrorism on legitimate business; and environmental crimes. The site provides numerous publications related to research topics along with links to other Internet sources.
6. <www.un.org/peacekeeping/>: This, the official United Nations website, describes its peacekeeping operations. Lists peacekeeping principles and guidelines, current and past missions, and the latest news of peacekeeping missions, both successes and failures.

# CRIMINOLOGICAL THEORY

CHAPTER 4

# INVENTING CRIMINOLOGY: CLASSICISM, POSITIVISM, AND BEYOND

**4.1 The Enlightenment and Classical Criminology**
- Beccaria: *Of Crimes and Punishments* (1764)
- Bentham: Punishment and the Panopticon
- Toward the Disciplinary Society

**4.2 The Emergence of Positivist Criminology**
- The Crisis of Classicism: The Dangerous Classes
- Quetelet's Social Mechanics of Crime

**4.3 Criminal Anthropology: Lombroso's "Born Criminal"**
- Lombroso's *Criminal Man* (1876)
- Goring's *The English Convict* (1913)

**4.4 Neoclassical Criminology**
- Penal Dilemmas
- Neoclassical Compromises

## PREVIEW

Chapter 4 introduces:
- The original and enduring key principles of classical criminology.
- The key analyses of the early positivist criminologists.
- A comparison of classical and positivist criminologies.
- The neoclassicism that represented a compromise between the excesses of classicism and positivism.
- The status of classicism and positivism today, including the importance nowadays of recent writings on rational choice and routine activities theories of crime

## KEY TERMS

born criminal
classical criminology
dangerous classes

deterrence theory
Enlightenment
eugenics

neoclassical criminology
Panopticon
positivism
positivist criminology

rational choice
routine activities theory
social contract
social mechanics

The ideas and concepts of the first criminologists originated in response to a variety of social conditions. These conditions included the legal and penal practices of the era and the concerns of government and influential sections of European society regarding the perceived dangers posed by the "dangerous classes." We do not assess directly the merits of these writings here. Worthwhile though that task is, our chief focus is on the background and social context of the era in which modern criminology was created.

## 4.1 THE ENLIGHTENMENT AND CLASSICAL CRIMINOLOGY

The origins of modern criminological theory can be traced to the writings of **Enlightenment** philosophers in the second half of the eighteenth century. To understand why these writings arose when they did, we begin with the notorious case of Jean Calas, a prosperous French cloth merchant who was wrongly convicted and then executed in 1762 for the murder of his son. The sentence of execution required that Calas

> in a chemise, with head and feet bare, will be taken in a cart, from the palace prison to the Cathedral. There, kneeling in front of the main door, holding in his hands a torch of yellow wax weighing two pounds, he must make the amende honorable, asking pardon of God, of the King, and of justice. Then the executioner should take him in the cart to the Place Saint Georges, where upon a scaffold his arms, legs, thighs, and loins will be broken and crushed. Finally, the prisoner should be placed upon a wheel, with his face turned to the sky, alive and in pain, and repent for his said crimes and misdeeds, all the while imploring God for his life,

> thereby to serve as an example and to instill terror in the wicked. (quoted in Beirne, 1993:11–12)

The Enlightenment theorists opposed Calas' execution because they saw it as cruel and inhumane. They also disagreed with prevailing views of the relation between crime and punishment. At that time in much of Europe, crime was defined as that which opposed the Word of God as it was revealed in the dogma of Roman Catholicism. Serious crimes were often seen to result from a pact made by individual sinners with supernatural forces such as the devil, demons, and evil spirits. Catholic doctrine held that the role of lawful authorities was to eradicate the devil from the body of the condemned so that others would not be infected with their sins. The application of physical pain took a great variety of forms and was widely used both as a method of punishment and as a form of inquisition to establish the innocence or guilt of the accused.

Throughout Europe those accused of crimes were overwhelmingly poor and enjoyed little or no protection from legal systems unashamedly designed to serve monarch, government, church, and men of property. In England, for example, even as late as 1820 there were as many as 200 capital offenses, the great majority for crimes against property. During these judicial dark ages, the precise punishments for many crimes were not even contained in the legal codes. The enormous discretionary powers of judges were exercised arbitrarily, and the judges were often open to bribery and corruption.

The Enlightenment's reforming spirit emerged in the mid-eighteenth century in France and grew into a widespread philosophical and

---

**BOX 4.1  ANIMALS ON TRIAL**

Even nonhuman animals were occasionally subjected to judicial irrationalities. Indeed, there is much evidence that until about 1800 in Europe and in colonial America pigs, horses, and a variety of other species were formally prosecuted in criminal courts for crimes and, if convicted, were executed with the full majesty of the law. One such example is the public execution in 1386 of an infanticidal sow in the French city of Falaise. Having been duly tried in a court of law presided over by a judge with counsel attending, the sow was dressed in human clothes, mutilated in the head and hind legs, and executed in the public square by an official hangman on whom had been bestowed a pair of new gloves befitting the solemnity of the occasion. (Beirne, 1994)

---

humanist movement. The movement believed that reason and experience, rather than faith and superstition, must replace the excesses and corruption of feudal societies. The Enlightenment's demands were guided by several new doctrines, one of the most important of which was the doctrine of the social contract. The Enlightenment's chief theorists included Voltaire, Montesquieu, Helvétius, Rousseau, and Diderot in France; Kant in Germany; and Ferguson, Adam Smith, and Hume in Scotland.

The doctrine of the **social contract** was an attempt to avoid Thomas Hobbes' (1588–1679) belief that society was based on the nasty and brutish fact of *bellum omnium contra omnes* ("the war of all against all")—all citizens pursuing their own narrow self-interests. How then could government be justified? What was the role of law in such a society? Enlightenment philosophers responded to such questions by asserting that society was held together by a contract between citizens and property owners. The fulfillment of this contract required a governmental authority. Only with such a contract could society exist. Citizens must surrender some measure of their individuality so that the government can enact and enforce laws in the interests of the common good; the government, in return, must agree to protect the common good but not to invade the natural, inviolable liberties and rights of individual citizens. The lives of the citizenry were to be regulated and protected not by theology but by "the rule of law." This utilitarian view further asserted that those who challenged the social contract, those who decided to break its rules, and those who pursued harmful pleasures and wickedness were liable to be punished for their misdeeds.

Some writers at this time also began to protest the specific barbarities and inequities characteristic of feudal systems of justice, such as the continued use of capital punishment. This classical criminology was part of the broad Enlightenment movement. We now examine the writings of the two most influential classical theorists: Cesare Bonesana Beccaria (1738–1794) and Jeremy Bentham (1748–1832).

### BECCARIA: *OF CRIMES AND PUNISHMENTS* (1764)

At first glance it could not have been suspected that Cesare Beccaria's *Of Crimes and Punishments* (1764) would become so influential. Little of his book was original. Its proposals for reform borrowed heavily from the existing humanist and rationalist texts of Enlightenment philosophers. Even the idea for his book was suggested to Beccaria by his friend Pietro Verri. Beccaria knew very little about criminal law and punishment when he began to write *Of Crimes and Punishments,* and his ideas consisted less of reasoned arguments for change than of a controversial program of reform.

Because of Beccaria's singular and continuing importance in the history of criminology, we quote at length major points from *Of Crimes and Punishments* (and see Figure 4.1).

2. *The Origin of Punishments, and the Right to Punish.* No man ever freely sacrificed a portion of his personal liberty merely in behalf of the common good. That chimera exists only in romances. If it were possible, every one of us would prefer that the compacts binding others did not bind us; every man tends to make himself the center of his whole world....

Laws are the conditions under which independent and isolated men united to form a society.

**FIGURE 4.1**   This engraving of "Justice" appeared at the beginning of the 1765 edition of Beccaria's *Of Crimes and Punishments*. It was probably completed by Beccaria himself in the same year. Notice that Justice herself recoils from the executioner's offering of three decapitated heads. Instead she gazes approvingly at various instruments of labor, of measurement, and of detection. (Photo by Piers Beirne)

Weary of living in a continual state of war, and of enjoying a liberty rendered useless by the uncertainty of preserving it, they sacrificed a part so that they might enjoy the rest of it in peace and safety. The sum of all these portions of liberty sacrificed by each for his own good constitutes the sovereignty of a nation, and their legitimate depositary and administrator is the sovereign. But merely to have established this deposit was not enough; it had to be defended against private usurpations by individuals each of whom always tries not only to withdraw his own share but also to usurp for himself that of others. Some tangible motives had to be introduced, therefore, to prevent the despotic spirit, which is in every man, from plunging the laws of society into its original chaos. These tangible motives are the punishments established against the infractors of the laws....

It was, thus, necessity that forced men to give up part of their personal liberty, and it is certain...that each is willing to place in the public fund only the least possible portion, no more than suffices to induce others to defend it. The aggregate of these least possible portions constitutes the right to punish; all that exceeds this is abuse and not justice.... (pp. 11–13)

6. *Imprisonment.* Detention in prison is a punishment which, unlike every other, must of necessity precede conviction for crime, but this distinctive character does not remove the other which is essential—namely, that only the law determines the cases in which a man is to suffer punishment.... (p. 19)

12. *Torture.* A cruelty consecrated by the practice of most nations is torture of the accused during his trial....No man can be called guilty before a judge has sentenced him, nor can society deprive him of protection before it has been decided that he has in fact violated the conditions under which such protection was accorded him.... (p. 30)

16. *The Death Penalty.* It is not the intensity of punishment that has the greatest effect on the human spirit, but its duration, for our sensibility

is more easily and more permanently affected by slight but repeated impressions than by a powerful but momentary action.…The death penalty becomes for the majority a spectacle and for some others an object of compassion mixed with disdain; these two sentiments rather than the salutary fear which the laws pretend to inspire occupy the spirits of the spectators. But in moderate and prolonged punishments the dominant sentiment is the latter, because it is the only one.…(pp. 46–47)

19. *Promptness.* The more promptly and the more closely punishment follows upon the commission of a crime, the more just and useful will it be.…(p. 55)

20. *The Certainty of Punishment.* One of the greatest curbs on crimes is not the cruelty of punishments, but their infallibility and, consequently, the vigilance of magistrates, and that severity of an inexorable judge which, to be a useful virtue, must be accompanied by a mild legislation. The certainty of punishment, even if it be moderate, will always make a stronger impression than the fear of another which is more terrible but combined with the hope of impunity.…(p. 58)

23. *Proportion Between Crimes and Punishments.* It is to the common interest not only that crimes not be committed, but also that they be less frequent in proportion to the harm they cause society. Therefore, the obstacles that deter men from committing crimes should be stronger in proportion as they are contrary to the public good, and as the inducements to commit them are stronger. There must, therefore, be a proper proportion between crimes and punishments. (p. 62)

24. *The Measure of Crimes.* The true measure of crimes is…the harm done to society.…(p. 64)

41. *How to Prevent Crimes.* It is better to prevent crimes than to punish them. This is the ultimate end of every good legislation, which, to use the general terms for assessing the good and evils of life, is the art of leading men to the greatest possible happiness or to the least possible unhappiness.…

Do you want to prevent crimes? See to it that the laws are clear and simple and that the entire force of a nation is united in their defense, and that no part of it is employed to destroy them. See to it that the laws favor not so much classes of men as men themselves. See to it that men fear the laws and fear nothing else. For fear of the laws is salutary, but fatal and fertile for crimes is one man's fear of another.…

Do you want to prevent crimes? See to it that enlightenment accompanies liberty. (pp. 93–95)

The image of crime and punishment in Beccaria's book is not one based exclusively on a single assumption about human nature. Beccaria believed—as did many others of his era—that human action was based on both free will and determinism. Indeed, attached to his humanism was Beccaria's attempt to apply to the study of crime and punishment some of the deterministic principles found in natural science, mathematics, probability theory, and the early forms of psychology. This project Beccaria termed the "science of man." From the perspective of this new science, Beccaria identified some of the causes of crime as "tyranny," "inequality of wealth," and "poverty."

In Beccaria's recommendations are the seeds of policies present in **criminal justice system**s around the world today, including the system in the United States. His book was the first widely read text to urge that the machinery of criminal justice use rules of due process, that sentencing policies reflect the harm inflicted on society by a given crime (essentially, that punishment "fit" the crime), and that punishment be prompt and certain and contain a measure of deterrence. His major recommendations can be summarized as follows:

• The right of governments to punish offenders derives from a contractual obligation among its citizens not to pursue their self-interest at the expense of others.

- Punishment must be constituted by uniform and enlightened legislation.
- Imprisonment must replace torture and capital punishment as the standard form of punishment.
- Punishment must fit the crime. It must be prompt and certain, and its duration must reflect only the gravity of the offense and the social harm it caused.

*Of Crimes and Punishments* had a great impact on much of Europe and colonial America. Part of Beccaria's fame doubtless derived from the fact that in 1766 his book was condemned for its extreme rationalism and placed on the *Index Prohibitorum* (the Papal Index of forbidden books) by the Catholic church. Beccaria's influence was most visible in the new classical legal codes of Austria, Denmark, France, Poland, Prussia, Russia, and Sweden. In the fledgling United States of America, the Constitution embraced Beccarian principles, as did the Bill of Rights. Beccaria's ideas were widely quoted by Thomas Jefferson, John Adams, and others. Upon reading *Of Crimes and Punishments*, English reformer Jeremy Bentham was driven to declare: "Oh! my master, first evangelist of Reason...you who have made so many useful excursions into the path of utility, what is there left to do?—Never to turn aside from that path" (cited in Paolucci, 1963 [1764]:x–xi). These words bring us to the other pillar of classical criminology, Jeremy Bentham, and to his writings on punishment and prisons.

## BENTHAM: PUNISHMENT AND THE PANOPTICON

Jeremy Bentham was a gifted and passionate young man who graduated from Oxford University at the age of 12 and who later became a law student in London. Bentham never practiced law but instead became the prolific author of numerous texts on moral philosophy, punishment, jurisprudence, prison reform, and the police. A keen critic of the British constitution and even more so of the U.S. Constitution, he traveled extensively throughout Europe and corresponded frequently with many leading intellectuals and political figures of his day.

Although much in his writing was original, Bentham owed intellectual debts to Beccaria, inevitably, and also to Scottish philosopher David Hume (1711–1776). Bentham was inspired by Beccaria to campaign for a rational, humane, and codified system of law. However, whereas Beccaria had simply compiled a list of humane reforms to the barbaric practices of criminal justice, Bentham intended to place these reforms on a solid philosophical foundation. While a law student, Bentham first read Hume's moral philosophy and was greatly impressed by it. Hume argued that the basic quality of moral action was its tendency to produce happiness—but that, as social beings with free will, members of a society derive pleasure from the happiness of others. Thus, individual members of society should pursue not only their own pleasure but that of others. He argued that the happiness, pleasures, and security of individuals are the sole ends that laws should protect and promote. This utilitarian principle—the greatest happiness to the greatest number—became the cornerstone of Bentham's writings. We now turn to his campaign to reform punishment and prisons.

*Punishment.* In his book *Introduction to the Principles of Morals and Legislation* of 1780, Bentham assumed that potential criminals consciously calculate the profits and losses that arise from committing a crime. Similarly, he suggested, lawmakers should calculate the measures required to prevent and punish crimes. Bentham argued that in promoting the law of utility, legislators should prevent mischiefs such as crimes by means of various sanctions, including punishment. Crimes, Bentham argued, could be prevented through either positive sanctions (rewards) or negative sanctions (punishment).

Bentham (1973:170–178) urged that legislators should follow four rules of utility in calculating the proportion (balance) between crime and punishment. First, the ultimate goal is the prevention of all crime. To achieve this goal, legislators should ensure that the pleasure derived from any crime always be outweighed by the pain inflicted by the punishment for its commission. Second, a person about to commit a crime should be persuaded by the very threat of punishment either not to commit that crime at all or to commit a lesser offense. Third, a person who has actually decided to commit a crime should be persuaded by the threat of punishment to do no more mischief than is necessary. In no case should punishment for a crime be more than is necessary to prevent its occurrence. Fourth, legislators should try to prevent crime as cheaply as possible (see Figure 4.2).

*The Panopticon.* In criminology, Bentham is most famous for the invention of his macabre Inspection House, otherwise known as the **Panopticon** (ancient Greek: "all seeing"). Bentham wrote in 1787 that the principles of his Panopticon represented an unequaled power of mind over mind. The Panopticon was explicitly created to be an engine of power that would discipline all of society.

We should remember that until the late eighteenth century, prisons were crudely designed and not intended for prolonged incarceration. Their uses were limited to act as holding institutions for torture before trial, for debtors, for confinement prior to execution, and (especially in England and France) for the period between conviction and transportation to a penal colony. Bentham argued that the prison must be transformed from its position as one among many marginal and temporary institutions within the system of criminal justice to its permanent center. His plan for a penitentiary Panopticon began with a three-storied circular or polygonal building. The circumference of the building contained the prisoners' cells, which were divided by partitions in the form of radii issuing from the circumference toward the center. The prisoners were thus isolated from one another. At the building's center was a three-storied tower, the Inspectors' Lodge, for the prison guards. Because the tower's windows were draped with blinds, the prisoners were unable to see the inspectors. The prisoners were to be seen without seeing, subject to "uninterrupted exposure to invisible inspection" (Bentham, 1973, III:88). Moreover, Bentham planned for the Panopticon to be built at a strategic location in a metropolitan area—a visible reminder to free citizens of the foolishness of their wrongdoing.

To these architectural principles Bentham added a strict regimen of visits by prisoners to the prison chapel for moral and religious instruction. Every minute of the prisoners' day was subject to discipline, order, and isolation to encourage self-reflection and moral reformation of character. Bentham's plans included rules for a crushing uniformity: in the segregation of inmates by sex and class; in diet, clothing, and bedding; in the ventilation, shading, cooling, and airing of

---

**BOX 4.2  THE PANOPTICON**

The objectives of the Panopticon were to punish the incorrigible, guard the insane, reform the vicious, confine suspects, employ the idle, maintain the helpless, cure the sick, and offer training in any branch of industry and education. These objectives therefore embraced not only prisons but also workhouses for the poor, factories, madhouses, hospitals, and schools. Bentham believed that the ingenious architectural principles of the Panopticon would enable morals to be reformed and "health preserved; industry invigorated; instruction diffused; public burdens lightened; Economy seated as it were upon a rock; the Gordian knot of the Poor-Laws not cut but untied—all by a simple idea in Architecture!" (1973, 1:i)

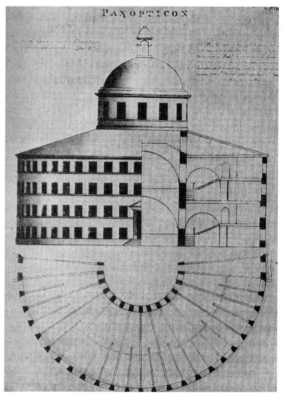

**FIGURE 4.3** The Panopticon: This figure shows an architectural cross section of the original Benthamite Panopticon. It depicts the central guard tower, in which the guards remained hidden from view, and the individual cells, in which inmates were exposed for inspection at any time of the day or night.

*Source:* University College London Library

**FIGURE 4.2** Jeremy Bentham (1748–1832): Jeremy Bentham was one of the chief architects of the "Inspection House," known as the Panopticon. In his will, he bequeathed his original manuscripts to the University College of London on the condition that the administrators there embalm his body and put it on permanent display for all to see. This photograph shows Bentham in his wood-and-glass box. There is no more perfect irony in the history of criminology! There is a rumor that Bentham's preserved body is wheeled into University College Council meetings and that his presence is recorded in the minutes; his vote is required, however, only when members are equally divided into ayes and nays, at which point Bentham's deciding vote is always cast in favor of the motion. (Photo by Piers Beirne)

cells; in the health, cleanliness, and exercise of prisoners; in the precise distribution of time; and in forms of punishment.

The prison governor was charged with ensuring that all prisoners were taught some marketable skill. The profits from what the prisoners produced through a system of contract labor were to contribute to the financial management of the prison. Bentham also offered suggestions for the conduct of prisoners' lives after prison: Their release was made conditional on "acceptance by a bondsman" (payment of bail) and on successful fulfillment of apprenticeship in a worthy trade or occupation.

At first, Bentham's innovative plans were praised; they were debated in Parliament, and in 1794 several sites in England were purchased for the construction of his penitentiary houses. But no Benthamite Panopticon was ever completed in England, partly because, according to some (Phillipson, 1975), King George III opposed it and Parliament deemed it too expensive. Moreover, no pure Benthamite Panopticon was built in continental Europe—despite a frenzied program of prison construction between 1780 and 1840—and the two Panopticons undertaken in the United States (one in Pennsylvania, the other in Illinois) were eventually abandoned as impractical.

Bentham's writings on crime and criminal justice were ignored and forgotten in the 50 years after his death. However, Bentham's lasting influence lay less in the actual implementation of his architectural plans than in the widespread acceptance of his principles of punishment and prison.

### TOWARD THE DISCIPLINARY SOCIETY

Significant questions remain about the nature of the reforms initiated by classical writers such as Beccaria and Bentham. How progressive was **classical criminology**? Whose interests did its ideas serve? Why did the proposals of Beccaria and Bentham gain widespread acceptance?

The origins of modern criminology begin with the writings of Beccaria and Bentham. Clearly, their ideas about penal reform gained official attention and were implemented in practice. But ideas about penal reform are rarely implemented simply because they are believed to be better somehow than those of their competitors; they are implemented also because they tend to serve certain interests and to achieve certain aims. Doubtless, the humanism of the classical writers commanded a measure of respect among most, if not all, sections of society in Europe and in America. The insistence that law be subject to rules of due process, for example, was a progressive idea, as was a revolutionary if rather primitive belief in the scientific study of

society that implicitly placed the classical writers at odds with the Catholic church and all those who believed that free will is the basis of human action.

At the same time, Beccaria and Bentham also championed ideas that were conservative even for their era. Though Beccaria's *Of Crimes and Punishments* was a plea for the supremacy of law rather than of religion and superstition, his proposed legal and administrative solutions to the problem of crime left untouched the social conditions in which it occurred. Bentham planned to extend Beccaria's proposals far beyond the criminal justice system. His Panopticon was to be an engine of regulation whose architectural principles would be used for the design not only of prisons but also of factories, hospitals, and schools (see Garland, 1997). The ultimate aim, then, of classical criminology was not to lessen punishment but to make it more efficient and to ensure that its principles applied to everyone.

### 4.2  THE EMERGENCE OF POSITIVIST CRIMINOLOGY

The second source of modern criminology was **positivism**, which is a method of analysis based on the collection of observable scientific facts. Its aim is to uncover, to explain, and to predict the ways in which observable facts occur in uniform patterns. Positivist analysis can thus be applied to such things as the movement of stars through the heavens, the fertility of rabbits, and, indeed, the entire subject matter of natural sciences such as physics, chemistry, and biology. Thus, the term **positivist criminology** is used generally to refer to the search for uniformities in the area of crime and criminal justice. Table 4.1 compares the major principles of classical criminology and positivist criminology.

Positivist criminology emerged in the writings and observations of various European authors in the nineteenth century. One of its forerunners

**TABLE 4.1 CLASSICAL AND POSITIVIST CRIMINOLOGY—A COMPARISON**

| Classical Criminology | Positivist Criminology |
|---|---|
| 1. The focus of criminological study should be the administration of justice and, especially, the prevention of crime. | 1. The focus of criminological study should be the criminal and the causes of crime. |
| 2. Human action is based on free will, the "motivation" for which can be determined by psychological factors. | 2. Human action is largely deterministic. |
| 3. Crime is an action voluntarily engaged in by free-willed individuals; their motivation can be determined by psychological and social factors. | 3. Crime is an action into which individuals are propelled by social, economic, and "mental" forces largely outside their control. |
| 4. The punishment should fit the crime. | 4. The punishment should fit the criminal. |

was *phrenology*, a movement that focused on the relationships among the organic structure of the brain, illness, and social behavior. But the phrenologists never regarded crime or criminals as the focus of their studies.

As a self-conscious effort to apply positivist principles to the study of crime, positivist criminology began with the ideas of French and Belgian statisticians in the 1820s. These ideas responded to a perceived crisis in classical criminology, and it is to this crisis that we now turn.

## THE CRISIS OF CLASSICISM: THE DANGEROUS CLASSES

The emergence of positivist criminology in early nineteenth-century France was an important response to changes in the system of criminal justice that occurred between the middle of the eighteenth century and the beginning of the nineteenth century.

On one side of this transformation were the barbaric practices of feudal society, especially in France. At the center of the new system was a network of institutions of confinement ushered in by classical writers such as Beccaria and Bentham. These institutions had been created to control and to oversee the entire population

of society and to operate on their inmates with the same monotonous precision as schools, barracks, and monasteries. Their expanding inventory included hospitals, workhouses, asylums, reformatories, houses of correction, and prisons. Their official aim was moral reformation through the deprivation of liberty and the prevention of crime through deterrence. Their "delinquent" and "pathological" inmates included syphilitics, alcoholics, idiots and eccentrics, vagabonds, immigrants, prostitutes, and petty and professional criminals. Inaugurated in 1810, the French prison system was based on a complex classification of inmates and included military prisons, debtors' prisons, agricultural colonies, and the galleys. These components operated in concert with a new criminal code, a professional police force (*gendarmerie*), a system of passport and identity cards, and an extensive network of paid informers and spies (Foucault, 1979).

Positivist criminology itself emerged from the convergence of two areas of government activity in France. From the criminal justice system, criminology acquired a secure position of status, financial support, and, because of its pronouncements about the social distribution and causes of crime, considerable interest among the citizenry. From the statistical movement, criminology acquired its intellectual orientation and the recognition by the scientific community of its methods of analysis. During the Restoration (1814–1830), the activities of the criminal justice system and the statistical movement had a common concern: the failure of the new institutions of confinement (such as prisons) to regulate the conduct of the **dangerous classes**—a derogatory term used by law-abiding citizens to describe those members of the working classes, the unemployed, and the unemployable who seemed to pose a threat to law and order.

Criminals, especially thieves, formed a large part of the dangerous classes. That the expanding network of prisons had significantly failed to control the criminal activities of the dangerous classes was apparent in at least three ways. First was the growing presence in urban areas of large numbers of poor, unemployed, and working-class thieves, whose desperate conditions were immortalized in such works as Victor Hugo's *Les Misérables* and Charles Dickens' *Oliver Twist*. For example, Paris, despite a doubling of its population between 1800 and 1850, remained structurally intact. It is not difficult to imagine how quickly this population explosion manifested itself in the incidence of infant mortality and related social problems of accommodation, food supplies, unemployment, public order, and crime (Chevalier, 1973; Beirne, 1993).

Second, the continued presence of the dangerous classes led to widespread fear of criminality. Reports of crime were widely circulated by newspapers and government inquiries—and eagerly devoured by their audiences. During certain winters of cold and destitution, the fear of crime turned to panic and terror. This widespread fear was heightened by working-class insurrections, and it quickly became an unquestioned tenet of middle-class thought that crime and revolution were symptoms of the same disease (Tombs, 1980).

Third, after 1815 increases in the official crime rate lent support to fearful public opinion.

For example, in that year a sudden increase was recorded in felony offenses, primarily in theft and disturbances of public order (Duesterberg, 1979; Wright, 1983). Between 1813 and 1820, the number of convictions in the criminal tribunals nearly doubled. Even more telling was the fact that many members of the dangerous classes were continually shuttled back and forth between incarceration and free society. This process was apparent in rising rates of recidivism, which implied that prisons were failing in their duty to reform the moral character of their inmates and that deterrence itself was a failure. In 1820 it was already understood that the prisons, "far from transforming criminals into citizens, serve only to manufacture new criminals and drive existing criminals ever deeper into criminality" (Foucault, 1980:40).

One question was central: "Should (or could) the prisoners be returned to society and, if so, how?" (Petit, 1984:137). Inquiry soon broadened to the larger population that passed through the criminal justice system. In 1825 the French government commissioned the first national statistical tables on crime, the annual *Compte général* (*General Account*). First published in 1827, the *Compte* reported the annual number of crimes against persons and property and whether those prosecuted were acquitted or convicted. It also recorded convicted criminals' age, sex, occupation, and educational level.

## QUETELET'S SOCIAL MECHANICS OF CRIME

To the French government the hard facts in the *Compte* promised to help pinpoint the causes of crime. These hopes were echoed by a group of social statisticians who were busy collecting data on such items as births, marriages, and deaths. Among this group was André-Michel Guerry, who in 1829 produced a one-page sheet of three maps that allowed the reader to see some elementary relationships between property crimes and personal crimes. The most influential member was the young Belgian astronomer Adolphe Quetelet (1796–1874). Quetelet's account of the "social mechanics of crime" is the place to begin an examination of the development of positivist analysis in criminology.

In 1823, during a visit to Paris, Quetelet learned of the potential for applying the principles of algebra, geometry, and astronomy to social conditions. This he termed **social mechanics**. In his book *Research on the Propensity for Crime at Different Ages*, Quetelet (1831) stressed that social mechanics could never pretend to discover laws verifiable for all individuals. But he argued that the phenomena of crime in society—when observed on a large scale using such statistical records as the *Compte*—obeyed the same lawlike regularities as existed in the heavens and the world of nature. Lo and behold! Dissecting the *Compte*, Quetelet uncovered astonishing regularities in French crime rates between 1826 and 1829 (see Table 4.2). He also noted constancy in the annual number of accused (tried) and convicted and in the ratios of accused to convicted, of accused to inhabitants, and of crimes against persons to crimes against property. The *Compte*

also suggested to Quetelet that young males, the poor, and those without jobs or in lowly occupations were more likely to commit crimes and to be convicted of them.

Quetelet reasoned that crime had three chief types of causes: (1) accidental causes, such as wars, famines, and natural disasters; (2) variable causes, such as free will and personality, that can oscillate between greater or smaller limits; and (3) constant causes, such as age, gender, occupation, and religion. Moreover, because he saw crime as a constant and inevitable feature of social organization, Quetelet (1842) further claimed that society itself caused crime:

> Every social state presupposes, then, a certain number and a certain order of crimes, these being merely the necessary consequences of its organization....Society prepares crime, and the guilty are only the instruments by which it is executed. (pp. 6, 108)

Quetelet's placement of criminal behavior in a formal structure of causality was a remarkable advance over the unsystematic speculations of his contemporaries. Flying in the face of the theory that criminals freely chose to engage in wickedness, Quetelet's intuition that society somehow caused crime marked a profound theoretical departure from the crude realism of public opinion and classical criminology.

However, in the 1840s Quetelet began to contrast the virtues of the average law-abiding citizen with the criminality of vagabonds, vagrants, "primitives," "gypsies," "inferior classes," certain races with "inferior moral stock," and persons of low moral character. Eventually, he came to believe that unhealthy morality was manifest in biological defects and that those with such defects had high criminal propensities. Crime, he concluded, was "a pestilential germ...contagious...[sometimes] hereditary" (Quetelet, 1848:214–215).

**TABLE 4.2  THE CONSTANCY OF CRIME, FRANCE, 1826–1829**

| Year Accused | Number Accused (Tried) | Accused of Crimes Against | | Disposition | |
|---|---|---|---|---|---|
| | | Persons | Property | Guilty | % Guilty |
| 1826 | 6,988 | 1,907 | 5,081 | 4,348 | 62 |
| 1827 | 6,929 | 1,911 | 5,018 | 4,236 | 61 |
| 1828 | 7,396 | 1,844 | 5,552 | 4,551 | 61 |
| 1829 | 7,373 | 1,791 | 5,582 | 4,475 | 61 |
| Totals | 28,686 | 7,453 | 21,233 | 17,610 | 61 |

Source: Quetelet (1984 [1831]:20), amended.

## 4.3 CRIMINAL ANTHROPOLOGY: LOMBROSO'S "BORN CRIMINAL"

Into this climate the invention of the **born criminal** was first introduced by Italian army physician Cesare Lombroso (1835–1909). When he began to study delinquents in the 1860s, Lombroso was convinced that only a scientific criminology (anthropometry) could avoid classical criminology's superstitious belief in free will.

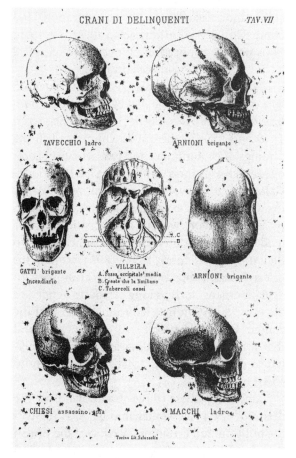

**FIGURE 4.4** Skulls of criminals, from Cesare Lombroso, *L'Uomo delinquente*, 1876: These skulls were collected by the Italian army doctor Cesare Lombroso (1836–1909) and reproduced in his book *Criminal Man*. Lombroso believed that the signs of criminality are manifest in certain bodily deformities and in physical and mental illnesses.
(Slide provided by Piers Beirne, from Cesare Lombroso, *Criminal Man*)

### LOMBROSO'S *CRIMINAL MAN* (1876)

Lombroso's book *Criminal Man* was written from within a diverse positivist landscape that included the new prominence of the scientific method in social investigations, the claim by statisticians that science is objective and therefore factual and free of values, and the evolutionism in Darwin's *Origin of Species*. According to Lombroso's own account, he believed that scientific criminology had to be based on an analysis of the individual criminal. This he realized after a series of revelations, one of which came during his postmortem examination of the convicted thief Vilella:

> On [Vilella's] death one cold grey November morning, I was deputed to make the postmortem, and on laying open the skull I found on the occipital part, exactly on the spot where a spine is found in the normal skull, a distinct depression which I named *median occipital fossa*, because of its situation precisely in the middle of the occiput as in inferior animals, especially rodents....
>
> At the sight of that skull, I seemed to see all of a sudden, lighted up as a vast plain under a flaming sky, the problem of the nature of the criminal—an atavistic being who reproduces in his person the ferocious instincts of primitive humanity and the inferior animals. Thus were explained anatomically the enormous jaws, high cheekbones, prominent superciliary arches, solitary lines in the palms, extreme size of the orbits, handle-shaped or sessile ears found in criminals, savages, and apes, insensibility to pain, extremely acute sight, tattooing, excessive idleness, love of orgies, and the irresistible craving for evil for its own sake. (Quoted in Lombroso and Ferrero, 1972:xxiv–xxv; and see Gibson and Rafter, 2006)

The arguments of *Criminal Man* stemmed from Lombroso's autopsies of 66 male delinquents in Italian anatomical museums (see Figure 4.4). He examined several aspects of the skulls of these corpses and found them to be similar to those of insane persons examined in his clinic, to those of "blacks" in the United States, to those of the Mongolian races, and, above all, to those of "prehistoric man." Lombroso also studied the physiognomy of 832 living Italian delinquents. This second group of delinquents included both males and females selected from among the "most notorious and depraved" Italian criminals. Of this group, 390 of its members were compared with 868 Italian soldiers and 90 "lunatics." From these data Lombroso (1876) concluded that

> many of the characteristics found in savages, and among the colored races, are also to be found in habitual delinquents. They have in common, for example, thinning hair, lack of strength and weight, low cranial capacity, receding foreheads, highly developed frontal sinuses, ... darker skin, thicker, curly hair [and] large or handle-shaped ears. (p.86)

Lombroso's discoveries of the born criminal established his new school as an academic science. With the publication of its own journal and key texts by his disciples, Lombrosianism soon dominated public discussion of crime in Italy. Its reputation quickly extended to Germany, Russia, and France. Lombrosian findings were tested in the late 1880s and early 1890s and received favorably by converts in France and Italy (Gibson, 2002) and the United States (Rafter, 1992; and see Horn, 2003).

## GORING'S *THE ENGLISH CONVICT* (1913)

Lombrosianism exercised little influence in England, but it was there that its most renowned refutation occurred: Charles Goring's (1913) *The English Convict: A Statistical Study*.

Goring's book combined the focal concerns of three hitherto more or less separate areas of activity. First, *The English Convict* continued the English tradition of prison research pursued by medical doctors. This involved the empirical calculation of "criminal propensities," often couched in the language and rhetoric of psychiatry: What mental and psychological factors distinguished prisoners from the law-abiding citizenry? Second, *The English Convict* extended the work of the British statistical movement. From the 1830s onward, the primary mission of many statisticians had been the quantification of social facts in order to address a wide range of controversial issues having to do with public health, child labor, factory conditions, education, and crime. Goring's contribution to these two traditions was the application of innovative statistical techniques to the study of criminals.

Goring's work was also strongly influenced by a third tradition, one that began with the publication of Darwin's *On the Origin of Species* in 1859 and that, in the 1890s, culminated in the findings of evolutionary and mathematical zoologists such as Francis Galton and W. F. R. Weldon. Galton's (1889) work on ancestral resemblance in sweet peas, for example, had shown that peas of a certain type, weight, and genetic structure tended to pass on their specific characteristics to their progeny. Weldon (1894–1895) found in his research on shrimps and crabs that creatures with deviant organs, such as long carapaces, tended to die early. Such findings led to the belief that the content of social action was itself inherited and that those with a genealogically deviant inheritance would be unable to adapt adequately to social life.

Straddling these three traditions was the desire of the professional middle class to stem the political and economic decline of the British Empire through rejuvenation of the physical stock and moral character of the British people. One platform in this social and political agenda was **eugenics** (ancient Greek: "good genes"). It was hoped that eugenist principles could be used to eliminate a broad spectrum of social undesirables, including the physically unfit, alcoholics,

**BOX 4.3** THE SCIENCE OF EUGENICS

The basic assumption of the eugenists was that the distribution of social, moral, and intellectual qualities could be discerned in humans with the same procedures used to identify the distribution of physical qualities in the world of nature. Francis Galton pioneered the view that in any nation the natural human talents that compose "civic worth" are distributed according to certain statistical laws. Galton assumed further that the distribution of worth was spread throughout society and that its presence or absence was manifest in such indicators as wealth and pathologies, respectively. In *Hereditary Genius* (1869), Galton argued—seeking retrospective confirmation from his cousin's *On the Origin of Species*—that it was almost exclusively the "naturally" worthy who achieved social prominence; conversely, the naturally "worthless" never succeeded in rising above their lowly positions, and this despite all government or private supports.

---

the very poor, the morally and mentally depraved, and habitual criminals.

Eugenist proposals were of two sorts. *Positive eugenics* suggested that the middle and upper classes should be provided with incentives to intermarry and produce offspring, on the grounds that ordinarily only in these strata were intelligent and hard-working citizens found. *Negative eugenics* demanded that social undesirables (such as habitual criminals) be isolated, sterilized, or occasionally castrated, because their useless offspring were a drain on national resources.

These diverse traditions merged in Goring's *The English Convict*. In 1903, Dr. Charles Goring was appointed coordinator of a government-sponsored project to test the factual reality of the concept of born criminals. Goring's tests involved three phases: (1) a statistical analysis to determine the presence of 37 Lombrosian characteristics in the criminal population, a group represented by 2,348 male convicts; (2) a comparison of the findings in the first phase with the characteristics of the "noncriminal public," represented by control groups, including a company of soldiers, English and Scottish undergraduate students, and the staff and inmates of two separate hospitals; and (3) an analysis of the general physique of criminals. Goring (1913) concluded that in

the present investigation we have exhaustively compared...criminals as a class, with the law-abiding public....No evidence has emerged confirming

the existence of a physical criminal type, such as Lombroso and his disciples have described—our inevitable conclusion must be that there is no such thing as a physical criminal type. (p. 173)

However, Goring did report that most criminals were physically inferior (in height and weight) to the general population. He reasoned that such differences could be explained perhaps by the process of "selection"; for example, those with inferior physiques were less likely to avoid arrest, given that the police were appointed only from among those with superior physiques. However, Goring suggested further that

this physical inferiority, although originating in and fostered by selection, may tend with time to become an inbred characteristic of the criminal classes, just as, with the passage of generations, the upper classes of the noncriminal community have become differentiated in physique from those lower on the social scale. (p. 200)

By the early twentieth century, most European criminologists distinguished firmly between biological and sociological causes of crime. Although most eugenists dismissed altogether the relevance of sociological factors, Goring nevertheless engaged in an analysis of the relative importance of several "adverse environmental conditions"— including employment, education, family life, and social class—and of mental defectiveness and heredity on the recidivism of convicts and the types of their crimes. In this second line of analysis, Goring assumed that sociological factors, on the one hand, and mental capacities and heredity, on the other, were independent of each other. For Goring it followed that to measure the effect of one factor, the effect of others must be controlled or eliminated. He therefore assumed that maladaptive, deviant, or defective qualities of individuals in a given species were not influenced by social environment. "Our interim conclusion," he argued,

> is that, relative to its origin in the constitution of the malefactor, and especially in his mentally defective constitution, crime in this country is only to a trifling extent (if to any) the product of social inequality, of adverse environment, or of other manifestations of what may be comprehensively termed the "force of circumstances." (p. 288)

Goring also noted that as many as 68 percent of the male offspring of criminals became criminal themselves. Was this the result of the genetic inheritance of criminal propensities or of the influence of family? Controlling for the influence of family contagion—by eliminating it from his calculations—Goring found the intensity of the inherited factor in criminality to be extremely significant and the intensity of family contagion to be almost negligible. "Criminality," Goring concluded, is inherited "at much the same rate as are other pathological conditions in man....The influence of inheritance and of mental defectiveness [are] by far the most significant factors we have been able to discover in the aetiology of crime" (p. 368).

In sum, *The English Convict* failed to refute Lombroso's concept of the born criminal. Indeed, Lombroso's concept of born criminality still had fervent followers in the United States even in the 1930s. Goring's dubious achievement was simply to replace Lombroso's atavistic criminal with one born with inferior weight, stature, and mental capacity.

## 4.4 NEOCLASSICAL CRIMINOLOGY

Thus far we have described the origins of the two most influential forms of modern criminology, namely, classicism and positivism. These two versions of criminology competed strongly for legislative and popular attention throughout Europe and North America. Yet in combination they produced unworkable dilemmas for the machinery of criminal justice.

### PENAL DILEMMAS

Classical and positivist criminology harbored fundamental differences of perspective on four key points (see Table 4.1). Especially after the rise of Lombrosianism in the mid-1870s, the classicists and the positivists engaged in a heated, bitter, and prolonged dispute. The outcome of this dispute—the precise contours of which varied from one country to another—had great significance for assumptions about criminal responsibility and the objectives and styles of punishment. In short, the intractable differences between classical and positivist criminologies, far from being confined to an academic arena, caused practical penal dilemmas whose resolution entailed a series of compromises agreed on by the major institutions of criminal justice.

The serious implications of the conflict between the classicists and the positivists were best understood by Gabriel Tarde. In his book *Penal Philosophy*, Tarde (1890) took issue with the debate between the classicists and the positivists over the respective merits of free will and determinism. Neither doctrine, he argued, was justified either theoretically or practically. The doctrine of free will held that the individual, uninfluenced by any external factors, chose to do one thing rather than another with complete freedom and foresight. This position was clearly absurd, Tarde indicated, given the obvious truth of the positivist insight that crime varied according to such factors as gender, age, and socioeconomic position. The doctrine of determinism had arisen, Tarde continued, largely as a reaction to the exaggerated free-willed individualism of the classicists. Determinism viewed the individual as a machine incapable of free choice. But Tarde replied that quite apart from such factors as gender, age, and socioeconomic position, individuals were authentic beings who somehow were the "authors" of their actions. Tarde therefore concluded that neither doctrine was adequate as a basis for a coherent system of penal responsibility.

Tarde attacked certain effects classicism had on the style of criminal justice. First, he denied that free will as such should be the basis of criminal responsibility. Individuals should be held accountable for their actions whether or not they exercise free will. Every individual, Tarde asserted, has unique psychological, social, and familial characteristics. Therefore, the basis of criminal liability and the relation between liability and punishment should be a combination of the social harm caused by accountable offenders and the offenders' unique personal characteristics. Second, Tarde objected to many classical legal reforms as impractical. If individuals had unique characteristics, they should not be subjected to uniformity of treatment by the criminal justice system. Legal distinctions should be made, for example, between men and women, children and adults, violent offenders and property offenders, first-time offenders and habitual criminals, and the sane and the insane.

Tarde also attacked the positivists, chiefly because their determinism greatly contributed to the ineffectiveness of the criminal justice system. If the positivists' concept of the criminal was accepted as the basis of criminal law, Tarde believed, only two unacceptable strategies would be available for dealing with criminals: complete forgiveness of a crime or extermination of the criminal. Clearly, if the actions of criminals were caused by factors outside their control,

rehabilitation was not a practical possibility—certainly not in the case of "born criminals." The influence of determinism was found in the increasing laxity with which prosecutors, judges, and juries treated criminals. Such leniency was apparent in the judicial tendency to reduce criminal charges from felonies to misdemeanors, which artificially reduced the crime rate and, in its turn, caused more than a threefold increase in the number of misdemeanors.

The key dilemma facing judges, legislators, and the criminal justice system, then, was this: How can justice be administered on a coherent and systematic basis? How can the partial truths of classicism and positivism be recognized without accepting the most dangerous implications of their respective extremes?

## NEOCLASSICAL COMPROMISES

The typical response of the criminal justice system to these two critical questions was doctrinal and procedural compromise. The compromise, devised roughly between 1880 and 1920, is known as *neoclassicism*. In effect, **neoclassical criminology** has become the basis of criminal responsibility and punishment in most Western countries.

The exact terms of the neoclassical compromise between classicism and positivism varied from one country to another; nonetheless, wherever it was instituted the compromise has had six general features (Garland, 1985; Beirne, 1993):

1. The concept of character has replaced the extremes of free will and determinism as the source of criminality. An offender's character is open to analysis by experts from the fields of law, medicine, psychiatry, probation, criminology, and social work. Because the links between character and crime can be influenced by an infinite variety of factors, crime should be

understood through multicausal (multifactorial) analysis.

2. There should be an equivalence between the seriousness of crime and the degree of punishment pronounced. Punishment should be exemplary but not vengeful.

3. Imprisonment must be the normal method of punishment, and a variety of penitentiary systems should be used. The criminally insane and the recidivists should be segregated from other prisoners. There should be increased use of visitation and probation.

4. The treatment of the criminal character should not be uniform but individualized. Specific treatment, both in prison and during postrelease programs, should be administered to offenders according to the nature and the degree of an individual's incorrigibility of character.

5. Every punishment should include a measure of deterrence for future miscreants. Deterrence is unworkable only for the insane.

6. The death penalty should be abolished for nearly all crimes.

## ASSESSMENT: CLASSICISM AND POSITIVISM TODAY

Classicism and positivism were the two great systems of early criminological theory. In some ways they were quite different enterprises. Each identified a different object of analysis for criminology: the one, the application of criminal law; the other, the criminal. Each provided a different focus on punishment: Classical criminology demanded that punishment fit the social harm caused by the crime, whereas positivist criminology demanded that punishment fit the criminal. At the same time, as we have suggested, both were part of the same broad movement to apply scientific principles to the study of society. However, whereas Beccaria's criminology (and classicism in general) held that human action is based simultaneously on both free will and determinism, the positivists of the next century insisted that crime and criminality are determined, patterned, and regular events in which an individual's will is more or less irrelevant.

As the remaining chapters of Part II suggest, the intellectual history of modern criminology is largely one of positivism's triumph over classicism. So thoroughgoing has been this triumph that even neoclassical criminology—which emerged as a compromise to the extremes of both classicism and positivism—has developed in positivist terms. Most criminological theory is modeled on the positivist methods of the natural sciences. Thus, criminal behavior tends to be viewed rather like the behavior of billiard balls (they move, predictably, according to certain laws of motion): The subject of criminology—the criminal—behaves according to certain sociological, historical, psychological, or economic laws. Most crime policies, likewise, are based on the assumption that individuals can be redirected toward lawful behavior, given changes in the sociological, historical, psychological, and economic causes that propel an individual into crime. The appeal of positivism in criminology is overwhelming.

But the fortresses of criminological positivism are not altogether impregnable. Put simply, if positivist criminology has accurately identified the causes of crime, why do state anticrime policies repeatedly fail? Reflecting the pessimism that seems the obvious answer to this question (anticrime policies fail because we have failed to grasp the true causes of crime), criminologist James Q. Wilson (1985) once famously argued that the search for the causes of crime should perhaps be abandoned. As policymakers, he reasoned, all that criminologists can do is devise anticrime policies that assume that potential criminals are rational actors who weigh the costs and benefits of engaging in crime. Wilson therefore suggested that we return to the rational calculus of classical criminology. Let us devise policies that deter free-willed, rational actors from committing crimes! Reenter **rational choice** as the motivating force of criminal behavior.

Wilson's plea for the prudent use of the classical criminology of Bentham and Beccaria has coincided with the rise, in the last two or three decades, of numerous studies that look for successful crime reduction strategies and that are based on the image of criminals as rational, calculating actors. These studies can be categorized in a variety of ways, though by convention they are associated either with **deterrence theory** or else with **routine activities theory**. Though we cannot explore either of these perspectives in this book, we note the significant influence, first, of classical deterrence in current research on topics as diverse as mandatory arrest for domestic violence, the death penalty for murder, the impact of gun control on violent crime, and on the use of shaming tactics against drivers who drink alcohol (for example, see J. Fagan, Zimring, and Geller, 2006; Unnithan, Pogrebin, and Stretesky, 2008; and Bertelli and Richardson, 2008).

Routine activities theory, second, is less a theory of the causes of crime than a statement about victimization—and a rather misleading one at that, because it fails to provide much or any of the sociological context of criminogenic situations, such as how and why crime is related to class, gender, race, and age.

We end this chapter with a provocative conclusion from Charles Tittle (1995; and see Section 7.5). About their lack of attention to the sociological contexts of crime, Tittle has argued that rational choice theories in general, including routine activities theory, resemble little more than a mechanical gearbox that transforms inputs into outputs. "Without knowing how and why the inputs take on particular values," he points out, "understanding the gearbox is of limited use in explaining and predicting behavior" (p. 12). It must be said that some attempts are now under way (Wilcox, Madensen, and Tillyer, 2007) to develop routine activities theory by grafting other theories of criminal behavior onto it, such as theories of criminal opportunity and social disorganization.

## REVIEW

This chapter introduced classical criminology and positivist criminology, each of which has had a great impact on the subsequent development of criminological theory. Each in its own way, these two criminologies set the tone for the ways in which criminologists understand crime today.

## THE ENLIGHTENMENT AND CLASSICAL CRIMINOLOGY

1. Classicism was the first form of modern criminology. It began as part of the Enlightenment's opposition to barbarism and arbitrariness in the criminal justice system.

2. Its principles are based in the belief that social action is influenced by both free will and determination.
3. The principles of utilitarianism were developed by Bentham. His views on punishment and imprisonment were widely accepted in theory, if not always in practice. Bentham is best remembered for his model prison, the Panopticon.

## THE EMERGENCE OF POSITIVIST CRIMINOLOGY

1. Positivist criminology began in France in the 1820s as a response to a breakdown in the classical penal system, chiefly evident in the failure of the new systems of incarceration to regulate the conduct of the dangerous classes. Positivist criminology was (and is) based on the belief that criminal behavior is as regular, patterned, and predictable as is behavior in the world of nature and that it should be examined with the scientific method.
2. The most influential form of early positivism was Quetelet's social mechanics of crime, which derived from the convergence of the concerns of criminal justice, astronomy, and statistics.
3. Quetelet's criminology employed natural science methods to identify the constancy of crime rates, criminal propensities, and the causes of crime.
4. Although his criminology was in some respects far in advance of his time, Quetelet ultimately believed that crime has biological causes.

## CRIMINAL ANTHROPOLOGY: LOMBROSO'S 'BORN CRIMINAL'

1. In 1876, Lombroso popularized the concept of the "born criminal" in his book *Criminal Man*. This biological concept radically opposed the supposed free-willed individual of classicism.
2. Lombroso believed that born criminals have primitive features that distinguish them from the law-abiding citizenry.
3. Goring's *The English Convict* tried to disentangle the respective influences of heredity and social environment on the activities of criminals. Goring's analysis of the physical features of English convicts and his comparisons between them and control samples of nonconvict populations, led him to decisively reject Lombroso's concept of born criminality. Through assumptions derived from eugenics, Goring also found that English criminals engaged in crime because of alleged mental deficiencies rather than for sociological reasons. This finding was quite compatible with Lombrosianism.

## NEOCLASSICAL CRIMINOLOGY

1. By the 1890s it was clear that a serious dilemma faced the machinery of criminal justice. Conflict between the classical and the positivist schools created a dangerous vacuum in penal policies.
2. The neoclassical school of criminology attempted to fill this vacuum with a coherent system of criminal responsibility based on accountability, individualization of punishment, and treatment programs.

3.  Although the exact terms of the compromise between classicism and positivism varied from one country to another, today its general outlines remain the dominant features of most Western systems of criminal justice.

## QUESTIONS FOR CLASS DISCUSSION

1.  Refer again to the grisly execution of Jean Calas in France in 1762, recounted at the beginning of this chapter. Less than a century later, in the 1830s, a very different penal style is visible in rules for the House of Young Prisoners in Paris. Some of these rules were as follows (cited in Foucault, 1979:6–7):

    Art[icle] 17. The prisoners' day will begin at six in the morning in winter and at five in summer. They will work for nine hours a day throughout the year. Two hours a day will be devoted to instruction. Work and the day will end at nine o'clock in winter and at eight in summer.

    Art. 18. Rising. At the first drumroll, the prisoners must rise and dress in silence, as the supervisor opens the cell doors. At the second drumroll, they must be dressed and make their beds. At the third, they must line up and proceed to the chapel for morning prayer. There is a five-minute interval between drumrolls.

    Art. 19. The prayers are conducted by the chaplain and followed by a moral or religious reading. This exercise must not last more than half an hour.

    Art. 20. Work. At a quarter to six in the summer, a quarter to seven in winter, the prisoners go down to the courtyard, where they must wash their hands and faces and receive their first ration of bread. Immediately afterwards, they form into work teams and go off to work, which must begin at six in summer and seven in winter.

    Art. 21. Meal. At ten o'clock the prisoners leave their work and go to the refectory; they wash their hands in their courtyards and assemble in divisions. After the dinner, there is recreation until 20 minutes to eleven.

    Art. 22. School. At 20 minutes to eleven, at the drumroll, the prisoners form into ranks and proceed in divisions to the school. The class lasts two hours and consists alternately of reading, writing, drawing, and arithmetic.

    Art. 23. At 20 minutes to one, the prisoners leave the school, in divisions, and return to their courtyards for recreation. At 5 minutes to one, at the drumroll, they form into work teams. . . .

    Art. 28. At half-past seven in summer, half-past eight in winter, the prisoners must be back in their cells after the washing of hands and the inspection of clothes in the courtyard; at the first drumroll, they must undress, and at the second get into bed. The cell doors are closed and the supervisors go the rounds in the corridors, to ensure order and silence.

    A.  What are the major differences between the assumptions of the two styles of punishment characterized respectively by the execution of Calas (in 1762) and by the rules for the House of Young Prisoners in Paris (circa 1837)?

    B.  This transformation of penal styles largely reflects changing theories on the causes of crime. Describe the broad transformation in such theories between the Enlightenment and Goring's *The English Convict* (1913).

      C. Is one penal style more "humane" than the other?

      D. What do these different penal styles imply about the possibility of the treatment and correction of criminals?

2. In *Crime and Everyday Life,* Marcus Felson (2006a:183–184) pinpoints the high risk of campus parking areas to property and violent victimization. Identify the assumptions about social interaction that he makes in recommending each of the following designs for safer college campuses:

- Arrange for nighttime students and workers to have parking near building doors, but not so close that they block the view of the parking area from the building.
- At low-use times, close off unneeded parking areas or sections of large parking areas to concentrate cars and people for supervision.
- Require students and staff to sign up by name and have a sticker, even for nighttime or free areas.
- Get visitors in cars to sign in and give them time limits.
- Fence parking areas.
- Eliminate nooks and corners in parking structures.
- Build parking structures on slopes so people on foot will have clear sight lines.
- Make parking structure stairwells easy to see into.
- Orient buildings to face parking areas.
- Trim hedges and the lower limbs of trees around parking areas, and avoid thick foliage.
- Post signs and organize the flow of traffic so neither cars nor pedestrians will get lost.

## FOR FURTHER STUDY

### READINGS

Beirne, Piers. 1993. *Inventing Criminology.* Albany: State University of New York Press.

Einstadter, Werner, and Stuart Henry. 2006. *Criminological Theory.* Fort Worth, TX: Harcourt Brace.

Foucault, Michel, ed. 1975. *I, Pierre Rivière, having slaughtered my mother, my sister, and my brother.* Translated by Frank Jellinek. Lincoln: University of Nebraska Press.

Gibson, Mary. 2002. *Born to Crime: Cesare Lombroso and the Origins of Biological Criminology.* Westport, CT: Praeger.

### WEBSITES

1. <http://www.wsu.edu/~dee/ENLIGHT/ENLIGHT.HTM>: This site provides a history of the European Enlightenment as an intellectual and scientific revolution, including more detail on Descartes, Rousseau, and the philosophes.

2. <http://www.deathpenaltyinfo.org>: This is the site for the Death Penalty Information Center. Capital punishment was and remains one of the key points of debate between classical and positivist criminologists.

# SOCIAL STRUCTURE, ANOMIE, AND CRIME

**5.1 Durkheim's Sociology of Law and Crime**
- Law and Social Solidarity
- The Nature of Crime
- Anomie, Egoism, and Crime
- The Evolution of Punishment
- Evaluation of Durkheim

**5.2 Social Structure, Anomie, and Deviance**
- Merton's Typology of Modes of Individual Adaptation
- Evaluation of Merton

**5.3 Revised Strain Theory**
- Agnew's General Strain Theory
- Evaluation of General Strain Theory
- Messner and Rosenfeld's Institutional Anomie Theory
- Evaluation of Institutional Anomie Theory

**PREVIEW**

Chapter 5 introduces:
- The abiding importance of Emile Durkheim's sociological approach to law and crime.
- Robert Merton's theory of social structure and anomie, a theory that seems to offer a good sociological explanation for the apparently high rates of deviance and crime in the United States.
- Two notable revisions to Mertonian strain and anomie theory: general strain theory and institutional anomie theory

**KEY TERMS**

anomie
class structure
conformity
innovation
institutional anomie theory
institutionalized means
norms

rebellion
repressive law
restitutive law
retreatism
social classes
social solidarity

## 5.1 DURKHEIM'S SOCIOLOGY OF LAW AND CRIME

Émile Durkheim (1858–1917) was one of the founders of sociological criminology, and his analyses of crime and punishment exert a powerful influence in the world of criminology today. Durkheim was a prodigious scholar whose innovative concepts and arguments spanned a great diversity of topics. The breadth of his interests is best seen in the titles of his major books: *The Division of Labor in Society* (1893), *The Rules of Sociological Method* (1894), *Suicide* (1897), *Professional Ethics and Civil Morals* (1900), and *The Elementary Forms of Religious Life* (1912).

Durkheim's writings on law and crime have had tremendous intellectual influence on the development of criminology. In much of his sociology, Durkheim tried to answer the difficult questions about how order and stability could be restored to France as it made the disruptive transition from a preindustrial social structure to modern and more complex forms of social organization in the nineteenth century: What are the

**FIGURE 5.1** Public execution in Paris, May 1, 1871: This photograph depicts the execution of sixty-two police officers by the communards of the Paris Commune during the civil war between the Third Republic and the Paris Commune. Events such as this aggravated the French public's fear of crime and fed into Durkheim's search for the conditions of social order.
*Source*: Hulton-Deutsch Collection / Corbis

preconditions of an ordered, stable, and moral society? What conditions produce social disorder? A logical consequence of Durkheim's search for the sources of social order was a concern with situations in which order and stability seemed to be lacking and that were manifest in such "pathologies" as crime and deviance (see Figure 5.1).

Before outlining Durkheim's writings on law and crime, we emphasize a theme that spanned his entire work: a sociological method. For Durkheim, societies can be analyzed properly only through the scientific method of positivism. Like Quetelet's social mechanics (see Section 4.2), Durkheim's positivism involved a search for lawlike regularities in social behavior. He insisted that generalizations about social behavior can be made independent of individual variations in free will, psychological state, and motivation.

Durkheim's positivist method stemmed from his insistence that "the first and most basic rule is *to consider social facts as things*" (1982:60). Durkheim's chief intention here was to distinguish sociology from such sciences as biology, politics, and psychology by making the "social fact" its object of study. But for Durkheim social facts were not to be confused with the psychic phenomena that exist only in individual consciousness; in reality, although we are often victims of the illusion that we act with free will, our actions are usually imposed on us externally. Durkheim defined social facts as "manners of acting, thinking, and feeling external to the individual, which are invested with a coercive power by virtue of which they exercise control over him" (p. 52). Social facts are thus obligatory and coercive. They have this character not because they are practiced by many people but because they are practiced collectively. "Social phenomena," Durkheim wrote, should thus "be considered in themselves, detached from the conscious beings who form their own mental representations of them" (p. 70).

For Durkheim, then, social phenomena (such as law and crime) have an objective existence of their own and exist quite independent of the individuals who experience them. This is a crucial insight, as we shall learn.

## LAW AND SOCIAL SOLIDARITY

Durkheim analyzed law in many of his writings. His most extended treatment occurs in *The Division of Labor in Society* (1984 [1893]). Here he tried to find the sources of social order ("social solidarity") in modern industrial societies and to determine the changes they undergo during evolution from lower to higher stages of civilization.

Durkheim argued that social development lies along a continuum, with primitive societies of "mechanical solidarity" at one end and modern societies of "organic solidarity" at the other. Mechanical solidarity is typical of simple societies with only a limited role specialization or division of labor. Members of such societies are quite similar to each other in their ways of acting, thinking, and feeling. They live within a shared consensus of beliefs and values—the "collective conscience"—in which collective life dominates and replaces individualism. During the course of social evolution, as roles within the division of labor became more specialized, **social solidarity** is transformed from a mechanical to an organic basis. Organic solidarity is thus typical of societies with an advanced division of labor and with members who have diffuse ways of acting, thinking, and feeling. Individualism dominates and replaces collective life. The cohesion of such societies derives from complex patterns of interdependence among the members and is based on the morals of various occupational categories and also on increasing respect for individual differences.

In his search for the sources of social order, Durkheim realized that social solidarity, which is abstract and internal to consciousness, does not lend itself to exact observation or precise measurement. Thus, to classify and compare the various forms of social solidarity he believed that it was necessary to use another, more visible aspect of social life that varies directly with solidarity. Durkheim argued that "to arrive at this classification, as well as this comparison, we must therefore substitute for this internal datum, which escapes us, an external one which symbolizes it, and then study the former through the latter" (1984:24). That visible symbol, he asserted, is law.

Durkheim never explicitly defined the essential qualities of law, but he implied that law differs from other forms of social regulation (including custom, ritual, ceremony, and professional obligation) because it alone exercises an organized pressure on individuals to conform to its commands. This pressure appears in the form of sanctions. To classify the different types of law, which themselves correspond to the different types of social solidarity, Durkheim reasoned that one must only classify different types of sanctions. Two forms of legal sanction correspond to the two forms of social solidarity: repressive sanctions and restitutive sanctions, which Durkheim termed, respectively, repressive law and restitutive law.

Durkheim held that **repressive law** is found chiefly in societies of mechanical solidarity. It is religious in origin and largely identical with penal and criminal law. The violation of repressive law results in the use of repressive sanctions. These sanctions consist of inflicting suffering or loss on individuals for having offended the strong sentiments of the collective conscience. Because repressive sanctions tend to be enforced by the whole of society, no special or organized institution (lawyers, courts, police, and so forth) is needed to enforce them. Durkheim provided numerous examples to show that the vast majority of the commands of ancient legal systems—such as the last four books of the Pentateuch (Exodus, Leviticus, Numbers, and Deuteronomy)—are solely directed to sentiments offended by crimes.

During the evolution from mechanical to organic solidarity, Durkheim argued, the volume of penal law in legal systems declines relative to other forms of law. He noted that certain crimes, such as those offending sexual and traditional sentiments, have nowadays almost disappeared (1984:109–110). With the decline of collective sentiments and the growth of individualism, repressive law is gradually ousted by **restitutive law**. This law consists not in the infliction of pain but in *"restoring the previous state of affairs, reestablishing relationships...disturbed from their normal form"* (p. 29). Restitutive law, growing continually in volume and intensity, results not from breaches of the collective conscience but from conflicts among occupational groups (for example, guilds, unions, and professional associations). Its violation involves enforcement of the *status quo ante* (previously existing state of affairs). Moreover, in contrast to repressive law, restitutive law is specialized through its two basic forms: (1) *Positive law* reflects the cooperation required in a complex division of labor and includes contract, administrative, domestic, and commercial legislation. (2) *Negative law* involves the rules between persons and objects that enjoin others not to interfere in certain proprietary rights of the owner and includes property and tort legislation.

## THE NATURE OF CRIME

Durkheim's analysis of relationships between law and sanctions was a critical tool for understanding social solidarity. In pursuing this goal he was led to analyze the nature of crime. As a sociologist, Durkheim rejected definitions of crime based on legalistic criteria. Such criteria—as well as criteria based on notions such as evil, social harm, violations of justice, and so forth—he regarded as inadequate for a scientific sociology.

What, then, is crime? To begin, no action is intrinsically or universally criminal. For Durkheim in *The Division of Labor in Society*, the common denominator of all crimes is that they are "acts repressed by prescribed punishments" (1984:31). This is what distinguishes a crime from a minor offense such as a tort or a breach of etiquette. In societies of mechanical solidarity, an act is defined as criminal because of the universal social reaction that condemns it. As Durkheim argued, "An act is criminal when it offends the strong, well-defined states of the collective consciousness....We should not say that an act offends the common consciousness because it is criminal, but that it is criminal because it offends that consciousness" (pp. 39–40). From this it seemed to follow that to investigate the nature of crime one must examine the nature of punishment.

What functions, then, does punishment serve? Central to Durkheim's criminology is his linking of crime and punishment. Thus: "If our definition of crime is exact it must account for all the characteristics of...punishment" (1984:44). Durkheim defined *punishment* as "a reaction of passionate feeling, graduated in intensity, which society exerts through the mediation of an organized body over those of its members who have violated certain rules of conduct" (p. 52).

Durkheim rejected popular beliefs that the function of punishment is simply revenge, deterrence, or the reformation of the character of criminals. The true function of punishment is to maintain and strengthen social solidarity. Each time a crime is committed, the subsequent condemnation of it by penal law reaffirms the values of the collective conscience or the shared consensus of a community's beliefs and values. In this way "honest people" are convinced of the moral righteousness of their conformity to law and of the "inferiority" of criminals. With great insight, Durkheim therefore concluded that "punishment is above all intended to have its effect upon honest people" (p. 63).

Durkheim made three specific claims about the nature of crime: (a) Crime is normal, (b) crime is inevitable, and (c) crime is useful.

*Crime is normal.* Durkheim caused considerable outrage by claiming that crime is a normal phenomenon, as normal as birth and marriage. Durkheim's discussion of this seemingly unusual claim is found in his 1894 book *The Rules of Sociological Method* (1984), in which he tried to restructure "the fundamental facts of criminology." Durkheim's starting point—like the starting point of his sociology in general—was his concept of the social fact: "*A social fact is normal for a given social type, viewed at a given phase of its development, when it occurs in the average society of that species, considered at the corresponding phase of its evolution*" (p. 97; emphasis in original).

In other words, in a given social context and against the background of a given level of social development, the very generality of social facts indicates that they must be normal phenomena. At any given moment society has a "normal," or statistically average, volume of births, for example, or of marriages and deaths. For Durkheim, it is only statistical deviations from such averages that are abnormal. Because crime is a social fact, Durkheim complained that criminologists err in seeing it only as a pathological or morbid phenomenon. Generally, crime should not be viewed as deviance or as sickness—what is abnormal to the biologist or to the pathologist is not necessarily so to the sociologist.

For Durkheim, then, crime as such is rarely abnormal. Crime occurs in all societies, it is tied closely to the facts of collective life, and its volume tends to increase as societies evolve from lower to higher phases. However, he was careful to add that although crime is a normal social fact, in a given context its rate might be abnormal.

*Crime is inevitable.* Durkheim admitted that his idea about the normality of crime surprised him. Eventually, he reasoned that no society can ever be entirely free of crime. To illustrate this point, Durkheim asked that we imagine a community of saints in a perfect and exemplary monastery: "In it crime as such will be unknown, but faults that appear venial to the ordinary person will arouse the same scandal as does normal crime in ordinary consciences" (1982:100). Moreover, universal and absolute conformity to rules is impossible because each member of society faces variation in "the immediate physical environment,...hereditary antecedents,...[and] social influences" (p. 100). Crime is therefore inevitable. Even if all the actions regarded as criminal at one moment suddenly disappeared, new forms of crime would be created at once.

*Crime is useful.* Durkheim first claimed that crime is normal and inevitable in *The Division of Labor in Society*. But in *The Rules of Sociological Method* he took the argument a step further in suggesting that "to classify crime among the phenomena of normal sociology is not merely to declare that it is an inevitable though regrettable phenomenon arising from the incorrigible weakness of man; it is to assert that it is a factor in public health, an integrative element in any healthy society" (p. 98).

Besides claiming that crime is normal and inevitable, Durkheim thus argued that crime is useful because crime is indispensable to the normal evolution of law and morality. Indeed, if crime is not a sickness, punishment cannot be its remedy. The nature of crime and punishment must therefore lie somewhere else than in the area of wrongdoing and its correction. If there were no crimes—if there was no deviation from social norms—Durkheim reasoned, then the collective conscience would have reached an intensity, an authoritarianism, unparalleled in history. In other words, a society with "no crime" must be an extremely repressive one.

For Durkheim, crime is useful because it is often a symptom of individual originality and a preparation for changes in law and morality.

He cited the fate of Socrates as an example of crime's utility. Socrates, perhaps the most original of all Greek philosophers, committed the "crime" of independent thought. Having been convicted of not believing in the official gods of the Athenian state and of corrupting the minds of the young, Socrates committed suicide by drinking hemlock. Durkheim suggested that "Socrates' crime served to prepare the way for a new morality and a new faith—one the Athenians...needed [inasmuch as] the traditions by which they had hitherto lived no longer corresponded to the conditions of their existence" (1982:102). Today's criminal may be tomorrow's philosopher!

## ANOMIE, EGOISM, AND CRIME

Durkheim applied his sociological insights to the analysis of two specific forms of deviance: suicide and homicide. First, he tried to show that suicide—usually regarded as the supreme act of individual deviance—has profoundly sociological rather than psychological or biological causes. Indeed, Durkheim (1951) claimed that variations in suicide rates can be explained only sociologically. His general concern was to show that the suicide rate of any society depends on the type and extent of social organization and integration. In any society each social group

> really has a collective inclination for the act, quite its own, and the source of all individual inclination, rather than their result. It is made up of the currents of egoism, altruism, or anomie running through the society under consideration.... These tendencies of the whole social body, by affecting individuals, cause them to commit suicide. (pp. 299–300)

Durkheim's explanation of varying suicide rates hinges on four types of suicide:

1. *Egoistic suicide* results from a weakening of the bonds between an individual and society. It is a special type of suicide caused by excessive individualism. It recedes only with the sort of increase in collective sentiments produced by wars and political crises. Social groups prone to egoistic suicide include Protestants (whose religious beliefs foster individualism), the unmarried, the childless, and the widowed.

2. *Altruistic suicide* results when individuals have insufficient inner strength to resist the demands of a social group into which they are overly integrated. Examples include Hindu widows, who place themselves next to their husbands on their funeral pyre, and slaves, who are expected to die with their masters.

3. *Anomic suicide* results from a sudden crisis in economic or familial life. Thus, in situations such as sudden impoverishment or unexpected riches, or immediately after family members are divorced, an abrupt change in expectations causes massive personal or social upheaval. In the aftermath of these situations, those who cannot adjust to their suddenly altered position become more suicide-prone.

4. *Individualized suicide* has particularized characteristics, either in the mental state that leads to the act or in the way it is achieved. These characteristics include melancholy, passion, and irritation, though these might also have social causes.

In addition to suicide, Durkheim (1958) analyzed the offense of homicide. He suggested that civilized peoples always consider three broad moral attitudes as duties: respect for life, respect for property, and the honor of others. In primitive societies, homicide is the most serious breach of moral duty because it is viewed as an offense against the whole of society, against what is sacred. Offenses against individual property or individual honor are seen as far less serious than offenses against the social order as a whole—and sometimes they are not considered offenses at all. In ancient Greece, Rome, and Judea, for example, victims of crimes other than homicide had to pursue their own redress and could allow the guilty party to pay a sum of money as a form of satisfaction.

Durkheim suggested that during social evolution, especially with the onset of Christianity, something of a reversal occurs in the hierarchical order of these duties. With the growth of modern societies, collective sentiments are generally reduced in intensity and sentiments centering on the individual achieve prominence. Homicide therefore remains the supremely forbidden act because it violates the individual. Given that homicide is so abhorred, Durkheim (1958) claimed that homicide rates tend to decline relative to the advance of civilization. At the same time, rates of other offenses against the individual, whether against person or property, tend to increase.

Durkheim was confident that homicide rates decreased with modernization because of the growth of the "cult of the individual" (namely, the great respect afforded the person by public opinion). But Durkheim knew that this explanation was too general:

> The decline in the rate of homicide at the present day has not come about because respect for the human person acts as a brake on the motives for murder or on the stimulants to murder, but because these motives and these stimulants grow fewer in number and have less intensity. (1958:117)

How, then, does one explain cases in which the general rule about declining homicide rates does not apply? To explain counterexamples, Durkheim introduced statistical evidence showing how other variables—including rural/urban differences, wars, religious membership, political crises, and state power—influence homicide rates. For example, he argued that Catholic countries tend to have higher homicide rates than Protestant ones because the latter's religious beliefs are more individualistic and, therefore, promote greater respect for the sanctity of individual life.

## THE EVOLUTION OF PUNISHMENT

In his 1901 (1983) essay "Two Laws of Penal Evolution," Durkheim offered a sophisticated theory of the history of punishment, returning squarely to his earlier concern with law and crime in *The Division of Labor in Society*. This final theory on the sources of punishment and of changes in its justifications and forms was a marked improvement on earlier analyses. Indeed, in his entire criminology it was only here that Durkheim considered that political factors sometimes influence the way in which certain behavior is defined as criminal.

In the essay, Durkheim modified his earlier argument to suggest that forms of punishment have varied historically in two ways, quantitatively and qualitatively. Each form is governed by a separate law, one quantitative in scope, the other qualitative (see Box 5.1).

Durkheim's first law contains two propositions. First, societies are more or less advanced according to their level of social complexity or to the intensity of their division of labor. Here Durkheim repeated his argument that less developed societies are dominated by repressive laws and barbaric forms of punishment, especially capital punishment. In such societies punishment is severe because most crimes are seen as religious violations that threaten the collective conscience. The second proposition concerns absolutist forms of political power: the exercise of governmental power without checks and balances. This authoritarian form of power (hypercentralization) exists in different types of society, early and modern, but occurs only when it is seen

---

**BOX 5.1** DURKHEIM'S TWO LAWS OF PENAL EVOLUTION

**Law 1:** The intensity of punishment is greater the more closely societies approximate to a less developed type—and the more the central power assumes an absolute character.

**Law 2:** Deprivations of liberty, and of liberty alone, varying in time according to the seriousness of the crime, tend to become more and more the normal means of social control.

---

as a right: "Such was the state of the criminal law until the middle of the eighteenth century. There then occurred, throughout Europe, the protest to which Beccaria gave his name" (1983:113).

Durkheim's first law implies that with social development the severity of punishment generally declines. This decline occurs not because authorities become more lenient but because the type of crime changes. In less developed societies, crime is seen as a threat to collective life, and, therefore, punishment is severe; in more developed societies, crime is seen as a threat to individuals only, and punishment is correspondingly less severe. However, by identifying the importance of the relationship between state power and punishment, Durkheim could now explain certain factual counterexamples to his earlier analysis. For example, he now claimed, interestingly, that in societies dominated by political absolutism, crimes retain a primarily sacrilegious character (1983). In other words, authoritarian societies act punitively and repressively not because they are not socially developed but because their organs of political power regard crime religiously—as an attack on the social order as a whole.

Durkheim's second law refers to qualitative changes in punishment. Durkheim illustrated the workings of the second law with examples from ancient Greece and modern France. He established that the death penalty had disappeared completely from some legal codes and had been taken over by incarceration. Durkheim explained this change by arguing that there is no need for incarceration in less developed societies. There, a crime affects the entire community, and, because responsibility for it is communal, all members of the community ensure that the offender does not escape before trial. However, with the disintegration of ancient societies—after which crime became more of an offense against an individual rather than against society as a whole—some method of pretrial detention was needed to ensure that offenders were held accountable.

Thus, Durkheim advanced the brilliant argument that the prison emerged from changing forms of crime. But he realized that this explanation was incomplete: "To explain an institution, it is not enough to establish that when it appeared it served some useful end; for just because it was desirable it does not follow that it was possible" (1983:117). Hence Durkheim proceeded to explain the growth of the prison in terms of his first law concerning the less repressive nature of punishment. Prisons arose because of the transformation in criminal responsibility from a collective to an individual basis. Some of the first prisons were "hole[s], in the form of a pit where the condemned wallow in refuse and vermin" (p. 119). But prisons, responding to the changed basis of criminal responsibility, gradually became milder, reflecting the general decline in the severity of punishment. As punishment as a whole became less severe, these new prisons became the typical form of punishment in developed societies.

Durkheim therefore concluded that "the qualitative changes in punishment are in part dependent on the simultaneous quantitative changes it undergoes" (1983:120). His two laws of penal evolution thus turn out to be interdependent. The very facts that bring about changes in the bases of criminal responsibility in early societies also create the apparent need for widespread use of imprisonment in modern societies!

## EVALUATION OF DURKHEIM

Quite aside from the power and scope of its analysis of crime, Durkheim's criminology has exerted tremendous influence on the development of sociological criminology. This influence has been most obvious in the writings of the Chicago school of criminology (see Section 6.1), Merton's theory of anomie and social structure (see Section 5.2), and Hirschi's theory of control and crime (see Section 7.3). Moreover, criminologists today continue to draw on Durkheim's insights.

More than anyone before him, Durkheim identified the sociological links among crime, law, punishment, and social organization. He showed that in any given society the amount and types of crime relate directly to the basic ways in which that society is organized. And societies, he insisted, should be understood historically. Durkheim also suggested that crime must be explained sociologically rather than in terms of an individual's psychological state or biological nature. Sociologically, crime is a normal and inevitable feature of social organization. Its functions lie not only in the area of sanctions but also in the creation and enforcement of solidarity.

Assessments of Durkheim's criminology tend to focus on three questions. Did he correctly describe the historical transformation in styles of punishment? Have homicide rates declined with modernization? How did his own personal and political agenda influence the propositions set forth in his various theories?

The first question has been debated largely in terms of whether the facts of the evolution of punishment fit Durkheim's theory of crime. In a well-known study that examined legal evolution in fifty-one societies, Schwartz and Miller (1964; see also Garland 1990) concluded that in simple societies restitutive law is more common than penal sanctions. This conclusion contradicts Durkheim's account of the evolution from repressive to restitutive sanctions. Therefore, it is reasonable to conclude that

> Durkheim may have derived his idea [of the evolution of punishment] from the fact that punishments in European societies were becoming much less severe at the time, because of the reforms introduced by Beccaria and other classical theorists. But the extremely harsh punishments that had been imposed prior to those reforms were associated not with simple, undeveloped societies, but rather with absolute monarchies. (Bernard, Snipes, and Gerould, 2010:124)

In answering the second question, empirical researchers have reached quite opposing results. Whereas some have found that homicide rates have declined with modernization, others have found an increase. Still others claim that most researchers have not really tested Durkheim's theory at all. Instead, as Bruce DiCristina (2004) points out, most commentaries on Durkheim's theory of homicide have been rather careless in understanding exactly what Durkheim meant by concepts such as *societal complexity* and *modernization*. Moreover,

> Overall, the empirical studies that attempt to assess Durkheim's theory of homicide require extensive reinterpretation since they misrepresent his theory and/or neglect its complexity. Indeed, in view of its complexity, its potential for extensive elaboration, and the considerable data limitations researchers face when testing it,...Durkheim's theory is not readily "falsifiable." (DiCristina, 2004:83)

Finally, we note that Durkheim is also frequently criticized for the biases that allegedly entered his sociological method in general and his criminology in particular. Durkheim has thus been scolded because his preoccupation with the sources of social order apparently led him to neglect the sources and expressions of social conflict. It is indeed true that Durkheim's criminology is based on certain assumptions: for example, that law tends to stem from and reflect widely held social values, that crime is a breach of these shared values, and that an examination of the political factors that influence the definition of certain actions as criminal is not necessary.

## 5.2 SOCIAL STRUCTURE, ANOMIE, AND DEVIANCE

It is hard to exaggerate the importance of Robert Merton's 1938 (1969) article "Social Structure and Anomie." Strongly opposed to biological and individualistic explanations of deviance and crime, Merton focused on the rates of such conduct. In developing this focus, Merton relied on Durkheim's concept of **anomie** to explain how and why "some social structures exert a definite pressure upon certain persons in the society to engage in nonconforming rather than conforming conduct" (p. 255). But whereas Durkheim had stressed that anomic states arise from unregulated human desires, Merton pinpointed the importance of the relationship between means and goals.

Merton's central hypothesis was that, sociologically, deviant behavior is a symptom of a specific sort of social disorganization: a lack of fit between culturally prescribed aspirations and socially structured avenues for achieving them. Although his essay could in principle be applied to many other societies, it is clear that Merton had in mind chiefly the United States and, especially, the goals enshrined in the American Dream.

Merton's argument began with two important elements of social and cultural structures. The first element is made up of the culturally defined goals that are held out as legitimate objectives for all members of a society. These goals are "the things worth striving for." The second element is made up of the regulations, controls, and procedures for moving toward goals, which are termed **institutionalized means**, or **norms**. A well-regulated, or stable, society has a balanced equilibrium between means and goals. In a stable society, both means and goals are accepted by everyone and are available to all. Social integration occurs effectively when individuals are socialized into accepting that they will be rewarded for the occasional sacrifice of conforming to institutionalized means and when they actually compete for rewards through legitimate means. Malintegrated, or unstable, societies stress the goals without stressing the means, or vice versa. In some societies, institutionalized means are not integrated with important social values. In societies such as the United States, provisions for making the means of achieving the goals available to all are insufficient.

Certain means, such as vivisection and medical experimentation, although perhaps technically more efficient in achieving goals, are sometimes unacceptable. Yet people often turn to technically more efficient means if other institutionalized means are unavailable. The more widespread the practice of using noninstitutionalized means, the more a society destabilizes or, put another way, the more widespread anomie becomes.

Competitive sports illustrate the processes that lead to anomie. If success in sports is construed as "winning the game at all costs" rather than as winning by the rules, the use of illegitimate but technically more efficient means is more attractive to participants. As Merton (1969) put it:

> The star of the opposing football team is surreptitiously slugged; the wrestler incapacitates his opponent through ingenious but illicit techniques; university alumni covertly subsidize "students" whose talents are confined to the athletic field. The emphasis on the goal has so attenuated

the satisfactions deriving from sheer participation in the competitive activity that only a successful outcome provides gratification. Through the same process, tension generated by the desire to win in a poker game is relieved by successfully dealing one's self four aces or, when the cult of success has truly flowered, by sagaciously shuffling the cards in a game of solitaire. (p. 259)

Moreover, Merton suggested that if "concern shifts exclusively to the outcome of competition, then those who perennially suffer defeat may, understandably enough, work for a change in the rules of the game" (1969:257). Merton believed that the United States is a society in which great emphasis is placed on certain success-goals without a corresponding emphasis on institutionalized means.

This lack of fit occurs in three ways. First, as in competitive sports, means are often elevated to ends (for example, money is commonly viewed as an end in itself rather than as a means to achieve a goal); moreover, its acquisition is a goal that can never be met. People in all income brackets want more money, and when they get more of it, they want still more. In other words, the goals of the American Dream are beyond nearly everyone's reach. Second, the lot of the multitudes who never achieve success-goals is made doubly worse because they not only fail to succeed but tend to endure penalties for such–supposed failure. Through the socializing agencies of family, school, and peer groups we are bombarded constantly with such slogans as "There is no such word as *fail*"; "Never be a quitter"; and "You can make it if you try." Coupled with this pressure to maintain lofty goals are very real penalties paid by those who draw in or reduce their ambitions. The cultural manifesto, Merton argued, is clear: Never quit, never stop trying, never lower your horizons.

Merton never fully articulates the third description of the lack of fit between means and goals in the United States, although at several points it reaches the surface of his argument. Merton hints that because of a maldistribution of power, certain segments of the population—such as individuals in the lower social strata—are continually denied access to legitimate, institutionalized means. Despite such slogans as "Anyone can be president" and "Work hard and you will be rewarded with monetary success," these goals are almost impossible to achieve for those at the bottom or at the margins of society. Tragically, failure tends to be defined as a consequence not of social inequality but of individual ineptitude or lack of ambition.

Merton's scenario of the American Dream contemplates a society that is egalitarian in its ideology but unequal in terms of the availability of the means of achieving success-goals. American society, therefore, is imperfect and badly integrated; its social and cultural structures inevitably produce **strain** and tension.

## MERTON'S TYPOLOGY OF MODES OF INDIVIDUAL ADAPTATION

What are the consequences of this strain on the individual? Merton identified five responses to the strains and tensions of social life in the United States (see Table 5.1): conformity, innovation, ritualism, retreatism, and rebellion. We stress that Merton did not conceive of these responses as psychological conditions but as structural responses to the strain of anomie. The ways in which individuals respond to anomie in part vary, in Merton's formulation, according to their position in the **class structure**.

I. *Conformity*. **Conformity** is the most common practice. Although Merton did not explain why the majority of the members of society typically conform, he suggested that "were this not so, the stability and continuity of the society could not be maintained" (1969:264). However, Merton was concerned chiefly with the four

**TABLE 5.1 A TYPOLOGY OF MODES OF INDIVIDUAL ADAPTATION**

| Mode of Adaptation | Culture Goals | Institutionalized Means |
|---|---|---|
| I Conformity | + | + |
| II Innovation | + | − |
| III Ritualism | − | + |
| IV Retreatism | − | − |
| V Rebellion | ± | ± |

Source: Merton (1969:263).

Note: + signifies acceptance, − signifies rejection, ± signifies rejection of prevailing values and substitution of new values.

deviant adaptations to the tensions generated by the gap between means and ends.

*II. Innovation.* The combination of a cultural emphasis on success-goals and the rigidity of the U.S. class structure, Merton insisted, produces an innovative deviant adaptation. Innovation is the most common deviant response and the most important for criminology. **Innovation** is deviant behavior that uses illegitimate means to achieve socially acceptable goals. Many crimes against property (such as burglaries, robberies, and larcenies) are clear examples of innovative acts. Because innovative responses are distributed throughout the U.S. class structure, there is, Merton suggested, no simple correlation between crime and poverty. The pressures to succeed operate at all points in the class structure; innovative deviance occurs throughout the social structure—from robber barons and white-collar criminals to common criminals in the lower social strata. However, Merton continued, innovative deviance in the United States is concentrated largely in the skilled and unskilled working class. It is there, more than at any other class location, that the gap between goals (which all are urged to achieve) and means is most acute.

In his theory of innovative deviance, Merton assumed that innovators are persons who have been improperly socialized. Had they been socialized properly—had they internalized the need to follow institutionalized norms—their behavior would, by definition, be conformist. An alternative for those who have fully internalized the institutionalized values but who still harbor the impossible-to-achieve aspirations of the American Dream is a dogged involvement with institutionalized norms at the expense of success-goals. This alternative Merton terms *ritualism*.

*III. Ritualism.* Merton (1969) defined **ritualism** as "the abandoning or scaling down of the lofty cultural goals of great pecuniary success and rapid social mobility to the point where one's aspirations can be satisfied" (pp. 273–274). It is the response of conformist bureaucrats who "take no chances." Ritualism is expressed in such clichés as "I'm not sticking my neck out" and "Aim low and you'll never be disappointed." Ritualism is practiced most often by members of the lower middle class, where "parents typically exert continuous pressure upon children to abide by the moral mandates of society, and where the social climb upwards is less likely to meet with success than among the upper middle class" (p. 275).

*IV. Retreatism.* **Retreatism** is an adaptation (or maladaptation) that relinquishes culturally prescribed goals and does not conform to institutionalized means. It is an escape mechanism that often arises when, after having internalized the importance of following legitimate means toward acceptable goals, an individual suffers repeated failure in goal achievement and is unable to resort to proscribed means. Retreatists constitute the "true aliens": They are "in the society but not of it" (1969:277). They include psychotics, autists, pariahs, outcasts, vagrants, vagabonds, tramps, chronic drunkards, and drug addicts. The retreatist adaptation, Merton insists, is by and large a private and isolated response rather than a public one.

*V. Rebellion.* **Rebellion** involves alienation from legitimate means and values. In contrast to retreatism, rebellion is a collective activity. For a rebellious disposition to be transformed into organized political action, legitimate means and values must be viewed as arbitrary or mythical, loyalty to them must be withdrawn, and an allegiance must be developed to new groups possessed of a new myth. The new myth has two functions. First, it must identify the source of large-scale frustration in society itself rather than in the individual. Second, it must be directed to the founding of a society with closer links between merit, effort, and reward. The precise mix of these criteria, Merton could have added, is subject to almost infinite variety and includes anarchists, communists, and the Ku Klux Klan.

## EVALUATION OF MERTON

Merton's analysis of the pressures and strains in the United States and of the way in which they lead to different deviant responses, including crime, is a brilliant polemic against those who believe that the causes of crime are found in such individualistic factors as defective personality and malformed biology. It is also a solid indictment of the tremendous social inequality in the United States; though he was always silent in this regard, it is certain that Merton was greatly influenced by Karl Marx's condemnation of capitalism, as Merton himself once admitted (Merton in a personal interview, cited in Cullen and Messner, 2007:26–27). Merton's argument about strain and anomie remains one of the most powerful sociological explanations of deviance and crime. Moreover, as Baumer (2007:85; and see Baumer and Gustafson. 2007) has recently suggested, there are doubtless numerous other still-to-be-explored lines of inquiry quite consistent with Merton's original reasoning, such as whether some individuals (e.g., those committed to community service or to being a good parent) might be somehow immunized from the stressful effects of a culture with materialistic success goals.

However, several criticisms must be made of Merton's analysis of the relations between social structure, anomie, and deviance. First, crucial parts of his argument hinge on unstated and unproven assumptions. For example, it is questionable whether acceptance of middle-class norms and values is as widespread in the United States as Merton depicts. Accepted by whom? For what reason? Are middle-class norms and values in Manhattan the same as those in rural Wisconsin and in Flagstaff, Arizona? Again, Merton's argument that deviance is a response to structural strain assumes that no form of deviant activity has authenticity in its own right. Yet some deviant activities are engaged in for no apparent reason other than that they are enjoyable.

Second, although Merton's analysis focuses on the psychic effects of strain on individuals at different points in the class structure, there is no indication of the structural causes of strain. Of course, we should not criticize Merton for not outlining something he never intended to examine—but this remains an important omission in his theory of social structure and anomie. It is especially important if we are concerned with issues of social policy and crime. If crime is caused by tensions and strain generated by a society that, for most people, routinely fails to deliver the promises of the American Dream, then how can crime be reduced? Should structural strain be seen as the starting point of a chain of causation that ends in crime and deviance? What are the causes of strain? Can nonconformist conduct be reduced by psychiatric counseling or prescription medications?

Third, recall that Merton's analysis was directed explicitly to success-oriented societies such as the United States. In such societies, the structural strain that produces nonconformist responses and that culminates in anomie derives from the gap between the availability of means and the ideology of equal opportunity. Strain is most intense for those with the least opportunity to partake in the promises of the American Dream (namely, lower-class individuals). Merton therefore suggests that nonconformist conduct (essentially, crime and deviance) is concentrated in the lower class.

But this conclusion is at best tentative and at worst false. It is true that crimes of lower-class individuals are far more likely to be detected by the police and to lead to arrest. Yet only in this limited sense is the (property) crime rate of the lower class greater than that of other classes. This reality does not mean, however, that the actual volume of crime committed by the lower class is greater than that of other classes. Indeed, if the strains of life really operate as suggested, Merton is left with the problem of explaining why it is that most members of society engage in law-abiding activities far more than they do in deviance.

## 5.3 REVISED STRAIN THEORY

The search for a general theory of crime is also present in various revisions to strain theory. We have already discussed Merton's arguments on strain and anomie, and we have seen how original and important they have been in criminology. But we have also seen that crucial parts of Merton's arguments hinge on assumptions that are unstated and unproven. For example, it is highly questionable whether the acceptance of middle-class norms and values—whatever they might be—is as widespread in the United States as Merton depicted. Moreover, although Merton's analysis focused on the psychic effects of strain on individuals at various points in the class structure, he tended to assume that strain is unidimensional in its origins and that it transfers in a rather straightforward way from the social structure to individuals.

In what follows we outline the two most influential attempts to fill in some of the gaps in Merton's original formulation. These are, respectively, Robert Agnew's general strain theory and Steven Messner and Richard Rosenfeld's institutional anomie theory.

## AGNEW'S GENERAL STRAIN THEORY

In his article "Foundation for a General Strain Theory of Crime and Delinquency," Agnew (1992) has suggested that, with suitable revisions, strain theory has a central role to play in explaining crime and delinquency. Agnew tried to develop this role with new insights from research on stress in medical sociology and psychology, on equity and justice in social psychology, and on aggression in psychology. Agnew's approach focuses on the individual and his or her immediate social environment.

Whereas Merton's strain theory focused on the ways in which an individual is barred from achieving conventional goals, Agnew expands strain theory to include the analysis of "relationships in which others present the individual with noxious or negative stimuli" (1992:49)— relationships, for example, in which an individual is not treated in the way(s) she or he would like to be. Strain may therefore result from failure either to achieve conventional goals or to escape from painful relationships.

Agnew pinpoints three chief sorts of strain. First, strain can be brought on by *failure to achieve positively valued goals*. This failure can happen in many ways, including disjunctions between aspirations and expectations/actual achievements, disjunctions between expectations and actual achievements, and disjunctions between just/fair outcomes and actual outcomes. Adolescents may experience stress when they perceive their own position in life as unjust, for example, and as a result they may engage in delinquency in order to reduce their inputs (e.g., by playing truant) or to increase the inputs of others (e.g., by being disorderly). Alternatively, they may try to increase their outcomes (e.g., by theft) or to reduce others' outcomes (e.g., by vandalism, theft, and assault). Some individuals may perceive their situation as so unjust that they remove themselves altogether from it (by running away or, we might add, by suicide).

Second, strain results from *the removal of positively valued stimuli from the individual*. Examples of this situation include the loss of a boyfriend/girlfriend, a friend's serious illness or death, and the separation of one's parents. According to Agnew, such events can lead to delinquency "as the individual tries to prevent the loss of the positive stimuli, retrieve the lost stimuli or obtain substitute stimuli, seek revenge against those responsible for the loss, or manage the negative effect caused by the loss by taking illicit drugs" (1992:58).

Third, strain occurs through *the presentation of negative stimuli*. By *negative stimuli* Agnew means such stressful life events as child abuse/neglect, criminal victimization, verbal threats and insults, and negative relations with parents, peers, and at school. Each of these events can cause a negative emotion, such as anger, and then trigger an aggressive response. Negative stimuli might also include physical pain, heat, noise, and pollution, all of which may be experienced as noxious for biological reasons.

Animal abuse is an example of crime to which Agnew (1998; and see Agnew, 2005) applies his general strain theory. He suggests that strain may lead both directly and indirectly to animal abuse, particularly to its socially unacceptable forms. The negative behavior of our companion animals, such as when they bite us or chew our possessions, may sometimes cause us to be angry. Sometimes individuals who abuse animals do so to seek revenge on an animal that has caused them stress. At times, strain resulting in abuse may occur when animals threaten crops or livestock or when endangered species halt economic development.

Some of the animal abuse that is attributed to stress is often viewed as socially acceptable. How many of us protest farmers who shoot coyotes? Who spares the mosquito that bites one's arm?

Agnew argues that animal abuse, particularly of the type that most people believe to be unacceptable, may also be fostered by strain that is not caused by animals. This type of abuse occurs, first, when people are so stressed that their awareness of how they abuse has become dulled. Here, an individual might have a general propensity to lash out at all other beings, including animals. Second, animals may sometimes be used as weapons by one party against another in a domestic dispute, as has become quite well documented (see Section 12.2).

Two further aspects of Agnew's analysis of stress and animal abuse have considerable bearing on his general strain theory. The first is that Agnew recognizes that strain may sometimes reduce the likelihood of animal abuse. To illustrate this tendency, Agnew pointed out that in the eighteenth century, English some members of English working class were motivated out of sympathy—for creatures in similarly wretched conditions—to take part in the early antivivisection movement. We might note, as does Agnew himself, that nowadays feminist members of the animal protection community stress that they and animals often have a common oppressor (i.e., men).

Second, when he brings his theory of strain to bear on animal abuse, Agnew displays his willingness to admit the relevance of numerous other factors, both sociological and psychological (see Figure 5.2). Among these other factors—which might in principle be infinite—are an individual's social position; psychological traits, such as empathy; level of stress and strain; socialization; social control; and the nature of the animal under consideration. It remains to be seen whether this flexibility dilutes or strengthens the explanatory power of Agnew's, rather, general theory.

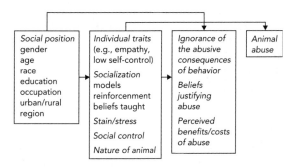

**FIGURE 5.2** A Social-Psychological Model of Animal Abuse
*Source*: Agnew (1998:182).

## EVALUATION OF GENERAL STRAIN THEORY

The scope of Agnew's general theory of strain and delinquency is much broader than earlier theories of anomie and strain. In particular, its reach extends far beyond the confines of social class. Though some key problems exist both with how best to test Agnew's theory and with what its advantages are compared with Mertonian anomie theory, it has received widespread support and confirmation (Tittle, Broidy, and Gertz, 2008). Agnew (1995) has himself said that at heart his theory is very simple: "If we treat people badly, they may get mad and engage in crime" (p. 315), a conclusion with which many criminologists will agree.

General strain theory will undoubtedly continue to generate further empirical testing. Undoubtedly, too, some of its propositions need further refinement. Thus, one study (Pérez, Jennings, and Gover, 2008; and see Kaufman, Rebellon, Thaxton, and Agnew, 2008) has found that, although the theory is basically correct, it needs to be modified in terms of its application to racial inequalities in the United States. In particular, Hispanics are subject to strains not found in the general population—these include, especially, the pressures to assimilate and the lack of social support

networks (p. 567). Another study has found that it remains unclear whether general strain theory can explain white-collar crime (Langton and Piquero, 2007:11).

## MESSNER AND ROSENFELD'S INSTITUTIONAL ANOMIE THEORY

Whereas Agnew extends Merton's anomie theory by applying it at a social-psychological level, Steven Messner and Richard Rosenfeld have extended it to the macro level of social organization. In their book *Crime and the American Dream*, Messner and Rosenfeld (2007) state that the American Dream refers to "a commitment to the goal of material success, to be pursued by everyone in society, under conditions of open, individual competition" (p. 6). The American Dream contains the basic values of American culture, in particular its commitment to achievement, individualism, universalism, and the glorification of materialistic success associated with the fetish for money. Messner and Rosenfeld claim that despite how it is filtered differentially through race and through gender, the American Dream is composed of values that are agreed on by a large majority of U.S. citizens.

Messner and Rosenfeld usefully extend Merton's analysis with their argument that U.S. society is unable to deliver the American Dream to a proportion of its citizens because in the United States—far more so than in other technologically developed societies—the capitalist economy has a lopsided dominance over all other major social institutions. This dominance of the economic realm in the institutional balance of power occurs in three interrelated ways.

First, *noneconomic institutional functions and roles are devalued*. Education, for example, tends to be seen not as end in itself but as a route to a well-paying job. Also, the chief tasks of families, such as parenting and nurturing, are not highly valued. Thus, homemakers do not have a high status; however, because of the fetish with material success, homeowners do, and, we might add, they are even rewarded with tax breaks by the government.

Second, *other social institutions are forced to accommodate to economic requirements*. For example, whereas societies such as Japan and some western European countries are strongly committed to family welfare, family life in the United States is dominated by the schedules and rewards of the labor market. Moreover, both schools and government depend heavily on private financial support.

Third, *economic norms penetrate most other institutional areas*. Thus "husbands and wives are 'partners' who 'manage' the household 'division of labor' in accordance with the 'marriage contract'" (2007:83). Schools are increasingly forced to be "accountable" to taxpayers, and students are sometimes described as "products" or even as "raw material" for the labor market.

Messner and Rosenfeld argue that the culture and the institutional structure of the United States—its social organization, in other words—lead directly to high levels of crime (see Figure 5.3). Crucially, the anomic forces in U.S. society that encourage crime are not opposed by the forces of social control that are meant to be nurtured by noneconomic institutions such as families and schools. Precisely because the power of capitalist economic values has devalued the prosocial messages of these noneconomic institutions, the latter are relatively powerless to create the sort of cooperative community that opposes crime. Hence, anomie is exacerbated and a vicious cycle occurs. According to Messner and Rosenfeld, the resultant generalized anomie helps explain not only the high rate of predatory crime in the United States but also white-collar and corporate crimes as well as the pervasive inclination in the United States to own guns and to use them in illegal ways.

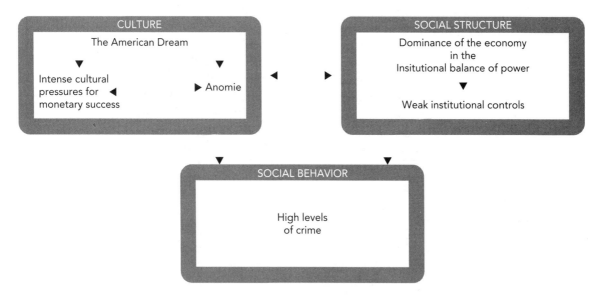

**FIGURE 5.3** An Analytical Model of the Linkages Between Macrosocial Organization and Crime
*Source*: Messner and Rosenfeld (2007:85).

## EVALUATION OF INSTITUTIONAL ANOMIE THEORY

Messner and Rosenfeld's account of the links among anomie, the decay of major social institutions, and the type and amount of crime in the United States has striking similarities to Durkheim's account of the same phenomena in France 100 years earlier. Moreover, like Durkheim, Messner and Rosenfeld have responded to this crisis by searching for the causes of social order, and, like Durkheim, they lament the rise of egoism, the decline of community, and the loss of faith in, or the lack of influence of, certain social institutions, such as the family and the school. Messner and Rosenfeld's analysis is also similar to those conflict and Marxist explanations of crime that focus on the distorting effects on social life of the dominance of capitalist relations of production (see Chapter 8; and see Chamlin and Cochran, 2007).

Messner and Rosenfeld's solution to the problem of crime entails two broad movements for social change. In combination, these movements—one institutional, the other cultural—would amount to a radical restructuring of American society. The first is the rebalancing of the major social institutions so that the economy is no longer dominant—with the effect that the polity, the family, the school, and the system of social stratification are all democratized and given an egalitarian thrust. This is not a novel proposal, although it is an important one.

The second movement entails what Messner and Rosenfeld term *cultural regeneration*—a proposal that is, regrettably, found only rarely in contemporary criminology. Cultural regeneration involves a radical reappraisal of the American Dream. In order to reduce strain, money and material possessions must no longer serve as the chief gauges of social worth. Parenting, "spousing," teaching, learning, and serving the community must become meaningful ends in themselves. Moreover, Messner and Rosenfeld warn that such a society will have to develop a cultural receptivity to restraints (2007:112–113). By this they mean that significantly lower levels of crime are unlikely to occur unless we become less obsessed with individual rights, interests, and privileges and more concerned with collective obligations and mutual support.

We note, too, that the authors of institutional anomie theory have admitted that one of the most basic questions still to be unanswered by institutional anomie theory is the origin of economic dominance and other institutional imbalances. "One approach to this issue," Messner, Thome, and Rosenfeld write (2008:178), "is to direct attention to the decreasing power of the nation-state and other political institutions to regulate economic processes or to compensate for certain dysfunctional consequences they produce in other spheres of social life."

Enter globalization—and imbalances between international economic markets, on the one hand, and, on the other, an adequate system of international regulation and international criminal justice (and return to Chapter 3).

## REVIEW

### DURKHEIM'S SOCIOLOGY OF LAW AND CRIME

1. In Durkheim's sociology lay an extremely successful attempt to integrate a theory of law with a theory of crime and punishment.
2. Durkheim's sociological method was based on the idea that societies can be fully understood only by the scientific method of positivism. Like Quetelet's social

mechanics, Durkheim's criminology attempted to find regularities in criminal behavior.

3. Durkheim's criminology began with the belief that types of law and types of social solidarity were intimately connected. Mechanical solidarity is associated with repressive law; organic solidarity is associated with restitutive law. During the evolution from mechanical to organic solidarity, the volume of repressive law declines relative to other forms of law. This is one way of explaining the broad transformation in penal strategies that accompanied the Enlightenment and classical criminology (see Section 4.1).

4. Durkheim argued that the function of punishment is to maintain and strengthen social solidarity rather than to repress crime. Crime is a normal, inevitable, and useful form of social activity. Detailed analyses of crime in Durkheim's works concentrate on suicide and homicide. Both of these crimes testify to the sociological causes of crime and, especially, to the effects of anomie and egoism on them.

5. Durkheim argued that forms of punishment have varied in history according to two laws. Quantitatively, punishment has tended to be more repressive the less developed the society and the more absolute the power of the central authority. Qualitatively, the more developed the society, the more imprisonment tends to become its dominant form of social control.

## SOCIAL STRUCTURE, ANOMIE, AND DEVIANCE

1. This section examined Merton's influential article "Social Structure and Anomie" (1938 [1969]). Merton's analysis of deviance and crime in part developed from the work of Durkheimian sociology.

2. Merton argued that certain societies, such as the United States, are unstable because of a lack of fit between socially approved means and socially approved goals.

3. According to Merton, failure to achieve socially approved goals leads to various structural responses: conformity, innovation, ritualism, retreatism, and rebellion.

## REVISED STRAIN THEORY

1. Whereas Merton's strain theory focused on the ways in which an individual is barred from achieving conventional goals, Agnew expands strain theory to include the analysis of relationships in which others present the individual with noxious or negative stimuli.

2. Agnew's social-psychological theory pinpoints three chief sorts of strain: failure to achieve positively valued goals; the removal of positively valued stimuli from the individual; and the presentation of negative stimuli. Agnew has said that at heart his theory is very simple: "If we treat people badly, they may get mad and engage in crime."

3. In his analysis of animal abuse, Agnew admits the relevance of numerous other factors, both sociological and psychological. These include an individual's social

position; psychological traits, such as empathy; level of stress and strain; socialization; social control; and the nature of the animal under consideration.

4. Despite the narrow demographic makeup of the populations that have been used to test it so far, Agnew's theory has gained some preliminary empirical support.

5. Messner and Rosenfeld's institutional anomie theory extends Merton's theory at the macro level. They argue that the American Dream in unachievable for some because of the lopsided dominance of the capitalist economy in the institutional balance of power.

6. This dominance of the economic realm occurs in three ways: Noneconomic institutional functions and roles are devalued; other social institutions are forced to accommodate to economic requirements; and economic norms penetrate most other institutional areas. In combination and in the absence of social control and cultural counterweights, this leads to high crime rates.

7. Messner and Rosenfeld's radical solution to the problem of crime in the United States involves both a rebalancing of the major social institutions and cultural regeneration.

## QUESTIONS FOR CLASS DISCUSSION

1. What did Durkheim mean when he wrote that "crime is normal"?
2. Is crime inevitable? If so, under what circumstances?
3. Does Merton's typology of deviance actually explain variations in crime rates?
4. How does the American Dream contribute to high crime rates?
5. Are societies with high crime rates necessarily worse off than societies with low crime rates?

## FOR FURTHER STUDY

### READINGS

Special issue on "Anomie/Anomia," 2008. *International Journal of Conflict and Violence* 2(2).
Special section on Robert K. Merton. 2007. *Theoretical Criminology,* 11(1). Essays by Cullen and Messner; Chamlin and Cochran; and Baumer.
Sumner, Colin. 1994. *The Sociology of Deviance*: An Obituary. New York: Continuum.

### WEBSITES

1. <http://durkheim.itgo.com/>: This is the website for the Emile Durkheim Archive, an online source designed for undergraduate students where Durkheim's major theories are explained. The site contains a glossary of Durkheim's terms and over seventy quotations from his work.

2. <http://www.sad.ch/sid/forschung/anomieresearch.html>: This site summarizes current research on anomie as well as its application. Students should be able to see how a given theoretical perspective influences a particular social policy.
3. <http://www.criminology.fsu.edu/crimtheory/agnew.htm>: This website provides a biography of Robert Agnew and an in-depth explanation of his general strain theory and its policy applications.

# DELINQUENT SUBCULTURES, SUBCULTURES OF DELINQUENCY, AND THE LABELING PERSPECTIVE

**PREVIEW**

Chapter 6 introduces:
- The innovative methods and concepts of the Chicago school of criminology, which culminated in the findings of Shaw and McKay's *Juvenile Delinquency and Urban Areas*.
- The ways in which criminologists have attempted to explain the origins, beliefs, and activities of different sorts of male, lower-class, delinquent subcultures.

- The antipositivist theory of David Matza, which argues that delinquents are not nearly so committed to their activities as subcultural theorists have supposed.
- The labeling perspective, among whose major concepts are primary and secondary deviance, deviance amplification, and stigmatization.

**KEY TERMS**

Chicago school of criminology
deviance
deviance amplification
drift
labeling perspective
middle-class measuring rod
primary deviance
reaction formation
secondary deviance

social constructionism
social control
social disorganization
social ecology
status frustration
stigma
subculture
techniques of neutralization

## 6.1 THE CHICAGO SCHOOL OF CRIMINOLOGY: SOCIAL DISORGANIZATION AND DELINQUENCY

No introduction to criminology could be complete if it failed to outline the originality and the importance to subsequent studies of juvenile delinquency of the **Chicago school of criminology**. This school of thought flourished between the end of the 1914–1918 war and the late 1940s, though its influence is still very much felt.

The Chicago school was part of the post-Progressive Era social science movement, many aspects of which evolved at the University of Chicago. Between 1915 and the early 1940s, sociological research in the United States was dominated by various academic disciplines at the University of Chicago, especially those of political science and sociology. This domination resulted from several factors, chief among them the nature of the city of Chicago itself. By the 1920s and 1930s, slightly more than a century after its founding, Chicago had changed beyond all recognition. From a small town of little more than two square miles and 200 inhabitants, Chicago had expanded to become the second-largest industrial metropolis in the United States, with a corporate area of 211 square miles and a

population of over 3.3 million. The city extended some 25 miles along Lake Michigan and from 8 to 10 miles inland.

During this expansion, tremendous changes occurred in the social composition of many neighborhoods in the city. These changes were especially visible in neighborhoods in and adjacent to the central business district and in areas of rapid industrial growth. "About the only thing that could be thought beautiful about…Chicago," a Chicago sociologist commented pointedly, "was fresh and lively Lake Michigan" (Faris, 1970:21). To journalists, social reformers, and sociologists, the ever-changing and fascinating patterns of daily life in Chicago were a barometer of the human condition itself. German sociologist Max Weber, visiting the city in 1904, found it "incredible and compared it to a man whose skin had been peeled off and whose intestines were seen at work" (Bulmer, 1984:xvi; and Beirne, 2006).

In this stimulating atmosphere, many creative scholars combined their talents and applied their energies to a sociological analysis of the harsh consequences of urbanism. Many members of the Chicago school came from a common background that can be summarized as rural or small

---

**BOX 6.1** THE RISE OF SOCIOLOGY IN THE UNITED STATES, 1890–1910

Three major factors fostered the intellectual and institutional rise of sociology in the United States (Schwendinger and Schwendinger, 1974; Ross, 1991; Camic and Xie, 1994):

1. The Progressive Era (1890–1910)—a combination of secular and Christian (especially Protestant) reform movements inspired by the professional middle classes (lawyers, doctors, teachers, and so on) and designed to improve the lot of the poor in the wake of the problems associated with the ill effects of industrialization and urbanization.
2. The rapid expansion of the university system in the United States and the institutionalization of the

social sciences and of statistics at elite universities (Columbia, Johns Hopkins, Yale, Harvard, University of Chicago) between the mid-1870s and 1915. The first course in sociology was probably offered in 1876 by Sumner; the first book on sociology was Lester Ward's *Dynamic Sociology* (1883). The first book on criminology to use sociology specifically as one of its multifactorial perspectives was probably Kellor's *Experimental Sociology* (1901).
3. The government's recognition, between 1865 and 1905, of new academic associations—including the American Social Science Association, the American Economic Association, the American Historical Association, and the American Sociological Society—for the professional security and advancement of the social science community.

---

town, midwestern, Christian in upbringing, and reform-oriented or even liberal in its political views; their investigations therefore led directly to policies for social reform.

The Chicago school brought innovative, vigorous, and eclectic methods of analysis to its research on urbanism. In the history of empirical research, these methods fell, chronologically, midway between (although curiously unrelated to) investigations that relied on large social surveys and those that used scientific measurement techniques. Members of the Chicago school employed a dazzling array of methodological techniques in their research. Their quantitative methods included advanced statistical analyses. Their qualitative techniques included the use of life-history documents, case studies, investigative journalism, media materials, in-depth interviews, and participant observation. Above all, Chicago sociologists believed in following Park's recommendation to get their feet wet with real research (Bulmer, 1984; and see Beirne, 2006); they took great pride in conducting research not in laboratories, faculty offices, or libraries but in "the open" or in "the field"—on the streets, in opium dens, in brothels, and in parks.

In effect, the Chicago school firmly believed that the new methodological techniques of fieldwork would enable factual, theory-free analysis of society: "Facts speak for themselves" quite independent of theoretical interpretation. However, the Chicago school's "facts" did not speak for themselves. Behind their facts lay the guiding hand of an important theoretical assumption: that the **social ecology** of urbanism could proceed within the same framework as the ecological study of plant and animal life. This assumption was present, sometimes beneath the surface and sometimes quite overtly, in numerous writings of the Chicago school, from the early research of Park (1915) and Burgess (1925) on urban spatial analysis to Shaw and McKay's famous book *Juvenile Delinquency and Urban Areas* (1942). The assumption was used to help describe how industrial and commercial expansion invades and disturbs the "metabolism" of "natural areas" (local communities) in the city.

After the 1914–1918 war, Chicago sociologists turned their ecological attentions to a variety of social problems. Exacerbated by the severe hardships of the Great Depression, by Prohibition, and by the well-publicized rise of gangland warfare and union racketeering, crime itself came to be seen as a major social problem. Crime, therefore, was one of the chief topics studied by members of the Chicago school. For example, W. I. Thomas and Florian Znaniecki's *The Polish Peasant in Europe and America* (1918–1920) used personal documents and life histories to examine how hard it was for immigrants to adjust to life in America. W. I. Thomas' *The Unadjusted Girl* (1923) collected information from 3,000 interviews to establish that all social behavior, including that of female delinquency, apparently derived from one or all of four motives, or "wishes": the wishes for new experience, for security, for response, and for recognition. As such, implied Thomas, delinquency and lawful activity were merely "functional alternatives" directed to the satisfaction of the same goals. *The Unadjusted Girl* marked a rare concern among criminologists with the behavior of young females. However, feminists find scant value in Thomas' book; the analysis is thoroughly sexist (females are entirely incidental to Thomas' concern with the four "wishes"). Thrasher's *The Gang* (1927) strongly implied that, although there are many gang types, delinquent gang activity represented a normal part of the process of adjustment between adolescence and adulthood. Delinquency, Thrasher found, was the best method of adjustment available to adolescents in deprived inner-city areas.

Clifford Shaw contributed two directions of research to the Chicago school before completing his famous *Juvenile Delinquency and Urban Areas* with Henry McKay in 1942. First, in *Delinquency Areas* Shaw (et al., 1929) argued that the physical destruction and social deterioration of inner-city areas leads to the disintegration of the community and, ultimately, to the loss of the community's ability to police itself. **Social disorganization**, in other words, causes increases in juvenile delinquency.

Second, Shaw showed how seemingly important it was for a researcher to listen to delinquents'

own definitions of their activities. Why did juveniles, according to their own explanations, engage in delinquency? To answer this question Shaw collected more than 200 life histories of juvenile delinquents. In 1930, Shaw published *The Jack-Roller*, a widely read account of "a delinquent boy's own story." This book was followed by *The Natural History of a Delinquent Career* (1939), a book that contradicted the public condemnation of a convicted rapist and armed robber widely depicted as a brute and a beast. Instead, insisted Shaw, this felon should be understood in terms of the values transmitted to him by numerous juvenile institutions and by his economically insecure and disorganized community in Chicago.

We turn now to what was, in some respects, the greatest achievement of the Chicago school's contribution to criminology: Shaw and McKay's (1942) *Juvenile Delinquency and Urban Areas*.

## SHAW AND MCKAY'S *JUVENILE DELINQUENCY AND URBAN AREAS* (1942)

Shaw and McKay's research applied to the city of Chicago the detailed statistical analyses pioneered a century earlier by Quetelet and Guerry (see Section 4.2). Its sophisticated analyses tried to untangle the links among the dynamics of urban growth, community problems, and rates of juvenile delinquency. Among the crucial questions about juvenile delinquency that Shaw and McKay sought to explore were:

1. Do juvenile delinquency rates and adult crime rates vary together in different types of cities?
2. Do rates of juvenile delinquency correlate with the rates of juvenile recidivism; with the economic, social, and cultural characteristics of local communities; and with patterns of immigration?
3. How do economic and social conditions influence the development of juvenile

delinquency as a cultural tradition in certain neighborhoods?

4. How can juvenile delinquency be prevented and treated?

Shaw and McKay approached these questions in four stages. First, they identified various physical and sociodemographic changes in Chicago neighborhoods. On the one hand, the physical changes comprised such factors as the growth of the central business district and the invasion of traditional local communities in the course of industrial and commercial expansion. During this expansion, Chicago landlords typically failed to repair rented dwellings in surrounding areas because of expectations that rising property prices—caused by the increased demand of industry and commerce for scarce land—would eventually yield fat profits. As a result, "zones of transition" surrounding the central business district and the industrial developments of Chicago were subject to increasing physical deterioration that, in turn, was manifest in the number of substandard and dangerous buildings that survived in the zone of transition.

On the other hand, the changes in Chicago's social composition derived largely from the fact that from the 1880s to the 1930s the population in Chicago's zone of transition was in relative decline while the population in its expanding suburbs was increasing. Using census data, Shaw and McKay found that a disproportionate number of those in professional and clerical occupations resided in the affluent suburbs, far from the central business district and industrial development. Correspondingly, a disproportionate number of industrial workers and the poor were concentrated in areas of physical deterioration. These deteriorated areas also contained the greatest number of families on welfare.

In combination, the physical and social changes in Chicago led to a far-reaching geographic segregation of the population. Shaw and McKay discovered further that patterns of immigration were part of a related process of economic and occupational segregation. The native white population not only enjoyed the highest economic status but tended to live in comfortable suburban houses; the residents of deteriorated zones of transition tended to have the lowest economic status. This latter group included (1) white European immigrants (especially from Czechoslovakia, Germany, Greece, Ireland, Italy, Poland, and Russia) and (2) African Americans, many of whom were "internal immigrants" who had migrated to Chicago from rural areas in the South.

Each immigrant group tended to be concentrated in a particular section of Chicago, although African-American families were more dispersed throughout the deteriorated neighborhoods than were European immigrants. Upon arrival in the "New World," each impoverished immigrant group tended to be pushed into the areas of lowest economic status. Eventually, however, most groups (but not African Americans, Latinos, or Native Americans) worked their way to the suburbs; their places in the deteriorated neighborhoods were simply filled by subsequent arrivals. To paraphrase the jargon of social ecology: As industry and commerce extend their habitat, the metabolism of existing natural areas is dominated or destroyed; surviving areas, in succession, are organically reconstituted as part of another natural area. Shaw and McKay inferred that this complicated process led to differential rates of delinquents.

Second, Shaw and McKay focused on the distribution of delinquency in Chicago. The juveniles in their data were of three types:

1. Alleged male juvenile delinquents (namely, those under age 17) brought before the Juvenile Court of Cook County.
2. Juveniles actually committed to correctional institutions.
3. All boys dealt with by the juvenile police probation officers.

Although the objection could be made that these three types represented a sample only of those apprehended rather than of all juvenile delinquents, this sample was larger than that for any previous study. Moreover, the data were compiled from different periods of time: (1) 9,860 alleged Chicago juvenile delinquents for the period 1934–1940; (2) 8,411 for 1927–1933; (3) 8,141 for 1917–1923; and (4) 8,056 for 1900–1906. Their use of time-series data, Shaw and McKay reasoned, permitted comparisons of delinquency rates not only in the same area for different periods but also in other areas, some of which had undergone great sociodemographic changes and some of which had remained relatively stable.

Their findings, displayed with spectacular diagrams and shaded maps, were most revealing. Using a series of spot maps that located the homes of all the delinquent boys reported in their data, Shaw and McKay showed that certain areas of Chicago had large concentrations of juvenile delinquents, whereas in other areas the delinquents were greatly dispersed. The areas of heaviest concentration were generally those near the central business district or those within or near areas zoned for industry and commerce.

Shaw and McKay divided the map of Chicago into 140 units, each approximately one square mile in size. They then computed delinquency rates for each unit (a delinquency rate was the number of delinquent boys in any given unit expressed as a percentage of the total number of boys in that unit). Significantly, the units with the highest delinquency rates were found to be those near the central business district and those adjacent to areas zoned for industry or commerce.

Shaw and McKay showed further that delinquency rates throughout Chicago varied in a strikingly uniform pattern (see Figure 6.1): The center of the city had the highest delinquency rates and the units at the extreme periphery the lowest; in between, the rates decreased regularly the farther away from the center. This finding—that delinquency rates actually declined as one moved from the center to the periphery of the delinquency zones in Chicago—is analyzed in greater detail later in this section.

Shaw and McKay theorized that juvenile delinquency would diminish as more conventional social structures replaced the "disorganized" inner-city societies of new immigrants. Yet other factors were clearly in play, as evidenced by the continued presence of juvenile delinquency throughout society.

Third, Shaw and McKay showed that juvenile delinquency was not an isolated social problem: area by area, juvenile delinquency rates were strongly correlated with such other community problems as high rates of school truancy, young adult offenders, infant mortality, tuberculosis, and mental disorders. In other words, Shaw and McKay found that areas in Chicago with certain social problems also tended to have higher rates of juvenile delinquency. Moreover, these same areas had the highest juvenile recidivism rates and relatively more delinquents who were later arrested as adults (1942: 138–139).

Shaw and McKay stressed that their analyses were correlational, not causal. The high correlation between delinquency rates and certain sociodemographic characteristics of Chicago neighborhoods did not mean that these characteristics cause delinquency. For example, Shaw and McKay saw that although the proportion of the foreign-born and the African-American population was higher in areas with high delinquency rates, this fact did not mean that the delinquency rates of these populations were higher because they were foreign-born or African American. They were higher, in part, because the high turnover of immigrant populations caused a withdrawal of residents' identification with their community and, correspondingly, a lack of pride in their neighborhood. Curiously, areas with high

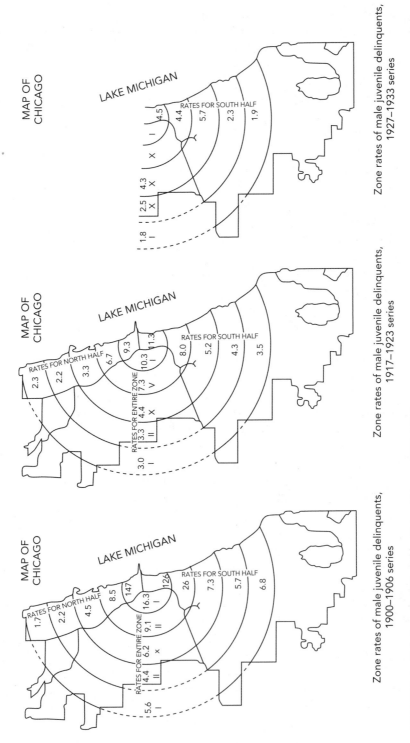

**FIGURE 6.1** Male Juvenile Delinquency Rates, Chicago. 1900–1933
*Source:* Adapted from Shaw and McKay (1969:69).

delinquency rates continued to have high rates irrespective of which groups inhabited them. Thus, between 1884 and 1930, eight inner-city Chicago areas underwent no changes in delinquency rates relative to other areas, despite the fact that the dominant population in these eight areas changed from Germans, Irish, English/Scots, and Scandinavians to Italians, Poles, and Slavs. This stability in delinquency rates, in the face of changing ethnic compositions, meant that "the delinquency-producing factors are inherent in the community" (1942:315).

Finally, Shaw and McKay tried to extend the importance of the relationship between "social values" and "larger economic and social processes" to the causes of juvenile delinquency. In areas with low delinquency rates (i.e., generally middle-class areas and those with high economic status), on the one hand, Shaw and McKay suggested that there was a general consensus about conventional values and attitudes toward such things as the welfare of children, the desirability of education, constructive leisure-time activities, and conformity to law. In such middle-class areas, moreover, respect for social values was expressed and cultivated by a variety of voluntary social control organizations, such as parent–teacher associations, women's clubs, service clubs, churches, and neighborhood centers. Children who lived in such environments tended to be insulated from direct contact with deviant forms of adult behavior and, in general, were "exposed to and participate[d] in a significant way in one mode of life only" (1942:171).

In areas with high delinquency rates (generally, working-class areas and those with low economic status), on the other hand, there was found to be wide diversity in norms and standards of behavior. This diversity resulted from the different cultural beliefs and practices of migrant groups and unassimilated immigrant groups, as well as from the moral values of predatory youth gangs and organized crime. Concerning these areas, Shaw and McKay (1942) summarized:

> Moral values range from those that are strictly conventional to those in direct opposition to conventionality as symbolized by the family, the church, and other institutions common to our general society. The deviant values are symbolized by groups and institutions ranging from adult criminal gangs engaged in theft and the marketing of stolen goods...to quasi-legitimate businesses and the rackets through which partial or complete control of legitimate business is sometimes exercised....Thus, within the same community theft may be defined as right and proper in some groups and as immoral, improper, and undesirable in others. In some groups wealth and prestige are secured through acts of skill and courage in the delinquent or criminal world, while in neighboring groups any attempt to achieve distinction in this manner would result in extreme disapprobation. Two conflicting systems of economic activity here present roughly equivalent opportunities for employment and for promotion. (pp. 171–172)

For Shaw and McKay, in other words, areas with high delinquency rates were those whose children were exposed to (1) conflicting sets of moral values, (2) adult role models whose material success derived from participation in criminal activities, and (3) a social tradition of delinquency that was a hallmark of the life of the local community. Boys constantly surrounded by this social milieu were thus routinely exposed to delinquent lifestyles. However, the mere existence of criminal organizations did not explain why some boys were tempted to join and others were not. So, what causes juvenile delinquency?

In their conclusion, Shaw and McKay (1942) attempted to answer this question. Once again, they emphasized that the major difference between areas with high and low rates of officially recorded delinquency was that the former tended to be more impoverished and the latter more affluent. Despite this difference, boys in all areas of Chicago—both rich and poor—were "exposed [in school and elsewhere] to the luxury values and success patterns of our culture" (p. 319). However, success by legitimate means was difficult to achieve for boys in low-income areas because they usually lacked the opportunities and skills required to be successful. Boys from low-income families thus calculated that the best way to achieve success lay in acts of delinquency and crime. Juvenile delinquency is therefore rational activity, and delinquent boys are by no means necessarily disorganized, maladjusted, or antisocial. As Shaw and McKay explained:

> In the low-income areas, where there is the greatest deprivation and frustration, where, in the history of the city, immigrant and migrant groups have brought together the widest variety of divergent cultural traditions and institutions, and where there exists the greatest disparity between the social values to which the people aspire and the availability of facilities for acquiring these values in conventional ways, the development of crime as an organized way of life is most marked. Crime, in this situation, may be regarded as one of the means employed by people to acquire, or to attempt to acquire, the economic and social values generally idealized in our culture, which persons in other circumstances acquire by conventional means. (p. 319)

### EVALUATION OF THE CHICAGO SCHOOL

Shaw and McKay's findings in their famous study have had enormous influence on criminology, as has the methodological legacy of the Chicago school in general. Doubtless a tribute to Shaw and McKay's signal importance, the method and findings of *Juvenile Delinquency and Urban Areas* have been reinterpreted and reworked endlessly by successive generations of criminologists (for example, see M. Felson, 2006b).

Now let us consider several criticisms of Shaw and McKay's work. First, consider the relationship between the source of their data and their finding that rates of juvenile delinquency tend to be highest in the low-income and working-class neighborhoods of cities. These data came from records of such official agencies as juvenile courts and juvenile probation officers. Although Shaw and McKay realized that many juveniles commit serious offenses that go undetected or for which they are not apprehended, they did not acknowledge that crime rates are not pregiven, objective facts. Crime rates are always socially constructed (see Chapter 2). Delinquency rates, for example, reflect not only the illegalities of juveniles but also the reporting activity of the public and the decision to accept an act as an offense by a police officer. Delinquency is so often found in working-class areas partly because working-class adolescents are more likely to have their offenses reported to the police, and, if their offenses are reported, they are more likely to be arrested, to enter the criminal justice system, and to leave it as officially defined delinquents.

Moreover, recent self-report studies and victimization surveys show that although lower-class neighborhoods contain a disproportionate amount of violent crime, delinquency as a whole is not concentrated among working-class adolescents. Status offenses and property crimes, in particular, are far more evenly distributed throughout the class structure.

Second, consider that Shaw and McKay's data on delinquency distribution derived from the residences of juveniles who entered the criminal justice system. Subsequent research on urban social spaces, beginning with Newman's *Defensible Space* (1973), has demonstrated the critical importance of the locations where crimes are committed rather than the residences of those who commit them—a fact of obvious importance in the case of syndicated, white-collar, and political crimes.

Third, consider Shaw and McKay's claim that delinquency rates remained stable despite great changes in the social composition of Chicago neighborhoods. If we ignore such factors as class bias in the construction of delinquency rates, it is possible that this claim was true for the specific period investigated (namely, 1906–1940). Yet there is no good reason to suppose, as Shaw and McKay did, that delinquency rates will be stable in other places and times. Indeed, it is likely that in Chicago itself delinquency rates after 1945 did not conform to the pattern predicted for them by Shaw and McKay (Bursik, 1984). Ultimately, we cannot be sure of the exact meaning of any claim about the stability of socially constructed crime rates. Does such a claim mean that the rate of actual illegalities remained stable? Does it mean, instead, that the actions of police officers remained constant? In posing these questions we are forced to raise anew a central question of the discussion in Chapter 2: What, precisely, do crime rates measure?

Some critics of *Juvenile Delinquency and Urban Areas* have complained that its findings were deeply structured by theoretical assumptions that lurked below the surface of their argument (Valier, 2002). In respect of the concept of **social disorganization**, for example, although Shaw and McKay were quite aware of the great diversity of lifestyles in Chicago, they nevertheless tended to start with an image of conventional lifestyles and then went on to describe those that deviated from convention as disorganized and, occasionally, as socially pathological. Sociologically, however, societies and communities can never be disorganized as such. *Disorganization* is a label that is always conceived of, explicitly or implicitly, in relation to some theoretically conceived yardstick of organization. Sometimes this conception is quite explicit (such as when someone says that unregulated industrial expansion is immoral because it destroys the communality of residential neighborhoods or that, compared

with the orderly lifestyles of the residents of Chicago's fashionable Gold Coast, life in the slums is disorganized). At other times, the concept of social organization is implicit only. Shaw and McKay assumed implicitly, and wrongly so, that the lifestyles and values of those in natural areas of transition were disorganized. Ultimately, Shaw and McKay assumed that juvenile delinquency was necessarily disorganized or deviant activity.

Moreover, their causal chain leading to delinquency suffered from theoretical confusion. Shaw and McKay made no attempt to follow through on the implications of their original insight—that industrial expansion, neighborhood destruction in zones of transition, and juvenile delinquency might be parts of the same causative process. In other words, although they correctly identified the socially harmful effects of unregulated industrial and commercial expansion on community life, they instead argued that these effects were generated by a breakdown in the values of the affected communities. For Shaw and McKay it was not dilapidated housing, overcrowding, poor hygiene, and inadequate leisure facilities (all effects of unregulated urban growth) that caused delinquency. Delinquency was caused by a breakdown in the values of the delinquents, in those of their families, and in those of their communities as a whole. Their analysis failed to view delinquency and capital movements as anything other than aspects of a temporary; coincidental process.

## 6.2  DELINQUENT SUBCULTURES

In the 1950s many criminologists began to examine the subcultural settings in which deviant values coexist with dominant social values. The central question of the subcultural theorists repeated Durkheim's question: Given the widespread persistence of deviance, what functions do deviant values serve for those who subscribe to them? This section outlines the key answers given to this question. As research on delinquent subcultures developed, it gradually recognized the importance of a variable never properly examined by the Chicago school—the influence of social class. We begin our outline of subcultural theory with Albert Cohen's book *Delinquent Boys* (1955).

## A. K. COHEN'S *DELINQUENT BOYS* (1955)

Cohen's *Delinquent Boys* begins with the premise that juvenile delinquency is a major problem of every sizable American community. All attempts to control delinquency had failed, Cohen argued, because none had accurately identified its causes. Cohen stressed that the Chicago school had overemphasized the social disorganization of the zones of transition and that these areas were not nearly as lacking in community spirit as researchers such as Shaw and McKay had imagined. Moreover, Cohen was critical of Mertonian anomie theory because it had failed to come to grips with the content of juvenile gangs. Cohen believed further that Merton had ignored the fact that delinquent gangs do not simply use deviant means to achieve culturally approved goals. Far from it, he insisted, delinquent gangs often seem to engage in violence simply for "the hell of it." And Sutherland's theory of differential association, too, failed to explain why some juveniles join gangs and others do not (see Chapter 7). Moreover, Cohen felt that Sutherland had taken for granted the existence of juvenile gangs and had failed to ask certain questions: Where do gangs come from? What are their origins? Why do delinquent gangs exist in some social settings but not in others?

About Sutherland, with whom he had done graduate study at Indiana, Cohen recorded his feeling that the theory of differential association

> has to do with how people come to acquire the delinquent or criminal culture through a process

of association. But, I asked, Where does it come from? How do you explain the existence of the culture?...But [Sutherland] didn't think that was much of a question. Somewhere he said, actually he wrote it too, that the southern practice of dropping the r's is explained by the southern practice of dropping the r's—that's all you have to know—which incidentally is wrong. It sounds on the face of it that it might say something but the point is, some speech practices become extinct, others spread and you get novelties linguistically. Some catch on, others don't. So it really wasn't a very good answer. (quoted in Laub, 1983:189)

For Cohen, then, existing theories in criminology did not explain much about delinquent behavior. No theory had seriously examined the values and beliefs of juvenile gang members and the nature and causes of their activities. Why do some juveniles, and not others, join delinquent gangs? Why do gangs do what they do? Why do gangs persist in urban neighborhoods?

Cohen's *Delinquent Boys* tried to answer such questions by beginning with the idea that the world of juvenile delinquents is enveloped in a subculture. Although the term *subculture* had been in use among anthropologists at least since the 1870s, it was Cohen who first applied it to the study of delinquency (Wolfgang and Ferracuti, 1967). *Culture*, for Cohen, refers to the knowledge, beliefs, values, codes, tastes, and prejudices that persist in the social relations people have regularly in their interactions with each other. A **subculture**, then, is a set of beliefs (and so forth) that differs in some way from those of the main or dominant culture. Taking part in delinquent acts is a major aspect of delinquent subcultures. As Cohen himself defined it, a delinquent subculture is "a way of life that has somehow become traditional among certain groups in American society. These groups are the boys' gangs that flourish most conspicuously in the 'delinquency neighborhoods' of our larger American cities" (1955:13).

---

**BOX 6.2** A. K. COHEN'S SUBCULTURE OF DELINQUENT BOYS

According to Cohen (1955), the subculture of delinquent boys has six major characteristics in the United States:

1. Its activities are *nonutilitarian, malicious,* and *negativistic*: Gang members are nonutilitarian because, for example, they sometimes steal simply for the hell of it; they are malicious because they take delight in others' discomfort, in terrorizing "good" children, and in flouting teachers and their rules (such as defecating on a teacher's desk); and they are negativistic because their delinquent conduct is right by the standards of the subculture precisely because it is wrong by conventional standards.
2. *Versatility*: Gang members rarely specialize in types of illegalities in the way that adult criminals and solitary delinquents do.

3. *Short-run hedonism*: Gang members have little interest in long-term goals, a fact that reflects their lower-class origins. Typically, they "hang around," "chew the fat," and "wait for something to turn up."
4. *Group autonomy*: Gang members are intensely loyal to their own gang, are very hostile to others, and resist even the efforts of their families to control them.
5. *Working-class membership*: Although cautious about relying on official crime statistics, Cohen nevertheless agrees that juvenile delinquents and juvenile subcultures are overwhelmingly concentrated in the working class.
6. *Male*: Although Cohen recognized the existence of female gangs and of solitary delinquency engaged in by females, he agreed with official statistics showing that delinquent subcultures are male-dominated.

---

Cohen reasoned that a good theory of delinquent subcultures must explain the existence of the six subcultural characteristics displayed in Box 6.2. But it must also explain why subcultures typically flourish where they do in the class structure. Cohen argued that subcultures exist because they provide a solution to certain problems of adjustment shared by a group of individuals. Why, then, is the delinquent subculture found mostly in working-class environments? In his explanation, Cohen began with the position of the family unit in the local community. He noted that, although the boundaries between working-class and middle-class families are sometimes indistinct, childrearing practices do vary between different classes. Crucially, children are not equally prepared to satisfy the standards by which U.S. society evaluates their passage to adulthood. Working-class parents, for example, place less emphasis than middle-class parents on development of analytical skills, education, self-denying discipline, and long-term planning for adult status and career; they place more emphasis on physical prowess in groups and learning through "having fun." However, because all children are evaluated by middle-class

standards, some children are doomed to be seen as failures in middle-class terms.

The prevailing middle-class standards (the **middle-class measuring rod**) by which all children are evaluated, especially in schools, include ambition; individual responsibility; outstanding achievement, especially academic or athletic; industry and thrift; foresight; manners, courtesy, and personality; control of physical aggression; constructive leisure; and respect for property. Because middle-class children tend to acquire these skills from their parents and peers far more than working-class children do, most adolescent failures are drawn from the working class. Above all, it is in the school—that supremely middle-class institution—that working-class boys fail. Failure in school often results in **status frustration**, which causes feelings of "guilt, self-recrimination, anxiety, and self-hatred" (A. Cohen, 1955:126). Because the working-class boy finds himself at the bottom of the status hierarchy, he is now in the market for a solution.

According to Cohen, it is within the working-class delinquent subculture that the otherwise-unadjusted working-class boy finds a solution to his lack of status in middle-class life. The delinquent subculture, therefore, operates as an "adjustment mechanism" for many working-class adolescents. Adjustment occurs through a process of **reaction formation**, in which the academic success typically denied working-class boys is contemptuously redefined as the "bookish knowledge" of "sissies," whereas "street knowledge," which is learned from friends in the delinquent gang, is regarded as superior to other forms of knowledge. In general, the virtues of the working-class gang include the practices regarded by the middle class as vices: nonutilitarian, malicious, and negativistic activities. The gang confers a much-needed high status on members who practice these activities; this status is typically denied working-class adolescents when they participate in an alien middle-class world.

Additionally, Cohen addressed two further problems about delinquency that were almost completely ignored in his era and are largely so in ours: female delinquency and middle-class delinquency.

Regarding female delinquency, Cohen suggested that because females are not socialized into being successful in the male-dominated realms of society, young females do not have the adjustment problems characteristic of male, working-class "failures." Although young females can eventually find additional satisfaction in a career, successful relationships with the opposite sex are the primary means by which they derive status. Their activities focus, therefore, on popularity with boys, dating, beautification, charm, clothes, and dancing. Although involvement in a delinquent subculture can increase the masculine status of a boy, it can only do harm to the feminine status of a girl. Cohen concluded that for a boy the delinquent response, " 'wrong' though it may be and 'disreputable,' is well within the range of responses that do not threaten his identification of himself as a male" (Cohen, 1955:140).

Regarding middle-class delinquency, Cohen rightly pointed out that its very existence must embarrass those who argue that a poor or working-class background is the chief cause of delinquency in general. He therefore speculated that this embarrassment may stem from inadequate concepts of social class (namely, because lower-class and middle-class families may in fact be culturally closer to each other than is usually admitted, boys from both groups might be responding to the same cultural tensions). Another possibility, according to Cohen—which ties in well with other aspects of his theory—is that middle-class delinquent subcultures respond to the same tensions of gender identification as their working-class counterparts. As Cohen (1955) argued in sociopsychological terms:

> Because of the structure of the modern family and the nature of our occupational system, children of both sexes tend to form early feminine identifications. The boy, however, unlike the girl, comes later under strong social pressure to establish his masculinity, his difference from female figures. Because his mother is the object of the feminine identification which he feels is the threat to his status as a male, he tends to react negativistically to those conduct norms which have been associated with mother and therefore have acquired feminine significance. Since mother has been the principal agent of indoctrination of "good," respectable behavior, "goodness" comes to symbolize femininity, and engaging in "bad" behavior acquires the function of denying his femininity and therefore asserting his masculinity. This is the motivation to juvenile delinquency. (p. 164)

Consequently, Cohen reasoned that males from middle-class homes may join delinquent gangs as well.

It is appropriate now to mention three problems in Cohen's analysis. First, much of the importance of Cohen's work lies in the original way in which it extended to delinquent boys an explanation of Merton's category of the rebellious deviant. At root, however, both Merton and Cohen shared the view that deviance (Merton) and delinquency (Cohen) arise as a reaction of the lower classes to their failure in middle-class terms. In this view, working-class activities, such as boys' delinquency, are wholly parasitic on middle-class practices. Indeed, what this view of delinquency ignored was precisely what the Chicago school of criminology had emphasized (at least in principle): the importance of granting authenticity to the values of the deviants themselves. In other words, at issue is whether working-class delinquents themselves regard their activities as a response to "failure".

Second, like nearly all his contemporaries, Cohen did not refer to the importance of race in his explanations of juvenile subcultures in the United States. As Colin Sumner (1994) has complained:

> No one seemed to notice the point that if the delinquent culture was so common in U.S. cities perhaps it was not so "sub," and few made anything of the fact that its occupants were mostly black. Their blackness, and the blackness of the so-called subculture, was completely glossed over in the theory....The subculture was truly an abstraction from reality....There was to be a stark awakening in the sixties, one which would render the abstraction of the subculture somewhat farcical. (p. 181)

Third, Cohen failed to provide empirical evidence that working-class delinquents accept middle-class success goals. In what sense, we are compelled to ask, does the subculture of working-class juvenile delinquency actually reject middle-class values? This question was soon addressed by other subcultural theorists, to whom we now turn.

## DELINQUENCY AND LOWER-CLASS CULTURE

Cohen's *Delinquent Boys* stimulated numerous responses from criminologists and inaugurated a wealth of new research into the diverse origins, functions, and forms of delinquent subcultures. We will outline the most influential arguments of this research.

The first major criticism of Cohen's findings was developed by Walter Miller in his article "Lower-Class Culture as a Generating Milieu of Gang Delinquency" (1958). The bulk of Miller's data came from reports of daily contact with ghetto youth in a large eastern city during a three-year project into the control of juvenile delinquency. The subjects of the study were both black and white, male and female, and in early, middle, and late adolescence.

Miller suggested that adolescent members of delinquent gangs, and of other forms of "street-corner society," are not psychopaths, nor are they physically or mentally defective. Far from it. Gang members are often drawn from the most "able" sections of the community. Why, then, do they commit crimes? Reasoned Miller: "The most general answer is that the commission of crimes...is motivated primarily by the attempt to achieve ends, states, or conditions which are valued, and to avoid those that are disvalued within their most meaningful cultural milieu" (Miller, 1958:346).

For achieving these ends, gang members tend to choose the most accessible means available. Miller argued that the lower-class way of life has a set of ends, or focal concerns, that include trouble, toughness, smartness, excitement, fate, and autonomy. These focal concerns differ greatly from those of the middle class. For example, whereas the middle class might value achievement in high school examinations, the lower class values the smartness embodied in the capacity to outfox, outwit, or con others. The distinctive focal concerns of the lower class derive from aspects of its structural position in U.S. society. According to Miller, 40–60 percent of the United States is influenced directly by lower-class culture, and of this, 15 percent composes the "hard-core lower-class group." Above all, this latter group is characterized by its distinctive family unit—the female-headed household (see Section 10.2). The female-headed household is one that "lacks" a permanent male parent or that has no male parent involved in child care and family support.

According to Miller, the major factor that pushes lower-class boys into joining delinquent gangs is the widespread presence of female-headed households in their cultural milieu. Why is this so? Miller depicted the lower-class boy as the victim of a female web of neglect. Because he is surrounded by females, the lower-class boy suffers from acute identity crises, especially those crises associated with problems of gender-role identification. Miller argued that the female-headed household does not provide "a range of essential functions—psychological, educational, and others"—for the lower-class boy (Miller, 1958:342). These functions, Miller concluded, are typically provided by the most accessible means available: the corner group and the gang. The focal concerns (such as smartness) of the gang parallel those of lower-class life in general. But the gang also embraces two further concerns that in combination explain their territoriality and their positive values: (1) belonging, or adherence to the rules of the gang, and (2) status (derived from smartness and related characteristics) as it is defined within the cultural framework of lower-class society.

Miller therefore reasoned that the delinquent gang functions to resolve crucial problems generated by the cultural, and especially the family, milieu of lower-class boys. But for Miller, unlike Cohen, the gang resolves these problems in its own cultural framework rather than in reaction to the cultural standards of the middle class. As an aside, we note that there is no evidence that boys in single-parent (female- or male-headed) households, for example, are more likely to be deprived emotionally or psychologically than boys in two-parent households (see Section 10.4).

Despite the antifeminist leanings of his argument, Miller casts serious doubt on the validity of Cohen's theory in one important respect. Recall that Cohen assumed that lower-class boys react to failure in middle-class worlds (such as school) and, as a result, seek status in the more familiar setting of the delinquent subculture. What Miller questions, quite correctly, is Cohen's assumption that the lower-class boy has no authentic values that identify gangs as good things to belong to simply because they are good things to belong to.

## DELINQUENCY AND OPPORTUNITY

Miller was part of a group of delinquency theorists (the Chicago school, Merton, and Cohen) who took the style and direction of delinquent subcultures, or gangs, very much for granted. However, this great simplification was uncovered by Richard Cloward and Lloyd Ohlin in their book *Delinquency and Opportunity* (1960). To explain why some juveniles violate conventional norms does not explain variations in the particular form of their deviant actions (such as theft, violence, drug use/abuse, and so forth). Why, for example, do some gangs allegedly focus on violence, some on theft, and still others on drug use/abuse? Following Merton's theory of anomie, Cloward and Ohlin asserted that delinquent subcultures arise because of a gap between the aspirations of lower-class youth and the possibility of their achieving those aspirations through legitimate means. However, the effects of the gap between aspirations and frustrated achievement vary from one individual to another. The direction of variation depends on two basic types of legitimate aspiration: aspirations for higher status (achieved by membership in the middle class) and for greater economic success. Table 6.1 outlines Cloward and Ohlin's four major categories of male lower-class youth.

According to Cloward and Ohlin, both Type I and Type II boys aspire to middle-class status.

**TABLE 6.1  CLOWARD AND OHLIN'S CLASSIFI-
CATION OF LOWER-CLASS YOUTH**

| Categories of Lower-Class Youth | Orientation of Lower-Class Youth | |
| --- | --- | --- |
| | Toward Membership in Middle Class | Toward Improvement in Economic Position |
| Type I | + | + |
| Type II | + | − |
| Type III | − | + |
| Type IV | − | − |

Source: Cloward and Ohlin (1960:95).

However, Type II boys regard a change in their reference groups as more important than greater economic success. Cloward and Ohlin agree with Cohen that when faced with frustrated opportunities for upward social mobility, boys of these two types are those most likely to react against middle-class values, because these boys are the ones who most want to be accepted by the middle class. Type III boys, who want more economic success (namely, money) but who are not interested in middle-class values or in becoming middle class, seek higher status in their own cultural milieu. They want " 'big cars,' 'flashy clothes,' and 'swell dames' " (1960:96). It is this group that composes the majority of delinquents. Type IV boys are street-corner boys who are not interested in social mobility in any sphere. These boys drop out, in other words, without dropping into anything else. Although they are sometimes criticized for lack of ambition, these boys rarely get into trouble with the law.

Cloward and Ohlin's astute analysis of delinquent subcultures clearly avoided an error made by Cohen. It did not assume, as Cohen had, that the cause of most juvenile delinquency is the failure of lower-class youth to succeed in middle-class institutions such as schools. Even though they may fail and even though they may be alienated from the school, lower-class delinquents do not become delinquent solely because of failure in school. The causative factors in delinquency are likely to be more complicated than the process suggested by Cohen. As Cloward and Ohlin (1960) indicated:

> Type III youth are alienated from the school because of a conflict regarding appropriate success-goals; this conflict simply reinforces their own definitions of criteria of success [i.e., making money versus making it into the middle class]. If these youngsters subsequently become delinquent, it is chiefly because they anticipate that legitimate channels to the goals they seek will be limited or closed. (p. 97)

Finally, Cloward and Ohlin argued that the illegitimate means of achieving success are not evenly distributed within working-class communities. They identify three sorts of delinquent subculture participated in by Type III boys:

1. *The criminal subculture.* The legitimate aspirations of delinquency-prone boys are satisfied illegitimately in neighborhoods where a criminal subculture already exists. A criminal subculture has its own success models, learning techniques, and gradations of status (mainly by age). Its leading members are also part of the conventional culture of the community, thus lending the subculture a measure of stability and legitimacy. Its focus is the rational, albeit illegal, provision of opportunities for income through activities such as theft. In areas where no established criminal subculture is available, the typical avenue for potential delinquents is membership in either a conflict subculture or a retreatist subculture.
2. *The conflict subculture.* The environs of the conflict subculture are typically poor, disorganized, transient, and unstable. The

activities of the conflict subculture make it extremely visible to the media and to the public. These activities focus on interpersonal violence, gang warfare, and the physical destruction of property.

3. *The retreatist subculture.* The retreatist subculture is the last avenue for boys who experience failure in both legitimate activities and in the illegalities of the criminal and conflict subcultures. The focus of the retreatist subculture is the retreat into persistent drug use/abuse. Of course, not all lower-class youth who experience status and economic deprivation engage in drug use/abuse. But those who choose to use and abuse drugs persistently are those who either (1) experience the double failure just described or (2) cannot revise their aspirations downward yet continue to experience the strain of frustrated opportunities.

The apparent implications of certain of the findings of Cloward and Ohlin's study were actively pursued as policy by the federal government. As Bernard, Snipes, and Gerould (2010) describe:

> After Robert Kennedy, who was then attorney general of the United States, read Cloward and Ohlin's book, he asked Lloyd Ohlin to help develop a new federal policy on juvenile delinquency. The result was the passage of the Juvenile Delinquency Prevention and Control Act of 1961, which was based on a comprehensive action program developed by Cloward and Ohlin in connection with their book. The program included improving education; creating work opportunities; organizing lower-class communities; and providing services to individuals, gangs, and families. The program was later expanded to include all lower-class people and became the basis of Lyndon Johnson's War on Poverty. (p. 162)

Billions of dollars were spent on the War on Poverty and other social welfare programs, but the war was eventually abandoned by President Nixon on the grounds that it showed no clear results. In fact, the reasons the program was abandoned are many and complex, including conservative objections that government should not be in the business of eliminating social inequalities. It must be considered seriously whether the subcultural theorists, because they had failed to identify the causes of juvenile delinquency, misunderstood the set of policies that should be implemented to contain it.

## EVALUATION OF SUBCULTURAL THEORY

As noted, theories of delinquent subcultures arose in the 1950s largely as an attempt to answer various questions ignored by the Chicago school. Yet, like their predecessors in the Chicago school, the subcultural theorists continued either to ignore the delinquency of young females or typically to view it in masculine terms. Additionally, they ignored the delinquency of middle-class youth.

How much of an advance was the new subcultural criminology of the 1950s over the Chicago school? As David Matza (1964) reported, the sociologists of delinquent subcultures provided two basic insights about delinquency. First, they showed that it typically is not a solitary enterprise but a group activity. Second, they showed that delinquent activities, rather than being engaged in by biologically or psychologically deformed individuals, typically develop in the sociological context of particular territorial locales. Often they develop in neighborhoods with cultural traditions associated with established gangs.

The criminology of the subcultural theorists was a real advance over earlier work in at least two respects. First, the subcultural theorists explicitly raised what the Chicago school left dormant: the relation between lower-class opportunities and the social and economic inequality of the U.S. class structure. Moreover, the subcultural theorists implicitly condemned the economic inequalities, the blocked opportunities, and the strains that result from class structure. The problem remains, however, as to whether they were correct in concluding that benevolent social programs could contain the juvenile delinquency that resulted from these economic conditions. Second, in some cases subcultural theory displayed considerable sensitivity to issues not previously raised. It recognized, for example, that juvenile delinquency took a number of forms and was engaged in for a variety of reasons.

In assessing the merits of subcultural theory, we also note that its findings provoked widespread criticism. Certain early critics, in particular Kitsuse and Dietrick (1959), argued that Cohen, for example, overemphasized the extent to which the delinquency of lower-class boys is a reaction to failing in middle-class terms. Perhaps most working-class boys simply do not care about middle-class values. Do working-class boys have no authentic cultural traditions of their own? Other critics objected that the activities of delinquent gangs are utilitarian rather than nonutilitarian and are far more diverse than the subcultural theorists allowed. Still other critics objected that not enough emphasis had been placed on the deviant psychological characteristics of juvenile gang leaders. For example, Lewis Yablonsky (1962) charged (without evidence) that gang leaders are typically sociopaths.

Clarence Schrag (1962) argued that the theory of differential opportunity is too general in the face of real-world complexities. Schrag objected that Cloward and Ohlin's theory fails to explain why, even in Type II and Type III communities, a substantial number of working-class boys do not join delinquent gangs. Why do some working-class boys but not others join gangs? Schrag also pointed out that, especially in neighborhoods with high delinquency rates, delinquent gangs are far more diverse, more fluid, and less organized than Cloward and Ohlin maintain.

Moreover, David Matza and Gresham Sykes (1961) disagreed with the subcultural theorists' portrayal of middle-class values as being centered on the Protestant ethic of hard work and abstemiousness. There are, they argued, numerous respectable subterranean values that both the middle class and the working class have in common, including the search for kicks and the identification of masculinity with toughness. In other words, Matza and Sykes questioned whether the activities of delinquent gangs really are deviant if those same activities find cultural support within the middle class.

## 6.3 MATZA'S DELINQUENCY AND DRIFT (1964)

In what at the time seemed like a complete annihilation of subcultural explanations of delinquency, David Matza eloquently complained that subcultural theory failed altogether to understand the causes of juvenile delinquency. In his book *Delinquency and Drift* (1964), Matza forcefully attacked the core assumptions of the lengthy positivist tradition that stretched from Quetelet's social mechanics (see Section 4.2) to the ideas of the subcultural theorists. At the same time, in this book, as well as in his *Becoming Deviant* (1969) and in his writings with Gresham Sykes (Sykes and Matza, 1957; Matza and Sykes, 1961), Matza offered an alternative theory of delinquency.

The key concepts in Matza's theory of delinquency are (1) the "positive delinquent"; (2) the "subculture of delinquency"; and (3) "delinquency and drift" (neutralization, will, and preparation and desperation). To these we now turn.

### THE POSITIVE DELINQUENT

According to Matza, positivist criminology made three explicit assumptions about crime and criminality. Each assumption, he argued, was wrong. Matza pointed out that positivist criminology assumed that the proper focus of criminological study should be the criminal rather than the criminal law. This assumption had led to a search for all sorts of motivational and socioeconomic causes of crime. However, the assumption ignored that crime is, above all, not only an action but also an infraction (namely, law breaking). In neglecting to study the legal and other institutions that define certain actions as infractions (in essence, crime and deviance), positivist criminology had "for close to a century display[ed] little concern for the essence of crime-infraction" (1964:5).

Moreover, positivist criminology had been unduly preoccupied with copying the methods of the natural sciences. Rejecting the free-will philosophies of classical criminology (see Section 4.1), the positivists had assumed, as a matter of faith, that all human action is determined by scientific law and that, therefore, humans are largely incapable of choosing between different paths of action. "The positive delinquent does not exercise choice," Matza (1964) wrote. "His action is constrained [and he] must behave in a delinquent manner because of the determinants that have shaped him" (p. 11). Matza admitted that this approach of hard determinism, found especially in biological theories of crime, had given way in recent times to soft determinism. This modified analysis of delinquent subcultures endowed individuals with the capacity to exercise choice, but, Matza continued, advocates of soft determinism still basically believed that criminality is caused. This more subtle form of determinism is at the heart of linking crime with poverty, differential association, and the values of delinquent subcultures.

Further, argued Matza (1964), positivist criminology assumed that criminals are fundamentally different from the law-abiding citizenry. With the exception of eighteenth-century classical criminology, this assumption had been a central feature of all previous criminology. From this assumption it follows that criminals are thus constrained by a set of circumstances that simply do not apply to the law abiding. However, Matza objected: "A reliance on differentiation, whether constitutional, personal, or sociocultural, as the key explanation of delinquency has pushed the standard-bearers of diverse theories to posit what have almost always turned out to be empirically undemonstrable differences" (p. 12).

Matza concluded that this doomed attempt to distinguish between the criminal and the law-abiding had resulted in, or perhaps paralleled, several other errors by the positivists. Because subcultural theorists had assumed that the values of delinquents differ from those of nondelinquents, for example, insufficient attention had been paid either to the values of society at large or to smaller units within it, such as the family. To study crime, Matza (1964) implied, we must look far beyond the immediate social environment where infraction is detected. Moreover, positivist criminology accounted for too much delinquency. It had been an "embarrassment of riches" that predicted far more delinquency than actually occurs. If delinquents really were as different from the law-abiding and as committed to the values of their subculture as the positivists had assumed, then

> involvement in delinquency would be more permanent and less transient, more pervasive and less intermittent than is apparently the case. Theories of delinquency yield an embarrassment of riches which seemingly go unmatched in the real world. This accounting for too much delinquency may be taken as an observable consequence of the distorted picture of the delinquent that has developed within positive criminology. (p. 22)

Matza's criticisms of the positivists' skeletal assumptions are most revealing. *Delinquency and Drift*, however, did much more than simply criticize the explanations of subcultural theorists; as with several other texts in the emerging societal reaction and labeling perspectives, it also put forward an alternative image of delinquency.

## THE SUBCULTURE OF DELINQUENCY

The basis of Matza's alternative theory of delinquency is that there is a subculture of delinquency but that it is not a delinquent subculture. Matza began by saying that subcultural theorists were wrong to see the relationship between the values of a subculture of delinquency and the values of mainstream culture as one of opposition. Things are not so neat and tidy. By and large, the vast majority of delinquents are children; it would therefore be surprising indeed if the subculture of delinquency were made up of children opposed strongly to the values of conventional mainstream culture. Matza believed, in other words, that juvenile delinquents are typically not very different from other juveniles and that their values are likely to be quite similar to those of nondelinquent youths.

These similarities between the conventional culture and the subculture of delinquency Matza termed *subterranean convergence*. In many of their basic ideas the subculture of delinquency and the conventional culture converge: in cowboy masculinity, in the search for kicks and excitement, in the Bohemian celebration of the primitive, and in the persistence of territorial sentiments in certain localities of large cities.

Matza suggested that the subculture of delinquency is of two minds regarding delinquency: One frame of mind allows and encourages its members to behave illegally and to gain prestige from doing so; the other reveals that the subculture remains basically committed to the important values of conventional culture. Both frames of mind must be examined if the subculture of delinquency is to be understood accurately. Moreover, Matza continued, conventional culture is often not quite as conventional as it is made out to be. Conventional culture is complex and many-sided. Its features

consist not only of ascetic Puritanism, middle-class morality, the Boy Scout oath, and the like, but also of hedonism, frivolity, and excitement.

Matza suggested that the way to understand the two-mindedness of the subculture of delinquency is to assess the posture of delinquents in a variety of circumstances, especially in what he terms *the situation of apprehension* and *the situation of company*. By the *situation of apprehension* Matza referred to the problem created if the subculture of delinquency and the conventional culture hold oppositional values: Delinquents will offer radical defenses of their activities when they are arrested by the police or when they are brought before a juvenile court. If the members of a subculture of delinquency are committed to their delinquent activities and values, they will feel almost no shame or guilt on detection by authority. Yet juveniles commonly express feelings of genuine contrition on apprehension. Such feelings cannot simply be dismissed as a manipulative tactic designed to appease authority. The contrition of juveniles, Matza (1964) concluded, "cannot be ignored if we are to avoid the gross stereotype of the delinquent as a hardened gangster in miniature" (p. 41). With the exception of a few bizarre oddities—regarded by ordinary delinquents as crazy—delinquents rarely desire either to attack the values of conventional culture or to defend those of the subculture of delinquency. Moreover, if delinquents are so different from nondelinquents, why do the vast majority of them desist from delinquency at the end of their adolescence?

By *the situation of company* Matza referred to the understanding of delinquents when in the company of their peers. Matza suggested that the values of the subculture of delinquency are far more fluid and less clear than usually thought. He argued that these values are not, as such, learned formally by novice delinquents, because there is no written or formal code of delinquent values to be learned. Actually, many things are not discussed openly and must be inferred (often wrongly!) by novices from the hints and cues of their friends. During entry into the subculture of delinquency, boys—there are very few females in Matza's *Delinquency and Drift*—suffer status anxiety about their masculinity. How can they learn the values of the subculture of delinquency without revealing that they are not yet the fully committed delinquents they believe all the other boys to be? Matza suggested that they do so by cautiously sounding out other boys about masculinity and appropriate delinquent acts. Thus: "Do I really like you? Yeah, come here and such and I'll show you how much I like you." Or: "Do I think that stealing a car is a good thing? Man, you a fag or something? Ain't you one of the boys?" Serious discussion of delinquency is almost always impossible for delinquents because of the anxiety it would produce about their own masculinity. Whatever the motive, Matza (1964) concluded, "The function of such remarks is to mislead the delinquent into believing that his subculture is committed to delinquency" (p. 54).

However, Matza was keenly aware that this comedy of errors cannot continue indefinitely. Most boys discover eventually, often from one close friend in whose company their anxieties can be relaxed, that almost no one is actually committed to the subculture of delinquency. They discover, in other words, that all along they were wrong to believe that delinquents are committed to their misdeeds. The importance of this eye-opening information is reinforced as juveniles become adults (as boys become "real men"). The achievement of real masculinity is marked by such new signs of status as jobs, wives, children, and mortgages. The acquisition of these "obvious" signs of masculinity allows the ex-delinquent to reject the values and activities of the subculture as "kids' stuff." Dwindling remnants of the old gang mix with the company of younger cohorts. But

the great majority of members of the subculture of delinquency do not become adult criminals.

## DELINQUENCY AND DRIFT

Recall that, against the determinism of the positivist tradition, Matza was eager to assert the presence of a certain degree of choice and free will in human action. This assertion is found in his concept of **drift**. Matza suggested that the delinquent is committed neither to the subculture of delinquency nor to the conventional culture. Instead, the delinquent chooses, more or less consciously, to drift between the one and the other, often many times in the course of a single day:

> Drift stands midway between freedom and control. Its basis is an area of the social structure in which control has been loosened [and where it is] coupled with the abortiveness of adolescent endeavor to organize an autonomous subculture....The delinquent transiently exists in a limbo between convention and crime, responding in turn to the demands of each, flirting now with one, now with the other, but postponing commitment, evading decision. Thus, he drifts between criminal and conventional action. (Matza, 1964:28)

Matza's theory of delinquency and drift has three components: neutralization, will, and preparation and desperation. *Neutralization* is the process by which potential delinquents are freed from conventional social and moral controls, and because of which they are then able to engage in delinquency (Sykes and Matza, 1957). With Gresham Sykes, Matza argued that most juvenile delinquents are not nearly as committed to delinquent values and activities as subcultural theorists have supposed. Indeed, precisely because they are not really opposed to mainstream values, juveniles often display feelings of shame and guilt when their delinquency is detected and exposed. To shield novice delinquents from such feelings, experienced delinquents teach them a variety of techniques to rationalize and justify their behavior. For example, they teach them to say such things as "I didn't mean it"; "I didn't really hurt anybody"; "They had it coming to them"; "Everybody's picking on me"; "I didn't do it for myself." These techniques operate to deflect or to neutralize the disapproval of such authority figures as judges, juvenile police officers, and probation workers.

**Techniques of neutralization**, then, generally reduce the effectiveness of social and moral controls (see Box 6.3). They allow juveniles to engage in delinquency despite the disapproval of authority figures or of their conforming peers. At the same time, Sykes and Matza were careful to note that such techniques are not powerful enough to shield all delinquents from feelings of shame and guilt. Moreover, some delinquents are so isolated from the conforming world of the dominant culture that neutralization techniques are not even useful.

Matza (1964) argued that the neutralization of the values of conventional culture is insufficient to ensure that a juvenile will actually drift into delinquency. For a delinquent act to occur, the juvenile must *will* it. Two factors that activate the will are preparation and desperation. Preparation provides the will to repeat old infractions of law; desperation provides the will to commit new ones.

By *preparation* Matza meant the skills a juvenile must have before committing a crime. To commit a robbery successfully, for example, a youth must have a certain rudimentary level of strength, dexterity, speed, agility, and cunning. Also, a youth must not be apprehensive or "chicken" when about to violate the law; or, in the language of classical criminology, he must not be deterred by the threat of the imposition of law. Youths must believe that

---

**BOX 6.3** TECHNIQUES OF NEUTRALIZATION

According to Sykes and Matza (1957:664–669), there are five basic techniques of neutralization:

1. **Denial of responsibility.** Insofar as the delinquent can define himself as lacking responsibility for his deviant actions, the disapproval of self or others is sharply reduced in effectiveness as a restraining influence. It may also be asserted that delinquent acts are due to forces outside of the individual and beyond his control, such as unloving parents, bad companions, or a slum neighborhood.

2. **Denial of injury.** The delinquent frequently, and in a hazy fashion, feels that his behavior does not really cause any great harm, despite the fact that it runs counter to the law.

3. **Denial of victim.** Even if the delinquent accepts the responsibility for his deviant actions and is willing to admit that his deviant actions involve an injury or hurt, the moral indignation of self and others may be neutralized by an insistence that the injury is not wrong in light of the circumstances. The injury, it may be claimed, is not really an injury; rather, it is a form of rightful retaliation or punishment.

4. **Condemnation of condemners.** The delinquent shifts the focus of attention from his own deviant acts to the motives and behavior of those who disapprove of his violations. By attacking others, he feels the wrongfulness of his own behavior is more easily repressed or lost to view.

5. **Appeal to higher loyalties.** Internal and external social controls may be neutralized by sacrificing the demands of the larger society for the demands of the small social groups to which the delinquent belongs, such as the sibling pair, the gang, or the friendship clique. The conflict between the claims of friendship and the claims of law, or a similar dilemma, has of course long been recognized. If the juvenile delinquent frequently resolves his dilemma by insisting that he must "always help a buddy" or "never squeal on a friend," even when it throws him into serious difficulties with the dominant social order, his choice remains familiar to the supposedly law-abiding public.

the police are relatively incompetent and that they are only relatively potent. In their preparation for delinquency, youths also learn that, even if their delinquency is detected, incarceration is unlikely.

By *desperation* Matza referred to what he suspected to be the primary motive in the will to delinquency: that youngsters feel they have no control over their lives. For youngsters with anxieties about their masculinity and about membership in their peer group, a mood of fatalism and desperation is the natural consequence of experiencing a lack of control. To assert control, a boy cannot just do anything ("Shit, man, anybody can do that"). He must master his fate. He must make something happen. Often the subculture of delinquency stresses the importance of delinquency as a means of making things happen; sometimes it stresses the time-honored method of exploiting and conquering females. However, Matza (1964) concluded, the will to crime may be "discouraged, deterred, or diverted by countless contingencies" (p. 191).

## EVALUATION OF *DELINQUENCY AND DRIFT*

One way of evaluating *Delinquency and Drift* is to see it as an attempt to restore to juveniles a degree of free will denied them by the determinism of the positivist tradition.

In criticizing the unwarranted determinism of positivist criminology, Matza tried to force us, instead, to appreciate the way in which deviants themselves view their activities. If certain youths consciously choose to drift between convention and delinquency, then clearly their accounts of why they drift become an essential part of explaining their actions. Deviants have voices that should be heard!

Although Matza's work has inspired few full-length studies, a notable exception is Jack Katz's phenomenological *The Seductions of Crime* (1988). Katz believes that positivist explanations that focus on "background" correlations—like socioeconomic factors or whether criminals were dropped on their heads when they were babies—do little to help us understand what motivates criminals to commit crime. As Katz wrote:

> The statistical and correlational findings of positivist criminology provide the following irritations to inquiry: (1) whatever the validity of the hereditary, psychological, and social-ecological conditions of crime, many of those in the supposedly causal categories do not commit the crime at issue, (2) many who do commit the crime do not fit the causal categories, and (3) what is most provocative, many who do fit the background categories and later commit the predicted crime go for long stretches without committing the crimes to which theory directs them. (pp. 3–4)

Expanding on the work of Matza, Katz argued that we need to understand the "foreground" of experience, the thrill, the magic, and the emotions that "seduce" persons to commit crime. Katz extended his ethnographic method to such crimes as murder, robbery, and shoplifting.

Although Katz has managed to develop Matza's insights in important ways, the question remains: Is Matza's reformulation successful, or does his reformulation merely shift the causes of delinquency from one positivist area to another—from status frustration to masculine anxiety, for example? This is a difficult question. Although Matza's basic thesis that delinquents drift between conventional and delinquent activities has been tested extensively, generally these tests have focused on the importance that Matza has attributed to techniques of neutralization.

Using data on cannabis users from the European School Survey on Alcohol and Other Drugs, one study (Pereetti-Watel, 2003) of young French cannabis users has found that, in addition to Matza's techniques of neutralization, deviants may use three other techniques to deny that their behavior entails much risk. In particular, suggests Pereetti-Watel, cannabis users may scapegoat others, such as users of hard drugs such as heroin, cocaine, and crack cocaine; they may display self-confidence, particularly in their ability to control their own drug consumption; and they may offer comparisons between the low risks of cannabis use and the higher risks of alcohol and other drugs.

But most tests of neutralization theory have explored two main questions: Do techniques of neutralization come before delinquent acts? Where do delinquents stand relative to delinquent and conventional values? It is fair to conclude that some delinquents use techniques of neutralization before and others after their behavior has been detected and defined as deviant. For example, many people who cheat on their income tax returns rationalize their behavior beforehand by claiming, "Everyone else is cheating the IRS, and I'm stupid if I don't do it."

Carl Klockars (1974) and Darrell Steffensmeier (1986) have shown, in their biographical studies of professional fences, that certain thieves can neutralize their past and their future illegalities—if they are involved in a continuing criminal career—by reasoning, "I'm not hurting anyone when I steal, because insurance will always pay the loss" Listen to Sam, Steffensmeier's fence:

> I don't feel I hurt any little people 'cause most of the stuff did come out of business places and big places, which were insurance write-offs and which they will many times mark it double what it was. In a roundabout way, yes, the individual is going to pay for it, like with the higher transport and that. I would not feel bad about this. It's the same as, say, chiseling on income tax. You cheat Uncle Sam, but that's not the same as cheating this here person. (1986:241)

However, such partial confirmations of Matza's thesis on the use of neutralization techniques have been challenged by Michael Hindelang

(1970, 1974). In his earlier study, Hindelang (1970) obtained the confidential information of 346 boys from a middle-class area of Oakland, California. In this study Hindelang asked his subjects to record the number of times they had committed any of twenty-six offenses (including theft, drug use/abuse, fighting, sexual deviance, and truancy) in the previous year. In addition, the youngsters were asked whether they strongly disapproved, disapproved, were indifferent to, approved, or strongly approved the act. If Matza was correct and delinquents are not committed to their misdeeds, then delinquent approval of an act should be similar to approval expressed by nondelinquents. Hindelang found that thirteen of fifteen activities he examined showed a significant association between delinquent involvement and the approval of delinquent acts. These findings clearly contradict Matza's thesis that delinquents do not differ substantively from nondelinquents in their commitment to conventional culture.

Recall Matza's point that if delinquents really were so influenced by their subculture, it would be extremely difficult to explain the fact that most members of the subculture eventually abandon their delinquency. In other words, how can we account for the maturational reform of juvenile delinquents? Why do most juvenile delinquents become conformist adults? A possible explanation of maturation is in fact precisely the one suggested by Matza himself: Most delinquents are never seriously committed to their delinquency in the first place. But as David Greenberg (1993) has argued, it is in fact unclear why most subculture carriers abandon activities so highly prized within the subculture. Why do gang members eventually desist from delinquent activities? Greenberg is quick to point out that, as valuable as Matza's insight is, it opens up other nagging questions:

> Why does desistance from violen[t] offenses occur later and more slowly than [from] theft offenses?

Why are some juveniles so much more extensively involved in delinquency than others? Matza's remarkable presentation of the subjective elements in delinquency must be supplemented by an analysis of the objective, structural elements in causation, if such questions are to be answered (p. 120; also see.

According to Greenberg, then, Matza did not adequately consider the relation between social class and socioeconomic status on the one hand and the distribution of values on the other. Are working-class youths, for example, more likely to engage in neutralization techniques than youths from other sections of society? If so, why? Indeed, why do some youths not commit delinquent acts? Or, to ask the same question differently, why do some youths conform to positive culture whereas others do not? This question has been explored within the context of control theory, to which we now turn.

## 6.4 THE LABELING PERSPECTIVE

During the 1960s, the legitimacy of political authority was challenged by many college students, liberal intellectuals, women's movements, and members of minority racial groups. Questions about U.S. foreign policy in Vietnam and elsewhere, about domestic civil rights, and about the stark social, economic, racial, and gender inequalities in the world's richest society quickly filtered through to sociological perspectives on crime and criminal justice. Certain radical intellectuals (such as Marcuse, 1964) argued that social inequality and injustice in the United States could be removed only by the powerless, deviant, outcast, criminal populations typically studied by criminologists. These populations, it was thought, had nothing to lose and everything to gain from a revolutionary overthrow of the existing social order. Reflecting this turbulent political climate, sociologists and criminologists opened a Pandora's box, using a key provided by Robert S. Lynd's (1939) famous question: "Knowledge for what?" In such an inegalitarian society as the United States, why is criminology typically concerned with crimes of the powerless rather than with crimes committed by the government, white-collar executives, and corporations? Who defines certain behavior as criminal? Whose side are we on (the "we" who study crime with detached objectivity)?

The criminologists who first examined such politicized questions were mainly younger scholars attached to the labeling perspective and conflict theory. As the labeling perspective developed, its neutral posture toward deviants became a celebration of deviant activity as evidence of the virtue of social diversity. Many deviant activities began to be seen in a different and more interesting light. The "opening up" and "demystifying" implied by the concept of **deviance** involves a very different relationship between the deviant and the student of deviance. In coming out of their criminological closets, labeling theorists tended to see in alcoholism, criminality, and mental illness, for example, individuals who are victimized by society and who are potential rebels against its values.

It is not easy to pin down the key concepts of the **labeling perspective**. There is even disagreement about the term itself. The labeling perspective has also been described as societal reaction, "sociology of deviance," "social interactionism," "the neo-Chicago school," and "the new deviancy theory." For convenience, we use *the labeling perspective* for all these terms.

Three key concepts are held by a majority of those using this perspective: (1) the social meaning of deviance, (2) societal reaction, and (3) stigma.

### THE SOCIAL MEANING OF DEVIANCE

Following in the footsteps of the Chicago school of the 1920s and 1930s—and drawing on the social psychology (phenomenology and symbolic interactionism) of George Herbert Mead, his student Herbert Blumer, and others—those researching deviance from the labeling perspective agree on the central importance of meanings in everyday life. Social reality itself is seen as an ongoing, fluid process that is constructed according to the outcome of the meanings that we attach to our interaction with others, on the one hand, and the meanings that they, on the other, attribute to us. Crime and deviance, then, are not pregiven, objective categories but negotiable statuses. Thus, in interactionist or participant observation studies, the researcher participates in the social interaction of drug users, alcoholics, mental patients, and others in order to "appreciate" the meanings that those people defined as deviant attribute to their own activities. As we saw in Section 6.3, this was partly the view of deviance advocated by David Matza.

The emphasis on meanings takes a number of twists and turns in the labeling perspective. At one level, the labeling perspective is skeptical that our knowledge can ever be objective and value-free. Because social behavior means different things to different people, one cannot have the sort of complete knowledge about social interaction that, for example, a natural scientist may have about the movement of inanimate objects such as billiard balls. Many of the studies in the labeling tradition have thus rejected the use of the scientific method. At another level, because they do not exist in a social vacuum, the meanings, perceptions, and opinions of certain individuals or groups are taken more seriously than those of others. Therefore, although reality is socially constructed, not all members of society have an equal voice in deciding precisely how it is constructed. Taking a sympathetic cue from the way in which society devalues deviants and outsiders, the labeling perspective typically sides with the underdog and the outcast.

A well-known example of the centrality of meaning in the labeling perspective is provided by Howard Becker's book *Outsiders* (1963). Becker argued (relying somewhat on learning theory) that marijuana users must learn to experience the meanings and effects of using marijuana if they are to get high "properly." He emphasized that social reality is constructed by the meanings embedded in everyday life. Indeed, Becker even claimed that the subjective experience of drugs is structured much more by social meanings and perceptions than by biological and pharmacological factors! If a situation is perceived and defined as real, then it is real in its consequences.

Moreover, as human and social beings, each of us differs in the meaning we attach to our own behavior and to that of others. At different times, and to different people, our behavior (such as having a tattoo) may be perceived as interesting or exotic or daring. The very same behavior may also be seen as dangerous, abnormal, sick, delinquent, or criminal. The labeling perspective insists that such perceptions are the only real difference between normal and deviant behavior.

Becker argued that it is a mistake to see deviance simply as the breaking of some agreed-on rule. To look at deviance in this way is to ignore the fact that what counts as deviance is largely a function of the ability of groups with political power to impose their concept of right and wrong on the behavior of other groups. Because great diversity exists in the values of groups with political power, great cross-cultural and cross-temporal variety exists in what officially (let alone unofficially) counts as deviance.

Homosexuality, for example, is perceived as morally deviant in some cultures but is tolerated in others; in still others, such as classical Greece and Rome, its practice was regarded as a positive virtue. In other words, suggested Becker, to understand deviance one must recognize that typically a given form of deviance is only statistically abnormal. As Becker (1963) argued:

> Social groups create deviance by making the rules whose infraction constitutes deviance, and by applying those rules to particular people and labeling them as outsiders. From this point of view, deviance is not a quality of the act the person commits, but rather a consequence of the application by others of rules and sanctions to an "offender." The deviant is one to whom that label has successfully been applied; deviant behavior is behavior that people so label. (p. 9, emphasis in original)

### SOCIETAL REACTION

In arguing that "deviant behavior is behavior that people so label," Becker does not claim that such acts as homicide would not exist without the label that is often attached to them. Rather, he points to the important role of **societal reaction** in the designation of certain acts as deviant or criminal. For example, although the act of killing another human being can occur without societal reaction to it, whether a given killing is labeled as murder, manslaughter, accidental death, or justifiable homicide depends crucially on the meaning attributed to it by a social audience. From Becker's perspective, it follows that society itself "creates" deviance because society defines it as such.

Half a century ago, Frank Tannenbaum (1938) pointed out that there is often a shift in society's reaction to delinquency and to delinquents, a process he described as the "dramatization of evil." Tannenbaum argued that the community's condemnation of delinquent behavior changes into a view of the offender as a delinquent person. Boys who vandalize schools are seen as "bad boys." In attempting to understand the mechanisms of this transformation, Edwin Lemert distinguished between primary and secondary deviance.

### PRIMARY AND SECONDARY DEVIANCE

In his books *Social Pathology* (1951) and *Human Deviance, Social Problems, and Social Control* (1967), Lemert used the sociopsychological concepts of primary and secondary deviation to understand the process of deviance. Lemert proposed this distinction in order to draw attention to the difference between the "original" and the "effective" causes of the deviant attributes and actions "associated with physical defects and incapacity, crime, prostitution, alcoholism, drug addiction, and mental disorders" (1967:40).

According to Lemert, **primary deviance** can be caused by a host of social, cultural, and psychological events. Primary deviants undergo no change in their psychological makeup or in the way they act as members of society. **Secondary deviance** is caused by the way in which society reacts to some of the people who engage in primary deviance. After they are apprehended, primary deviants suffer a variety of consequences, many of which focus on the application to them of such deviant labels as "sick," "cripple," "criminal," "insane," and so on. Such labels can have important consequences—for friendship, for job opportunities, and for self-image. Sometimes the effect of deviant labels is so powerful—either through a self-fulfilling prophecy or through the negative consequences of stigmatization—that labeled individuals are forced to reorient their lives around the label. Secondary deviants accept their new identity as a "deviant" and act in accordance with the societal reaction to their primary deviance. Secondary deviance is thus a powerful tool for explaining recidivism.

Labeling theorists do not study the causes of crime in the same way that most theories we have examined thus far do. Indeed, labeling theorists tend to evade altogether questions of individual causation. It is clear that labeling theorists are concerned chiefly with the way society itself causes deviance. They are interested in how and why society labels certain behaviors deviant. Lemert, for example, argued that, whereas previous studies of deviance tended to rest heavily on the idea that deviance leads to social control, "I have come to believe that the reverse idea, i.e., social control leads to deviance, is equally tenable and the potentially richer premise for studying deviance in modern society" (1967:v).

According to the labeling perspective, the response to certain behavior, rather than the behavior itself, is the crucial element in the designation of behavior as deviant. The diverse ways in which society reacts to and actually creates deviance have been examined in many studies. For example, Stanley Cohen's (1972) book *Folk Devils and Moral Panics* examines how the media, the police, and various moral entrepreneurs conspired to create a panic over the activities of two youth gangs (the Mods and the Rockers) in southern England in the mid-1960s. In this case the media and agencies of social control knowingly or otherwise created more deviance where none might have existed at all. This process has been termed *deviance amplification.*

## DEVIANCE AMPLIFICATION

One well-known study illustrates the major features of the process of **deviance amplification** (Young, 1971). The subjects of Young's participant observation study were marijuana users in west London in the late 1960s. Young showed how the socially harmless activity of marijuana use was transformed into a social problem through the complicated web of interaction among the mass media, the public, the police, and the users themselves (see Figure 6.2).

Young described how the mass media made marijuana use a social problem through sensationalistic and lurid accounts of the lives of marijuana users. The media's portrayal of marijuana users as sick, unwashed, promiscuous weirdos completely committed to drug use was a stereotype that inflamed popular indignation during 1967. Young showed how this media pressure led police to amplify the very problem they vigilantly sought to curb. Intensive police action led to an organized defensive posture in the drug-using community. Drug users united around a shared sense of injustice concerning harsh sentences and mass media stereotypes. Drug use became a symbol of defiance against an unjust and intolerant society.

The media used the rising number of drug convictions to fan public indignation about marijuana use even further. Increased pressure was then put on the police to stamp out this new evil. Expanded police drug units ensured greater

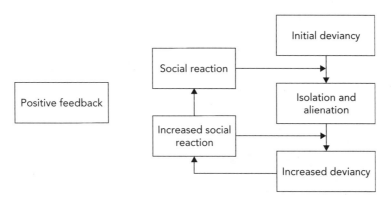

**FIGURE 6.2** The Amplification of Deviance
*Source*: Young (1971:34).

detection of marijuana users. Once again the number of drug convictions soared. The vicious cycle was firmly established. Young's research demonstrated, then, that the police actually amplify the deviant activities they mean to control. Moreover, Gary Marx (1981) has shown that there are three types of interdependence between rule enforcers (such as police, prosecutors, and judges) and deviants that involve the possibility of deviance amplification: (1) escalation, (2) nonenforcement, and (3) covert facilitation.

First, the situation of *escalation* can arise from initial attempts at social control. Marx pointed out, for example, that "police involvement in family conflict, crowd, and automobile chase situations can contribute to violations where none was imminent, or it can increase the seriousness of these situations" (Marx, 1981:223). The mere presence of police officers at the scene of a domestic disturbance, for instance, can easily escalate a potentially dangerous situation into an overtly violent one. High-speed police vehicle chases, which sometimes result in injuries or death, can lead to manslaughter charges where none would otherwise have existed.

Second, there is the situation of *nonenforcement*, which is less direct than escalation. According to Marx, the nonenforcement of rules is difficult to identify because it is often hidden and illegal. Marx documented that police may adopt a policy of nonenforcement with respect to informants, for example, who provide information about the law breaking of others or help facilitate a controlled commission of a crime or with respect to vice entrepreneurs who agree to keep their own illegal behavior within agreed-on limits.

Third, in a situation of *covert facilitation*, rule enforcers take an active role in encouraging others to break rules. The police go undercover to buy or sell illegal goods and services, for example, or the police may pose as johns in order to arrest prostitutes or try to buy drugs in order to

arrest drug dealers. Or the police may use a decoy, such as a female police officer in civilian clothes, to create a robbery or assault, or they may pose as the representatives of a foreign country in order to trap unwitting members of Congress into taking a bribe to secure political influence in Washington.

## STIGMATIZATION

As noted, whether or not individuals are regarded as deviant depends on societal reaction to their behavior. Moreover, partly because of this reaction to their behavior (primary deviance), some deviants are pushed into further (or secondary) deviance. This redirection of behavior occurs in a variety of ways. We now consider why societal reaction to deviance often results in, and can actually stem from, the fact that those who deviate from the norm tend to be stigmatized. Goffman (1963) related that, for the ancient Greeks, *stigma* referred to

> bodily signs designed to expose something unusual and bad about the moral status of the signifier. The signs were cut or burnt into the body and advertised that the bearer was a slave, a criminal, or a traitor—a blemished person, ritually polluted, to be avoided, especially in public places. Later, in Christian times, two layers of metaphor were added to the term: the first referred to bodily signs of holy grace that took the form of eruptive blossoms on the skin; the second, a medical allusion to this religious allusion, referred to bodily signs of physical disorder. (p. 1)

A **stigma** is therefore a sign of disgrace imposed on an individual. It is a way of spoiling a person's real identity, marking him or her as someone to be avoided. The stigmatizing process operates in numerous settings, and a stigma can be applied as a label to numerous persons: in medicine, to those with physical deformities (cripples, gimps, dwarfs, giants) or mental deviancy (weirdos, lunatics, crazies); in education, to those who achieve low grades in school (retards, dumbos, failures) or, sometimes, to those who achieve high grades (egg-heads, nerds, brains); in religion, to those who do not believe in the "one and true" God (witches, heretics, pagans); and in the criminal justice system, to those convicted of crimes (ex-cons, recidivists, career criminals). In these examples a stigma is a sign denoting someone who is disqualified, by varying degrees, from full social acceptance. It can affect self-esteem, self-concept, and future behavior. Returning to the central importance of meaning, we emphasize that a stigma can vary in the meaning that it has both to the person stigmatized and to the social audience.

What are the effects of the stigmatizing process? According to one study (R. Schwartz and Skolnick, 1964), the effectiveness of legal sanctions against stigmatized individuals often varies with the social position of the defendant penalized. This study showed that unskilled workers suffer much more from the stigma that goes with accusations of assault than do doctors from the effects of accusations of medical malpractice. This finding is supported by a similar study in Holland (Buikhuisen and Dijksterhuis, 1971). This study found that two groups of convicts—one convicted once for theft, the other for drunken driving—received significantly less positive responses than nonconvicts in their job applications to seventy-five large companies.

However, another study, with a somewhat different focus, found that the effects of a stigma are not quite so straightforward. In this study Terance Miethe and Richard McCorkle (1997) set out to test whether prosecutors and judges are biased in their perceptions of gang members. If the "master status" of gang members includes their stereotypical designation as "vile, dangerous, detached, and unpredictable youths" (p. 411), as it did in this study of 168 gang and 202 nongang felony cases in Las Vegas in 1993, we would expect the criminal justice system to deal relatively harshly with gang members. The study found that the master status was at work, in that sentencing decisions for gang members were far less likely to be affected by other offender and offense characteristics than for nongang members. But the study also found that charges against the sentencing of gang members were more lenient than in nongang cases! This is so, the authors speculated, because of additional images that are attached to the master status of gang membership. For example, prosecutors may be so keen to secure convictions of gang members that they "give up more" to do so, perhaps by plea bargaining or by being more likely to dismiss cases with unreliable witnesses.

What are the ways in which people respond to being stigmatized? How do stigmatized individuals—to pose Goffman's (1963) graphic question—"negotiate" their "spoiled identities" (p. 9)? Research addressing these two questions is inconclusive. The response to stigmatization clearly varies. Sometimes it is relatively easy for stigmatized individuals to hide or to "correct" their stigma. For example, persons with certain forms of deviant attributes, such as physical deformities or illiteracy, can seek surgical or educational remedies to reform or hide their apparent defects. However, as Goffman suggested, these strategies are not always completely successful: "Where such repair is possible, what often results is not the acquisition of fully normal status, but a transformation of self from someone with a particular blemish into someone with a record of having corrected a particular blemish" (1963:9).

The effects of a stigma also depend partly on the institutional context in which it is conferred. In his book *Asylums*, for example, Goffman (1961a) reports that in "total institutions"—such as mental hospitals, where "a large number of like-situated individuals, cut off from the wider society for an appreciable period of time, together lead an enclosed, formally administered round of life" (p. xiii)—it is difficult to shrug off the effects of a stigma. Goffman reported that in the mental institution he studied for three years (St. Elizabeth's Hospital in Washington, D.C.), whenever patients exhibited "normal" behavior, the staff often interpreted that very normalcy as a sign that they were "abnormal"! According to some research (for example, Link, Cullen, Frank, and Wozniak, 1987), former mental patients often encounter public preconceptions that they are dangerous—not on the basis of their behavior but because of the label attached to them.

It is reasonable to conclude that responses to stigmatization are associated strongly with social class and relative powerlessness. The exact nature of this association, however, is unclear. Allen Liska (1981), for example, noted:

> Since blacks occupy a negative social status and are not well integrated into society, they are not very sensitive to official reactions of society. Labeling may have its maximum effect on people well integrated into society; hence, the effects of labeling should be maximal for first offenders, the middle class, and whites and minimal for prior offenders, the lower class, and blacks. (pp. 132–133)

Although negative labeling arguably can be seen as affecting those with higher social status more than those with lower social status (for example, African Americans), it is also true that the former have greater resources for counteracting stigmatization. The question of whether certain social groups are better equipped to counteract the effects of labeling returns us to another question raised by Lemert's distinction between primary and secondary deviance: Is the person on whom the label "criminal" is conferred likely to be propelled into more crime or deterred from future criminal behavior?

Hirschfield (2008) has looked at the effects of arrest on a group of African-American and Latino inner-city, disadvantaged youth in Chicago. Hirschfield found through in-depth personal interviews that, according to their own

perceptions, these juvenile arrestees had suffered no obvious negative effects from their contact with the justice system—either in their own self-image or in how they were perceived by family and peers. This was so because arrest was such a frequent phenomenon in their impoverished neighborhoods that the label "juvenile arrestee" appeared as a normal, almost unremarkable if unwarranted part of their social lives. Indeed, the arrestees' families and friends remained vital sources of support after arrest.

However, a quite different result has been found in a longitudinal study of 870 public school students in Rochester, New York, aged 13.5–15 years (Bernburg, Krohn, and Rivera, 2006). The study found, based on arrest data, that juvenile justice intervention significantly increased the odds of (1) subsequent gang membership compared with those youth who had experienced no such intervention and (2) subsequent involvement in serious delinquency. This study is a good example of a relatively new direction in labeling theory, namely, that the effects of labeling are not direct but mediated through the triggering of other processes—for example, through labeling's effect on increased membership in delinquent gangs and in other deviant networks. Bernburg et al. (p. 82) point out, too, that labeling theory probably complements other theories of crime, such as differential association and learning theory, which stress that delinquency is partly a product of associating with delinquent peers and learning delinquency from them. At the same time, the authors argue,

> Labeling theory broadens the viewpoint of this [other] research, pointing out that deviant groups provide social shelter from stigma as well as providing collective rationalizations, definitions, peer pressure, and opportunities that encourage and facilitate deviant behavior....The exclusionary processes triggered by deviant labeling may...explain the individual's movement into a deviant group,

as well as the isolation of deviant groups from mainstream social life. (p. 82)

One of the great unsolved puzzles is whether recidivism is due to some propensity to crime attributable to such sociological factors as class, gender, race, and age or to the effects of labeling (in most U.S. jurisdictions the many negative consequences that are imposed on convicted felons include loss of voting privileges, holding public office, loss of the privilege to own a gun, and difficulties with employment, income, and housing). One answer to this puzzle has been provided by the Florida-based research of Chiricos, Barrick, Bales, and Bontrager (2007; and see Kubrin and Stewart, 2006). Chiricos and colleagues' study looked at reconviction data of 95,919 men and women convicted of a felony in Florida courts and who were facing a period of probation. In respect of these particular convicted defendants, Florida law allows judges the option of withholding formal adjudication of guilt, thus allowing them truthfully to state that they had not been convicted of a felony. It was found that the effect of a criminal label (a judge's formal adjudication of guilt) is (1) significantly higher on recidivism than for those who have had that adjudication withheld and (2) stronger for whites than for blacks or Hispanics, for females than for males, and for those aged 30 or more who have no prior convictions. These somewhat surprising findings can perhaps be explained, Chiricos et al. (p. 571) suggest, in one of two ways. Either recidivists are typically less disadvantaged by a formal label, or the more socially advantaged have more to lose from a criminal stigma. We await the next round in this debate.

## EVALUATION OF LABELING THEORY

The labeling perspective remains quite influential in criminology today. Its influence continues largely because it reminds us that labels such as "crime" and "deviance" are applied selectively to social phenomena. Moreover, the labeling perspective has uncovered the ironic ways in which the process of societal reaction sometimes amplifies the very problems it seeks to eliminate through the stimulation of moral panics and the effects of stigmatization.

It must be said, too, that the adherents of the labeling perspective have never fully pursued its own ambitious agenda. If terms such as "crime" and "deviance" are applied selectively to social behavior, it is crucial to explore the criteria of selection. Such an examination would involve thoroughgoing questions about the interests served by criminal law. In his book *Controlology*, Jason Ditton (1979) therefore complains:

The total rejection of positivism by followers of the labeling perspective either had no effect at all on the institutionalized study of crime or, at best, the massive theoretical critique was distilled into an additional factor ("the reaction") to be henceforth coopted in the unchanged rhetoric of mathematical calculation. It has always been content instead to snipe at convention from the theoretical sidelines—happy to stand on the lunatic fringe and lob distracting stories of strippers, nudists, gays, teddy boys, nutters, dwarfs, and druggies at the central juggernaut of state-sponsored criminology. (p. 5)

In this assessment Ditton bemoans the fact that the labeling perspective never became labeling theory. If criminal behavior really is what agents of social control define it as, then, concludes Ditton, the term *controlology*, rather than *criminology*, better reflects what we should be studying!

Although the labeling perspective has failed to travel as far as its logical conclusion—what Ditton refers to as *controlology*—nevertheless, its great insights continue to contribute to the development of criminology in at least two respects. First, because its emphasis on the harmful effects of labels has been widely recognized as correct, it has led, with mixed results, to certain changes in criminal justice policy. These changes embrace decriminalization, diversion, decarceration, and restitution. They also include the New Zealand–Australian-based movement toward "reintegrative shaming" and "restorative justice" (e.g., Braithwaite, 2002; Daly and Stubbs, 2006; and see Einstadter and Henry (2006).

Second, because of its inclination to demystify powerful label-conferring institutions in areas such as criminal justice, mental health, and medicine, the labeling perspective nourishes a climate for the growth of *social constructionism* in criminology. **Social constructionism** encourages a healthy sociological disrespect for how knowledge of social problems such as crime is phrased, manipulated, defined, and disseminated in the mass media and in other public forums (see Section 1.2). In criminology its influence can be found in numerous studies of how moral entrepreneurs, social movements, and the mass media mold—or ignore—the public perception of the causes, prevalence, and seriousness of crimes such as serial murder, child abuse, drug use, prostitution, drinking and driving, pedophilia, and terrorism (e.g., Jenkins, 2003; Best, 2004, 2007). Like that of the labeling perspective, the motto of social constructionism might be "Question authority!"

## REVIEW

This chapter outlined subcultural perspectives on delinquency. First, we looked at the key themes emerging in the sociology of delinquent subcultures during the 1950s; this sociology was influenced strongly by earlier traditions of anomie and differential association. Second, we summarized David Matza's criticism of the positivist approach to juvenile delinquency. In his alternative formulation, Matza emphasized that juveniles consciously drift between the conventional culture and the subculture of delinquency. Third, we examined various theories that focus on the causal importance of the notion of control.

### THE CHICAGO SCHOOL OF CRIMINOLOGY, DISORGANIZATION, AND DELINQUENCY

1. Initially, sociological criminology in the United States was almost exclusively identified with the perspective of social ecology developed by the Chicago school from 1920 onward. Chicago was an important site of the progressive movement, and the city naturally lent itself to the study of social problems, including crime.

2. The Chicago school adopted and spread several innovative research techniques, including both quantitative and qualitative methods. The latter involved life-history documents, case studies, investigative journalism, media materials, in-depth interviews, and participant observation. These methods, it was believed, would produce objective, value-free knowledge.

3. Shaw and McKay's *Juvenile Delinquency and Urban Areas* (1942) concluded that many social problems, including juvenile delinquency, were concentrated in zones of transition populated by white, lower-class immigrants and by blacks. This concentration was correlated with such factors as rates of adult crime, school truancy, disease, and mental disorders, and it remained highly stable despite resident turnover in the zones of transition. Certain of these problems, it was felt, could be alleviated by a change in the local community's values.

4. The Chicago school has been extremely influential in the development of socio-logical criminology. Nevertheless, it has been criticized for its factual errors and its empiricist theory.

## DELINQUENT SUBCULTURES

1. Albert Cohen's *Delinquent Boys* (1955) suggested that delinquent boys inhabit a sub-culture whose activities are nonutilitarian, malicious, and negativistic. Lower-class boys (rather than middle-class boys, or girls in general) are doomed to fail in terms of middle-class standards, especially in school, and they react by participating in the creation of a delinquent subculture or by joining a bearer group of such a subcul-ture. This reaction provides the status that the middle-class world denies them.

2. Cohen's findings were criticized by numerous scholars, including Miller (1958) and Cloward and Ohlin (1960). Miller suggested that Cohen had overemphasized the extent to which lower-class youth internalized middle-class values. Lower-class delinquent subcultures should therefore be understood in terms of the focal con-cerns of lower-class life, especially the female-headed household.

3. In *Delinquency and Opportunity* (1960), Cloward and Ohlin responded that earlier theorists had simplified both the reasons that lower-class youth join delinquent subcultures and the variety of such subcultures. Delinquents tend to be boys who desire greater economic success but who, uninterested in becoming middle class, seek higher status in lower-class terms. Boys generally join a criminal subculture, if available; if not, they join a conflict subculture. Boys who fail in these subcultures or for whom they are unavailable tend to join the retreatist subculture.

## MATZA'S DELINQUENCY AND DRIFT (1964)

1. *Delinquency and Drift* offered powerful criticisms of the lengthy positivist tradi-tion stretching from Quetelet's social mechanics of crime to the subcultural the-ories of delinquency discussed in this chapter. Matza argued that this tradition wrongly argues that all activities of juveniles are determined by social and environ-mental forces over which they have absolutely no control. Matza claimed, rather, that juveniles exercise rational choice over their activities, whether delinquent or conformist.

2. Matza stressed the existence of a subculture of delinquency but that is not a delin-quent subculture. Because most delinquents are children, it is not surprising that the values of the subculture of delinquency are not opposed to those of the con-ventional culture. For this reason, most delinquents mature into conformist adults rather than adult criminals.

3. Delinquents drift in and out of delinquency and conventional behavior. They rationalize their delinquent activity by means of five main techniques of neutrali-zation: denial of responsibility, denial of injury, denial of victim, condemnation of condemners, and appeal to higher loyalties. These techniques are supplemented by situations of preparation and desperation.

4. Matza identified serious problems in the positivist tradition. However, there is little conclusive evidence that his image of a less constrained deviant is actually closer to social reality. Some critics have suggested that Matza paid insufficient attention to constraints of social class and racial inequality.

### THE LABELING PERSPECTIVE

1. The labeling perspective claims that deviance and crime are in the eye of the beholder. It is not the quality of an act that makes it deviant or criminal but the perception of it as such by a social audience. The labeling perspective emerged very much as a creature of the social and political unrest of the 1960s.
2. Its underlying themes are a romantic attachment to the underdog, a reflexive concern with the role of the criminologist in an inegalitarian society, an opposition to scientism, and an emphasis on the importance of meanings in social interaction.
3. The distinction between primary and secondary deviance highlights how the societal reaction to deviance creates and amplifies the very behavior it seeks to control.
4. Deviance amplification also occurs through stigmatization. The stigmatizing effect of the label attached to primary deviation is one of the most important factors in secondary deviation. The handling of stigmatization requires skill and power that many individuals do not possess.
5. The labeling perspective has never been carried through to its logical conclusion. If crime and deviance are only categories conferred on behavior by agents of social control, then criminology should be reoriented and renamed *controlology*.

### QUESTIONS FOR CLASS DISCUSSION

1. To what extent does Albert Cohen's *Delinquent Boys* (1955) represent a rejection of the findings of Clifford Shaw and Henry McKay's *Juvenile Delinquency and Urban Areas* (1942)?
2. How do the respective explanations of the causes of juvenile delinquency advanced by Walter Miller (1958) and Richard Cloward and Lloyd Ohlin (1960) represent an advance over Cohen's *Delinquent Boys*?
3. Do delinquents drift?
4. Does David Matza's *Delinquency and Drift* mark a return to assumptions of classical criminology described in Chapter 4?
5. In his book *Outsiders*, Howard Becker wrote that "deviance is not a quality of the act the person commits, but rather a consequence of the application by others of rules and sanctions to an 'offender'" (1963:9). Do you agree with Becker's view? Why or why not?

### FOR FURTHER STUDY

#### READINGS

Bernard, Thomas J., Jeffrey B. Snipes, and Alexander L. Gerould. 2010. *Vold's Theoretical Criminology.* New York: Oxford University Press.

Matza, David. 1964. *Delinquency and Drift*. New York: John Wiley.

Special Issue: The Jack-Roller at 100. 2007. *Theoretical Criminology* 11: 4. Essays by Marunna and Matravers; Gadd and Jefferson; Bereswill and Browne; and Koesling and Neuber.

## WEBSITES

1. <http://www.sonoma.edu/cja/info/Edintro.html>: This site is constructed in memory of Edwin Lemert and features a professional and personal biography of this influential criminologist.

2. <http://www.sad.ch/index.php/en/Youth-and-Anomie/Fields-of-Activity/Jugend-und-Anomieforschung.html>: This webpage, hosted by the Swiss Academy of Development (SAD), summarizes current research on youth and anomie as well as its relevance. It claims that findings from SAD's research projects lay the foundation for the creation of national youth policies.

3. <http://socialecology.uci.edu/about>: This is an overview of the study of social ecology provided by the School of Social Ecology at the University of California at Irvine. Click on the "In the news" link to find a list of recent news articles relevant to social ecology.

4. <http://www.law.ed.ac.uk/cls/esytc/>: This is the home page for the Edinburgh Study of Youth Transitions in Crime (ESYTC), which investigates youth offending and antisocial behavior. The longitudinal study follows over 4,000 youth who started secondary school in Edinburgh in the autumn of 1998. The website is updated regularly with the most recent findings from the study.

5. <http://www.mysiconsulting.org/index.php>: This is the home page for the Missouri Youth Services Institute (MYSI), a nonprofit organization committed to reforming juvenile justice systems. It has received recognition for being the "model" state juvenile justice system.

6. <http://www.hirenetwork.org/>: This is the website for the National H.I.R.E network, which aims to increase employment opportunities for people facing the stigma of a criminal record by changing public policies, employment practices, and public opinion. The site offers related publications, state resources for ex-offenders, and a statement of the organization's policy initiatives.

# SOCIAL LEARNING THEORY AND SOCIAL CONTROL THEORY

**PREVIEW**

Chapter 7 introduces:
- The theories of differential association and differential social organization.
- Social learning theory.
- Two general theories of crime and deviance: the theory of self-control and the theory of control balance.

**KEY TERMS**

control balance
control deficit
control surplus
differential association
differential social organization
general theory

integrated theory
reinforcement
self-control
social control
social disorganization

## 7.1 DIFFERENTIAL ASSOCIATION

No introduction to modern criminology would be complete without a recognition of the enduring theoretical contributions made by Edwin Sutherland (1883–1950), a sociologist who also coined the term *white-collar crime*. By his own account, Sutherland began an academic career with primary training in political economy and political science and a major interest in the study of labor problems (1956). In 1921 he began serious work in criminology by drafting an overview of the field. This project led, in 1924, to the first reasonably systematic textbook in U.S. criminology, Sutherland's cautious yet progressive *Criminology*. In it, Sutherland claimed that the criminologist should not assume the correctness of such popular and legal categories as "crime," "criminality," and "crime rates." Instead, he argued, sociology should provide the primary perspective of criminology, the focus of which should be both law and crime.

In the early editions of *Criminology*, Sutherland stressed that the causes of crime are, in principle, infinite. However, his belief in multicausality weakened as further study convinced him to integrate existing findings about the causes of crime into a general theory of crime. What Sutherland termed the theory (or "principle") of **differential association** resulted from this ambitious agenda.

Sutherland's theory of differential association was influenced by a number of preceding theories, including the Chicago school's concept of social disorganization and George Herbert Mead and W. I. Thomas' socio-psychological emphasis on the importance of meanings in social interaction. Although we do not address social psychology as such, it is worth quoting Bernard, Snipes, and Gerould's (2010) summary of the elements in Mead's theory that influenced Sutherland's theory of differential association:

> In Mead's theory a cognitive factor—"meanings"—determines behavior. Mead then argued that people construct relatively permanent "definitions" of their situation out of the meanings they derive from particular experiences. That is, they generalize the meanings they have derived from particular situations and form a relatively set way of looking at things. It is because of these different "definitions" that different people in similar situations may act in different ways. To cite an old example, two brothers may grow up in identical terrible situations, but one becomes a criminal while the other becomes a priest. (p. 181)

Sutherland meant for the theory of differential association to explain both the process by which a given person learns to engage in crime and the content of what is learned.

The theory of differential association can be summarized as follows (Sutherland, 1947):

1. Criminal behavior is learned, like all other behavior, within intimate personal groups in an interactive process of communication. This means that criminality is not inherited biologically.
2. The learning of criminal behavior includes instruction in the techniques of crime and in the motivational values favorable to committing it. These values are learned from definitions that state whether legal codes are favorable or unfavorable. The principle of differential association asserts that a person becomes criminal when definitions favorable to the violation of law exceed the definitions unfavorable to violation and when contacts with criminal patterns outweigh contacts with anticriminal patterns. Exposure to such definitions and contacts varies in frequency, duration, priority, and intensity.
3. Although criminal behavior is an expression of general needs and values, it is not explained by those general needs and values, since noncriminal behavior is an

expression of the same needs and values. As Sutherland (1947) wrote:

> Thieves generally steal in order to secure money, but likewise honest laborers work in order to secure money. The attempts by many scholars to explain criminal behavior by general drives and values, such as the happiness principle, striving for social status, the money motive, or frustration, have been and must continue to be futile since they explain lawful behavior as completely as they explain criminal behavior. (p. 8)

Although Sutherland's theory of differential association was crafted to apply to the criminal behavior of individuals, he was also concerned with the question of why crime tended to be concentrated in certain groups in society. In his recollection of the development of the theory of differential association, Sutherland (1956) referred to the importance of three questions:

> One of these questions was, Negroes [sic], young-adult males, and city dwellers all have relatively high crime rates: What do these three groups have in common that places them in this position? Another question was, Even if feebleminded persons have a high crime rate, why do they commit crimes? It is not feeblemindedness as such, for some feebleminded persons do not commit crimes. Later I raised another question, which became even more important in my search for generalizations. Crime rates have a high correlation with poverty if considered by areas of a city but a low correlation if considered chronologically in relation to the business cycle; this obviously means that poverty as such is not an important cause of crime. How are the varying associations between crime and poverty explained? (p. 15)

Sutherland ([1924] 1947) began to examine these sociological questions, albeit tentatively, in the context of his last version of differential association. Although almost wholly unintegrated,

Sutherland's argument was that social organization in the United States had moved from a simple to a more complex and differentiated type as a result of the industrial revolution. At the same time, there had been a relaxation in the uniformity of **social control**. Traditional social controls, such as those exercised uniformly within the family and local community and by religion, were increasingly challenged by the rise of economic and political individualism, increased social mobility, and material acquisitiveness. In the United States this process of **social disorganization** or, more accurately, reorganization, had been exacerbated by successive waves of immigration and had resulted in culture conflict between different communities. Crime was one expression of this conflict. Crime rates would be higher in communities that lacked traditional social controls and that contained some social groups organized for criminal behavior. Crime was also, therefore, an expression of such **differential social organization**.

Through these remarks, Sutherland was trying to convey the idea that differential social organization explains the origin of crime and that differential association explains its transmission from one person to another. A final twist appeared in Sutherland's last major book, *White Collar Crime* (1949), in which he attempted, briefly and tantalizingly, to integrate his incoherent combination of differential association and differential social (dis)organization with Merton's concept of anomie:

> Differential association is a hypothetical explanation of crime from the point of view of the process by which a person is initiated into crime. Social disorganization is a hypothetical explanation of crime from the point of view of the society. These two hypotheses are consistent with each other and one is the counterpart of the other. Both apply to ordinary crime as well as to white-collar crime.

Social disorganization may be either of two types: anomie, or the lack of standards which direct the behavior of members of a society in general or in specific areas of behavior; or the organization within a society of groups which are in conflict with reference to specified practices. Briefly stated, social disorganization may appear in the form of lack of standards or conflict of standards. (1983:255)

## EVALUATION OF DIFFERENTIAL ASSOCIATION

Sutherland's theory of differential association has enjoyed great popularity among criminologists because its basic argument seems to offer a precise sociological explanation of why some people engage in crime and others do not. Persons commit crime because they have associated, socially and culturally, more (in frequency, duration, priority, and intensity) with procriminal patterns than with anticriminal patterns. Crime is learned by normal persons who have been influenced by a specific cultural process. In support of differential association theory, one recent study (Church, Wharton, and Taylor, 2009), for example, has found that association with delinquent peers is the strongest predictor of future delinquency.

The theory of differential association has also generated substantial controversy (see, for example, Costello, 1997; Matsueda, 1997). We can summarize the major criticisms of the theory in three ways:

1. The terms of the theory are so deliberately abstract that testing them has proven extremely difficult. How, for example, can we actually measure an "excess" of definitions favorable to violation of law over definitions unfavorable to violation of law? What, precisely, are "associations" with "criminal patterns"? Should such associations include the influence of deep-rooted, socially harmful tenden-

cies such as racism and sexism—some of which have even been expressed in law and espoused by government officials and law enforcement officers? Questions such as these reveal clearly that the terms of Sutherland's theory are insufficiently precise.

2. The actual causal chain in Sutherland's theory arguably rests on a tautology. Logically, if we assume that human beings are not automata, to say that crime is engaged in by persons who are motivated to engage in it or who learn to engage in it is not to say very much at all.

3. The premises of Sutherland's theory are highly controversial. The image of the social actor postulated by Sutherland is that of an empty vessel with no history, no beliefs, no preferences, and no capacity for choice. Into this vessel Sutherland sought to pour "pro-" and "anti-" criminal tendencies. If (for some unstated reason) there is an excess of procriminal tendencies poured into this human vessel, then, the theory of differential association suggests, the vessel engages in crime. Because of this rigid determinism, the theory cannot explain why certain persons associate more with procriminal patterns than with anticriminal patterns. Yet this must certainly be incorporated into any theory that seeks to generalize about the causes of crime.

## 7.2 SOCIAL LEARNING THEORY

Sutherland's focus on the origins and the transmission of delinquent values stimulated new lines of inquiry, one of which is social learning theory. With Sutherland's original insight in mind, subsequent empirical studies indeed seem to have confirmed that the more serious a juvenile's delinquent involvement, the more likely he or she will be to have friends who are also delinquent. This finding, however, does not explain how or why associational patterns influence involvement in delinquency.

In arguing that Sutherland's theory of differential association and differential social organization cannot account for the process leading to individual criminality, Robert Burgess and Ronald Akers (1966:130) urged that criminologists try to use the genetic explanations of social behavior found in behavioral psychology. When these explanations are combined with structural explanations, such as subcultural and anomie theories, criminologists have termed them *social learning theory*.

The basic premise of **social learning theory** is that social behavior is determined neither by inner personality drives nor by outer sociological and environmental factors. Rather, it is a cognitive process in which personality and environment engage in a continuous process of reciprocal interaction. Modern learning theory, especially the operant conditioning theory of such behavioral scientists as B. F. Skinner (1953), was pioneered in laboratory settings. Operant (or active) conditioning theory begins with the empirical fact that animal behavior is affected by its consequences, both negative and positive. Animals are easily trained to perform certain actions if they are rewarded for doing so. For example, dogs usually learn to sit following the command "Sit!" if, after every time they sit, they receive positive **reinforcement** in the form of a treat or a friendly pat from their trainer. Desired behavior, in other words, is reinforced through a process of conditioned learning that emphasizes rewards or (for dogs that do not sit on command) punishments.

However, Bandura (1973) has shown that the process of social learning would be extremely tiring and hazardous if it depended solely on rewards and punishments. Although some behavior patterns are acquired through the process of rewarding and punishing direct experience, other behavior patterns are acquired by observing the behavior of significant others (family and peer group).

## DIFFERENTIAL REINFORCEMENT

Several criminologists have indicated the importance of learning theory as an explanatory tool for understanding crime. For example, in a direct application of Skinnerian theory, Clarence Ray Jeffery (1965) claimed that, in any given social situation, whether someone commits a crime depends largely on his or her past conditioning history—namely, whether the individual has been *reinforced* (or rewarded) for crime. Jeffery's theory of *differential reinforcement* states: "A criminal act occurs in an environment in which in the past the actor has been reinforced for behaving in this manner, and the aversive consequences attached to the behavior have been of such a nature that they do not control or prevent the response" (p. 295).

Crime is therefore a response to reinforcing stimuli. For example, the crime of robbery may produce either money or imprisonment (and often both). If only money is produced, the behavior is likely to continue; if only imprisonment is produced, the aversive consequence is likely to deter the act. Thus, according to this explanation, crime depends chiefly on the process of differential reinforcement.

For Burgess and Akers (1966), social behavior (including criminal behavior) responds chiefly to a complicated network of rewards and punishments. Any given behavior is likely to continue or to increase if it is followed more by rewards than by punishments; the same behavior is likely to decrease or to end if it is followed more by punishments than by rewards. Paraphrasing Burgess and Akers, criminal behavior is actually learned in seven stages (see also Akers, 1973; and

Akers, Krohn, Lanza-Kaduce, and Radosevich, 1979):

1. Criminal behavior is learned through direct conditioning or through imitation.
2. Criminal behavior is learned both in non-social reinforcing situations (for example, the physical effects of drug use) or nonsocial discriminative situations and through social interaction in which the behavior of others is either for or against criminal behavior.
3. The principal component of learning criminal behavior occurs in groups that compose the individual's major source of reinforcements: peer friendship groups, the family, schools, and churches.
4. Learning criminal behavior—including specific techniques, attitudes, and avoidance procedures—depends on effective and available reinforcers and the existing reinforcement contingencies.
5. The specific type and the frequency of learned behavior depend on the reinforcers that are effective and available and on the norms by which these reinforcers are applied.
6. Criminal behavior is a function of norms that are discriminative for criminal behavior, the learning of which occurs when such behavior is more highly reinforced than noncriminal behavior.
7. The strength of criminal behavior is a direct function of the amount, frequency, and probability of its reinforcement.

For Akers, all seven stages in this process must be examined. However, the central part of his theory lies in two factors that concern the learning of acts and definitions: (1) differential reinforcement and (2) positive and negative definitions (Akers, 1973, 1997). All social behavior is either strengthened by reward (positive reinforcement)

and avoidance of punishment (negative reinforcement) or weakened by aversive stimuli (punishment) and lack of reward (negative punishment). Whether a deviant act or a conforming act occurs depends on differential reinforcement (essentially, the cumulative effect of past and present rewards or punishments both for the act and for alternative acts). However, besides learning an act, a person learns whether the act is defined as good or bad. The more a person defines an act as good or as justifiable, the more likely he or she is to engage in it and the less likely he or she is to engage in alternatives. As Akers summarized: "A person participates in deviant activity, then, to the extent that it has been differentially reinforced over conforming behavior or defined as more desirable than conforming alternatives, or at least justified" (1973:287–288).

As with Sutherland's theory of differential association, Akers' social learning theory is intended as a general theory of crime. The broad scope of this theory is best seen in Akers' book *Deviant Behavior: A Social Learning Approach* (1973). Here Akers tries to apply social learning theory to all deviant behavior—"the principal forms of which...[include] drug use and addiction; homosexuality; prostitution; white-collar, professional, organized, and violent crimes; suicide; and mental illness" (p. vii). In this book Akers applies the general principles of social learning theory to each aspect of deviance: (1) how a person first engages in the deviant act, (2) how that person progresses to more frequent engagement, (3) the substantive events that reinforce the act, and (4) the content of the definitions favorable to the act.

Consider two examples of Akers' use of learning theory: suicide and drug use. Suicide presents an interesting test case for a learning theory of deviance that relies on reinforcement as the major motivating element because, without exception, the act of taking one's own life cannot be reinforced for one's future behavior (one has none!). Moreover, on the whole, U.S. culture condemns suicide, which means that there are very few definitions favorable to it. But Akers is confident that the act of suicide is based on social learning, and he offers a four-stage model as evidence (1973):

1. People learn that suicide appears to be a solution to personal problems. Everyone knows, or learns, that some people eliminate their problems successfully by hanging themselves, jumping off bridges, or overdosing on drugs. A terminal illness, the loss of a loved one, financial ruin, and existential angst are all situations in which suicide can be rationalized, justified, excused, or forgiven. These rationalizations are not defined as definitions favorable to the act of suicide, but they often operate to neutralize unfavorable definitions.

2. People learn about specific techniques of suicide. We learn that a drug overdose (which sometimes can be interrupted after the drug is taken) is less likely to be successful than suicide by shooting. We also learn, according to Akers, that certain techniques are considered more appropriate for one sex than another: the violence of shooting, for example, is a "masculine" technique, whereas a drug overdose is more "feminine."

3. People learn that the act of suicide receives considerable attention. Thus, some proportion of suicidal behavior is actually intended to result not in death but in gaining attention from loved ones. Suicide resulting from previously learned nonfatal suicidal behavior is common. In some cases of suicide without prior attempts, the act of suicide derives from imitation—psychiatrists, therefore, have

high rates of suicide compared with most other occupations.

4. Whether a person tries to commit suicide again depends in part on the reaction of others. "They may increase their attention to him without necessarily solving the crises and thus reinforce further attempts, or they may reinforce his belief that there is no hope. In either case he is likely to attempt again, and one of these attempts may be fatal" (p. 251).

A study of drug (marijuana) and alcohol use among teenagers was conducted by Akers et al. (1979) to test social learning theory. This study was based on a self-report questionnaire administered to 3,065 male and female teenagers attending grades 7 through 12 in seven communities in three midwestern states. It strongly confirmed social learning theory: The probability of abstinence from drug and alcohol use decreased and the frequency of use increased when individual teenagers (1) associated more with using rather than abstaining peers and adults, (2) were more rewarded than punished for use, and (3) were exposed more to favorable than to unfavorable definitions of use. Akers and his colleagues concluded that these three factors explained 55 percent of the differences between users of and abstainers from alcohol, and 68 percent of the differences between users of and abstainers from marijuana.

In a his book *Social Learning and Social Structure: A General Theory of Crime and Deviance*, Akers (1998; and see Akers and Jensen, 2007) offered a useful personal history of the development of his theory and presents a slightly revised version of it. Here, Akers proposes a "social learning and social structure" (SSSL) model of crime. Figure 7.1 shows that social learning mediates the relationship between social structure (the independent variable) and criminal behavior and crime rates (the dependent variable).

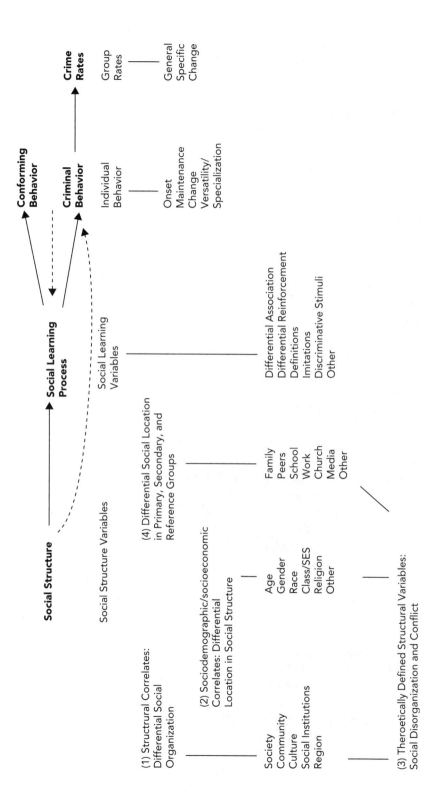

**FIGURE 7.1** The SSSL Model: Social Structure and Social Learning in Crime
*Source:* Akers (1998:331).

Although Akers acknowledges here that many of the variables in this model have been tested extensively, he bemoans the fact that there has been little research on the relationship between social learning and social structure. He suggests, for example, that imitation will likely turn out to be a key factor in the learning of criminal behavior. Moreover, he points to the need for more research on social learning and serious crime, such as white-collar crime, in adult samples in many areas of noncriminal deviance, such as sexual deviance and problem drinking.

Finally, we note that, except for a symposium in the journal *Theoretical Criminology* in 1999, there have been few major developments in social learning theory in the new millennium. In that symposium, Akers and some mostly polite critics of social learning theory debated the status and future of the theory. Robert Sampson (1999), first, believing social learning theory to be deeply flawed, pointed out that empirical evaluations of the theory have concentrated too much on statistical modeling and not enough on the theoretical and conceptual aspects of their research designs. Sardonically, Sampson complained "[I]t is perhaps emblematic of the field of delinquency research that so much turns on semantics, renaming, and an ex post reading of what teenagers really mean when they agree that 'suckers deserve to be taken advantage of'" (p. 441). Merry Morash (1999), second, criticized social learning theory chiefly because its focus on individuals and on motivation has ignored the gender-related distribution of power, resources, and opportunities. She complained that "the research support for the connection of gender structure to social learning variables that are predictive of delinquency is quite incomplete, complex, and controversial" (p. 456). And Marvin Krohn (1999), third, hoped that more attention would be paid to the role of differential association within the theory and to integration with other theories, such as social control.

Akers (1999; and see Akers, 2008) offers spirited replies to these three critics. To Morash, for example, he responded that there is not much in his book about feminism because there is not much in the feminist literature about social learning theory. Additionally, Akers (1999, p. 492) suggested three chief areas where the theory might be developed:

> First is the SSSL model going beyond links to the structural and sociodemographic covariates of crime to better propositional integration with theories such as social disorganization. Second is improved operationalization of the four major social learning concepts and of the structural concepts in further tests of social learning and the SSSL model. Third is going beyond these main concepts to specify additional social learning variables.

## EVALUATION OF SOCIAL LEARNING THEORY

Apart from his own sustained research and that of a small group of followers, the basic principles of Akers' social learning theory and its explanations of why some persons commit criminal and deviant acts have still not been tested widely or deeply.

It is probable that some criminologists shy away from social learning theory because of the ethical difficulties associated with its policy implications. If criminal tendencies, including violence, are chiefly learned, it seems to follow that they can just as easily be unlearned through behavior modification. Controversial examples of behavior modification treatment include drug-based therapy, electrocardiac treatment, chemotherapy, and confrontational juvenile correctional programs such as boot camps. Although none of these strategies has proven very effective, all arouse widespread ethical controversy because they appear to foreshadow a return to the violent criminal justice system of the dark and distant past.

## 7.3 SOCIAL CONTROL THEORY

The concept of *social control* was pioneered in the United States by sociologists and social psychologists. At first, social control was understood broadly as all institutions and processes that guarantee social order. In some writings, it was depicted as a coercive device by which the will of the powerful was imposed on society. However, during the 1940s the concept of **social control** was given a much narrower reading. Two aspects of this narrower view were soon adopted as guiding themes in criminology. First, social control was stripped of its critical content and declared a functional necessity that contributed to the well-being of society. Without social control, functionalists claimed, anarchy and chaos would prevail in any society. Second, the concept was narrowed to include small groups (such as families, schools, and peers). The focus here was on how these groups socialized their members.

These narrower perspectives on social control are vividly present in the studies to which we now turn. These studies proceed on the central assumption that crime is likely to occur when the social bonds between an individual and society are weakened or severed. In what follows we present the best-known versions of **social control theory** in criminology, namely, Travis Hirschi's (1969) social control, or "social bonding," theory.

Hirschi's *Causes of Delinquency* (1969) is a prominent landmark in the developing literature on the sociology and social psychology of social control. Hirschi thought that most sociological theories had failed to show that delinquency actually is caused by such factors as the strains of "sex, race, social class, neighborhood, mother's employment, the broken home, size of family, and so forth" (p. 65). Although these factors might be correlated with delinquency, Hirschi reasoned, there is no evidence they actually cause it. Instead of looking for the causes of delinquency, he argued, it is much more fruitful to look for the causes of conformity. Perhaps delinquency is merely an absence of the causes of conformity.

Hirschi therefore started with the seemingly biological proposition that most people have antisocial tendencies. These tendencies are actualized, he continued, only if various sorts of social control are relaxed. Whether individuals are law abiding or deviant depends on the extent of variance from the four factors that are critical in bonding them to society: (1) attachment to parents, school, and peers; (2) commitment to conventional lines of action; (3) involvement in conventional activities; and (4) belief in conventional values.

Let us look at Hirschi's theory in a little more detail. First, Hirschi theorized that juveniles will be law-abiding if they have strong attachments to positive role models or significant others—their parents, schoolteachers, and law-abiding friends. Weak attachments to expectations of significant others can derive from a lack of discipline by parents and teachers, poor intellectual and social skills exhibited by the juvenile, disrespect for or indifference to expectations and opinions of significant others, and differential association with juvenile delinquents.

Second, Hirschi maintained that for a system of social control to be effective, juveniles must fear punishment. He reasoned that delinquents are likely to be juveniles who, during their difficult passage to adulthood, are less committed to completing their education or achieving a high-status career. Hirschi therefore disagreed with subcultural theories that identified frustrated aspirations as the main provocation for delinquency, although he did not identify the factors that cause variance in juvenile attachment to conventional lines of action.

Third, juvenile attachments and attitudinal commitments to positive role models and to conventional goals are likely to be reflected in juveniles' daily involvement in conventional activities. The more juveniles are involved in such conventional activities as education and school-related activities, the more they are discouraged from engaging in delinquency, and vice versa.

Fourth, Hirschi argued that belief in the goodness of certain values—such as respect for the law and for the police and belief in the wrongness of such actions as juvenile delinquency—operates as a brake on delinquency.

Finally, Hirschi implied that all four factors (attachment, commitment, involvement, and belief) are strongly interrelated:

> In general, the more closely a person is tied to conventional society in any of these ways, the more closely he is likely to be tied in the other ways. The person who is attached to conventional people is, for example, more likely to be involved in conventional activities and to accept conventional notions of desirable conduct (1969:27).

In his book *Causes of Delinquency*, Hirschi also attempted to test his theory empirically. The testing was based on a study of school records, police records, and questionnaire responses gathered from a large sample of juveniles (stratified by race, sex, school, and grade) in the San Francisco–Oakland area in the mid-1960s. Self-report items included many questions about attitudes toward family, school, and peers. Six items in the questionnaire were meant to serve as an index of delinquency. Three questions asked whether in the last year the juvenile had stolen anything worth less than $2, worth $2–$50, and worth over $50. Three questions asked whether he or she had ever "taken a car for a ride without the owner's permission," "banged up something that did not belong to you on purpose," and (not counting fights with brothers and sisters) "beaten up on anyone or hurt anyone on purpose" (1969:54).

From these data Hirschi made a variety of generalizations about the links between social control and delinquency, each of which seemed remarkably at odds with previous theories. Here are the seven most important of these generalizations:

1. Juveniles engage less in delinquency the more they are attached to their families.
2. Juveniles engage less in delinquency the better they perform in school.
3. The greater a youth's stake in conformity, then, irrespective of the delinquency of his or her peers, the less likely he or she is to be delinquent.
4. Members of delinquent gangs do not have cohesive or warm associations with fellow gang members.
5. The importance of techniques of neutralization in delinquency is inconclusive.
6. There is no significant causal link between delinquency and social class.
7. In the United States, no section of society encourages delinquency more than any other.

Hirschi later (1983) reformulated his theory somewhat and extended its scope to focus on child socialization rather than on adolescence. In this revised version Hirschi borrowed from the Oregon Social Learning Center's treatment of families with problem children. He reported the Center's "commonsense" finding that "children must be punished for their misdeeds" (p. 53). If inadequate childrearing techniques and lax discipline are allegedly the chief factors in juvenile delinquency, these factors are especially present, Hirschi argued, among working mothers, in situations of child abuse, among parents with criminal records, in large families, and in single-parent families: "The single parent (usually a woman)...is less able to devote time to monitoring and punishment, and is more likely to be involved in negative, abusive contacts with her children" (p. 62).

Continuing forcefully to reject theories of crime that stress such factors as poverty, social class, and unemployment, Hirschi asserted that good childrearing techniques and proper discipline are the chief ways to prevent or control juvenile delinquency. Good techniques include monitoring children, recognizing problems, and punishing misbehavior. Hirschi proposed, somewhat vaguely, three policies for the control of problem children. First, childrearing classes should be standard fare in high school so that future parents learn the rudiments of sound childrearing techniques. Second, parents and teachers should combine their knowledge and their supervisory roles in order better to address childrearing issues. Third, there must be appropriate governmental commitment to ensuring that families have incentives to raise law-abiding children. However, as Hirschi (1983) recognized, these proposals are highly controversial. For instance, should the government penalize parents (and guardians) who do not use sound childrearing practices? If so, how severe a penalty is appropriate? Where should the dividing line be drawn between family privacy and governmental responsibility?

Research has shown that some of Hirschi's key concepts need to be refined. For example, Stephen Cernkovich and Peggy Giordano (1987) complain that Hirschi's concept of attachment is too vague. What exactly is attachment? How does one measure it? They suggest that to understand the subtle dynamics of family interaction, future researchers should (1) recognize the importance of different measures of attachment—including control and supervision, identity support (during adolescent crises), caring and trust, forms and degrees of intimate communication, parental disapproval of peers, and conflict—and (2) explore the effects on delinquency of the variety of intact and broken family units, including both-parent, mother-only, father-only, father/stepmother, and mother/stepfather homes.

Other researchers have complained that there is very little about gender in Hirschi's theory.

Thus, a study by Booth, Farrell, and Varano (2008) of social control and gender has found, not surprisingly, that males and females have somewhat different paths to delinquency. It was found, in particular, that involvement in church and nonsport school activities significantly reduced serious delinquency for young men but not for young women (p. 447). Moreover, their involvement in delinquency was reduced for young females when they participated in non-traditional female activities in schools, such as sports (though why this is so remains to be explained).

The relation between Hirschi's concept of conformity, on the one hand, and his other key concepts (attachment, involvement, commitment, and belief), on the other, has also been criticized strongly. As discussed earlier, Hirschi asserted that juveniles are law-abiding or conforming if they have strong attachments to their positive role models. But Hirschi's statement confuses a definition of conformity with an explanation of conformity. As Thomas Bernard (1987) wrote: "If conformity is defined as acts controlled by attachments, involvements, commitments, and beliefs, conformity cannot be explained by the same statement without simply restating the definition" (p. 417). In other words, Hirschi's reasoning appears to be circular, and it is therefore not at all clear that the concepts of control theory explain anything at all.

Still other criminologists have raised serious doubts about the validity of Hirschi's findings. Robert Agnew (1985), for example, found in his longitudinal study of 2,213 boys between 1966 and 1968 that Hirschi's theory cannot explain serious forms of juvenile crime. In other words, even if control theory can explain minor crimes such as petty theft, it does not and cannot explain why some juveniles commit very violent offenses. Some other explanation is needed for such crimes. Agnew also found that although at any given point in time delinquency may appear strongly correlated with Hirschi's control variables, in the long run, rather than delinquency's being caused by weak social controls, delinquency itself can causally affect control! Agnew therefore concluded that "the explanatory power of Hirschi's social control theory has been exaggerated" (p. 58).

Some researchers have tried to combine social control theory with other elements of other theories of crime. For example, Payne and Salotti (2008; and see Capaldi, Kim, and Owen, 2008) have compared how well social control theory and social learning theory together and separately enabled them to predict college students' deviant behavior. Their study obtained data from 747 self-report surveys by college students at a liberal arts college in New Jersey. They concluded that elements in both theories were strongly correlated with alcohol and drug use, in particular, but that the strongest correlations were when elements in both theories were combined.

### EVALUATION OF SOCIAL CONTROL THEORY

Among many criminologists, the control theory of crime continues to be extremely influential. In Hirschi's version, especially, it is a formalized theory whose several propositions lend themselves easily to empirical tests. It is a major source of current research and has consistently received strong empirical support from some researchers (see Goode, 2008; Laub and Sampson, 1988).

Moreover, it has motivated other researchers to pinpoint the apparent importance of strict control—and the dire consequences of lax discipline—in institutions such as schools, about which we will have more to say soon.

### 7.4 SELF-CONTROL THEORY

We now describe two theories that are intended to be general theories of crime: in turn, the theory of **self-control** and the theory of **control**

balance. Their common focus is the concept of control.

### GOTTFREDSON AND HIRSCHI'S THEORY OF SELF-CONTROL

In recent years Travis Hirschi has radically narrowed or refocused, though not entirely abandoned, the theory of social control he presented in *Causes of Delinquency*. This change of emphasis was signaled in Michael Gottfredson and Hirschi's wide-ranging and influential book *A General Theory of Crime* (1990), in which the two authors put forward a theory of self-control and crime.

Gottfredson and Hirschi argued that individual differences in criminal behavior stem from differences in "self-control." Finding much merit in classical criminology's emphasis on the relationships between pleasure and pain, they defined the problem of self-control as "the differential tendency of people to avoid criminal acts whatever the circumstances in which they find themselves" (1990:87). Low self-control coupled with opportunity increases an individual's propensity to commit crime, especially crimes involving force or fraud. High self-control effectively reduces the likelihood of committing crime. Moreover, those with high levels of self-control are significantly less likely throughout their lives to commit crime.

Clearly, this claim about the importance of self-control in the generation of crime has two crucial features: first, the characteristics of self-control and, second, the factors that promote or retard the level of self-control.

Gottfredson and Hirschi assumed that the characteristics of self-control can be derived from the nature of crime itself, which has five chief aspects:

1. Because crime offers immediate gratification of desires, people with low self-control wish to give in to their desires at

once. They live in the here and now. For this reason, those with low self-control also tend to indulge in a variety of other immediate pleasures that are not criminal, such as smoking, drinking, using drugs, gambling, having illegitimate children, and engaging in illicit sex.

2. Because crime is exciting, risky, and thrilling, people with low self-control tend to be adventuresome, active, and physical rather than cautious, cognitive, and verbal.

3. Because crime provides few or meager long-term benefits and because engaging in crime interferes with jobs, marriages, family, and friends, people with low self-control tend to have marriages, friendships, and job profiles that are also unstable.

4. Because crime requires little skill or planning, people without self-control need not have or need not value cognitive or academic skills.

5. Because crime often causes victims pain or discomfort, people with low self-control tend to be self-centered and indifferent to others' suffering and needs.

To these five major characteristics of crime and self-control Gottfredson and Hirschi added that for those with low self-control, crime is not an automatic occurrence. For crime to occur, low self-control must be coupled with an opportunity to commit it. The opportunity for crime usually dictates whether any given person with low self-control actually commits a crime. Because crime is not a specialized activity, a potential criminal (in other words, a person with low self-control) will tend to commit a crime if the opportunity presents itself. Thus, a rapist is more likely than a nonrapist to (mis)use drugs and to commit robberies and burglaries. Moreover, if the opportunity to commit a crime is absent, persons with

low self-control are more likely to engage in other acts that are "psychologically or theoretically equivalent to crime." Thus, in areas where property is secure and guarded, persons with low self-control will tend not to commit property crimes but are more likely than nonthieves to smoke, drink, and play truant from school.

What, then, are the sources or causes of low self-control? Gottfredson and Hirschi argued that the major cause is ineffective childrearing. As such, they continued, crime can be predicted from evidence of low self-control at very early stages in life. Children without self-control are children whose parents or guardians (1) do not monitor their behavior; (2) do not recognize deviant behavior when it happens; and (3) do not punish such behavior. By the time of the age of responsibility (eight years), most, if not all, children have attained—or failed to attain—a level of self-control that will remain constant for the rest of their lives:

> All that is required to activate the system is affection for or investment in the child. The person who cares for the child will watch his behavior, see him doing things he should not do, and correct him. The result may be a child more capable of delaying gratification, more sensitive to the interests and desires of others, more independent, more willing to accept restraints on his activity, and more unlikely to use force or violence to attain his ends. (1990:97)

Gottfredson and Hirschi asserted that many of the conventional causes of crime are in fact not causes of crime but consequences of low self-control. Persons with low self-control sort themselves into and are sorted into circumstances that are correlated with crime. For example, consider the longstanding finding that one of the causes of delinquency is that delinquents tend to have friends who are delinquent. This finding is rejected by Gottfredson and Hirschi; they believe that young persons with low self-control are attracted to the pleasures of delinquent activities and that the delinquent gang provides the opportunity for crime.

## EVALUATION OF SELF-CONTROL THEORY

In formulating the theory of crime and self-control with Gottfredson in *A General Theory of Crime*, Hirschi apparently abandoned his earlier, multifaceted theory of social control in favor of a monocausal theory whose core concept is intended to explain all crime. Recently, Hirschi and Gottfredson have bluntly stated that their theory of crime "is a choice theory" (2008:223), strongly implying that it is akin to rational choice theories of crime (see Section 4, pp. 101–102).

Hirschi and Gottfredson have insisted that the theory of self-control can explain such diverse behaviors as delinquency, white-collar crime, and organized crime. The theory of self-control has been criticized because of this claim, among others. The never-ending search for a **general theory** leaves itself open to the continuing objection that a theory that attempts to explain everything ultimately explains very little or even nothing at all.

Nevertheless, Gottfredson and Hirschi's theory of crime and self-control has led to some excitement among criminologists in the United States, and it has been subjected to a great amount of empirical testing. The results have been mixed. Some researchers have rejected the theory as almost irrelevant to certain relationships, such as to gender and crime (Iovanni and Miller, 2008) and to the apparent decline of crime with age (D. Greenberg, 2008). Others have found that its key terms should be specified more clearly; and still others have lent it modest support (e.g., see Pratt and Cullen, 2000; Chapple, 2005; Antonaccio and Tittle, 2008). Perhaps a key reason for this mixed reception is that Gottfredson and Hirschi did not originally spell out precisely what they meant by "self-control" and by "opportunity" (Simpson and Geis, 2008).

Indeed, C. Hay and Forrest (2008), complaining that low self-control does not exist in a sociological vacuum, have studied the effects on crime of the relationship between low self-control and criminal opportunity. Using data from the National Longitudinal Study of youth, they report, somewhat tentatively, that opportunities to commit crime interact with low-self control: The more opportunities for crime there are, the more likely are those with low self-control to commit crime. Other researchers have tried to integrate self-control explanations with aspects of other criminological theories. For example, one study has found that both low self-control and social learning are involved in the formation of students' intentions to engage in movie piracy (Higgins, Fell, and Wilson, 2007; and see R. Felson and Messner, 2008). Another study, which examined the influence of language skills on low self-control, suggests that sociological factors and genetic factors interact to explain covariation between language and self-control (Vaughn, DeLisi, Beaver, and Wright, 2009).

Let us now point to various problems with self-control theory that return us squarely to important themes we raised earlier in this book.

First, the theory of self-control and crime seems to be based on a tautology: If low self-control increases the propensity for crime, and if high propensity for crime is defined as low self-control, the theory is saying that low self-control causes low self-control (Geis, 2000; but see Hirschi and Gottfredson, 2008). What is needed, in short, are reliable indicators and measures of self-control that are separate from both the propensity to commit crime and crime itself. To this Hirschi and Gottfredson (2000) have replied that as logical systems, all theories contain tautologies and that the very heart of their theory contains not one but two "successful" tautologies: "deviant behavior predicts deviant behavior" and "self-control causes deviant behavior"!

Second, it is impossible, if not downright arrogant, to characterize all criminal behavior as involving individuals with low self-control. Indeed, most criminologists would agree that persons with high levels of self-control who practice deferred gratification are precisely the individuals who engage in the numerous types of political, white-collar, syndicated, and state crimes (Friedrichs and Schwartz, 2008)! At the very least, many crimes require a specific rather than a general explanation, and numerous others have nothing to do with self-control. In this regard, there is an emerging tendency to try and integrate self-control theory with other theories of crime, such as situational action theory (see Wikström, 2007), institutional anomie theory, and social disorganization theory (Matsueda, 2008), and with other key variables, such as the influence of morality (Antonaccio and Tittle, 2008) on an individual's decision to engage in crime.

Third, if crime is an individual matter of self-control, how does one explain that some societies have much greater crime rates than others? Why does the United States have a homicide rate three to five times higher than the rate in most European countries? Is it because the U.S. population somehow has less self-control, or does it have something to do with the nature of social organization in the United States?

Finally, it is worth identifying, in respect of the high violent crime rates in the United States, the sorts of social policies that tend to stem from or be associated with both self-control theory and social control theory. In the view of these conservative theories, high rates of violence are caused by permissive, lax, or absent parents and by the decline of religious values, the collapse of order in high schools, governments that are too generous with the poor and with welfare recipients, and criminal justice systems that are too soft on criminals. Typical conservative policies

for controlling crime include compulsory religious instruction from the elementary school upward, restoration of strict discipline (including corporal punishment) in the nation's high schools, reduction or elimination of government welfare programs in order to cultivate individual responsibility and to foster initiative among the "undeserving poor," and increased severity of penal sanctions (such as longer prison sentences and determinate sentencing).

On the other side of this dispute are the liberal critics of control theory. Elliott Currie (1997), for example, has argued that the high violent crime rates in the United States have little to do with lax social control and much to do with the logic of free economic enterprise and its unfortunate consequences. Chief among these consequences are (Currie, 1997; and see Young, 2007, in Chapter 9):

- The progressive destruction of jobs and livelihood.
- The growth of extremes of economic inequality and material deprivation.
- The withdrawal of public services and supports, especially for families and children.
- The erosion of informal and communal networks of mutual support, supervision, and care.
- The spread of a materialistic, neglectful, and "hard" culture.
- The unregulated marketing of the technology of violence.
- The weakening of social and political alternatives.

Moreover, liberal critics of control theory counter that strict discipline neither deters nor controls crime and delinquency. Stricter discipline (including corporal punishment) may actually encourage delinquency, they continue, because its use teaches children that physical force is the appropriate way to solve interpersonal problems. It is no accident, the liberal argument concludes, that the United States has both the highest rate of violent crime and the highest rate of incarceration of all industrial nations. Punitive control and high rates of violent crime are both symptoms of the same problem: The United States is a thoroughly violent society, even, ironically, in its response to violent crime. In the liberal scenario, the causes of crime must be attacked by social policies that seek alternatives to imprisonment, that foster community spirit, that create employment for the poor, and that make adequate provision for the children of poorer families.

We now turn to another exploration of the importance of the concept of control, namely, the theory of control balance.

## 7.5 CONTROL BALANCE THEORY

For a while after the great success of labeling theory in the 1960s and 1970s, the concept of deviance never played as significant a role in the theoretical development of criminology. However, with Charles Tittle's book *Control Balance* (1995), the concept of deviance reemerged as an innovating force in criminology. Like Gottfredson and Hirschi's theory of self-control, Tittle's theory is focused on control, with an aim of nothing less than a general explanation of its subject matter. Indeed, the subtitle of his book is *Toward a General Theory of Deviance*. Tittle's theory tries to combine aspects of numerous other theories, including differential association, anomie, Marxism/conflict, social control, labeling, rational choice, and routine activities.

Tittle (1995) states that although what counts as deviance is subject to great variation, deviance is "any behavior that the majority of a given group regards as unacceptable or that typically evokes a collective response of a negative type" (p. 124). It is thus not the number of people who engage in an act that makes it deviant but the number of people who view it as such. Crime is merely a specialized form of deviance, one that is regarded as such by criminal law. Tittle identifies six forms of deviance, distinguished by how serious they are:

1. *Predation.* Acts of direct physical violence, manipulation, or property extraction, including theft, rape, homicide, robbery, assault, fraud, and individual price gouging, as well as acts such as parents' use of guilt to get a child's attention.
2. *Exploitation.* Acts of indirect predation, such as corporate price-fixing, unsafe workplaces, influence peddling, and contract killings.
3. *Defiance.* Acts of hostility or contempt for social norms—including vandalism, sullenness by a marital partner, and political protests—that bring the actor no obvious benefit.
4. *Plunder.* Acts of autocratic behavior, ethnic cleansing, and the destruction of the environment, rarely committed with an awareness of their harmfulness.
5. *Decadence.* Acts of undisciplined excess, such as group sex with children, humiliating others for entertainment, sadistic torture.
6. *Submission.* Acts in which one allows oneself to be physically abused, humiliated, or sexually degraded.

Tittle's theory begins by accepting the basic premise of other control theories. This premise is that the main variable in explaining individual acts of deviance or crime is control of the ability to act. The theory's central premise is that "the amount of control to which an individual is subject, relative to the amount of control he or she can exercise, determines the probability that deviance will occur as well as the type of deviance likely to occur" (1995:135).

The "amount of control to which an individual is subject, relative to the amount of control he or she can exercise" is known as the *control ratio* for that individual. Individuals are in **control balance** if the amount of control they exercise is the same as the amount of control they experience. If one controls more than one experiences control, then one has a **control surplus.** If one experiences control more than one controls, then one has a **control deficit.**

Individuals with a control balance tend to conform. Those who have more control and those who have less control both tend to engage in more deviance than those in control balance—and the extent of their deviance is proportional to how far out of balance they are. Individuals with control surpluses are likely to want to extend them; they will tend to do so by engaging in acts of exploitation, plunder, or decadence. Individuals with the smallest control surpluses are most likely to engage in exploitation, those with the largest surpluses are most likely to engage in decadence. Those with control deficits are likely to wish to remove them or to minimize their effects; they will tend to do so by engaging in acts of predation, defiance, or submission. Individuals with marginal control deficits are most likely to engage in acts of predation; those with the most deficits, in acts of submission.

Under what conditions are individuals with an unbalanced control ratio motivated to engage in deviance? What provides the push, reason, impulse, or urge for them to deviate? Tittle says that motivating factors are of two basic sorts, one predispositional, the other situational. *Predispositional* factors include bodily and psychic needs; the desire for autonomy, which we all learn at a very early age; and the control ratio, which varies from one individual to another and depends on such factors as age, class, status, race, and gender.

But being predisposed to deviance does not necessarily mean that deviance will happen: "For deviant motivation to emerge, those predisposed toward it by an imbalanced control ratio must comprehend, or perceive, the possibility that deviance will alter their control ratios in an advantageous way" (Tittle, 1995:162). The *situational* influences on deviant motivation include provocations, such as verbal insults and racial slurs, and challenges from or displays of weakness by others. Adolescent subcultures, for example, are acutely aware of repression and encourage their members to resist it.

Tittle added a third and a fourth factor to this complex theory. The third is *constraint*, which refers to the probability, or perceived probability, that control will actually be exercised. Fourth, and finally, is *opportunity.* Clearly, one must have access to another person in order to assault him or her and access to another's property in order to steal it.

### EVALUATION OF CONTROL BALANCE THEORY

Tittle's theory of control balance is clearly regarded by its author as a work in progress. Tittle himself has written that "it was unveiled like a roughly shaped clay statue with a sign saying 'bring your tools and your ideas and refine or reshape this'" (1997:99). In a broader context it must be seen as part of a movement in criminology toward an **integrated theory** (e.g., Bernard and Snipes, 1996; G. Barak, 1998; Bernard, Snipes, and Gerould, 2010:327–345), a key aspect of which is to model the process of theory building on the natural sciences. An integrated theory such as control balance seeks to be both as simple and as general as possible, which sometimes invites objections that its basic assumptions are too simple or wrong and that its scope is too general or too ambiguous (Short, Savelsberg, Jensen, and Tittle, 1999).

Modifications to some of the key components of control balance theory have been proposed by John Braithwaite (1997; and see Tittle, 1997, 1999; A. Piquero and Hickman, 1999; and see

N. Piquero and Piquero, 2006; K. Williams, 2008). Braithwaite believes that the differences among exploitation, plunder, and decadence are not clearly defined. Moreover, there is perhaps no great difference between predation on the deficit side of control balance and exploitation on the surplus side. For example, predation might easily include shakedowns, bribery, extortion, and price-fixing. Indeed, Braithwaite recommended that most of Tittle's categories of deviance be abandoned in favor of a simplified theory of predatory deviance. In addition, Braithwaite (1997; and see Braithwaite and Pettit, 1990) advanced four implications of the theory of control balance, each of which makes an important statement about what a democratic and egalitarian society would look like:

1. Societies with greater equality of control will be better off because of reduced predatory deviance and reduced withdrawal from social and political life.

2. For any level of inequality of control, control that is exercised respectfully, without humiliation or debasement, will generate less predatory deviance.

3. When control is distributed with equity and exercised with virtuous respect, acceptance of that control is desirable because, especially for men, this acceptance will defuse predatory deviance.

4. When social bonds, social support, and communities are strong, equality of control is likely to increase, as is the respect with which control is exercised and the willingness of citizens to accept equitable, virtuous, and public-regarding controls.

## REVIEW

This chapter examined five influential theories about the causes and transmission of crime: differential association, social learning theory, social control theory, self-control theory, and control balance theory. Each offers a rather different view of the processes that culminate in crime.

### DIFFERENTIAL ASSOCIATION

1. Sutherland's general theory of differential association attempted to explain both conformity and deviation. It held that a person engages in crime because of an excess of definitions favorable to violation of law over definitions unfavorable to violation of law. Crime is thus learned behavior. By merging social disorganization theory with differential association theory, Sutherland attempted, largely unsuccessfully, to explain the origins of crime and its cultural transmission.

2. Sutherland's theories of the causes of crime have proven difficult to test, largely because their content is imprecise and their scope so general. Yet they remain the starting point for much analysis of crime today.

### SOCIAL LEARNING THEORY

1. Social learning theory begins with the idea that social behavior is a cognitive process in which personality and environment interact reciprocally. It was pioneered in laboratory settings under the influence of B. F. Skinner's operant conditioning

theory, according to which desired behavior can be reinforced by conditioned learning based on rewards and punishments.

2. Some criminologists have argued that whether individuals commit crime depends on their past conditioning history (namely, whether they have been reinforced [or rewarded] for having committed crime). Akers' social learning theory attempts to revise Sutherland's theory of differential association. Its major concepts are (1) differential reinforcement and (2) positive and negative definitions.

3. Social learning theory is a general theory of crime: It attempts to explain all crime.

## SOCIAL CONTROL THEORY

1. Hirschi's theory of social control is based on the idea that it is better to look for the causes of conformity than for the causes of delinquency. Delinquency is an absence of the causes of conformity. Whether individuals are law-abiding or deviant depends on variation among four factors that bond them to society: attachment to parents, school, and peers; commitment to conventional lines of action; involvement in conventional activities; and belief.

2. Hirschi argued that good childrearing techniques and proper discipline are the chief means of preventing and controlling delinquency.

3. The policy implications of control theory are the subject of heated debate among criminologists. Conservatives argue that stern discipline and family values are the best means of delinquency prevention; liberals reply that such discipline has never been shown to deter crime. Liberals argue that to reduce crime, we must attack its causes with policies that seek alternatives to prison, foster community spirit, create employment for the poor, and provide adequately for children of poorer families.

## SELF-CONTROL THEORY

1. Gottfredson and Hirschi's theory of self-control suggests that individual differences in criminal behavior are the results of differences in "self-control." Low self-control coupled with opportunity increases an individual's propensity to commit crime, especially crimes involving force or fraud.

2. The major cause of low self-control is ineffective childrearing. The characteristics of self-control can be derived from the nature of crime itself, of which Gottfredson and Hirschi outline five chief aspects.

3. Empirical tests of self-control theory have had mixed results, with some critics characterizing its core proposition as a tautology.

## CONTROL BALANCE THEORY

1. The main premise of Tittle's theory of control balance is that the amount of control to which an individual is subject relative to the amount of control he or she can exercise determines the probability and type of deviance. The theory identifies six types of deviance: predation, exploitation, defiance, plunder, decadence, and submission.

2. Individuals are in control balance if the amount of control they exercise is the same as the amount of control they experience. If one controls more than one experiences control, then one has a control surplus. If one experiences control more than one controls, then one has a control deficit. Individuals with a control balance tend to conform. Those who have more control and those who have less control both tend to engage in more deviance.

3. Some modifications to Tittle's theory have been proposed, including simplifying it into a theory of predatory deviance.

## QUESTIONS FOR CLASS DISCUSSION

1. Can social learning theory adequately explain the causes of suicide?
2. In the area of crime, do birds of a feather flock together?
3. Should a search for the causes of conformity be as important to criminology as analysis of the causes of crime?
4. Is suicide evidence of low self-control or, rather, of high self-control?

## FOR FURTHER STUDY

### READINGS

Symposium on Control Balance. 1999. Essays by Short, Savelsberg, Jensen, and Tittle. *Theoretical Criminology* 3 (3): 327–352.

Symposium on Social Learning Theory. 1999. Essays by Sampson, Morash, Krohn and Akers. *Theoretical Criminology* 3 (4): 438–493.

### WEBSITES

1. <http://www.aber.ac.uk/media/sections/tv07.html>: This Media and Communication Studies site compiles information regarding television viewing and violent behavior, with links to social learning theory.

# THE CONFLICT TRADITION

**8.1 Marxism, Law, and Crime**
- Key Concepts of Marxism
- State and Law
- Criminalization as a Violation of Rights
- Crime and Demoralization
- Evaluation of Marxism

**8.2 Conflict Theory**
- Crime and Criminalization
- Criminal Law and Crime
- Toward an Integrated Conflict Theory
- Evaluation of Conflict Theory

**8.3 Radical Criminology**
- Left Realism
- Evaluation of Radical Criminology

**PREVIEW**

Chapter 8 introduces:
- The major approach to state, law and crime as found in the works of the founders of classical Marxism.
- The approach of conflict theory towards an understanding of crime, criminal law and criminalization.
- The major theoretical developments of radical criminology, including left realism.

**KEY TERMS**

conflict theory

consensus theory

criminalization

ideology

integrated theory

left realism

means of production

mode of production

radical criminology

social classes

## 8.1 MARXISM, LAW, AND CRIME

An introduction to criminology would be seriously incomplete without an analysis of the perspectives of the authors of classical Marxism: Karl Marx (1818–1883) and his colleague and friend Friedrich Engels (1820–1895). Before outlining the various claims Marx and Engels made concerning the nature of crime, we briefly consider certain key concepts of their writings.

### KEY CONCEPTS OF MARXISM

The development of Marxian theory can be traced to Marx and Engels' initial acceptance, subsequent rejection, and ultimate transcendence of early-nineteenth-century German idealist philosophy. In his very first writings in the 1840s, Marx strongly opposed the idea that history and social change reflect such idealist factors as God, the intellect, reason, the spirit, and the progress of civilization. Marx gradually developed a materialist concept of historical change. His materialism combined the ideas of English political economists (such as Malthus, Ricardo, Bentham, and Say) and French socialists (including Saint-Simon, Lassalle, and Fourier), forging them into a new theory termed *historical materialism*.

Marxism is based on the concept that although human beings make their own history, they do not do so entirely as they choose. "The history of all hitherto existing society," Marx and Engels famously declared, "is the history of class struggles" (Marx and Engels, 1848:108). During such struggles **social classes** actively create and recreate the conditions of their existence. At the same time, the very existence of social classes means that members of a society cannot live exactly as they would choose. Social classes, therefore, also constrain social relationships. Class position is an important determinant of such basic life events as social mobility, consciousness, level and types of education and income, leisure patterns, and (as we see later) the likelihood of incarceration.

What, then, did Marx and Engels understand by the term *social classes*? To grasp this term properly we begin with their concept of **mode of production**, which Marx analyzes carefully in his lengthy book *Capital* (1868). Analytically, the concept *mode of production* entails two major elements: the means of production and the social relations of production.

*Means of production* refers to specific types of technology, capital, labor, tools, machinery and equipment, monetary systems, and land. In combination, these items are the necessary raw materials for producing commodities. All these materials, combined in various ways, are required to produce commodities as different as bicycles and criminology textbooks. They are subject to almost infinite variety. Commodities such as reading materials, for example, can be produced on stone tablets, papyrus, parchment, biodegradable paper, and computer discs. Commodities can also be produced, exchanged, and sold on a small or a large scale and by capital-intensive or labor-intensive means.

*Social relations of production* refers to the many ways in which members of a society relate both to the possession (legal or otherwise) of the means of production and to the distribution of the commodities that result from the process of production. For example, the productive process can occur in the institutional context of private or communal relationships; it can occur at home, in fields, or in factories; its participants can be slaves, free laborers, white-collar workers, bankers, landed gentry, industrialists, or state bureaucrats. The productive process can be more or less influenced by gender. It can be unaffected by or be dominated by political authority.

The means of production and the social relations of production, in combination, compose a mode of production. In their theory of history, Marx and Engels identified several distinct modes of production: primitive communal, slave, feudal, Asiatic, capitalist, socialist, and communist.

Engels usually, but Marx almost never, saw such modes of production as definite stages through which all societies evolved. Several modes of production can exist in one society. For example, until at least the Civil War in the 1860s, slave, feudal, and capitalist modes of production all coexisted in the United States. Again, during the 1920s, feudal, capitalist, and socialist modes of production all coexisted in the USSR. However, in any given society, one mode of production tends to dominate and lend its character to other aspects of social relationships.

Any given society, depending on its dominant mode of production, has typical social classes. Under capitalism—Marx's primary focus—typical classes include the *lumpenproletariat* (the perennially unemployed, those "unfit" for work), the *proletariat* (skilled and unskilled workers), the *middle class,* and the capitalist class (those who own capital: industrialists, financiers, commercial speculators, and landlords). In capitalist societies the basic class struggle is between the capitalist class (bourgeoisie) and the working class (proletariat). The economic site of this particular struggle is the productive process; the struggle occurs over the distribution of the fruits of this process. The capitalist class, on the one hand, strives to maximize profit from the unpaid labor of the working class. Its income lies in rent, interest, and industrial profit. The working class, on the other hand, strives to maximize wages. It attempts to do so by reducing the length of the working day, by compelling employers to pay higher wages, and by wresting from the capitalist class such concessions as health insurance, work-safety regulations, and job security. The goals of the capitalist class and the working class are thus mutually exclusive. Typically, the one maximizes its return from the productive process at the expense of the other.

For Marx and Engels, then, social classes are determined chiefly by their economic position within a given mode of production. Interclass relationships are rarely fixed; they vary according to changes in the political and economic power of one side or another. However, in Marxian analysis the basic class conflict in capitalist societies is between those who own the means of production and those who have no source of income other than their labor. This exploitive situation is inherently unstable and, Marx and Engels asserted, tends to lead toward socialism. Under socialism the means of production are socialized and class struggles begin to evaporate.

We note here the great importance of political power to the maintenance, development, or rupture of a mode of production and the class relationships associated with it. Maintenance of class relationships ultimately depends on coercion. Sometimes this coercion is quite naked; usually it is a subtler process. The relationship between economic position and political power—and, indeed, between economic position and many other aspects of social life—Marx often depicted in terms of the metaphorical "base and superstructure." He once described the relationship between economy and politics in the following terms:

> In the social production of their life, men enter into definite relations that are indispensable and independent of their will, relations of production which correspond to a definite stage of development of their material productive forces. The sum total of these relations of production constitutes the economic structure of society, the real foundation, on which rises a legal and political superstructure and to which correspond definite forms of social consciousness. The mode of production of material life conditions the social, political, and intellectual life process in general. It is not the consciousness of men that determines their being, but, on the contrary, their social being that determines their consciousness. (1959:503–504)

The mode of production thus conditions the life process in general. It does so with a mechanism Marx and Engels term *ideology.* **Ideology** has several meanings in their writings. First, it refers to any set of structured beliefs, values, and ideas. Examples include bourgeois ideology, proletarian ideology, and legal ideology. *Bourgeois ideology,* for example, refers to beliefs and values—such as thriftiness and respect for private property—typically held by bourgeois (capitalist) classes. In capitalist society, the ideas of the capitalist class tend to be the ruling ideas.

Second, ideology refers sometimes to a set of mistaken or false beliefs. "Ideology is a process," wrote Engels, "accomplished by the so-called thinker consciously, it is true, but with a false consciousness" (1888:496). Marx often attacked religious beliefs ("the opium of the masses"), not only because he believed they alienated people from each other but also because religious beliefs wrongly assumed the existence of God. In the same context, Marx sometimes contrasted ideology with science: Ideology is false belief; science is correct belief.

Finally, and most difficult, the term *ideology* refers to a set of beliefs that both reflect social reality and simultaneously distort it. To help understand this dual process, think of a straight stick standing upright in a pool of water. In this situation the image conveys the appearance that the stick is bent. Thus, the image is both a reflection of physical matter (governed by the laws of optics) and a distortion of it (the stick is not actually bent). This final meaning of ideology, then, refers to a process whereby beliefs, deriving from real social relationships, hide or mask the precise nature of such relationships. Certain ideas, such as those associated with justice, fulfill the ideological function of masking from exploited classes the nature of their oppression and its precise source.

This final meaning of ideology was especially important for Marx and Engels' analysis of state and law. Here the institutions and doctrines of state and law play a key role in the dominance of bourgeois ideology.

## STATE AND LAW

Marx and Engels used the term *state* to refer broadly to the organs of political authority and to the ideological processes that underpin the legitimacy of this authority, including the standing army, police, bureaucracy, clergy, and judicature. Generally, Marx and Engels saw the state both as a product of society at a certain level of development and as an institution that seemingly stands above society. However, this apparent ability to stand above society and represent itself as neutral and independent of class struggles is in fact an ideological distortion, inasmuch as the state and its various components are actually manipulated by the dominant class.

*The state thus has a class character.* In capitalist societies the state is typically a weapon or instrument manipulated by the capitalist classes, though Marx realized that state activities are not always so simple. For example, in one analysis of French politics, Marx (1952) described how the French state represented the interests of millions of smallholding peasants. In this sort of scenario, the state can be a prize actively pursued by contestants in the class struggle.

*Law is a crucial component of the state apparatus.* In class societies, according to Marx and Engels, law is endowed with several functions. First, law tends to reflect and promote the interest of the dominant class in private property. It does so by promoting and protecting all private property, thereby obscuring the fact that the vast majority of property is owned by only a tiny fraction of the population. Law fulfills this function through constitutions, through statutory and case law, and, with support from agencies of the criminal justice system, by enforcing compliance with its commandments. Second, law operates as a central mechanism of bourgeois ideology. Through such notions as *justice* and *fair play*, law promulgates the idea that it is independent of economic and political interests and that it can mediate conflicts in the interests of the whole society. But in class societies law cannot do this: To apply law fairly and equally in a society of inequality is merely to perpetuate inequality. Legal doctrines such as "the rule of law" and "equality before the law" are thus no more than fictions designed to lull the populace into believing that law truly does stand above society as an impartial arbiter. Finally, law acts as a repressive apparatus. Typically, this function is activated when the legal system represses the working class and its organized political movements.

## CRIMINALIZATION AS A VIOLATION OF RIGHTS

In certain of Marx's writings the process of criminalization was described somewhat moralistically as a violation by the state of some natural or inalienable human rights. Thus, in commenting on a decrease in the official crime rate in Britain between 1855 and 1858, Marx complained:

> This apparent decrease of crime, however, since 1854, is to be exclusively attributed to some technical changes in British jurisdiction; to the Juvenile Offenders' Act...and to the Criminal Justice Act of 1855, which authorizes the Police Magistrates to pass sentences for short periods, with the consent of the prisoners. Violations of the law are generally the offspring of economical agencies beyond the control of the legislator...[but] it depends to some degree on official society to stamp certain violations of its rules as crimes or as transgressions only. This difference of nomenclature, so far from being indifferent, decides on the fate of thousands of men and the moral tone of society. (Quoted in Cain and Hunt, 1979:189)

In one of his very first articles—written in 1842, when he was a radical journalist in Prussia—Marx (1942a) attacked censorship laws because they violated real freedom of expression. By "real" freedom Marx meant not only freedom

to do certain things but also freedom not to be exploited by others. In another 1842 article— which led him eventually to study economic relationships—Marx (1842b) discussed a Prussian law, enacted by the Rhineland Assembly, on the theft of wood. Despite a serious shortage of firewood and a depression in the local wine industry, this draconian law made it a criminal offense for anyone to collect and pilfer fallen wood in private forests. Marx attacked this law as a blatant undermining of what had been a customary right of the Rhenish peasantry since the sixteenth century.

## CRIME AND DEMORALIZATION

There is another way in which Marxian writings argued that criminalization violates rights. Many of Marx and Engels' writings analyzed the capitalist mode of production, and it is difficult not to believe that they thought capitalist production was unjust. Thus Marx (1859) wrote in the *New York Daily Tribune*, commenting on the lot of the Irish peasantry: "There must be something rotten in the core of a social system that increases its wealth without diminishing its misery, and

**FIGURE 8.1** How is public order possible? A late-nine-teenth-century industrial scene. Friedrich Engels commented in harsh terms about the terrible effects of unbridled industrialization on the English working class in the 1840s: dangerous working conditions, poverty, open sewers, air- and water-borne diseases, and street crime.
*Source*: Factory Interior, CA./ Stock Montage

increases in crimes even more rapidly than in numbers." For Marx, the social system associated with capitalist production was unjust partly because it permitted others (namely, capitalists) to profit from workers' labors.

It is a simple matter of historical record that from the birth of industrialization to the time when Engels wrote *Condition of the Working Class* (see Figure 8.1) *in England* (1845), British capitalism spawned gruesome living and working conditions for the mass of the population. Sometimes these conditions led to competition among members of the working class, and hence to crime In Marxian analysis these conditions led to massive demoralization. This psychological condition, in its turn, led either to crime or to rebellion.

The linking of crime and demoralization is a vivid and recurring theme in many of Marx and Engels' more polemical passages. Thus Engels wrote that the working class

> is cast out and ignored by the class in power, morally as well as physically and mentally. The only provision made for them is the law, which fastens upon them when they become obnoxious to the bourgeoisie. Like the dullest of brutes, they are treated to but one form of education, the whip, in the shape of force, not convincing but intimidating. There is, therefore, no cause for surprise if the workers, treated as brutes, actually become such. (*Condition of the Working Class in England* 1845: 411–412)

In another passage, Engels blamed the appalling conditions at home and at work for the criminality of the working class in Manchester. These conditions produced demoralization that, in turn, fostered widespread "drunkenness, sexual irregularities, brutality, and disregard for the rights of property" (*Condition of the Working Class in England* 1845: 421). Engels also suggested a different form that demoralization might take:

> True, there are, within the working class, numbers too moral to steal even when reduced to the utmost extremity, and these starve or commit suicide;…numbers of the poor [actually] kill themselves to avoid the misery from which they see no other means of escape. (p. 412)

One alternative to demoralization was rebellion. In *Capital* (1868), Marx documented the rebellion of the British working class against the harsh emergence of industrial capitalism. As a class, British workers first manifested opposition to the bourgeoisie by resisting the introduction of machinery; the Luddites even smashed it or attempted to assassinate manufacturers. "Theft," said Engels "was the most primitive form of protest" (*Condition of the Working Class in England* 1845:502–503).

Although Marx and Engels identified certain working-class crime as rebellion, they did not look on it favorably. Doubtless they shared with their contemporaries a puritan assessment of the activities of the dangerous class. In addition, Marx and Engels condemned such forms of rebellion as having no value for working-class revolutionary consciousness. Thus, Engels (1885) lamented that working-class crime is "the earliest, crudest, and least fruitful form of this rebellion" (p. 502). Elsewhere, Marx and Engels analyzed the class allies on which the working class could realistically depend for the growth of its revolutionary movement. Within that context, they complained:

> The "dangerous class," the social scum, that passively rotting mass thrown off by the lowest layers of the old society, may, here and there, be swept into the movement by a proletarian revolution; its conditions of life, however, prepare it far more for the part of a bribed tool of reactionary intrigue. (1848:118)

## EVALUATION OF MARXISM

Marx and Engels' writings are an important part of the development of sociological criminology.

Their writings, like Durkheim's, have endured among criminologists because they offer a radical, sociological approach to crime in capitalist societies. Crime, in their view, is not caused by moral or biological defects in individuals but by fundamental defects in a society's social organization.

Marx and Engels saw crime, as Durkheim did, as an inevitable feature of existing social organization. Unlike Durkheim, they believed that crime is inevitable because it is an expression of basic social and class inequalities. Working-class crime, especially, results from demoralization and occasionally turns to primitive rebellion. The extent of crime and its forms, they suggested, should be understood in the context of the specific state, legal system, and class relationships associated with a given mode of production. Yet Marx and Engels did not explain crime simply by reference to economic factors. They clearly understood that crime involves a political process in which the state criminalizes certain conduct and in so doing often reflects the interests not of society as a whole but of certain groups within it. Crime, Marx and Engels sometimes suggested, was a form of rebellion against this process. (Marx and Engels never seriously addressed certain basic questions about the nature of crime). Why, for example, are some actions defined as criminal but others are not? Because they did not consider this definitional question, Marx and Engels, like most of their Victorian contemporaries, tended to accept that crime is a violation of moral or good conduct. In arguing, therefore, that the lumpenproletariat and the unskilled working class engage in the great bulk of this conduct, they generally ignored the different types of crime committed by different classes. Finally, the writings of Marx and Engels contain no analysis of the links between crime and other forms of social inequality (see Chapter 10)

## 8.2 CONFLICT THEORY

In this section we examine conflict theory, a theory of crime that overlaps with both Marxism and the labeling perspective. To understand what conflict theory says about crime, criminalization, and criminal law, we review certain general ideas that conflict theorists hold about the nature of social conflict.

**Conflict theory** usually is approached by thinking of it in relation to its polar opposite, **consensus theory**. The debate over consensus and conflict theories pivots on three questions: How is social order possible? What is the nature of power? What is the nature of authority? The many answers given to these questions often hinge on the answers to certain other questions: What is human nature? What are the causes of social inequality? What is a "good" or a "just" society?

According to consensus theory, on the one hand, a democratic society is held together by its members' common acceptance of such basic values as virtue, honor, right, and wrong. These are the basic values on which most people agree most of the time. Because of this common agreement, social order proceeds in a harmonious and predictable fashion. This means that social change occurs only slowly and in a nondisruptive, evolutionary fashion. In such a situation power and authority tend to be invested in persons with intellectual or moral capabilities—persons knowledgeable about and attentive to the public good and the national interest.

According to conflict theory, on the other hand, there is little agreement on basic values. Society is made up of many competing groups, each with different interests. Conflict is the paradoxical feature of social order, and social change occurs in disruptive ways. Power and authority tend to be self-perpetuating domains of life that reflect deep-seated patterns of social, economic, and political inequality. In this conflict scenario, law is a weapon that the powerful use to enforce their private interests, often at the expense of the public interest.

## CRIME AND CRIMINALIZATION

The best introduction to conflict criminology is the pioneering work of Thorsten Sellin. We have already noted (Section 1.2) the importance of Sellin's (1938) concept of conduct norms in the continuing debate over the proper definition of crime. We now focus on another aspect of Sellin's argument in his book *Culture Conflict and Crime*—namely, the role of conflict in understanding crime. Sellin suggested that the advance of civilization (i.e., of urbanization and industrialization) vastly increases the potential for social and cultural conflict. Instead of the well-knit social fabric of less technologically developed cultures, modern society contains many competing groups, poorly defined interpersonal relationships, and, especially in cities, social anonymity. The rules (conduct norms) of such a society increasingly lack the sort of moral force possessed by the rules that grow out of deep-rooted, unified community sentiments.

For Sellin, crime was one of the many consequences of the conflicting conduct norms and social disorganization of modern society. Culture conflict exists when a person is caught between conflicting cultural rules. Two forms of cultural conflict in particular tend to result in crime. *Primary culture conflict* arises when there is a clash between the norms of different cultures. This type of conflict can occur when the law of one group is extended to cover the territory of another group or when members of one cultural group migrate to the territory of a different group. *Secondary culture conflict* arises from the process of differentiation and inequality in the parent culture. An example of secondary culture conflict is the clash between law enforcement and the second generation of immigrant families over the rules governing views of gambling, prostitution, and liquor.

Whereas Sellin emphasized the importance of cultural conflict as a cause of crime, George Vold (1958) pointed to the roles of what he termed *group conflict* and *political organization*. Vold believed that in any society people in similar social situations tend to group together to further their interests through collective action. Groups conflict with other groups when the goals of one can be achieved only at the expense of others: "The prohibitionist wishes to outlaw the manufacture and sale of alcoholic beverages; the distillers and brewers wish unrestricted opportunity to make and sell a product for which there is a genuine economic demand" (p. 208). In turn, distillers and brewers face competition over goals from other groups, such as trade unionists (who want to raise wages and improve working conditions) and environmentalists (who do not want distillery chemicals to pollute the atmosphere, the soil, or the land). Environmentalists, in turn, face competition from groups who claim that economic progress should not be restricted by undue government interference.

In a democratic society, Vold pointed out, each of the many interest groups attempts to secure its own interests by lobbying the legislature to enact laws in its favor. Groups that muster the greatest number of votes effectively enact new laws that enforce their interests and that, at the same time, curb the behavior and goals of competing groups. In other words:

> The whole political process of law making, law breaking, and law enforcement becomes a direct reflection of deep-seated and fundamental conflicts between interest groups and their more general struggles for the control of the police power of the state. Those who produce legislative majorities win control over the police power and dominate the policies that decide who is likely to be involved in violation of the law. (Vold, 1958:209)

For Vold, therefore, crime is behavior committed by minority groups whose regular actions and goals have not been secured by legislative process. Juvenile delinquency, for example, is minority behavior unacceptable to the more powerful adult world. Those who reject the majority view tend to be criminalized. Because patterns of criminalization reflect the different degrees of political power wielded by different social groups, Vold argued that much crime should be understood as having a political nature. This is obviously the case for crimes that result, for instance, from political revolution and social protest movements. But it is also true for other, less obvious cases, such as the clash of interests between management and workers and the struggle of racial minorities and women to secure their interests in racist and sexist societies. Vold (1958) concluded:

> There are many situations in which criminality is the normal, natural response of normal, natural human beings struggling in understandably normal and natural situations for the maintenance of the way of life to which they stand committed. (p. 218)

Vold's focus on the role of power in the process of criminalization was expanded by the influential contributions to conflict theory of Richard Quinney (1970, 1977; Quinney and Wildeman, 1977), to whose writings we now turn.

Quinney applied his theoretical perspective on the social reality of crime to a variety of situations: the religious and political foundations of criminal law; the behavior of judges, the judiciary, and the police; and such diverse conduct as that defined by the laws of theft, antitrust laws, food and drug laws, sexual psychopath laws, and legislation protecting morality and public order (see Box 8.1 and Figure 8.2).

Austin Turk has also made influential contributions to conflict theories of crime, especially

---

### BOX 8.1  RICHARD QUINNEY'S CONFLICT THEORY OF CRIME

In his book *The Social Reality of Crime*, Richard Quinney (1970) stated the six propositions of his conflict theory of crime:

1. The defining quality of crime lies in the definition of crime rather than in criminal behavior as such. This definition is applied by legislators, police, prosecutors, and judges; it is always applied in the context of a society characterized by diversity, conflict, coercion, and change. Society is divided along political lines rather than being an entity based on consensus and stability. Persons become criminal when others define their behavior as criminal.

2. Criminal definitions exist because the interests of some segments (or groups) of society are in conflict with the interests of others. Segments with greater power can have their definitions formulated in law and imposed on those with lesser power. According to Quinney, the greater the degree of social conflict, the more likely it is that the powerful will criminalize the behavior of powerless groups that conflict with their interests.

3. The content of laws and their application tend to reflect the interests of the powerful because the powerful typically control or manipulate members of law enforcement and judicial machinery.

4. Different societal groups typically learn to do different things. The less frequently people engage in law making and law enforcing, the more frequently their actions are defined as criminal. Moreover, increased experience with criminal definitions increases the likelihood that people will do things that are subsequently defined as criminal.

5. There are many conceptions or opinions about which actions should be criminalized. However, Quinney pointed out that the opinions of the most powerful are in fact the most powerful opinions. Through the mass media the opinions of the powerful are communicated to others as the opinions that must be obeyed.

6. The social reality of crime is a composite of these propositions.

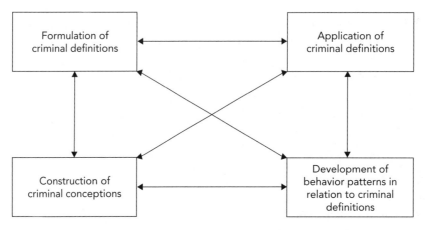

**FIGURE 8.2**  A Model of the Social Reality of Crime
*Source*: Quinney (1970:25).

in his book *Criminality and Legal Order* (1969). Turk's theory is most insightful in showing how conflict theorists understand the process of criminalization. Turk's intricate argument begins with the assumption that the social order of modern societies is based on the relationships of conflict and domination between authorities and subjects (1969). *Authorities* are those who make the most important legal decisions about the social order; *subjects* are those who have little or no influence on the process of decision making or on its substantive content. Slum dwellers, for example, have virtually no control over decisions affecting their life chances in such vital areas as tenancy and welfare. Conflicts between authorities and subjects occur over a wide range of social and cultural norms. Law is a crucial mechanism for resolving (essentially, treating but not curing) many conflicts over acceptable values and behavior. **Criminalization** is the process by which authorities, for any reason, confer an illegal status on certain behaviors of subjects (resisters). Authorities are either first-line (police) or higher-level enforcers (prosecutors, trial court judges, and appellate court judges).

Turk's theory of criminalization is designed to answer two questions: (1) Under what circumstances do subjects become criminals? (2) When are subjects dealt with harshly? Turk's answer to these questions has three parts. First, the more significant a law is to authorities, the more likely it is that resisters will be criminalized. This scenario, of course, assumes that the various enforcers agree to waive their respective discretionary powers not to arrest, not to prosecute, and not to find mitigating circumstances.

Second, Turk argued that the probability of criminalization varies according to the respective power of enforcers and resisters. Turk pointed out that "power differences between enforcers and norm resisters vary from relationships in which the enforcers are virtually all-powerful to cases where enforcers and resisters are about equal in resources, including effective organization, manpower, skills, funds, weaponry" (1969:67).

One would expect perhaps that the relatively greater the power of enforcers, the more likely they are to criminalize offensive behavior. Paradoxically, for Turk the probability of criminalization has a curvilinear relationship with power differences between enforcers and resisters. Turk suggested that the degree of criminalization of resisters depends largely on how threatened the enforcers feel by resisters. He argued that the greater the power of enforcers relative to resisters, the less likely it is that conflict results in criminalization; the closer their respective amounts of power, the more likely that the enforcers resort to criminalization.

Finally, Turk asserted that the probability of criminalization is influenced by what he termed *the realism of conflict moves*. By this Turk meant that the criminalization of resisters' activities sometimes serves the interests of neither enforcers nor resisters. Because realism depends on knowledge of what it takes to be successful in a conflict, the act of criminalization is often a sign of failure. It would not be particularly astute on the part of the police, for example, if arrests created martyrs that increased the size of the opposition. By the same token, from the point of view of resisters, arrests might be very useful! Again, criminalization is less likely to occur the more sophisticated the resisters.

## CRIMINAL LAW AND CRIME

We have seen that criminalization is one of the key concepts of conflict theory. Crime is behavior that is criminalized through the application of criminal law. For conflict theory, then, we cannot understand crime without simultaneously understanding the role of criminal law in society (see Section 1.3). We now examine how conflict theorists have understood criminal law.

One of the best-known conflict accounts of criminal law is found in William Chambliss and Robert Seidman's *Law, Order, and Power* (1982). This book contains a comprehensive application of conflict theory to (1) the creation of law, (2) the general principles of law, and (3) the implementation of law. The analysis of law is approached with the underlying assumption that "the central myth about the legal order in the U.S. is that normative structures of the written law represent the actual operation of the legal order" (3). The law in the books, in other words,

is not at all the same thing as the law in action. Chambliss and Seidman continued:

> This myth of the operation of the law is given the lie daily. We all know today that blacks and the poor are not treated fairly or equitably by the police. We know that judges have discretion and in fact make policy (as the Supreme Court did in the school desegregation cases). We know that electoral laws have been loaded in the past in favor of the rich, and the average presidential candidate is not a poor man, that one-fifth of the senators of the United States are millionaires.
>
> It is our contention that, far from being primarily a value-neutral framework within which conflict can be peacefully resolved, the power of the state is itself the principal prize in the perpetual conflict that is society. The legal order…is in fact a self-serving system to devise and maintain power and privilege. (p. 7)

As nineteenth-century philosopher Anatole France once remarked: "The majestic equality of the law allows both the rich and the poor to sleep under bridges if they so choose!"

Chambliss and Seidman's detailed analysis of the relationships among conflict, power, and the purposes of law is extended to such institutions as legislatures, appellate courts, and the police. But perhaps the most telling sections of their analysis concern appellate courts. Although many citizens see how easily the decisions of Congress can be swayed by lobbyists and special-interest groups, most of us reject the idea that appellate courts are open to such persuasion. Yet Chambliss and Seidman suggested that the various inputs into the rule-making processes of the appellate courts are "necessarily biased in favor of ensuring that courts as institutions are more available to the wealthy than to the poor, and tend to produce solutions in the interests of the wealthy" (1982:113). These biases cluster around several variables, the two most important of which are (1) the selection of issues with which judges are confronted and (2) their personal characteristics and socialization.

Because most appellate cases are initiated by individual litigants, it follows that the majority of such appeals are actually brought by those with sufficient funds to afford them. Thus, most appellate cases, such as those in the area of trusts and corporate law, concern legal problems of the relatively wealthy. Conversely, legal problems of the poor rarely come to the attention of appellate courts. Nowhere is this bias reflected more than in the area of criminal law and police powers. The poor tend to be arrested, interrogated, abused, and incarcerated much more often than any other societal group. But the problems the poor routinely encounter throughout the criminal justice system almost never reach appellate courts. Moreover, the poor lack the funds to hire lawyers to initiate the necessary legal proceedings. Indeed, to protect themselves from the abuse of police powers, the poor must rely almost exclusively on the charitable endeavors of such groups as the American Civil Liberties Union.

For their accounts of the links among power, law, and crime, conflict criminologists have drawn examples from diverse historical periods and a variety of societies. An excellent example concerns a change in the law of theft in medieval England: the *Carrier's Case* of 1473, in which an English court in effect altered the definition of larceny in order to convict a cotton carrier of stealing the contents of several bales that he had been hired to transport (see Box 8.2).

The *Carrier's Case* is an example of the crude power and conflict that lie behind the majesty of the law. The case is important not only because it shows how judges in fact make law but also because it shows how extralegal factors influence judges when they make law.

Jerome Hall (1969) identified various political and economic conditions that thrust themselves on the court in the *Carrier's Case*. It is interesting to note that when the carrier was indicted for larceny, no specific mention was made of the contents of the bales he had opened. Hall produced evidence, however, to show that these contents were almost certainly either wool or cloth—no ordinary commodities during the fifteenth century. Indeed, wool and cloth were the products of the most important industry in

---

**BOX 8.2  THE CARRIER'S CASE**

As reported in Jerome Hall's account of the *Carrier's Case* of 1473 (1969; and see Chambliss, 1964), the facts of the case were as follows. A "carrier" had been hired as a bailee to transport certain bales of cotton to the English port of Southampton. However, during the journey he took the bales to another place, broke them open, and took the contents. The bailee was apprehended, charged, and convicted of larceny by a majority of judges in the Court of Star Chamber.

This innocent-looking case marked an important innovation in the English law of larceny. Prior to the *Carrier's Case*, the element of trespass had to be demonstrated by the prosecution in order for a defendant to be convicted of larceny. At that time, legal opinion agreed that (1) trespass was an essential element of larceny, (2) a person having possession of property could not commit a trespass upon that property, and (3) a bailee has possession (Hall, 1969). The common law recognized no criminal liability if a person who was legally entitled to the possession of an item later converted it to his or her own use (the rationale being that owners should protect themselves by selecting a trustworthy carrier). These three precedents therefore created a serious problem: Because the carrier had been legally consigned the bales, they were in his possession. There was, then, no legal precedent by which the carrier could be convicted of larceny! However, by clever intellectual juggling (known as a legal fiction), it was ruled that the mere opening of the bales ended the carrier's legal possession of them. In this way some of the most important English judges who were hearing the case ruled that the carrier was in fact guilty of larceny. The law of larceny was thus expanded to include this and similar factual situations.

England at that time, an industry encouraged by a king deeply committed to solidifying his rule at home by gaining the economic and political support of European merchants who traded in these commodities. According to Hall, King Edward IV (the reigning monarch of England) desperately needed to regulate and elevate the standards for security and honesty in the transportation of commodities bound for foreign markets. It is therefore quite likely that the king persuaded the court to expand the law of theft even though legal precedent did not permit it to do so.

Why did the judges expand the law? According to Hall, it was a matter of simple political expediency. During the fifteenth century the court of Star Chamber, like most other judicial bodies, was subject to the political will of the king. Thus, although judges at the time of the *Carrier's Case* wanted to assert their independence from the monarch, they were politically unable to do so. The result was a legal decision dictated by political interests.

The *Carrier's Case* illustrates the conflict theorists' claim that behind the majestic impartiality of the law often lies the power of an elite or a ruling class. When the situation requires, as in the *Carrier's Case,* and in numerous other cases from antiquity forward, the criminal law's thin veneer of neutrality is readily stripped away.

## TOWARD AN INTEGRATED CONFLICT THEORY

A two-pronged tendency has appeared in order to integrate the many propositions of the conflict tradition and the empirical studies that have sought to test them. On the one hand, this integration has been furthered by a somewhat formal synthesis of the various concepts used in existing conflict theory. Thus Edmund McGarrell and Thomas Castellano's (1991) integrative model applies ideas about structural conflict, the influence of the mass media, fear of crime, and victimization to the formulation and enforcement of criminal law. Bernard and Snipes (see Bernard, Snipes, and Gerould, 2010:256–258) have also offered a unified conflict theory of crime. This theory combines an understanding of how the diverse values and actions in modern societies intersect with political and economic power to influence the enforcement of criminal law and the distribution of official crime rates. On the other hand, there has been a movement to integrate aspects of existing conflict theory with concepts derived from the other traditions in criminology and elsewhere.

In his book *Structural Criminology,* John Hagan (1989) and his colleagues developed what is variously termed *power-control theory* and *structural criminology.* In his analysis of crime Hagan combined insights from the labeling perspective, control theory, Marxism, feminism, and a criminology that recognizes the importance of the macro level of social structure. Hagan's core claim is that the vertical relations of power (e.g., parents over children, men over women) are more important in understanding patterns of crime and exploitation than horizontal relations (e.g., peer pressure). In his book Hagan extended this core claim to white-collar and corporate crime; sentencing and punishment; perceptions of (in)justice by different social classes and by race; and delinquency and the family.

One example of Hagan's approach was his integration of studies of labor force participation with those of household structures in order to examine why delinquency rates for males are almost universally higher than for females. Hagan argued that in Western industrialized societies, an instrument–object relationship exists between parents and children. Parents are the instruments of control, the objects of which are children. This relationship shapes gender patterns. However, these power relations vary with class and gender. In particular, Hagan noted, women gain new power in the family as they enter the labor market. He identified two family structures based on women's participation in the paid labor market: "patriarchal" and "egalitarian." In the former, the husband/father works outside the home in an authority position and the wife/mother works at home. Through socialization, daughters "focus their futures around domestic labour and consumption, as contrasted with sons who are prepared for participation in direct production" (1989:156). In the latter, the husband/father and wife/mother both work in authority positions outside the home. These egalitarian families "socially reproduce daughters who are prepared along with sons to join the production sphere" (p. 157).

Thus, although daughters are less delinquent than sons in both types of family because daughters are more controlled by their mothers, Hagan argued that daughters in patriarchal families are more often taught by parents to avoid risk-taking activities; in egalitarian families both daughters and sons are taught to be open to risk taking. It is this combination of the instrument-object relationship and the corresponding social psychology of risk taking that affects delinquency. According to Hagan, patriarchal families are characterized by larger gender differences in delinquency: "Daughters become more like sons in their involvement in such forms of risk taking as delinquency" (1989:158).

Hagan must be applauded for integrating some feminist insights into a framework for understanding girls' youth crime and for developing a theory that takes gender seriously as an explanatory variable. Although Hagan's original formulation of power-control theory seems to conclude that "mother's liberation causes daughter's crime" the theory is important because it demonstrates that gender is constructed differently in diverse family structures and social classes.

Besides the construction of gender, conflict theorists have also shown great differences in the respective attitudes of white and black Americans toward imprisonment, punitiveness, and discrimination. In particular, differences in beliefs about why black men are disproportionately incarcerated have been found to derive from the vastly different lived realities of those with different social positions in a racist society (Hagan, Shedd, and Payne, 2005; and see Buckler and Unnever, 2008; Unnever, 2008).

Integrating concerns with both gender and race, a study in St. Louis, Missouri, has examined how life in a disadvantaged inner-city neighborhood affects the respective risk-avoidance strategies of young African American men and women. (Cobbina, Miller, and Brunson, 2008). With the use of in-depth interviews, the authors found, on the one hand, that young men's risks were structured by their greater participation in neighborhood life, which tended to include gang membership, the sale of drugs, and the carrying of drugs (pp. 698–699). Young women's particular risks, on the other hand, were governed by their interaction in public spaces with strange(r) young males in public spaces, who tended to sexualize their encounters with women and to regard them as prey who are physically and psychologically weaker (p. 699).

## EVALUATION OF CONFLICT THEORY

Conflict explanations of crime, criminal law, and criminalization have been tested often and, to a certain extent, have been confirmed by criminologists. Confirmatory test cases include such diverse examples as laws concerning vagrancy, alcohol, drugs, prostitution, and bias in court decisions. In each case the ability of one segment of society to impose its moral view on another was a crucial element in the passage of a given law.

As a cautionary note, it should be pointed out that it requires a great leap of faith to assume either that law always arises from conflict or that crime always expresses conflict or that the process of criminalization always serves the interests of the powerful. Most criminologists today realize that arguments based on such general assumptions are seriously open to doubt. Moreover, conflict theory has rarely been precise in defining such crucial terms as *power* and *conflict*. What, precisely, is *conflict*? Do all conflicts involve *power*? But quite apart from whether the claims of conflict theory should be seen as confirmed, disconfirmed, or simply too abstract to be testable, its chief legacy is its introduction of a political dimension largely lacking in earlier criminology.

## 8.3  RADICAL CRIMINOLOGY

Earlier in this chapter we outlined Marx and Engels' writings on crime. As noted, neither Marx nor Engels devoted much time to the analysis of crime; however, several European socialist writers of the late nineteenth and early twentieth centuries did—attempting to apply Marxist theory to an understanding of crime and law. Foremost among these socialists was Willem Bonger (1905; and see Antonaccio and Tittle, 2007), the influential Dutch author of *Criminality and Economic Conditions*. Bonger reasoned that a capitalist economic system promotes egoism at the expense of altruism in all members of society and that certain people in all social classes develop a "criminal thought" from such egoism, which eventually leads to crime and to a criminal class. All crimes—economic, sexual, political, and pathological—committed by both the economically powerless and the powerful, Bonger argued, were the result of egoism engendered by a capitalist economic system (and see Ruschke and Kircheimer, 1939).

Not until some 70 years later was Marxist theory first applied to an understanding of crime in the United States. This was at once known as **radical criminology** (Schwendinger and Schwendinger, 1975, 1977; Chambliss, 1975; Quinney, 1973; Platt, 1974; Michalowski and Bolander, 1976; Lynch and Michalowski, 2006). In Britain, Taylor, Walton, and Young's (1973) book *The New Criminology* assembled a devastating critique of mainstream criminology and called for a social theory capable of explaining both the wider and immediate origins of the criminal act as well as the effect of societal reaction on criminal behavior. Although it did not develop an explicit theory of its own, this book prompted theorists in the United States to form various radical perspectives on crime during the 1970s and 1980s.

Steven Spitzer (1975) devised probably the most intriguing Marxist theory of crime and deviance. Assuming that capitalist societies are based on class conflict and that harmony is achieved through the dominance of a specific class, Spitzer reasoned that deviants are drawn from groups who create problems for those who rule. Although these groups largely victimize and burden people in their own classes, "their problematic quality ultimately resides in their challenge to the basis and form of class rule" (p. 640). In other words, populations become problematic for those who rule when they disturb, hinder, or call into question any of the following:

1. Capitalist modes of appropriating the product of human labor (called into question when the poor "steal" from the rich).
2. Social conditions under which capitalist production takes place (questioned by those who refuse or are unable to perform wage labor).
3. Patterns of distribution and consumption in capitalist society (questioned by those who use drugs for escape and transcendence rather than sociability and adjustment).
4. The process of socialization for productive and nonproductive roles (questioned by

youth who refuse to be schooled or people who deny the validity of family life).

5. Ideology that supports the functioning of capitalist society (questioned by proponents of alternative forms of social organization).

Spitzer argued that problem populations are created in two ways: directly, through fundamental contradictions in the capitalist economy, and indirectly, through contradictions in social control institutions. An example of the direct creation of a problem population is the inherent production of surplus labor (as technological innovation replaces workers with machines) in capitalist economies. Surplus populations are necessary for capitalism because they help support continued capital accumulation. A surplus population provides a mass labor pool that can be drawn into wage labor when necessary and that simultaneously keeps wages down by increasing competition for scarce jobs. However, this surplus population is also problematic, in that it must be neutralized and controlled (since it may rebel) if capital accumulation and, therefore, profit making are to continue. Thus, members of this group become eligible for processing as deviants.

Spitzer used mass education as an indirect example of the creation of a problem population. The widespread education of youth from all social classes was developed initially to withhold large numbers of young people from the labor market until they could later be absorbed into wage labor. Yet education simultaneously provides many youth with critical insights into the oppressive character of capitalism. These insights ultimately lead to hostilities toward the system and subsequent mobilization against it (for example, by dropouts and radicals). These youths then become eligible for deviant processing.

Spitzer identified two problem populations: social junk and social dynamite. *Social junk* are those who represent a control cost—the handicapped and mentally ill—but who are relatively harmless to society. Their deviant status arises from their failure or inability to participate adequately in the capitalist marketplace. *Social dynamite* are those who might challenge capitalist relations of production and who are thus a political threat to the capitalist class. Modern-day examples of social dynamite would include anarchists who protest the globalized workings of the International Monetary Fund and activist animal rights groups whose members are willing to damage research laboratories that cause animals pain and suffering.

In *Class, State, and Crime*, Richard Quinney (1977a) also developed a Marxist perspective on crime. He focused on four major areas: (1) the development of the capitalist political economy, the forces and relations of production, the capitalist state, and the class struggle between the owners of capital and the working class; (2) the systems of domination and repression wielded to benefit the capitalist class; (3) the forms of accommodation and resistance to capitalism by oppressed people; and (4) the dialectical relationship of accommodation and resistance to capitalism, because it is here that crimes of domination and crimes of accommodation are created.

Quinney identified several types of crimes of domination that result from the workings of capitalism. *Crimes of control* include crimes by the police and the FBI, such as misdemeanors, felonies, brutality, illegal surveillance, and violation of civil liberties. *Crimes of government* involve political crime, such as the Watergate break-in and CIA assassinations of foreign political leaders. *Crimes of economic domination* consist primarily of corporate crimes ranging from price fixing to pollution but also including the close connections between syndicated crime and criminal operations of the state. Finally, *social injuries* are harms not defined as illegal in legal codes, such as the denial of basic human rights resulting from sexism, racism, and economic exploitation. *Crimes of accommodation* are acts of adaptation by the lower and working classes in response to the oppressive conditions of capitalism. *Predatory crimes* include parasitical acts such as burglary, robbery, and drug dealing. *Personal crimes*—such as murder, assault, and rape—are directed at other members of the lower and working classes and result from the brutalized conditions of capitalism. Finally, *crimes of resistance* are actions conducted by members of the working class that are specifically directed at the workplace, such as sabotage and machine breaking. As Quinney summarized:

> Crimes of accommodation and resistance thus range from unconscious reactions to exploitation, to conscious acts of survival within the capitalist system, to politically conscious acts of rebellion. These criminal actions, moreover, not only cover the range of meaning but also actually evolve or progress from *unconscious reaction* to *political rebellion*. Finally, the crimes may eventually reach the

ultimate stage of conscious political action—*revolt*. (1977a:65–66, italics in original)

Another version of radical theory was put forward by William Chambliss (1988a). His *structural contradictions* theory of crime held that all historical eras and all societies, while constructing their means of survival, create contradictory forces, dilemmas, and conflicts. Under capitalism, the basic contradiction is between capital and labor. This contradiction results in worker demands for better working conditions and higher wages, even as capitalists resist these demands. The dilemma for capital, labor, and the state is how to reconcile the conflict, inasmuch as the fundamental contradiction is ignored. Resolving the conflict can result either in further conflicts—because the fundamental contradiction persists—or in an additional contradiction (as shown in Figure 8.3).

Chambliss also identified two fundamental contradictions in a capitalist political economy that lead to crime. The first is the "wages, profits, and consumption contradiction." If, on the

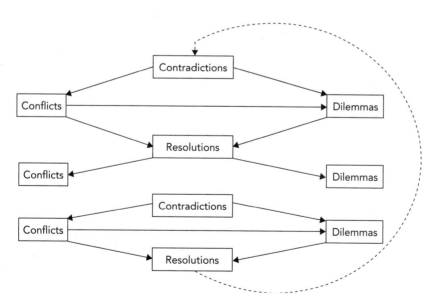

**FIGURE 8.3** Structural Contradictions Theory
*Source*: Chambliss (1988a:305).

one hand, workers have insufficient money to purchase commodities (because capitalists do not pay them enough in wages), the economy becomes sluggish. If, on the other hand, workers are paid high wages, this cuts into profits, and less money is available for reinvestment. This inherent contradiction of capitalism culminates in crime. Chambliss identified, second, a "wages–labor supply contradiction." Capitalism maintains a surplus labor force that helps keep wages down and provides a supply of labor from which capital can draw whenever the demands of workers threaten profits. Workers who push their demands are let go, and fresh labor is brought in. However, this reserve army of labor simultaneously

> forms an underclass that cannot consume but nonetheless is socialized into a system in which consumption is the necessary condition for happiness. Criminal behavior offers a solution for the underclass: What they cannot earn legitimately they can earn illegitimately. (1988a:309)

## LEFT REALISM

In the mid-1980s, radical and Marxist criminologists continued to refine their understanding of crime, especially of conventional crime. This new approach they termed **left realism**. As Matthews (1987; and see Lea and Young, 1984, 1986) put it, crime is not a heralded revolt but "tends to extend the fragmentation of urban life, mimic individualistic and acquisitive values, and limits public space and social and political participation" (p. 373). Because of this disorganizing effect, left realists argued that conventional crime must be examined seriously by radical criminologists.

Indeed, rather than viewing crime as the result of absolute deprivation and as a form of rebellion, left realists argued that conventional crime is driven by relative deprivation as well as by reactionary, selfish, and individualistic attitudes.

Conventional crime is a serious problem in working-class communities. Crime control must therefore be taken seriously. Certain elements of a realist crime control program were outlined by Lea and Young (1986). First, they argued for *demarginalization*. Instead of marginalizing offenders in prison, much greater use should be made of community service orders and victim restitution schemes. Widespread decarceration should be encouraged. Incarceration should be used only in cases of extreme danger to the community. Second, they advocated *preemptive deterrence* (deterring crime before it is committed) through citizen groups who cooperate with the police as well as through evening youth patrols such as the Guardian Angels. Third, criminologists must look realistically at the circumstances of both offender and victim. Fourth, criminologists must be realistic about policing. The police "force" must be transformed into a police "service" accountable to the public. Finally, Lea and Young proposed the pursuit of "alternative politics that harness the energies of the marginalized," helping create a "politics of crime control" that is part of other grassroots movements and combating "the tendency of a divided and disillusioned public to move to the right" (p. 363).

Walter DeKeseredy (2003) has suggested the following as core elements of a left-realist program for curbing crime:

- Job creation and training programs, including publicly supported, community-oriented job creation.
- Higher minimum wage level.
- Government-sponsored day care so that poor single parents can work without the bulk of their paychecks going to pay for child care; some unemployed single parents today do not look for work because they cannot afford child care.
- Housing assistance, which not only helps the poor but also enables abused women and

children to escape their environments without ending up destitute and on the streets.

- Introduction of entrepreneurial skills into the high school curriculum.
- Creation of links among schools, private business, and government agencies.
- Universal health care.

## EVALUATION OF RADICAL CRIMINOLOGY

Using Marxist social theory, radicals in the 1970s and 1980s developed theories that give priority to historical and structural analyses of crime, focusing on economic relationships, class struggle, capital accumulation, and the role of the reserve army of labor. In sum, the foregoing approaches have used Marxist theory to understand the relationship between the political and economic realms of a capitalist society. These perspectives advance our understanding of why certain behaviors are criminalized by the state, whereas others are not, and of how capitalism itself generates certain class patterns of crime.

Radical criminology has not been without its critics. To some critics, left realism remains unidimensional; that is, its concentration on relative deprivation as a source of crime is linked solely to social class and tends to exclude questions to do with how gender, race, and age might affect street crime. To some leftist critics, a radical criminology grounded in Marxist theory is actually impossible, inasmuch as crime is not an explicit Marxian concept like, for example, *mode of production* or *capital accumulation*. Moreover, mainstream criminologists have criticized radical criminology for being unscientific, moralistic, utopian, and one dimensional. Radical criminology, it is claimed, attempts to explain all crime in economic terms; it has made the mistake, in particular, of saying that other social relationships, such as those involving gender and race, are less important to the understanding of crime than are economic relationships.

## REVIEW

### MARXISM, LAW, AND CRIME

1. Marx and Engels' writings on state, law, and crime were set in the context of their sociological analysis of modern capitalist societies.
2. The key concepts of Marx and Engels' sociology are *social classes, mode of production, means of production, social relations of production,* and *ideology.* The articulation of these concepts defines the movement of social relationships throughout history, although their primary concern was with relationships in capitalist societies.
3. Marx and Engels generally insisted that the institutions of state and law and the doctrines that emerge from them serve the interests of the dominant economic class. The state arises from class struggles and gives the false appearance of independence from social classes. Law is endowed with several functions: It defends and enforces existing property relationships, and in class societies it does so in the context of unequal ownership of property; it acts as an ideological mechanism, promoting respect for private property; and in moments of acute class struggle, it acts as a mechanism of repression.
4. Marx and Engels offered a view of crime and capitalism that differed greatly from the social contract and free-will theorists of the Enlightenment. They defined crime in three ways: as a violation by the state of natural or human rights, as a result of

the demoralization caused by the gruesome conditions of industrial capitalism, and as a form of primitive rebellion.

## CONFLICT THEORY

1. Conflict theory, often contrasted with consensus theory, overlaps with the labeling perspective. Its key idea is that to understand crime we must also understand the interests served by criminal law. In this view, crime is a category applied to some persons after a politico-legal process of criminalization. Theoretically, then, crime and criminal law are merely different sides of the same coin.
2. According to conflict theory, crime and criminal law are the two basic aspects of the process of criminalization. It is this process that criminologists should study.
3. The most influential examples of conflict theory are Vold's theory of group conflict and crime, Quinney's theory of the social reality of crime, and Turk's theory of criminalization.
4. Chambliss and Seidman have applied many insights of conflict theory in an attempt to understand the creation of law, the general principles of law, and the implementation of law. Law typically reflects the interests of the powerful.
5. Many assumptions of conflict theory have been revealed as overly generalized. Conflict theory, as such, has been most influential in the continuing popularity of the labeling perspective and in the emergence of radical criminology.

## RADICAL CRIMINOLOGY

1. Although Marx and Engels never gave crime concerted attention, several European socialist writers, such as Willem Bonger, applied Marxist theory to crime in the late nineteenth and early twentieth centuries.
2. In the 1970s and 1980s, radical criminology developed various Marxist perspectives on crime and social control.
3. These approaches use Marxist theory to understand (1) why some behavior is criminalized and other behavior is not and (2) how a capitalist economic system generates class patterns of crime.
4. Since the mid-1980s, some radical criminologists have developed a left-realist approach to crime. They argue that crime and its control must be taken seriously, and they have developed a program for curbing conventional crime.

## QUESTIONS FOR CLASS DISCUSSION

1. Can crime be studied properly without simultaneously studying the process of criminalization?
2. Compare the various Marxist perspectives on crime with some of the other theories discussed in this book.
3. Can you describe the social organization of a future society in which crime has disappeared entirely?

## FOR FURTHER STUDY

### READINGS

Bernard, Thomas J., Jeffrey B. Snipes, and Alexander L. Gerould. 2010. *Vold's Theoretical Criminology.* New York; Oxford University Press.

Greenberg, David F., ed. 1981. *Crime & Capitalism: Readings in Marxist Criminology.* Mountain View, CA: Mayfield.

Lynch, Michael J., and Raymond J. Michalowski. 2006. *Primer in Radical Criminology: Critical Perspectives on Power, Crime and Identity.* Monsey, NY: Criminal Justice Press.

### WEBSITES

1. <http://marx.eserver.org/>: This online list of writings is provided by "eserver," based at the University of Washington. The list includes full-text documents of Marx and Engels' work spanning many years and different stages of their thought.
2. <http://www.ijcv.org/>: This is the online publication of the *International Journal of Conflict and Violence*. Published in volume 2, issue 2, are several articles that assess social conflict and anomie theory.

CHAPTER 9

# FEMINIST AND CRITICAL CRIMINOLOGIES

**PREVIEW**

Chapter 9 introduces:
- Feminist criminologies.
- A variety of critical criminologies, including constitutive criminology, cultural criminology, critical humanist criminology (peacemaking criminology and convict criminology), and green criminology.

**KEY TERMS**

abolitionism

anarchism

constitutive criminology

convict criminology

cultural criminology

feminism

green criminology

liberal feminism

Marxist feminism

patriarchy

peacemaking criminology

radical feminism

restorative justice

socialist feminism

speciesism

In this chapter we outline a variety of approaches to crime and harm whose politics may broadly be described as leftist, liberal, and committed to social change and social justice. We divide them into the two main categories of *feminist criminologies* and *critical criminologies*. They include several feminist perspectives, constitutive criminology, cultural criminology, green criminology, and what we term *critical humanist criminology* (peacemaking criminology, convict criminology, and the movement toward restorative justice).

## 9.1 FEMINIST CRIMINOLOGIES

The feminist movement has had an important impact on the social sciences, including sociology and criminology. The term **feminist** is commonly and broadly used to refer to all those who consciously maintain that women are discriminated against because of their gender and who seek to end women's resulting subordination through social change.

Kathleen Daly and Meda Chesney-Lind (1988b) have outlined five core elements of feminist thought that help distinguish feminism from other forms of social theory:

1. Gender is not a natural fact but a complex social, historical, and cultural product; it is related to, but not simply derived from, biological sex differences and reproduction capacities.
2. Gender and gender relations order social life and social institutions in fundamental ways.
3. Gender relations and constructs of masculinity and femininity are not symmetrical but are based on an organizing principle of men's superiority and social and political-economic dominance over women.
4. Systems of knowledge reflect men's views of the natural and social world; the production of knowledge is gendered.

5. Women should be at the center of intellectual inquiry, not peripheral, invisible, or appendages to men.

Contemporary feminist contributions to criminology can be divided into two phases; the first extends from the late 1960s to the mid-1980s and the second from the late 1980s to the present (Daly and Maher, 1998).

### THE FIRST PHASE

In the first phase, feminist criminologists concentrated on criticizing criminological theory for either being gender-blind or misrepresenting women. Feminist criminologists also conducted investigations of women's experiences as offenders, victims, and workers in the criminal justice system, and they used popular feminist theories of the time—liberal, Marxist, radical, and socialist—to explain women's and men's involvement in crime. Let us briefly consider the feminist theoretical perspectives on crime that emerged in the 1970s and 1980s.

As Jaggar and Rothenberg (1984) point out, **liberal feminism** has its roots in the eighteenth- and nineteenth-century social ideals of liberty and equality. Liberty came to be understood as freedom from interference by the state, primarily in the private sphere. The ideal of equality required that each individual should be able to rise in society just as far as his or her talents permit, unhindered by restraints of law or custom. What qualities should count as talents and how they should be rewarded is to be determined by the supply and demand for those talents within a market economy. To guarantee that the most genuinely talented individuals are identified, it is necessary to ensure that everyone has an equal opportunity to develop his or her talents. Within the liberal tradition, therefore, equality has come to be construed as equality of opportunity.

The formulation of the ideals of liberty and equality created the conditions that motivated women to demand that these ideals be applied to them as well as to men. From Mary Wollstonecraft's *A Vindication of the Rights of Women* in 1792 and John Stuart Mill's *The Subjection of Women* in 1851 to *Ms.* magazine and the publications of the National Organization for Women (NOW), the roots of women's subordination, for liberal feminists, are embedded in the denial to women of civil rights and social opportunities. Liberal feminists argue that women should receive the same rights and have the same opportunities as men. Women are oppressed because of gender discrimination, which deprives them of the same opportunities and rights that men enjoy. Consequently, women are effectively kept outside the mainstream of society (politics, business, finance, medicine, law, and so forth). Liberal feminists argue that this problem can be resolved by letting women into the mainstream. The liberal feminist program calls for state reform to bring about those changes necessary to promote women's rapid integration into the backbone of society.

One of the reasons for women's discrimination, according to liberal feminists, is gender-role socialization. Liberal feminists argue that conventional family patterns structure masculine and feminine identities. Girls and women, on the one hand, are socialized to be patient, understanding, sensitive, passive, dependent, and nurturing. The female role, liberal feminists continue, centers on functions reflecting these personality traits; such functions are found specifically in the family (women's identity resides in the domestic sphere) but also in the labor market, where women take gender-specific jobs such as clerical, service, and sales positions. Boys and men, on the other hand, are socialized to be self-confident, independent, bold, responsible, competitive, and aggressive. The male role reflects these traits, as a man is encouraged to find an identity in the public sphere (the workplace), thus providing money and security for

"his" family. Because the role and the traits associated with femininity are defined as inferior, sexist ideologies arise that consider women to be second-class persons. Accordingly, because of the emphasis on both equality and socialization, liberal feminists have called for policies providing women with equal opportunities and androgynous socialization.

Some criminologists have used liberal feminist theory to explain the relationships between opportunity, socialization, and crime. Rita Simon (1975), for instance, argued that until the 1970s women's crime was quite limited because women's opportunities were restricted. With the rise of the second wave of the feminist movement in the 1960s and the subsequent liberated woman of the 1970s, women were provided with more opportunities to act like men. Simon alleged that this increased equality in the labor market resulted in increased opportunities for women to commit occupationally related crimes, such as embezzlement. However, as we note later, increased women's crime is made up primarily of nonoccupationally related crimes, such as larceny (mostly shoplifting) and petty forms of fraud.

A more sophisticated formulation of liberal feminist opportunity theory was provided by Josephina Figueira-McDonough (1980), who hypothesized that similar levels of strain (resulting from high success aspirations and low legitimate opportunities) lead to similar criminal behavior patterns by both genders if they have equal knowledge of and comparable access to illegitimate means.

Liberal feminists also attempt to explain crime in terms of gender-role socialization. In the 1970s several liberal feminist writers emphasized the relationship between gender role and crime. For example, Dale Hoffman-Bustamante (1973) explained how patterns of crime are related to the different role expectations of men and women and thus to gender differences in socialization patterns. Ann

Oakley (1972) was more explicit, contending that "the patterns of male and female crime are tied to cultural patterns of masculinity and femininity, so that the type and the amount of crime committed by each sex express both sex-typed personality and sex-typed social role" (p. 68). Oakley saw crime as specifically masculine, which helps explain women's lower crime rate:

> Criminality and masculinity are linked because the sorts of acts associated with each have much in common. The demonstration of physical strength, a certain kind of aggressiveness, visible and external "proof" of achievement, whether legal or illegal—these are facets of the ideal male personality and also of much criminal behavior. Both male and criminal are valued by their peers for these qualities. Thus, the dividing line between what is masculine and what is criminal may at times be a thin one. (p. 72)

Oakley (1972) went on to argue that although crime may be a specific manifestation of masculinity and, therefore, predominantly male, "the sex difference has narrowed considerably in recent years, suggesting that, as some of the differences between the sex roles are reduced by the conditions of modern life, the deviance of male and female becomes more alike" (p. 70). This point was later emphasized by Freda Adler in her book *Sisters in Crime* (1975). Adler argued that because of the women's movement, by the mid-1970s gender roles had so merged that women became more masculine and, thus, engaged in more violent crime.

Specific types of female crime have also been analyzed by liberal feminists in terms of gender-role socialization. For example, Karen Rosenblum (1975) argued that important parallels exist between the attributes of the female gender role and prostitution, so the latter can be interpreted simply as a consequence and extension of fundamental aspects of the former. Women are defined as sex objects—either of lust or chastity—yet are socialized to be passive sexually and also to use sex as a means to status. Consequently, "the difference between the utilization of and expectations regarding sexuality is only one of degree. The decision to become a call girl simply requires an exaggeration of one aspect of the situation experienced as a nondeviant woman" (p. 180).

**Marxist feminism** differs considerably from liberal feminism. Marxist feminists theorize, following Engels (1970a), that the class and gender divisions of labor together determine the social position of women and men in any society, but they see gender division of labor as resulting from the class division of labor. According to Marxist feminists, as private property evolved, males began to dominate all social institutions. Thus Marxist feminists view the capitalist mode of production as the basic organizing mechanism of Western societies; this mode of production determines the social relations between classes and genders. Gender and class inequalities result from property relations and the capitalist mode of production.

For Marxist feminists, masculine dominance is an ideological manifestation of a class society in which women are dominated primarily by capital and only secondarily by men. The latter form of domination, however, results from the mode of production. Although most Marxist feminists examine masculine dominance and sexism in society, they comprehend the roles of men and women in relation to capital, not in relation to a separate system of masculine power and dominance. Women's labor in the home is analyzed not in terms of how it benefits men but, rather, how it provides profits for the capitalist class.

An excellent illustration of a Marxist feminist approach to crime is the work of Sheila Balkan, Ron Berger, and Janet Schmidt in their book *Crime and Deviance in America* (1980). Discussing women's crime, they argued that a capitalist mode of production "lays the foundation for a theory of women's criminality" (p. 211).

To understand female criminality, they continued, we must understand the ideology of sexism and how it legitimizes the structure of the family under capitalism. By reason of the needs of a capitalist society—in particular the reproduction of labor power—women's social position has been centered on the family, sexuality, and the home. Sexism, they argued, is an ideological result of capitalist relations that structure women's position and women's crime. Consequently, nonviolent crimes by women—such as shoplifting and prostitution—reflect such conditions. Moreover, when women commit violent crimes such as murder, their victims are usually family members, relatives, or lovers. Women are also less likely to use guns and more likely to use such household implements as kitchen knives as weapons. Thus women's crime reflects their oppressed position in a capitalist economic system.

Similarly, Julia and Herman Schwendinger's (1983) Marxist feminist analysis of rape contended that the level of male violence in any society is determined primarily by class relations and the mode of production. The Schwendingers argued that societies without commodity production are gender egalitarian, women are deemed equal to men in most aspects of social life, and violence against women is almost nonexistent. When such societies begin to produce for exchange (either voluntarily or because of the imposition of colonial power), men control the production system and women are confined to the home. This new division of labor results in an increase in male authority, a decrease in women's social position, and violence against women. Hence, gender inequality and violence against women become closely tied to and rooted in the mode of production. Indeed, the Schwendingers concluded that exploitative modes of production in class societies either produce or intensify gender inequality and violence against women (p. 179).

Whereas Marxist feminism emphasizes the structural conditions of a class society (more specifically, a capitalist society) as the root cause of masculine dominance, women's special oppression, and thus crime, **radical feminism** sees masculine power and privilege as the root cause of all social relations and inequality. For radical feminists, the most important relations in any society are found in **patriarchy** (masculine control of the labor power and sexuality of women); all other relations (such as class) are secondary and derive from male–female relations. Radical feminists also assert the following (Jaggar and Rothenberg, 1984):

- Women were, historically, the first oppressed group.
- Women's oppression is the most widespread, existing in virtually every known society.
- Women's oppression is the deepest, in that it is the hardest form of oppression to eradicate and cannot be removed by other social changes such as the abolition of class society.

Catharine MacKinnon (1984), a prominent radical feminist, adds that the control of women's sexuality by men is central to masculine dominance. Sexuality, the primary social sphere of male power, entails the expropriation of women's sexuality by men, and this expropriation structures men and women as social and sexual beings within society. For MacKinnon, power is maintained over women through compulsory heterosexuality and sexual violence (rape, wife beating, sexual harassment, and pornography).

It follows that when discussing crime, radical feminists concentrate on violence against women. Certain segments of radical feminism emphasize biological determinism in their discussion of crime. For example, writing about rape, Susan Brownmiller (1975) argued that "by anatomical fiat—the inescapable construction of their genital organs—the human male was a *natural* predator and the human female served as his *natural* prey" (p. 16, emphasis added). For Brownmiller, gender inequality is the result of the anatomical and biological makeup of men and women. Male anatomy and biology provide men with the apparatus to rape women; by the very nature of their anatomy and biology, women "cannot retaliate in kind" (p. 14). Women's overall subordination and men's criminality—particularly male violence against females—result from these biological facts.

Many radical feminists disagree with Brownmiller's extreme biological determinism, arguing instead that women's victimization by men results from their social position rather than their biology. For example, Elizabeth Stanko (1985) argued in her book *Intimate Intrusions* that because of masculine dominance and female powerlessness, the "normal" male is physically aggressive and the "normal" female experiences this aggression in the form of sexual violence. For Stanko, violence against women seems to be universal across time and place: "To be a woman—in most societies, in most eras—is to experience physical and/or sexual terrorism at the hands of men" (p. 9). Thus, male violence is a reflection of the universality of male dominance and the secondary status of women. Moreover, following MacKinnon's position on sexuality, Stanko argued:

> Women learn, often at a very early age, that their sexuality is not their own and that maleness can at any point intrude into it. Sexuality, then, is a form of power, and gender, as socially constructed, embodies it, not the reverse. As such, male sexual and physical prowess takes precedence over female sexual and physical autonomy. (p. 73)

According to Stanko (1985), women, as appendages to men, are "expected to endure or alternatively have been seen as legitimate, deserving targets of male sexual and physical aggression because that is part of what men *are*. Women, as connected to men, are then violated" (p. 74). Male violence is customary in patriarchal culture; therefore, it is also customary that women

endure it. Thus, this ideology helps maintain male dominance and control over women. As Stanko concluded: "Forced sexuality for women is 'paradigmatic' of their existence within a social sphere of male power" (p. 75).

In short, radical feminists view the basic structure of social reality as a total system of male domination. This form of domination is constructed by men and enables them to control women's bodies and thereby to trap women as forced sexual slaves (Jaggar, 1983).

Finally, **socialist feminism** differs from both Marxist and radical feminism: It prioritizes neither class nor gender. Socialist feminists view both class and gender relations as interacting and co-reproducing each other in society. For socialist feminists, class and gender interact to determine the social organization of society at any particular time in history. To understand class, socialist feminists argue that we must recognize how it is structured by gender; conversely, to understand gender requires an examination of how it is structured by class. Consequently, people's overall life experiences are shaped by both class and gender relations, and the interaction of these relationships structures crime in society.

An example of a socialist feminist explanation of crime is James W. Messerschmidt's book *Capitalism, Patriarchy, and Crime* (1986b). Messerschmidt argued that the United States is a patriarchal capitalist society and that the interaction of patriarchy and capitalism patterns the types and seriousness of crime. This interaction creates a powerless group of women and the working and lower classes, on one hand, and a powerful group of men and the professional-managerial (traditional middle) and capitalist classes on the other. For Messerschmidt, power constituted by both gender and class is critical to understanding crime:

> It is the powerful (in both the gender and class spheres) who do most of the damage to society,

not, as is commonly supposed, the disadvantaged, poor, and subordinate. The interaction of gender and class creates positions of power and powerlessness in the gender/class hierarchy, resulting in different types and degrees of criminality and varying opportunities for engaging in them. Just as the powerful have more legitimate opportunities, so they have more illegitimate opportunities. (p. 42)

Given that men and members of the professional-managerial and capitalist classes have the most power, they have greater opportunities to engage in crime, not only more often but also in ways that are more harmful to society. Males of all social classes therefore commit more crime than females, their class position determining the type of crime they may commit (for example, lower- and working-class males have no opportunity to commit corporate crimes, whereas professional- and managerial-class males have no need to resort to conventional crimes). In Messerschmidt's view, low female crime rates are related to women's powerless position in the United States. Their subordinate position relegates women to fewer legitimate as well as fewer illegitimate opportunities and to fewer resources with which to engage in serious forms of crime. Thus, overall, socialist feminists argue that crime is related to the opportunities a gender/class position allows, and they attempt a simultaneous explanation of the gender and class patterns of crime.

## THE SECOND PHASE

In the second phase of feminist contributions to criminology—extending from the late 1980s to the present—two specific directions of theorizing about women and crime have occurred (Daly and Maher, 1998). These two directions involve (1) the examination of how women are constructed in and by particular discourses such as the law and (2) the exploration of women's

actual lives and how their specific problems and responses to these problems influence involvement in crime. Daly and Maher contrast these two directions in feminist theorizing in the following way: The first "often characterizes women as effects of discourse" and the second "tends to characterize women as subjects of their own lives" (p. 4).

The work of Carol Smart (1998) is an example of what it means to examine the effects of discourse (language and symbolic representation) on women. Smart argues that the law can be understood as a discourse that produces gender identities. In particular, Smart shows that the law constructs both different "types of Woman" and "Woman as distinct from Man." Smart uses the example of the prostitute to explain this distinction more fully: "In legal discourse the prostitute is constructed as the bad woman, but at the same time she epitomizes Woman in contradistinction to Man because she is what any woman could be and because she represents a deviousness and a licentiousness arising from her (supposedly naturally given) bodily form, while the Man remains innocuous" (p. 28).

Smart (1998) also examines how legal discourse constructs the "bad mother." Taking us back to seventeenth-century England, Smart points to a statute of 1623 that made it unlawful for a mother to kill her bastard infant. With the introduction of this new law, the burden of proving innocence was placed on the mother alone. Then in 1803 the first statute on abortion was enacted in Britain, criminalizing abortion at any stage of pregnancy. In 1882 the age of consent was raised to 13 and in 1885 to 16, thus exposing young women who became pregnant—yet who were too young to marry—to legal control; and in 1913 the Mental Deficiency Act resulted in the incarceration of unmarried mothers on grounds of moral imbecility or feeblemindedness. According to Smart, this set of laws established a type of woman (the bad mother) as well as Woman distinct from Man because motherhood was constructed as "natural":

> Means of avoiding motherhood were denied to women, and the inevitability of the link between sex and reproduction was established through the harsh repression of those deploying traditional means of rupturing this link. We see the rise of compulsory motherhood for any woman who was heterosexually active. The "bad mother" reinforced notions of proper motherhood and, therefore, is constructed by legal discourse as a type of woman. Yet simultaneously this legal discourse establishes the "bad mother" as Woman because "she invokes the proper place of Man." She is the problem (supposedly) because she does not have a man. (p. 30)

In contrast to Smart's postmodern feminism, the work of Meda Chesney-Lind explores women as subjects of their own lives. For example, in a study of gang members in Hawaii, she examined the personal and familial characteristics, self-reported delinquency, and the gang activities of both boys and girls (Joe and Chesney-Lind, 1998). The evidence (based on interviews) reveals significant differences between boy and girl gang members. Although both boys and girls came from high-crime and economically depressed neighborhoods, 75 percent of the girls (as opposed to 55 percent of the boys) reported being victims of parental physical and/or sexual abuse. Thus, although the gang provides a surrogate family role to most youth who join, this is especially so for girls who have been victimized by a family member. In other words, the reasons for joining a gang are not the same for girls and boys: Girls are more likely to be runaways from physical and sexual victimization at home who eventually approach a gang for solace as an alternative family. Chesney-Lind (1995) concludes that to understand female crime, it is important to focus on the "real" lives of women and girls and on how their real-life specific problems—based

on gender, race, and class inequalities—and their response to these problems are related to eventual delinquent and criminal behavior. Obviously, this focus is quite different from Smart's focus on women as the effects of discourse.

Since the early 1990s, feminist scholars have examined the relationship between masculinities and crime, resulting in numerous works being published, from individually authored books (Messerschmidt, 1993, 1997, 2000, 2004; Polk, 1994; Collier, 1998; Winlow, 2001; Mullins, 2006) to edited volumes (Newburn and Stanko, 1994; Bowker, 1998; Tomsen, 2008) to special academic-journal issues (Carlen and Jefferson, 1996) to a variety of scholarly articles (Peralta and Cruz, 2006; Whitehead, 2005; Hearn and Whitehead, 2006; Cohen and Harvey, 2006). Like the work on girls and women by feminist criminologists, the examination of masculinities and crime developed in two similar directions: men as effects of discourse and men as subjects of their own lives.

An example of the former is the work of Richard Collier's *Masculinities, Crime, and Criminology* (1998). The bulk of this book describes the ways in which various types of men—lawyers, criminologists, youth offenders, mass murderers, and fathers—have been constructed by discourse. As an example, Collier explores the discursive production of the "dangerous" male child in contemporary Britain. In particular, he focuses on how adolescent male offenders have been produced through discourse. Collier discusses the "rat boy" media discourse that emerged in Britain in the early 1990s because of growing concern over "what to do" with persistent adolescent male offenders. Rat boys would engage in "crime sprees" and then "hide in the maze of ventilation shafts, tunnels, and roof spaces . . . while trying to evade capture by the police"—hence, the name *rat boy*. Various media discourses characterized these working-class boys as "monsters," "animals," and "vermin" and "as beyond the social, outside society, as venal" (p. 91). According to Collier, what emerged through this characterization was an offending adolescent male who is simultaneously masculine "like other boys and yet also appeared as other, as less than human, as *different* from other boys" (p. 91).

An example of exploring men as subjects of their own lives is the book *Crime as Structured Action* (1997) by James W. Messerschmidt. Here, Messerschmidt explores the relationship among masculinities as they are constructed by men differentiated through race, class, time, and social situation. As one example, Messerschmidt examines the changes in Malcolm X's masculine identity within a range of race and class contexts: a childhood in which he constantly battled for acceptance as a young man; a zoot suit culture that embraced him without stigma as a "hipster" and "hustler"; and a spiritual and political movement that celebrated him as father, husband, and national spokesperson. Across these sites and through shifting currencies of his sense of masculine, race, and class identity, Malcolm X moved in and out of crime. Malcolm X simply appropriated crime as a resource for "doing masculinity" at a specific moment in his life, a period when gender, race, and class relations were equally significant. Thus, Messerschmidt provides information about why Malcolm X "chose" crime at a certain stage of his life and how that engagement relates to his gender, race, and class position in society.

As with feminist theorizing on women and crime, then, current efforts to theorize men and crime maintain two tendencies: Postmodern work investigates how men and boys are constructed by discourse, whereas other efforts explore men as active agents who construct masculinities and crime in particular social contexts.

Although the social construction of masculinities has now come under careful criminological scrutiny, in approaching the relationship between masculinities and crime, criminologists have concentrated on men and boys and ignored women and girls. Concentrating exclusively on men and boys neglects the fact that women and girls occasionally engage in masculine practices and crime. Given that masculinities and femininities are not determined biologically, it certainly makes sense to identify and examine possible masculinities by women and girls and femininities by men and boys and their relation to crime.

Jody Miller (2001, 2002) initiated this in her important book *One of the Guys*, in which she shows that certain gang girls identify with the boys in their gangs and describe such gangs as "masculinist enterprises." These girls differentiate themselves from other gang girls by engaging in "gender crossing" and "embracing a *masculine* identity that they view as contradicting their bodily sex category (that is, female)" (Miller, 2002:443). Similarly, Messerschmidt's (2004) life-history study of adolescent assaultive violence—reported in his book *Flesh and Blood*—discovered numerous gender constructions by violent girls and found that some girls "do" masculinity by in part displaying themselves in a masculine way, by engaging primarily in what they and others in their milieu consider to be authentically masculine behavior, and by rejecting outright most aspects of femininity (see Flavin and Desautels, 2006; and Renzetti, 2009).

## EVALUATION OF FEMINIST CRIMINOLOGIES

Feminist criminology of the 1970s and 1980s made significant contributions to the field of criminology, and, as we have seen, it continues to flourish. Most concerns about first-phase feminist criminology centered on the feminist theories used to explain crime. For example, liberal feminism has been criticized for its inability to "explain the emergence of gender inequality, nor can it account, other than by analogy, for effects of race and class stratification on the conditions

**BOX 9.1**  HOLDING YOUR SQUARE

Christopher W. Mullins (2006) opens his important book, *Holding Your Square*, with an anecdote about a 43-year-old man stumbling through a crowded tavern who predictably yet accidentally spills his drink on another man seated at the bar. The seated man immediately responds by slapping the disconcerted 43-year-old across the face, leaving a glowing handprint on his cheek. Utterly humiliated, the 43-year-old swiftly exits the tavern, grabs a handgun from his car, waits in hiding for the soon-to-be-victim to leave the tavern, and then sneaks up behind him and puts seven bullets in his head. To help conceptualize such a "senseless" crime, Mullins takes us on a scholarly journey through the culture of street life in St. Louis and argues how this particular social milieu both structures rules of masculine interaction and sanctions interpersonal violence as an appropriate response to masculinity challenges.

There are several exceptional qualities to this study. First, Mullins presents an important account of how and why a specific form of hegemonic masculinity is embedded in the street life of St. Louis. His analysis not only supports previous theoretical work on masculinity and street crime but also extends the work by demonstrating that street-life hegemonic masculinity can be understood only in its relationship to subordinated "punk" masculinities—masculinities that likewise are constructed in the same street life culture—and in relation to particular femininities in that street culture. Second, Mullins' exposition of street violence is solid, confirming previous theoretical work that considerable violence among men in public settings results from masculinity challenges.

Mullins explores how men within specific social situations—such as the earlier example of spilling beer—come to view certain practices of other men as a threat to their masculinity, a threat that requires a culturally supported masculine response: physical violence. Moreover, he clarifies how such masculinity challenges can subsequently escalate, resulting all to often in the death of one or more of the male interactants. Third, Mullins' analysis adds two new and intriguing dimensions to our understanding of men involved in street violence. First, he presents an incisive discussion of interaction among street men and the various women in their lives. Previous work on masculinities and street crime unaccountably ignores this salient component of gender relations. Mullins, however, uniquely explicates that such men tend to construct *hegemonic* masculinities—or those masculinities that fashion power relations between men and women and among men—over women on the street and/or over those sharing domestic households, yet these same men simultaneously construct *protective* masculinities when interacting with mothers, grandmothers, sisters, and female cousins. Second, Mullins examines one of the most underexplored areas of research on masculinities in general—the contradictions involved in masculine constructions. The author lucidly illustrates how the men in his study vacillated among multiple meanings of masculinity according to their interactional needs.

Mullins' book makes timely, salient, and novel contributions to the literature on gender and crime, on masculinities and violence, on masculinities in general, and on street culture—it is the best study to date on masculinities and street violence.

---

of women's lives. Its analysis for change tends to be limited to issues of equal opportunity and individual choice" (Andersen, 1993:318).

A critique of Rita Simon's position on crime supplies another example of the kind of criticism leveled at liberal feminism. Simon (1975) argued that the women's movement has increased women's opportunities in the labor market and that this advancement explains their increasing involvement in property crimes. But this argument ignores the fact that the sharpest increases

in property crimes are found in nonoccupational theft, such as larceny (mostly shoplifting) and minor fraud (such as check and welfare fraud). Moreover, most female property offenders are adolescents who have had little if any contact with the labor market (Belknap, 2007).

The liberal feminist emphasis on gender-role socialization has also been criticized. Smart (1976) argued that liberal feminism failed to place the discussion of gender roles "within a structural explanation of the social origin of those roles" (p. 69). In other words, liberal feminists did not account historically, socially, and economically for women's subordinate position in the gender division of labor and, therefore, did not explain the broader reasons for the current patterns of socialization. Smart also criticized role theory for not discussing female motivation or intent. As she pointed out: "Role theory does not explain why, even though women are socialized into primarily conforming patterns of behavior, a considerable number engage in crime" (p. 69).

Both Marxist feminism and radical feminism have been criticized for being reductionist. Marxist feminists have been faulted for reducing all social phenomena—including male and female crime—to economic conditions and for being unable to explain gender divisions and power relations between men and women. Radical feminist theory has been criticized for its view that social classes are simply an epiphenomenon of gender inequality. Moreover, a major problem with radical feminist theory is that it assumes universal female subordination. Yet anthropological research has shown that in many hunting-and-gathering societies, gender relations were quite equal and men did not control the labor power and sexuality of women (Reiter, 1975; Shostak, 1983). Radical feminists have also been criticized for explaining male violence against women in biological terms or as simply a reflection of masculine power and dominance. Finally, the term *patriarchy*, which both radical and socialist feminists use to label masculine dominance, has been criticized for its timeless characterization of masculine power and prestige. In other words, neither radical nor socialist feminists have adequately accounted for historical changes in patriarchy and its various forms.

The second phase of feminist criminology is extremely promising, in particular because of its continuing critique of "malestream" criminology, its own theoretical diversity, its particular varieties of feminist research methodologies, and its welcome inclusion of the study of masculinities. But more importantly, second-phase feminist criminology embraces a social justice perspective that demands we respect diversity; reject male-centered biases; be thoughtful in what we study, how we study it, how our findings are presented, and the actions we recommend; understand the interconnections among gender, race, class, and age; and share criminological information with students, scholars, community members, practitioners, lawmakers, journalists, victims, people with criminal records, and advocates (Flavin and Desautels, 2006).

## 9.2 CRITICAL CRIMINOLOGIES

Critical criminology developed from the radical, conflict, and feminist criminologies of the 1960s, '70s, and '80s. It is also an umbrella term for several other perspectives that began to emerge in the mid- to late 1980s and that continue to develop and flourish today. Although these perspectives differ in significant ways—which we outline shortly—critical criminology tends commonly to reject the following (MacLean and Milovanovic, 1998):

- Usage of the legalistic definition of crime.
- Prevailing usages of linear, nondialectical notions of "causation."
- Correctional penal policy.
- The increasing investment of energy in more punitive responses to crime.
- The limited attention paid to political economy in the contribution to crime.
- The targeting of selected groups, informally or formally, for official police intervention.
- The resistance to entertaining (i.e., examining) gross inequalities in living standards, alienating working conditions, and dilapidated communities.
- The continued and often systematic practices of sexism, racism, and classism (and their

intersecting effects), often disguised as neutral and objective or factual categories.

Critical criminology is self-consciously committed to the making of theories that provide better avenues for understanding the difference between what is and what can be. It is always interested in the quest for positive social change and social justice. In this section we summarize the approaches of four critical criminologies: constitutive criminology; cultural criminology; critical humanist criminologies, including peacemaking criminology and convict criminology; and green criminology. We now look at each of these in turn.

## CONSTITUTIVE CRIMINOLOGY

At its most abstract level, **constitutive criminology** is a postmodernist reaction to the scientific rationalism and positivist certainty of the Enlightenment. It rejects scientific notions of "cause," just as it rejects the idea that crime is a simple or fixed category. Bruce Arrigo (2006; and see Henry and Einstadter, 1998; Henry and Lanier, 2006; and Henry and Lukas, 2009) has suggested that postmodern thought in criminology has three main characteristics:

1. *The centrality of language.* Written and spoken language shapes reality because it is the "source and product" of our social actions. Words define who we are, our interaction with others, and the institutions of society in which we participate. Language is not neutral but contains implicit values and hidden assumptions.
2. *Partial knowledge and provisional truth.* Because language structures thought and action in ways that are not neutral, the meanings of daily life are limited by the language in use. Inevitably, certain forms of understanding are devalued, and what is regarded as meaningful is always already incomplete. Thus, "truth" and "knowledge" are at best partial and provisional.
3. *Deconstruction, difference, and possibility.* As language filters the way people think, feel, and act in partial and provisional ways, there exists a degree of "undeniable relativity" to being human. Deconstruction is a postmodern method used to decode a written or spoken text and thereby unveil the implicit values and hidden assumptions embedded in particular narratives. Deconstruction reveals the privileging in certain contexts of particular "truth claims" and how others are dismissed or ignored. Postmodernists attempt to embrace articulated differences by highlighting all voices involved in any social interaction.

Constitutive criminology is a self-consciously political position that seeks to get behind or to lay bare the rhetoric, the dogma, and the mystification that goes into the public discourse about crime. In other words, constitutive criminology examines how crime is constituted by public discourse. For present purposes, we can strip away the complex philosophical and linguistic wrappings of their labors and reduce constitutive criminology to three major propositions.

First, crime is not simply what the criminal law says it is. Rather, crime is the ability or the power to impose one's will on others in any particular social context: Crimes "are nothing less than moments in the expression of power, such that those who are subjected to them are denied... their own humanity, the power to make a difference" (Henry and Milovanovic, 1996:116; and see Henry and Milovanovic, 1991, 1994, 2003; but see Cowling, 2006; S. Russell, 2006). Henry and Milovanovic thus redefine crime "in terms of the power to create harm (pain) in any context" (1996:118). This redefinition of crime identifies two major forms of harm: "harms of reduction," which occur "when an offended party experiences a loss of some quality relative to their present standing," and "harms of repression," which occur "when an offended party experiences a limit or restriction preventing them from achieving a desired position or standing" (p. 103).

Second, Henry and Milovanovic reject modernist notions of causality, arguing that crime is "discursively constructed through human processes" in which "people lose sight of the humanity and integrity of those with whom they interrelate and whom their actions and interactions affect" (1996:170, 175). The "psycho-socio-cultural matrix" provides the "discursive medium" through which individuals construct "meaningful harms to others" (p. x). In short, some individuals become "excessive investors" in the expression of power and control, resulting

in "thought processes which objectify others as separate, dehumanized entities" (p. 175).

Third, Henry and Milovanovic construct a policy for curbing crime. They argue that any human relationship that involves the actual or potential infliction of harm must be analyzed carefully in its discursive context, exposed, and restructured in nonharmful ways. Thus, their policy includes the development of alternative "replacement discourses" (primarily in the mass media) as well as "narrative therapies" in which excessive investors are assisted in developing "liberating life narratives" (1996:224).

## CULTURAL CRIMINOLOGY

The critical perspective known as **cultural criminology** first emerged in a collection of essays

**FIGURE 9.1** Base jumping off the New River Gorge Bridge, West Virginia
*Source*: Ferrell, Hayward, and Young (2008:167).

edited by Jeff Ferrell and Clint Sanders (1995; and see Ferrell, 2004, 2007; Ferrell, Hayward, Morrison, and Presdee, 2004; Ferrell and Hamm, 1998; Ferrell and Websdale, 1999; Presdee, 2000). One of the key themes of this collection, entitled *Cultural Criminology*, is the meaning and imagery of such diverse living-at-the-edge (*edgework*) practices as base jumping (see Figure 9.1), anti-abortion violence, fast motorcycle riding, binge drinking, and media and legal constructions of gender, drug dealing, graffiti, music, and fashion and style. The conceptual focus of edgework is the immediacy and the excitement of risk taking in a world dominated by the boredom and pointless drudgery of late modernity. Edgework finds patterns of power and excitement and harm in such diverse sites as urban back alleys, garbage dumps, walls and cliff tops, and corporate boardrooms (Lyng, 2005; Milovanovic, 2006; Williams, 2007).

A recent book in the emerging perspective of cultural criminology is Jeff Ferrell, Keith Hayward, and Jock Young's (2008) *Cultural Criminology: An Invitation*. Approaching the many themes of this book, one cannot miss the constant vehemence that its authors reserve for mainstream criminology (read "quantitative criminology" and "survey research"). In this view mainstream criminology is irrelevant, boring, lifeless, and navel-gazing. Against method! In particular, they direct their onslaught to the methods of survey research. In so doing they complain generally about the enforced need for young academics, driven by considerations of tenure and job security, to write numerous grant applications to undertake more and more quantitative research on matters of less and less significance. Nowadays, in the United States especially, it is true that the politics of college Institutional Review Boards (IRBs) make it almost impossible to do serious research with live human subjects, with the result that what is left to work with is a seemingly endless mass of demographic numbers totally devoid of thinking and feeling

humans. Imagine what would have happened to Howard Becker's famous participant observation research in the 1960s on marijuana use among college students (Section 6.4) if, instead, it was today rather than four decades ago that he was seeking IRB permission to get stoned with his subjects in order to discover how they learned to get high and what it meant to them! To take another example, would IRBs nowadays permit the sort of fascinating participant observation research of three decades ago on social interaction among nature lovers undertaken on nude beaches in La Jolla, California (Douglas and Rasmussen, 1977)? Probably not.

*Cultural Criminology: An Invitation* is an important book. It is provocative and challenging in its social criticism. It is intensely political. Its intellectual origins of cultural criminology are intentionally several and diverse. The authors (Ferrell, Hayward, and Young, 2008) travel backward and forward and include: (1) a return to the understanding of meanings in social interaction emphasized by 1960s phenomenology and some of the sociologists and social psychologists working in the labeling perspective (Section 6.4; see also Katz, 1988); (2) a return to the analysis of culture and subcultures initiated by Albert Cohen and others (Section 6.2); (3) a return to the Chicago school of criminology (of the 1918–1945 era). Get out of your armchair! Leave the library! Mix with real people! Embrace ethnography! (Section 6.1); and (4) an embrace of 1960s French situationism and the anarchism of Munich, 1918, and of Berkeley, London, and Paris in 1968. Smash the state! Thus: "[W]e seek to revitalize political critique in criminology, to create a contemporary criminology—a cultural criminology—that can confront systems of control and relations of power as they operate today" (p. 7).

One of the earliest scenarios in *Cultural Criminology: An Invitation* is a section entitled "Meaning in Motion: Bloody Knuckles." "Amidst

**BOX 9.2** THE AESTHETICS OF AUTHORITY

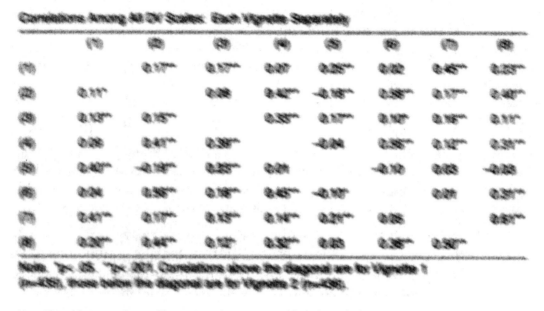

Note: This table is not only out of focus, it's made up. How would you know if others were made up? And what exactly does "made up" mean in the current criminological climate?

*Source*: Ferrell, Hayward, and Young (2008:170).

---

the cultural motion of late modernity," write Ferrell, Hayward, and Young (2008), "here's one movement you may not think of as cultural at all," namely,

> the quick, snapping trajectory of arm, elbow, and fist as a punch is thrown. That movement seems more a matter of bone and muscle than culture and meaning—and if that punch strikes somebody in the mouth, there are the bloody knuckles that are pulled back in the next motion. (p. 7)

The authors then suppose that perhaps someone reports this event to the police. Perhaps the punch-thrower ends up in jail, gets bailed out, or doesn't, gets convicted, or doesn't, and then returns to prison, or perhaps goes home. These are the everyday rhythms of skin and blood and criminal justice.

Further supposition: Was the person who got hit in the mouth a boyfriend? A girlfriend? A cop? A boxer in the ring? Whichever, each situation *means* something different to each of the actors involved. Still more: When did it happen? In the 1940s? In the 1940s domestic violence had not even been invented as a concept. Now? Both in the 1940s and today, in a sadly warped rationalization, men sometimes claim that "a swollen lip and bloody knuckles mean 'I love you'" (p. 8). But again: "maybe its not so much the bloody knuckles and the swollen lips as whose lips and knuckles they are, and who gets to decide what they mean" (p. 8.).

In a few sentences that set the tone of much of the rest of their book—of their cultural criminology—the authors then argue that the meaning of physical violence may stop and start but that its meaning is fluid and continues to circulate. Always the context of bloody knuckles and swollen lips is power and inequality. Sometimes, the sequence is bought and sold and offered as a televised pay-per-view show. Sometimes, in our globalized world, it is in the frontlines of terror, war, and ideology. If that is the case, then

> if we hope to confront the *politics* of violence—that is, to understand how violence works as a form of power and domination, to empathize with the victimization that violence produces—we must engage with the *cultures* of violence. Even this most direct of crimes...is not direct at all. It's a symbolic exchange as much as a physical one, an exchange encased in immediate situations and in larger circumstances, an exchange whose meaning is negotiated before and after the blood is spilt. (pp. 8–9)

One has, first of all, to read the pages of this giddy and rambling book to appreciate its originality and to understand why cultural criminology has drawn such a devoted following of late. Still more, one has to see *Cultural Criminology: An Invitation*, be seduced by its anarchic drawings and carnivalesque photos and its stirring list of recommended films at the end of each chapter. At times, its images and messages practically explode off the page. One almost expects the book to be sold with an accompanying music CD (Pink Floyd or gangsta rap, perhaps?).

A book that can be placed side by side with *Cultural Criminology* is *The Vertigo of Late Modernity* (henceforth, *Vertigo*), by Jock Young (2007). Though it is undoubtedly a big, bold book of critical criminology, it is rather a difficult work to classify. On the one hand, *Vertigo* is greatly influenced by Merton's concepts of anomie and social strain. Its scope, however, including throughout a concern for the highs and lows of late modernity and globalization, is even greater than that of the Mertonian tradition. On the other hand, in that its major intellectual and political points are interwoven with small-scale cultural encounters

and clashes that cry out for further ethnographic analysis (edgework, especially), it is also a book of cultural criminology.

> In a world where pleasure is increasingly commodified and control of one's life extremely limited: going to the edge and grasping control out of chaos can be both reassuring and immensely pleasurable....Armed robbery fits this bill, as does hard drug use, and even the more minor crimes of shoplifting and casual violence can have their satisfactions. (p. 57).

Though it is possible to open Young's book at random and begin reading at any page—rather like one can with the sociologist Erving Goffman's (1961b) book *Encounters*—its starting point, not unsurprisingly, is that of *vertigo*, which is

> the malaise of late modernity: a sense of insecurity, of insubstantiality, of uncertainty, a whiff of chaos and a fear of falling. The signs of giddiness, of unsteadiness, are everywhere, some serious, many minor; yet once acknowledged, a series of separate seemingly disparate facts begin to fall into place: the obsession with rules, an insistence on clear uncompromising lines of demarcation between correct and incorrect behavior, a narrowing of borders, the decreased tolerance of deviance, a disproportionate response to rule-breaking, an easy resort to punitiveness and a point at which simple punishment begins to verge on the vindictive (p. 12).

To simplify greatly, Young applies Robert Merton's notion of anomie to the new economic and cultural realities of globalization. During the 1950s and 1960s and prior to the last decade or so, Western societies were for the middle class comfortable and secure places: Their jobs were assured, as too were rising incomes and guarantees of provision for health, education, retirement, and so on. Cultural goals were mostly agreed on by most of the citizenry, even among those who are excluded from economic security. Identities were simple and largely uncontested. Tolerance was the rule rather than the exception, though

But in late modernity the forces of globalization are attacking this happy security with all the destructive power of a sledgehammer. Globalized turbo market capitalism ensures that many manufacturing jobs leave their original sites in the First World and are relocated in the more profitable Third World. In Western societies the widespread sense among the upper and middles classes of security and comfort is shattered and replaced by deep-seated anxieties, a precariousness of being, fractured identities, fragile families and weaker communities, and a widespread process of "othering" problem populations—especially drug users, sexual deviants, immigrants, the unemployed, and foreigners. Citizens of affluent countries are increasingly prone to vertigo—to a giddying fear of downward social mobility, a fear of falling. Thus, the American gulag: the mass incarceration of problem populations. Those in the Third World—who see the consumerist lives of affluent Westerners on TV—feel increasingly frustrated, humiliated, and angry with their lots in life. Thus, global jihad. "If there is one thing a critical criminology can tell us," Young (2007) writes, "it is how the experience of injustice can lead to further injustice" (p. 172).

> Nowadays we may talk of a "global Merton," a ubiquitous situation of anomie where widespread aspirations have been generated by the forces of globalization and where massive relative deprivation is engendered in the Third World, giving rise to a discontent which is unlikely to be allayed. For how conceivably can one justify on a meritocratic basis such disparities of income which occur merely because of the arbitrary factor of place of birth?...But it is not relative deprivation alone which foments discontent: The hubris of Western culture, its world dominance, challenges the tra-

> ditional and the local; the political and economic power of the First World sidelines and denigrates the "developing" nations. (p. 156)

The direction we are going looks bleak, and the traditional notions of family and community are being swept away by the juggernaut known as globalization. But Young (2007) ends his analysis of late modernity with questions about the politics of the future. Where are we headed? Is it toward a better sense of self-worth and greater equality within and among nations? Or is it, rather, toward something even worse and more worrisome than we have now?

By way of summary, there is no doubt that cultural criminology marks an innovative contribution to critical criminology. Strongly opposed to the quantitative methods of mainstream criminology, including survey research, cultural criminology instead emphasizes edgework, meaning, and the complex effects of globalization on everyday life.

### CRITICAL HUMANIST CRIMINOLOGIES

Under the umbrella of critical criminology are several perspectives that focus on humanizing the institutions of criminal justice. **Peacemaking criminology** is one tendency in this movement. Its eclectic theoretical basis lies in a flexible mixture of perspectives drawn from left realism (see Section 8.3), a reverence for nonviolence, humanism, feminism, and humanistic education. This combination is most visible in Harold Pepinsky and Richard Quinney's anthology *Criminology as Peacemaking* (1991b; and see Pepinsky, 2006; Sullivan, 2008). At the beginning of their book, Pepinsky and Quinney state:

> The peacemaking perspective is steadily making its way into criminology. In recent years there have been proposals and programs that foster mediation, conflict resolution, reconciliation, and community. They are part of an emerging criminology of peacemaking, a criminology that seeks

to alleviate suffering and thereby reduce crime. This is a criminology that is based necessarily on human transformation in the achievement of peace and justice. (p. ix)

The various authors of the twenty chapters in this anthology address a wide variety of practical issues that converge on the need to use more humane and more caring approaches to the problem of crime. Although all the authors seem to agree with other critical criminologists that it is economic, political, and social inequalities that foster crime, the emphasis here is less on the causes of crime than on how to resolve the conflicts of which crime is an expression. The key policies of peacemaking criminology thus involve such terms as *responsiveness, reconciliation, conflict resolution, harmony,* and *community.*

Some critical criminologists have expanded the peacemaking perspective. For example, Susan Caulfield and Angela Evans (1997) have argued that at its core "peacemaking has a reverence for life, for the connectedness of all beings" (p. 103). To help reduce human suffering, including the suffering that results from crime, Caulfield and Evans call for the criminal justice system to address the "essence," rather than the "appearance," of being human:

Much of criminology and criminal justice focuses on the appearance of a human being: what they did, ascriptive characteristics, and the like. Rarely is there concern with understanding the essence of a person: how they feel, what they fear, how they see themselves in reference to the universe. We surmise, as do others, that this avoidance of one's essence is a part of self-defense or self-denial on the part of both individuals and criminal justice....Knowing only the appearance, rather than the essence, of harm, how can criminal justice keep from being fragmented and in search of some form of control, no matter how illusory? (p. 105)

Similarly, Pepinsky (2006) has argued that peacemaking criminology allows for the construction of a compassionate discourse that will heal rifts in the social fabric and weave all societal members "back into accepted, responsible, safe social relations, rather than identifying, condemning, punishing, and separating offenders from the community." He concludes by urging the following:

Peacemaking, like the paradigm of making war on crime and criminality, is an attitude. The attitude of peacemaking keeps arising in my mind and soul in the words of a song David Mallett wrote in 1975: "Inch by inch, row by row, I'm gonna make this garden grow./ All it takes is a rake and a hoe and a piece of fertile ground." Let's go for it. (p. 192)

Quinney (1997) has maintained that current responses to crime by the criminal justice system are a form of "negative peace." That is, the purpose of the criminal justice system is to deter or process acts of crime through the threat and application of force. Thus the criminal justice system's response to crime is a form of violence in itself, which subsequently begets further violence. Quinney therefore views peacemaking criminology as part of the movement toward "positive peace," which exists when the sources of crime—such as poverty, inequality, racism, and alienation—are no longer present. As Quinney concludes:

There can be no peace—no positive peace—without social justice. Without social justice and without peace (personal and social), there is crime. And there is, as well, the violence of criminal justice....Criminal justice keeps things as they are. Social policies and programs that are positive in nature—that focus on positive peacemaking—create something new. They eliminate the structural sources of violence and crime. A critical, peacemaking criminologist is engaged in the work of positive peace. (p. 117)

John Fuller (1998, 2003) has developed what he terms a "Peacemaking Pyramid Paradigm" as a first step toward a more coherent peacemaking theory. This pyramid involves six stages that should be considered when constructing solutions to criminal justice system problems:

1. *Nonviolence.* Peacemaking criminology argues against state violence as a criminal justice policy, such as use of the death penalty.
2. *Social justice.* Peacemaking criminology opposes any form of racism, sexism, and classism in the criminal justice system, such as racial profiling.
3. *Inclusion.* The criminal justice system must be all-inclusive of community members, such as allowing a voice by family members of victims and offenders as well as other interested individuals from affected neighborhoods.
4. *Correct means.* It should be ensured that offenders and victims are not coerced into settlement of their cases—due process must be preserved.
5. *Ascertainable criteria.* It should be ensured that all parties involved in criminal justice proceedings understand the procedures, including clearly written legal guidelines.
6. *Categorical imperative.* Responses to crime should reflect a philosophy of nonviolence and social justice that is extended throughout the criminal justice system. All involved in the criminal justice process must be treated with respect and dignity.

A second movement within critical humanist criminology is **convict criminology.** Most of this perspective's adherents are ex-convicts who have become sociologists and criminologists. Convict criminology's starting point is the awesome size of the prison system in the United States and the misery that goes with it. Its humanist and ameliorative promise is to "tell it like it is" from the inside in ways that are not available to those who have never been incarcerated. A good example of

convict criminology at work is Stephen Richards' (2008a; and see Richards, 2008b) account of the horrendous conditions at the first federal supermax prison, the U.S. Penitentiary in Marion, Illinois. He documents how the high-security detention confinement at Marion has routinely and violently inflicted physical and psychic harm on inmates there.

A combination of diversity in perspective and leftist politics also lies at the heart of several other humanist tendencies in critical criminology. Among these are abolitionism, anarchism and restorative justice.

- **Abolitionism.** The perspective of **abolitionism** focuses on the oppressive and faulty logic of incarceration as a solution to the problem of crime. Here, prison and many other institutions of social control are typically seen not as a solution but as key parts of the problem. The classic abolitionist text is Willem de Haan's (1990) *The Politics of Redress: Crime, Punishment, and Penal Abolition.*
- **Anarchism.** Anarchist approaches focus on the state, its agencies and institutions, as the primary source of most social ills, including crime. Particular objects of attack include the state machinery of prisons, police, courts, judges, and lawyers (for example, see Ferrell, 1997; Tifft and Sullivan, 2006).
- **Restorative justice.** "Reintegrative" or "constructive" shaming is the central tactical mechanism in the movement of **restorative justice,** which began in New Zealand and Australia and which is based on conferencing with victims and offenders (Braithwaite, 1989; and see Daly, 2002). During conferences offenders are confronted by their victims and by their victims' friends and families in an effort to help them understand the harm they have caused others through their wrongful actions or omissions. At the same time, victims are encouraged not to see offenders as vile and fixed objects of

punitiveness but to understand them as existing somewhere between authentic beings and beings with damaged identities who likely did what they did because of sociological and psychological circumstances over which they had little or no control. Whether the process of reintegrative shaming succeeds and, if so, at what psychic costs is an open question (Gadd and Jefferson, 2007:163–181).

## GREEN CRIMINOLOGY

Criminology has been slow to recognize the finite nature of the Earth's resources and how overexploitation and abuse generate new problems of criminological concern (conflict, corruption, lawbreaking, rule-avoidance, manslaughter and murder, and so on). The most recent addition to critical criminology is therefore a green perspective on the environment, on humanity, and on animals other than humans (henceforth, "animals").

For **green criminology** the starting point of analysis is a reappraisal of traditional notions of crimes, offenses, and injurious behavior; it then proceeds to examine the role played by human societies, including corporations and governments, in generating harms to the environment of planet Earth and to all species who live and breathe in it (Beirne, 2009; Beirne and South, 2007; Carrabine, Cox, Lee, Plummer, and South, 2009:313–330; M. Lynch, 1990; South and Beirne, 2006; White, 2008).

According to green criminologists, there are at least four major sites of green harms (and see Beirne and South, 2009): (1) global warming and air pollution; (2) deforestation and other environmental harms; (3) water pollution; and (4) harms against animals other than humans. We now outline each of these in turn.

**1. Global warming and air pollution.** The burning of fossil fuels by automobiles and to generate electricity in factories and in residential homes releases about 6 billion tons of carbon into the air each year, adding about 3 billion

tons annually to the 170 billion tons that have settled there since the industrial revolution. The rate of growth in carbon emissions is around 2 percent per year. The people who commit these harms here may be those who ignore laws, regulations, and international treaties and controls, contributing to or causing global warming pollution of the air. Here, potential criminals are governments and big business as well as consumers.

According to a report in 2008 by the Intergovernmental Panel on Climate Change (IPCC), the evidence for warming of the climate system is unequivocal, as is evidence about increases in global average air and ocean temperatures, widespread melting of snow and ice, and rising global average sea levels (IPCC, 2008:2). Indeed, 11 of the last 12 years (1995–2006) are among the 12 warmest years since the beginning of instrumental records of the global environment (see Figure 9.2).

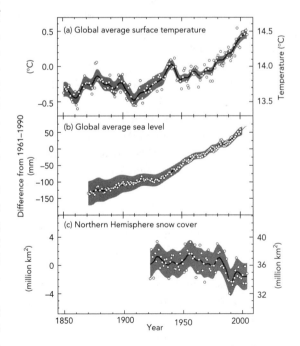

**FIGURE 9.2** Changes in Temperature, Sea Level, and Northern Hemisphere Snow Cover, 1850–2007
*Source*: Intergovernmental Panel on Climate Change (2008).

According to the IPCC, human activities in the Arctic (such as the Inuit's ability to hunt and travel over snow and ice) have been adversely affected by temperature increases. What are the causes of these increases? According to the IPCC, at a very high level of confidence the major cause of temperature increase is human-induced greenhouse gases, produced above all by the increased use of fossil fuels. The Inuit complain, among other things, that the United States government has committed crimes and human rights violations against them because they—especially, the U.S. Department of Environmental Protection—have failed to curtail the growth of carbon emissions in greenhouse gases.

**2. Deforestation and other environmental harms.** Since the seventeenth century, much of the world has become increasingly urbanized. Between 1960 and 1990 about 20 percent of the world's tropical forest was lost. New crimes and criminals here would include those who deal in the destruction of rain forests and other natural habitats with little regard for environmental impact; those who exploit natural resources for their own ends; and illicit markets that develop around the sale of many of these valuable commodities.

The extent and financial cost of some of the major forms of environmental and ecological harms are staggering. One estimate is given in an editorial in *Environmental Health Perspectives* (2004:A80):

> As far as we know, the total value of the major forms of international environmental crime—illegal logging and fishing, illegal trade in wildlife and in ozone-depleting substances, and illegal dumping in hazardous waste—may be on the order of $20 billion to 40 billion a year, about 5–10 percent of the size of the global drug trade. Compared to the "war on drugs," however, the resources and political will that are being devoted to tackling the problems of international environmental crime

are derisory; yet, also unlike the drug trade, they threaten every citizen of the world.

A concept that unifies a now considerable body of work in green criminology is the idea of justice: justice for tiny planet Earth, for the environment, for the biosphere, and for animals other than humans (Beirne, 2009; Benton, 2007; White, 2008; Lynch and Stretesky, 2007). Many studies have drawn attention to the environmental victimization of communities of the poor and powerless due to the frequency with which their locations are also the sites of polluting industry, for instance, and of waste processing plants or other environmentally hazardous facilities. One author has argued, in addition, that women are at greater risk of male violence in the wake of climate change (Wachholz, 2007). Environmental injustices also include cases where local, indigenous populations have been forcibly removed from land to which they are spiritually attached or where their land has been exploited for military, agribusiness, or other purposes in circumstances depriving them of any control or say. Usually, the consequences are damaging, if not devastating, and lead to community dislocation, relationship breakdowns, mental health and substance misuse problems, among numerous other harms. Hence, White (2008:38) usefully suggests that green constructions of justice involve both environmental and ecological rights and also species' rights.

**3. Water pollution.** Some 25 million people die every year from consuming contaminated drinking water. Oceans are polluted and the ecosystems of coral reefs and freshwater rivers are under threat. Oil pollution is an excellent example of a high-profile and enormously damaging problem that ought to have been reduced to a rare risk by the start of the twenty-first century. Yet such is the power of the vested interests and the dependence of the global economy on oil that, "since the notorious *Exxon Valdez* incident in Alaska's Prince William Sound in 1989, at least 1.1 million tons of oil have spilled worldwide—equivalent to some 30 Valdez accidents" (Carrabine, Iganski and Lee,. 2004:318).

**4. Harms against animals other than humans.** Though criminology has been very slow to confront **animal abuse**, there is nonetheless a growing body of work that addresses it. The increased visibility of animals in criminology reflects a number of factors, the most important of which is the animal rights movement. The theoretical heart of this movement began with the writings of a small group of moral philosophers, among which by far the most influential are Peter Singer's (1975) *Animal Liberation* and Tom Regan's (1983) *The Case for Animal Rights.* Their chief goal has been the elimination of **speciesism**, namely, those practices and ideologies that promote the satisfaction of human interests at the expense of animals and, largely through the vehicles of utilitarianism and liberal-rights theory, the creation of a nonspeciesist discourse that might more justly govern our relationships with animals. Side by side with these founding philosophical statements are pioneering feminist contributions, especially the writings of Carol Adams and Josephine Donovan (e.g., Adams and Donovan, 1995).

In those cases where the animal rights movement has managed to enlist public opinion to influence legislatures—in the United States, in the U.K., and in other western European societies and in Canada, Australia, New Zealand, and elsewhere—pro-animal gains seem to have been impressive. The most obvious pro-animal legislative protections include the regulation of conditions in agribusiness (mass production of animals for food and clothing in stockyards and slaughterhouses), in scientific and commercial laboratory experimentation on animals, and in zoos and aquaria. Other positive developments range from the protection of endangered exotic species, especially popular species such as whales, eagles, and wolves, to a greater concern with diet—less meat and more grains, vegetables, and fruit, and with what not to wear—less animal products such as fur and leather.

Animal rights theorists and others have shown that animal abuse takes numerous forms. Animals are first and foremost abused by the speciesist language we humans use to refer to them. *Speciesist language* we define as utterances that express a prejudice or an attitude of bias in favor of one's own species and against those of members of other species. Historically, the distinction between *Homo sapiens* and animals carries with it a heavy cultural baggage. Implicitly, it tends to be voiced as if humans were somehow not animals and as if all animals other than humans were insapient ("dumb animals"). At root, the distinction is based on the prejudice that nonhuman animals are necessarily the Other. Indeed, the earliest-known use of the word *animal* referred to diabolical or inferior traits typically associated with the Devil, with the Antichrist, and with feral animals.

The often-violent images and metaphors of speciesist language are filled with implicit

---

**BOX 9.3  APPROACHING ANIMAL ABUSE**

Animal abuse typically refers to those diverse human actions that contribute to the pain, suffering, or death of animals or that otherwise adversely affect their welfare. Animal abuse may be physical, psychological, or emotional. It may involve active maltreatment or passive neglect and may be direct or indirect. Sometimes, of course, animals are harmed when their environments are degraded through the sheer chaos wrought by natural disasters such as earthquakes, hurricanes, and tsunamis or through human-induced causes such as wars, climate change, oil spills, and road construction. (See further Cazaux and Beirne, 2001) declarations about how worthwhile lives differ from lives with little or no intrinsic value. Speciesism and sexism clearly often operate together and in tandem, with women and animals depicted as objects to be controlled, manipulated, and exploited. Thus, when men describe women as "cows," "bitches," "(dumb) bunnies," "birds," "chicks," "foxes," or "fresh meat" and their genitalia as other species, they use derogatory language essentially to relegate both women and animals to the inferior statuses of "less than male" and, even, "less than human." Some forms of speciesist language are seemingly more subtle. *Fisheries*, for example, refers not to an objective reality but to diverse species that are acted on as objects of commodification by humans and, as such, trapped or otherwise "harvested," killed, and consumed. The same sort of egregious misdescription appears in many other categories as well, including *laboratory animals* (instead of *animals used in laboratories*), *pets, circus animals, racehorses*, and so on.

In the same way that we nowadays use language that is neutral with respect to gender, race, age, and physical and mental disability, for example, so we need to develop an awareness of speciesist language. Clearly, radical revision of speciesist language is long overdue. In some cases, new descriptions altogether are needed—for example, *animal sexual assault* for *bestiality*, and *theriocide* for the *killing of animals by humans*.

Humans harm animals in numerous ways (in Section 12.2 we will look in particular at animal abuse within families and then examine in some detail animal sexual assault). Sometimes the infliction of abuse is unintentional; at other times it results from ignorance or inattention to animals' needs. There is, too, almost certainly, a strong association between those who abuse animals as children—or those who witness their parents or guardians abusing animals—and those who grow up subsequently to abuse humans (but

see Beirne, 2009:Ch. 5). Perhaps this association or ("progression") can be explained by social learning theory. Perhaps it can be explained by some psychosocial insight into how in at-risk situations some children and adolescents are unable to retain or to develop a sense of compassion for their fellow creatures.

One-on-one cases of individual cruelty certainly command our attention, and deservedly so. But, depending on one's viewpoint of whether animals are persons who should or should not be eaten, then we must stress that by far the greatest amount of animal abuse occurs not in families but in institutional contexts, where animal abuse is widespread, invisible, and often defined as socially acceptable. Indeed, by the time you finish reading this page roughly 8,000 animals will have been slaughtered for human consumption. Consider, too, what the psychosocial effects of their daily work might be on those who work in laboratories that practice vivisection or on those who labor in zoos, circuses, and the like. Although the empirical evidence here is very difficult to obtain, the psychological toll on this group of victims is graphically uncovered in Gail Eisnitz's *Slaughterhouse* (2007). A slaughterhouse worker interviewed by Eisnitz—"Van Winkle"—believed that "it was not uncommon" for slaughterhouse workers to be arrested for having assaulted humans. Describing the mental attitude developed from *sticking* hogs (i.e., slitting hogs' throats in the often-botched attempt to kill them), he divulged that

> The worst thing, worse than the physical danger, is the emotional toll. If you work in that stick pit for any period of time, you develop an attitude that lets you kill things but doesn't let you care. You may look a hog in the eye that's walking around down in the blood pit with you and think, God, that really isn't a bad-looking animal. You may want to pet it. Pigs down on the kill floor have come up and nuzzled me like a puppy. Two minutes

later I had to kill them—beat them to death with a pipe. I can't care. (Eisnitz, 2007:87)

Van Winkle continued:

I've had ideas of hanging my foreman upside down on the line and sticking him. I remember going into the office and telling the personnel man I have no problem pulling the trigger on a person— if you get in my face I'll blow you away.... Every sticker I know carries a gun, and every one of them would shoot you. Most stickers I know have been arrested for assault. A lot of them have problems with alcohol. They have to drink; they have no other way of killing live, kicking animals all day long. (p. 88)

We can conclude this section on green criminology by noting that many issues here are intertwined. Some issues centrally concern both the environment and animals at the same time, among which the most important is probably the production and consumption of beef. As Dale Jamieson has rightly complained:

The addiction to beef that is characteristic of people in the industrialized countries is not only a moral atrocity for animals but also causes health problems for consumers, reduces grain supplies for the poor, precipitates social divisions in developing countries, contributes to climate change, leads to the conversion of forests to pasture lands, is a causal factor in overgrazing, and is implicated in the destruction of native plants and animals. (2003:46)

## EVALUATION OF CRITICAL CRIMINOLOGIES

In this section we have outlined four perspectives in critical criminology: constitutive criminology, cultural criminology, critical humanist criminology, and green criminology. There is considerable overlap in the concerns of each of these critical criminologies. All four are united, for example, by their opposition to the inequalities generated by many of society's master institutions.

Constitutive criminology, which has been quite influential in the development of other critical criminology perspectives, seems somewhat to have run its course of late. Undoubtedly, it poses a challenge to modernist criminology, especially in respect of the latter's concentration on the scientific study of crime and social control. However, important questions remain about the texts of constitutive criminology: Has it simply replaced a modernist truth with a postmodernist one? From a postmodernist stance, constitutive criminology is one among many discourses that declare that it frames the "true" picture of crime, How, then, is constitutive criminology somehow excluded from this self-interestedness?

Cultural criminology has bloomed in the past decade and has acquired a considerable following. Especially in the form of Ferrell, Hayward, and Young's (2008) *Cultural Criminology: An Invitation* and Young's (2007) *The Vertigo of Late Modernity*, it is an exciting and innovative contribution to critical criminology. With its self-stated dismissal of the stale methods of mainstream criminology, cultural criminology instead emphasizes edgework, meaning, and the complex effects of globalization on everyday life. By some feminists it has been accused—rather unfairly—of concentrating on activities (e.g., base jumping) that are most often only available to young white males. Moreover, some fellow travelers in the critical criminology community have accused cultural criminology of ignoring the effects of capitalism's master institutions on the degradation of the lives of the poor and of minorities. We expect the flowers of cultural criminology to continue to blossom. Whether its disavowal of a coherent focus is a refreshing blessing or will turn out to be a curse, the future alone will tell.

Critical humanist criminology has attempted to sensitize the discipline to the importance of more humane and more caring approaches to the criminal justice system. This is as true for peacemaking criminology as it is for convict criminology. Perhaps both are less critical criminologies, as such, than they are critical approaches to the criminal justice system. Though laudable in their ideologies, neither peacemaking criminology nor convict criminology has as yet offered a blueprint for achieving a humanistic criminal justice system. Perhaps the very term *humanistic criminal justice system* is an oxymoron. How, given the widespread presence of deep-seated inequalities in the United States, does society move from a criminal justice system based on repression to one that concentrates on cooperation, compassion, and respect?

This section also briefly referred to abolitionism, to anarchist criminology, and to the restorative justice movement. Like other forms of critical humanist criminology, these offer valuable insights on the many problems of criminal justice institutions, though it is unclear quite what they contribute to the study of crime. In recent years, it must be said, both abolitionist and anarchist tendencies have largely disappeared as entities in their own right—though they continue to exert an important influence on and within cultural criminology and restorative justice.

Green criminology is the newest member of the community of critical criminologies. Like all other critical criminologies, it begins its analysis with a rejection of state-defined notions of harm ("crimes"). Green criminology combines the theoretical and political insights of two social movements, namely, the leftist-liberal environmental movement and the animal rights movement. Criminology has been notoriously slow to address either environmental questions or speciesism. The four constituent parts of green criminology are the study of (1) global warming and air pollution; (2) deforestation and other environmental harms; (3) water pollution; and (4) harms against animals other than humans. Can green criminology, as it is now constituted, survive the schisms and splits that have plagued both the environmental and the animal rights movements? Time will tell.

## REVIEW

In this chapter we have introduced a variety of criminological theories that have been developed in the last decade. Each will no doubt be developed further in the next decade. Several of these theories embody a movement toward general and integrated theory, yet they are remarkably diverse in their basic assumptions about human sociality and the causes of crime.

### FEMINIST CRIMINOLOGIES

1. In its first phase, feminist criminology developed four major perspectives in the 1970s and 1980s—liberal, Marxist, radical, and socialist. Each feminist perspective looks at gender relationships in a distinct way, asks different questions, and explains crime differently.
2. In the second phase of feminist contributions to criminology, two specific directions of theorizing have occurred: the exploration of women's and men's actual lives and an examination of how women and men are constructed in and by discourse. In addition, feminist criminologists have begun to examine the variable relationship among masculinities, femininities, men, women, and crime.

### CRITICAL CRIMINOLOGIES

This section outlined the differing contributions to critical criminology of constitutive criminology, cultural criminology, critical humanist criminology, and green criminology.

In combination these criminologies reject state definitions of crime and conventional policies for curbing crime and other social harms. They attempt, too, to humanize the institutions of criminal justice by emphasizing cooperation, compassion, and community among humans and across species lines rather than mass incarceration, punishment, condemnation, and exclusion.

## QUESTIONS FOR CLASS DISCUSSION

1. Choose several crimes, and discuss how, respectively, the four feminist perspectives (of the first phase of feminist criminology) explain them.
2. Discuss possible masculinities by women and femininities by men that may be related to crime.
3. "What if you only had space to leave a hundred words on a hacked criminal justice website? What if you only had 15 minutes to speak at a criminology conference? What would you say?" (Ferrell, Hayward and Young, 2008:204). Well, what would you write and say?
4. Is a "Peacemaking Pyramid" actually possible in Western industrialized societies?
5. Consider the plight of 155,000 Arctic Inuit, whose six indigenous groups inhabit the northernmost parts of Canada, Denmark, Finland, Iceland, Norway, Russia, Sweden, and the United States. In 2005 the Inuit sought a ruling—and in late 2009 were still seeking it—against the U.S. government from the Inter-American Commission on Human Rights. In their suit the Inuit claimed that, because it tolerated heat-trapping smokestacks and automobile exhaust emissions, which directly cause global warming, the melting of the Arctic ice cap, and environmental degradation, the United States has been contributing not only to the deaths of individual Inuit but also to the possible extinction of their culture. With a considerable body of scientific evidence to support them, the Inuit further complain that rising temperatures, disappearing glaciers and ice caps, and wind-borne toxic pollution have adversely affected the health of Arctic seals and of the Inuit who regularly eat them. Seal hunting, it should be added, the Inuit see as an essential part of their culture and traditions and, indeed, of their physical survival.

   In the preceding paragraph, what harms (or crimes) have been committed, by whom, and against whom?
6. Why are some harms to animals defined as criminal, others as abusive but not criminal, and still others as neither criminal nor abusive? Illustrate each possibility with several examples.

## FOR FURTHER STUDY

### READINGS

Beirne, Piers. 2009. *Confronting Animal Abuse: Law, Criminology, and Human-Animal Relationships.* Lanham, MD: Rowman & Littlefield.

DeKeseredy, Walter S., and Barbara Perry. 2006. *Advancing Critical Criminology: Theory and Application*: Lanham, MD: Lexington Books.

Ferrell, Jeff, Keith Hayward, and Jock Young. 2008. *Cultural Criminology: An Invitation*. Los Angeles: Sage

Renzetti, Claire. 2009. *Feminist Criminology*. New York: Routledge.

Tomsen, Stephen, ed. 2008. *Crime, Criminal Justice, and Masculinities*. Burlington, VT: Ashgate.

White, Rob. 2008. *Crimes Against Nature: Environmental Criminology and Ecological Justice*. Uffculme, Devon, UK: Willan

Young, Jock. 2007. *The Vertigo of Late Modernity*. Los Angeles: Sage.

## WEBSITES

1. <http://www.asc41.com/dir4/>: This is the site of the Division on Women and Crime in the American Society of Criminology. The Division promotes research and theory development that enhances the links among gender, crime, and justice.

2. <http://www.critcrim.org/>: This is the website for the American Society of Criminology (ASC) Division on Critical Criminology and contains a newsletter of summary essays about radical and feminist criminological perspectives.

3. <http://www.albany.edu/scj/jcjpc/index.html>: The *Journal of Criminal Justice and Popular Culture* is available at this website and provides full access to its peer-reviewed articles, many of which discuss how offenders are portrayed in the mass media and how this portrayal relates to their age, gender, race, or ethnicity.

4. <http://www.culturalcriminology.org>: This is the website of the Cultural Criminology team at the University of Kent, U.K. Its aim is to provide a general introductory resource for those interested in cultural criminology.

5. <http://www.cas.usf.edu/criminology/ccjcorpcrime.htm>: This University of South Florida website provides links to the major agencies in the United States responsible for corporate behavior in a number of fields, including the environment, occupational health and safety, consumer protection, and food and health.

6. <http://www.peta.org>: This is the website of the activist organization People for the Ethical Treatment of Animals. Many of the videos available at this site are extremely graphic. Be warned!

# INEQUALITIES AND CRIME

# INEQUALITY, CRIME, AND VICTIMIZATION

**PREVIEW**

Chapter 10 introduces:
- Social inequality and its relation to crime.
- How social position both permits and prevents criminal opportunity.
- Patterns of crime and victimization in the United States.

**KEY TERMS**

| | |
|---|---|
| age | social class |
| gender | social inequality |
| race | social position |

As emphasized in Chapter 1, crime is a sociological problem. To understand the varieties of crime, then, it is essential to establish their sociological context—how crime is shaped by the social factors of society. Accordingly, in this chapter we discuss the considerable sociological research that is necessary to grasp the patterns of crime in the United States.

The chief social factor underlying crime is structured **social inequality**. All industrialized societies are marked by social inequalities. Critical aspects of life—such as economic benefits, life chances, social privileges, and political power—are intimately connected to the social inequalities that structure society. Inequality is a sociological question, a product of human history.

At least four major forms of inequality influence crime: class, gender, race, and age. These inequalities create different life experiences for people, depending on their class, gender, race, and age characteristics, and they also shape patterns of crime and victimization. In other words, criminal opportunities and victimization are intimately related to social position in the class, gender, race, and age hierarchies of society. **Social position** thus refers to one's individual location in society based on the social characteristics of class, gender, race, and age.

Some scholars try to explain why one individual commits crime and another individual in the same social position does not. Although this is an intriguing question, our focus is on explaining sociological patterns of crime. Why do members of one class disproportionately commit a certain type of crime? Why do men commit more crimes than women? To answer such questions we must analyze those inequalities in the social structures that shape our lives. Social position—in terms of class, gender, race, and age—influences, limits, and structures human behavior, whether that behavior is legal or illegal, harmful or safe. Social position permits and precludes criminal opportunities. The patterns of crime therefore reflect the broader inequalities embedded in society.

In this chapter, for analytical purposes, we discuss class, gender, race, and age separately. However, in the real world, social inequalities are interrelated. As participating members of society, all of us have simultaneously class, gender, race, and age social positions. All four positions interact to structure society and its accompanying patterns of crime and victimization. In what follows, our discussion is limited to an examination of why and how general patterns of crime and victimization occur in the United States.

## 10.1 CLASS AND CRIME

In the United States sharp class divisions exist, and inequalities structure the patterns of crime and victimization. Although class position is associated with level of income, occupation, and education, it is determined chiefly by the way in which the production system of a society is organized. Historically, societies have organized production in different ways, which in turn has created different types of social classes. Class, then, is an important sociological concept for understanding patterns of crime. We define a **social class** as a group of people who share the same position in the same economic system. Class influences both economic relationships and economic inequalities as well as the *type* and *seriousness* of crime.

### PATTERNS OF CRIME AND VICTIMIZATION

The Uniform Crime Reports do not rank the crime rates for various social classes. However, over 25 years ago John Braithwaite (1981) reviewed a significant number of studies that used official statistics to generate data on the relationship between class and crime, and he concluded that they all "showed lower-class juveniles to have substantially higher offense rates than middle-class juveniles. Among adults, all... studies found lower-class people to have higher crime rates" (p. 38). Moreover, Braithwaite's earlier review (1979b) of nearly 300 studies based on official statistics *and* self-reports concluded that

1. Lower-class adults commit those types of crime handled by the police (conventional crimes) at a higher rate than middle-class adults do.
2. Adults living in lower-class areas commit those types of crime handled by the police at a higher rate than adults living in middle-class areas.
3. Lower-class juveniles commit crime at a higher rate than middle-class juveniles.
4. Juveniles living in lower-class areas commit crime at a higher rate than juveniles living in middle-class areas.

Regarding specific offense types, self-report studies indicate that class differences exist for both serious property crime and interpersonal crimes of violence. A delinquency study by Elliott and Huizinga (1983) is of particular importance because it analyzed both the percentage of a social class committing certain offenses at a specific time (*prevalence*) and the frequency with which these class members commit crimes (*incidence*). For status offenses and general delinquency, class differentials in prevalence were practically nonexistent. Elliott and Huizinga did, however, find significant class differentials for youth in the serious conventional crimes: Middle-class youths were far less likely to report committing such crimes than lower- and working-class youths were. Regarding incidence, the same pattern held: Both male and female middle-class youth were much less likely than other youths to report committing serious crimes.

More recent studies confirm the conclusions just outlined. For example, in a study of high school students, it was found that violent offenses and more public forms of youth crime were relatively high among lower-class students (mostly boys), whereas covert types of youth crime were high among middle- and upper-class students (Gutierrez and Shoemaker, 2008).

But conventional crimes are only one aspect of the entire range of crimes. Unfortunately, criminological studies of class and crime have concentrated on class differences in conventional crimes, ignoring white-collar and political crimes. Although poor and working-class people may commit the more serious conventional crimes handled by the police, members of the professional-managerial class (traditionally seen as the middle class) have greater opportunities to commit white-collar and political crimes. In fact, when we consider this class/crime link, it is clear that the vast bulk of avoidable harm and economic loss originates from the professional-managerial class. Consequently, the *type* and *seriousness* of crime are associated with social class position: Conventional crimes tend to be committed more often by the poor and working classes; white-collar and political crimes tend to be committed more often by the professional-managerial class.

The National Crime Victimization Survey provides information on victimization and in so doing helps us understand the *intra-* and *inter-class* nature of conventional crimes. For rape, robbery, assault, and purse snatching/pocket-picking in 2007, the NCVS data show that the lower the family income, the greater the chance of victimization. The most frequent victims of such crimes were those with an annual family income of less than $15,000. We can conclude that such crimes tend to be *intraclass*: Both the *offenders* and the *victims* are usually members of the same class.

Moreover, according to the NCVS for 2007, the victimization rates for the category termed *property crimes*—household burglary, motor vehicle theft, and theft—show a different pattern: Household burglary victimization declines with annual family income; motor vehicle theft victimization remains relatively stable between incomes of $15,000 and $35,000; and theft victimization remains relatively stable throughout all income levels (Department of Justice, 2008).

With the exception of theft and motor vehicle theft, conventional crime victimization is therefore an intraclass phenomenon. In other words, the poor tend to victimize the poor, but they are *also* more susceptible to syndicated, corporate, and political crime victimization. Consequently, the poor face crime from all directions.

In Chapter 2 we outlined some longitudinal data sets with which criminologists are trying to determine why some offenders continue to offend while others desist from doing so. On the other side of this equation, research has been conducted to determine why some victims are repeatedly victimized and others are not (Farrell and Pease, 2001; Tseloni and Pease, 2003). Using data in the National Crime Victimization Survey, these authors have identified two factors that are crucial in repeat victimizations. One is what they term *event dependence*, in which an initial victimization increases the probability of subsequent victimizations. Simply, offenders are more likely to prey on victims if they have already successfully victimized them. The other is *heterogeneity*, by which they mean that some households are more likely to be victimized irrespective of their past history of victimization. The victimization-prone households are characterized by factors related to gender, race, age, marital status, lone parenthood, educational level, employment status, and length of residence. But they also include lifestyle indicators, such as patterns of shopping and evenings outside the home. Using cross-national data, other researchers have found that residence in large cities in developing countries is also an important factor in repeat victimization (van Dijk, van Kesteren, and Smit, 2007; van Dijk, 2008).

Let us now consider theory and research on class and crime.

## CLASS AND VARIETIES OF CRIME

Unequal class relationships help explain the class patterns of crime and victimization in the United States. Regarding the conventional crimes handled by the police, research has shown that economic conditions associated with the poor and working classes—in particular, unemployment and income inequality—play a significant role in the perpetuation of these crimes. Notwithstanding the inconsistencies in research on the relationship between unemployment and conventional crime, the majority of studies report a link between the two. M. Harvey Brenner's (1976) pioneering work in the 1970s, for instance, found that when the unemployment rate increased 1 percentage point, a corresponding 4 percent increase occurred in homicides and a 6 percent increase occurred in robberies.

In the 1980s, research again uncovered a link between unemployment and conventional crime. James DeFronzo's (1983) study of thirty-nine U.S. metropolitan areas found that "unemployment rates had statistically significant positive effects on rape, burglary, and larceny" (p. 128). Thornberry and Christenson (1984) investigated the employment history of 1,000 boys born in 1945 and related this to the boys' involvement in conventional criminality. They concluded that "unemployment has significant instantaneous effects on crime" (p. 408). In other words, crime seems to follow the onset of unemployment.

Cook and Zarkin (1985) investigated the business cycle and its relationship to conventional crime from 1933 to 1980. They concluded that "an increase in the unemployment rate from, say, 7 percent to 8 percent will result in a 2.3 percent increase in the robbery rate and a 1.6 percent increase in the burglary rate" (p. 126). More recent studies have shown a positive and significant relationship between unemployment and conventional crime (Carlson and Michalowski, 1997; Shihadeh and Ousey, 1998;

Gould, Weinberg, and Mustard, 2002; Oster and Agell, 2007). Consequently, when large numbers of people are unemployed, there appears to be an increase in the conventional crime rate.

In addition to the foregoing, some studies examining the relationship between unemployment and crime suggest that although unemployment increases the *motivations* for crime, it may simultaneously decrease the actual *opportunities* to offend (Britt, 1997; Elliott and Ellingsworth, 1997). That is, unemployment increases the incentive to engage in crime, yet because of the downturn in the economy, fewer concrete targets of crime exist. However, Kleck and Chiricos (2002), in the most rigorous study to date, show that "opportunity levels" are specifically unrelated to property crime rates and, therefore, do not mediate the relationship between unemployment and crime.

Given the correlation between unemployment and conventional crime, we cannot forget that other characteristics—such as gender and age—play an equally significant role in the patterning of conventional crime. Indeed, as we discuss later in this chapter, both the elderly and women have high unemployment rates yet do not commit conventional crimes at the rate, for instance, that young males do. Consequently, gender and age mediate the unemployment/crime association.

In addition to unemployment, income inequality significantly affects conventional crime. Braithwaite's (1979b) study of 193 U.S. metropolitan areas found "strong and consistent support for the hypothesis that cities in which there is a wide income gap between poor and average-income families have high rates for all types of crime" (p. 216). Jacobs (1981) studied property crimes and income inequality in some 200 cities and established a strong relationship between economic inequality and the crimes of burglary and larceny. Jacobs' study is important because it helps us understand why high rates

of property crime victimization occur in higher-income groups. As Jacobs points out:

> When there are large differences in resources in a metropolitan area, those with little to lose and much to gain will find that potential victims with more to steal are located only a limited distance away....The less successful can readily observe the fruits of affluence in unequal metropolitan areas. It follows that in a society where there is a great cultural emphasis placed on economic success, pronounced differences in resources seem to result in more property crimes. (pp. 22–23)

In other words, relative class deprivation and inequality seem conducive to higher rates of conventional property crime, and recent studies confirm this conclusion (Choe, 2008; Patterson, 2006).

Other research demonstrates that income inequality directly affects both the rate of property crimes and the rate of violent crimes. Blau and Blau's (1982) classic study found that in the 125 largest metropolitan areas, high rates of interpersonal violence result largely from economic inequalities. Income inequalities in cities promote interpersonal violence because "in a society founded on the principle 'that all men are created equal,' economic inequalities rooted in ascribed positions violate the spirit of democracy and are likely to create alienation, despair, and conflict" (p. 26). Other studies have made similar conclusions about violent crime. For instance, Stack and Kanavy (1983) investigated the relationship between economic conditions and rape, reporting strong support "for an economic theory of crime based on unemployment as well as income inequality. Both variables exert positive, independent effects on rape" (pp. 71–72). More recent work (e.g., Shover, 1996; LaFree, 1999; Lee and Bankston, 1999; Thacher, 2004; Wozniak, 2008) likewise shows a relationship between neighborhood poverty, relative deprivation, and convention crime.

These unequal economic conditions are also associated with crimes of the *hidden economy*—those economic transactions that are unreported and often illegal. For instance, babysitting for a friend is a *legal* part of the hidden economy. Illegal transactions of the hidden economy consist of conventional property crimes—from robbery to fencing—and such crimes as illegal drug distribution, gambling, prostitution, and employee theft. The hidden economy entails large numbers of people participating in economic activity—working, buying, selling—outside the view and control of the state. Employee theft and the amateur trade in stolen goods are examples of activities within this hidden economy. Moreover, when the legitimate labor market offers few attractive alternatives, illicit work—selling drugs, running numbers rackets, engaging in prostitution, and organizing criminal syndicates—likewise becomes relatively inviting.

Conventional crimes of the hidden economy are not found solely on the street. Most crime actually occurs in the workplace. Economic conditions such as inflation can affect the working class by pushing people into higher tax brackets and reducing the overall purchasing power of their remaining income. The result is that those who experience reduced standards of living and are not prepared to endure it sometimes turn to tax evasion, embezzlement, fraud, and other forms of occupational crime and off-the-books income.

However, occupational crimes cannot be explained solely by economic deprivation. Closer examination of crimes such as employee theft reveals that the *internal* structure of the workplace is equally important. Hollinger and Clark's (1983) study of employee theft in three industries concluded that this crime "is best understood within the social context of the work environment that includes perceived job dissatisfaction as a principal component" (p. 86). Dissatisfaction includes not only job quality

but also such issues as *perceived inequality*. Many workers, when belittled by employers and thus reminded of the inequality in the workplace, turn to employee theft to "get back" at the boss or company.

Jerald Greenberg (1997; and see Tomlinson and Greenberg, 2009) has called employee theft "the motive to even the score" (p. 94). In other words, employee theft is designed to bring harm to employers who are believed to have harmed employees. Thus employee theft is used to establish equity in an unequal relationship. Indeed, in a series of studies, Greenberg demonstrated that the more inequality in the workplace between employer and employee, the greater the likelihood of employee theft. Moreover, the *amount* of employee theft depends on the nature of interpersonal treatment: Inequality is "magnified by the insult of insensitive treatment" by employers to employees (Greenberg, 1997:96). The unequal relationships within the workplace and the workers' resentment of that inequality often trigger employee theft.

Thus far we have looked at crimes largely associated with the poor and working classes and how social position permits and precludes opportunities for committing conventional crimes. However, with the development of large corporations, financial institutions, and the state, a corresponding consolidation of a professional-managerial class has emerged. Members of this class can of course commit conventional crimes, but their structural position also provides the opportunity to engage in corporate and political crimes. The remainder of this section is devoted to a brief discussion of each of these crimes.

Corporations in a capitalist economy endure only if they make a profit. Yet profit making is not simply a matter of individual corporate greed. Rather, the pressure to make profits is created and enforced by the competitive structure of capitalism as an economic system. Corporations that do not continually reinvest their capital are likely to be "eaten up" by those that do. This pressure for profit drives corporate executives to engage in corporate crime. Moreover, in the pursuit of profit, corporate executives must overcome several obstacles, such as minimizing costs and creating demand, to succeed at profit making. Corporate executives can increase profits by keeping costs down. The lower the cost to the corporation for labor, tools, machinery, and so on, the higher the profits. Many corporate executives secure profits by minimizing the costs of worker, consumer, and environmental safety. The pressure to minimize costs helps create the conditions for corporate crimes (such as unsafe working conditions, unsafe products, environmental pollution, and subminimum wages) and global corporate crimes (such as dumping unsafe products and moving unsafe working conditions to more favorable environments).

A corporation has difficulty making a profit if it fails to sell what it produces. Thus, in addition to minimizing costs, corporate executives must create a demand for their product. This necessity is conducive to corporate deception in marketing, especially when demand for the product is erratic and variable. Corporate executives thus may conquer this obstacle by engaging in such corporate crimes as consumer fraud, false advertising, and other deceptive practices.

In sum, then, although not every corporation is criminal, in a profit-driven society corporations are inherently criminogenic because of the intrinsic aspects of profit making and the obstacles a corporation must overcome to achieve its primary goal. Because of such corporate priorities, incentives exist that make corporate crime the logical outcome. In fact, sociological studies have shown that when corporate profits decline, corporate crime occurs more often (Friedrichs, 2007). Thus, the structural position of corporate executive's in the professional-managerial class and the necessity of profit making help us understand corporate crime.

The constant requirement for profit making is also related to the corporate association with criminal syndicates (traditionally known as *organized crime*). Profits from the illegal sale and distribution of goods and services are often laundered through large financial institutions, providing profits for both the syndicate and these corporations. There is, then, a close relationship between the hidden economy and the formal economy. Through labor racketeering, criminal syndicates also serve corporate interests by providing a means for preventing unionization and for controlling labor organizing, which helps minimize costs. In short, the symbiotic relationship between criminal syndicates and legitimate businesses serves both interests by helping them achieve their common goal of profit making (Simon, 2007).

Members of the professional-managerial class employed in the political arena can use their position for personal ends. For instance, politicians can gain financially by engaging in a variety of corrupt practices, such as bribery and the misuse of state funds. Political crimes for personal economic gain provide another example of how class position influences the type of crime.

We must note, too, that the state operates in certain ways to serve the economic interests of corporations. Although the managers of the state have historically come from the professional-managerial classes, the state is not simply an *instrument* of any class. In a capitalist economy the state operates to protect and support a corporate-dominated economy. The state came into being with the development of social classes in agricultural societies; since then, the economically dominant class has usually been the most politically powerful class. However, this does not mean the state operates in a monolithic manner. Rather, state actions result from political conflicts among classes and also within the professional-managerial class. Nevertheless, these conflicts are embedded in an overall state policy of maintaining a viable capitalist economy.

Inasmuch as the major corporations (Fortune 500) dominate the U.S. economy, the state has a particular interest in their viability. This intimate relationship between the state and the economy often leads to political crime. For example, those who manage the state are interested in bolstering a healthy capitalist economy, not only for generating state revenues but also for their own continued political futures. Consequently, state managers take actions that facilitate corporate investment.

Corporations base their foreign investment decisions on such things as the cost of labor and raw materials, the size of the market, and the political climate (stability) of the society receiving the capital. Is the working class under control? Will the state raise taxes? Does the state support business freedom? If the answers to such questions are negative, it is unlikely that corporations will invest. Consequently, U.S. foreign policy has supported global practices that permit the greatest opportunity for corporations to invest in other countries. Revolutionary movements in Africa and Central and Latin America, for example, that challenge the status quo also threaten corporate profits. The result is that the U.S. government has supported reactionary and oppressive regimes to quell such movements—as in Iran under the Shah and in Chile under Pinochet—and the CIA and National Security Council have moved to overthrow democratically elected governments. In other words, the state sometimes engages in global political crimes because of its inherent need to protect and maintain a capitalist economy.

The preceding discussion has provided selected examples of the relationship among class inequality, social position, and the types and seriousness of crime. Class position and inequality, however, provide only a partial understanding of how the patterns of crime and victimization

occur in the United States. We now turn to a second, although equally important, sociological factor—gender inequality and crime.

## 10.2 GENDER AND CRIME

**Gender** refers to historically and culturally developed behavior resulting from relationships between males/males, females/females, and males/females. Gender relations have developed sociologically into unequal relationships between males and females. This inequality has profound consequences for patterns of crime and victimization. In fact, gender is probably the best predictor of crime and victimization.

### PATTERNS OF CRIME AND VICTIMIZATION

Arrest data, self-report studies, and victimization surveys help us form a picture of which gender commits the greatest number of conventional crimes and what *types* of conventional crimes are associated most often with each gender. Consider arrest data. According to the Uniform Crime Reports (UCR), for 2007 males clearly outnumber females in terms of arrest numbers. Men comprise the overwhelming majority of those arrested for the eight major felonies. Indeed, in every case except larceny, men account for 78 percent or more of the arrests. The most significant crimes committed by females, according to the arrest data, are larceny (40 percent), forgery and counterfeiting (38 percent), fraud (44 percent), embezzlement (51 percent), and prostitution and commercialized vice (68 percent) (Federal Bureau of Investigation, 2008).

Numerous researchers have used self-report studies to generate data on gender and crime. Although we cannot discuss all aspects of this work here, Douglas Smith and Christy Visher (1980; also see Steffensmeier and Allan, 1995a; Broidy and Agnew, 1997) reduced a large portion of this research (forty-four studies) to a single database from which they determined the magnitude of the relationship between gender and crime. Smith and Visher concluded that the findings of the self-report studies are remarkably similar to arrest data. Thus, males reported much more involvement in conventional crimes, especially in serious felonies. Moreover, in number and type, the female contribution to conventional crimes was found to be quite similar to the arrest data. However, Smith and Visher established that arrest data underreport women's involvement in nonserious property crimes, such as shoplifting and fraud, particularly for female youth. In other words, according to self-report studies, adult involvement in conventional crimes seems more male dominated than youth crime, especially for property crimes (see also Spunt, 2002).

Thus, arrest, self-report, and victimization data all suggest that both male adults and youths commit more conventional crimes and more serious types of conventional crimes than female adults and youths. When women commit conventional crimes, they are primarily less serious offenses against property. Women are most likely to commit larceny, fraud, and embezzlement (Belknap, 2007; Chesney-Lind and Pasko, 2004). Males disproportionately commit interpersonal crimes of violence and property crimes, especially the more serious ones. Moreover, males have a virtual monopoly on the commission of syndicated, corporate, and political crime. Thus males commit the greatest number of crimes and the most serious types of them.

According to the National Crime Victimization Survey for 2007, males also have the highest rate of victimization for interpersonal crimes of violence (except rape/sexual assault and purse snatching/pocket picking). Consequently, for interpersonal crimes of violence, the highest victimization rate is *intragender:* males victimizing males. Nevertheless, there is substantial *intergender* victimization: males violating women

through such offenses as rape and violence against women in the family.

## GENDER AND VARIETIES OF CRIME

The patterns of crime and victimization just identified reflect broad social inequalities between men and women. Unequal relations between men and women are evident most clearly in the fact that men control the institutional structures of society and therefore also control women. Patterns of crime and victimization in contemporary U.S. society reflect these unequal gender relations. We consider first how these gender relations are structured and then relate that structure theoretically to the empirical evidence on gender and crime.

As industrialization has developed, women have been drawn out of the home and into the labor market in increasing numbers. More women today work in the labor market than ever before. For example, in 1970, 32 percent of all women 16 years and older were in the labor force; by 2008 this figure had risen to 46 percent (*Statistical Abstract of the U.S.*, 2009). Yet, as women enter the labor market they are segregated into certain "feminine" occupations. Most women are concentrated in service, retail, and clerical jobs. These occupations are among the lowest-paid positions in the labor market and provide little opportunity for advancement. Women make up 92 percent of nurses, 97 percent of prekindergarten and kindergarten teachers, 76 percent of cashiers, 97 percent of secretaries and administrative assistants, 90 percent of clerks, 88 percent of bank tellers, 95 percent of child-care workers, and 74 percent of waiters and waitresses. At the other end of the job hierarchy, women make up only 15 percent of engineers, 28 percent of dentists, 30 percent of physicians and surgeons, and 33 percent of lawyers (*Statistical Abstract of the U.S.*, 2009).

Women's position in this unequal-gendered labor market helps explain their patterns of crime. For example, as women experience economic pressure from increasing inflation and low pay, they are more likely to engage in crimes such as embezzlement. Moreover, the gender division of labor just identified determines the type of embezzlement women are most likely to commit. Although women make up slightly more than one-third of all embezzlers, they are primarily petty embezzlers (Chesney-Lind and Pasko, 2004). The gendered nature of embezzlement relates to women's subordinate position in the gender division of labor. As is clear from the foregoing evidence, the occupations in which women are employed today are ones that handle large quantities of money. Not surprisingly, research on gender and bank embezzlement shows that since women are more likely to be bank tellers and men bank officers, women embezzlers tend to "take cash from the till," whereas men have greater opportunity to "manipulate the books." In addition, women's motivation to engage in bank embezzlement and other white-collar crimes differs from that of men:

> Although women and men do share motives, women are more likely than men to commit their crimes to improve their family's economic status, fulfill a caretaking role, or maintain a love relationship. They are less likely than men to commit their crimes to advance a career or to obtain some long-desired status symbol. (Bartol, 2001:284)

Women's position in the gender division of labor also helps explain their involvement in other property crimes, such as larceny and fraud. The literature on the *feminization of poverty* indicates that "the fastest-growing population living in poverty today is made up of women and children" (Sidel, 2006). The increasing impoverishment of women is caused by such factors as (1) rising divorce rates and the attendant rapid development of female-headed households; (2) the gender division of labor, which continues to discriminate against women; (3) the lack of adequate child care; and (4) a welfare system that maintains its recipients below the poverty line. Not surprisingly, most female offenders are either unemployed or working in low-paying, menial jobs (Belknap, 2007). Research has confirmed this relationship between the feminization of poverty and women's property crimes. For example, increasing economic marginalization of women places them in circumstances where they are more likely to offend. In particular, Holtfreter, Reisig, and Morash (2004) have found that poor women are most likely to commit crimes if they do not receive government-sponsored benefits, such as subsidized housing and training for jobs, that raise the quality of their lives.

Although segregation into the "pink-collar ghetto" structures women's conventional criminality, women are largely absent from the major professions. Even though more women have become corporate managers in recent years, women managers are still systematically segregated into such lower-status managerial positions as personnel, research, affirmative action, and equal employment (*Statistical Abstract of the United States*, 2009). These jobs do not lead to decision-making positions within the corporation. In other words, the gender division of labor within the corporate managerial structure effectively segregates women from, but places men in, positions of power where corporate crimes are contrived. This process is often referred to as the *old-boy network*, a sponsorship system that recruits junior male executives into the upper ranks of the managerial divisions of the corporation. Consequently, corporate crime is a male-dominated activity. And studies examining gender and corporate crime have found that men's financial gains from such crimes are much larger than women's, that women usually work alone when committing these crimes whereas men usually work with others, and that women's share of corporate crime is only 1 percent of women's white-collar crime cases (compared to

**BOX 10.1  GETTING PLAYED**

Jody Miller's *Getting Played: African American Girls, Urban Inequality, and Gendered Violence* (2008) notes that there has been a lack of scholarly attention to violence against lower-class African American young women in the United States. Indeed, criminological research on crime in lower-class racial-minority communities generally has been gender-blind; and when African American young women in these communities have been the subjects of research, the focus has been on their commission of crime, not on their being victims of crime.

Drawing on in depth interviews of lower-class African American boys and girls, Miller helps to rectify this shortfall, demonstrating that African American young women face widespread gendered violence, primarily because the public spaces in the communities where they reside is dominated by men—their male peers, adult men, and male offenders—who maintain a specific "masculine street code that emphasizes respect, interpersonal violence, and heterosexual prowess demonstrated via sexual conquest" (p. 191). Consequently, the girls Miller interviewed talked of adopting numerous strategies in their attempt to remain safe, such as avoiding public spaces in their neighborhoods by staying close to home and relying on the company of others for protection. However, these strategies simultaneously were limiting, in the sense that staying home obviously hindered their ability to be fully participating members of their communities, and relying on the company of others was complicated by the residential instability in their neighborhoods and the fact that the greatest risk of victimization was at the hands of acquaintances.

The young women Miller interviewed also discussed their experiences of sexual harassment at school—which occurred more often in this institution than on the street. Sexual harassment occurred throughout the corridors of the school—in hallways, in classrooms, in the cafeteria and gym, and on the grounds outside the school buildings. The girls experienced a variety of gendered forms of name-calling, sexual comments and rumors, and touching, groping, and grabbing. Moreover, because their schools are chronically understaffed, underfunded, and "primarily concerned with weapons and gang violence, school personnel rarely saw sexual harassment for the serious problem that it was" (p. 194).

In addition to sexual harassment, the young women reported being coerced into unwanted sex and actual or attempted sexual assault, including gang rape and dating violence—one in three of the interviewees experienced multiple sexual victimizations.

Miller's book is an important contribution to the criminological literature because it demonstrates the agency of the young women—they were not simply "passive victims"—through their various strategies in attempting to prevent sexual mistreatment as well as showing how the intersection of unequal class, gender, race, and age relations are implicated in both crime and victimization.

14 percent of men's) (Belknap, 2007; Friedrichs, 2007).

In the political arena, the gender division of labor likewise guarantees that political crime is dominated by men. There has never been a female president or vice president of the United States, and in 2009 only 75 of the 435 representatives in Congress and 17 of the 100 senators were women. Thus, women constitute more than 50 percent of the U.S. population yet hold approximately 17 percent of the seats in Congress. This absence of women from top governmental positions also results from an old-boy network. The gender division of labor within mainstream political parties—the Democratic and Republican parties in the United States—makes it extremely difficult for women either to reach positions of party responsibility or to be supported as candidates by parties. Thus, historically, women have been involved in political crimes from "below"—such as Susan B. Anthony's conviction for voting in 1872 (women were not granted the right to vote in the United States until 1920) and Angela Davis's arrest for conspiracy to free revolutionary George Jackson (she was acquitted in 1972 in a highly publicized political trial) (Turk, 2000).

An old-boy network also functions in criminal syndicates and street gangs. Steffensmeier's (1983) classic work has shown that women are excluded or underrepresented in criminal syndicates and, if present, are allocated less valued roles. Criminal syndicates are masculine dominated because of what Steffensmeier termed *homosocial reproduction, sex-typing,* and *the task environment of crime.*

*Homosocial reproduction* refers to the ways in which those in powerful positions fill positions with men like themselves. Because men dominate (control and populate) criminal syndicates, they prefer to work, associate, and do business with other men. This homosocial reproduction works in tandem with *sex-typing.* According to Steffensmeier (1983), males in criminal syndicates stereotype women and criminal work in certain ways that effectively discriminate against women. Males in criminal syndicates, for example, see their work as (1) too hard, heavy, and dangerous for women and (2) too degrading and cheapening for women, leading to a loss of women's dignity. Steffensmeier added that men view "women as not as *capable,* or not as skilled, or not as stable; and believe that, while women *take orders* from men, men do not take orders from any woman" (p. 1013). Finally, the *task environment of crime* refers to the fact that to survive in the world of crime, a criminal syndicate must deal with the threat of arrest and imprisonment as well as threats from other criminal groups. Consequently, because both *secrecy* and *violence* are inextricable aspects of criminal syndicates, they recruit people who the leaders feel certain can help satisfy these needs. As Steffensmeier stated:

> A premium is placed on attributes such as trust and reliability and on physical characteristics such as strength and "muscle"—the capacity for force or violence. These characteristics have not been the prerogative of females. Furthermore, there is an almost inexhaustible pool of males to fill openings in crime groups; there are few empty places left for females. (p. 1014)

The three factors identified by Steffensmeier show that the structure of criminal syndicates tends to reflect the broader gender inequalities of society.

All this does not mean, of course, that women are never involved in important roles within professional and syndicated crime. Clearly, throughout history some women have been involved in such criminal activities. The important point is that these activities are highly dominated by men, a phenomenon that is socially determined by gender relations in the broader society. Nevertheless, more recent research indicates that women involved in syndicated crime are not simply subordinate to men but engage in a variety of activities in syndicated crime. For example, women who are wives, daughters, or sisters to men who are involved in syndicated crime often are not happy with their life, feel manipulated by "their men," and often rebel against their lifestyle, usually through arguments, separations, divorces, and occasional violence (Albanese, 2007). Moreover, some women have become involved in criminal syndicates without any type of dependent status to men—such as operating in the illegal gambling, loan sharking, and drug markets (Carson, 2000).

Not surprisingly, males also dominate street gangs. Within a culture based on gender inequality, parents tend to control the spare time of young females more closely than that of males, leaving males freer to explore the outside world and to come into contact with one another (Hagan, McCarthy, and Foster, 2002). Young male criminality is therefore much more likely than female criminality to be collective in nature. And as Box (1983) pointed out, females are seen by male gang members as emotional, unreliable, illogical, and untrustworthy—"not the type of person you want along on an armed robbery" (p. 182). Thus the old-boy network also infiltrates street gangs. When girls are members of street gangs, they usually inhabit powerless positions. For example, Jody Miller (2001) reported in her book *One of the Guys* that gender inequality is rampant in mixed-gender gangs, such as male leadership, a double standard with regard to sexual activities, the sexual exploitation of some girls, and most girls' exclusion from serious gang crime.

Interpersonal violence against women is also closely associated with gender inequalities. Although some rapists actually may be psychopathic, research indicates that the vast majority are not emotionally disturbed (Walklate, 2004). Moreover, most assumptions about rape held by the public—such as that rape is impossible, that women want to be raped, that "no" means "yes"—have been disproven by research (Belknap, 2007). Most criminologists therefore view rape as the result of the structural subordination of women in contemporary society.

The United States has been described as a rape-prone society. In her research of 186 tribal societies, social anthropologist Peggy Sanday (1981) found that high rape rates occur in societies that are dominated by males and that feature male violence. Rape-prone societies, then, are those in which males dominate politically, economically, and ideologically and that glorify male violence. Rape-free societies, Sanday found, are marked by relative gender equality, the belief that the sexes are complementary, and a low level of interpersonal violence overall. Thus Sanday's work helps us understand why the United States can be considered a rape-prone society. Not only is U.S. society dominated politically, economically, and ideologically by males, but it also glorifies male violence in the street, in sports, in the state, and so on.

Indeed, the assertion of dominance enables rape. The rapist uses sex as a violent attack on the integrity of the woman as a person. In a rape, what is normally understood as an act of affection becomes an act of hate. This act destroys the woman's integrity by denying the victim her own will to engage or not to engage in sexuality as she pleases. By prohibiting this freedom, the rapist creates conditions of dominance and subordination.

Rape reflects the dominance/subordination gender relationships in society. This was evident in Philippe Bourgois' (2003) study of inner-city Puerto Rican men. Because of economic marginalization, these men were unable to become "head of the household" as in their grandfathers' generation. Consequently, Bourgois found that many of these men took "refuge" in a drug economy that celebrated misogyny and in a predatory street culture that normalized gang rape. As Bourgois stated, "Marginalized men lash out against the women and children they can no longer support economically or control patriarchally" (p. 412).

Like rape, violence by men in the family (wife rape, wife battering, and child sexual abuse) reflects gender power and inequality. The structure of the traditional nuclear family encourages the husband/father to view "his" wife and children as under his control. Violence in the family is intimately linked to the cultural expectation that males are authority figures within monogamous relationships. Some men therefore feel they have the right to dominate and control their wives, and wife battering serves to ensure continued compliance with their commands. If a wife questions such authority in any way, a violent husband turns to force simply to "get his way" (Ptacek, 1998).

Women's subordinate social position reinforces masculine dominance and violence in the family. If a wife is unemployed or works in a low-paying job, as is all too typical nowadays, it is easier for a husband to control her. In this type of society a husband usually has the economic power and the wife is dependent, often even if she works outside the home. Such conditions make it difficult for her to leave a violent relationship, especially if she has children.

Economic dependency and powerlessness in the family also affect the likelihood of wife rape. Because of this unequal economic familial relationship, wife rape may not be physically violent.

If she is unwilling to "oblige" him, a husband can obtain access to "his" wife's body by threatening a beating, loss of affection, or loss of economic support. The wife may thus conclude that unwanted sexual intercourse is not as harmful as the alternative—poverty and distress. This situation is exacerbated for women with children or without skills.

Gender inequality is also related to wife killing. For example, Bailey and Peterson (1995) found that the rate of women being killed by their husbands is significantly higher in cities where the college education gap between males and females is greater, where women experience higher levels of unemployment than men, and where a positive association exists with male–female inequality in income. As Bailey and Peterson concluded, "The overall pattern of findings for wife killings suggests that gender inequality breeds violence against wives" (p. 202).

Similarly, child sexual abuse results from the powerlessness of children (especially young girls) in the family and their economic and emotional dependence. Children are essentially a captive population; they are economically and emotionally dependent on parents. Particularly at young ages, children do what is necessary to maintain a supportive relationship with their parents, even to the extent of keeping the assault secret. Consequently, this dependency and powerlessness makes child sexual abuse highly exploitive and nonconsensual. In other words, to understand child sexual abuse it is essential to understand power within the family. This type of abuse primarily entails a father as perpetrator and his daughter as victim. The power and authority claimed by the father structures the offender/victim relationship. Believing that women's role is to serve the needs of men—including their sexual needs—the male authority figure uses his power to assault his daughter incestuously.

Our discussion points to the fact that analysis of gender inequality adds considerably to our understanding of the patterns of crime and victimization in U.S. society. As with class position, gender position structures the opportunities for engaging in crime and the possibilities of being victimized by crime.

In addition to class and gender, racial inequality structures patterns of crime and victimization. Let us now turn to this topic.

## 10.3  RACE AND CRIME

Genetic differences in skin color assume social significance when they are used to justify unequal treatment of one race by another. **Race** relations, like class and gender relations, have developed into unequal relations in which one race (white) uses skin color to legitimize domination and control of other races. Simultaneously, this inequality has important consequences for the patterns of crime and victimization in the United States.

Although whites continue to dominate several racial and ethnic groups in the United States—such as Native Americans, Asians, Mexican Americans, and African Americans—we focus on the inequality between whites and African Americans and the relationship of that inequality to crime and victimization. We concentrate on these two groups because, unfortunately, criminologists generally have ignored other racial and ethnic groups; therefore, insufficient data are available with which to make comparisons. We begin with a discussion of racial patterns of crime and victimization and then turn to a discussion of race and varieties of crime.

### PATTERNS OF CRIME AND VICTIMIZATION

The UCR indicates that whites account for approximately 70 percent of all arrests; African Americans account for 28 percent; the remainder are of other races (Federal Bureau of Investigation, 2008). Racial arrest disparities are evident when we take population into account.

African Americans constitute only 13 percent of the U.S. population (Current Population Reports, 2009), yet they account for 39 percent of violent crime arrests and for over 30 percent of property crime arrests (Federal Bureau of Investigation, 2008).

Although arrest data show striking differences in rates for adults, self-report studies show that African American and white youths report similar involvement in youth crime (LaFree and Hussong, 2001). When specific offenses are analyzed, however, it appears that African American adults and youths report more involvement in the most serious conventional crimes, especially crimes of interpersonal violence. Summing up their analysis of arrest, self-report, and victimization data on race and crime, Hagan and Peterson (1995) stated the following: "These data reflect a crucial aspect of crime and race in America: Not only are rates of offending and arrest high in African American communities, but so too are rates of victimization. That is, crime is predominantly intraracial" (p. 23).

Thus, the higher *arrest* rate for African Americans is probably the result of *both* the criminal justice system's selection bias and a greater involvement of African Americans in conventional crimes. Criminologists have known for quite some time that when individuals of different social classes and races come into contact with the criminal justice system *for the same crime,* young, lower-class, minority males are more likely to be arrested, prosecuted, convicted, and sentenced to prison for longer terms (Reiman, 2006. Moreover, this criminal justice system racial bias seems to occur at an even higher frequency in cities with the most pronounced racial segregation (Stolzenberg, D'Alessio, and Eitle, 2004). Because of racial inequality in U.S. society, African Americans indeed suffer considerable discriminatory and oppressive conditions that whites do not. It is this disadvantageous social position that most likely results in a higher crime rate by African Americans than might otherwise be expected for their population size.

African Americans are also more often the victims of violent crime. According to the National Crime Victimization Survey, in 2007 African Americans were victimized at a greater rate for all personal crimes—in particular, for robbery and assault. And African Americans are victimized at a higher rate than whites for all household property crimes—in particular, for both household burglary and motor vehicle theft. Thus we can conclude that conventional crimes—especially crimes of interpersonal violence and property crimes—are *intraracial.* Nevertheless, there seems to be an increasing rate of *interracial* violence directed by whites *against* African Americans (see Section 12.1).

Conventional crimes are only one aspect of criminality, and, unfortunately, criminologists have concentrated their analysis of race and crime only on racial differences in rates of conventional crimes. However, whites clearly dominate in corporate and political positions, where corporate and political crimes are committed. Therefore, although conventional crimes may be committed more often by African Americans than by whites, the more harmful and economically damaging white-collar and political crimes are disproportionately committed by whites.

## RACE AND VARIETIES OF CRIME

As we point out in our discussion of "hate crimes" (see Section 12.1), African Americans are among the most frequent victims of interracial violence. However, they are also the primary victims of conventional crime. Discrimination continues to worsen the disadvantages African Americans already suffer, creating conditions for high rates of intraracial crime. Obstacles experienced by the white working class are greater for African Americans because of racial discrimination. Numerous studies have shown that racial discrimination, segregation, and concentrated poverty produce pervasive social and economic disadvantages, which lead to criminal behavior among young minority males (Peterson, Krivo, and Hagan, 2006; Kaufman, Rebellon, Thaxton, and Agnew, 2008).

The relationship between unemployment and crime we discussed in Section 10.1 is especially helpful in understanding the high crime rates of African American male and female youth. Research has shown consistently that the overrepresentation of African American adults and youths in conventional crime statistics is the result of racial and economical inequalities (Anderson, 1999; Hawkins, 2003; Sampson and Wilson, 1995; Gabbidon and Greene, 2008). Indeed, the 1954 official unemployment rates of African American and white 16- to 19-year-olds were almost identical: 15.4 and 14.0 percent, respectively (Duster, 1987). By 2008, however, 35 percent of African American 16- to 19-year-olds and 21 percent of white 16- to 19-year-olds were officially unemployed (Department of Labor, 2009). In other words, economic inequality between white and African American youth has increased since the mid-1950s. The high rate of crimes committed by African American youths has thus stemmed from their deteriorating economic situation (McNulty and Bellair, 2003).

Nevertheless, an interesting study by Lee and Ousey (2007) found that when disadvantaged African Americans experience high neighborhood integration with affluent non-African Americans, violent crime rates are lower than when neighborhoods consist of only disadvantaged African Americans and disadvantaged non-African Americans. Thus, as Lee and Ousey conclude, neighborhood integration that crosses race and class boundaries has an important violence-constraining impact, yet neither racial neighborhood integration among class disadvantaged nor social class integration within African American communities yields a violence-constraining effect.

Although the African American female violent crime rate is high, within the African American community, the vast majority of criminal violence is committed *by* African American men *against* African American men. For African American men ages 15–44, homicide is the leading cause of death, and African American men are eight times more likely to die by murder than are white males.

The work of Bruce, Roscigno, and McCall (1998) and Bruce and Roscigno (2003) has likewise shown the relationship between racial inequality and violence by African Americans. Specifically, they demonstrated that a link exists between structural racial disadvantage and the perpetuation of interpersonal violence in inner-city African American communities. Growing up in disadvantaged communities, African Americans become aware of the structural constraints of their existence, such as the lack of educational and job opportunities. Bruce and his colleagues argued that these constraints shape social and psychological well-being and lead to anger, frustration, and despair.

Moreover, because of the lack of legitimate economic opportunities, many poor inner-city African Americans participate in the informal economy of drugs and weapons trafficking. The combination of illegal activities and the availability of weapons increases the potential for gun use to solve conflicts. The result is the transformation of nonviolent neighborhoods into communities gripped by the ever-present threat of violent confrontation. Such a threat of danger can result in interactional rituals that lead to violence:

The reality of living in an area where individuals have to depend on illegitimate activities for survival can have negative consequences for social psychological processes, which, in turn, may increase the potential for violence.... Because gang members hold such grim prospects for life, minor incidents such as accidentally bumping into someone or wearing a particular color create the possibility that an individual will be attacked. (Bruce, Roscigno, and McCall, 1998:44)

Thus, these authors have shown how violence among African Americans results from the intersection of racial and economical disadvantage, local context, and individual social action.

In summary, racial inequality structures conventional crime, both interracial and intraracial. Interracial violence results from extreme racist beliefs in a racially segregated and unequal society. Crime by African Americans is the product of their positions in class and racial hierarchies, which are, of course, mediated by gender.

Still, we must remember that the vast majority of those who commit interpersonal violent crimes are young white males and that every year approximately 70 percent of *all* conventional crimes are committed by whites (Gabbidon, 2009).

Moreover, combined class, gender, and racial inequality also determine who can engage in white-collar and political crimes. African Americans hold only 8 percent of executive, administrative, and managerial positions and only 9 percent of professional positions (*Statistical Abstract of the U.S.*, 2009). Additionally, although in 2009 the United States elected the first African American president, there has never been an African American vice president; and in 2009, African Americans held one seat in the U.S. Senate and only 42 of the 435 seats in the House. Thus, racial inequality determines that whites hold more of those positions in which the most serious and harmful crimes occur—white-collar and political crimes. Racial inequality—as with class

---

### BOX 10.2  WHITENESS AND CRIME

An unexamined aspect of criminological discussions about race is the relationship between "whiteness" and crime. Although white people commit the most *amounts* of crime and the most serious and dangerous *types* of crime (see Chapter 13), "whiteness" is an invisible variable throughout criminological research and theory. Indeed, "whiteness" is deemed unproblematic as an ethnicity except as a possible source of racism (Webster, 2008). However, in the 1990s numerous scholars in a variety disciplines began to examine "whiteness" (Frankenberg, 1993; Morrison, 1992; Roediger, 1991), and now some criminologists have launched into this important area of study. For example, Messerschmidt (2007) analyzed the relationship among whiteness, masculinity, and lynching during U.S. Reconstruction (1865–1877), concluding that white supremacist men "were doing a specific type of whiteness and masculinity simultaneously as they were doing lynching—the three merged into one entity" (p. 91). In addition, Webster (2007) pointed out that because notions of race can only be conceptualized as relational (as with gender, class, and age), attention by criminologists should likewise be paid to the ethnicity and ideology of "whiteness." Thus, the different ways in which "whiteness" comes to be constructed in society is as important to criminologists as is the construction of racial minority identity in understanding race and crime (p. 6). Following his own suggestion, then, in an important article—"Marginalized White Ethnicity, Race and Crime"—Webster (2008) examined different types of "whiteness" in working-class communities—the "underclass," "white niggers," the "new" migrants, and "white trash"—and showed that certain whites are seen as "less white" than other whites within a hierarchy of "whiteness." Class contempt for such marginalized white working-class ethnicities as those just noted, Webster argues, has unleashed a "chain of signifiers": "familial disorder and dysfunction, dangerous masculinities, dependency, fecund and excessive femininities, antisocial behavior, moral and ecological decay, and quick resort to criminality" (p. 307). Consequently, Webster concludes his article by pointing out that the intersection of race/ethnicity, gender, and class has resulted in marginalized white working-class ethnicities being "criminalized in ways not dissimilar from the criminalization of visible working-class minorities" (p. 293). (See also, Gabbidon, 2010.)

and gender inequality—governs social position in society and, therefore, criminal opportunities.

## 10.4 AGE AND CRIME

Economic benefits, social privileges, and political power are based not only on class, gender, and race but also on **age**. Even such basic rights as sexual activity, voting, and drinking alcohol are conferred by age. Thus, age inequality and age discrimination exist in U.S. society. These phenomena are most pronounced for youth, but they also affect the elderly. Unequal generational divisions between young and old are prevalent, and social behavior—including crime—is linked to the aging process. One's position in the age hierarchy permits or precludes opportunity for engaging in crime. Consider the patterns of crime and victimization based on age.

### PATTERNS OF CRIME AND VICTIMIZATION

According to arrest data in the UCR (Federal Bureau of Investigation, 2008), participation in conventional crime rises with age, peaks in the teenage and early adulthood years, and then declines. Two important age patterns for conventional property and violent crimes emerge: (1) Property crime arrest rates peak between the ages of 17 and 18 and then decline rather quickly, and (2) for violent crimes the rate peaks at around the ages of 18–19 and declines much more slowly.

Some criminologists have questioned arrest data on age. For example, because youths tend to commit conventional crimes in groups, they are allegedly more visible to the police and thus more likely to be arrested. Also, some criminologists argue that youths are less skilled than are adults in committing crime and, therefore, more likely to be arrested. It may be, then, that arrest statistics on age are biased; this would explain the overrepresentation of youth in UCR data. However, self-report studies report similar age patterns for conventional crimes (Warr, 2001). We conclude therefore that arrest data are reliable evidence of the age distribution of conventional crime.

Victimization rates for conventional crimes by age show that for crimes of violence, young persons aged 16–19 have the highest rates of victimization (Department of Justice, 2008). For victims over the age of 19, violent crimes decline with age, so those aged 65 and older have the lowest victimization rates for violent crimes. Moreover, property crime victimization rates are highest for the youngest heads of household and decline with age. For conventional crimes, then, the highest victimization rates are *intra-age*.

### AGE AND VARIETIES OF CRIME

David Greenberg (1977) has shown in his classic work on age and crime that during the transition from childhood to adolescence, the links between children and parents decrease (yet economic dependence remains), while receptivity to peers and peer evaluation increases. Being popular and connected with the "right" groups becomes critically important for most youths. The partial disengagement from family and the heightened closeness to peers, combined with advertising directed toward the teenage market, create the conditions for youthful involvement in pleasure-seeking, consumption-oriented social lives. Indeed, participation in this teenage social life requires money for buying the "right stuff": clothing, cosmetics, cigarettes, alcoholic beverages, narcotics, CDs, CD players, gasoline for cars and motorcycles, tickets to films and concerts, and meals in restaurants. However, because teenage labor force participation has declined drastically, youths are finding it more and more difficult to support their participation in teen life. Thus, the high rate of property crimes for teenagers is, according to Greenberg, "a response to the disjunction between the desire to participate in social activities with peers and the absence of legitimate sources of funds needed to finance this participation" (p. 197). Because of teenage social position, property crimes increasingly serve as an alternative to work.

When youths leave high school—and when their social position changes accordingly— peer evaluation decreases and opportunities for becoming financially self-sufficient expand. This situation reduces teenagers' motivation to engage in property crimes, and their involvement in property crimes drops off rapidly at post– high school ages. As Greenberg (1983) stated: "Employment, leaving school, military enlist- ment, and marriage eliminate major sources of criminogenic frustration, and at the same time supply informal social control" (p. 33).

Steffensmeier and Allan (1995b) expanded on Greenberg's thesis, arguing that five major changes mark the transition from late adoles- cence to early adulthood:

1. Greater access to legitimate sources of material goods and excitement: jobs, cred- it, alcohol, sex, and so forth.
2. Age-graded norms: externally, increased expectation of maturity and responsibil- ity; internally, anticipation of assuming adult roles, coupled with reduced subjec- tive acceptance of deviant roles and the threat they pose to entering adult status.
3. Peer associations and lifestyle: reduced orientation to same-age/same-sex peers and increased orientation toward persons of the opposite sex and/or persons who are older or more mature.
4. Increased legal and social costs for devi- ant behavior.
5. Patterns of illegitimate opportunities: with the assumption of adult roles, opportuni- ties increasing for crimes (for example, gambling, fraud, and employee theft) that are less risky, more lucrative, and/or less likely to be reflected in official statistics.

Greenberg also attempted to explain the high rates of interpersonal violence committed by youth and young adults. As discussed earlier in this chapter, interpersonal crimes of violence are committed primarily by males. Traditional gen- der ideology calls for males to work outside the home and support a family. However, lower- and working-class males have less of a chance than other males of fulfilling these activities. This sit- uation, Greenberg (1977) reasoned, generates a masculine-status anxiety in which such men

> may attempt to alleviate their anxiety by exagger- ating those traditionally male traits that *can* be expressed. Attempts to dominate women (includ- ing rape) and patterns of interpersonal violence can be seen in these terms. In other words, crime can…provide a sense of potency that is expected and desired but not achieved in other spheres of life. (p. 207)

Greenberg pointed out that arrest rates for interpersonal crimes of violence peak in the immediate post–high school age brackets, when primarily lower- and working-class males—who do not attend college—anticipate or actively seek full-time work. He argued that masculine- status anxiety helps us understand not only age variations in interpersonal crimes of violence but class, gender, and race as well. Greenberg con- cluded that the variable relationship between age and crime depends on historical, cultural, and economic factors. Patterns of crime in the United States therefore reflect the particular develop- ment of age segregation and of the social posi- tion of youth in U.S. society.

Not everyone agrees that age is an impor- tant factor in explaining patterns of crime. Hirschi and Gottfredson (1983), for example, have agreed that the age distribution of crime depicted in the UCR is accurate and that it "rep- resents one of the brute facts of criminology" (p. 552). But, whereas Greenberg argued that the age distribution of crime varies with social conditions, Hirschi and Gottfredson have contended that the age distribution of crime is *invariant* across all social and cultural conditions. For them the shape and form of the age distribution remains "virtually unchanged" from time to time and place to place. Criminological theory and research therefore need not consider age as an important variable in explaining crime.

Greenberg (1985) has countered this argument with considerable historical and cross-cultural evidence. He has shown that today there is less adult crime relative to juvenile crime in the United States than there used to be. Similarly, an analysis of other societies—both industrial and preindustrial—displays a noticeable shift toward younger ages involved in criminality once industrialization occurs. For example, in contemporary Norway, the age distribution of crime is similar to that in the United States. Yet as criminologist Nils Christie pointed out, speaking of Norway: "Police statistics for 1870 showed no peak for teenagers. They did not exist at that time. A hundred years ago, the peak was somewhere in the middle twenties and with a *slow decrease* in criminal activity among the older groups" (cited in Greenberg, 1985:12, emphasis added). For the Banyoro and Basoga (two preindustrialized Bantu-speaking peoples of Uganda), the peak age of those who commit homicide is 35, and rarely are homicides committed by teenagers (Greenberg, 1985).

The emergence of the life-course perspective in criminology has encouraged further discussion of the link between age and crime (Warr, 2001). For example, Sampson and Laub (1993, 2003) and Warr (2002) argue that the transition to adulthood and its accompanying conforming practices—e.g., marriage and employment—"wean" youths from teenage peer influence and encourage desistance from crime. More recently, Verrill (2004) argues that the onset, continuance, and desistance of criminal behavior, manifest in the age–crime curve discussed earlier, is a function primarily of differential association; Fagan and

Western (2005) show that the age/crime curve is not a unitary phenomenon but actually varies by type of crime, gender, and exposure to the criminal justice system; and Greenberg (2008:43) demonstrates that biological aging of the human body does not explain the decline in crime with years—the decline in crimes of violence is slower than the decline in property crimes, "which is not what one would expect if physiological aging accounts for the drop in crime."

In addition, race and class can affect an individual's ability to move out of crime; that is, race and class inequality limit access to legitimate resources—such as college attendance and employment at adequate wages—that allow "maturation" out of crime (Shover and Thompson, 2006). Steffensmeier and Allan (1995b) provided one example:

> For black inner-city youths, the high level of youth inequality that characterizes modern societies is compounded by the problems of living in a racist society, and they are less able to leave behind the inequality of youth status. As they move into young adulthood they continue to experience limited access to the adult labor market. (pp. 103–104)

In a similar vein, Hagan (1991) and Uggen and Massoglia (2003) have shown that crime rates for working-class youth decline less slowly than rates for middle-class youth.

The segregation and subordination of youth in society as a whole are not the only factors that generate specific age patterns of crime. The subordination of youth within specific institutions also plays a role. Unequal relationships between parents and children can set the stage for generational conflict and at least three types of crime: child physical abuse, child sexual abuse, and youth crime. Child abuse results from power relations across generations and the accompanying ideology that children should at all times be subordinate to parents. A thin line separates authoritarian, punitive, and harsh forms of discipline, on the one hand, and child abuse, on the other; indeed, they seem to coexist.

Moreover, research reveals a strong relationship between child sexual abuse and future delinquency. The vast majority of victims of child sexual abuse (both girls and boys) report severe forms of trauma, leading many to run away from home. In particular, girls on the street report high rates of physical abuse and sexual abuse (Chesney-Lind and Pasko, 2004). Running away from sexual abuse and a violent home, these young women and men turn to crime to survive. After reviewing the literature on young women, Meda Chesney-Lind and Lisa Pasko pointed out that sexually abused female runaways are "significantly more likely than their nonabused counterparts to engage in delinquent or criminal activities, such as substance abuse, petty theft, and prostitution" (p. 27).

Consequently, the powerlessness of children in the home and the extreme results of that subordination (child physical abuse, child sexual abuse, and neglect—along with the lack of community social services for homeless youth) contribute to crime both quantitatively and qualitatively. These findings demonstrate the important ties between social position, victimization, and subsequent crime.

In addition to the home, the school is an institution that structures how age impacts social position, victimization, and subsequent crime. For example, in the 1990s several school homicides occurred in the United States, and nearly all the "school shooters" were boys. These boys had all been bullied consistently, primarily concerning their bodily appearance, by bigger and stronger boys. Research on these shootings has concluded that the killers viewed their subsequent violence as a means of retaliating against the peer abuse at school and thereby a way of gaining masculine respect (Kimmel and Mahler, 2003).

Although the social position of youth presents young people with opportunities for committing certain crimes, it also precludes them from committing others. Systematically denied access to the labor market, youths are effectively segregated from positions where workplace-related crimes—such as embezzlement and corporate crimes—and political crimes occur. For corporate and political crimes, the ages 30–60 clearly dominate; these are the prime ages of employment, and individuals of these ages make up the most powerful age group in society.

As we stated earlier, the elderly are also increasingly segregated and subordinated in the United States. Not surprisingly, in the 1980s criminologists became interested in the topic of crime and the elderly. An important article by Cullen, Wozniak, and Frank (1985), for example, concluded that the majority (78 percent) of elderly arrests are for larceny, which is almost six times higher than the next-highest category, aggravated assault. Elderly males and females seem to commit larceny in equal proportions (Mandino, 2000). Moreover, the elderly tend to steal household and personal necessities of low value—such as toothpaste, cigarettes, and tools (Brogden and Nijhar, 2000). It should be noted, however, that although larceny seems to be the crime most frequently committed by the elderly, they are much less likely to commit larceny than any other age group (Klemke, 1992). And as would be expected from our earlier analysis, elderly property crime rates are correlated with adverse economic conditions (Wahidin and Cain, 2006).

## REVIEW

This chapter discussed considerable empirical research to help explain the patterns of crime and victimization in the United States. Of primary importance is structured inequality: Class, gender, race, and age hierarchies determine social position and thus criminal opportunities.

## CLASS AND CRIME

1. Arrest data, self-report studies, and victimization surveys all show that conventional crimes by adults and youth are disproportionately concentrated in the lower and working classes.
2. White-collar and political crimes are disproportionately committed by members of the professional-managerial class.
3. Victimization data show that all conventional crimes—except personal larceny without contact and motor vehicle theft—are likely to be intraclass.
4. Unemployment and income inequality are associated both with conventional crimes and with nonoccupational crimes of the hidden economy.
5. Both economic conditions such as inflation and perceived inequality within the workplace itself are conducive to occupational crimes such as employee theft.
6. Corporate crimes are caused chiefly by the desire of corporate executives to overcome obstacles to profit making.
7. Because of their position within the state, politicians have opportunities to gain financially by engaging in a variety of corrupt practices.
8. The close association between the state and the economy creates conditions for systematic state crimes—such as global political crimes.

## GENDER AND CRIME

1. Arrest data, self-report studies, and victimization surveys show that male adults and youths are the chief perpetrators of almost all forms of conventional crime.
2. Males have a virtual monopoly on the commission of syndicated, corporate, and political crimes.
3. When females commit crime, they engage mostly in petty forms of theft, such as shoplifting, fraud, and minor embezzlement, and in prostitution.
4. Victimization data on conventional crimes suggest that males victimize other males.
5. Women's subordinate position in the gender division of labor structures the type of embezzlement women commit.
6. The feminization of poverty is associated with female fraud, shoplifting, and other forms of petty theft.
7. Males dominate in syndicated, corporate, and political crimes because of their power to exclude women systematically from positions where these crimes originate.
8. Male violence toward women derives from gender inequality, the structural subordination of women, and the power and dominance accorded men in U.S. society.

## RACE AND CRIME

1. Data on race and crime suggest that African American adults and youths commit a disproportionate amount of conventional crimes for their population size—especially interpersonal crimes of violence.

2. Whites clearly commit the vast majority of conventional crimes and dominate the more harmful and economically damaging white-collar and political crimes.

3. Victimization data show that conventional crimes are intraracial (e.g., African Americans typically victimize African Americans and whites typically victimize whites).

4. Because racial oppression multiplies African Americans' disadvantages, they experience a disproportionate number of economic and social obstacles.

5. Overrepresentation of African American adults and youth in conventional crime statistics—both property crimes and interpersonal crimes of violence—is the result of racial economic inequality.

6. The racial hierarchy results in white domination of the positions where white-collar and political crimes occur.

## AGE AND CRIME

1. Conventional crime arrest rates vary with age. Property crimes peak between 13 and 17 years of age and decline rapidly with age; violent crimes peak at around 18 or 19 years of age and decline much more slowly.

2. Victimization rates for conventional crimes show that young persons ages 12–24 have the highest rates of conventional crime victimization.

3. The high rate of property crime for youths results from their desire to participate in social activities and from a lack of adequate funds to pay for them.

4. Not all criminologists agree that age is an important factor in crime; the life-course perspective has added new insights to this relationship.

5. Power and inequality within institutions, such as the family and the school, can create social positions leading to the victimization of youths. This victimization has implications for future involvement in crime.

6. White-collar and political crimes are committed by the most powerful age group, those 30–60 years of age.

7. Elderly crime consists mostly of petty forms of theft, such as shoplifting, and is caused by adverse economic conditions.

## QUESTIONS FOR CLASS DISCUSSION

1. Choose several crimes, and then explain how social position permits and prevents opportunities for their commission.

2. Discuss how the interaction of class, gender, race, and age affects criminal opportunities. Cite several examples.

3. How does the discussion of the varieties of crime in this text differ from those offered by the media?

4. Identify other forms of inequality in society that have not been examined in this chapter (e.g., urban/rural), and then discuss how they may be related to crime and victimization.

## FOR FURTHER STUDY

### READINGS

Davies, Pamela, Peter Francis, and Chris Greer, eds. 2007. *Victims, Crime and Society*. Thousand Oaks, CA: Sage.

Gabbidon, Shaun. 2010. *Criminological Perspectives on Race and Crime*. New York: Routledge.

Grover, Chris. 2008. *Crime and Inequality*. Portland, OR: Willan.

Miller, Jody. 2008. *Getting Played: African American Girls, Urban Inequality, and Gendered Violence*. New York: New York University Press.

### WEBSITES

1. <http://www.americanhumane.org>: The American Humane Association operates this website, which provides reliable information on child abuse and neglect. It also provides information on the abuse of animals.
2. <http://www.interactivetheatre.org/mav/>: This site, titled "Men Against Violence Webring," offers some action-oriented solutions to male violence. Useful links are provided, with a goal for men to take greater responsibility for violence.
3. <http://www.fbi.gov/ucr/ucr/hc2007/index.html>: This site provides the most up-to-date statistics on hate crimes reported to the police. The data cover incidents, offenses, victims, offenders, and location type that were motivated by bias against the victim's perceived race, religion, ethnicity, sexual orientation, or disability.

CHAPTER 11

# PROPERTY CRIME

**11.1 Robbery and Burglary**
- Robbery
- Typologies of Robbery
- Robbery as Transaction
- Robbers on Robbery
- Burglary
- Burglars on Burglary

**11.2 Varieties of Larceny**
- Shoplifting
- Motor Vehicle Theft
- Fraud

**11.3 Dealing and Damage**
- Fencing
- Arson

**PREVIEW**

Chapter 11 introduces:
- What sociologists mean by property crime.
- The various types of property crime.
- The difference between amateur and professional property offenders.
- The nature, extent, and costs of property crime.

**KEY TERMS**

armed robbery
arson
automobile theft
burglary
carjacking
check fraud
credit-card fraud
fencing

identity theft
income-tax fraud
larceny
motor vehicle theft
property crime
robbery
shoplifting
strong-arm robbery

Most conventional "street crimes" entail the taking of property. Indeed, according to National Crime Victimization Survey (NCVS) data, property crimes make up more than 78 percent of all victimizations (Department of Justice, 2008).

In addition to being more frequent, property crimes differ from crimes of interpersonal violence in another significant way: Offender and victim are, in most cases, strangers. For crimes such as burglary, automobile theft, and arson, no direct interaction between offender and victim usually takes place. And in those crimes where interaction does exist—such as check fraud—it is not immediately apparent that a crime has been committed.

We define **property crime** as the unlawful damage to or taking of the property of another, regardless of whether the threat of or actual use of physical violence occurs. In this chapter we discuss seven types of property crime: robbery, burglary, shoplifting, automobile theft, fraud, fencing, and arson. While discussing each, we examine the similarities and differences between professional and amateur property offenders. Professional and amateur property offenders are similar in that each commits the same type of crime. In other words, there are both professional and amateur robbers, burglars, auto thieves, and so forth. However, professionals and amateurs differ in important ways. Professionals carefully plan and execute their crimes, using sophisticated techniques and skills. They are committed to crime as a lifestyle and tend to specialize in one particular form of property crime. Amateurs engage in crime when the opportunity arises, do not extensively plan their crime, do not always think of themselves as criminals, and do not usually specialize in one type of property crime.

## 11.1 ROBBERY AND BURGLARY

Our discussion of property crime begins with what most of us—including criminologists—consider

to be the two most serious forms of theft: robbery and burglary.

## ROBBERY

**Robbery** has been defined in various ways. Some states define it as a property crime, although other states and the FBI see it as a violent crime. The FBI defines robbery as "the taking of or attempting to take anything of value from the care, custody, or control of a person or persons by force or by threat of force or violence and/or by putting the victim in fear" (Federal Bureau of Investigation, 2008). In historical fiction and in contemporary media, robbers are often depicted as romantic heroes—professional thieves who are willing to go all the way in their quest for gold and booty.

Robbery ranks among the most feared of crimes because it entails both threatened and actual use of violence and loss of property to the victim. Moreover, unlike the other property crimes discussed in this chapter, robbery involves a direct confrontation between offender and victim. Robbery also differs significantly from other interpersonal crimes of violence, in that it is more likely to involve two or more offenders; the majority of robberies are committed by strangers to the victim, and robbers are more likely to use weapons. Moreover, the primary motive of the robber is not violence but economic gain.

If priority is given to an offender's motive, as most sociologists do, it makes sense to see robbery as a property crime rather than as a violent crime. In robbery, violence is secondary to the taking of property: When violence is used, it is a means to an end.

More than 90 percent of robbers are male, and their often-unsophisticated crimes are disproportionately committed by members of minority groups, such as African Americans in the United States and Franco-Canadians in Canada (Desroches, 2002). The robbery rate has been steadily declining in the United States since 1990; part of this "decline" may be because street robbers' victims are nowadays more likely themselves to be criminals, such as drug dealers, and thus are unlikely to report their victimization to the police (Jacobs and Wright, 2008). In 2007, 445,125 robberies were reported to the police, or 148 per 100,000 inhabitants (Federal Bureau of Investigation, 2008), though the NCVS reveals that about 57 percent of all robberies are never reported to the police (Department of Justice, 2008). About 53 percent of all robbery victims require some form of medical treatment; 25.1 percent are either treated in a hospital emergency room or admitted to hospital (Simon and Mercy, 2001).

## TYPOLOGIES OF ROBBERY

Scholars have developed several typologies of robbers. Some typologies focus on the level and type of violence used by robbers, some on robbers' skill and foresight, and some on whether the victim is an individual or an institution, such as a bank or a commercial enterprise (Gill, 2000). Smith and Hung (2008) recently examined the research on "commercial" versus "street" robberies, noting that a bank robbery occurs in the United States every 52 minutes, yet almost 60 percent of such commercial robbers are caught and convicted; thus, although bank robberies are frequent, they are also losing propositions. Street robberies usually take place on the street, yet "fringe areas" of large cities also seem to be popular, such as small parking lots, stairwells, ATMs, and public restrooms.

Whether violence and personal injury occur during a robbery depends on the type of robbery. **Strong-arm robbery** (sometimes referred to as *unarmed robbery* because the offender robs without the use of a weapon) is actually much more dangerous than **armed robbery** (the display of a deadly weapon to carry out the robbery).

Approximately twice as many strong-arm robbery victims, compared to armed-robbery victims, are injured. And armed robberies are not only less dangerous than strong-arm robberies, they also occur more often and are more likely to be successful (Department of Justice, 2008; Willis, 2006).

One of the most successful typologies is Conklin's (1972) classic separation of *professional robbers* and *opportunist robbers*. Both types can be involved in similar robbery scenarios. But professional robbers carefully plan and execute their crimes, exhibiting greater skill than other robbery offenders and, usually, operating with accomplices (Conklin, 1972). Walsh (1986) found that when professionals operate with accomplices, they commonly are people "recommended" to them. The professional commits to robbery as a lifestyle, engages in sophisticated planning, neutralizes security, and investigates all possible escape routes. Thus, professional robbers are considerably more skilled and conduct more extensive planning than other robbers.

Conklin identified two types of professional robbers. The first commits robbery almost exclusively. The second commits other types of crimes but occasionally commits robbery with professional skill. In addition to these *solo professionals*, Walsh (1986) found two other types of professionals: *criminal syndicates*, which assemble teams of robbers, and independent, small, professional *teams* of two or three robbers. McCorkle and Miethe (2003) report that professional robbers tend to rely on three to four "big scores" per year to support a hedonistic lifestyle, and their average take is approximately $5,000 higher than that of amateur opportunist robberies.

The *opportunist* robber is probably the most common type of robber (Smith and Hung, 2008). Opportunists do not commit to robbery on a long-term basis such as professionals do. Rather, these individuals rob infrequently, choosing such easily accessible and vulnerable victims as the elderly, public drunks, taxi drivers, and people walking alone on unlit streets. Opportunists are sometimes involved in other forms of conventional property theft, such as burglary. When we commonly think of "street crime" or "muggings," we have opportunistic robbery in mind. Such haphazard, random, and spur-of-the-moment robberies generally net only small amounts of cash (McCorkle and Miethe, 2003; Calder, 2001).

Four of every five opportunistic robberies are the work of strangers to the victim(s), and opportunists rob their victims—more than half the time—on the street or in some outdoor area near their own home, such as a park, a playground, or a parking lot. Opportunistic robberies occur more often in inner districts of the largest cities. As shown in Table 11.1, street/highway robberies reported to police increase as size of city population increases. The table also shows

that although street robberies increase with city size, other forms of robbery actually decrease with city size.

## ROBBERY AS TRANSACTION

Robbery is similar to murder and assault, in that it involves a face-to-face confrontation between offender and victim. In fact, Luckenbill's (1981) classic research on robbery suggests that it involves a four-stage *transaction* between offender and victim. Each stage consists of important tasks that the offender and victim execute together. First, once a victim has been selected, the offender *creates copresence* with the victim by moving into striking range without causing suspicion. In other words, the robber attempts a "normal appearance" while maintaining an appropriate position for the imminent robbery. Second, after establishing copresence, and after the offender decides

**TABLE 11.1   ROBBERY, LOCATION. PERCENT DISTRIBUTION BY POPULATION GROUP, 2007**

| Type | Group I (61 cities, 250,000 and over; population 38,190,834) | Group II (162 cities, 100,000 to 249,999; population 24,273,026) | Group III (426 cities, 50,000 to 99,999; population 29,252,848) | Group IV (724 cities, 25,000 to 49,999; population 24,940,391) | Group V (1,599 cities, 10,000 to 24,999; population 25,356,536) | Group VI (6,425 cities, under 10,000; population 20,816,186) | County agencies (3,612 agencies; population 82,797,741) |
|---|---|---|---|---|---|---|---|
| Total[1] | 100.0 | 100.0 | 100.0 | 100.0 | 100.0 | 100.0 | 100.0 |
| Street/highway | 52.5 | 44.8 | 39.5 | 37.1 | 30.1 | 25.5 | 33.8 |
| Commercial house | 11.9 | 14.7 | 15.6 | 14.8 | 16.7 | 13.1 | 16.2 |
| Gas or service station | 1.9 | 2.5 | 3.0 | 3.3 | 3.9 | 4.0 | 3.4 |
| Convenience store | 4.1 | 5.8 | 6.4 | 6.7 | 8.0 | 8.8 | 6.8 |
| Residence | 14.0 | 14.5 | 13.7 | 13.6 | 15.6 | 14.7 | 21.2 |
| Bank | 1.4 | 2.0 | 2.6 | 2.9 | 3.6 | 3.3 | 2.3 |
| Miscellaneous | 14.1 | 15.7 | 19.3 | 21.6 | 22.1 | 30.7 | 16.3 |

Source: *Crime in the United States, 2007.*
*U.S. Department of Justice—Federal Bureau of Investigation* September 2008.

[1] Because of rounding, the percentages may not add to 100.0.

and subsequently initiates the robbery, the victim determines whether to resist. At the same time, the offender considers how much force, if any, is required to obtain the desired property. It is this interaction, and acknowledgment by both offender and victim, that *creates a common robbery frame* to which each, Luckenbill argues, most likely adheres. Third, once a common robbery frame is established, the *property is transferred.* Although the transfer is usually controlled by the offender, several obstructions may occur: The victim may not adhere to the robbery frame, outsiders may disrupt the robbery, or the offender may not have the knowledge and skill required to complete the transfer. Assuming transfer of the property is successful, in the fourth stage the offender tries to *escape,* such as by jumping into a getaway car or containing the victim in some fashion.

Luckenbill's research shows that robbery is more than just an offender's illegal behavior. It is an interaction involving joint contributions by both offender and victim. However, although both offender and victim contribute, it is hardly a simple *transaction* between equal partners, as Luckenbill suggests. The key point in a robbery scenario is that the interaction is coercive. One party—the offender—exercises dominance over the victim. *Transaction* implies equality, yet equality does not exist between robbery victim and offender.

It is also questionable whether Luckenbill's model applies to all robbery types. For instance, it does not apply especially well to the robbing of banks and armored cars, to muggings and purse snatchings, and to robbery during a burglary. Yet these robbery types constitute the majority of all robberies (Smith and Hung, 2008). More than half of all robberies are committed against persons who, as part of their employment, are in charge of money and goods (for example, banks and armored cars); 20–25 percent of robberies occur in the open following a sudden attack (such as muggings and purse snatchings);

and 12–17 percent of robberies occur on private premises (for instance, during a burglary) (Walsh, 1986; Gill, 2001). Recent research on "moralistic street robbery" likewise does not support Luckenbill's perspective, given that such robbers engage in the crime because of disputes with partners in trade, because their character has been challenged, or because the offender's belief in a just world has been jeopardized (Jacobs and Wright, 2008). And research by Porter and Laurence (2006) show that interaction between offender and victim must take into consideration the type of victim—commercial versus personal robberies—as well as interpersonal themes—such as dominance, submission, hostility, and cooperation—during the robbery incident.

Moreover, Luckenbill's research ignores the similarities and differences between male and female robbers. In an important study, Jody Miller (1998) found that male and female robbers have similar motives: Both want to obtain money to purchase status-enhancing commodities, such as jewelry and illegal drugs. Male and female robbers differ, however, in the way they accomplish the robbery transaction. Males use guns placed on the body of the victim or in close proximity to the victim, in a confrontational manner. Female robbers engage in three much less confrontational forms of interaction. First, they are more likely than male robbers to choose females as victims because, from their point of view, they are easier to rob—i.e., women victims rarely fight back. Second, female robbers often promise men sexual favors and, when the male is in a vulnerable position and his guard is down, run off with his money or goods. Finally, female robbers will work with male robbers as subordinate accomplices to robbery.

## ROBBERS ON ROBBERY

Richard Wright and Scott Decker's (1997) classic study of "active armed robbers" sheds light on the processes involved in committing the crime of armed robbery. Unlike previous studies of robbery, which focused on incarcerated offenders, these criminologists interviewed 86 offenders who were actively involved in robbery on the streets of St. Louis, Missouri. The interviews generated data from the robbers' perspective on (1) why they commit robbery, (2) how they choose the target, and (3) how they commit the offense. Regarding the first, the vast majority of the offenders committed robbery because of deep involvement in self-indulgent activities promoted by street culture, such as gambling, alcohol use, and drug use. When faced with a pressing need for cash, these individuals turned to robbery as the quickest and easiest way out of financial difficulties.

In choosing a target, most of the robbers reported that they preferred victims in close proximity to where they lived, typically preying on local criminals, especially street-corner drug dealers. Drug dealers are "good robbery victims" because they carry plenty of cash and are in no position to report their victimization to the police. Of course, these robbers also robbed law-abiding citizens, choosing victims who indicate through their demeanor and dress that they have a supply of easily available cash. A few of the robbers Wright and Decker interviewed victimized small commercial establishments, such as liquor stores, gas stations, taverns, and pawn shops. These businesses were chosen because they also had cash readily available.

Having decided to rob and having settled on a particular target, the robber must next "pull it off"—that is, commit to the robbery and carry it out. Here Wright and Decker's data correspond with Luckenbill's perspective discussed earlier. First, robbers approach the victim, announcing the robbery and allowing victims no room for negotiation by "creating an illusion of impending death" (p. 96). Robbers attempt to catch victims off guard and, through tough talk, a fierce

demeanor, and the display of a deadly weapon, usually scare people into compliance. Once dominance over the victim is established, the robber attempts to manage the transfer of goods. Many armed robbers simply order victims to "hand over the money," whereas some choose to search their victims. Only if victims fail to comply with demands do robbers turn to violence. As Wright and Decker explain,

> faced with a recalcitrant victim, most of the offenders responded with severe but nonlethal violence in the hope of convincing the person to cooperate. Often this violence involved smacking or beating the victim about the head with a pistol. (p. 113)

Finally, the offender must escape. Most of the robbers in this study preferred to be the first to depart the robbery scene. However, before making their escape, these robbers once again made verbal threats, such as "If you come out of this alley ... I'm gonna shoot the shit out of you" (Wright and Decker:116). Such threats are designed to continue the illusion of impending death from the beginning of the robbery to its completion.

In many accounts, robbers seem to be involved in a precisely calculated strategy of cause and effect. They appear as actors who, despite the illegality of their actions, pursue their aims with considerable choice and rational calculation. However, this image of the reasoning criminal is far less neat and tidy in the messiness of real life. For example, from their reading of 5,000 police statements and from several interviews and group discussions with perpetrators of street robbery in the city of Amsterdam, de Haan and Vos (2003) show that "rationality" is not the only thing to consider when trying to understand what robbers do. Robbers routinely act inconsistently. They stumble around impulsively. They operate with emotions such as guilt and shame. Moreover, from interviews with 350 armed robbers in Britain, Roger Matthews (2002) concluded that many robbers are drunk or on drugs just before or during their robberies. Indeed, in addition to consuming drugs and/or alcohol prior to offending, establishments traditionally targeted by professional robbers are now being victimized by offenders characterized as "drug involved," who are desperate and thus volatile and who are robbing to finance a need for illicit drugs (Willis, 2006). Nevertheless, in addition to a life focused on drug use, robbers engage in this crime to accumulate street capital through status-enhancing items (e.g., jewelry and money) to increase their masculine image in a street culture (Brookman, Mullins, and Bennett, 2007).

## BURGLARY

**Burglary** is defined as unlawful entry of a house, business, or other structure with the intent to commit a felony. Whereas robbery entails theft through the threat or actual use of violence, for burglary to occur someone must actually enter a structure unlawfully with the intent to commit a felony. Moreover, burglary—like the other property crimes to be discussed in this chapter—differs from robbery in another critical way: It seldom involves a direct, face-to-face confrontation between offender and victim.

In 2007, 2,179,140 burglaries were reported to the police, or approximately 722.5 per 100,000 inhabitants (Federal Bureau of Investigation, 2008). However, the NCVS reported that only about 50 percent of all burglaries are reported to the police. Consequently, the NCVS typically reports almost 1 million more burglaries than the FBI, for a total of 3.5 million. As with robbery, the police probably know about no more than 50 percent of all burglaries.

Burglars can also be classified as amateurs or professionals. Both are similar in that they may burglarize houses or businesses and may operate alone or work with others in a team (Cromwell and Jolicouer, 2001). However, they also differ in important ways. *Amateur burglars* enter a structure when they "feel the need." Their style of intrusion is unsophisticated—perhaps simply breaking a window or breaking down a door. Because amateurs are more interested in volume of burglaries than in quality, little planning is involved. Amateur burglars rarely specialize in theft of specific items but, rather, steal a variety of merchandise as opportunities arise, usually accessible goods such as televisions, stereos, VCRs, CD players, silverware, jewelry, and money. Thus, amateurs are usually juveniles or young adults who lack a commitment to crime and do not think of themselves as "thieves." Moreover, the vast majority come from economically deprived backgrounds, are undereducated, and are often addicted to drugs (Mawby, 2001).

*Professional burglars* are specialists who use considerable skill and planning. Professionals have "external contacts" about specific goods to steal, are systematic in their offenses, and plan their crimes carefully (Cromwell and Jolicouer, 2001). A good example of a professional burglar is Harry King, a *box-man* (safecracker) who reported to Chambliss (King and Chambliss, 1984) all the intrigues and skill required to enter a building successfully, open or "kidnap" a safe, and efficiently escape. King learned his trade from another professional box-man, working initially as an apprentice. He eventually made his living from burglary, engaging in extensive planning and never feeling the need to carry a weapon during a "caper." Moreover, he kept up with the latest technology applicable to his trade. According to King, it is essential for the professional to be familiar with the latest "burglary tools," such as drills and saws, and to spend time practicing and preparing for future capers (p. 35).

Professional burglars also rely on contacts with tipsters, or persons who identify possible targets for the burglar. In addition to tipsters, professional burglars establish important contacts with police, attorneys, and judges. This liaison with members of the criminal justice system frequently allows professional burglars to "fix" their cases prior to committing the burglaries. King found it easy to fix cases because "the only people that really profit from theft are the fix, the judge, and the district attorney" (King and Chambliss, 1984:84).

Burglary is usually classified as either residential or commercial. The majority of residential burglaries (60 percent) occur during the day, when residents are not usually at home, whereas the majority of commercial burglaries (65 percent) take place in the late evening or early morning, when businesses are closed (Coupe and Blake, 2006). Moreover, whether residential or commercial, 60 percent of all burglaries involve forcible entry, 27 percent involve attempted forcible entry, and the remainder entail an illegal entry with no force (Cromwell and Jolicouer, 2001).

## BURGLARS ON BURGLARY

Several researchers have interviewed active residential burglars (Cromwell, Olson, and Avary, 1991; Wright and Decker, 1994; Nee and Meenaghan, 2006). The major conclusions of these studies of "burglars on burglary" include the following:

- Need for money is the primary motivation for involvement in burglary. A legitimate job, when available, does not adequately satisfy the immediacy of desire of cash.
- The majority of burglars cannot compete in the labor market, because they are poorly educated, unskilled, and heavy illicit drug and alcohol users.
- Burglars use their proceeds for food, shelter, and clothing, yet most of their gain goes toward the maintenance of a "partying" lifestyle based in illicit drug and alcohol use.
- Burglary is a means for a burglar to "be somebody" by successfully completing a dangerous act.

- Most burglars decide to commit a burglary away from the scene of the crime, they then search for a suitable neighborhood until they find an attractive target, and then they watch this potential target before committing a burglary.
- Burglars choose residences to burglarize because of "external cues"—such as the size and condition of the dwelling and type of cars in the driveway—suggesting that there are goods worth stealing inside.
- Once a residence is chosen as a possible target, burglars use a decision-making strategy consisting of three questions: (1) Can the residence be entered without the burglar's being seen and reported? (2) Is the residence currently occupied? (3) Can the residence be broken into easily? If the answer is "yes" to all three questions, the burglar will probably proceed.
- Most burglaries are committed during daytime hours, when victims usually are at work, and burglars typically, but not always, work alone.
- Situational factors, such as the presence of a dog, an alarm system, and alert neighbors, are the most effective deterrents to burglars.

None of the studies cited so far examines how gender affects residential burglary. However, a study by Mullins and Wright (2003) compared the similarities and differences between male and female burglars. Their data are drawn from interviews with currently active (not incarcerated, and interviewed on the street) young adult residential burglars—eighteen females and thirty-six males—and reveal some interesting findings. First, the vast majority of all burglars were initiated into burglary through interaction with intimate groups, committing their first burglary with friends, family members, or street associates. However, men were more likely to have been introduced to burglary by same-sex friends,

## BOX 11.1 PERSISTENT PROPERTY OFFENDERS

An important question asked by criminologists is why offenders persist in committing crime, that is, why, even after arrest, conviction, and incarceration, many continue to engage in property crime?

Kenneth Tunnell, in his classic book *Choosing Crime* (1992), examined this question by interviewing sixty chronic repeat property offenders. These were individuals who had committed a great number of crimes (mostly robbery and burglary) and with considerable frequency. In questioning these offenders about their motivation to commit property crimes continually, Tunnell found that 88 percent engaged in crime for "quick, easy money" to be used for living expenses and pleasurable commodities, such as illicit drugs (p. 39). In addition, many property offenders commit these crimes for a sense of accomplishment, to gain power over someone, for revenge, or simply as a sport.

This engagement in property crime primarily for money is related to their class position and, therefore, limited access to legitimate alternatives. As Tunnell (1992) found through his interviews, repetitive offenders choose "the best alternative available to them since crime often allowed them to obtain satisfaction of their immediate needs" (p. 70). Indeed, these offenders spent money as quickly as it came in and therefore had little to show for their risky criminal activity. Since the immediate need for drugs and easily consumable commodities continued, along with a lack of legitimate legal options, these criminals persisted in property crime.

An interesting aspect of this study considered whether the decision to commit crime was related to possible negative consequences of their illegal actions—getting caught. As Tunnell reported:

> Nearly all sixty reported they rarely considered the threat of capture, arrest, and imprisonment and that risk was considered a nuisance rather than a real, tangible threat. Risk-related thoughts were considered distracting from their prime objective—committing the crime. Thus, many were simply able to not think about risks and put them out of their minds. (1992:100)

Thus, crime control policies based on severe penalties (such as lengthy prison sentences) that attempt to scare criminals to "go straight" do not seem to have an impact on persistent property offenders.

In his more recent work, *Living Off Crime*, Tunnell (2006) concentrates his analysis more centrally on the issue of social class, in particular how persistent property criminals are embedded within "class-based opportunities, lower-class criminal subcultures, and lower-class criminal lifestyles" (p. 6). Tunnell shows how these class conditions structure forms of consciousness conducive to persistent property offending, such as an overwhelming rejection of wage labor and a desire for fashionable clothing to project the coolest, masculine look; indeed, involvement in persistent property crimes constructs a "public masculinity" that is simultaneously "widespread and inseparable from their ongoing, hedonistic, autonomous, trouble-filled lives" (p. 52).

An interesting earlier study of street robbers and burglars is Neal Shover's (1996) similar exploration of why property offenders persist in committing crime. Shover likewise shows how the class background of persistent robbers and burglars limits their legitimate occupational options and, therefore, their ultimate choices. Born into a life of poverty, lower-working-class children are prepared to accept these limited legitimate choices. After dropping out of school, many are attracted to the local street culture, making it even more difficult for them to "defer gratification" in favor of long-term goals. Shover has shown that the street culture is much too attractive because of its emphasis of "life as party":

> The hallmark of life as party is enjoyment of "good times" with minimal concern for obligations and commitments external to the person's immediate social setting. Those who pursue life as party are determined to suspend concern for serious matters in favor of enjoying the moment.... Life as party is enjoyed in the company of alcohol and other drugs. In bars and lounges, on street corners, or while cruising in automobiles, party pursuers celebrate and affirm values of spontaneity, independence, and resourcefulness. (pp. 93–94)

The pursuit of life as party quickly exhausts one's meager financial resources. Consequently, members of the street culture oscillate in and out of financial desperation. Robbery and burglary, then, become solutions for obtaining the badly needed "fast money" to participate adequately in the party. Thus, the cycle continues, and members of the street culture become persistent property offenders.

while the women often were initiated to burglary through interaction with their boyfriends. Second, both male and female burglars reported similar motives for engaging in residential burglary—to finance a "party" lifestyle that centers on illicit drug use and flamboyant display of designer clothing and jewelry. However, once again differences were found: Female burglars committed the crime also to help provide the basic necessities for others (such as food, shelter, and clothing for children), whereas the male burglars emphasized protecting their street status by satisfying their own needs.

Third, during the commission of the crime, males prefer to burglarize alone or with other men because they feel that women are untrustworthy. When men and women work together on a burglary, the female usually takes on a subordinate role, seldom planning the crime or entering the residence but, rather, serving as the "lookout" and the "get-away driver." Finally, regarding desistance from residential burglary, the men claimed that a good legal job or a stable relationship with a woman would deter them from committing this crime. In contrast, the vast majority of female burglars stated that for them to refrain from engaging in this crime they would need to sever their relationship with criminally involved males. Thus, Mullins and Wright conclude that the social processes involved in residential burglary—initiation, commission, and potential desistance—are heavily structured by gender and that, in particular, women must "negotiate male-dominated networks and landscapes in accomplishing their crimes" (2003:833).

## 11.2 VARIETIES OF LARCENY

In Section 13.1 we discuss employee theft—workers who take merchandise and job-related items from their workplace. Our concern here, however, is with nonoccupational theft, or what is commonly referred to as larceny. **Larceny** is the unlawful taking of property from the possession of someone other than one's employer. A larceny does *not* involve the threat of actual use of force (robbery)—with the exception of carjacking—or breaking and entering (burglary). In 2007, 6.5 million larcenies were reported to the police, or approximately 2,178 per 100,000 inhabitants (Federal Bureau of Investigation, 2008).

The NCVS does not use the term *larceny* but, rather, *theft*, which refers to personal larcenies without contact, such as theft of an umbrella from a restaurant, a radio from a beach, or a bicycle from a schoolyard. Only 17 percent of such thefts valued at less than $50 were reported to the police in 2007. However, in the same year, for thefts of $250 or more, 56 percent were reported to the police. Thus, the greater the value of the merchandise stolen, the greater the likelihood the theft will be reported to the police. Finally, given these reporting figures, we should not be surprised to find that the NCVS reported more than twice as many victimizations as the UCR: In 2006 there were 14.3 million (Department of Justice, 2008).

In this section we discuss three major types of larceny: shoplifting, motor vehicle theft, and fraud.

## SHOPLIFTING

One particular type of larceny—shoplifting—has been accorded considerable attention by sociologists and criminologists. **Shoplifting**—theft of property from a retail store by "customers"—results in approximately $31 billion of lost merchandise each year (Klemke, 2001; Caputo, 2008).

One of the earliest efforts by a sociologist to study shoplifting is the classic work by Mary Owen Cameron (1964), *The Booster and the Snitch.* Cameron divided shoplifters into two types: *boosters*, who steal merchandise to sell it, and *snitches*, who steal for their own consumption. In other words, the booster is a professional who steals for the purpose of making money, and the snitch is an amateur who steals for personal use. According to Cameron, boosters—comprising about 10 percent of shoplifters—possess five characteristics:

1. Boosters work a large number of stores rather than a few large stores.
2. Boosters use considerable planning and skill to execute their theft.
3. Boosters steal only expensive merchandise and, like professional robbers and burglars, sell it to a professional fence.
4. Boosters often easily "fix" their cases if caught.
5. Boosters use sophisticated methods and devices for engaging in shoplifting.

These devices include *booster bloomers*, garments especially designed to hold stolen merchandise, and *booster boxes*, specifically designed to look like wrapped packages but that actually contain secret openings into which items can be placed quickly and easily.

Other studies of boosters found that they usually operate as a team, in which one member distracts sales associates, a second takes the item and surreptitiously passes it to a third, who then takes the item(s) out of the store (Klemke, 2001; Cromwell, 2002).

The other 90 percent of shoplifters, according to Cameron, are snitches, or amateurs, who possess the following characteristics:

1. They are "respectable" members of the community.
2. They do not think of themselves as criminals.
3. They have no criminal associations or connections.
4. They steal from a store when the opportunity arises.
5. They do not plan extensively but enter the store "prepared" to shoplift (equipped with "shopping lists," large handbags, briefcases, shopping bags, and scissors and razor blades for snipping off price tags).

Snitches simply place items in pockets or inside coats, sometimes actually wearing the stolen merchandise under their clothing, or engage in such activities as price-tag switching, in which they pay less for merchandise. Recent examinations of snitches confirm Cameron's initial insights (Klemke, 2001; Cromwell, 2002).

Cameron's findings about boosters and snitches are important because they show shoplifting to be a frequent crime and one that is not primarily committed by professionals, "lower-class" people, or a unique "criminal element." Rather, shoplifting is committed by "normal" and "ordinary" individuals. However, the most active shoplifters seem to be teenagers, with activity peaking at age 17, when approximately 39 percent of males and 23 percent of females admit having engaged in this crime at least once during the previous year. The percentage declines rapidly with age, so that by age 23 only 11 percent of males and 7 percent of females admit having shoplifted in the previous year (Klemke, 2001). And the most frequently shoplifted items are cigarettes, cosmetics, meat, batteries, film, jewelry, clothing, and music disks (Cromwell, 2002). More recent research confirms what was just discussed but also indicates that persistent property offenders are more likely to engage in a variety of property crimes, such as shoplifting and burglary (Schneider, 2005), and first-time shoplifters tend to engage in "moral reasoning" prior to offending, such as considering the risk involved, the offender's actual need for the item(s), and the opinion of peers (Forney, Forney, and Crutsinger, 2005). Gail Caputo's (2008) recent research also sheds light on the notion of the "booster," arguing that the drug-addicted women she interviewed engaged in shoplifting primarily for economic gain to pay for the desired drugs as well as for the necessities of life (food, shelter, clothing, etc.). The women sold the merchandise they shoplifted to individuals as well as to small "mom and pop" stores, thereby viewing their shoplifting as work that involved habit, ethic, technique, and skill. Thus, these drug-addicted women shoplifters can be considered contemporary professional boosters in terms of both criminal motivation and method, whose crime is embedded in a supportive and organized illicit economy in their neighborhoods.

## MOTOR VEHICLE THEFT

**Motor vehicle theft** is the unlawful taking of or attempting to take a motor vehicle, such as an automobile, a van, a truck, or a motorcycle. In 2007, 1,095,769 motor vehicle thefts were reported to the police, or approximately 433 per 100,000 inhabitants (Federal Bureau of Investigation, 2008). In 2007, the estimated national loss from reported motor vehicle theft was $7.6 billion, and at the time of the theft the average value per vehicle stolen was $4,713.

The NCVS found that for 2007, 89 percent of completed motor vehicle theft victimizations were reported to the police. Not surprisingly, the NCVS reported a figure close to the FBI total: approximately 992,260 motor vehicle thefts in 2007.

Most scholars have concentrated on one type of motor vehicle theft, **automobile theft.** This is probably the best reported of all property crimes (90 percent) because of (1) the high value of vehicles, (2) insurance requirements, (3) the assistance needed from police to recover stolen cars, and (4) the high probability that stolen cars will actually be located.

As with robbery, burglary, and shoplifting, sociologists have divided auto thefts into the primary types of amateur and professional. One of the earliest applications of this typology is in

Jerome Hall's (1952) well-known book, *Theft, Law, and Society.* For Hall, most auto thieves are amateur joyriders who steal automobiles for excitement and to "show off," quickly abandoning the car after a short time. According to Hall, joyriders mostly steal cars with unlocked doors, open windows, keys in the ignition, and sometimes even the motor running. Professional auto thieves steal automobiles in more indirect and skillful ways. According to Hall, many simply work with repair-shop employees who secure duplicate keys for the thief. Others steal cars advertised in newspapers by providing the owner with a "down payment," never to be heard from again. Once an automobile is stolen, many professionals work with or personally control a *chop-shop*, in which stolen automobiles are stripped of all sellable accessories. These accessories are sold to dealers, repair shops and garages, and professional fences.

McCaghy, Giordano, and Henson (1977) argue that Hall's typology is too simplistic for this crime. According to these sociologists, auto thieves "are a more complex lot" (p. 377), and they have suggested a typology that includes five categories: (1) joyriding, (2) short-term transportation, (3) long-term transportation, (4) commission of another crime, and (5) profit. We now examine each.

McCaghy, Giordano, and Henson agree with Hall that joyriding auto theft signifies recreational, nonutilitarian, short-term use of cars. For the joyrider, the primary goal is not to obtain transportation; rather, "automobile symbolism is predominant: The car is stolen not for what it does, but for what it means" (McCaghy, Giordano, and Henson, 1977:378). The second type—short-term transportation—is similar to joyriding, in that it clearly involves short-term use of a stolen automobile. It differs, however, in that the thief's primary interest in the car is its ability to provide transportation from one location to another—from one place in the city to another or even from one state to another. As with joyriding, many juveniles are involved in short-term auto theft.

The third type—long-term transportation—involves thieves stealing the vehicle with the intent of keeping it for long-term personal use. This type of auto thief usually steals automobiles outside his or her state of residence and, on returning home, if not before, repaints the vehicle. Most long-term auto thieves are adults. Some auto thieves—the fourth type—steal cars to aid them in the commission of another crime, such as robbery or burglary. This fourth type represents only a small portion of all auto thefts, even though the scenario is depicted over and over again on prime-time television. Once again, the motivation is the utility of the automobile.

Finally, the fifth type identified by McCaghy, Giordano, and Henson is theft for profit, which is somewhat similar to Hall's professional theft. However, for McCaghy, Giordano, and Henson, this fifth type of automobile thief includes a wide variety of individuals whose motive is not to keep the car but, rather, to resell it or its parts for profit. They identify two forms of this type: amateurs and professionals. Amateurs steal a car to strip it of easily accessible components such as batteries, tires, and a variety of engine parts. They sell these parts to friends, acquaintances, or amateur fences, or they re-equip their own cars using some of the parts. Professionals, however, are highly organized, reselling expensive stolen cars in the United States and internationally. Professionals alter the vehicle registration numbers and falsify registration papers. Many purchase expensive wrecked vehicles and their ownership documents for a low cost and then steal an identical car (year, make, model), replacing the vehicle identification number plate with that of the wrecked vehicle and making other minor alterations. Subsequently, the converted vehicle is sold to an unsuspecting party who registers and retitles the vehicle in his or her name, giving it a legitimate

identity virtually impossible to trace to the thief. McCaghy, Giordano, and Henson argue that professionals are also involved in the chop-shop business, specializing in the sale of specific parts to fences: hoods, fenders, bumpers, grills, and other hard-to-obtain parts.

Although amateurs and professionals clearly differ in skill and quality of theft, they both consider the automobile a valuable piece of property. Auto theft for profit differs from the other types of auto theft identified by McCaghy, Giordano, and Henson—joyriding, short-and long-term transportation, and aiding in the commission of another crime—because those who commit these latter types consider the automobile either a symbol or a form of transportation.

Ronald Clarke and Patricia Harris (1992) have provided a typology of auto theft that includes three types:

1. Thefts for temporary use, such as joyriding and short-term transportation.
2. Professional thefts intended to deprive the owner permanently of the vehicle, which is used for resale, for export, or for chopping.
3. Thefts from vehicles, such as CD players, radios, and batteries.

Clarke and Harris' typology differs from those of other researchers in one basic way: It includes "theft from vehicles" as a category of auto theft.

Claire Corbett (2003) constructed the most recent typology of auto theft (similar to Clarke and Harris's) that includes the following three types:

- Theft for contents and parts.
- Joyriding.
- Professional theft.

In the past, auto thieves stole "internal parts" of the automobile—such as CD players and speakers—but Corbett records that today "external parts," such as bumpers, wheels, and license plates, are the parts mostly targeted by auto thieves. Regarding joyriding, Corbett notes that this form of auto theft does not actually maintain much joy for the rider once it is recognized that joyriders are 200 times more likely than other drivers to become crash-involved. Moreover, teenage males are by far the most frequent offenders, being six times more likely to have stolen an automobile than any-age female. Finally, professional auto thieves usually began as joyriders, work together in teams, and normally have some type of connection with the legitimate auto trade. In addition, most auto theft occurs in lower-class neighborhoods, and increasing numbers of auto thieves steal the keys first—through burglary, robbery, and fraud—prior to engaging in this particular theft (Walsh and Taylor, 2007; Copes and Cherbonneau, 2006).

All of the foregoing examples of auto theft usually occur without direct contact between offender and victim. However, during and since the 1990s a new type of auto theft began to be discussed in the media, **carjacking**, in which the auto thief uses direct physical force to steal a car from a driver. In a carjacking, automobiles are stolen from drivers at such places as rest stops, service stations, car washes, red lights, and shopping mall parking lots. Some facts on carjacking include (Copes and Wallace, 2001):

- The rate of carjacking is approximately 25 per 100,000 population.
- Fifty percent of carjackings are successful.
- Victims are injured in 23 percent of completed carjackings and in 10 percent of attempted carjackings.
- Offenders use a weapon in 83 percent of all attempted and completed carjackings.

### FRAUD

In Sections 13.1 and 13.2 we discuss occupational fraud and corporate financial fraud; here we focus on nonoccupationally related frauds, such as check and credit-card fraud and income-tax fraud. We begin with an examination of check fraud.

*Check fraud.* The crimes thus far analyzed—robbery, burglary, shoplifting, and motor vehicle theft—are clearly recognizable as crimes by an offender against a victim. In contrast, **check fraud**—deliberately deceiving someone for personal economic gain by producing a counterfeit or forged check—has little in the act to identify it as a crime. In other words, check fraud is not at the time of its commission easily recognizable as a crime. Indeed, this holds true for all forms of fraud discussed in this section; it is not until sometime later that the event is determined to be a crime.

Individuals can even engage in check fraud without knowing it. For instance, if someone continually writes checks against his or her account at a time when that account does not hold sufficient funds to cover the checks, the checks are normally returned with the designation "Nonsufficient Funds" (NSF), and the individual could be prosecuted for fraud. Other forms of check fraud include altering checks, forging someone else's personal checks, producing counterfeit personal and payroll checks, stealing government checks (checks rendering a salary, tax refund, pension, welfare allotment, and/or veteran benefit), forging a signature, and *check kiting*, or gaining access to funds deposited in a bank before they are collected from the bank from which they are drawn (Scarpitti and Lenhart, 2001; Walsh, 2005).

Lemert's (1967) classic study of "naive" and "systematic" check forgery remains the most extensive examination of check fraud. *Naive check forgers* are amateurs who commit the crime only when they have an urgent need for money and who are unfamiliar with "criminal techniques." The naive check forger, Lemert found, ordinarily has completed more years of school than the general population and works in a clerical, skilled, or professional occupation. Lemert also established that a majority of naive check forgers reside in the community in which their crimes are committed.

*Systematic check forgers* view themselves as forgers, regularly use a special technique to pass bad checks, and organize their lives around check fraud. Some systematic check forgers view their fraud as a "regular business," but most do not, engaging in it for the alleged "fast and luxurious" life. These forgers give special attention to such details as banking hours and the best places to present checks; yet, according to Lemert (1967), such details serve only as "guides" for the fraud. Moreover, systematic check forgers are less likely than other professional property offenders to use the "fix," because they simply have "too many bad checks outstanding and too many victims to mollify by offering restitution" (p. 111). The systematic check forger is different from other professional property offenders in another way. According to Lemert, check forgery requires neither a high degree of technical skill nor a long learning "apprenticeship"; you simply "learn as you go." However, systematic check forgery does require the ability to impersonate someone else, and therefore success is based on development of expertise in assuming fictitious roles. Finally, although systematic check forgers tend to be migratory (like other professional property offenders), most tend to work alone, avoiding contact with a network of illegitimate and legitimate people. Lemert found that some systematic check forgers work in "check-passing gangs" and a few "contract out" their services; however, the majority operate on a solitary basis. These forgers manufacture or steal checks (usually personal or payroll checks) and then work alone to pass them illegally.

**Credit-Card and Related Fraud.** Lemert's discussion of check fraud identified fraudsters as amateurs and professionals; the same classification holds for **credit-card fraud.** The typical perpetrator of credit-card fraud is someone of modest means who finds himself or herself in need of money and subsequently views illegal credit-card use as the easiest way of satisfying that need (Scarpitti and Lenhart, 2001). Professionals usually work in groups who move from town to town in order to avoid detection and who concentrate on elaborate methods of stealing and manufacturing illegal credit cards.

Other methods of professional fraudsters include check guarantee fraud, purchase credit-card fraud, and purchase check fraud. The first, *check guarantee fraud,* occurs when individuals "ride" a stolen credit card—or several cards—by cashing checks (also stolen) in numerous bank branches in the shortest possible time. The term *ride* refers to the total number of banks visited by fraudsters with just one credit card; "the take" is the total amount of cash withdrawals per ride. *Purchase check* and *purchase credit-card fraud* simply entail using stolen checks and credit cards to purchase goods from retail stores. A group network of fraud usually consists of thieves (people who steal the checks and cards), riders (people who use the checks and cards in banks and stores), and fences (who buy the fraudulently obtained merchandise). Research indicates that large organized schemes account for half the total dollar loss due to credit-card fraud (Scarpitti and Lenhart, 2001). The fastest-growing type of credit card fraud is *counterfeiting cards,* whereby fraudsters use the Internet and other forms of technology to create a fictitious card or to duplicate information from a valid card—obtaining names, account numbers, credit limits, and other identifying information—and thus create a fraudulent credit card with ease (Ross, 2005a).

*Income-Tax Fraud.* The government is also a potential victim of fraudsters. Indeed, the potential for defrauding the government is actually limitless because of the vast number and variety of government programs. To fraudsters, the

**BOX 11.2  IDENTITY THEFT**

**Identity theft** occurs when someone adopts another person's identity, usually to facilitate further crime. The identity thief essentially steals the personhood of another by asserting in various ways to be that person. Thus, identity theft entails the fraudulent use of personal information to pretend to be someone else.

Emily Finch (2003) has developed an interesting typology of identity theft. She distinguishes two types of identity theft that differ in three major ways: duration, level of immersion, and motivation. *Duration* refers to the amount of time one fraudulently adopts another identity—from a few minutes to lifelong use. *Level of immersion* is "the depth with which the imposter delves into the victim's life and to the range and extent of the personal details that are misappropriated" (p. 90). Level of immersion, then, varies from illegally possessing and using someone's name and date of birth to more complex situations involving financial, employment, and education details to masquerade as the victim.

A combination of duration and level of immersion establishes the two major types of identity theft—*total identity theft* and *partial identity theft*. When someone permanently adopts all the details of another persons life, the offender has engaged in total identity theft, whereas the temporary use of someone's personal information is classified as partial identity theft.

*Motivation* is related to both types of identity theft in various ways. For example, partial and total identity theft often involve the adoption of the victim's identity solely for the commission of a crime, such as fraudulently obtaining access to goods and services. According to

Finch (2003), this is "the most prevalent form of identity theft as it accounts for the vast majority of partial identity theft and a significant proportion of cases of total identity theft" (p. 90). Moreover, adopting another person's identity—either for temporary or lifelong duration—can help an offender avoid detection by ensuring that his or her criminal acts (otherwise unrelated to the identity theft) are attributed to someone else. In these types of cases the motivation is to use another's identity to avoid detection should the identity thief be caught engaging in other criminal activities.

Nevertheless, identity theft does not always entail attempts to avoid detection or to facilitate fraudulent behavior; it also can provide a means to escape an unsatisfactory life and obtain the opportunity to begin anew. As Finch (2003) puts it:

> This urge to reinvent oneself may derive from a general sense of dissatisfaction with one's own identity or be a way to escape from some particularly problematic aspect of life such as debt or a traumatic relationship. Identity theft provides both a practical and symbolic respite from a life that has gone wrong by enabling the individual to escape the problem and to acquire a legal identity that is in accord with his or her perceived or desired individual identity. (p. 91)

Given that everything the identity thief requires to select a victim and fraudulently appropriate his or her identity is now available on the Internet, identity theft has been labeled by the Federal Trade Commission as "the fastest-growing crime of our time" (Finch, 2003:94) (see also, Finch and Fafinski, 2009).

---

federal government is a bottomless financial pit. **Income-tax fraud**, however, is probably the most prevalent form of defrauding the government. Cheating on one's income tax is made possible in the United States because of the following (Mattera, 1985):

1. The complexity of the tax codes.
2. The seemingly infinite number of deductible expenses.
3. The Internal Revenue Service's reliance on a system in which taxpayers calculate their own tax bill.

4. The small number of returns actually scrutinized by the IRS.

Two major forms of income-tax fraud are tax avoidance and tax evasion. In *tax avoidance,* individuals may underreport wages by, for example, working a second job—for which earnings are paid in cash—but filing an income-tax return only for wages earned from the first job. Another type of tax avoidance is to earn wages and salaries in a variety of ways but to file no income-tax return for *any* portion of it. This completely off-the-books employment is not uncommon among restaurant and construction workers as well as among providers of personal services, such as house painters and appliance repair persons.

*Tax evasion* involves intentionally paying less of one's tax bill than is legally required, through the understatement of tax liability (Thurman and Vose, 2001). Approximately 80 percent of lost federal tax revenue results from underreporting of income, while overstating deductions and failing to file a return account for the remaining 20 percent. The most recent research on income-tax fraud indicates that (Desnoyers, 2005):

- It is one of the most serious types of fraud because of the size of the tax gap it produces.
- Most taxpayers do not engage in income-tax fraud.
- Taxpayers are most compliant when they feel a moral obligation to pay what they owe.
- Taxpayers who engage in tax avoidance and evasion usually subscribe to excuses to neutralize any moral guilt.

## 11.3 DEALING AND DAMAGE

Fencing and arson, although property crimes, are somewhat different from robbery, burglary, and larceny. Fencing is buying and selling—or dealing in—stolen goods, and arson involves damage to property of another.

### FENCING

As stated earlier, **fencing** is buying, selling, or dealing in stolen goods. A fence's sources of goods include robbers, burglars, shoplifters, auto thieves, fraudsters, and employee thieves (whom we examine in Section 13.1). Once a thief successfully steals "the goods" and does not plan to make personal use of them, he or she must dispose of the goods as quickly as possible. Some thieves engage in *self-fencing*—that is, selling the stolen goods to people who do not know the goods are stolen or selling them to consumers

who are unconcerned with their origin. Many people jump at the opportunity to buy items at a discount; consequently, thieves find accessible outlets for stolen merchandise in friends, acquaintances, and on the street generally.

In their interviews with burglars, Cromwell, Olson, and Avary (1991) found that the market for stolen property is both diverse and ubiquitous, including

> schoolteachers, social workers, plumbers, operators of small business establishments, attorneys, bail bond agents, drug dealers, systems analysts, college professors, high school and college students, and other individuals who regularly or occasionally purchased merchandise they knew or believed to be stolen. (p. 80)

Most of the individuals interviewed in this study reported that they bought stolen goods for personal use—and did not resell the goods—and, thus, technically, can be considered "receivers," rather than fences.

Some thieves, however, sell their goods to amateur fences. Stuart Henry's (1976, 1978) classic work on the amateur trade in stolen goods is interesting in this regard. Henry (1976) defined amateur fencing as "the activity of regular part-time purchase of genuine quality merchandise (usually, though not necessarily, stolen) for the purpose of selling cheaply for the interest of those involved" (p. 794). Most amateur fences *say* they participate in the trade of stolen goods for personal economic gain. Notwithstanding, it seems that amateur fences rarely make money. Henry found this to be the case because amateur fences are unlikely to come into contact with either highly valued articles or large quantities of these items, or, if they do, they find it is difficult to resell them. But more important, the price charged by the fence is determined by the nature of the relationship between the fence and the buyer. Most stolen goods go from the amateur fence to relatives and friends, who "are often given the goods and not even charged cost price," and when friends and relatives are charged, it is rarely more than the fence actually paid for the items (p. 798).

Thus, even though amateur fencing is structured in terms of economic exchange, Henry concluded that in actuality, the majority of deals are made for the purpose of reaffirming established relationships. Amateur fencing provides the individual fence with status, prestige, and reciprocal social favors. As Henry (1976) stated, "The social content of the relations surrounding amateur exchange outweighs the material value of the goods involved" (p. 801). Amateur trade in stolen goods becomes a means of sustaining a network of communal relations among relatives, friends, and acquaintances. Consequently, amateur trade in stolen goods is quite informal and even takes place in people's homes. Henry (1978) provided an example: "Whenever Jim, a shoplifter, supplied cheap goods to Freddy, a plumber, there would be a Sunday-morning knock at the door: 'I got some suits: Do you want them?'" (p. 18).

Many thieves, however, sell their stolen merchandise to a professional fence. For example, burglars prefer a professional fence because professionals can purchase large amounts of merchandise, tend to ask fewer questions than other buyers of stolen goods, and are motivated to be discreet about their business dealings (Wright and Decker, 1994).

Several classic studies have examined professional fencing operations in relation to property theft. Within such literature the consensus seems to be that most professional fences have strong ties to the legitimate business community. As Hall wrote in his book *Theft, Law, and Society* (1952), the professional fence is "an established participant" in the legitimate "economic life of society" (p. 155). Professional fences are "offshoots from legitimate businesses," frequently specialize in a chosen field, and thus are "able to evaluate merchandise expertly and to compete

generally on the basis of their special skills" (p. 157).

Marilyn Walsh (1977) reported that the average professional fence in her study was "a 45- to 55-year-old white, male businessman. As such, he looked strikingly similar to most managers and administrators in wholesale and retail trades." For Walsh, then, the professional fence is "strikingly dissimilar" to the thief and is "demographically a very ordinary man" (p. 15).

Finally, a study by Darrell Steffensmeier (1986) confirms that the "overwhelming majority of fences…are simultaneously proprietors or operators of a legitimate business which provides a cover or front for the fencing" (p. 20). "Sam Goodman," the main character of Steffensmeier's book, is a legitimate and successful businessperson who also—as part of his business—sells stolen merchandise. In Sam's view, it is difficult for anyone to succeed in business without "chiseling" in some form or fashion; professional fencing is simply his type of chiseling.

The legitimate business identity of the professional fence covers the comings and goings of thieves, making thieves indistinguishable from customers and legitimate delivery persons (Klockars, 1974). In short, the evidence on fencing shows that, as Henry (1977) put it,

> It is not the case that one species of actor, the "fence," buys stolen goods, whereas another, the "businessman," buys legitimate ones. Rather, it demonstrates that businessmen buy cheap goods in order that they may sell at a profit; a greater or lesser proportion of their purchases may be illicit. (p. 133).

The professional fence is "in the shadow of two worlds" (the subtitle of Steffensmeier's book), providing legitimate and illegitimate goods in the business world while simultaneously buying stolen goods in the criminal world. Professional fencing is in fact indistinguishable from legitimate business activity. The professional fence may also develop a special relationship with the police:

> Fences are able to offer various "perks" or payoffs to the police and other legal officials....In return for these perks, the police may be less zealous in responding to complaints against the fence or may sabotage an ongoing investigation. (Steffensmeier, 1986:152)

Most detectives who frequented Sam's shop were simply recipients of Sam's generosity, yet a few were "actively on the take" (p. 153).

In Klockars' (1974) earlier case study of the fence "Vincent Swaggi" it was found that the largest single group of buyers were in some way connected to the criminal justice system: police officers, detectives, lawyers, judges, customs officials, insurance adjusters, and crime reporters. The relationship between Swaggi and these buyers was quite comfortable and friendly. As Klockars pointed out,

> A joking atmosphere prevails, with "What's hot today, Vince?" as a standard opening from Vincent's law enforcement customers. Although Vincent has heard that question a thousand times he always answers, "Everything," and laughs. (p. 104)

Thus, both amateur and professional thievery, as well as amateur and professional fencing, must be understood as being embedded in a network of relations with other legitimate and illegitimate people.

More recent discussions of fencing confirm the conclusions of this earlier research, suggesting that both amateur and professional fences continue to exist (Head, 2001). However, the role of the professional fence may be changing as most thieves today dispose of their stolen merchandise themselves. Moreover, an increased reliance on "anonymous outlets" such as the Internet "may unintentionally lead to the demise of traditional fencing operations, or it may serve to enhance the ability of fences to dispose of merchandise more efficiently and effectively" (p. 229).

## ARSON

**Arson** is the willful or malicious burning of a house, public building, motor vehicle, aircraft, or other property of another. In 2007, 64,332 arson offenses were reported to the police, or approximately 25 per 100,000 inhabitants (Federal Bureau of Investigation, 2008). The vast majority of arsons occur in cities with populations of over 250,000. However, it should be pointed out that only fires determined through investigation to have been willingly or maliciously set are classified as arsons by the FBI. Fires of suspicious or unknown origins are excluded. In addition, it is not simply in big cities but specifically in the economically declining inner-city neighborhoods of big cities that the most common arsons occur.

When we think of arson, what commonly comes to mind is the deranged pyromaniac depicted on prime-time television. Clearly, there are cases of individuals who engage in this behavior for the excitement and mere "pleasure" of setting fires and watching structures burn; however, their number is indeed small when compared with other types of arsonists. Excluding pyromaniacs, four major types of arson have been identified by sociologists, police officials, and firefighters. The types are based on arsonists' motives and include crime concealment, revenge, vandalism, and profit. We briefly consider each type.

*Crime concealment* refers to the use of fires to destroy evidence—for example, of a burglary, a larceny, or a murder. In such cases individuals use arson to remove any evidence connecting the perpetrator to the crime or to prevent identification of the victim. In addition, people set fires to destroy records that contain evidence of other crimes, such as fraud and white-collar crimes such as embezzlement and corporate crime.

*Revenge arsons* result from quarrels, hatred, and jealousy among lovers, neighbors, employees, family members and relatives, and persons motivated by racist or religious contempt. Children sometimes express resentment against siblings who receive greater attention by burning a brother's or sister's bed; they may indicate incest victimization by setting afire the bed in which they were victimized. Similarly, women who are the victims of physical or sexual abuse in the home may obtain revenge by setting the bed afire. The church arsons that occurred in the mid-1990s are examples of arson resulting from racial or religious contempt. According to the National Church Arson Task Force (1997), between 1995 and 1997 approximately 429 church arsons were committed. Of these incidents, 162 involved African American churches, more than three-quarters were located in the southern United States, and the vast majority of offenders were white.

The third type of arson—*vandalism*—is usually associated with youths who set fires in schools, automobiles, and vacant buildings. Vacant buildings often serve as playgrounds for inner-city youths, some of whom may rationalize that a fire in such a building will not hurt anyone. Watching the building burn, as well as the fire department's extinguishing it, can be "exciting" to some youth. However, it is difficult to determine whether such fires are actually the result of arson. Determining criminal intent of youth is based on age and the motive behind the fire setting. If the youth is under the age of consent and there is insufficient evidence indicating malicious and willful fire setting, the youth most likely will not be labeled an arsonist (Garry, 1997).

Finally, the most costly arson—in terms of property damaged and lives lost and injured—is for *profit*. Individuals can profit from arson in

several ways: *stop-loss* arson—in which businesses on the verge of great financial loss or even financial ruin "sell" the business to an insurance company by setting it ablaze to obtain the coverage proceeds; *property improvement or rehabilitation* arson—in which property owners improve a structure or replace deteriorating furnishings from the proceeds of small fire insurance claims; *elimination of competition* arson—where a business eliminates its competition by setting it afire; and *extortion, coercion, and intimidation* arson—in which criminal syndicates use the threat of arson to extort money from businesses. However, arguably the most lucrative and destructive form of arson-for-profit occurs when individuals purchase a particular property—usually in an economically depressed area of a city—and insure the property for more than its value. By setting the property ablaze, the owner can reap a substantial profit.

Brady's (1983) classic study of arson concentrated on this latter type of arson-for-profit. His research went considerably beyond an examination of individuals, connecting arson-for-profit to major banks and criminal syndicates in one particular city, Boston. Brady showed that there was, in the late 1970s and early 1980s, a pattern to the fires occurring in Boston, with arson being demographically concentrated within certain poor Boston neighborhoods, such as Roxbury, North Dorchester, East Boston, and Jamaica Plain. Within these economically depressed areas, arson was more common in buildings owned by absentee landlords than in either owner-occupied tenements or public housing projects. Many of these privately owned buildings had been abandoned, and between 1978 and 1982 more than half of Boston's 3,000 arsons occurred in abandoned buildings. These buildings were not abandoned because of a "natural process of neighborhood evolution" but because of "discriminatory mortgage-lending policies of banks that deny credit to certain districts of the inner city in order to invest in more profitable suburban real estate" (p. 10). This latter practice, known as *redlining*, devastates neighborhoods by forcing small businesses to close because they cannot secure bank loans. Moreover, landlords fail to repair their buildings, eventually abandoning them, because property values decline drastically. This type of situation sets the stage for arson-for-profit. For example, property owners hire a criminal syndicate to "torch" their buildings as a way to avoid losing on unprofitable property. Since the criminal syndicate offers to buy the building at a price far greater than market value—which the bank has agreed to mortgage—the syndicate arranges for insurance well above the actual value of the property. The overmortgaged and overinsured property is then set fire, and both the criminal syndicate and the bank profit because "the new mortgage paid by the insurance company greatly exceeds the old bad debt assumed under foreclosure" (p. 11).

A recent discussion of arson confirms that the different types just discussed—concealment, revenge, vandalism, and profit—continue to be committed (Goetz, 2001). Yet it seems that "many arsons-for-profit go unchecked, with local law-enforcement agencies unwilling or unable to do much about this problem" (p. 27). Nevertheless, Goetz argues that much of the arson-for-profit identified by Brady and others occurred in the 1970s and 1980s, in which a postindustrial transformation was taking place in local real estate economies (such as massive gentrification), which wreaked havoc on many working-class and poor neighborhoods. Thus, it remains unclear whether arson-for-profit will be as widespread in the future as it was in the 1970s and 1980s.

### REVIEW

This chapter examined seven types of property crimes: robbery, burglary, shoplifting, motor vehicle theft, fraud, fencing, and arson. These property crimes are different from crimes of interpersonal violence in certain ways:

- They occur much more frequently.
- Offender and victim are usually strangers.
- In many cases no direct interaction occurs between offender and victim.
- In some cases—as in most frauds—it is not immediately apparent that a crime has been committed.

### ROBBERY AND BURGLARY

1. Robbery is a unique property crime involving direct interaction between offender and victim. It also entails both the threatened or actual use of physical violence and property loss to the victim.
2. Because robbery differs from crimes of interpersonal violence in significant sociological ways, it is labeled a property crime.
3. Strong-arm robbery is considerably more dangerous than armed robbery.
4. Robbery can be classified in terms of both incidents and offenders. The two major types of robbery offenders are professionals and opportunists.
5. Burglars can be classified as professionals and amateurs.

6. Important information on robbery and burglary has come from interviews with criminals who are not incarcerated but are actively involved in these crimes.

7. Property offenders persist in their crimes because of their desperate economic situation and pursuit of "life as party."

## VARIETIES OF LARCENY

1. One type of larceny—shoplifting—has received the most attention by criminologists.

2. There are two major types of shoplifters: boosters (professionals) and snitches (amateurs).

3. Individuals steal automobiles for joyriding, for short- and long-term transportation, for commission of another crime, and for profit.

4. Check fraud consists of drawing checks on insufficient funds in a checking account, forging someone else's personal checks, producing counterfeit personal and payroll checks, altering payroll checks, and stealing government checks and forging a signature.

5. Two major types of check fraud are naive forgers (amateurs) and systematic forgers (professionals).

6. Systematic forgers differ from other professional property offenders in significant ways.

7. Check and credit-card fraudsters may work alone or in groups.

8. The government is the victim of substantial fraud, such as income-tax fraud.

9. Identity theft is the fastest-growing crime of our time.

## DEALING AND DAMAGE

1. Fencing is the buying and selling of stolen goods and is conducted by both professionals and amateurs.

2. The majority of amateur fences sell their goods to relatives, friends, and acquaintances—not for purposes of economic gain but to enhance established relationships.

3. Most professional fences have strong ties to the legitimate business community and are part of a loosely structured, yet mutually supportive, network of individuals involved in acquiring and distributing stolen property.

4. This network consists of thieves, fences, criminal justice personnel, criminal syndicates, goods transporters, and buyers.

5. Arson causes more injury, death, and property loss than any other of the UCR index offenses.

6. There are four major types of arson: crime concealment, revenge, vandalism, and profit.

7. The most costly type of arson—in terms of property damage and lives lost and injured—results from profit-making ventures.

## QUESTIONS FOR CLASS DISCUSSION

1. This textbook argues that robbery is a property crime. Examine that assessment of robbery, and present an argument for or against its conclusion.
2. Most research on property offenders comes from incarcerated individuals. However, we presented research of "robbers on robbery" and "burglars on burglary." What are some of the advantages and disadvantages of this type of approach to gathering data on crime and criminals?
3. What are the major differences between professional and amateur property offenders?
4. Using examples, describe how "dealing" and "damage" are different from the varieties of larceny discussed.
5. How have modern forms of technology—such as computers and the Internet— changed the nature of property crime?

## FOR FURTHER STUDY

### READINGS

Caputo, Gail A. 2008. *Out in the Storm: Drug-Addicted Women Living as Shoplifters and Sex Workers.* Boston: Northeastern University Press.
Finch, Emily, and Stefan Fafinski. 2009. *Identity Theft.* Portland, OR: Willan.
Jewkes, Yvonne, and Majid Yar, eds. 2009. *Handbook of Internet Crime.* Portland, OR: Willan.
Tunnell, Kenneth. 2006. *Living Off Crime.* Lanham, MD: Rowman & Littlefield.

### WEBSITES

1. <http://www.ojp.gov/bjs/gvc.htm#Property>: From the Department of Justice, this graphic shows the rates of property crime declining, according to the National Crime Victimization Survey.
2. <http://www.usfa.dhs.gov>: From the U.S. Fire Administration, this site identifies prevention efforts in the United States. There are also links to community programs aimed at preventing arson.
3. <http://www.privacyrights.org/identity.htm>: This site educates users about identity theft. It contains numerous fact sheets on identity theft in the United States.

# INTERPERSONAL VIOLENCE

**PREVIEW**

Chapter 12 introduces:
- The various types of interpersonal violence.
- The nature and extent of interpersonal violence.
- The varying definitions of interpersonal violence.

**KEY TERMS**

| | |
|---|---|
| aggravated assault | murder |
| animal abuse | professional murder |
| battering | rape |
| child abuse | serial murder |
| elder abuse | sexual harassment |
| hate crimes | social coercion |
| interpersonal coercion | victim precipitation |
| manslaughter | wife rape |
| mass murder | |

Interpersonal crimes of violence have affected the way many of us live. We fear the streets, fear being home alone, fear being by ourselves in the center of the city, and fear specific acts, such as murder, assault, and rape. Fear of crime alters our lifestyles significantly.

Moreover, we are particularly afraid of strangers. In 1967 the President's Commission on Law Enforcement and the Administration of Justice reported that "the fear of crimes of violence is not a simple fear of injury or death or even of all crimes of violence, but, at bottom, a fear of strangers" (President's Commission, 1967a:52). There is no reason to believe this situation has changed. Many of us assume that most violent crimes are committed on the streets by strangers. We fear most of all the random, unprovoked attack on the street by a stranger.

Much of this fear (see Chapter Section 1.1) is created by the mass media, for it is from the media that most people develop their comprehension of where, by whom, and how often violent crime is committed. Magazines, newspapers, and television focus on dramatic, violent crimes such as murder; "prime-time criminals," usually strangers to their victims, commit their crimes on the street. A distorted view of crime is thus encouraged.

Indeed, most conventional crime is not violent. There are many more crimes against property than crimes of interpersonal violence. And crimes of interpersonal violence occur most frequently indoors and, therefore, are more or less invisible to the public; the perpetrators—although sometimes strangers—are usually relatives, friends, or acquaintances of the victims. This is not to say, however, that crimes of interpersonal violence in the United States are not a substantial problem. As citizens, we are rightly concerned about a major social cancer: The United States has one of the highest levels of interpersonal violence in the industrialized world.

With this in mind, we turn now to a discussion of certain specific acts of interpersonal violence.

We discuss the nature, extent, and types of three categories of interpersonal violence: (1) murder, assault, hate crimes, and rape; (2) violence in the family; and (3) violence in the workplace. These crimes are often referred to as *one-on-one* or *person-to-person* crimes because one person inflicts violence on another. Interpersonal violence therefore differs from other types of violence—such as corporate violence (see Section 13.2)—that inflict harm on larger numbers of people and do not entail direct, face-to-face interaction.

## 12.1 MURDER, ASSAULT, HATE CRIMES, AND RAPE

When we think of violent crimes, what commonly comes to mind are the crimes of murder, assault, and—for women, in particular—rape. In this section we look at the nature and extent of four forms of interpersonal violence. We begin with a discussion of murder and aggravated assault.

### MURDER AND AGGRAVATED ASSAULT

**Murder** is defined as "the willful (nonnegligent) killing of one human being by another" (Federal Bureau of Investigation, 2008). Individuals can also be charged by the state with manslaughter for killing another person through gross negligence. The difference between murder and manslaughter is based on intent, or what is referred to as *mens rea* (a guilty mind is present in the offender)—the conscious intent of the murderer is to kill. In murder, malice is always present, although the degree of murder is based on the level of premeditation (essentially, to what extent the murder is plotted beforehand). **Manslaughter** is divided into two types: voluntary and involuntary. *Voluntary* manslaughter occurs when the death is the result of a sudden passion arising from an immediate adequate cause. If the victim does not die but sustains serious injury, the crime is defined by the state as assault. *Involuntary* manslaughter results when one individual unintentionally kills another through recklessness or gross negligence, such as might happen during an automobile accident.

As we noted, the most comprehensive source for determining the number of murders in the United States is the Uniform Crime Reports (UCR), published by the Federal Bureau of Investigation. Obviously, it is impossible to conduct victimization surveys on murder. Although it is difficult to conceal a killing from official investigation, a number of murders may be ignored, overlooked, or disregarded; coroners may err in ruling an accidental death or a suicide as a murder, and some bodies simply may be hidden. Thus, although we must rely on police data as our source for determining the nature and extent of murder in the United States, these data must be viewed with some degree of skepticism.

In 2007 there were 16,929 murders in the United States. This means that approximately 6 of every 100,000 people were victims of murder (Federal Bureau of Investigation, 2008). Although murder is the most serious form of crime, it fortunately occurs the least often, accounting for only 1.2 percent of all index crimes. Moreover, the murder rate continues to decline in the United States—in 2007 it was approximately 50 percent lower than the rate recorded for 1993.

Murder also occurs primarily in big cities and in the South. Generally, the larger the city in terms of population, the higher the violent-crime rate. Studies over several decades have consistently shown a close relationship between city size and murder rates. That is, the larger the city, the higher the murder rate.

The typical killing—whether in large cities or small—results from a disagreement between individuals who know each other. Approximately 43 percent of murders involve family members, friends, or acquaintances, while 13 percent involve strangers; in the remaining 44 percent the relationship between victim and offender is unknown.

Moreover, most murders involve arguments over romantic triangles, property and money, and other issues. The typical murder, then, involves family, friends, or acquaintances who are engaged in an argument—usually over a trivial matter—that eventually leads to a killing. Consequently, we have more to fear from those to whom we are close than from strangers.

It is therefore not surprising to find that the typical murder is also related to routine social activities among family, friends, or acquaintances. Murder is most likely to occur during times when routine activities are more concentrated around the home. For example, murder occurs most often during summer vacations (July and August) and holiday seasons (December and January), which are traditionally a time when family members, neighbors, and friends are together (Federal Bureau of Investigation, 2008). Moreover, weekend murders are more likely to occur at home, among family members, and during the early evening hours.

Although the typical murder discussed thus far is characteristic of the largest proportion of murders, there are other types. For example, **professional murder** takes place when one individual kills another for personal profit. An unwritten "contract" is arranged, such as over the telephone or the Internet, between people who have never met personally. The victim, or "hit," is normally unknown to the killer, which makes it easier for the killer to engage in the crime. By conceptualizing the killing as a "business" or as "just a job," professional murderers can deny wrongfulness and thus justify their behavior even further.

Another type of murder, **serial murder**, occurs when an individual kills two or more people over a period of time. In serial murder there is generally no prior relationship between offender and victims, the subsequent murders often have no connection to the initial murder, and the victims usually hold some type of symbolic value to the murderer (e.g., prostitutes, homosexuals, hospital patients, children) (Egger, 2001). Moreover, serial murder may actually have increased: between 1900 and 1924 there were 13 serial killers known to the police, yet from 1990 to 2004 there were 163 (Renzetti, 2008).

There are two types of serial murderers. First, there are those killers who murder within the general area of their residence. An example of this type of serial murderer is John Wayne Gacy, who in 1979 murdered thirty-three young boys in or near his home and then hid their bodies in the crawl space of his home, inside the walls, and under the patio and driveway. Another example is Donald Harvery, a nurse's aide in Cincinnati. In the late 1980s, Harvery systematically killed twenty-one patients to allegedly relieve them from their suffering. Second, there are murderers who kill outside the proximity of their own residences. Examples of this type are Ted Bundy, who was found guilty of killing more than twenty women in Washington, Utah, and Colorado, and Henry Lee Lucas, who *admitted* killing 365 people in twenty-five states. According to some researchers, at least 142 of Lucas' killings have been verified (Holmes and DeBurger, 1985). More recent examples include the case of the "Unabomber," or Ted Kaczynski, who over the course of 17 years (1978–1995) killed three people and injured twenty-two by sending bombs through the mail (in 1998 he pleaded guilty to thirteen federal bombing offenses), the "sniper" case of Lee Boyd Malvo and John Allen Muhammed, who in 2002 killed ten people in the Washington, D.C., and northern Virginia suburbs, and the case of Dale Hauser, who in Phoenix over a 14-month period (2005–2006), randomly shot and killed six strangers and injured another nineteen, most of whom were pedestrians and bicyclists.

Finally, a **mass murder** is committed when an individual kills two or more people at once, rather than singly over time. Some recent cases of mass murder include Jiverly Wong, who in April 2009 killed thirteen people at the American Civic Association in Binghamton, New York; Robert Stewart, who in March 2009 killed eight people at Pinelake Health and Rehab in Carthage, North Carolina; and Devan Kalathat, who also in March 2009 killed his two children and three other relatives at his home in Santa Clara, California. The various in-school killings of students and teachers that occurred in the 1990s provide another example. Some of the better-known of these "school shootings" include the following.

- On February 2, 1996, in Moses Lake, Washington, Barry Loukaitus (age 14) shot and killed a teacher and two students at his junior high school.
- Eight months later, in Pearl, Mississippi, Luke Woodman (age 16) shot and killed two students in his high school.
- Two months later, in West Paducah, Kentucky, Michael Carneal (age 14) shot and killed three students in his high school.
- On March 24, 1998, in Jonesboro, Arkansas, Michael Johnson (age 13) and his accomplice, Andrew Golden (age 11), shot and killed a teacher and four students in their junior high school.
- On April 20, 1999, in Littleton, Colorado, Eric Harris (age 18) and Dylan Klebold (age 17) shot and killed a teacher, twelve students, and themselves.

In a study of these "school shooters," Kimmel and Mahler (2003) show that the media distorted the facts regarding these killings by suggesting that (1) they resulted from an increase in violent media content (when in fact school violence has actually decreased as violent media content has increased), (2) the school shooters came from unstable/dysfunctional families (the truth being that almost all the school shooters came from intact "stable" families with no history of child abuse), and (3) the killings were simply "kids killing kids" (yet all the school killings involved *boys* killing boys and girls). Kimmel and Mahler go on to show that the vast majority of the school shooters were victims of severe in-school bullying because they were defined as "different," such as being shy, bookish, artistic, nonathletic, and geekish. Kimmel and Mahler conclude that the bullying challenged the school shooters' masculinity and thus motivated them to adopt a practice that is culturally defined as "acceptable" for restoring their masculinity—interpersonal violence (see also Klein, 2006; Fast, 2008).

More recently, two mass murders occurred on college campuses: on April 16, 2007, Seung-Hui Cho killed thirty-two people in a dorm and in two classrooms on the Virginia Tech campus, and then he killed himself in the deadliest mass murder by a single killer in U.S. history; on February 14, 2008, Steven Kazmierczak opened fire in a lecture hall at Northern Illinois University, killing five students and then himself.

Undoubtedly the most horrific and unique case of mass murder in the United States (because of the number of people killed and because it also entailed mass suicide) occurred on September 11, 2001. On that day, nineteen individuals connected to the Al Qaeda terrorist network hijacked four U.S. commercial airplanes and murdered close to 3,000 people by flying the airplanes into the twin World Trade Center towers in New York City, the Pentagon Building in Arlington, Virginia, and a field in rural Pennsylvania. We will discuss and contextualize this mass murder/suicide more thoroughly in Chapter 14 because it also represents an example of political crime.

The most common weapon used to commit murder in the United States is a firearm. In 2007, approximately 68 percent of all murders were committed with a firearm, 53 percent with a handgun (Federal Bureau of Investigation, 2008). Many people argue that because of the relationship between firearms and murder, firearms (especially handguns) should be controlled rigidly by the state. Others, in particular members of the National Rifle Association (NRA), argue that "Guns do not kill, people do."

Although the debate over firearm ownership and murder is likely to continue for some time, sociologists and criminologists have generated some interesting information that sheds light on the subject. First, firearm ownership varies by region, which correlates with the regional murder rates. The South, on the one hand, has both the highest murder rate and the highest rate of firearm ownership. The Northeast, on the other hand, has the lowest murder rate and the lowest rate of firearm ownership (Federal Bureau of Investigation, 2008). Second, the chance of dying from a firearm wound is much higher than from assault with a knife, club, or fist. In fact, assaults with firearms are two to six times more likely to result in death than assaults with knives. Third, increases in murder are correlated with increases in firearm ownership. Fourth, because of easy availability of firearms, more accidental deaths and injuries occur.

All of this does not mean that firearms *cause* murder. However, it is obvious that households with firearms present are more likely—during a family argument, for instance—to experience a firearm death than households without firearms. Thus, although scant evidence exists to suggest that firearm ownership deters crime, by assuming it does and then purchasing guns, households actually become less, rather than more, safe and secure.

In 1958 criminologist Marvin Wolfgang coined the term *victim-precipitated murder*, applying it to those murders in which "the victim is a direct, positive precipitator in the crime" (p. 252). In victim-precipitated murder, the victim is the first to display and use a deadly weapon or to strike a blow and, therefore, "the first to commence the interplay of resort to physical violence" (p. 252). For example, such a murder may involve two people having an argument during which the victim threatens the offender with a knife. Responding, the offender pulls out a gun and fires a fatal bullet. Wolfgang estimates that in one of every four murders, the victim precipitates the killing.

Some criminologists have questioned the thesis of **victim precipitation**, suggesting that the interaction between offender and victim actually involves challenges and provocations by *both* participants that lead up to the killing. In his classic research, David Luckenbill (1977) found that murder results from an "intense interchange" between offender, victim, and sometimes an audience and parallels a "character contest" wherein both offender and victim attempt to maintain "face" at the other's expense. This interchange between offender and victim takes place as follows:

1. The victim makes what the offender perceives as an offensive move, gesture, or remark.
2. The offender then retaliates with a verbal or physical challenge.
3. The victim then retaliates, creating a "working" agreement that commits both parties to a violent resolution of the conflict.
4. The battle eventually results in the death of the victim.

In 63 percent of Luckenbill's cases such an exchange between offender and victim took place. Additional research has reported similar results, concluding that the typical murder involves contributions to the violent conflict by both offender and victim (Polk, 1994).

Although Luckenbill's theory is intriguing, it is certainly not applicable to all forms of murder. Obviously, it offers little help in understanding professional, serial, and mass murder. Moreover, Nancy Jurik and Peter Gregware (1992) have shown that for female-perpetrated murder, the idea of a character contest does not seem to hold in many cases, such as murder resulting from child abuse and killing in self-defense (to avoid wife beating). Thus, Luckenbill's theory may help us understand some male offender/male victim murder but is inadequate when applied to typical female offender/male victim murders. Whereas Luckenbill emphasizes a character contest, Jurik and Gregware's data on women "suggest the salience of strategic, life-saving dimensions and an imposed—rather than consensual—characterization of the violence in these homicides" (p. 196).

**Aggravated assault** is "an unlawful attack by one person upon another for the purpose of inflicting severe or aggravated bodily injury" (Federal Bureau of Investigation, 2008). Aggravated assault is usually accompanied by the use of a weapon or by other means likely to produce death or great bodily harm.

Aggravated assault and murder are closely related crimes. In fact, much of what has already been discussed regarding murder can also be applied to aggravated assault. However, there are some differences between the two crimes. The first and most obvious difference is that an assault does not result in an actual death. Although the typical aggravated assault and the typical murder are similar in most major respects, it is the existence of a dead body that creates the major difference between them. If a killing does not occur, the crime is some type of assault.

A second difference is that there are more aggravated assaults in the United States than murders. In 2007 there were approximately 855,856 reported aggravated assaults, resulting in a rate of about 284 per 100,000 individuals (Federal Bureau of Investigation, 2008). This rate is nearly fifty times the murder rate. However, in its National Crime Victimization Survey (NCVS), the Department of Justice (2008) found that only 60 percent of the victims of aggravated assault reported the crime to the police. Consequently, aggravated assault occurs more often than the UCR data indicate. Indeed, the NCVS estimates that almost 1,344,280 aggravated assault victimizations occurred in 2007.

Finally, according to the NCVS, aggravated assault—unlike murder—involves strangers more often (51 percent of the time) than relatives, friends, or acquaintances (Department of Justice, 2008). However, victims may be less likely to report assaults by people they know. Thus, it could well be that regarding the victim/offender relationship, aggravated assault is similar to murder. Nevertheless, studies of aggravated assault show that males are more likely to be victimized by strangers and females victimized by husbands and boyfriends (Bachman, 2001). Moreover, the location of assault victimization corresponds to the gender patterns just noted: Females are more likely to be assaulted at or near a private residence, whereas males are usually assaulted in a public setting. Despite this pattern, more recent research on assault by girls and women suggests that it occurs in a variety of settings and differing pathways, all depending on the context and relationships involved (Miller and Mullins, 2006; Mullins and Miller, 2008; Jones, 2008).

## HATE CRIMES

A pervasive fact of life in industrialized societies is the existence of **hate crimes**, or violence perpetrated on people because of their perceived race, religion, disability, ethnicity, or sexual orientation. Hate crimes differ from other forms of interpersonal violence in at least three distinct ways (Martin, 2001): (1) Victims face greater difficulty coming to terms with their victimization, (2) communities face higher levels of fear and heightened intergroup tensions, and (3) labeling such incidents "hate crimes" increases the amount of attention paid to these harms by the criminal justice system.

In 2007, 7,624 hate crimes were reported to the FBI, of which 51 percent were motivated by racial bias, 18 percent by religious bias, 17 percent

by sexual-orientation bias, 13 percent by ethnicity/national origin bias, and 1 percent by disability bias (Federal Bureau of Investigation, 2008). Moreover, a study by the National Coalition of Anti-Violence Programs (2008) found that in 2007 there were 2,430 reported incidents of violence against lesbian, gay, bisexual, transgender, and HIV-positive people (see Figure 12.1 for a recent hate crime against a transgender person). This represents a 24 percent increase in hate crimes over the previous year, yet only approximately 50 percent were reported to the police. Moreover, in 2007, 64 percent of all victims identified as lesbian or gay men and heterosexuals comprised only 9 percent of the reported victims of anti–lesbian, gay, bisexual, and transgender violence. Nevertheless, this shows that hate crimes are crimes of perception: Victims are chosen not necessarily because they are, for example, lesbian or gay but because the perpetrator perceives them to be such (Girshick, 2008a). Moreover, gay men are significantly more likely

**FIGURE 12.1** Angie Zapata was beaten and killed in 2009 by Allen Andrade (pictured) because she was transgender. Andrade was convicted of first-degree murder in the case, the first U.S. trial in which a hate-crime statute was used to prosecute the killing of a transgender person. Only twelve states and the District of Columbia have hate-crime statutes that include gender identity.
*Source*: Newscom

than lesbians or bisexuals to experience hate violence (Herek, 2009).

Despite the many positive changes resulting from the civil rights movement, racism persists in the United States, expressing its extreme form in racist attacks on African Americans and other racial and ethnic minorities. The 1970s saw increasing reports of racial violence against African Americans by white youth. In 1980, the Subcommittee on Crime of the U.S. House of Representatives investigated this violence. In its report, *Increasing Violence Against Minorities,* the subcommittee found anti–African American attacks both by individuals (primarily young white males) and by groups such as the Ku Klux Klan. The report concluded that there "is abundant evidence of a marked increase in the incidence of criminal violence directed against minority groups" (U.S. House Subcommittee on Crime, 1980:2). Today, 51 percent of reported hate crimes are motivated by racial bias (Federal Bureau of Investigation, 2008).

Consider racist skinheads, who hold extremely conservative and neo-Nazi views. They routinely target racial and ethnic minorities and homosexuals for violent attacks. Indeed, Mark Hamm's (1993) important study *American Skinheads: The Criminology and Control of Hate Crime* reported that the defining characteristics of skinhead ideology are racism, homophobia, and anti-Semitism. Although African Americans are the most frequent victims of racist violence, other racial groups are also victimized, such as whites, Native Americans, Hispanics, Asians, Jews, and Arabs, as well as immigrants and the homeless (Perry, 2008a; Shenoy, 2008, Wachholz, 2005; Wooden and Blazak, 2001).

Moreover, according to the Southern Poverty Law Center's (2009) recent study *The Year in Hate*, the number of hate groups in the United States increased from 888 in 2007 to 926 in 2008. In addition to the publicity surrounding immigration in the United States, the report noted two other reasons for this increase in the number of hate groups: the worsening economic recession and the election of Barack Obama as the first African American president of the United States. The report also pointed to Ku Klux Klan groups, neo-Nazis, and racist skinheads as being the three most active and dangerous white supremacist hate groups in 2008. But the report also identified a new 2008 hate group trend: the increasing militancy of the extremist fringe of the Hebrew Israelite movement, whose members believe that Jews are creatures of the devil and that whites deserve death or slavery. As the report detailed (p. 1): "These radical black supremacists have no love for Barack Obama, calling him a "house nigger" and a puppet of Israel. They preach to inner-city blacks that evil Jews are solely responsible for the recession."

Hate crimes differ from other forms of interpersonal violence in three important ways: They are more vicious, extremely brutal, and frequently perpetrated at random on total strangers (commonly a single victim) by multiple offenders (usually groups of white, working-class male teenagers). For hate crimes perpetrated in 2007 against specifically lesbian, gay, bisexual, transgender, or HIV-positive people, offenders were strangers in 31 percent of the incidents (National Coalition of Anti-Violence Programs, 2008).

Why do hate crimes occur? One of the better explanations is offered by Levin and McDevitt (1993), who have argued that this type of crime is the result in the United States of a "growing *culture of hate:* From humor and music to religion and politics, a person's group affiliation—the fact that he or she *differs from people in the in-group*—is being used more and more to provide a basis for dehumanizing and insulting that person" (p. 34). Although this "culture of hate" does not actually cause hate crimes, in a social context of growing unemployment and hard economic times, coupled with an influx of recent immigrants from eastern Europe, Southeast Asia, Africa, and Latin America, as well as a visible gay/lesbian rights movement, a culture of hate provides "support and encouragement to those who seek to express their personal version of bigotry in some form of criminal behavior" (pp. 42–43). Indeed, Barbara Perry's (1998) research on hate groups in the United States found that such groups facilitate a negative politics of difference:

> Hate groups have mobilized in an effort to reassert a narrow, exclusive understanding of national identity. In particular, they provide a menu of ideologies which presume the hegemony of white, heterosexual, Christian male power.…To the extent that hate groups define their collective identity as the norm, they necessarily engage in a politics of difference which seeks to negate, exclude, and repress those groups that fall outside of that norm, namely non-Whites, non-Christians, non-heterosexuals, even non-males. And they do so by invoking ideological claims to superiority and power. (p. 32)

And as Stephen Tomsen (2002; see also Tomsen, 2009) has reported in his important work on antihomosexual homicides:

> Savage gang attacks that are carried out in public locations with an expected availability of homosexuals often closely approximate the typical pattern of hate crime. But perpetrators are also preoccupied with attaining a heightened male status for themselves and with policing the acceptable patterns of public male sexual identity. (p. 99)

## RAPE

**Rape**, as traditionally defined in criminal law, is "the carnal knowledge of a female forcibly and against her will" (Federal Bureau of Investigation, 2008). By concentrating on "against her will," the criminal law makes it imperative that the threat or actual use of physical violence by the offender be present to constitute proof that the victim did not consent. Consequently, this traditional definition of rape actually means, in practice, sexual intercourse obtained by the threat or actual use of physical violence. Hence, the criminal law labels rape "forcible rape."

However, many scholars have argued that the traditional criminal law definition of forcible rape is inadequate, for it recognizes only one type of force—sexual intercourse obtained through the threat or actual use of physical violence. Some scholars argue that this definition does not provide for rape resulting from intimidation or pressure other than the threat or actual use of physical force. For example, a rape omitted from this traditional definition involves a woman who is coerced economically—"If you don't 'put out' you'll be fired"—where her overt genuine consent is absent.

Moreover, some criminologists have pointed out that the traditional definition of rape does not include *all* rapes that occur through the threat or actual use of physical violence. These criminologists note that in many states the violent forcible rape of a wife is simply not considered rape. Although in 1993 wife rape became a crime in all fifty states, in thirty states wife rape is treated as a lesser crime than rape; in the majority of these states a husband cannot be prosecuted for wife rape if the woman is unable to consent because she is mentally or physically impaired, asleep, or unconscious; and in most of these states husbands may be exempt from charges if the crime is not reported to the police in a "timely" manner (Bergen, 2008a).

Nevertheless, because of feminist criticism, state definitions of rape have been expanded in certain ways: They are now gender neutral, meaning either men or women can be victims of rape; they cover anal and oral penetration by a penis or other objects; and they include nonforcible intercourse with someone unable to consent (e.g., unconscious, mentally incapacitated).

Not everyone agrees with expanding the definition of rape to include "economic coercion," however. Some argue that an important distinction should be made between those who are coerced physically and those who may be coerced in other ways. For example, David Finkelhor and Kersti Yllö (1985) have argued that although labeling sexual assault obtained through economic force as rape highlights how oppressive and coercive sex is under certain circumstances, it simultaneously expands, and therefore dilutes, the meaning of the word *rape*. Moreover, they have argued, it is extremely difficult to determine when force or coercion is being used in a relationship. For these two reasons, then, Finkelhor and Yllö have contended that the term *rape* should be used only for situations of actual or threatened physical force. This does not mean that other kinds of force are not used. Indeed, Finkelhor and Yllö held that

> a woman whose husband tells her he is going to humiliate her publicly if she won't perform some sexual act, for instance, may be making a more fearsome and devastating threat than a man who threatens only to push himself on his wife. We would be prepared to call this type of coercion forced sex, but not rape. (pp. 89–90)

Thus, Finkelhor and Yllö suggested that there are two types of sexual coercion in the United States but that sexual coercion, although frightening and traumatic, is clearly not, and should not be considered, rape. They distinguished *social coercion* from *interpersonal coercion*. **Social coercion** occurs, for example, when women feel they should have sex with their husbands because it is their wifely "duty." Many women feel they cannot say no because they are married or because the husband pays the bills or because of religious authority. Thus, there exist social pressures on women to have sex with their husbands even if

they do not want to do so. **Interpersonal coercion** occurs when a woman has sex with her husband or an employer in the face of nonviolent threats. For example, a wife may have sex with her husband "to keep peace in the house," or an employee may have sex with her boss to gain a promotion or just simply to keep a job.

Whether we agree with Finkelhor and Yllö or with the expanded definition of rape, the important point to understand is that sexual coercion can, and in fact does, occur in ways other than through the threat or actual use of physical violence.

In 2007 there were 90,427 reported forcible rapes, representing a rate of 30 per 100,000 people (Federal Bureau of Investigation, 2008). However, we must view the police data with caution, inasmuch as the majority of rapes are not reported to the police. Indeed, only approximately 43 percent of rapes and attempted rapes are reported each year to the police (Department of Justice, 2008). This situation is due not only to fear of retaliation but to the trauma that rape victims experience, the shame they are often made to feel, and the perception that getting involved with the criminal justice system would itself be traumatic and possibly futile. Moreover, women have a far greater chance of being raped by someone they know than by a stranger, which clearly affects the victim's decision to report the crime to the police. Victims may feel (1) embarrassed, (2) that they should have been able to prevent the rape, (3) that they want to protect the offender, or (4) that they will not be believed. Consequently, for all these reasons, the number of rapes in U.S. society is much larger than statistics in the Uniform Crime Reports indicate. Indeed, the National Crime Victimization Survey estimated that 260,940 forcible rapes occurred in 2007, suggesting that only about 30 percent of incidents were reported to the police (Department of Justice, 2008). Paralleling murder, then, rape is more likely to be committed by someone the victim knows. Women are more likely to be raped by a husband, an ex-husband, a boyfriend, an acquaintance, or a date than by a stranger.

Popular culture often represents rape as *victim precipitated*—that is, the eventual victim is seen as "attracting" victimization by, for example, wearing certain clothing (e.g., a miniskirt), frequenting particular places (e.g., a fraternity party), or engaging in specific practices (e.g., hitchhiking). However, the concept of *victim-precipitated rape* asks us to identify with the rapist because it fails to acknowledge the victim's rights—in particular, the right to change one's mind whenever one pleases. This situation is collusion, which is exactly what the rapist has done—namely, refused to recognize the victim's right to change her or his mind. Moreover, by shifting blame from offender to victim, the idea of victim-precipitated rape diverts attention from the rapist as well as from the broader social factors forming the context in which rape occurs. Thus, although the idea of victim precipitation may be relevant to the crime of murder, it is mistaken to apply the concept to rape.

In addition, the idea of victim-precipitated rape is based on the pervasive myth in our society that men have a special and overwhelming "urge" or "drive" toward heterosexual intercourse. According to this myth, men have virtually an uncontrollable sexual need that, once "sparked," must find instant satisfaction, regardless of the consequences. Thus, if a woman awakens this sexual desire by engaging in provocative behavior, it is argued, the man cannot be held responsible for his behavior because the "urge" will be too strong for him to control. However, rapists rarely randomly and spontaneously assault their victims. Most stranger rapists spend time looking for women in locations most likely to be immune from surveillance, such as inside a home, an apartment, or a motor vehicle. Thus, stranger rape and date rape are not explosive acts, the result of sudden and uncontrollable sexual desire. Rape is an act of violent sexual domination intended to devalue and humiliate the victim. It is not simply an expression of sexual desire.

Rapists are also portrayed in popular culture as "crazy." However, empirical research has been unable to confirm this belief, as Joanne Belknap (2007) points out:

> Just as with sexual-assault victims, rapists come from every racial, ethnic, and economic group. They include doctors, lawyers, ministers, priests, professors, politicians, and many others. Thus, just as anyone can be a rape victim, so too can anyone be a rapist. (p. 274)

An example is the case of a group of teenage middle-class white male athletes who lured a "retarded" girl into a basement in Glen Ridge, New Jersey (Lefkowitz, 1997; Messner, 2002). The rapists were the most popular high school athletes in the town, and the gang rape was carefully planned. Chairs were set up in the basement for an "audience" of boys (thirteen boys were involved as rapists or voyeurs) to watch other boys induce the victim into various sexual acts. Eventually six of the thirteen boys left—but did not notify the police—and seven remained in the basement. Messner (p. 31) explains what happened next:

> While the girl was forced to continue giving oral sex to the boy, other boys laughed, yelled encouragement to their friends, and derisively shouted, "You whore!" at the girl. One boy decided it would be amusing to force a baseball bat up her vagina. When he did this (and followed it with a broomstick), the girl heard one boy's voice say, "Stop. You're hurting her," but another voice prevailed: "Do it more." Later, the girl remembered that the boys were all laughing while she was crying. When they were done, they warned her not to tell anyone. (p. 31)

Messner points out that four factors enabled this gang rape to occur:

1. The key role of competitive, homophobic, and misogynistic talk and joking as the central, most honored form of dominance-bonding in the athletic male peer group.
2. The group practice of "voyeuring," whereby boys set up situations where they seduce girls into places and situations in which their friends can watch the sex act and sometimes take an active part in it.
3. The suppression of empathy toward others—especially toward the girls who are the objects of their competitive dominance-bonding—that boys learn from each other.
4. The enabling of some men's sexual violence against women by a "culture of silence" among peers, in families, and in the community.

Approximately 30 percent of reported rapes involve more than one perpetrator, and such gang rapes are more often committed by stranger assailants and result in greater physical injury to victims than single-offender rapes (Ullman, 2008).

In the traditional definition of rape, the victims of forcible rape are always female. However, there are cases of males being forcibly raped by both males and females. When women are arrested for forcible rape, they are usually an accomplice to a man, assisting him in raping a female.

Male rape of another male is also rare, except in prison. In prison a male's chances of being a rape victim increase. It has been estimated that in U.S. prisons approximately one of every four male inmates has been raped (Kupers, 2001). Rape as an act of violent sexual domination intended to devalue and humiliate the victim is a widespread practice in male prisons. Young men in U.S. prisons must seek protection from stronger, older, and more powerful inmates, and many of them become sexual slaves to their "protectors." Others are forced into prostitution and are traded for such prison commodities as cigarettes. Rape in prison is a masculine confirming act. Stephen Donaldson (2001) argues that at the top of the prisoner classification system are the

> so-called "Men," and they are defined by a successful and continuing refusal to be sexually penetrated. A single instance of being penetrated, whether voluntary or not, is universally held to constitute an irreversible "loss of manhood." The "Men" rule the roost and establish the values and behavioral norms for the entire prison population; convict leaders, gang members, and the organizers of such activities as the smuggling of contraband, protection rackets, and prostitution rings must be and remain "Men." (p. 118)

Rape in male prisons involves a power dynamic among men. A "Man" who engages in rape is considered a "booty bandit," and a "real man," not a homosexual. Booty bandits rape "punks"—those who are young, small in stature, inexperienced in personal combat, and first-timers—who are forced into sexually submissive roles and thus become slaves to the booty bandits, who in turn have the power to sell, trade, rent, or lend them at whim. In other words, the social dynamics of prison rape are extremely instructive in understanding the rape of women in the larger society.

Moreover, it is quite unlikely that a male will be the victim of a rape unless he is incarcerated, and even then, once he has reached adulthood, he is virtually safe from any form of sexual assault.

Finally, the discussion in Box 12.1 points to the fact that certain institutions—such as college campuses—may create forms of social interaction conducive to rape and other types of violence against women. Another institution is the military. As Peter Iadicola and Anson Shupe (1998)

**BOX 12.1 COLLEGE MALE ATHLETE VIOLENCE AGAINST WOMEN**

Violence is a common feature in men's sports culture. "Legitimate" forms of violence are characterized through such practices as tackles, blocks, body checks, collisions, hits, and jabs and are officially sanctioned in a variety of college sports. Some acts that are prohibited by official rules of a given sport are still accepted and occur routinely, such as fistfights and avoidable boarding in hockey, the late hit in football, the wandering elbow in basketball and soccer, and the "beanball" and "knockdown" pitches in baseball.

In addition, athletes are encouraged to ignore pain ("no pain, no gain"), and college sports reward men for physically dominating others, hiding their fears, and distinguishing themselves from all that is feminine. Consequently, the world of college male sports *may* motivate men to construct a violent masculinity, because such sports are predicated on the successful utilization of violence; that is, sport activities routinely turn the human body into a weapon to be used against other bodies, resulting in pain, serious injury, or death. Men's college sports are key institutional sites for the reflection of violent masculinity (Messner and Stevens, 2002).

Although college male sports culture institutionalizes a hypermasculinity in which violence is an essential part, does the empirical research support the conclusion that it is simultaneously a breeding ground for rape and other forms of violence against women? Some studies, using both official college police data as well as self-reports, have concluded that male college athletes are more likely to be violent toward women than other college males are (Fritner and Robinson, 1993; Koss and

Gaines, 1993; Boeringer, 1996; Crosset, Ptacek, McDonald, and Benedict, 1996; Sawyer et al., 2002; Forbes et al., 2006; O'Toole, 2007). However, other studies have found no significant difference between college male athletes and nonathletes in sexual violence reports to campus police and self-report studies (Crosset, Todd, Benedict, and McDonald, 1995; Schwartz and Nogrady, 1996). Thus, it is difficult to conclude simply that athletic participation in college predisposes men toward violence against women.

Nevertheless, researchers have also investigated whether specific types of male college athletes are more often violent against women. The conclusion of several studies is that college males involved in especially high-contact sports—such as football, hockey, and lacrosse—have higher rates of violence against women (in particular, group rape) than other athletes and nonathletes (Koss and Gaines, 1993; Crosset, Ptacek, McDonald, and Benedict, 1996; Sanday, 1996; Nixon, 1997; Curry, 2000; Messner, 2005). The conclusion of this research is straightforward: Male college athletes who participate in the foregoing high-contact sports use violence as a customary and institutionalized strategy during competition, and this violence *may* carry over to other social situations outside the sporting context. However, these studies still leave unanswered the important question of which male college contact-sport athletes are also involved in violence against women outside the sport context. Do you think certain college contact-sport males are violent toward women whereas other college contact-sport male athletes are not? If so, why do those who are violent toward women engage in different types of violence?

---

have shown, throughout history rape has often been an institutionalized component of war:

> The systematic rape by soldiers of innocent women in towns and villages in the United States during the American Revolution, during the conquest and attempted genocide of native people on the North American continent, during the American Civil War, during World Wars I and II in Belgium, France, China, and Germany, and during the most recent wars of our time in Korea and Vietnam,

Bangladesh, Nicaragua, El Salvador, Russia, and the former Yugoslavia are just a few examples. Rape has been used to punish the enemy and as a reward for the victors. (p. 127).

The rape–war connection is not limited to the battlefield, for women in the U.S. military are also subject to this crime. Some recent incidents include (Courtois, 2008: 654):

- Sexual assaults on female trainees at Aberdeen, Maryland, resulted in charges against numerous instructors and reprimands against several officers.

- Female cadets reported being raped by male cadets at the Air Force and Naval academies and facing retaliation when they reported it—leadership knew of the sexual misconduct for years but failed to address it.
- Female combat troops in Afghanistan and Iraq reported sexual assaults during training and having their complaints ignored.

## 12.2 INTERPERSONAL VIOLENCE IN THE FAMILY

The family is, on the one hand, a "haven in a heartless world," a place where love and security prevail. On the other hand, it is a site of conflict among its members. Unfortunately, for many family members this conflict turns into violence. Although considerable violence occurs among family members (as we have seen), violent crimes such as murder, assault, hate crimes, and rape are not specific to the family and can occur outside its boundaries. In this section we focus on those types of interpersonal violence that occur only within the family setting. An accurate measure of interpersonal violence specific to the family is difficult to establish, but sociologists estimate that the problem is widespread for families throughout Western industrialized societies. We discuss five types of interpersonal violence specific to the family: wife rape, battering, child abuse, elder abuse, and animal abuse.

### HETEROSEXUAL WIFE RAPE AND BATTERING

"It is within marriage," wrote sociologists Russell Dobash and Rebecca Dobash over 30 years ago, "that a woman is most likely to be slapped and shoved about, severely assaulted, killed, or raped" (1979, p. 75). In fact, sociologists and criminologists have shown since 1977 that wife rape is more common than rape by dates, acquaintances, and strangers. Following Patricia Peacock (1998), we define **wife rape** as any sexual activity by a legal spouse that is performed against and without the consent of the other spouse. In the section on rape we showed that women are more likely to be raped by someone they know. Adding to this, women can likewise be raped by an acquaintance, friend, date, relative, authority figure, or stranger. However, wife rape is different, in the sense that *only* women who have ever been married can actually be raped by their husband or ex-husband. Thus, Russell (1990), in her classic work on this crime, calculated rates of rape and attempted rape based on the percentage of women who had ever been married—rather than as a percentage of the entire sample—and found that "the prevalence of wife rape increases from 8 percent to 12 percent. This percentage places rape and attempted rape by husbands second only to rape and attempted rape by acquaintances" (p. 62).

When Russell looked only at *completed* rapes (rather than the combination of completed and attempted rapes), she found that more women had been victimized by their husbands than by any other type of perpetrator. Although only 3 percent of the women in her sample were victims of a completed rape by a stranger, 5 percent were victims of a completed rape by lovers or ex-lovers, and 8 percent were victims of a completed rape by husbands or ex-husbands. One could therefore conclude from Russell's data that the more intimate the relationship between the victim and the offender, the greater the chance that a rape attempt will be completed.

Similarly, Finkelhor and Yllö (1985) surveyed 323 Boston-area women to determine the extent of wife rape there. They found that 10 percent of these women had experienced a rape by a husband or ex-husband, whereas only 3 percent had been raped by a stranger. In addition, another 10 percent of the women had been raped by a date. Finkelhor and Yllö concluded that "sexual assaults by intimates, including husbands, are by far the most common type of rape" (p. 7). It is estimated that 14 percent to 25 percent of married women are forced by their husbands to have sexual intercourse against their will during the course of their marriage (Belknap, 2007).

In Patricia Peacock's (1998) survey of 278 women, she found that 40, or 14 percent of the sample, reported at least one incident of wife rape. The following are the sexual activities that husbands forced their wives to participate in: intercourse (88 percent); perpetrator fondling victim (48 percent), victim forced to fondle perpetrator (45 percent), victim forced to perform oral sex on perpetrator (45 percent), perpetrator engaging victim in anal sex (40 percent), and perpetrator performing oral sex on victim (17 percent).

Moreover, the victims of wife rape report not only that the rape by their husbands is frightening and brutal but that it involves humiliation, degradation, and hatred (Bergen, 2008b; Peacock, 1998). And a large proportion of wife rapists use "sexual coercion"—"If you don't 'put out' I'll divorce you"—rather than direct physical violence to obtain sexual access to a wife's body, and because of such coercion many women "give in" to unwanted sex with their husbands for the following reasons (Basile, 1999; Belknap, 2007:293):

1. *Unwanted turns to wanted.* The woman did not initially want to have sex but was able to enjoy it ultimately.
2. *It's my duty.* The woman has sex because she believes it is her marital obligation, not because she wants to have sex.
3. *Easier not to argue.* The woman has sex because she can't tolerate any more verbal or nonverbal behavior from her partner, and sex is the easiest way out of the situation.
4. *Don't know what might happen if I don't.* The woman has sex because she is afraid of a negative consequence if she doesn't.

5. *Know what will happen if I don't.* The woman knows from experience that if she doesn't comply, she will be raped and/or experience other serious forms of violence.

In an interesting study on separation/divorce sexual assault—or the victimization of women who want to leave, are in the process of leaving, or who have left their marital or cohabiting partner—it was found that in addition to rape or attempted rape: 80 percent of the victims experienced at least two forms of nonsexual abuse, such as physical violence, harm to pets and prized possessions, and psychological abuse; 74 percent were sexually abused when they expressed a desire to leave; 49 percent were sexually abused when attempting to leave; and 33 percent were sexually abused after they left (DeKeseredy, 2008).

It is clear, then, that the sexual assault of a wife may occur as well in marriages with little or no physical violence. However, there also seems to be a close relationship between wife rape and wife beating. Studies indicate that between 30 and 50 percent of all wife beating involves some form of sexual abuse (Bergen, 2008b; Belknap, 2007). This physical violence against women was not always illegal. Throughout the seventeenth, eighteenth, and nineteenth centuries in western Europe, it was legal for men to beat their wives, as long as the method used and the extent of the violence remained within certain limits. For example, in eighteenth-century France the law restricted violence against wives to "blows, thumps, kicks, or punches on the back if they leave no traces." Moreover, the law did not allow for the use of "sharp-edged or crushing instruments." The phrase "rule of thumb" allegedly derives from English common law, which specified that a man could beat his wife—for disciplinary reasons—as long as he used a stick no thicker than his thumb.

Although ideas on wife **battering** have changed considerably—it is now socially abhorred and illegal—it still occurs more frequently than most people believe. It is impossible to generate useful statistics on wife battering, because the beating most likely has taken place in isolation from the community and because most victims are too embarrassed to report the assault to the police, social service agency, or shelter. Therefore, to understand the prevalence of wife battering, we must rely on estimates provided by researchers in the field.

Estimates of the amount of wife battering in the United States vary. For instance, *Time* magazine reported in 1983 that 6 million women are physically abused each year by their husbands, battery being the "single major cause of injury to women, more significant than auto accidents, rapes, or muggings" (p. 23). According to the National Coalition Against Domestic Violence, approximately 50 percent of women will be battered in their lifetime, and every 15 seconds a woman is battered in the United States (Bloom, 2008; Belknap, 2007). However, most women battered by their husbands do not report the incident. Thus, the amount of wife battering is higher than these figures indicate.

Research on battering in heterosexual couples suggests there are four major types (Johnson and Ferraro, 2000; Johnson, 2001, 2007):

1. *Common couple violence.* This type is not connected to a general pattern of control but arises in the context of an argument in which both partners lash out at each other. Common couple violence has a low per-couple frequency, does not escalate over time, does not involve severe physical violence, and is likely to be mutual.
2. *Patriarchal terrorism.* This type involves violence as only one aspect of a general pattern of control—the violence is one of the means to control a partner. Patriarchal terrorism has a high per-couple frequency and is likely to escalate over time, to

**TABLE 12.1  INDIVIDUAL VIOLENT BEHAVIOR IN HETEROSEXUAL COUPLES**

| Types of Violence | Husbands | Wives |
| --- | --- | --- |
| Common couple violence | 56% | 44% |
| Patriarchal terrorism | 97% | 3% |
| Violent resistance | 4% | 96% |
| Mutual violent control | 50% | 50% |

Source: Johnson (2001:1000).

involve serious physical injury, and to be perpetrated by exclusively only one of the partners. Men represent approximately 97 percent of patriarchal terrorists.
3. *Violent resistance.* This type is perpetrated almost entirely by women who are primarily the victims of patriarchal terrorism.
4. *Mutual violent control.* This type involves partners in which both are controlling and physically violent. This type is rare (see Table 12.1), and little research has been done on mutual violent control.

The vast majority of research on battering in heterosexual couples has concentrated on patriarchal terrorism. This research indicates that, although patriarchal terrorism transcends class, race/ethnicity, and neighborhood boundaries, not all groups of women are equally at risk of victimization. Indeed, a recent study of how each of these variables plays a role in patriarchal terrorism concluded the following (Benson and Fox, 2004):

- Patriarchal terrorism occurs more often and is more severe in economically disadvantaged neighborhoods. Women living in disadvantaged neighborhoods are more than twice as likely to be the victims of intimate violence, compared with women in more advantaged neighborhoods.
- For the individuals involved, both objective (being unemployed or not making enough

money to meet family needs) and subjective (worrying about finances) forms of economic distress increase the risk of intimate violence against women.

- Women who live in economically disadvantaged communities and are struggling with money in their own relationships suffer the greatest risk of patriarchal violence.

- African Americans and whites with the same economic characteristics have similar rates of patriarchal violence, but African Americans have a higher overall rate due in part to higher levels of economic distress and their location in disadvantaged neighborhoods.

- Women whose male partners experienced two or more periods of unemployment (during the 5-year study) were almost three times as likely to be victims of patriarchal terrorism as women whose partners were in stable jobs.

- Women in disadvantaged neighborhoods are more likely to be victimized repeatedly or to be injured by their domestic partners than women who live in more advantaged neighborhoods.

An important question always asked by students of patriarchal terrorism is "Why doesn't she leave?" In fact, most victims of battering do leave violent relationships (Johnson and Ferraro, 2000). Nevertheless, Angela Browne (1995) has argued that asking "Why don't battered women leave?" assumes that leaving an abusive relationship will end the violence. Indeed, battered women who leave a violent relationship are more likely to experience more violence. Yet several researchers have answered this question, reporting that women stay in a violent relationship for a number of reasons. First, of course, is fear. The wife fears that if she leaves, the husband will find her and injure her even more severely. As Browne reported, based on interviews with battered women: "Many of the women stayed because they had tried to escape and been beaten

for it, or because they believed their partner would retaliate against an attempt to leave him with further violence" (p. 232). Many women also fear for the safety of others (such as children), and they fear being without a home and losing the status of "wife."

Second, most battered women do not have the material resources to survive. Many are normally full-time homemakers, with few marketable skills and several children to provide for. Third, Browne (1995) reported "practical problems" faced by battered women in effecting a separation from an abusive relationship, such as where to live, how to obtain legal help, and how to plan for continued safety (e.g., can she go to work, or will the batterer find her there and cause her further harm?). Finally, women in abusive situations adopt "coping" strategies—similar to prisoners of war—evaluating which particular method will allow survival with the least amount of violence. As Browne found in her study of battered women,

> the women . . . often attempted to appease the aggressor by compliance, and to work through the relationship to obtain leniency and safety. Their primary concern during assaultive incidents was to survive. Their main concern after abusive incidents was to avoid angering the partner again. (p. 239)

However, because of the existence of shelters, more and more women are able to leave such situations. There are more than 2,500 women's shelters and service programs in the United States offering short-term refuge for women and their children, and every state has legislation against wife battering. Moreover, in 1994 Congress passed the Violence Against Women Act, establishing the Office of Domestic Violence within the Department of Justice and appropriating $1.5 billion to eliminate violence against women. The Act was reauthorized in 2000 and in 2005, expanding its services each time; it is due to be endorsed again in 2010.

We should mention, also, that wife battering is related to spouse killings. The case of O. J. Simpson serves as an example. In 1995 O. J. Simpson was found not guilty for the murders of his ex-wife, Nicole Brown Simpson, and her friend Ronald Goldman. However, in a subsequent civil trial, Simpson was found liable for the two deaths and ordered to pay $33.5 million in damages to the Brown and Goldman families. The heart of the civil case against Simpson was that the deaths resulted from a pattern of continued wife battering, with Goldman caught in the crime by chance. As one example of this wife battering, on New Year's Day 1989, Nicole Brown Simpson suffered a split lip, a red welt over one eye, and scratches and bruises, including a handprint on her neck. Police charged Simpson with wife battering, he pleaded no contest to the charge, and the judge found him guilty (Berry, 1998).

The Simpson case is not unique, for husbands/boyfriends are much more likely to murder wives/girlfriends than wives/girlfriends are to murder husbands/boyfriends (Federal Bureau of Investigation, 2008). Moreover, husbands often kill wives after lengthy periods of prolonged physical violence, yet the roles in such cases are seldom if ever reversed for wives. Husbands and wives also do not initiate similar acts of murder, because men are more likely than women to kill their spouse and children together, to stalk and kill a spouse who has left them, to kill their spouse as part of a planned murder-suicide, or to kill their spouse in response to a revelation of wifely infidelity. Unlike husbands, wives kill their spouses after years of suffering physical violence, after all attempts for assistance have been exhausted, when they feel trapped by the violence, or because they fear for their own and/or others' lives.

---

### BOX 12.2 OFFLINE AND ONLINE STALKING

*Offline stalking* normally refers to repeatedly pursuing someone offline (or physically) in a way that would cause a reasonable person to feel fear. In popular culture, offline stalking is frequently associated with celebrities—such as the case of Jody Foster being stalked by John Hinckley—but criminologists have shown that the most common victim of offline stalking is an ex-intimate partner (Belknap, 2007:323).

One study has revealed the following information regarding offline stalking (Tjaden and Thoennes, 1998):

- Over 1 million women are stalked each year in the United States.
- One in 12 women are stalked in their lifetime.
- 77 percent of women know the stalker.
- 87 percent of stalkers are men.
- 59 percent of women are stalked by a current or former intimate partner.
- 81 percent of women stalked by an intimate partner are also physically assaulted by that partner.
- The average duration of stalking involving intimate partners is 2.2 years.

- 61 percent of stalkers make unwanted phone calls; 33 percent send or leave unwanted letters or items; 29 percent vandalize property; and 9 percent kill or threaten to kill a family pet.
- 56 percent of women stalked take some type of self-protective measure, such as relocating.
- 26 percent of women stalked lose time at work.
- Gay men are more likely to be stalked than straight men.

A study (McFarlane et al., 1999) that examined women who have been stalked offline and then became victims of attempted or actual femicide, found that

- 76 percent of femicide victims and 85 percent of attempted femicide victims were stalked by the person who killed them.
- 67 percent of femicide victims and 71 percent of attempted femicide victims had been physically abused by their intimate partner, and 89 percent of all victims were stalked in the 12 months prior to the murder.
- 79 percent of physically abused victims reported stalking during the same period as the physical abuse.

The foregoing studies concentrate exclusively on offline stalking, yet recently the NCVS published a special report—*Stalking Victimization in the United States*—concluding that every year approximately 3.4 million people age 18 or older (14 in every 1,000) are victims of offline *and/or* online stalking (Department of Justice, 2009). The report identified seven major types of stalking: making unwanted phone calls (66.2 percent), posting information or spreading rumors on the Internet, in a public place, or by word of mouth (35.7 percent), following or spying (34.3 percent), showing up at places without a legitimate reason (31.1 percent), sending unsolicited or unwanted letters or e-mails (30.6 percent), waiting at places for the victim (29.0 percent), leaving unwanted items, presents, or flowers (12.2 percent). The NCVS report went on to point out that, almost half (46 percent) of stalking victims experienced at least one victimization per week; 11 percent reported being stalked for 5 years or more; women (20 per 1,000 people) were at a much greater risk than men (7 per 1,000 people) for stalking victimization; men were identified 70 percent of the time as stalkers; the highest victimization rate was for women divorced or separated (34 per 1,000 people); and 1 in 4 stalking victims reported some form of offline stalking, such as e-mail (83 percent) or instant messaging (35 percent) (see also Kernsmith, 2008).

*Online stalking*, or "cyberstalking," then, refers to repeatedly pursuing someone online in a harassing or threatening manner. Online stalking takes many forms in addition to those above, such as unsolicited hate, obscene, or threatening e-mail, malicious messages posted in newsgroups, "mail bombs," e-mail viruses, and electronic junk mail or "spam" (Joseph, 2003; Barak, 2007). The vast majority of online stalkers seem to be men, and their victims are women (Finn, 2008). Online stalking has a more global dimension than offline stalking—the cyberstalker and victim may even be located in different countries when the stalking takes place. Moreover, in online stalking a victim may not even know who the perpetrator is. Joseph (2003) provides an example of how "cyberstalking hackers" can "mask" their identities:

> A hacker may gain access to an e-mail account of an "innocent" user and use this address to send messages that may be threatening or offensive. From his or her home computer in Toronto, for example, a person can hack into the computer server at a university in Australia. From the account at the university in Australia, he or she can hack into a university in Japan.

From this new account he or she can then hack into the University of Arizona, choose a user name and send threatening messages to his or her next-door neighbor in Toronto. The message will appear to have come from Arizona, but in fact it is coming from their neighbor in Toronto. (p. 108)

Popular culture suggests that another form of online stalking—Internet-initiated sex offenses against young people—is primarily committed by strangers who are pedophiles and who (1) pretend to be peers to victims, (2) initiate relationships with very young children, and (3) persistently stalk these children into abduction and then rape them. However, a study examining 129 sexual offense cases involving juvenile victims that originated through online interaction found that the victims primarily were 13- to 15-year-old girls who met adult male offenders in online chat rooms (Wolak, Finkelhor, and Mitchell, 2004). The offenders therefore were not found to be pedophiles, since pedophilia is defined as having a sexual attraction to prepubescent children. Although the offenders did manipulate the youths in various ways, only 5 percent represented themselves as peers; thus, the vast majority did not deceive victims about being older men (76 percent were older than 25) who were interested in sexual relationships. Moreover, the vast majority of offenders did not use physical force or coercion to abuse victims, and they did not abduct victims. Rather, victims "typically agreed to meet these adults, knowing of their sexual interest. They engaged in sexual intercourse, or other sexual activity, with the adults, often on multiple occasions" (p. 16). Finally, the authors of this study argue that it is misleading to characterize these offenders as "strangers," because in the majority of cases they had communicated extensively with victims (both online and offline), establishing "romantic or otherwise close relationships before they first met victims face-to-face" (p. 16). Consequently, most of the Internet-initiated sex crimes in this study involved teenagers who were too young to legally consent to sexual intercourse.

The newest form of stalking is referred to as "high-tech stalking," which involves stalking individuals with forms of technology other than computers, such as intercepting phone calls via listening devices or tracking a victim's movements through cameras, global positioning satellite (GPS) instruments, and/or video imaging technologies (Southworth, Tucker, Fraser, and Shulruff, 2008).

## GAY AND LESBIAN PARTNER BATTERING

Most research on battering concentrates on heterosexual relationships. However, recent studies suggest that battering is found not only in heterosexual monogamy but also in other family forms, such as gay and lesbian relationships.

Like heterosexual wife battering, homosexual partner battering is difficult to document, especially because homosexuals remain an even more hidden population. Nevertheless, the studies that have been done (and based on small samples) report rates of domestic violence within lesbian and gay families as similar to those found in heterosexual families (Mahoney, Williams, and West, 2001; McClennen, 2005). In 2007 the National Coalition of Anti-Violence Programs documented 3,319 cases of lesbian, gay, bisexual, and transgender domestic violence. Of these cases, the vast majority involved lesbians and gay men (67 percent), males and females (as opposed to intersexed and transgender people), and white (44 percent) individuals between the ages of 30 and 39 (30 percent) (National Coalition of Anti-Violence Programs, 2008).

Additionally, the dynamics of homosexual partner battering are similar to those for heterosexual wife battering. For example, both involve similar types of violence, such as pushing, shoving, slugging, threats, and demeaning forms of behavior, as well as similar motives, such as manipulation, control, coercion, and punishment (Cruz, 2003; Renzetti, 2000; Girshick, 2008b). Moreover, as in heterosexual wife battering, in homosexual partner battering the violence increases in frequency and severity over time, and most victims of homosexual partner battering remain in abusive relationships for reasons similar to those for heterosexual wife battering victims (McClennen, 2005). Thus, overall, gay and lesbian partner battering is in many ways similar to heterosexual wife battering.

However, there is one important difference, which derives from the homophobic culture we live in: The abuser may threaten to reveal to others that the partner is lesbian or gay. This practice, labeled *outing*, can result in shunning by relatives and friends, the loss of a job, and a range of other discriminatory consequences, with little or no legal recourse for victims (Renzetti, 2000; Mahoney, Williams, and West, 2001). This form of abuse does not exist with heterosexual couples. Moreover, victims of same-sex partner battering have fewer services and less support available to them than heterosexual victims, and they must reveal not simply their victimization but their sexual identity to service providers, who may question that identity; indeed, there are no battered men's shelters for gay (or straight) men (Girshick, 2008b).

## CHILD AND ELDER ABUSE

Prior to the 1960s, no laws existed that criminalized child abuse—not because child abuse did not exist but because it was not in the interests of medical doctors to "see" it. According to Stephen Pfohl (1984), four factors impeded the recognition of child abuse by the medical profession:

1. Physicians were unaware of the possibilities of an abuse diagnosis.
2. Many physicians were unwilling to believe that parents would abuse their own children.
3. The "norm of confidentiality" created an obstacle for an abuse diagnosis.
4. Physicians were reluctant to become involved with the criminal justice system because it was time-consuming and hindered their ability to control the consequences of such a diagnosis.

However, for a specific specialty within medicine—pediatric radiology—these four barriers, Pfohl argued, did not apply. Abuse diagnosis was in fact an ultimate consequence of their mission: Pediatric radiologists constantly viewed children's X-rays and thus observed broken bones and other abnormalities. Pediatric radiologists were also removed from direct contact with the patient's family and thus had no need to be fearful of confidentiality. Most important, the "discovery" of child abuse provided pediatric radiologists—working in a low-profile specialty—the possibility of greater recognition within the medical community as well as an opportunity to coalesce with more academic segments of that community, such as psychiatrists. Thus, as Pfohl (1984) pointed out: "The organizational advantages surrounding the discovery of abuse by pediatric radiology set in motion a process of labeling abuse as deviance and legislating against it" (p. 61). Indeed, in a four-year period beginning in 1962, all fifty states passed laws against child abuse. Consequently, the "discovery" of child abuse "manifestly contributed to the advancement of humanitarian pursuits while covertly rewarding" pediatric radiology with enhanced status (p. 45).

After its discovery, public concern about child abuse increased dramatically, so that by the mid-1980s, 90 percent of the U.S. population considered it a serious national problem (Wolfe, 1985). Moreover, although more people today seem concerned about child abuse, the media have helped perpetuate the myth that most abuse of children—especially sexual abuse—occurs outside the home by day-care workers and child molesters lurking around elementary school playgrounds. However, most physical and sexual abuse of children actually occurs within the family (Finkelhor, 2008).

Researchers tend to agree that **child abuse** takes four forms—physical, sexual, emotional, and neglect (inattention to a child's basic needs for health, nutrition, shelter, education, affection, and protection). Approximately 1 million cases of child abuse are reported each year, or a rate of approximately 24 per 1,000 children, and more than half (52 percent) involve girls (U.S. Department of Health and Human Services, 2008). Of these cases, 16 percent entail physical abuse, 64 percent neglect, 9 percent sexual abuse, and 7 percent emotional abuse; the remainder are classified as "other" types of abuse.

Regarding the perpetrators of child abuse, the U.S. Department of Health and Human Services (2008) reports that 80 percent are parents; other relatives account for 7 percent, and unmarried partners account for 3 percent. The remaining perpetrators include people with other (e.g., camp counselor) or unknown relationship to victims. Regarding parents, both men and women commit child abuse. However, although women perform most of the child care in U.S. society, they commit only about 50 percent of the *physical abuse* and neglect of children. In other words, 50 percent of those who physically abuse and neglect children are men, who have on average little responsibility for children.

Important gender differences are found regarding abuse and neglect: Females are more likely to be abused and to suffer injuries due to abuse than males; females experience more abuse than males, whereas males experience more neglect than females; and for both males and females, abuse and neglect increase with age (U.S. Department of Health and Human Services, 2008).

Because sexual abuse has tended to be surrounded by extreme secrecy, it is hard to document its incidence. Nevertheless, it is estimated that approximately 20 percent of women and 10 percent of men in the United States were sexually abused as children (Finkelhor, 2008). In her classic work, *The Secret Trauma*, Diana Russell (1986) examined incestuous abuse and found that 16 percent of the 930 women interviewed reported at least one experience of incest before the age of 18. Of these women, 12 percent (152) had been sexually abused by a relative before their fourteenth birthday. More recent research shows that in the sexual abuse of girls, almost 50 percent of the perpetrators are family members and for boys almost 20 percent are family members (Kendall-Tackett, 2008). Thus, incestuous abuse is by no means rare.

Most incestuous abuse is committed by an adult male (usually the father), with the likely victim a child (usually the daughter) under the age of 18. Certain "typical characteristics" of incestuous assault include the following (Chesney-Lind and Pasko, 2004; Hunter, 2000):

- Approximately 70 percent of incestuous abuse victims are female.
- At least one-third of all female victims are younger than 11 years old.
- Incestuous abuse usually begins earlier for girls than for boys, and victimization of girls lasts longer than for boys.
- Assaults commonly take place repeatedly, lasting three years or more.
- The assault involves not only "sexuality" but also betrayal of trust by an adult on whom the child depends and exploitation of power differences in terms of gender as well as age.

As with other sexual assaults, victims experience incestuous abuse as coercive. At first—because of her young age—the victim may be unable to comprehend what is happening. However, as she suffers the assaults over time, she eventually understands that something "different" and wrong is happening to her. She feels guilty and humiliated and blames herself for the continued assaults. Many such victims not only experience fear, anxiety, depression, anger, and difficulties in school; they also often run away from home (Chesney-Lind and Pasko, 2004). Incestuously abused women also reveal that they remain frightened and upset years later (Kendall-Tackett, 2008). Moreover, prostitutes have informed sociologists that as victims of incestuous assault, they were first bribed by an adult

family male (sex for clothes, toys, and affection, for example), only later to be forced into sexual intercourse with him (Chesney-Lind and Pasko, 2004). Consequently, they learned they could obtain commodities by making their bodies available to men and thus turned to prostitution on the street to survive once they ran away from an incestuously abusive home.

Like child abuse, **elder abuse** involves physical abuse (use of physical force that may result in bodily injury, physical pain, or impairment), sexual abuse (nonconsensual sexual contact of any kind), and emotional abuse (infliction of anguish, pain, or distress through verbal or nonverbal acts), as well as neglect (refusal or failure to fulfill any part of a person's obligations or duties to an elderly person). But elder abuse differs from child abuse in that it also includes financial or material exploitation. This latter form of abuse involves illegal or improper use of an elder's funds, property, or assets (Wahidin and Cain, 2006).

There are two major types of elder abuse—domestic and institutional. *Domestic* elder abuse generally refers to any of the foregoing abusive behaviors committed by someone who is a spouse, sibling, child, friend, or caregiver in the elder's home or in the home of a caregiver. *Institutional* elder abuse involves any of the aforementioned forms of abuse that occur in a residential facility, such as a nursing home or group home, and committed by someone who has a contractual relationship with the victim (i.e., paid caregiver, staff, or professional).

According to the National Center on Elder Abuse (2005):

- Women disproportionately constitute the victims of elder abuse (56 percent).
- Of all victims, 66 percent are Caucasian and 17 percent are African American.
- Of elder abuse victims, 47 percent are 80 years of age or older.

- Of all victimizations, 66 percent are domestic and 10 percent occur in institutional settings (in the remaining 24 percent, the setting is unknown).
- The majority of victimizations entail neglect (49 percent), followed by emotional abuse (36 percent), financial/material exploitation (30 percent), physical abuse (25 percent), and sexual abuse (0.5 percent).
- The majority of perpetrators (52 percent) are males between the ages of 36 and 50.
- Typically, perpetrators are family members (for domestic elder abuse), with the highest percentage being a spouse to the victim, followed by an adult child.
- Domestic abusers tend to be dependent—usually financially—on the victim, which challenges the popular culture ideology that domestic elder abuse is primarily caused by frail elderly people who are dependent on others for care.
- In an institutional setting, the vast majority of perpetrators are "institutional staff."

Most domestic forms of elder abuse are similar to interpersonal violence in the family, in the sense that the husband or adult son uses the abuse to wield control over the wife/mother (Vinton, 2001). In addition, victims often are isolated from people to whom they might report the abuse, and victims fear further physical or emotional abuse should they mention it to others (Anetzberger, 2008).

Studies of elder abuse in nursing homes report practices that result in chronic neglect, substandard care, overcrowding, authoritarian practices, and failure to protect residents from abusive staff (Nerenberg, 2002; Gorgen, 2006). Regarding perpetrators, research shows that 10 percent of nurses and aides *admit* committing physical abuse, and 40 percent *admit* committing emotional abuse against nursing home residents. The most common forms of physical abuse in

nursing homes include unnecessary restraints, pushing, grabbing, shoving, punching, hitting with an object, and throwing something at a resident. The most common forms of emotional abuse in nursing homes are yelling at, swearing at, and insulting residents; denying them privileges; and threatening to throw something at or hit residents. Moreover, approximately 36 percent of nurses and aides report witnessing other employees physically abusing residents, and 81 percent have observed at least one incident of emotional abuse. The perpetrators tend to be much younger than nonperpetrators, and they view the victims as residents who "need to have everything done for them," "are waiting to die," and "are like children who sometimes need discipline." Finally, studies of sexual abuse in nursing homes suggest that most victims are women between the ages of 70 and 89, they need help with orientation to time and place, and the abuse involves primarily kissing and fondling by male residents (Roberto, 2008).

### ANIMAL ABUSE

**Animal abuse,** the cruel treatment of certain species of animal, has been outlawed in Maine since 1821, in England since 1822, and in most other U.S. states since the second half of the nineteenth century. Yet, as we saw in Section 1.2, criminal law is sometimes not a useful point of reference from which to look at this crime, let alone to understand it or to reduce its incidence. Indeed, animal anticruelty statutes are often species-biased and ineffective (and see Section 9.2 for our definition of animal abuse).

Anticruelty statutes are often species-biased (i.e., "speciesist" or "anthropocentric") because the range of animals they typically define as capable of being abused is narrow and highly selective. Among the numerous species excluded from the reach of many current anticruelty statutes are "wild" animals, birds, fish, reptiles, invertebrates, "vermin," and "pests." More favored species include popular, endangered, and exotic species, such as whales, wolves, and eagles, the abuse of which often carries considerable criminal sanctions.

Animal abuse is one of the least recognized forms of interpersonal violence in the family. When they are regarded as "pets," nonhuman animals (hereinafter, "animals") are typically treated as family members. Like other family members, they have names, they eat but are not eaten, they play and sleep indoors, they receive affection and love, and sometimes they are abused. Like humans, animals may be abused physically, sexually, emotionally, and psychologically, and they may be neglected. Like human infants and young children, domesticated animals are completely dependent on humans for food and shelter. Significantly, animals are for the most part unable either to deter humans who intend to abuse them or to report their abuse to authorities who might aid them.

Animal abuse tends to coexist with other forms of family violence. If one human member of a household is abusing another, animal abuse is also more likely there—and vice versa. Animal abuse has been found to be disproportionately present in situations of partner abuse (both heterosexual and homosexual), child physical abuse, child sexual abuse, and sibling abuse (Baldry, 2003; Beirne, 2009). Somewhat piecemeal findings about the presence of animal abuse in families have come from a variety of sources. These include the records of Societies for the Prevention of Cruelty to Animals, victimization surveys, and structured interviews with battered women and abused and neglected children. In addition, reports of animal abuse are made to veterinarians, women's shelters, animal shelters, animal control officers, police, and staff in various government agencies, such as the Department of Health and Human Services.

However, the exact prevalence of animal abuse is not known. Perhaps because animal abuse is not generally regarded as a serious crime, the amount of solid information on it is quite thin. We cannot analyze official (i.e., government-generated) data on animal abuse—there is none. In its compilation of crime data for 17,000 police departments, for example, the FBI's (2008) Uniform Crime Reports has no entries on animal abuse, although it does refer—next to "office equipment" and "televisions"—to "livestock" and "clothing and furs" stolen and recovered. In no technologically advanced societies do there exist large-scale, police-based data on the incidence and prevalence of animal abuse. There are no large-scale self-report studies of animal abuse. There are no household victimization surveys of animal abuse.

Our sociological knowledge of the hows, the whys, and the whens of animal abuse is therefore quite rudimentary. We know very little, for example, about how animal abuse is related to the key sociological variables of social class, gender, race/ethnicity, and age. At present, we can really only speculate that some of the sociological dimensions of animal abuse mirror those on interhuman violence. For example, young males probably commit animal abuse far more frequently than young females, and, when they do, their abuse is often considerably more violent (Flynn, 2008).

Animal sexual assault is one of the few crimes against animals that has gained some attention recently, although it is still regarded as so distasteful and controversial that even *The Jerry Springer Show* refused to air a segment filmed on it. Beirne (2009) argues that *bestiality* should be renamed *animal sexual assault*, because human–animal sexual relations almost always involve coercion and often cause animals pain and even death, and because animals are unable either to communicate consent to us in a form that we can readily understand or to speak out about their abuse.

There are at least four types of animal sexual assault, based on a combination of humans' motives and the degree of harm suffered by the abused animals (Beirne, 2009):

1. *Zoophilia.* This form of animal sexual assault occurs when animals are the preferred sexual partners of humans. This is probably the least common form of animal sexual assault.
2. *Commodification.* This is the main aspect of animal sexual assaults—packaged as commodities for sale in a market. It often involves a twofold assault: one by a man on a woman, who is assaulted and humiliated by being forced to have sex with an animal, the other on the animal, who is coerced into having sex with a human. Examples include live shows of women copulating with animals in bars and sex clubs or depictions of animal sexual assaults in pornographic films and at numerous Internet pornographic websites.
3. *Adolescent sexual experimentation.* This is probably the most prevalent form of animal sexual assault. It can occur either alone or with other adolescents, who either watch or participate. In a group context, some boys of necessity teach how it is done while others learn. It can be performed for a variety of reasons, including curiosity, cruelty, showing off for other boys, and acquiring the techniques of intercourse for later use on girls (or on boys).
4. *Aggravated cruelty.* Besides the possibility of cruelty during adolescent sexual experimentation, aggravated cruelty can be a major element in animal sexual assault in other ways. In mid-nineteenth-century England, for example, one case was reported in which 2-foot-long knotted sticks were thrust into mares' wombs, which were then vigorously rent, and another where the penises of cart horses and

donkeys were cut off (Archer, 1985). Multiple cases of such atrocities have been confirmed in several English counties from the early 1990s up till today (Beirne, 2009). Sometimes, aggravated cruelty against animals takes place in conjunction with the humiliation of women.

## 12.3 INTERPERSONAL VIOLENCE IN THE WORKPLACE

In Section 13.2 we will discuss some of the environmental hazards in the workplace, such as unsafe working conditions because of inadequate protection from dangerous substances. Although workplace dangers such as environmentally unsafe working conditions are impersonal, murder, assault, and sexual harassment are different, entailing violence perpetrated in a personal manner. For these reasons we discuss murder, assault, and sexual harassment as forms of interpersonal violence rather than as occupational crime.

### MURDER AND ASSAULT

There are four major types of workplace violence that may result in an assault and/or a murder:

1. *Criminal Intent*—the offender has no business relationship with the workplace and simply engages in some type of theft that may escalate into violence.
2. *Customer–Client*—the offender is a customer or client of the victim and the violent act occurs during normal duties at the workplace.
3. *Worker-on-Worker*—the offender is a current or former employee and attacks a coworker.
4. *Personal Relationship*—the offender has a relationship (e.g., family) with the victim (Riedel, 2008).

The vast majority of workplace murders are committed by men against men; both offenders and victims usually are between the ages of 25 and 44; guns are used 86 percent of the time; robbery is the most common initial motive that then results in workplace murder (Payne, 2005). Indeed, murder is the third leading cause of death in the workplace, and workplace murders increased by 13 percent in 2007 (Department of Labor, 2008). The highest rates of workplace homicides are found in retail trade businesses, especially food and beverage stores, transit and ground passenger transportation businesses, and leisure and hospitality businesses (p. 8).

The most common type of workplace violent crime, however, is simple assault (Duhart, 2001). Each year, approximately 1.3 million simple assault victimizations occur in the workplace, followed by 325,000 aggravated assaults and 900 murders. Workplace violence accounts for approximately 18 percent of all violent crime. Police officers experience workplace violent crime at rates higher than any other occupation, whereas university professors are victimized the least often. The workplace violent crime rate for whites is 25 percent higher than that for African Americans and 59 percent higher than the rate for other races (although most workplace victimizations are intraracial). Finally, the male workplace violent crime victimization rate is 56 percent higher than the female rate (and men and women are primarily victimized by men), and most people victimized are between the ages of 20 and 34 (Riedel, 2008).

Although a large majority of workplace violence occurs among strangers, personal disputes among coworkers have received the most attention from criminologists. Indeed, this type of workplace murder is classified by researchers as "murder by proxy," in which victims are chosen by a vengeful employee because of their association with the revenge target. The vengeful employee—usually a middle-aged white male who is "falling down" (was recently fired or reprimanded by a boss or lost his "status" or job to younger competitors, racial minorities, women, or immigrants)—responds by "getting back" at those seen as causing his frustration or as simply being an employee at his place of work where the painful event occurred. Some recent cases include the following:

- Three supervisors killed by a disgruntled employee at a jeep plant in Toledo, Ohio (January 2005).
- Three coworkers killed by a fired worker at a menu-printing plant in Signal Hill, California (March 2007).
- One woman killed because of a domestic dispute at a temporary staffing agency in Louisburg, North Carolina (April 2008).
- An employee shot by a coworker at a Randolph, Massachusetts, Alloy Fabricators plant (May 2008).
- Five people killed at a western Kentucky plastics plant after an employee argued with a supervisor (June 2008).

Regarding workplace assaults (both simple and aggravated) by occupation, law enforcement officers again suffer the largest amount of assault victimization on the job, followed by those working in mental health, retail sales, medical health, teaching, and transportation occupations (Duhart, 2001). Additionally, transportation workers (such as taxi drivers) suffer more aggravated, but not simple, assault than those who work in medical health and teaching (Riedel, 2008).

### SEXUAL HARASSMENT

Whereas males are much more often the victims of murder and assault at work, female workers have more often been victims of sexual harassment. But it was not until the mid-1970s that sexual harassment was recognized as a social problem (Benson and Thompson, 1982), and it was not until 1980 that sexual harassment actually became a crime. The Equal Employment Opportunity Commission issued guidelines in 1980 for determining sexual harassment as a violation of Title VII of the U.S. Civil Rights Act. This act was intended to prohibit discrimination on the basis of gender, and its guidelines apply to federal, state, and local government agencies as well as to private employers with 15 or more employees. The guidelines specify that employers have an "affirmative duty" to prevent and eliminate sexual harassment on the job and that "unwelcome sexual advances, requests for sexual favors, and other verbal or physical conduct of a sexual nature" are offenses if submission is explicitly or implicitly a condition of the individual's employment. When the submission or rejection affects one's employment or work performance by creating a working environment that is intimidating, hostile, and offensive, a violation of Title VII has also occurred. Thus, following this definition, **sexual harassment** includes not only attempted and completed forcible rape and "interpersonal coercion" but also sexist jokes and innuendos, "accidental" collisions and fondling, and constant ogling and pinches.

Myths about sexual harassment—that it affects only a few women, that women really "ask for it," and that charges of sexual harassment are commonly false, for example—continue to be perpetuated. However, studies of sexual harassment indicate the prevalence of *nonconsenting* interpersonal sexual violence in the workplace. For example, in 1981 the Merit System's Protection Board conducted a study of sexual harassment among federal employees for the Subcommittee on Investigations of the House Committee on Post Office and Civil Service (Russell, 1990). The board found (in their random sample of over 20,000 federal employees) that 42 percent of all female employees reported being sexually harassed at work. The number of sexual harassment complaints filed with the Equal Employment Opportunity Commission

jumped from 5,694 cases in 1990 to 10,900 cases in the first eight months of 1993, most likely because of the national "teach-in" on sexual harassment following the confirmation hearings of Supreme Court Justice Clarence Thomas. Surveys continue to show that prevalence rates of sexual harassment have not decreased over time—approximately 40 percent of U.S. women report every year that they experienced a legally actionable form of sexual harassment (Morgan, 2001; O'Toole et al., 2007). What this information reveals is that sexual harassment in the workplace is likely widespread.

Why does such harassment occur? Research shows that gender power is an essential component of much sexual harassment, especially in situations involving a male superior and a female subordinate, although women also are harassed by male coworkers and even male subordinates. For example, women who work in male-dominated institutions—such as policing, military, and athletic organizations—face much sexual harassment, and certain organizations maintain value systems, communicative processes, rituals, and organizational symbols that create a sexist culture at work (O'Toole et al., 2007). Many organizations use sexual metaphor in communicative processes that may be conducive to sexual harassment. For example, female employees at Stroh's Brewing Company brought a sexual harassment suit against the company, charging that the Swedish Bikini Team advertising campaign in the early 1990s contributed to a sexualized work environment in which women were subjected to daily verbal and physical abuse by male employees.

Studies of sexual harassment also indicate that rape and interpersonal coercion exist within the workplace. Approximately 37,000 rapes and sexual assaults occur at the workplace every year (Duhart, 2001). Interpersonal coercion (recalling our earlier discussion in this chapter) involves economic threats made by a male supervisor to the effect that, if the female employee or possible employee does not engage in sexual intercourse with him, she either will not be hired, retained, or promoted or else will be fired, demoted, or transferred to a more unpleasant position. If we assume that the female employee or possible employee does not secretly desire sexual intercourse with the male supervisor, such threats can be coercive. In other words, economic deprivation is a serious and expensive cost, even when set beside unwelcome and undesired coitus (Morgan, 2008).

Indeed, sexual harassment has similarities with incestuous assault: The victim of incest, like the sexually harassed woman, is economically, if not emotionally, dependent on the offender. Sexual harassment is likewise humiliating, and, paralleling incestuous assault, there is motivation to keep it a secret. In fact, only approximately 12 percent of sexually harassed women at the workplace report the offense (Morgan, 2008). Sexual harassment, like incestuous assault, often continues for a long time and is experienced as an abuse of power and a betrayal of trust.

Finally, the risk of sexual harassment is highest in male-dominated workplaces. For women in military, coal mining, construction, and criminal justice system occupations, the rate of sexual harassment is approximately 30 percent higher than in the general population.

Victims of sexual harassment suffer severe consequences. The majority of women report emotional stress, such as nervousness, fear, and sleeplessness, as well as interference with their job performance, and many also find it necessary to obtain psychological help. Moreover, victims of sexual harassment at work report higher rates of absenteeism and low productivity, thereby adversely affecting their own financial situation as well as that of their employer (Gutek and Koss, 2007).

## REVIEW

In this chapter we have discussed interpersonal crimes of violence—murder, assault, hate crimes, rape, wife and gay/lesbian partner battering, child abuse, elder abuse, animal abuse, and sexual harassment. These crimes create extensive public concern and fear—and rightly so, inasmuch as the United States has one of the highest levels of violent crime in the industrialized world. However, crimes of interpersonal violence occur most often indoors—not on the streets—and are usually committed by relatives, friends, and acquaintances of the victims.

## MURDER, ASSAULT, HATE CRIMES, AND RAPE

1. Murder is the most serious form of interpersonal violence; fortunately, it occurs the least often. Murder is primarily a big-city crime and occurs most frequently in the South. There is little evidence suggesting that owning a firearm is the chief cause of murder. In some cases the interaction between offender and victim involves threats and retaliation by both participants to the murder. There are important similarities and differences between murder and aggravated assault.

2. Hate crimes differ from other forms of interpersonal violence, in that they are more vicious, are excessively brutal, and are frequently perpetrated at random on total strangers (commonly a single victim) by multiple offenders, and victims face great difficulty coming to terms with their victimization. Evidence indicates an increase in hate groups in recent years.

3. Rape occurs much more often in the United States than most people recognize. Sociologists, criminologists, and feminists are currently debating the appropriate definition of rape. Women are more likely to be raped by someone they know than by a stranger. The idea of victim-precipitated rape is a myth. Although there are a few reported cases of women raping men, males are relatively safe from sexual assault, unless they are in prison. Throughout history, rape has been an institutionalized component of war, and institutions—such as universities—may create conditions conducive to rape.

## INTERPERSONAL VIOLENCE IN THE FAMILY

1. Women of completed rapes are victimized more by their husbands than by any other type of perpetrator. Victims of wife rape feel humiliated and degraded and experience psychological trauma for years afterward.
2. Between 30 and 50 percent of battered women are also raped by their husbands. Wife battering was legally and socially acceptable for centuries. Research on battering in heterosexual couples identifies four major types: common couple violence, patriarchal terrorism, violent resistance, and mutual violent control. Many women, because of social and economic pressures, feel they cannot leave an abusive relationship.
3. Stalking occurs both online and offline as well as through "high-tech" forms.
4. Homosexual battering—in lesbian and gay male relationships—seems to occur at a similar rate as wife battering in heterosexual relationships. The dynamics of battering in lesbian and gay male relationships are similar to those in heterosexual relationships, although there are some important differences.
5. Most physical and sexual abuse of children occurs within the family. Men and women each commit 50 percent of the physical abuse and neglect of children. Incestuous abuse is by no means rare in the United States; it is usually committed by an adult male (usually the father), and the victim is usually a child under 18 (generally a daughter). Incestuously assaulted girls and women find the encounter coercive, and years later many report still being frightened and upset.
6. Elder abuse involves physical, sexual, and emotional abuse as well as neglect and material and financial exploitation. There exists two major types of elder abuse—domestic and institutional.
7. As a form of family violence, animal abuse is one of the least recognized. Its several forms include cruelty, abuse, and neglect. There are no large-scale sources of data on animal abuse, though a discussion of some of the sociological characteristics of animal sexual assault has been presented in this chapter.
8. The chapter uses an animal rights definition of animal abuse as any act that contributes to the pain, suffering, or death of an animal or that otherwise threatens its welfare. Animal abuse may be physical, psychological, or emotional; may involve active maltreatment or passive neglect or omission; and may be direct or indirect, intentional or unintentional. Some forms of animal abuse are socially acceptable.

## INTERPERSONAL VIOLENCE IN THE WORKPLACE

1. The most common form of interpersonal violence in the workplace is assault; retail sales and law enforcement suffer the most victimizations. The typical violent person in the workplace is a vengeful middle-aged white male.
2. Sexual harassment includes behavior ranging from sexist jokes to interpersonal coercion and rape. Sexual harassment in the workplace is not uncommon. Sexual harassment causes emotional stress and interferes with job and nonoccupational performance.

## QUESTIONS FOR CLASS DISCUSSION

1. The media foster the image that most interpersonal violence occurs in the streets; as we have seen, it primarily takes place indoors. Discuss why you think the media distort the reality of interpersonal violence and why most violence occurs indoors.
2. Is there a "culture of hate" in North America? If so, what type of policy would you create to curb that culture?
3. Is the legal definition of rape too narrow, or is it satisfactory as it stands?
4. Identify the similarities and differences between child and elder abuse, and then explain why these forms of abuse exist.
5. Consider the problematic case of Deena the stripping chimpanzee reported in Adams (1990). For $100 Deena and her trainer would appear at a social gathering, during which Deena would perform a striptease act for the partygoers. Is this animal sexual assault?

## FOR FURTHER STUDY

### READINGS

Beirne, Piers. 2009. *Confronting Animal Abuse: Law, Criminology, and Human-Animal Relationships.* Lanham, MD: Rowman & Littlefield.

Finkelhor, David. 2008. *Childhood Victimization: Violence, Crime, and Abuse in the Lives of Young People.* New York: Oxford University Press.

Hattery, Angela J. 2009. *Intimate Partner Violence.* Lanham, MD: Rowman & Littlefield.

Tomsen, Stephen. 2009. *Violence, Prejudice and Sexuality.* New York: Routledge.

Wahidin, Azrini, and Maureen Cain, eds. 2006. *Ageing, Crime and Society.* Portland, OR: Willan.

### WEBSITES

1. <http://www.ovw.usdoj.gov/>: The Department of Justice Violence Against Women Office's website provides links to federal legislation and current research on violence against women.
2. <http://www.abanet.org/domviol/home.html>: The American Bar Association's Commission on Domestic Violence provides excellent and up-to-date statistics on intimate violence.

3. <http://www.ncavp.org>: The website of the National Coalition of Anti-Violence Programs provides useful information on violence committed against and within the lesbian, gay, bisexual, and transgender communities.

4. <http://www.hsus.org>: The website of the Humane Society of the United States (HSUS), a pro-animal organization. The website provides information about human–animal interaction, animal rights and animal welfare, and current campaigns against a variety of forms of animal abuse.

5. <http://childwelfare.gov>: This website of the U.S. Department of Health and Human Services provides information on research, legislation, and research related to child abuse and neglect.

6. <http://jan.ucc.nau.edu/~pms/icash.html>: The International Coalition Against Sexual Harassment website provides useful links to the most current issues related to sexual harassment, including "facts about sexual harassment."

# WHITE-COLLAR CRIME

**13.1 Occupational Crime**
- Occupational Theft
- Occupational Fraud

**13.2 Corporate Crime**
- Corporate Violence
- Corporate Theft

**13.3 Transnational Corporate Crime**
- Bribery
- Dumping
- Dangerous Working Conditions

**PREVIEW**

Chapter 13 introduces:
- What sociologists mean by white-collar crime.
- The various types of white-collar crime.
- The nature, extent, and costs of white-collar crime.
- How white-collar crimes differ from other crimes.

**KEY TERMS**

collective embezzlement
corporate crimes
corporate theft
corporate violence
deceptive advertising
embezzlement
employee theft
financial fraud

insider trading
occupational crimes
occupational fraud
occupational theft
physician fraud
price-fixing
transnational corporate crime
white-collar crime

When we think of crime, we usually focus on the types of crimes already discussed in this book—property crimes and interpersonal crimes of violence. This thinking is inevitable because official agencies of social control (police and courts) concentrate on these behaviors (thus attracting media attention) and because these crimes are the ones most frequently studied by sociologists and criminologists. However, although the crimes discussed in Chapters 11 and 12 generate considerable fear and suffering in society, the white-collar crimes discussed in this chapter are much more harmful.

Edwin Sutherland was the first sociologist in the United States to conceptualize the problem of **white-collar crime**. Given the contemptuous attitude toward the law and business ethics displayed by the "robber barons" (such as Daniel Drew and John D. Rockefeller) in the late 1800s and the widespread and publicized corporate fraud of the 1920s and 1930s, Edwin Sutherland (1949) focused his classic study on "crime committed by a person of respectability and high social status in the course of his occupation" (p. 2). The bulk of Sutherland's data in *White-Collar Crime* consisted of decisions of federal, state, and municipal courts and administrative commissions involving the seventy largest manufacturing, mining, and mercantile corporations in the United States. Among the worst corporate offenders were such giants as American Sugar Refining; American Tobacco; Armour; DuPont; Ford; General Electric; General Motors; Gimbel; A&P; International Harvester; Loew's; Montgomery Ward; National Steel; Procter & Gamble; Sears; U.S. Steel; Warner Brothers; Westinghouse Electric; and Woolworth. Sutherland reported in painstaking detail that in the preceding 20 years

> each of the 70 large corporations has one or more decisions against it, with a maximum of 50. The total number of decisions is 980, and the average per corporation is 14.0. Sixty corporations have

> decisions against them for restraint of trade, 53 for infringement, 44 for unfair labor practices, 43 for miscellaneous offenses, 28 for misrepresentation in advertising, and 26 for rebates. (p. 15)

Of the seventy largest industrial and commercial U.S. corporations, 97.1 percent were recidivists, in that they had two or more decisions against them. In addition, Sutherland also revealed that the Federal Trade Commission, by order of Congress, reported that during the 1914–1918 and 1939–1945 wars many corporations had violated wartime regulations. These violations included price regulation abuse, overcharging, and fraudulent profiteering in war-related materials, tax evasion, restraint of trade, illegal maintenance of competitive positions, violations of embargoes and neutrality, and even treason (for example, illegally revealing classified information to the enemy). As Sutherland concluded:

> The large corporations in time of war, when Western civilization was endangered, did not sacrifice their own interests and participate wholeheartedly in a national policy, but instead they attempted to use this emergency as an opportunity for extraordinary enrichment of themselves at the expense of others. (p. 191)

With these data Sutherland (1949) demonstrated that in order to maximize their profits, U.S. corporations routinely commit crimes against consumers, competitors, stockholders and other investors, inventors, employees, and the state itself. Corporations tend to commit more crimes the greater their age, the larger their size, and the more their economic position was monopolistic, antiunion, and dependent on advertising (pp. 258–263).

Demonstrating that white-collar crime was widespread and endemic to U.S. business, Sutherland was led to concentrate almost exclusively on one type of white-collar crime: corporate crime. However, sociologists and criminologists later expanded the definition of white-collar crime to include not only corporate crimes but also occupational crimes and transnational corporate crimes.

- **Occupational crimes** are committed by individuals in the course of their occupations for direct personal gain. These crimes are usually committed against an employer. Embezzlement is an example of an occupational crime.
- **Corporate crimes** differ from occupational crimes in that they are not committed for direct personal gain—although certain individuals may benefit indirectly from them. Rather, these crimes primarily benefit the corporation. We define corporate crimes as illegal and/or socially **injurious** acts of intent or indifference that occur for the purpose of furthering corporate goals and that physically and/or economically abuse individuals in the United States and/or abroad. Collusion of top executives of utility corporations to fix prices is an example of corporate crime.
- **Transnational corporate crimes** constitute the third type of white-collar crime. Many corporations conduct their business operations in more than one country. Consequently, this transnational character of U.S. corporations sometimes results in crimes perpetrated on the people of other societies, ranging from bribery to export of hazardous products to dangerous working conditions.

These three types of white-collar crime are both similar to and different from the crimes already discussed in Chapters 11 and 12. Like other crimes, white-collar crimes involve theft and violence. That is, commission of white-collar crimes results in loss of property and/or physical injury and death. But white-collar crimes differ from other crimes in two important ways. First, white-collar crimes entail far more victimization—in terms of economic loss and

lives injured and lost—than the crimes discussed earlier. Second, victimization resulting from white-collar crimes is less apparent—although, once again, far more severe—than the one-on-one type of victimization resulting from interpersonal crimes of violence. Indeed, most of us who suffer the pains of white-collar crimes—corporate crimes in particular—are unaware of our own victimization.

## 13.1 OCCUPATIONAL CRIME

Occupational crime occurs in the workplace and is motivated by direct personal gain; it has two main forms: occupational theft and occupational fraud. **Occupational theft** stems from an abuse of trust between the employee and employer. We examine two types of occupational theft: employee theft and embezzlement. Both types affect consumers by increasing the cost of goods and services; they also affect some businesses negatively. **Occupational fraud** is a deliberate workplace deception practiced for the purpose of obtaining personal financial gain. This type of fraud is ubiquitous; we explore the major aspects of occupational fraud with examples from the fields of medicine and securities.

### OCCUPATIONAL THEFT

In preindustrialized societies—such as feudal England in the seventeenth century—people had common rights to such necessities as the gathering of wood, the killing of game, and the grazing of animals. But with the transition from feudalism to capitalism, these "rights" were translated into "property." As Jason Ditton (1997b) has stated: The "annexation of common rights...naturally culminated in the simultaneous creation of 'property,' and the propertied classes, and the ultimate criminalization of customary practices" (p. 41). As land previously open to everyone's use became the private property of a few, wood gathering became wood theft, game rights became poaching, and grazing rights became trespassing. In addition, this privatization, as Ditton explains,

> released into urban life a working population not only used to receiving part of their "wages" in kind...but also one still stinging from the effects of the abrupt and cruel negation of those practices in the countryside. As one might expect, and empirical evidence supports this, a major source of irritation to factory owners who took on such "idle" rural labourers was their penchant for making off with parts of the workplace or the fruits of their labour there, in addition to their wages. (p. 43)

Indeed, the preindustrial cultural tradition of common rights was carried over into industrialized society. Workers expected "wages-in-kind"—extras to supplement their actual earnings. In eighteenth-century England, for instance, workers in manufacturing industries "constantly borrowed, bartered, and sold small quantities of materials among themselves," a good portion of which was stolen from the workplace (Henry, 1987:142). As Stuart Henry has argued,

> criminalization of the consumption of a part of one's daily labor was redefined in conjunction with capitalist development of the factory to become employee theft and embezzlement; the trading of embezzled goods came to constitute a hidden economy. (p. 142)

In other words, accompanying the rise of capitalism was the emergence of two major forms of occupational theft: employee theft and embezzlement. We consider each in turn.

**Employee theft**—stealing merchandise and job-related items from one's workplace—is one of the most pervasive and costly crimes in the United States. Self-report studies suggest that 75 percent of employees *admit* to some sort of theft from the workplace (Tomlinson and Greenberg, 2009).

The cost of employee theft is enormous. Most employees steal minor items; yet when these items are multiplied by many workers, the cost becomes substantial. *Inventory shrinkage* (loss from employee theft, shoplifting, poor paperwork, and vendor theft) adds approximately 15 percent to the price of all retail goods, and most of this loss is attributable to employee theft (Coleman, 2006). Overall, researchers estimate that employee theft costs $400 billion annually (Greenberg, 2002).

Research indicates that perceived unfairness in the workplace (i.e., being underpaid) is the main reason for employee theft. Moreover, interpersonally insensitive treatment on the part of managers and supervisors provides individuals with rationalizations for engaging in theft at the workplace. As Jerald Greenberg (2002) puts it, "People who feel underpaid are inclined to steal and to engage in other types of deviant behavior when company agents display indifference regarding the suffering they experience as a result of underpayment" (p. 986; see also Holtfreter, 2005).

Two classic studies, by Jason Ditton (1977a) and Gerald Mars (1983), enhance our understanding of the relationship between employee theft and occupation. Ditton considered employee theft a form of what he called *part-time crime*. However, part-time crime is not simply a matter of time commitment, inasmuch as a part-time criminal may well

> spend more hours and minutes breaking the law than somebody involved full time in crime. The crucial distinction is that whereas the full-time criminal's legitimate occupation is perceived by him [or her] to be merely nominal, the part-time criminal sees his [or her] illegitimate activities in the same way, as nominal. (p. 91)

In other words, part-time criminals may spend more hours planning and executing their crime than full-time criminals, but this activity is *perceived* by them as inconsequential to their full-time legitimate activity at work.

In a participant observation study of bread salesmen at "Wellbread Bakery," Ditton found that part-time employee theft entailed three activities: fiddling, stealing, and dealing. *Fiddling* is the practice by salespeople (those who sell and deliver bakery goods) of overcharging customers by either increasing the price or reducing the number of items for the standard price. Ditton found that fiddling was tolerated—even overtly recommended—by management because the loser is the customer rather than the company.

*Stealing* is theft from the company itself. Although production workers have *pilfering rights* to a daily loaf of bread, salespeople are excluded from this dubious privilege. As Ditton (1977a) explains:

> It is assumed that production staff have no outlet other than domestic consumption of pilfered loaves, and that this empirical feature of the practice will de facto limit the amount of bread that they will take. Salesmen, on the other hand, are assumed to have guaranteed occupational access to facilities (a round of customers) which would encourage them systematically to escalate their thefts beyond tolerable levels. Thus, for salesmen at Wellbread's, we may define a successful steal as the removal of some sort of asset skillfully, unobserved, and without permission. Salesmen steal both convertible consumer goods, for resale to their customers, and nonconvertible assets, such as plastic bags and clipboards, which, as tools of the trade, make occupational life easier. (p. 101)

*Dealing*—the third employee theft activity identified by Ditton (1977a)—is the clandestine unofficial "distribution of other people's goods to the mutual interest and profit of those covertly involved" (p. 106). Dealing involves the collusion of salespeople and other employee staff in arranging a profit-making venture. For example, the bread dispatcher may provide extra trays of bread to salespeople without "booking it." Subsequent to the sale of the extra trays, both the salespeople and the dispatcher share the profits. Dealing, then, involves the amateur trade (or fencing) in stolen goods from the workplace.

Ditton's book describes how crime can provide an outlet for creativity in monotonous and alienated work environments as well as challenge the official view of crime as being predominantly a lower-class, nonoccupational phenomenon.

Gerald Mars (1983) distinguishes between various types of employee theft and links these to types of jobs. Mars divided workers into four types (hawks, donkeys, wolves, and vultures), marked by such elements as the amount of job autonomy, extent of isolation from others, and degree of control over one's labor power. Mars also examined the amount of collectiveness in the workplace, which varies according to how a workplace prioritizes the interests of the group over the individual and is distinguished by such elements as the frequency with which people interact with others, whether contacts occur within a mutually interconnecting network, and the scope of group social life outside the workplace.

*Hawks* are professionals, executives, and small-business persons who maintain individuality, autonomy, and control over their labor power but have infrequent contact with others. Therefore, it is much easier for hawks to "bend the rules" to their personal advantage. Work-related expenses provide an example. A journalist, for instance, may claim first-class travel but actually go second class or may falsify costs of entertainment and meals as business expenses. More extreme, one journalist said: "It's not uncommon for you to say you're dashing…somewhere for a story. You look up fares plus a few beers for fictitious informants and a taxi or two and bang it in for expenses" (cited in Mars, 1983:47).

*Donkeys* have little autonomy, are not isolated from others, and have no control over their labor power. Moreover, donkeys do not work within a group setting with frequent interaction.

Supermarket cashiers and workers "on long and noisy mass-production belts" are examples of donkeys. Because of the structured nature of these jobs, employee theft is more restricted than it is for hawks. Supermarket cashiers, for instance, are limited to undercharging—or not charging at all—friends and family who frequent the store where they work or simply to "taking from the till." As one cashier expressed to Mars: A theft may occur "when your mother or friend comes in. Then they get away with a load of stuff and you put hardly anything through the till" (1983:66).

*Wolves* are similar to donkeys, in the sense of having little autonomy and lacking control over their labor power, but they differ in that their jobs require a group of workers. For both hawks and donkeys, control over theft belongs to the individual. For wolves, however, theft is under group control. Airport baggage handlers and longshoremen are examples of wolves. If dockworkers, for example, want to steal cargo, they need the support of the group to do so. This is so both because they work as a group and because they must divide their labor so that some workers steal cargo while others distract supervisors. As Mars (1983) explained:

> Theoretically, all these men can pilfer cargo. Yet supervision of unloading by the ships' officers at one end and the shed superintendent at the other greatly reduces *individual* opportunities. Those with *access* therefore need the *support* of those who do not have access, to distract the attention of the supervisors, to provide cover, to "clear" documents, and to enable the swift removal and distribution of goods once they have been pilfered. (p. 103)

Finally, *vultures* have considerable individual autonomy, yet that autonomy operates within a loosely structured work group setting. Waiters, truck drivers, and hotel workers are examples of vultures. Such occupations enjoy a degree of independence yet rely on support from coworkers.

For example, Mars found a coordinated group of truck drivers who arranged the "private delivery" of stolen company goods on company time.

Mars' work thus identifies how type of occupation and workplace setting help determine type of occupational theft. Indeed, his classification of hawks, donkeys, wolves, and vultures involves a combination of employee theft and embezzlement.

**Embezzlement**, like employee theft, involves a violation of employer–employee trust. However, embezzlement differs from employee theft in that it involves taking money—rather than merchandise and job-related items—for one's personal use. The supermarket cashier donkey, for example, has the opportunity to steal both merchandise (employee theft) and money (embezzlement).

Embezzlement ranges from simply "taking from the till" to "manipulating the books," but people in certain occupations can embezzle more easily than those in other jobs. Individuals who occupy top business or bank positions—such as loan officers, accountants, computer operators, and CEOs—have a much greater opportunity for embezzling large sums of money than cashiers, bank tellers, sales clerks, or other lower-level employees do. Consequently, individuals in a position to embezzle and who actually do embezzle large sums of money are frequently viewed by employers as some of the most important people in the company.

Most embezzlers turn to this crime because they are living beyond their financial means, and in some cases the problem involves large gambling debts or family emergencies (such as unexpected medical bills not covered by insurance) (Coleman, 2006).

Much embezzlement results from the use of computers: Computer technology makes it easier to manipulate books because manipulations are so difficult to detect and trace. Moreover, only about 15 percent of computer embezzlements

## BOX 13.1 COLLECTIVE EMBEZZLEMENT

The text identifies embezzlement as a crime committed by employees *against* the company. However, a new type of embezzlement emerged in the 1990s from the savings and loan scandal, what Kitty Calavita, Henry Pontell, and Robert Tillman (1997) term **collective embezzlement**. This type of embezzlement entails the theft of funds from savings and loan institutions for personal gain, at the expense of the institutions and with the approval of management. In other words, like traditional embezzlement, collective embezzlement is a crime against the company. Yet collective embezzlement differs from traditional embezzlement in that it is endorsed, approved, and accomplished by management itself. It is, in short, "crime by the corporation against the corporation" (p. 63).

The savings and loan scandal is the most expensive white-collar crime in U.S. history and will likely eventually cost the U.S. government between $300 billion and $500 billion. Ultimately, U.S. taxpayers are the victims of this crime because the money embezzled did not belong to the embezzlers. The reason that taxpayers are the victims is that in 1980, Congress increased the amount for which the Federal Savings and Loan Insurance Corporation (FSLIC) would insure S&L accounts from a maximum of $40,000 to $100,000 per deposit. Additionally, Congress phased out controls on interest rates. Subsequently, S&Ls raised their interest rates, thus attracting wealthy depositors, who did not face any risk of loss; should an S&L fail, the U.S. government (and therefore taxpayers) would reimburse depositors up to $100,000 per deposit. This new opportunity, when combined with the Reagan administration's deregulation policies of "getting government off our backs," created the perfect conditions for this new form of occupational crime.

According to U.S. government reports, crime or misconduct played a crucial role in 70 to 80 percent of the S&Ls bailed out. The vast majority of these bailouts were the result of embezzlement. The case of Erwin "Erv" Hansen's "shopping spree," or embezzling S&L funds to finance a lavish lifestyle, is one example of collective embezzlement. Hansen, president of Centennial Savings and Loan in northern California, embezzled S&L funds to purchase such things as antique furniture ($130,000), a penthouse in San Francisco ($773,487), a Mercedes limousine ($77,000), five cars for his family ($90,000), and a $137,000 Rolls Royce for himself. Hansen also gave a Christmas party for his friends based on the theme of a "Renaissance Faire." Couples were "proclaimed" as jesters announced their entry into the hall, which was transformed into an Elizabethan forest of 300 living trees sparkling with 75,000 tiny white lights. Candlelight shimmered through piped-in fog that simulated medieval moors and woods. Oriental rugs covered the floor. Because of this embezzlement, Centennial eventually became insolvent, costing the FSLIC an estimated $160 million.

Other types of collective embezzlement include such group behavior as "land flips," "nominee loans," "reciprocal lending," and "linked financing." A *land flip* is described as follows:

> A sells a parcel of real estate to B for $1 million, its approximate market value. B finances the sale with a bank loan. . . . B sells the property back to A for $2 million. A finances the sale with a bank loan, with the bank relying on a fraudulent appraisal. B repays his original loan and takes $1 million in "profit" off the table, which he shares with A. A defaults on the loan, leaving the bank with a $1 million loss. (Calavita, Pontell, and Tillman, 1997:49)

Thus, this type of collective embezzlement requires three participants: two people to "flip" the money and a corrupt appraiser.

In the case of *nominee loans*, the owner/officer of an S&L will extend a loan to a *straw borrower*—someone indirectly connected to the S&L—who receives a kickback for obtaining the loan and then returns the remaining money to the lender. One such owner/officer, Don Dixon (owner of all the stock in Vernon S&L in Texas), put together a network of some thirty companies for the purpose of making illegal loans to himself, costing taxpayers approximately $1.3 billion.

*Reciprocal lending* refers to executives from at least two different S&Ls making loans to each other. One investigation in Wyoming revealed a chain of reciprocal loans among four S&Ls that resulted in a $26 million loss to taxpayers.

Finally, in *linked financing* someone deposits money in an S&L (insured by the FSLIC) under the condition that the person receive a loan in return. Subsequently, the loan is defaulted on, the S&L becomes insolvent, and the federal government pays back the deposit because it was insured. Thus, both the depositor and the owner of the S&L make money.

The majority of perpetrators of this collective embezzlement were men, yet twenty-seven women also were involved—50 percent of whom were either a vice president or a manager of an S&L—who embezzled on average $508,000 (Dodge, 2009).

are ever reported. According to one estimate, the average computer crime nets approximately $500,000, and most computer embezzlement is committed by authorized users, trusted insiders, and skilled employees (Rosoff, Pontell, and Tillman, 2007). The most common method of computer embezzlement is to divert cash into fraudulent accounts. A variation of this method is called *salami slicing*, in which many small amounts of numerous private accounts are "sliced off" and diverted to the fraudulent account. Coleman (2006) provides an example of this technique of computer embezzlement:

> [T]wo computer programmers at a large New York garment firm instructed the company computer to increase each employee's income tax withholding by two cents a week and to deposit the money in the programmer's withholding accounts. At the end of the year, the embezzlers planned to receive their profits in the form of refund checks from the Internal Revenue Service. However, those giant-size refunds touched off an IRS investigation that uncovered the crime. (p. 22)

## OCCUPATIONAL FRAUD

In Section 11.2 we discussed various types of fraud committed against the government and through the use of checks and credit cards. We now discuss two types of occupational fraud— physician fraud and insider trading—committed for direct personal gain in the course of one's occupation.

Like most people, most physicians are honest. Some, however, commit **physician fraud** through unnecessary prescription of pharmaceutical drugs, unnecessary surgical procedures, and overtreatment of Medicare and Medicaid patients. Approximately 22 percent of all antibiotic prescriptions in U.S. hospitals are prescribed unnecessarily, and adverse drug reactions result in more than 100,000 hospitalized patient

deaths each year (Coleman, 2006). Some physicians even perform unnecessary surgeries, which cost the people of the United States approximately $4 billion annually, and it is estimated that 2.4 million unnecessary surgeries are performed in the United States each year. Moreover, estimated deaths each year from unnecessary surgeries range from 12,000 to 16,000, and from 44,000 to 88,000 patients die in hospitals each year from medical negligence (Reiman, 2006: Purdy, 2005).

Physician fraud occurs in Medicaid (for the poor) and Medicare (for the elderly) programs, costing an estimated $100 billion a year (Coleman, 2006). When physicians know that medical costs will be paid for the poor and elderly, there seemingly exists much to be gained by fraudulently increasing the amount of medical work performed and doing it at a minimum cost. A prominent example of Medicaid fraud is that of a California ophthalmologist found guilty of performing unnecessary cataract surgery on poor patients to obtain Medicaid fees. For the affluent the surgery was performed skillfully and successfully; for the poor it was performed in "slipshod fashion." In one case the physician totally blinded a 57-year-old woman when he performed unnecessary surgery on her one *sighted* eye (p. 28).

Paul Jesilow, Henry Pontell, and Gilbert Geis (1993), in their classic work, investigated Medicaid fraud in the early 1990s. For their book *Prescription for Profit*, they drew on case file material from California and New York (the two states with the largest number of violators) and found four primary categories of crimes committed by physicians caught violating Medicaid programs:

> (1) billing schemes, which include billing for services not rendered, charging for nonexistent office visits, or receiving or giving kickbacks; (2) poor quality of care, which includes unnecessary tests,

treatments, and surgeries as well as inadequate record keeping; (3) illegal distribution of controlled substances, which include drug prescriptions and sales; and (4) sex with patients whereby physicians under the guise of "therapy" received payments for sexual liaisons with their patients. (p. 105)

Psychiatrists constitute a disproportionate share (in relation to other medical specialists) of Medicare and Medicaid fraud. Examples of physician fraud by psychiatrists include charging patients for individual therapy when patients are actually involved in group therapy, charging a fee for "treatment" that is in reality sexual relations between psychiatrist and "patient," and charging for therapy that simply constitutes the prescription of pharmaceutical drugs (Jesilow, Pontell, and Geis, 1993). Moreover, psychiatrists represent approximately 8 percent of all physicians but about 20 percent of all physicians suspended from Medicaid for fraud (Rosoff, Pontell, and Tillman, 2007).

A second type of occupational fraud is insider trading, a form of securities fraud. **Insider trading** occurs when one uses *inside information* (information unavailable to the public) to gain a personal advantage over others in the buying and selling of stock. Individuals obtain such inside information because of their occupational position. For example, if one company plans to take over another, a large number of people are usually involved in the decision making (lawyers, corporate executives, and others). All these people know that if the takeover occurs, the value of each company's stock will change. Thus, prior to takeover, some of these people may take advantage of their inside information, using it to buy or sell stock prior to public disclosure. This trading is illegal.

One of the earliest insider trading cases involved the Texas Gulf Sulfur Company. In 1963 large deposits of copper and zinc were discovered by company engineers. Employees with access to this information (prior to public disclosure) abused that privilege to profit personally by buying considerable amounts of the company's stock. The employees were convicted of insider trading; the court concluding that all potential investors should have equal access to this type of information and that company employees—"insiders"—should not have an advantage over the public at large.

Some of the better-known insider trading cases in recent years include the following:

- Paul Thayer, official of LTV Corporation and former deputy secretary of defense, admitted committing insider trading in 1985.
- Thomas Reed, former Reagan national security aide, used inside information to convert a $3,000 stock option into a $427,000 gain in two days.
- Dennis Levine, managing director of Drexel Burnham Lambert (an investment banking firm), and Ivan Boesky, Wall Street's most successful arbitrageur—two of the major actors in an informal 1986 network—exchanged information on mergers, takeovers, and corporate restructurings in order to execute trades prior to public disclosure. It is alleged that Boesky profited more than $50 million and Levine almost $13 million from this insider trading network.
- Part of the Levine/Boesky network was Martin A. Siegel, who sold takeover information to Boesky from August 1982 until February 1986.
- In 1987 it was uncovered that Timothy Tabor (ex-vice-president of Kidder, Peabody), Richard Wigton (Kidder vice-president), and Robert M. Freeman (head of arbitrage at Goldman, Sachs) were also involved in the network, exchanging takeover information that allegedly earned its participants millions of dollars.

- In 1994 it was shown that an investor paid a Keystone mutual fund analyst $700,000 for insider information on the fund's future investments.
- In 1995, a Time Warner employee had advance information that company stock was about to fall in value. Subsequently, this employee sold 20,000 shares of Time Warner stock and avoided $413,700 in losses.
- In 2002, the founder of ImClone Systems, Inc., Sam Waksal, pleaded guilty to insider trading because he provided advance information to several family members that the FDA was about to disapprove for sale a new ImClone cancer drug. Waksal and his family made approximately $10 million through this insider fraud.

The case of Martha Stewart—the "queen of perfection"—who is a friend of Sam Waksal, increased public awareness of insider trading. On December 27, 2001, Stewart sold 3,928 shares of ImClone stock at $58 per share, earning $230,000 on the sale. The following day the FDA refused to approve ImClone's application for a new cancer drug, and ImClone's stock immediately dropped to $45 per share. Thus, Stewart had made $51,000 by selling her stock prior to the FDA's report becoming public.

Stewart was originally charged with insider trading because it was alleged that she—like Waksal's family members—had received inside information that Waksal was planning on selling a portion of his own stock. However, eventually Stewart was not charged with insider trading but, rather, of making false statements to investigators and obstruction of justice. In March 2005, she completed a sentence of five months in a minimum-security prison and, since her conviction, Stewart's shares in her company—Martha Stewart Omnimedia, Inc.—dropped in value by approximately $250 million, yet her company is now once again making a profit (Dodge, 2009).

---

### BOX 13.2   PONZI SCHEME

A *Ponzi scheme* is a form of fraud in which belief in the success of a nonexistent enterprise is fostered by the payment of quick returns to the first investors from money invested by later investors. Given that such frauds require an increasing flow of investments to keep the scheme going, inevitably investments become inadequate to pay earlier investors, and the fraudulent enterprise collapses.

The scheme is named after Charles Ponzi, who emigrated from Italy to the United States in 1903. Between 1919 and 1920 he began diverting investors' funds to support payments to earlier investors and his own personal wealth.

Some recent examples of Ponzi schemes include the following:

- The HomeStake fraud by Robert Trippet, involving the fraudulent selling of drilling rights to hypothetical oil wells, in which well-known celebrities, such as Candice Bergen, Faye Dunaway, Bob Dylan, and Liza Minnelli, were swindled out of large sums of money (Simon, 2008).
- Attorney Nikolai Tehin, who represented struggling poor immigrants in law suits against landlords and fraudulent physicians, used the settlement money to pay off earlier clients, diverting the majority to pay for a 73-foot yacht, a home worth $8 million, and a fleet of luxury cars (Rosoff, Pontell, and Tillman, 2007).
- Bernard L. Madoff pleaded guilty in 2008 to running a Ponzi scheme in which the cost to investors over 20 years was $65 billion—most likely Wall Street's biggest and longest fraud in history—and who stole large sums of money from celebrities such as Elie Wiesel and Steven Spielberg. The U.S. Government hopes to seek $170 billion in forfeited assets from Madoff's estate.

## 13.2 CORPORATE CRIME

We define *corporate crime* as (1) illegal and/or socially injurious acts of intent or indifference (2) that occur for the purpose of furthering the goals of a corporation and (3) that physically and/or economically abuse individuals in the United States and/or abroad. Thus, corporate crime includes not only illegal acts but also socially injurious acts that lie outside the jurisdiction of criminal or regulatory law. Moreover, corporate crime includes harmful acts that result from indifference to the consequences of certain actions as well as from the deliberate intent to harm. By including "indifference," we follow Steven Box (1983), who explained that if

> a person intends doing *someone* harm, it cannot be assumed that s/he displays a disdain towards humanity, although it is clearly directed towards the particular intended victim. However, if indifference characterizes the attitude a person has toward the consequences of his/her action, then s/he is indifferent as to who suffers—it could literally be anybody—and this does display disdain for humanity in general. In this sense, the intent to harm someone may be less immoral (or at least no more immoral) than to be indifferent as to whom is harmed. (p. 21)

Finally, our definition notes that corporations perpetrate violence and theft at home and abroad. Corporate crime victimizes large numbers of people throughout the world, and it is considerably more harmful and dangerous than the crimes we have already discussed in this and other chapters. We turn now to certain specific types of corporate violence and corporate theft.

### CORPORATE VIOLENCE

In this section we examine **corporate violence** against workers, consumers, and the general public. We begin with workers.

Every year approximately 30,000 workers die from work-related diseases and accidents, and approximately 3.6 million workers suffer new cases of job-related diseases and accidents in the United States (Friedrichs, 2007). Some criminologists have argued that workers are injured and die on the job not because of their own carelessness (although this does occur) but, rather, because of the conditions under which workers must labor, such as production quotas (Reiman, 2006). The organization of the workplace, then, primarily determines possible worker negligence and carelessness. However, we must note that all the preceding figures are based primarily on company reports. Because a company's insurance rating and costs are related to the frequency of injuries, illnesses, and deaths in the workplace, corporations have an incentive to hide accidents.

Consequently, the preceding figures most likely understate the seriousness of corporate violence. Even so, the figures clearly indicate that corporate violence in the workplace exceeds the amount of interpersonal violence in U.S. society. We pointed out in Chapter 12 that we are actually safer in the street than indoors; the evidence presented here suggests that we are safer almost anywhere than in the workplace.

An example of corporate violence caused by the intentional violation of safety standards is the case of Film Recovery Systems, Inc. (Frank and Lynch, 1992). Workers at the Film Recovery plant who worked around cyanide—poisonous if swallowed, inhaled, or absorbed through the skin—were not protected with adequate equipment (gloves, boots, aprons, and so on) and effective ventilation. In fact, the plant air was thick with an odorous "yellow haze" of cyanide fumes. On February 10, 1985, Stephen Golab, a worker at the plant, collapsed on the plant floor and died. The subsequent autopsy revealed that Golab died from inhaling large quantities of cyanide fumes from the plant air (Ross, 2005b). Three executives of Film Recovery were eventually convicted of murder and fourteen counts of reckless conduct. The conviction of the Film Recovery executives was the first of its kind in this country. Moreover, state courts have upheld the principle that employers can be criminally prosecuted for unsafe working conditions (Friedrichs, 2007).

In a more recent case, McWane, Inc., a large Alabama-based sewer and water pipe manufacturer, maintained unsafe working conditions for years that resulted in the death of nine workers and more than 4,600 injuries since 1995 (Mokhiber and Weissman, 2004). For example, one worker died when "an industrial oven exploded after he was directed to use it to incinerate highly combustible paint" and another "was crushed by a conveyor belt that lacked a required protective guard" (p. 19). Although McWane, Inc., had been cited for 400 safety violations and 450 environmental violations since 1995, it only had to pay a fine of $500,000, and no McWane executives have been charged with murder.

Corporations also continue to expose workers to dangers, such as the "silent killers." Workers are sometimes victims of corporate violence simply because they hold a job with a company that does not adequately protect them from such dangerous substances as asbestos fibers, cotton dust, and chemical compounds. Asbestos, for example, was a suspected "silent killer" as early as 1918, when a number of life insurance companies disallowed policies to asbestos workers because of their high death rate (Epstein, 1978). In the 1950s a connection between asbestos and lung cancer was found by British epidemiologist Richard Doll. The asbestos industry funded eleven studies in an attempt to rebut this link; however, fifty-two independent studies found asbestos to pose a major threat to human health (Coleman, 2006). For decades asbestos producers hid from workers and the public the known dangers of the product, which has resulted in 100,000 deaths each year from asbestos-related disease, and the medical costs for asbestos-related disease over the next 25

years is expected to reach $500 billion (Bowker, 2003). As sociologist James Coleman (2006) stated: "Such evidence suggests that the asbestos industry knowingly perpetrated a massive fraud on its workers and on the public" (p. 72). Finally, countless asbestos victims exist who have not had direct connection to its production, such as spouses who wash asbestos-laden clothes (Rosoff, Pontell, and Tillman, 2007).

Other examples of corporations concealing the dangers of "silent killers" abound. Since at least the 1960s, medical studies have shown that byssinosis (or brown lung disease) is a severe health problem for textile workers; yet the textile industry remains insensitive to worker health (Mokhiber, 1999). By the early 2000s textile workers continued to offer detailed testimony on the extreme levels of cotton dust that fills the mills (Friedrichs, 2007). Also, in the 1960s the chemical industry knew of research indicating that vinyl chloride is linked to a degenerative bone condition, acroosteolysis, as well as a rare form of cancer, angiosarcoma, in workers exposed to the chemical. To keep this information concealed from workers and the public, chemical companies signed a joint secrecy agreement not to reveal the conclusions of the research publicly (Markowitz and Rosner, 2002).

As consumers, we are also subject to victimization from corporate violence. According to the National Commission on Product Safety, 20 million U.S. citizens have suffered injuries from using unsafe products, in which 110,000 are permanently disabled and 30,000 die from the injuries (Simon, 2008).

The case of the Dalkon Shield, an IUD, is a telling example. The Dalkon Shield was manufactured, promoted, and marketed in the face of company files containing several hundred negative reports from physicians and others about its safety. Although these reports represented firm evidence linking the Dalkon Shield with seventy-five cases of uterine perforation, ectopic pregnancies, and at least seventeen deaths, they were never made public (Braithwaite, 1984). Approximately 2.86 million Dalkon Shields were distributed in the United States, and the vast majority of women who used this IUD developed the dangerous infection known as pelvic inflammatory disease (Mintz, 1986; Dodge, 2009).

Myriad products—from hazardous toys to dangerous automobiles—have been found harmful to consumers. A horrific example of corporate violence against youthful consumers is the drug thalidomide, which was marketed as a safe treatment for "morning sickness" during the early stages of pregnancy. Approximately 8,000 pregnant women who took the prescription drug gave birth to terribly deformed babies. The corporation that patented and distributed the drug deliberately falsified test data and concealed the facts about the drug's serious side effects.

Production of an unsafe automobile, the Ford Pinto, is a notorious illustration of corporate violence against consumers. As David Simon (2008) points out, Ford knew that this car had a defective gasoline tank that would ignite even in low-speed rear-end collisions, yet the company "reasoned that 180 burn deaths, 180 serious burn injuries, and 2,100 burned vehicles would cost $49.5 million (each death was figured at $200,000). But doing a recall of all Pintos and making each $11 repair would amount to $137 million" (p. 121). It is reported that as many as 900 burn deaths occurred as a result of the exploding Pinto (Dowie, 1979).

In the early 1970s the Firestone 500 steel-belted radial tire was produced and sold, and throughout that decade the company continued to receive evidence of the tire's danger to motorists. It was plagued with sudden blowouts and the separation of its tread from the steel-belted inner layer. Although the tire had been linked to thousands of automobile accidents and at least forty-one deaths, Firestone was fined only $50,000 (Simon, 2008).

In the 1990s, General Motors was found liable for gas tank defects in some of their pickup trucks, and at least 150 fatalities were attributed to unsafe General Motors pickup trucks (Friedrichs, 2007). Moreover, in the same decade it became known that the tobacco industry had committed a horrendous fraud on consumers by (1) hiding unfavorable research indicating that nicotine is an addicting drug, (2) hiding their own studies indicating that smoking causes lung cancer and heart disease, (3) manipulating the nicotine level in cigarettes to make sure each "smoke" had enough nicotine to keep smokers hooked, and (4) creating covert campaigns to addict teenagers to nicotine in order to create lifetime smokers. The percentage of high school students who smoke now exceeds the percentage of smokers in the adult population (Rosoff, Pontell, and Tillman, 2007).

We turn now to a discussion of violence against the general public, not just specific consumers. Corporate pollution provides an easy illustration of this type of corporate crime. The case of Love Canal is no doubt the most familiar. From the late 1930s until 1953, Hooker Chemical Company dumped hundreds of tons of toxic waste into the abandoned Love Canal, near Niagara Falls, New York (Tallmer, 1987). In 1953, Hooker sold the dump site to the local school board, which in turn sold it to a private developer. The canal was filled in, and eventually houses were built on top of the chemical dump. Some 20 years later, "as leaching wastes began to be linked to miscarriages, birth defects, and other ailments, more than 200 families fled their homes" (p. 113).

United States corporations produce approximately 292 million tons of toxic waste each year, and the Environmental Protection Agency (EPA) estimates that 90 percent of this waste is disposed of improperly. Thus, Love Canal is not unique. In Times Beach, Missouri, the EPA found dioxin levels 100 times those considered safe, forcing the federal government to purchase the entire town and move the people out.

Probably the worst hazardous waste condition in the United States—more serious than Love Canal and Times Beach—is, as Russell (1988) reported, the chemical contamination of a small Arkansas community, Jacksonville, referred to by local residents as "Dioxinville." Approximately twenty chemicals have been found in Jacksonville's air, twelve of which were also found in the Love Canal area. But the major problem in Jacksonville is dioxin, one of the most lethal substances ever produced. Dioxin has been found to cause cancer and fetus-malforming effects in animals at concentrations as low as 10 to 100 parts per trillion; the EPA considers dioxin dangerous to humans when it measures one part per billion. As Russell pointed out, just "one part per million is therefore 1,000 times more toxic. In Jacksonville, dioxin was measured...at concentrations as high as 111 parts per million," or 111,000 times as toxic as the EPA danger level (p. 9).

Jacksonville is contaminated with at least 30,000 barrels containing dioxin waste. From 1946 to 1957, Reasor-Hill Chemical Corporation buried drums of chemical waste in an open field near its plant in Jacksonville. In 1961 the plant was acquired by the Hercules Chemical Corporation, which continued to bury drums of chemical waste and began discharging processed wastewater—from production of chlordane and Agent Orange—into a nearby creek. By 1979 it became known that the plant and surrounding area were contaminated with dioxin. Today, dangerous levels of dioxin (higher than one part per billion) have been found in soil samples (taken from residents' yards) as well as in the air, the city sewer system and lagoons, the sediments of the nearby floodplain, and fish and wood ducks (Russell, 1988).

This disaster could have been avoided. Dow Chemical Company knew as far back as 1965 about the dangers of dioxin. As Green and Berry (1985a) reported:

> One memorandum from Dow's toxicology director warned then (1965) that the chemical could be "exceptionally toxic"; the company's medical director said that dioxin-related "fatalities have been reported in the literature." Dow's response was to discuss these problems with its competitors at a March meeting, but not to inform the government or public because the situation might "explode" and spur more federal regulation of the chemical industry. (p. 263)

Dow's cover-up contributed to the violence at Love Canal, Times Beach, and Jacksonville. Yet the story of hazardous waste does not end here. More recently, it has been estimated that approximately 30,000 waste sites pose significant health problems related to water contamination, and in Ponca City, Oklahoma, families were paid $40,000 to evacuate the town because of water contamination (Rosoff, Pontell, and Tillman, 2007).

Contaminated drinking water is only a tip of the corporate violence iceberg. As Jodi Seager (1993) noted, American chemical companies admitted that they annually leak or vent 196 "extremely hazardous" compounds into the air. The EPA cautiously estimates that as few as 15 to 45 of the hundreds of released air toxins directly cause up to 1,700 cases of cancer each year. American industry alone generates annually 280 million tons of lethal garbage and 10.3 billion pounds of toxic chemicals that are spewed each year into the air, discharged into public waters, and flushed into the sewers—enough to fill 8,000 Love Canals. Some recent examples of violence against the public are provided by Simon (2008):

- The Louisiana-Pacific Corporation was fined $37 million and convicted of eighteen felony counts, including conspiring to violate the Clean Air Act, lying to the Colorado

Department of Public Health, and submitting nonrepresentative samples to the American Plywood Association.

- The Colonial Pipeline Company was fined $7 million after pleading guilty to spilling 1 million gallons of oil into the Reedy River in South Carolina, killing approximately 35,000 fish.
- Royal Caribbean cruise line was fined $18 million for dumping oil and other hazardous wastes (some mixed with ordinary garbage) into U.S. harbors and coastal areas.

## CORPORATE THEFT

**Corporate theft** is similar to other forms of theft—in the sense that property is taken from people—yet it is significantly different, primarily because it does not entail a face-to-face confrontation and it is not easily apparent that a crime has been committed. Three of the most costly and prevalent forms of corporate theft are deceptive advertising, financial fraud, and price-fixing. We look briefly at each.

According to the Federal Trade Commission Act, **deceptive advertising** occurs when advertisements are "misleading in a material respect" (Coleman, 2006:24). This means that advertising can in fact be false, as long as it is not deceptive. In other words, it is illegal for advertising to be both false and deceptive or just simply deceptive. When Jell-O claims that "every kid in America loves Jell-O brand gelatin," that is clearly making a false statement. However, exaggerated claims (hype) such as this have been interpreted by the courts as not deceptive because it is believed that no reasonable person would take the statement seriously. Nevertheless, many corporations have simultaneously lied and deceived for decades. For example, Anacin was found to be the subject of deceptive advertising when its manufacturer claimed that Anacin (Simon and Eitzen, 1986):

- Relieved nervousness, tension, stress, fatigue, and depression.

- Was stronger than aspirin.
- Brought relief within 22 seconds.
- Was highly recommended over aspirin by physicians.
- Was more effective for relieving pain than any other analgesic available without prescription.

Moreover, corporations have also violated the law by engaging in deception without outright lying. For example, the bottom of a bowl of Campbell's "chunky style" soup used in a TV commercial was lined with marbles, creating the illusion that the soup was much thicker and chunkier than it actually was (Coleman, 2006).

More recent cases include the following (Mokhiber and Weissman, 2004; Rosoff, Pontell, and Tillman, 2007):

- The Home Shopping Network was fined $1.1 million by the Federal Trade Commission for advertisements making unsubstantiated claims for skin care, weight loss, and PMS/menopause products.
- The manufacturer of No Nonsense Pantyhose was penalized for wrongly claiming that its hosiery was virtually indestructible.
- The Federal Trade Commission obtained a settlement agreement from Jenny Craig, Inc., in response to charges of deceptive advertising regarding Jenny Craig diet program's claims about weight loss, price, and safety.
- Providian Financial, one of the largest credit card issuers in the United States, agreed to pay $300 million to consumers for its deceptive advertisements promising lower rates on balance transfers when in fact they were higher.
- The Federal Trade Commission charged Kentucky Fried Chicken with making false claims that its fried chicken is both nutritious and compatible with certain weight-loss programs. Kentucky Fried Chicken stated in advertisements that Original Recipe fried chicken

breasts are better for consumers' health than eating a Burger King Whopper, even though the chicken breasts have three times the trans fat and cholesterol and twice the sodium.

Corporate executives can engage in a form of fraud that serves the interests of the corporation, **financial fraud**. Such was the case with the firm E. F. Hutton and Company. Hutton officials pleaded guilty in 1985 to defrauding some 400 banks by writing checks in excess of amounts it had on deposit. Hutton officials then moved funds—to cover these amounts—from one bank to another, thereby avoiding overdrafts. In effect, what Hutton officials did was simply provide the company with interest-free loans (Nash, 1985; Claybrook, 1986). As Cullen, Maakestad, and Cavender (1987) pointed out, the entire "operation involved nearly $10 billion; on some days the company enjoyed $250 million in illegal 'loans'" (p. 56).

In 1988, E. F. Hutton pleaded guilty to two felony counts of laundering hundreds of thousands of dollars for criminal syndicate figures and businesspeople seeking to evade payment of taxes. According to the *Washington Post*, investigators found that "customers would bring suitcases full of cash to Hutton brokers," who would then transfer the money to secret overseas bank accounts (Kurtz, 1988:A3).

Both financial institutions and criminal syndicates profit from money laundering. It is against the law not to report cash transactions in excess of $10,000. Financial institutions evade this required federal disclosure by fraudulently converting large amounts of cash (sometimes provided by criminal syndicates) into bonds worth $9,999 or less, or they secretly launder it in foreign bank accounts. Financial institutions are attracted to obtaining money from criminal syndicates because large sums of money can be used for future investments or interest-earning loans, and criminal syndicates benefit from

money laundering because, in essence, this process changes "dirty" money into "clean" money.

A recent example of financial fraud involves the now-infamous Enron Corporation. Enron was formed in 1985 and quickly became the seventh-largest corporation in the United States. As an energy company involved in trading gas and electricity stock, Enron eventually found its profits squeezed from competing trading operations. After numerous years of complicated deals in an attempt to stay afloat, Enron was billions of dollars in debt. The entire debt, however, was concealed from shareholders by pumping up reported earnings and creating secret partnerships that "had the effect of grossly distorting the relationship between Enron's assets and profits and its losses and debt" (Friedrichs, 2007:78). The fraud was not revealed to the public until October 2001, when Enron announced that the company was actually worth $1.2 billion less than previously reported; as a result, in December of the same year, Enron filed for bankruptcy. Consequently, large numbers of Enron employees lost billions of dollars in retirement savings because their retirement accounts had been invested in Enron stock. Moreover, although employees knew Enron stock was drastically dropping in value, Enron executives prohibited them from withdrawing their retirement funds. At the same time, as Rosoff, Pontell, and Tillman (2007) point out, these same executives "literally made out like bandits." Indeed, twenty-nine executives at Enron sold $1.1 billion worth of stock, including the major fraudsters: Andrew Fastow sold stock worth $23 million, Jeff Skilling sold his holdings for $67 million, and Kenneth Lay earned $146 million from options trades.

The case of Enron was only the beginning of a "corporate crime wave" that opened the twenty-first century. Arthur Andersen & Company (a top accounting firm in the world), WorldCom (a large telecommunications company), Adelphia (a large cable company), Global Crossing (an international fiber-optic cable company), Qwest Communications (a long-distance telephone company), and Halliburton (an energy servicing company) are just a few of the corporations that have been implicated in various forms of financial fraud, though their cases are unresolved at this writing.

Finally, corporate theft may result in tremendous costs to unsuspecting taxpayers. For example, Wal-Mart has a notorious reputation for paying workers relatively low wages and inadequate benefits. Such practices harm workers directly but simultaneously harm taxpayers indirectly (Mokhiber and Weissman, 2004). As Mokhiber and Weissman point out, a 200-person Wal-Mart store costs taxpayers approximately $420,750 per year, or about $2,103 per employee, including:

- $36,000 a year for free and reduced lunches for just fifty qualifying Wal-Mart families.
- $42,000 a year for Section 8 housing assistance, assuming 3 percent of the store employees qualify for such assistance, at $6,700 per family.
- $125,000 a year for federal tax credits and deductions for low-income families, assuming fifty employees are heads of household with a child and fifty are married with two children.
- $100,000 a year for additional Title I [educational] expenses, assuming fifty Wal-Mart families qualify with an average of two children.
- $108,000 a year for the additional federal health care costs of moving into state children's health insurance programs (S-CHIP), assuming thirty employees with an average of two children qualify.

In other words, corporations engage in a hidden form of theft that imposes costs on communities and taxpayers.

**Price-fixing** is probably the most expensive form of corporate theft. The basic purpose of antitrust laws is to impede corporations from colluding to fix prices by ensuring that competition keeps prices as low as possible. Profits above those that would be produced in a competitive industry are illegal. Probably the most famous price-fixing incident is the case of Heavy Electrical Equipment, in which twenty-nine corporations—including General Electric and Westinghouse—conspired to fix prices, primarily on government contracts (Green, Moore, and Wasserstein, 1972; Pearce, 1976). The illegal costs paid by purchasers of the electrical equipment in this case alone totaled $1.75 billion per year for 7 years (Hills, 1987).

Recent cases of price-fixing indicate that this crime is widespread, occurring in such diverse industries as steel, glass, natural gas, infant formula, commercial explosives, athletic shoes, residential doors, scouring pads, plastic dinnerware, video games, white bread, and Passover matzo (Rosoff, Pontell, and Tillman, 2007). Some specific cases include the following (Friedrichs, 2007; Mokhiber and Weissman, 2004):

- Archer Daniels Midland Corporation paid a $100 million fine for fixing prices on feed additives, an illegal activity driving up prices of processed foods, soft drinks, detergents, and other widely consumed products.
- Two drug companies, Hoffman-LaRoche and BASF, were fined $752 million for fixing prices on vitamins.
- Nintendo, the video game maker, was fined $147 million for fixing prices on its products.
- Bayer agreed to pay the Federal Trade Commission $66 million to settle a price-fixing case related to chemicals used to make rubber.

## 13.3 TRANSNATIONAL CORPORATE CRIME

Transnationals—large corporations that maintain business operations in more than one country—are a major factor in globalization. Because of advances in communication and transportation technology as well as the establishment of "free trade" agreements (such as the Osaka Declaration and the North American Free Trade Agreement), transnationals have been able to accelerate the movement of capital over vast distances. Indeed, transnationals account for 75 percent of all world trade, and, as Sarah Anderson, John Cavanagh, and Thea Lee (2005: 9–70) have documented, transnationals—especially those based in the United States—are the key players in the global economy:

- Of the 100 largest economies in the world, 52 are now transnational corporations; only 48 are countries.
- The combined sales of the world's top 200 corporations are far greater than a third of the world's economic activity.
- The amount of money spent on cheap underwear and other discount goods at Wal-Mart is more than the gross domestic product of 174 countries.
- Despite the cancer risk, cigarette smokers helped push Philip Morris (now Altria Group) sales higher than the gross domestic product of 148 countries.
- Leaving countless boarded-up locally owned hardware stores in its wake, Home Depot grew from 200 stores to more than 1,500 in the past decade, with sales exceeding the gross national product of 147 countries.

By 1975 three-fourths of all U.S. companies with sales over 100 million dollars had manufacturing facilities in other countries (Michalowski and Kramer, 1987). By 1977 developing nations had surpassed developed ones in dollar value as locations for manufacturing by U.S. industries. Reimportation of overseas assembly by U.S. companies increased fivefold between 1969 and 1983, and in the textiles and electronics industries more than half of all sales

in the mid-1980s by U.S. corporations were assembled abroad. Transnationals expanded dramatically throughout the 1990s so that by now, well into the twenty-first century, few societies can claim isolation from the touch of transnational corporations.

A major aspect of this transnational global reach is **transnational corporate crime**. Indeed, criminologists have known since the early 1980s that transnational corporations are the worst corporate offenders. In one comprehensive study of corporate crime, Clinard and Yeager (1980) found that small corporations (annual sales of $300 million to $499 million) accounted for only 10 percent of corporate violations, and medium-sized corporations (annual sales of $500 million to $999 million) for 20 percent; however, large corporations (annual sales of $1 billion or more) accounted for almost 75 percent of all violations. Moreover, large corporations accounted for 72.1 percent of the serious and 62.8 percent of the moderately serious violations. Of the fifteen largest corporations in the world in 1978 (the time of Clinard and Yeager's study), three were car manufacturers, eight were oil companies, and one was a chemical producer. The largest corporations, then, are the worst offenders, in view of Clinard and Yeager's finding that "the oil, pharmaceutical, and motor vehicle industries" are the "most likely" to commit corporate crime (p. 119). Subsequent studies have likewise found that the largest corporations are the worst corporate offenders (Rosoff, Pontell, and Tillman, 2007). Indeed, it is the oil, auto, and chemical corporations that continue to dominate the top 200 transnationals list (Anderson, Cavanagh, and Lee, 2005).

Although transnationals are a *global* phenomenon, the most harmful consequences of transnational actions are found at the *local* level, victimizing real people and real environments far removed from U.S. society. Let us, then, turn to three major types of transnational corporate crime: bribery, the export of hazardous products, and the relocation of dangerous working conditions.

## BRIBERY

The transnational nature of U.S. corporations has resulted in considerable Third World corporate crime, ranging from bribery to export of hazardous products to dangerous working conditions. Regarding bribery, one study of thirty-four U.S. transnational corporations that admitted paying overseas bribes found that the bribes totaled $93.7 million and that the resulting sales revenues amounted to $679 billion (Coleman, 2006). As Coleman points out, "The bribe money constituted only 0.014 percent of the sales of those companies" (p. 41).

Because of the enormous volume of bribery, in 1977 Congress enacted the Foreign Corrupt Practices Act, which attempted to prevent such conduct. Yet transnational bribery continues. For example, a recent study found that during a 4-year period in the late 1990s, bribes influenced 239 U.S. international contract competitions, the majority of contracts given to those offering the bribes (Davis, 2005). The media continues to report violations of the Foreign Corrupt Practices Act (Simon, 2008).

Bribery is profitable for transnationals and the political elites in Third World countries, yet it perpetrates serious harm on a good portion of the rest of the people in these countries. Braithwaite (1979a) convincingly argued that transnational bribery is one of the most destructive and injurious crimes today because of its unequal and antidemocratic consequences:

> When a government official in a Third World country recommends (under the influence of a bribe) that his country purchase the more expensive but less adequate of two types of aircraft, then the extra millions of dollars will be found from the taxes sweated out of the country's impoverished citizens. For a mass consumer product, the million dollar bribe to the civil servant will be passed on in higher prices to the consuming public. Although it is conceivable that bribes can be used to secure the sale of a better and cheaper product, the more general effect is to shift the balance of business away from the most efficient producer and in favor of the most corrupt producer. The whole purpose of business–government bribes is, after all, the inegalitarian purpose of enticing governments to act against the public interest and in the interest of the transnational. (p. 126)

## DUMPING

Transnational corporations are also involved in "dumping" on other countries certain hazardous products banned or not approved for sale in the United States. United States–based transnationals frequently sell to other nations defective medical devices, lethal drugs, known carcinogens, toxic pesticides, contaminated foods, and other products ruled unfit for use and/or consumption in the United States. For example, the contraceptive Depo-Provera—banned in the United States because of its severe side effects—was dumped in seventy foreign countries, especially in the Third World (Simon, 2008).

A. H. Robbins dumped approximately 1.71 million Dalkon Shields in more than eighty foreign countries, and close to 1 million were actually implanted (Dodge, 2009). These IUDs were sold by Robbins to the Agency for International Development (AID) at a 48 percent discount and were packaged *unsterilized* (Braithwaite, 1984). They were then distributed by AID to a variety of countries in Africa, Asia, the Middle East, the Caribbean, and Central and South America, where medical techniques are mostly underdeveloped and consumer protection laws are practically nonexistent. Obviously, tens of thousands of women worldwide have been victimized by this corporate crime, especially once we consider the fact that the Dalkon Shield "is still in common use in some countries" (Simon, 2008:178).

**BOX 13.3  BHOPAL—1984 AND BEYOND**

In 1984, Union Carbide Corporation (UCC) was one of the largest chemical transnational corporations in the world. Based in Danbury, Connecticut, UCC operated numerous chemical plants around the globe. These plants manufactured and processed chemicals to produce pesticides, insecticides, and other consumer products (Doyle, 2004).

One of the plants owned by UCC was constructed in Bhopal, India, in 1980 to produce a highly toxic chemical—methyl isocyanate (MIC)—for use in UCC's various products. The plant produced substantially more MIC than it could immediately process, so UCC installed bulk-storage tanks in the Bhopal plant. However, there existed critical differences in the design of the safety standards for UCC plants in the United States and UCC plants elsewhere. The following table compares the safety measures realized in two UCC plants, one in Institute, West Virginia, and the other in Bhopal, India. In particular, storing MIC in large tanks for long periods of time, coupled with inadequate investment in safety measures—such as no emergency scrubbers to neutralize leaks, inappropriate cooling systems, and a lack of continued refrigeration—increased the possibility of a toxic leak's occurring.

| Institute, West Virginia, USA | Bhopal, Madhya Pradesh, India |
|---|---|
| **Capacity** | |
| High production of MIC matched with high processing capacity. MIC not stored for long periods of time. | High production capacity of MIC but low processing capacity. MIC stored in large quantities for long periods of time. |
| **Emergency Scrubbers** | |
| MIC storage tank equipped with emergency scrubbers (to neutralize any escaping MIC) designed to operate under emergency conditions. | No emergency caustic scrubber to neutralize any MIC leak. |
| **Computerized Monitoring** | |
| Computerized monitoring of instruments (gauges, alarms, etc.) and processes to support visual observation. | No computerized monitoring of instruments and processes. Relied solely on manual observation. |
| **Cooling System** | |
| MIC field storage tanks used a cooling system based on chloroform (inert and nonreactive with MIC). | MIC tanks used a cooling system based on brine (highly reactive with MIC). |
| **Refrigeration Unit** | |
| Refrigeration unit to control temperature in the tanks was never turned off. | Refrigeration unit had been turned off since June 1984. |
| **Nitrogen Pressure** | |
| MIC was always maintained under nitrogen pressure. | MIC tanks had not been under nitrogen pressure since October 1984. |
| **Emergency Plan** | |
| An elaborate four-stage emergency plan to deal with toxic releases, fires, etc., including a general public alert linked to community police, river and rail traffic, and local radio stations. Various emergency broadcast systems in place to alert and disseminate appropriate information to the public. | No system to inform public authorities or the people living adjacent to the plant. No emergency plan shared with communities living adjacent to the plant; no system to disseminate information regarding emergency to the public, with the exception of a loud siren. |

| Institute, West Virginia, USA | Bhopal, Madhya Pradesh, India |
|---|---|
| **Maintenance Program** | |
| A maintenance program to determine and evaluate replacement frequency for valves and instrumentation and alarm systems. Weekly review of safety valves and reviews and maintenance recorded extensively. | No evidence of an effective instrument maintenance program. Safety valve testing program largely ineffective, and no proper records maintained of reviews of instruments, valves and alarm systems, etc. |
| **Lab Analysis** | |
| A lab analysis of MIC was conducted to test quality and check for contamination prior to storage, processing, or distribution. | No lab analysis of quality was undertaken. MIC stored for long periods without testing for contamination. |
| **Training** | |
| Extensive employee training program to ensure high level of training and information among all employees of normal and emergency procedures. | Operators put in charge without sufficient training. |
| **Protective Equipment** | |
| Extensive provision of appropriate personal protective equipment to employees, including protective clothing, air respirators, etc. | Personal protective gear and breathing air equipment not easily accessible, inadequate, and of poor quality. |

Source: © Amnesty International (2004:46–47).

In addition to poor safety measures, UCC management ignored warnings of ongoing safety problems at the Bhopal plant. For example, from 1982 to 1984 occupational safety survey teams from UCC headquarters in the United States warned management numerous times of the potential release of toxic substances at the Bhopal plant—such as MIC—because of equipment failures, operating and maintenance problems, and deficiencies in safety valves. No measures were taken by management to confront these safety issues, and UCC failed to implement an emergency plan in Bhopal to warn the community about leaks, even though it had such a plan in place in the United States (Amnesty International, 2004).

On December 2, 1984, the predicted nightmare occurred: An estimated 54,000 pounds of deadly MIC—together with 26,000 pounds of reaction products—silently leaked out of one of the tanks, killing close to 8,000 Bhopal residents within three days of the leak. Between 1985 and 2003 an estimated additional 15,000 people died because of the gas leak, and exposure to the toxin has resulted in chronic, debilitating illnesses for at least 120,000 people, for whom treatment has proved largely ineffective (Amnesty International, 2004).

In response to the crime, UCC blamed India's "cultural backwardness" for the gas leak (Pearce and Tombs, 1999). This is an astonishing and racist claim, given the fact that, as Pearce and Tombs rightly point out, UCC "possessed" the Bhopal plant, in the sense that the parent company (1) dictated how and which chemicals were produced and stored, (2) monitored safety procedures at the plant, and (3) had the right to intervene if safety was ever affected. In short, UCC management is "responsible for both acts of commission and omission that created the Bhopal disaster" (p. 205).

The victims of this transnational corporate crime await just compensation and adequate medical assistance. The plant site has not been cleaned up, toxic waste continues to pollute the environment and the drinking water, and no one associated with UCC has ever been held responsible for the crime (Amnesty International, 2004).

Corporations also dump chemicals, such as pesticides, on foreign markets. For example, DDT—a pesticide banned in the United States—in the mid-1980s was being sold particularly in Central and South America, only to return home on such imported food as bananas and coffee (Asinoff, 1985). Overall, more than 150 million pounds of "blacklisted" products worth up to $800 million are dumped each year, representing approximately 25 percent of U.S. pesticide production (Simon, 2008).

## DANGEROUS WORKING CONDITIONS

Transnationals have also—in addition to bribery and dumping—relocated dangerous working conditions to other countries. Transnationals search for areas of the world where pollution controls and worker safety regulations are minimal or nonexistent. For example, in the United States it is now illegal to expose workers to carcinogenic agents, such as asbestos. However, in Mexico, the "law merely provides a light fine ($45 to $90) for the failure to warn workers that they are working around a health hazard" (Simon, 2008:179). Consequently, U.S. asbestos makers have increasingly relocated plants to Mexico and other Third World countries where little control exists over workplace hazards.

Additionally, Mexico provides a good example of the harmful consequences of relocating dangerous polluting plants. Indeed, the U.S.–Mexico border has become "a two-thousand-mile Love Canal":

These plants have filled the sky and water with a staggering amount of chemical pollution. With this contamination have come all the accompanying human miseries. A disturbing pattern of deformities and mental retardation has been observed among children of this area. Their mothers had all worked in the *maquiladoras* zone [border area where U.S. companies invest] and had been exposed to toxic chemicals. (Rosoff, Pontell, and Tillman, 2007:166–167)

Economists have argued that the North American Free Trade Agreement (NAFTA), signed by Canada, the United States, and Mexico in 1994, has accelerated the trend toward expansion of the Mexican *maquiladora* industrial sector. Whereas the U.S. economy has lost approximately 450,000 jobs since the signing of NAFTA, foreign direct investment rose 64 percent in 1994, the first year after NAFTA's activation. This investment resulted in the employment of approximately 750,000 Mexican workers in some 2,500 export *maquiladora* plants (Burgoon, 1996). Moreover, a study of the effects of NAFTA on Mexico 10 years after its implementation found, for example: (1) 1.5 million Mexican farm livelihoods were destroyed because cheap U.S. corn was "dumped" in Mexico, (2) migration to the United States more than doubled because of low-paying jobs (e.g., the average wage in Mexico for manufacturing workers actually *declined* from $5.00 to $4.00 per day following NAFTA), (3) migration to the "maquila zones" has likewise doubled, overwhelming the outdated sewage systems and resulting in dramatic contamination of drinking water (e.g., hepatitis A infection rates in the "maquila zones" is more than double the national rate), and (4) increasing industrialization in the "maquila zones" has massively intensified toxic dumping (e.g., rates of birth defects and lupus in these zones have doubled) (Public Citizen, 2004).

## REVIEW

This chapter examined various types of white-collar crime—occupational crime, corporate crime, and transnational corporate crime. These crimes are similar to crimes previously discussed because they also entail theft and violence. However, they differ from other crimes because (1) they cause far greater victimization and (2) the victimization they produce is less apparent.

## OCCUPATIONAL CRIME

1. There are two major types of occupational crime: theft and fraud. Occupational theft includes employee theft and embezzlement, which differ in what is stolen—merchandise and job-related items or money, respectively.
2. Employee theft and embezzlement—two of the most costly crimes in the United States—occur in different ways, depending on the type of job, and they range from simply stealing merchandise to "taking from the till" and "manipulating the books" to collective embezzlement.
3. Two types of occupational fraud are physician fraud and insider trading. The former occurs through prescription of pharmaceutical drugs, surgical procedures, and treating Medicare and Medicaid patients. Insider trading results when "insiders" gain special advantage in the buying and selling of stock.

## CORPORATE CRIME

1. Corporate violence causes considerable worker illness, injury, and death; corporations also perpetrate violence on consumers and the general public.
2. Three of the most costly and prevalent forms of corporate theft are deceptive advertising, financial fraud, and price-fixing.

## TRANSNATIONAL CORPORATE CRIME

1. Transnational corporations are the worst corporate offenders.
2. Three of the most costly and prevalent forms of transnational corporate crime are bribery, dumping, and relocating dangerous working conditions.

## QUESTIONS FOR CLASS DISCUSSION

1. Why is it valuable to study white-collar crime?
2. How do various types of work help determine specific types of occupational theft? How do the arguments of Ditton and of Mars relate to your own job? Your parents' jobs?
3. Describe how corporate violence and theft differ from the types of violence and theft discussed in Chapters 11 and 12.
4. Discuss the differences and similarities between transnational corporate crime and the other types of white-collar crime examined in this chapter.
5. Are there other forms of white-collar crime not covered in this chapter? If so, would they fit into one of the three categories identified here?

## FOR FURTHER STUDY

### READINGS

Dodge, Mary. 2009. *Women and White-Collar Crime.* Upper Saddle River, NJ: Prentice Hall.

Friedrichs, David O. 2007. *Trusted Criminals: White-Collar Crime in Contemporary Society.* Belmont, CA: Wadsworth.

Markowitz, Gerald, and David Rosner. 2002. *Deceit and Denial: The Deadly Politics of Industrial Pollution.* Berkeley: University of California Press.

Rosoff, Stephen M., Henry N. Pontell, and Robert Tillman. 2007. *Profit Without Honor: White-Collar Crime and the Looting of America.* Upper Saddle River, NJ: Prentice Hall.

### WEBSITES

1. <http://www.citizen.org/trade>: This site provides valuable information on corporate globalization and its effects on health and safety, environmental protection, economic justice, and democratic, accountable governance in selected countries.

2. <http://www.osha.gov/oshstats/work.html>: From the Occupational Safety and Health Administration, this site provides current statistics on workplace deaths and injuries. It should be kept in mind that these are conservative estimates from the Bureau of Labor Statistics.

3. <http://www.natlconsumersleague.org>: The National Consumers' League compiles recent information on consumer fraud.

4. <http://www.pirg.org>: Public Interest Research Groups are nonprofit organizations that monitor the safety of consumer products. This site offers PIRG reports on child deaths from unsafe toys as well as some deadly consequences of illegal dumping of toxic chemicals. Readers may be interested to find out the contact information for the PIRG in their own state.

5. <http://www.multinationalmonitor.org>: This site is an online magazine, Multinational Monitor, which has articles documenting cases of corporate crime. Every year the magazine announces its ten worst corporations of that year.

# POLITICAL CRIME

**14.1 Political Crimes Against the State**
- Violent Political Crimes Against the State
- Nonviolent Political Crimes Against the State

**14.2 Domestic Political Crimes by the State**
- State Corruption
- State Political Repression
- State-Corporate Crime

**14.3 Transnational Political Crimes by the State**
- State Terrorism
- The State, Terrorism, and Globalization

**PREVIEW**

Chapter 14 introduces:
- What sociologists mean by "political crime."
- The extent, nature, and costs of political crime.
- The various types of political crime, including crimes against the state and crimes by the state.

**KEY TERMS**

civil disobedience

corrupt campaign practices

election fraud

individual/group terrorism

international law

political bribery

political crime

political repression

state-corporate crime

state corruption

state terrorism

terrorism

transnational political crime

Criminologists rarely recognize the category "political crime." When they do, however, they usually conceptualize political crime as crime committed against the state. However, as we show in this chapter, the state and its representatives often *initiate* illegal attacks on legally functioning—albeit politically challenging—subordinate groups. Moreover, criminologists' failure to label this conduct as harmful serves to obscure the real nature of such actions. As we assert in the following argument, the state's political actions not infrequently result in violations of domestic and international law.

Accordingly, our definition of **political crime** is threefold, entailing not only crimes *against* the state (violations of law for the purpose of modifying or changing social conditions) but also crimes *by* the state, both domestic (violations of law and unethical acts by state officials and agencies whose victimization occurs inside the United States) and transnational (violations of domestic and international law by state officials and agencies whose victimization occurs outside the United States).

## 14.1 POLITICAL CRIMES AGAINST THE STATE

Political crimes against the state are carried out for the purpose of changing or modifying existing social conditions. When individuals or groups believe a particular social condition (or overall social structure) is problematic in some important way, they may attempt to modify the social order or to alter it entirely by means that violate criminal law. Political crimes against the state differ from other crimes discussed in this book in that they are not engaged in for personal gain. Rather, they are committed on behalf of a specific group (class, race, gender, political party, for example). Moreover, political crimes against the state are usually intentionally overt and public rather than covert and secret.

Political crimes against the state, then, involve intentional violations of criminal law for political purposes as well as various acts criminalized by the state for the purpose of curbing political dissent. Political crimes against the state may also be violent or nonviolent. We consider first some examples of violent political crimes against the state.

## VIOLENT POLITICAL CRIMES AGAINST THE STATE

Throughout U.S. history, social groups have turned to violence in a bid simply to modify the social order or perhaps to change it completely. In fact, the United States was born of politically violent crimes against the British government. By encouraging, and then engaging in, the Revolutionary War (1775–1783), colonists violated the British law of treason, which made it illegal to levy war against the king.

Native Americans in the United States have likewise resorted to violence to oppose state policies and to change social conditions. Although the examples are legion, consider briefly the case involving the Lakota Sioux and General George Armstrong Custer. In 1868 the U.S. government signed the Fort Laramie Treaty with the Lakota, guaranteeing them tribal sovereignty and assuring them perpetual control over "unceded Indian territory from which whites are excluded, stretching from the Missouri River west to the Powder River hunting grounds into the Wyoming Big Horn Mountains and from the Canadian border south into Nebraska" (Garitty, 1980).

However, the treaty was repeatedly broken by the U.S. government. In 1874 Custer trespassed onto Lakota land to confirm the existence of gold in the Black Hills of South Dakota. Gold was indeed found, and Custer's cavalry allowed thousands of "gold-hungry miners" to scrape the Black Hills clean (Johansen and Maestas, 1979). As a result, in 1876 the Lakota, Cheyenne, and Arapaho assembled at Little Big Horn in Montana. This gathering has been reported to be "the largest gathering of native peoples ever to have taken place in the hemisphere" (Garitty, 1980:263). Led by Gall, Two Moons, Dull Knife, and Crazy Horse, the Native Americans responded to the trespassers by killing Custer and 204 of his men because they had "violated the sanctity of the Black Hills" (Johansen and Maestas, 1979:29). This did not stop the U.S. government from violating the treaty; it continued to do so until 1889, when the Great Sioux Nation was reduced, in violation of the treaty, to five small reservations in western South Dakota (Ortiz, 1977).

Overall, between 1776 and 1871 the U.S. government ratified 371 treaties with native Indian nations (Weyler, 1982). Figure 14.1 traces the results of U.S. government violations of those treaties. The Lakota example is important not only for indicating the use of violence to change social conditions and to oppose state policy but also for understanding that groups often resort to violence *in response* to state violence or criminality.

Similarly, farmers in the United States have engaged in violence to change existing conditions. Prior to 1800, farmers were involved in numerous rebellions, the Shays' Rebellion being one of the most famous. In the late 1700s many farmers experienced severe social and economic problems, forcing many to borrow money at extremely high interest rates to survive. Moreover, in order to meet their growing debts "they mortgaged their future crops and went still deeper into debt" (Parenti, 2008:42). And, as Parenti pointed out:

> Among the people there grew the feeling that the revolution against the British crown had been fought for naught. Angry armed crowds in several states began blocking foreclosures and forcibly freeing debtors from jail. In the winter of 1787, debtor farmers in western Massachusetts led by Daniel Shays took up arms. Their rebellion was forcibly put down by the state militia after skirmishes that left eleven men dead and scores wounded. (p. 42)

Workers have also historically engaged in violence to change certain working conditions. The extraordinarily unsafe, lengthy, and alienating working conditions in the 1800s and early 1900s led many workers to turn to labor violence to make their grievances effective. A good example was the 1886 struggle for the eight-hour workday that resulted in substantial violence between striking workers and the police. In May of that year a major rally was held at Haymarket Square in Chicago; when the last speaker had finished, a bomb exploded among the police, killing one and wounding many others. The police responded by firing into the crowd. The labor movement in the

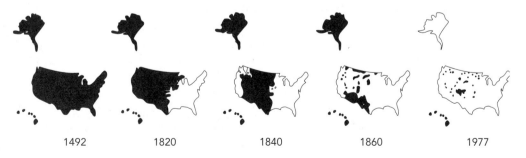

| 1492 | 1820 | 1840 | 1860 | 1977 |

**FIGURE 14.1** Native American Land Within the United States
*Source*: Weyler (1982:65).

late 1800s and early 1900s—for the eight-hour day and other job demands—resulted in many long and bloody battles (Lens, 1973; Brecher, 1980).

Women have also engaged in violence at times in an attempt to change social conditions. For example, during the U.S. suffrage movement (to secure for women the right to vote) a number of feminist marches turned to mob violence between the demonstrators and outside agitators (O'Neil, 1969). However, the suffrage movement in the United States was clearly not as militant as it was in England. The British suffragettes (the Women's Social and Political Union) engaged in a specific strategy of violence—such as arson and vandalism—to achieve political ends; their motto was "Deeds, Not Words" (Heidensohn, 1985).

In addition to the foregoing, many of the African American urban rebellions in the 1960s and 1970s were motivated by political concerns for civil rights. During the same period, groups such as the Weather Underground—an organization that broke off in 1969 from the Students for a Democratic Society—turned to violence as a means for political change. The Underground made the following announcement in 1969: "Kids know that the lines are drawn; revolution is touching all of our lives. Tens of thousands have learned that protest and marches don't do it. Revolutionary violence is the only way" (cited in Evans, 1983:255).

Certain feminist groups in the United States have engaged in such violent acts as setting afire or bombing shops selling pornographic materials. For example, in 1980 in Seattle, women's antipornography groups stink-bombed several pornography bookstores, and in that same year in New York City, "three porn movie houses were firebombed" (Morgan, 1980:138). In 1986, six members of the United Freedom Front were convicted of violent, politically motivated crimes. According to the *New York Times*, the six were found guilty of bombing (unoccupied) military centers and corporate buildings that housed either defense contractors or companies doing business in South Africa (Buder, 1986).

Certain antiabortion individuals and groups have engaged in various forms of violence against the people and/or the places that provide abortions. Some recent examples include the following:

- On September 13, 2006, David McMenemy crashed his car into the Edgerton Women's Care Center in Davenport, Iowa.
- On April 25, 2007, Paul Ross Evans left a package containing explosives at a women's health clinic in Austin, Texas.
- On May 9, 2007, an unidentified individual set fire to a Planned Parenthood clinic in Virginia Beach, Virginia.
- On January 22, 2009, Matthew L. Derosia drove his SUV into the front entrance of a Planned Parenthood clinic in St. Paul, Minnesota.

Today, when most people think about political crimes against the state they think of terrorism. We define **terrorism** as the use of force or violence to intimidate, coerce, or change a government or a civilian population for political reasons. Terrorism may be perpetrated by a state through its political policies or by individuals and groups (not necessarily supported by a state) to oppose certain state policies. In Section 14.3 we discuss *state terrorism*. Here we examine three types of **individual/group terrorism**: political assassination, domestic terrorism, and international terrorism.

Political assassination of members of the state for political reasons has occurred historically in the United States. Some of the better-known political assassins are John Wilkes Booth, Leon Czolgosz, Oscar Collazo and Griselio Torresola, and Sirhan Sirhan (Hagan, 1997). John Wilkes Booth murdered President Lincoln in 1865 in support of slavery and the Confederacy; Czolgosz murdered President McKinley in 1901 as part of an anarchist revolt; Collazo and Torresola's assassination attempt on President Truman in 1950 was in support of Puerto Rican independence; and Sirhan felt the assassination of Robert Kennedy in 1969 would help the Palestinian cause. Certainly the best-known political assassination in the United States is that of President John F. Kennedy. However, as David Simon (2008:306–309) pointed out, that assassination remains unsolved and is marked by considerable controversy.

- After the assassination, President Johnson, Assistant Attorney General Katzenbach, and FBI Director Hoover ordered a cover-up of the investigation. All three agreed that the public must be convinced that Lee Harvey Oswald was the lone killer.
- The House Special Committee on Assassinations found that President Kennedy's assassination most likely resulted from a conspiracy, not one individual. The committee pointed to syndicated crime as having the "means, motive, and opportunity" to assassinate the president, and/or anti-Castro Cubans killed the president because he did not support the Bay of Pigs invasion with air cover.
- Others have argued that the CIA killed President Kennedy because he was about to make peace with the Soviet Union, end the Cold War, and withdraw military personnel from Vietnam. Moreover, the CIA was allegedly upset because the Kennedy administration canceled covert operations against Cuba.

In addition to political assassinations, another type of individual/group terrorism is referred to as *domestic terrorism*, or violent acts committed against the U.S. state for political reasons by citizens of the United States. On April 19, 1995, the worst act of domestic terrorism was committed by Timothy McVeigh and Terry Nichols. As members of antigovernment paramilitary right-wing militia groups (approximately 850 such groups currently operate across the United States), these two conspired and carried out the bombing of the Alfred P. Murray Federal Building in Oklahoma City, killing 168 people and injuring more than 500. Some 4,000 pounds of homemade explosives were packed inside a rental truck and detonated in front of the federal building. A large number of those killed were federal employees as well as fifteen children under the age of 5 who were attending a day-care center in the building. McVeigh was found guilty of murder, conspiracy, and use of a weapon of mass destruction; Nichols was convicted of conspiracy and involuntary manslaughter in the bombing.

Recently, the U.S. Department of Homeland Security (2009) issued a report—*Right-Wing Extremism: Current Economic and Political Climate Fueling Resurgence in Radicalization and Recruitment*—indicating that domestic right-wing terrorist groups may be gaining new recruits by playing on the fears about several issues, such as the economic downturn and the election of the first African American president, Barack Obama. In addition, the report highlighted the possible passage of new restrictions on firearms, "and the return of military veterans facing significant challenges reintegrating into their communities" could lead to "the emergence of terrorist groups or lone-wolf extremists capable of carrying out violent attacks" (p. 2).

*International terrorism*, violent acts committed against the state for political reasons by citizens of other countries, is the most recent form of terrorism within the borders of the United States. The first bombing of the World Trade Center in New York City—which killed six people, injured over 1,000, and caused more than $500 million in damage—is a prime example. On November 12, 1997, Ramzi Yousef and Eyad Najim were convicted of the 1993 bombing. Yousef directed and helped to carry out the bombing; Najim drove the truck that carried the bomb. Four others had previously been convicted of the bombing. These men were working under the direction of Sheikh Omar Abdul Rahman (who was ironically recruited by the CIA to fight against the Soviet Union in Afghanistan in the 1980s, which we further discuss in Section 14.3) and allegedly bombed the World Trade Center building in order to punish the United States for its continued support of Israel (Hagan, 1997).

However, the most horrific international terrorist act in the United States occurred on September 11, 2001. As we pointed out in Section 12.1, this is a unique case of mass murder in the United States because of the number of people killed (almost 3,000) and because it also entailed a mass suicide (by 19 hijackers). These terrorists, who were connected to the Al Qaeda ("the base") network, hijacked four U.S. commercial airplanes and flew those planes into the twin World Trade Center towers in New York City, the Pentagon Building in Arlington, Virginia, and a field in rural Pennsylvania. Osama bin Laden—an exile from Saudi Arabia who also earlier worked with the CIA to fight the Soviets in Afghanistan—was the financier and mastermind behind this terrorist act. Bin Laden also organized the 1998 bombings of U.S. embassies in Kenya and Tanzania, killing 12 U.S. citizens and 300 Africans, as well as the 2000 bombing of the U.S.S. Cole, which killed 17 U.S. sailors. Most of the 19 hijackers were from Saudi Arabia, in their mid-20s, and well educated (Hewitt, 2003). Al Qaeda operates in at least 35 countries and maintains "sleeper cells" that can be activated to carry out specific attacks. The motive behind the bombings as well as the September 11 attack was to punish the United States for its support of corrupt and authoritarian regimes in several Arab states, including Saudi Arabia and Egypt, and for the global dissemination of Western values. We will have more to say about Al Qaeda, bin Laden, and the terrorist attack of September 11 in Section 14.3.

## NONVIOLENT POLITICAL CRIMES AGAINST THE STATE

Most political crime against the state is not violent. Individuals and groups in the United States historically have engaged in such actions as civil disobedience and demonstrations of a nonviolent nature, which sometimes result in criminalization by the state. Consider a few examples.

The efforts of Martin Luther King, Jr., and the civil rights movement of the early 1960s to end racial segregation in the United States were based on an explicitly nonviolent strategy. Dr. King's major weapon was **civil disobedience**, or refusing to obey certain laws seen as unjust. In his famous "Letter from Birmingham Jail," King put forth his arguments for such actions:

> There are two types of laws: There are *just* and there are *unjust* laws. I would agree with St. Augustine that "An unjust law is no law at all." Now what is the difference between the two? How does one determine when a law is just or unjust?...Any law that uplifts human personality is just. Any law that degrades human personality is unjust. All segregation statutes are unjust because segregation distorts the soul and damages the personality. It gives the segregator a false sense of superiority, and the segregated a false sense of inferiority....So segregation is not only politically, economically, and sociologically unsound, but it is morally wrong and sinful....So I can urge men to disobey segregation ordinances because they are morally wrong....I hope you can see the distinction I am trying to point out. In no sense do I advocate evading or defying the law as the rabid segregationist would do. This would lead to anarchy. One who breaks an unjust law must do it *openly, lovingly,* and with a willingness to accept the penalty. I submit that an individual who breaks a law that conscience tells him is unjust, and willingly accepts the penalty by

staying in jail to arouse the conscience of the community over its injustice, is in reality expressing the very highest respect for law. (Cited in Washington, 1986:293–294)

Individuals can also engage in civil disobedience, not for the purpose of changing the law being broken, but, rather, to protest—and hopefully put a stop to—particular state policies. For example, in 1976 members of the Clamshell Alliance engaged in civil disobedience by organizing a "sit-in" at the construction site of the Seabrook, New Hampshire, nuclear power plant. On May 1 of that year, 1,414 people occupied the construction site (for the purpose of halting construction of the plant) and were arrested for trespassing, more than half refusing bond and spending about two weeks in National Guard armories. The resulting publicity inspired other groups around the country, and a massive antinuclear movement eventually emerged (Dwyer, 1983).

Another example of this type of civil disobedience involved student and community demonstrators at the University of Massachusetts in the fall of 1986. The demonstrators—who included former President Carter's daughter, Amy, and ex-"yippie" leader Abbie Hoffman—engaged in a sit-in at a campus building used to recruit agents for the Central Intelligence Agency (CIA). Carter, Hoffman, and others, arrested for trespassing and disorderly conduct, were tried in April 1987. Although the demonstrators admitted at trial that they had trespassed on university property, they were nevertheless allowed by the judge to assert the criminal defense of "necessity" and won acquittal. This affirmative defense can be used to prove that a defendant's "illegal" acts were justified—in this case to stop a more dangerous crime: the recruiting of CIA agents who would, according to the demonstrators, most likely engage in significantly more heinous and illegal activities. After presenting the testimony of various experts on CIA criminality around the globe, the jury acquitted the demonstrators (Tushnet, 1988).

Individuals and groups may also engage in nonviolent protests and demonstrations against state policies that are not specifically directed at violating any law. Because the state regards such behavior as threatening, it enforces certain laws chosen for the purpose of curbing the dissent. For example, the trial of the Chicago Eight—which grew out of nonviolent demonstrations against the Vietnam War conducted at the 1968 Democratic convention—resulted in the demonstrators' being charged with "conspiracy." The state does not have to prove that an activity was actually planned, only that the conspirators communicated in some way (Clinard and Quinney, 1973). All Chicago Eight defendants were acquitted of conspiracy but received numerous contempt citations because of their behavior during the course of the trial. As Clinard and Quinney noted, "Whether or not the defendants are convicted, the conspiracy law is an effective form of political harassment whereby those who threaten the system can be detained for long periods of time at great personal expense" (p. 156).

The most recent nonviolent demonstrations have been the antiglobalization protests that began in Seattle in 1999 but quickly moved to a number of other cities throughout the world, such as Prague and Melbourne. Approximately 100,000 people take part in these demonstrations, protesting against the policies of the World Trade Organization, the International Monetary Fund, transnational corporations, and governments in the Western world. The antiglobalization movement consists of people from a wide range of political and cultural persuasions, yet their message is the same: "Globalization worsens economic insecurity and deepens social inequality" (Ruggiero, 2002:48).

What is ironic about this new type of social movement is that although it is antiglobalization, it is an example of "globalization from below," or a global movement that challenges the negative aspects of "globalization from above" (Kellner, 2003), and its organizing efforts have benefited from globalization. For example, Ruggiero (2002) examined one organization in France that is part of the antiglobalization movement—Attac—and found that it uses 200 translators who make information material available in ten languages through discussion lists that are available in six languages and accessible on their website:

> Attac's website was first seen as a source of information for experts, later as an activists' tool, and finally as the showroom of the association. Each month it hosts between 30 and 40 new documents and is contacted 800,000 times from 90 different countries. The site offers information about political activities and demonstrations, and also launches petitions and organizes conferences online. (p. 49)

Despite the fact that the vast majority of people demonstrate peacefully during antiglobalization protests, the police reaction to the protestors has grown stronger in terms of the number of police deployed and the tactics used. These demonstrations are now routinely met with police officers dressed in riot gear who outnumber the protestors and use pepper spray, tear gas, truncheons, water cannons, and mass arrests to "control" the protestors. And this has simultaneously resulted in global communication and cooperation among police and immigration authorities. For example, two weeks prior to the Prague demonstration, the Czech border police had received from police in other countries the names and photos of foreigners who had participated in earlier antiglobalization protests, and they turned back approximately 600 of these people at the border (Vayrynen, 2004).

Most recently, at the G20 summit (representatives from a group of 20 industrialized and developing nations) in London on April 1, 2009, thousands of antiglobalization protesters from around the world gathered to demonstrate, primarily through civil disobedience, against the meeting, and they called for economic justice and environmental accountability. And on November 2, 2008, former U.S. Vice President, Nobel Peace Prize winner, and environmental activist Al Gore, speaking at the Clinton Global Initiative in New York City, urged young people to engage in civil disobedience to stop the construction of coal plants.

Another example of nonviolent political crime against the state is spying. There exist different types of political spies, which Hagan (1997) argued can be classified according to motivation. For example, there are *mercenary spies*, who are the most common and provide intelligence secrets to a foreign government for monetary gain; *ideological spies*, who provide secrets to foreign governments because of strong political or ideological beliefs; *alienated/egocentric spies*, who provide secrets to a foreign government because they want to "get even" with the U.S. government or government agency; and finally, the *buccaneer spy*, who provides secrets to a foreign government for adventure and for excitement.

Probably the best-known recent case of illegal spying is that of Aldrich Ames, a 32-year veteran of the Central Intelligence Agency. Beginning in 1985 and continuing until 1994, Ames stole intelligence secrets and sold them to the Soviet Union, which became Russia in 1991. Ames is probably the highest-paid known Soviet spy, earning between $1.5 million and $2.5 million. He most likely got caught because of his lavish lifestyle—he paid $540,000 in cash for a home in Arlington, Virginia, bought two new cars, bought stock worth $165,000, and charged $455,000 on credit cards. Ames was sentenced to life in prison (Hagan, 1997).

*Computer spying* recently emerged as a growing security issue. Consider the following examples (Rosoff, Pontell, and Tillman, 2007:539):

- A 22-year-old former Harvard student allegedly used stolen university passwords to break into military computers.
- Two "hackers" penetrated seven computer systems, gaining access to all information at Griffiss Air Force Base in New York. The spies copied files—including sensitive battlefield simulations—and installed devices to read the passwords of everyone entering the systems.
- A Washington, D.C., "hacker" was arrested for breaking into the Pentagon computer system and subsequently demonstrated his computer skills by cracking the Air Force computer system within 15 seconds while military officials watched.

## 14.2 DOMESTIC POLITICAL CRIMES BY THE STATE

Domestic political crimes by the state are violations of law and unethical conduct by state officials or agencies whose victimization occurs within the boundaries of the United States. We discuss three types: state corruption, political repression, and state-corporate crime. **State corruption** is illegal or unethical use of state authority for personal or political gain. **Political repression** is illegal or unethical conduct by state officials or agencies for purposes of repressing domestic political dissent. **State-corporate crime** is illegal or socially harmful behavior that occurs at the intersection of state agencies and private corporations.

### STATE CORRUPTION

State corruption exists at city, state, and national levels and involves a wide range of state-directed activities—such as purchasing goods and services,

use of public funds and property, tax assessment and collection, regulation of commercial activity, zoning and land use, law enforcement, and so on. We focus on three types of state corruption: political bribery, election fraud, and corrupt campaign practices.

**Political bribery** is the accepting of money or property by state officials in return for favors. Politicians, for example, have myriad opportunities for involvement in bribery, accepting money for such services as introducing special forms of legislation, voting a specific way on already-introduced legislation, and voting in favor of a government contract. One of the best-known cases of bribery of politicians is the ABSCAM case. This FBI "sting" operation, which took place in the early 1980s, resulted in the conviction of seven members of Congress for accepting bribes from undercover FBI agents posing as Arab sheiks. The "sheiks" met the members of Congress in hotel rooms, offering them substantial amounts of money or stock for favorable legislation on business ventures. Only one of the eight politicians refused the bribe.

Five recent examples of this form of state corruption involved the cases of James Traficant, Jr., Vincent "Buddy" Cianci, Jack Abramoff, Randy "Duke" Cunningham, and Rod Blagojevich. Traficant is an ex-Democratic congressperson from Ohio who was convicted in 2002 on ten counts of bribery, tax evasion, and extorting money from his own staff. Cianci is the ex-mayor of Providence, Rhode Island, who in 2002 was convicted and sentenced to 5 years and 4 months in federal prison for soliciting bribes for city contracts, jobs, and tax breaks. Testimony at his trial indicated, for example, that Cianci received a $10,000 bribe for reducing an individual's $500,000 tax bill to $100,000, and he received $5,000 for ordering the hiring of a woman's son on the city police force. Cunningham, an eight-term Republican congressperson from San Diego, plead guilty in 2005 to supporting lucrative defense contracts in exchange for a mansion, a Rolls Royce, a $140,000 yacht, museum-quality antiques, $40,000 Persian rugs, and thousands of dollars in cash. As Rosoff, Pontell, and Tillman (2007:434) point out: "Between 2000 and 2005, the total of Cunningham's bribes was set at a stunning $2.4 million. In terms of dollar amount, that made Cunningham *the most corrupt member of Congress ever uncovered in U.S. history*." Abramoff is a former lobbyist who pleaded guilty on January 3, 2006, to three felony counts of defrauding Native Americans and corruption of public officials. Abramoff defrauded four Native American nations—the Saginaw Chippewas, the Agua Caliente, the Choctaws, and the Coushattas—of tens of millions of dollars related to gaming. On September 4, 2008, Abramoff was found guilty of trading expensive gifts, meals, and sports trips in exchange for political favors. Finally, Blagojevich was governor of Illinois from 2003 to 2009 and was arrested and charged on December 9, 2008, with federal crimes of conspiracy to commit mail and wire fraud and solicitation of bribery. Blagojevich allegedly conspired to commit several "pay-to-play" schemes, including the attempt to "sell" President Barack Obama's vacated U.S. Senate seat to the highest bidder. On January 29, 2009, Blagojevich was impeached and removed from office by the Illinois State Senate, and at this writing he currently is awaiting trial on the federal indictment.

State officials, other than politicians, are also in a position to accept bribes. The police, for example, have a long history of involvement in corruption. From at least the 1890s on, a legion of investigative committees has consistently unearthed substantial and wide-ranging forms of police bribery (Coleman, 2006). In the 1980s bribery in law enforcement once again came to national attention. In 1988, for example, seven Boston police detectives were convicted on fifty-seven counts of bribery totaling $18,000 over an 8-year period (*Boston Herald*, 1988). Moreover, over 100 law-enforcement drug-related bribery cases came before state and federal courts in the 1980s (Shenon, 1988). Most recently, an investigation uncovered numerous corrupt acts—including bribery—by some members of the Los Angeles Police Department (LAPD). Dozens of "antigang officers" were implicated in drug dealing, making false arrests, shaking down drug dealers, bribery, giving perjured testimony, and framing innocent people (Coleman, 2006). As a result of this police corruption, over 100 criminal convictions were overturned, and the responsibility for making police reforms at LAPD was placed in the hands of a federal judge.

Judges and lawyers have similarly been found to be involved in bribery. An investigation of the Circuit Court of Cook County, Illinois, for example, revealed that judges were providing specific dispositions or consideration to a case in exchange for money or other things of value, and "lawyers would pay off judges for permission to 'hustle' clients in large-volume criminal courtrooms" (Valukas and Raphaelson, 1988:4). In one particular court,

> a corrupt chief judge assigned other judges to the "big rooms" (courts where driving under the influence cases were heard) based on their willingness to accommodate the corrupt defense lawyers who practiced there. These defense lawyers were called "miracle workers" because they never lost a case. These same lawyers got their results by paying judges, often through middlemen, for favorable disposition of their clients' drunk driving cases. Often the arresting police officer was also paid to testify in a way that created a reasonable doubt. The weakened evidence gave the corrupt judge "something to hang his hat on" in finding the defendant not guilty. (p. 4)

Most recently, several Dade County, Florida, judges were found guilty of taking bribes from drug-trafficking defendants totaling $266,000; a federal district judge in Louisiana was convicted of accepting $16,500 from a convicted drug dealer to obtain a lighter sentence; and a judge in Chicago was found to have accepted eight automobiles and $400,000 in cash payoffs for dismissing drunk driving cases (Rosoff, Pontell, and Tillman, 2007).

Many politicians have also been involved in **election fraud**—illegal voting, false registration, stuffing ballot boxes, and the like—which had its beginning in the heyday of political machines in the late 1800s. Some presidential examples include the following (Douglas, 1977; Weld, 1988):

- Harry Truman likely would not have been elected senator from Missouri if he had not received 50,000 fraudulent votes provided by the "Pendergast Machine" in Kansas City.
- John Kennedy was assured victory in 1960 when Chicago Mayor Richard Daley and his machine stuffed ballot boxes with Kennedy votes.
- Lyndon Johnson won his 1948 Senate race in Texas by 202 fraudulently obtained votes.
- Approximately $5,000 was allegedly used to purchase black votes for Jimmy Carter in the 1976 California primary.

Election fraud can also occur through forgery and false accounting by election officials. As David Simon (2008) shows:

> Corrupt election officials can (1) complete ballots when the voter has failed to vote for a particular office, (2) declare ballots for the opposition invalid by deliberately defacing them or making two preferences for a single office, (3) destroy ballots for the opposition, (4) add premarked ballots to the total, and (5) simply miscount. (p. 226)

In the 2000 presidential election between Vice President Al Gore and Texas Governor George W. Bush, the outcome was determined by the vote in Florida, which it was assumed Bush eventually won. However, investigations of the voting process in Florida reveal that Bush "won" Florida through a deliberate preemption, prior to election day, of tens of thousands of Democratic votes by disenfranchising citizens, slanting the count of military voters overseas, and blocking a proper recount (DeHaven-Smith, 2008). Moreover, the 2004 presidential election between Democratic challenger Senator John Kerry and the Republican incumbent, President George W. Bush, was also most likely "won" through fraud, such as concocting at least 4 million phantom votes, the "hacking and stacking" of e-voting machines, and using electronic voting machines that failed to pass lab tests (Collins, 2008; Griscom, 2008; Richardson and Friedman, 2008).

Finally, **corrupt campaign practices** appear to be relatively widespread in the United States. Probably the most well-known form of such corruption occurred in June 1972, when a group of ex-CIA operatives was caught breaking into the Democratic Party's national headquarters in the Watergate Building in Washington, D.C. In what eventually became known as "Watergate," subsequent investigations revealed that the burglary was only part of an extensive campaign of political corruption involving political espionage, electoral sabotage, wiretapping, theft of private records, and illegal use of campaign funds—planned and directed by members of then-President Nixon's campaign staff and White House staff. In August 1974, in order to avoid an impeachment trial, Richard Nixon resigned from the presidency and eventually was pardoned of all crimes associated with Watergate by President Gerald Ford.

Most likely the bulk of this type of crime involves politicians who tend to be extremely loyal to those who contribute to their campaign. For example, during the last six years, Congressional candidates accepted $36.5 million in campaign contributions, yet: (1) in return, bankers were granted deregulation and bailouts that cost U.S. taxpayers over $1 trillion; (2) those congresspeople receiving contributions from tobacco companies were three times more likely to have voted against crackdowns on cigarette sales to minors; and (3) those congresspeople receiving the largest sums from defense contractors were twice as likely to support higher military spending than those who received little or nothing (Parenti, 2008).

One of the most controversial historical forms of possible corrupt campaign practices is outlined in Box 14.1.

## STATE POLITICAL REPRESSION

Federal agencies such as the FBI and the CIA have been involved in numerous illegal activities,

---

**BOX 14.1   OCTOBER SURPRISE**

Corrupt campaign practices may also have been part of the 1980 Reagan-Bush campaign for the presidency. On November 4, 1979, the U.S. embassy in Tehran, Iran, was taken over by a group of students loyal to the Ayatollah Khomeini. Sixty-six U.S. citizens were held captive until, mysteriously, January 20, 1981. Only two hours after President Reagan's inauguration on that day—the 444th day of captivity—the hostages were released. Why were the hostages released at that particular date and time? Abbie Hoffman and Jonathan Silvers (1988) think they know why. Fearing in the final weeks of the 1980 presidential campaign that President Carter would come up with an "October Surprise"—somehow bring home the hostages, thus almost guaranteeing his reelection—the Reagan-Bush campaign, Hoffman and Silvers argued, quite possibly managed to stop such an event from occurring. What follows is a summary of Hoffman and Silvers' argument.

In May 1984 the House Subcommittee on Human Resources found that by October 1980, senior Reagan advisers had informants at the CIA, the Defense Intelligence Agency, the National Security Council, the White House Situation Room, and military bases around the country for purposes of reporting any aircraft movements related to the hostages in any way. In short, by "the fall of 1980, the Carter White House was riddled with moles, spies, and informers" for the Reagan-Bush campaign (Hoffman and Silvers, 1988:151).

In addition to monitoring the possibility of a Carter "October Surprise," Reagan-Bush campaign officials may have attempted to deal directly with the Iranians themselves. In other words, prior even to taking office, Reagan-Bush campaign officials may have attempted to guarantee victory by "cutting a deal" with Iran. In exchange for keeping the hostages until inauguration day, Hoffman and Silvers argued, Reagan-Bush officials pledged that Iran would receive U.S. military arms and supplies. Others have supported Hoffman and Silvers' argument (Honegger, 1989; Sick, 1991). In particular, Gary Sick (1991) added that William Casey, Reagan's campaign manager, met with Iranian arms dealer Cyrus Hashemi in Madrid and Paris on July 26 and 27, 1980, to hammer out the deal.

The "October Surprise" argument is not without substance. The hostages were released on inauguration day, and that same year, on July 24, Israel contracted with Iran to sell them more than $100 million worth of U.S. arms (J. Marshall, Scott, and Hunter, 1987). Moreover, McFarlane, Casey, and Israel played important roles in the initial phases of the arms-for-hostages deal that eventually erupted as the Iran-Contra scandal.

The allegations we have outlined prompted investigations by both the U.S. Senate and the House. Neither inquiry found credible evidence of a secret deal. Yet Sick responded to the House report by arguing that William Casey's activities were not adequately substantiated. For example, Sick (1991) has claimed that "the report says Mr. Casey could not have attended a Madrid meeting the weekend of July 26–27 because he was at the Bohemian Grove outside San Francisco. And the committee's own evidence places him at the Grove the following weekend, from August 1 to August 3" (p. 17). Casey's passport mysteriously vanished—and was therefore not available to the task force—and crucial pages were missing from his loose-leaf calendar. Thus, Sick concluded that questions remained, and he hoped "the task force will open its files to outside independent investigators to the maximum extent permissible by law" (p. 17).

many of which relate to political repression. For instance, although legally the CIA has no domestic security or law-enforcement functions, it has (1) opened and photographed the mail of over 1 million private citizens; (2) broken into homes and offices, stealing documents and installing illegal surveillance devices; and (3) equipped, trained, and supported local police forces (Parenti, 2008).

Similarly, since its inception in 1938, the FBI has been involved in a variety of illegal activities related to the repression of political dissent. Historically, one of the first responsibilities of the FBI was to investigate "subversion," which was entirely unrelated to the enforcement of federal criminal laws (Church Committee, 1976). In 1938, for instance, the FBI *illegally* investigated subversion in (1) the maritime, steel, coal, clothing, garment, fur, automobile, and newspaper industries; (2) educational institutions; (3) organized labor; (4) youth groups; (5) African American groups; (6) government affairs; and (7) the military. Explicit illegality included wiretapping, bugging, mail openings, and breaking and entering. Through such illegal behavior the FBI gathered information on "radical" individuals and groups and forwarded it directly to the White House.

The major thrust of the FBI since at least 1941, however, has been its counterintelligence program, more commonly known as COINTELPRO. Although the FBI's counterintelligence function is restricted by law to "hostile foreign governments, foreign organizations, and individuals connected to them" (Churchill and Vander Wall, 1988:37), the FBI clearly went beyond that mandate to include not only intelligence gathering but also strategies and tactics for the purpose of disrupting and "neutralizing" organizations that the FBI felt were threatening to the social order. As William C. Sullivan, former head of the FBI Counterintelligence Division, stated in the mid-1970s (cited in Church Committee, 1976): "We

were engaged in COINTELPRO tactics, to divide, conquer, weaken, in diverse ways, an organization. We were engaged in that when I entered the Bureau in 1941" (p. 66).

Between 1940 and the early 1960s, COINTELPRO activities were primarily directed at the U.S. Communist Party and the Socialist Workers Party (Church Committee, 1976). In the 1960s and early 1970s the FBI investigated new groups, implementing some 2,370 separate COINTELPRO actions (Kunstler, 1978). Some of the groups embraced by COINTELPRO activities were the Puerto Rican independence movement, the civil rights movement, Students for a Democratic Society, and the Black Liberation movement. Because of space limitation, it is impossible to discuss the effects of COINTELPRO on each of these movements. Therefore, we focus on one particular case, the FBI's campaign against Martin Luther King, Jr.

In 1962 the FBI claimed that Dr. King and the civil rights movement had been duped by the Communists. This claim was eventually proved false (Garrow, 1981). Nevertheless, in December 1963—four months after the famous civil rights march on Washington and King's "I Have a Dream" speech—a 9-hour meeting was convened at FBI headquarters to discuss various "avenues of approach aimed at neutralizing King as an effective Negro leader" (Church Committee, 1976:220). Agents throughout the country were instructed to continue gathering information on King's personal life "in order that we may consider using this information at an opportune time in a counterintelligence move to discredit him" (p. 220). According to David Garrow (1981), the FBI went through the Southern Christian Leadership Conference's (SCLC's) trash in hope of finding incriminating evidence against that organization and King. The FBI investigated Dr. King's bank and charge accounts, instituted electronic surveillance of King's apartment and office, attempted to win cooperation with the Bureau from certain SCLC employees, sent threatening forged letters in King's name to SCLC contributors, and attempted to intensify the well-known mutual dislike between King and NAACP head Roy Wilkins. However, the FBI was unable to produce any incriminating evidence against the SCLC or King himself.

Undaunted, on January 5, 1964, FBI agents planted a microphone in King's bedroom at the Willard Hotel in Washington, D.C. Over the next two years the FBI installed at least fourteen additional bugs in King's hotel rooms across the country, sometimes accompanied by physical and photographic surveillance (Church Committee, 1976). Alleging that the resulting tapes revealed "meetings" with prostitutes, the FBI then fabricated an anonymous letter to King, enclosing a copy of one of the tapes, and sent them to King on the eve of his receiving the Nobel Peace Prize (pp. 220–221). The letter, in part, reads as follows (cited in Garrow, 1981):

> King,
>
> In view of your low grade...I will not dignify your name with either a Mr. or a Reverend or a Dr....No person can overcome facts, not even a fraud like yourself...I repeat—no person can successfully argue against facts. You are finished....
>
> King, there is only one thing left for you to do....You are done. There is but one way out for you. You better take it before your filthy, abnormal fraudulent self is bared to the nation. (pp. 125–126)

When this effort by the FBI failed to force King to commit suicide—as he himself allegedly interpreted the purpose of the message (Church Committee, 1976)—the FBI "leaked" the tapes and photographs to a number of leading newspapers in the United States (Wise, 1976; Bray, 1980).

Unhindered by the FBI's virulent attacks and efforts to halt his political movement, King traveled to Sweden to receive the Nobel Peace Prize. During his stay in Europe and on his return to the United States, the Bureau continued its activities (Church Committee, 1976). The "neutralization" program actually continued until King's death. As late as March 1968, FBI agents were instructed to neutralize King because he might, according to the Bureau, become a "messiah" who could "unify and electrify the militant black nationalist movement" (p. 223). Moreover, as Churchill and Vander Wall (1988) pointed out: "Given the nature of the Bureau's campaign to neutralize King, there remain serious questions—unresolved by subsequent congressional investigations—as to the FBI's role in King's assassination in Memphis on March 31, 1968" (p. 57). Indeed, the FBI had long previously (1964) determined that New York attorney Samuel R. Pierce (an extreme conservative) should be King's successor; he would be, according to one FBI document, the "'right kind' of leader" (p. 395).

Most methods used by the FBI under COINTELPRO were, according to the Church Committee investigating FBI illegalities, "secret programs...which used unlawful or improper acts" to carry out desired goals (1976:137). Beyond falsification of information and documents and illegal surveillance, the FBI conducted hundreds of illegal burglaries against "threatening" individuals and organizations, stealing private files and documents. Moreover, through COINTELPRO the FBI conducted disinformation campaigns, used "agent provocateurs" to disrupt political (primarily leftist) organizations, and was implicated in the assassination of such dissident political group leaders as Fred Hampton of the Black Panther Party (Churchill and Vander Wall, 1988).

In the 1980s, the FBI was involved in intelligence gathering and overall monitoring of the Committee in Solidarity with the People of El Salvador (CISPES). Through the Freedom of Information Act, the Center for Constitutional Rights in New York obtained FBI files on CISPES, documenting political intelligence gathering and

**BOX 14.2** **THE CASE OF LEONARD PELTIER**

Although COINTELPRO was allegedly abolished in 1971, FBI illegalities continued. The case of Leonard Peltier is extraordinary in this regard. Leonard Peltier is, and was in the 1970s, a member of the American Indian Movement (AIM), a national movement of Native Americans striving to restore their traditional culture and reclaim the rights guaranteed them by treaties entered into over a period of 100 years. In 1975, Peltier was living at the Pine Ridge Indian Reservation in South Dakota (along with approximately thirty other AIM members and supporters) when, on the morning of June 26, two armed FBI agents entered the reservation, allegedly in search of a young Native American accused of stealing a pair of cowboy boots. A firefight occurred between members of AIM and the FBI. Shortly thereafter, both agents and an AIM member were dead. There was never an investigation of the killing of the AIM member, yet four Native Americans were charged with the murder of the two agents. Only one, Leonard Peltier, was convicted. The charges against one of the original defendants were dropped, allegedly due to a lack of evidence; the other two were brought to trial in Cedar Rapids, Iowa, in the summer of 1976. Both were eventually acquitted amid controversy concerning FBI misconduct in the prosecution of their case (Messerschmidt, 1986a).

Prior to the Cedar Rapids trial, Peltier sought political asylum in Canada, where he was apprehended by the Royal Canadian Mounted Police at the request of the FBI. He petitioned the Canadian government to grant him status as a political refugee, contending that it would be impossible for him to receive a fair trial in the United States because of his political beliefs and activities. The FBI's response to Peltier's petition was to provide the Canadian authorities with two fabricated "eyewitness" affidavits signed by a Lakota woman, Myrtle Poor Bear. It was later revealed at Peltier's trial, but out of the presence of the jury, that Myrtle Poor Bear never knew Leonard Peltier, had never seen him before, was more than 50 miles away from the crime scene on the day of the firefight, and was most likely coerced by FBI agents to sign the affidavits. The Canadian government honored the U.S. extradition request.

Unhappy with the acquittal in Cedar Rapids and thus with the "performance" of the federal judge in that case, the federal government obtained a change of venue to Fargo, North Dakota. Here the FBI found the judge they wanted. Virtually the entire defense, which had justified an acquittal in Cedar Rapids, was ruled inadmissible by the judge in Fargo. But more important, according to a detailed examination of the trial record, the prosecution enjoyed free rein to manipulate highly inconsistent and contradictory circumstantial evidence, and the entire trial was saturated with the suppression of evidence, the coercion of testimony, and, quite possibly, judicial impropriety. It was under these circumstances that Leonard Peltier was convicted and sentenced to serve two consecutive life terms for the murder of two FBI agents.

Peltier appealed the conviction to the Eighth U.S. Circuit Court of Appeals in St. Louis. Although noting, for example, that the Myrtle Poor Bear affair was "disturbing," the court upheld his conviction. Several more appeals were heard, each fruitless. In the final appeal to the Eighth Circuit, the judges stated the following in their decision: "We recognize that there is evidence in this record of improper conduct on the part of some FBI agents, but we are reluctant to impute even further improprieties to them" (cited in Churchill and Vander Wall, 1988). As Churchill and Vander Wall responded, "Thus, it was deemed more appropriate that Leonard Peltier remain locked away in a maximum security cell rather than expose the FBI to further scrutiny concerning the way in which it had obtained its conviction, even after a clear pattern of Bureau misconduct had been demonstrated" (p. 326).

Because of the foregoing, many people worldwide believe that Peltier's arrest, prosecution, and continued confinement are the result of his political activities as a leader of AIM. Although Peltier remains behind bars, (1) he was selected to receive the International Human Rights Prize by the Human Rights Commission of Spain, (2) over fifty members of Congress have twice signed "Friend of the Court" briefs supporting Peltier's right to a new trial, (3) over fifty members of the Canadian Parliament signed a petition asking the U.S. government to order a new trial (six of the Canadian endorsers held cabinet posts at the time of Peltier's extradition), (4) human rights organizations, such as Amnesty International, have supported Peltier's request for a retrial and have recommended that an independent Commission of Inquiry be established to look into the case, and (5) over 14 million people worldwide have signed petitions demanding a new trial for Peltier. On August 20, 2009, Peltier was denied parole and he will not be eligible for another parole hearing until 2024, when he is 79 years old.

political harassment of individuals and groups associated with CISPES and working to change U.S. foreign policy in Central America. The files also reveal that fifty-two of the fifty-nine FBI field offices were involved in the massive investigation. Initially the FBI attempted to substantiate that CISPES was an agent of a foreign government and, therefore, in violation of the Foreign Agents Registration Act. When this failed, the FBI—with approval from then-Attorney General William French Smith—mounted a new investigation, on the premise that CISPES was probably a "terrorist" organization. The FBI, however, never found any evidence to support this thesis either. In fact, field reports came into FBI headquarters indicating that those involved in CISPES and related organizations were "legitimate" and "respectable" people involved in such activities as demonstrations, lobbying, protests, rallies, newsletters, and occasional nonviolent civil disobedience—all protected by the First Amendment.

The FBI, however, did not stop there but went on to develop two rationales that allowed the investigation to continue. Ann Buitrago (1988) summarizes the rationales:

> *The "Covert Programs" Rationale:* To explain away its negative results, the FBI reasoned that all the peaceful legal activities on which CISPES' broad support was based merely represented an *overt* program designed to cover a sinister *covert* program of which most CISPES members were unaware.
>
> *The "Front Groups" Rationale:* The old concept of "front groups" was dredged up to enable the investigation to expand beyond CISPES chapters and affiliates to any of the hundreds of organizations whose work brought them in touch with CISPES or its members. The usefulness to the FBI of the notion of "front groups" was that even though a given group was clearly not involved in terrorism but only in public education and/or protest, it could continue to be investigated because it might be a CISPES "front." (p. 3)

These rationales had the effect of driving the investigation further and deeper. Under the guise of looking for "fronts" and "covert terrorists," the FBI used the following techniques to investigate CISPES:

1. FBI informers infiltrated organizations and were sent to meetings and demonstrations.
2. Record checks were made of FBI files, other police records, school records, phone books, and student-faculty directories.
3. Frequent physical surveillance of people, residences, meeting places, offices, and demonstrations took place, often accompanied by photographic surveillance.
4. CISPES-related literature was collected and reviewed.
5. Radio programs were monitored.
6. License plate numbers of vehicles at or near demonstrations, public events, and conferences were traced, and the names of owners were investigated.
7. FBI interviews were attempted of CISPES leaders, members, former members, and members of other groups "knowledgeable" of CISPES.

In addition, the FBI worked closely with several right-wing groups, helping to develop further the privatization of intelligence gathering. For instance, right-wing groups—such as the Young Americans for Freedom (YAF) and CARP (followers of Sun Yung Moon)—would routinely gather "intelligence" and pass it on to the FBI. In one case a YAF document on the CISPES National Convention was sent to FBI headquarters, where it was disseminated to thirty-two field offices (Center for Constitutional Rights, 1988).

Ironically, the only "covert program" uncovered during this operation was conducted by right-wing groups and the FBI. In fact, the FBI's "terrorist" investigation was viewed by those investigating the case as simply a cover for conducting domestic security programs aimed at disrupting organizations critical of U.S. foreign policy. According to Buitrago (1988), hostility toward CISPES "pours out of these documents" (pp. 4–5). For example, the field office at "Dallas wrote frequently about the need to devise investigative activity '*against* this organization'; New Orleans fired off a tirade against CISPES and individuals who 'display contempt against the U.S. government,' calling for them to be deported or denied reentry if they ever left the country" (pp. 4–5).

At least one FBI agent refused to go along with this investigation. In January 1988, Jack Ryan, an FBI agent for 22 years, was fired because he refused to investigate peace groups opposed to U.S. policy in Central America. As Ryan stated: "Investigating this as domestic terrorism or domestic violence is absurd. . . . What our government's doing is wrong in Central America. I don't want to be a part of it" (cited in Hopkins, 1988:14). Ryan was fired just 10 months before his retirement.

In 1978 the Foreign Intelligence Surveillance Act (FISA) was established by Congress; it forbid wiretapping and eavesdropping on U.S. citizens without a warrant. Nevertheless, after the terrorist attacks of September 11, 2001, President George W. Bush argued that he was now allowed to violate the act, which he proceeded to do. In 2001 Bush signed a secret order establishing his "Terrorist Surveillance Program," which authorized the National Security Agency (NSA) to engage in warrantless eavesdropping on telephone and computer communications of U.S. citizens. Under the Bush administration, the NSA listened to as many as 500 conversations at any given time and secretly has listened to tens of thousands of private conversations since the program began. The NSA was also provided unsupervised access to U.S. telecommunication companies' fiber-optic lines to intercept the communications (Cohn, 2007).

The most politically repressive form of legislation in recent years is the Uniting and Strengthening America by Providing Appropriate Tools Required to Intercept and Obstruct Terrorism Act (USA PATRIOT Act), which was passed by Congress just six weeks after the September 11, 2001, international terrorist attacks. The act sacrifices political freedoms in the name of national security by (1) limiting freedom of speech and political association, (2) denying U.S. entry to noncitizens simply on the basis of political ideology, (3) granting the state enhanced surveillance powers, such as tracking e-mail and Internet use, conducting sneak-and-peek searches (by postal workers, for example), obtaining sensitive personnel records, monitoring financial transactions, conducting nationwide roving wiretaps, and even monitoring library records (Chang, 2001). Within only two months of the act's being signed into law by President Bush (on October 26, 2001), the Department of Justice admitted detaining more than 1,200 immigrants, none of whom were charged with terrorism. Moreover, most of these individuals were denied basic rights of due process, including the right to know the charges against them, the right to an attorney, and the use of prolonged solitary confinement (Platt and O'Leary, 2003). Nearly four dozen antiwar groups, such as the Vegan Community Project, the People for the Ethical Treatment of Animals, and various interfaith organizations for peace and justice, were subjected to FBI surveillance during the Bush administration (Cohn, 2007). Indeed, a 2006 Justice Department investigation found that in just 2004 and 2005, more than 100 violations of the Patriot Act occurred, including "incidents where agents tapped the wrong telephone, intercepted the wrong e-mails, or continued listening to conversations after the warrant had expired" (p. 98).

Moreover, during the Bush administration, it was uncovered by the Center for American

Progress that the White House had engaged in what they labeled, "Intimigate," or the development of a pattern of firing, intimidating, and defaming anyone who challenged the administration's perspective on the Iraq war. For example, White House advisor Larry Lindsey was fired when he told a newspaper that the Iraq war would cost $200 billion; General Anthony Zinni, President Bush's special Middle East mediator, was not reappointed because he indicated publicly that there were more pressing foreign policy issues than Iraq and that there could be a prolonged difficult aftermath to that war; and administration officials leaked the name of Valerie Plame, a CIA officer, to journalists after her husband, former ambassador Joseph Wilson IV, publicly challenged President Bush's claim that Iraq had attempted to buy uranium ore from Africa. In the latter example, Lewis "Scooter" Libby, Assistant to President Bush and Chief of Staff to Vice President Dick Cheney, was convicted on March 6, 2007, of obstruction of justice, perjury, and making false statements to federal investigators for his role in this "Intimigate" affair. Libby is the highest-ranking White House official in the Bush administration to be convicted in a governmental scandal.

## STATE-CORPORATE CRIME

State corporate crime generally is understood as illegal or socially harmful acts that occur at the intersection of state agencies and private corporations. However, research on state corporate crimes has uncovered two major types: (1) when a state agency utilizes a private corporation to achieve a state goal in an illegal or socially harmful way, and (2) when omissions by a state agency allow a private corporation to pursue illegal or socially harmful acts (Kramer and Michalowski, 1990; Aulette and Michalowski, 1993). We discuss two examples for each.

On January 28, 1986, the space shuttle *Challenger* took off on its last mission, tragically exploding just 73 seconds into flight, killing all seven crew members, including a New Hampshire school teacher. This case is an example of the first type of state-corporate crime because a state agency, the National Aeronautics Space Administration (NASA), utilized a private corporation, Morton Thiokol, Inc. (MTI), to launch *Challenger* despite solid evidence indicating it was unsafe to do so (Kramer, 1992; Maier and Messerschmidt, 1998).

In its final report, the Presidential Commission (1986) that investigated the *Challenger* tragedy found that it was in part caused by technical failure (of a rubber O-ring in one of the solid rocket boosters that failed to seal properly) due to freezing temperatures preceding liftoff. But the commission also concluded that the decision-making process that led to the fatal launch was "seriously flawed." The string of warnings unheeded, of recommendations ignored—from the early developmental stages years prior all the way through the final decision processes—culminated in the crime. Indeed, the managers at both NASA and MTI agreed to allow the launch because the former was required to "stay on schedule" (to continue receiving congressional economic support) and the latter wanted to preserve a lucrative contract (NASA was seeking bids from competitors for MTI's $1 billion contract). Thus, both NASA and MTI agreed to the dangerous launch in order to satisfy their individual organizational needs.

More recently, in 2005 the energy corporation Unocal agreed to settle a lawsuit against it for assisting and encouraging the torture, murder, and rape of Burmese citizens by government soldiers so that Unocal could build a gas pipeline (Eviatar, 2005). Indeed, the Burmese military was using forced labor to clear land Unocal needed to build its pipeline, and it is clear that Unocal was aware of the abuses, because their own consultants had repeatedly warned the company of the crimes being committed and both the U.S. State Department and the United Nations had documented the brutality of the Burmese military. Thus the Burmese state and the Unocal corporation were involved in assisting and encouraging human rights violations to facilitate their joint venture of building and profiting from the gas pipeline.

The second type of state-corporate crime involves omissions by state agencies that allow a private corporation to pursue harmful acts. An example of this type of state-corporate crime occurred on September 3, 1991, when an explosion and fire occurred at the Imperial Food Products chicken-processing plant in Hamlet, North Carolina, killing twenty-five workers and injuring another fifty-six (Aulette and Michalowski, 1993). Investigations of the explosion and fire revealed a pattern of failures by regulatory agencies—such as the Occupational Safety and Health Administration (OSHA)—that played a significant role in creating the conditions that led to this crime. As Aulette and Michalowski further point out: "This regulatory failure was facilitated by the state of North Carolina through its refusal to fund and support the state's Occupational Safety and Health Program even to the limits of *available* federal monies" (p. 1710).

The technical cause of the fire was a rupture in a hydraulic line near a deep fryer, which resulted in the explosion. However, the killing of twenty-five workers at the Imperial plant is more complex than simply a technical failure. Indeed, historically state agencies developed a pro-business and an antilabor climate in the state, resulting in underfunding and understaffing the North Carolina–OSHA program. In such a context, that state agency often overlooked dangerous working conditions in the interest of attracting business investments in the state. Consequently, it was such omissions by state agencies that led to the "single most important" cause of the killing: a lack of accessible routes to safety. In violation of OSHA regulations, Imperial plant managers had locked the exit doors to stop employees from stealing chicken nuggets. Consequently, twenty-five workers died from smoke inhalation.

The crash of ValuJet Flight 592 in 1996 is another example of this second type of state-corporate crime. Just prior to takeoff of Flight 592, expired chemical oxygen generators were placed in the cargo department below the passenger cabin, violating the rules of the Federal Aviation Administration (FAA) that forbids transportation of hazardous material in the cargo area of an airplane. The National Transportation Safety Board investigated the eventual fire that engulfed the entire plane, determining that both ValuJet—for not supervising properly the loading of such hazardous material—and the FAA—for its failure to enforce safety regulations—were culpable for the crime (Friedrichs, 2007).

## 14.3 TRANSNATIONAL POLITICAL CRIMES BY THE STATE

In 1947, President Harry Truman signed into law the National Security Act, providing not only for the Central Intelligence Agency (CIA) but also for the National Security Council (NSC). The primary responsibility of the CIA, according to this act, is to gather foreign intelligence and transmit it directly to the White House; the NSC was set up ostensibly as a civilian advisory group to the president on domestic, foreign, and military policies related to national security. However, both the CIA and the NSC have used their respective powers to go beyond their legislative mandates, engaging in a variety of covert operations almost from their inception. These covert operations have, at times, violated U.S. laws, such as the Neutrality Act, which makes it a crime to prepare a means for, or to furnish weapons for, military expeditions against any foreign country with which the United States is at peace.

In addition, both the CIA and the NSC have, at times, violated international law. **International**

**law** embodies a variety of treaties, agreements, customary law principles, and general legal principles that serve to judge the actions and behavior of various states that have agreed to them. For example, the United Nations Charter is an essential part of international law. In particular, Article 2(3) of the U.N. Charter obligates member states to settle international disputes through peaceful means, and Article 2(4) provides that no country has the right to use force or the threat of force against the territorial integrity or political independence of any state (Buergenthal and Murphy, 2002). These provisions impose a general prohibition on the use of force in international relations, but the Charter also outlines two exceptions when use of force is permitted: (1) as self-defense in response to an armed attack, and (2) through the specific authorization by the U.N. Security Council as a last resort to maintain international peace and security. If the use of force or threat of force by one state against another does not meet either of these two exceptions, a violation of international law has occurred.

In this final section we present examples of violations of international law by the U.S. state. These violations represent transnational political crimes by the state because they violate international law and because the resulting victimization occurs outside of the United States. More specifically, since these violations of international law entail the use of force or violence to intimidate, coerce, or change a government or civilian population for political reasons, they also constitute examples of **state terrorism**. We first discuss numerous examples of state terrorism perpetrated by the U.S. government through its foreign policy; then we end the chapter with a discussion of the state, terrorism, and globalization.

## STATE TERRORISM

In 1953 the U.S. state engaged in its first extensive operation to overthrow a democratically elected foreign leader. This situation occurred in Iran, where the legitimately elected and reform-minded prime minister, Mohammed Mossadegh, was toppled by the CIA. The CIA (along with British intelligence agencies) planned, funded, and implemented the operation (Gasiorowski and Byrne, 2004). Mossadegh had nationalized several large foreign-owned oil companies, thus challenging U.S. interests in the region (Prados, 1986). Even though Mossadegh offered compensation, Secretary of State John Foster Dulles and his brother, Allen Welsh Dulles (then director of the CIA) supported President Eisenhower's decision to reinstate the Shah as head of Iran. Once in power, the Shah—Reza Pahlavi—was considerably more favorable to U.S. economic interests. For example, he allowed U.S. oil companies to take over almost 50 percent of Iran's oil production, and U.S. arms merchants (such as Richard Secord, who would emerge as a leading figure in the Iran-Contra scandal in the 1980s) negotiated more than $18 billion in weapon sales over the next 20 years (Moyers, 1988).

In 1957 the CIA helped set up the Iranian secret police (SAVAK), which stalked Iranian dissidents and earned a worldwide reputation for extreme sadism and frequent use of torture. From its inception, SAVAK agents "received special training at the Marine base in Quantico, Virginia, and attended orientation programs at CIA headquarters in Langley, Virginia" (Chomsky and Herman, 1979:49). While the Shah was in power, close to 1,500 people were arrested *monthly*, and on only one day, June 5, 1963, SAVAK and the Shah's army allegedly killed as many as 6,000 citizens (Simon and Eitzen, 1986). Future Iran-Contra operative Richard Secord (working with Albert Hakim) was chief of the U.S. Air Force's Military Advisory Assistance Group in Iran in 1975, which represented U.S. defense contractors selling the technology of control to the Shah (Sheehan, 1988). Secord proved an excellent representative. In 1977 alone, Iran purchased $4.2

billion worth of arms, "making Iran the largest foreign buyer of U.S. arms"; in the entire decade, the Shah purchased more than $17 billion worth of military equipment (Marshall, Scott, and Hunter, 1987).

In addition, political prisoners (arrested and incarcerated because they disagreed with government policy) numbered as high as 100,000 each year in Reza Pahlavi's Iran. Amnesty International, the human rights organization, reported 20 years after the coup (when the Shah was still in power) that Iran "has the highest rate of death penalties in the world, no valid system of civilian courts, and a history of torture which is beyond belief. No country in the world has a worse record in human rights than Iran" (cited in Chomsky and Herman, 1979:13). Thus, this early operation in Iran violated the U.N. Charter and represents an example of state terrorism.

The Iranian people rebelled against the Shah in 1979, shouting such slogans during demonstrations as "Death to the Shah" and "Death to the American Satan." Historically, the emergence of the Shah's outrageous repression, the subsequent rise of Khomeini, the hostage crisis, and the subsequent Iran-Contra scandal can all be seen as direct outcomes of the 1953 U.S. state policy in Iran (see Box 14.3 later in this chapter).

In 1954 the U.S. state turned its attention to Guatemala, violating the U.N. Charter again by overthrowing its president, Jacobo Arbenz, who received 65 percent of the vote in a democratic election (Herman, 1982). Not only did Arbenz maintain democratic institutions—such as allowing workers the right to unionize—he also launched a massive land reform program. Given that less than 3 percent of the landowners held more than 70 percent of the land when Arbenz was elected, he nationalized more than 1.5 million acres—including land owned by his own family—and turned it over to peasants (Moyers, 1988).

A considerable portion of this land belonged to a U.S.-based corporation, United Fruit Company, which immediately worked with the Dulles brothers in Washington to remove Arbenz from office (Herman, 1982). The CIA organized a contingent of "rebels," led by Castillo Armas, who crossed over the Honduras border on June 18, 1954. Although Arbenz's military attempted to hold off the rebels, it was unable to defend against CIA B-26 and P-47 air raids on Guatemala City (McClintock, 1985). Arbenz fled the country, and on July 8, 1954, he was replaced by Armas, who immediately overturned the reformist policies of the Arbenz government, returning the land to United Fruit and other landowners. Virtually all beneficiaries of the agrarian reform movement under Arbenz were dispossessed, entire cooperatives dissolved, literacy programs suspended, teachers fired, and "subversive" books burned. As Moyers (1988) pointed out, the CIA's "Operation Success" was in reality an example of state terrorism:

> The CIA had called its covert action against Guatemala "Operation Success." Military dictators ruled the country for the next 30 years. The United States provided them with weapons and trained their officers.... Peasants were slaughtered, political opponents were tortured, suspected insurgents shot, stabbed, burned alive, or strangled. There were so many deaths at one point that coroners complained they couldn't keep up with the workload. (p. 10)

Approximately five years after Operation Success, the U.S. state began planning another covert action that violated the U.N. Charter, this time in Cuba. Prior to 1959, syndicate figures—in particular, Santo Trafficante, Jr.—were heavily invested in narcotics trafficking, gambling, and prostitution in Cuba. Fulgencio Batista, then dictator of Cuba, profited substantially from these syndicate ventures (Kruger, 1980). On January 1, 1959, however, Fidel Castro's revolution forced Batista, and much of syndicated crime, out of Cuba. Immediately the CIA moved to overthrow the Castro government, recruiting right-wing anti-Castro Cubans who had fled the country to do the dirty work (Hinckle and Turner, 1981). Under the title "Operation 40," this group organized by the CIA carried out terrorist acts against Cuba and conspired to assassinate various leaders in the Cuban government. Part of the program involved hiring Robert Maheu—an associate of Howard Hughes and a private investigator who worked for the CIA—to recruit syndicate figures John Roselli, Sam Giancana, and Santo Trafficante, Jr., to orchestrate the assassination of Castro for $150,000 (Wyden, 1979). Also involved in Operation 40 were people later identified with the Iran-Contra scandal, such as Rafael "Chi Chi" Quintero and Felix Rodriguez (both anti-Castro Cubans working for the CIA) (Marshall, Scott, and Hunter, 1987). Thus, Operation 40 consisted of a well-organized sabotage, invasion, and assassination force, later known as Brigade 2506, which was based and trained by the CIA in both the United States and Guatemala. In short, Operation 40 and Brigade 2506 were U.S. state–sponsored terrorist organizations.

In mid-April 1961 a major invasion of the Bay of Pigs in Cuba took place but was unsuccessful (Hinckle and Turner, 1981). At the last minute President John Kennedy—fearing the attack would be identified as a U.S. operation if air cover were provided to the anti-Castro Cubans—halted the air strike, leaving Brigade 2506 defenseless upon landing at the Bay of Pigs (Ranelagh, 1987). Nevertheless, the plan to assassinate Castro continued.

The assassination operation became known as JM/WAVE, was based in Miami, and consisted of some 300 agents and 4,000–6,000 Cuban exile operatives (Kruger, 1980). In addition to at least eight attempted assassinations of Castro, this CIA-directed unit was involved in *daily violations* of the law—from the National Security Act to the Neutrality Act—as well as statutes involving

firearms possession and perjury (Prados, 1986). JM/WAVE involved state terrorist attacks against Cuban infrastructure—such as railroads, oil and sugar refineries, and factories—as well as, for example, contaminating exported Cuban sugar with chemicals at San Juan, Puerto Rico, and at other ports and sabotaging shipments of machinery and spare parts en route to Cuba (p. 212). Raids against Cuban targets continued until 1965.

When JM/WAVE was dismantled in 1965, the CIA left behind a highly trained army of 6,000 fanatically anticommunist Cubans allied to syndicated crime, who eventually merged into international terrorist organizations such as Alpha 66 and Omega 7 (Kruger, 1980). These organizations ultimately became known as the "Cuban Refugee Terrorist Network," involving overlapping memberships in the different groups. According to Edward Herman (1982) in his examination of terrorism, this network was responsible for a substantial number of terrorist acts in the Western Hemisphere. Trained by the CIA in the "arts of bomb construction, demolition, and efficient murder as part of the secret war against Cuba," the network was found to be responsible for twenty-five to thirty bombings in Dade County, Florida, in 1975 alone. In addition, Herman has argued that this network has assassinated diplomats in Lisbon, Mexico City, New York City, and Washington, D.C.

Ironically, certain Bay of Pigs veterans in this network financed their underground terrorist operations through involvement in the illegal drug trade. Indeed, according to Kruger (1980), a primary reason JM/WAVE was closed down was "because one of its aircraft was caught smuggling narcotics into the United States" (p. 146). Criminologist Howard Abadinsky (1989) has added that certain of these anti-Castro Cubans "imported only enough cocaine to satisfy members of their own community, but by the mid-1960s, the market began to expand, and they began to import the substance in greater quantities" (p. 209). And, as Marshall, Scott, and Hunter (1987) have asserted:

> America's drug problem today is arguably, in large measure, an outgrowth of the "secret war" against Fidel Castro begun under Presidents Eisenhower and Kennedy....The connection isn't fanciful. Over the years, federal and local law enforcement officials have found CIA-trained Cuban exiles at the center of some of this nation's biggest drug rings. They had the clandestine skills, the Latin connections, the political protection and the requisite lack of scruples to become champion traffickers. (p. 134)

In 1965 many of those involved in the Miami JM/WAVE operation were transferred to Laos, where the CIA organized its secret Meo tribe army (Kruger, 1980). CIA offices were set up in Vientiane and Long Tieng, both cities becoming new centers of the heroin trade. During this time, one of the most active heroin laboratories was in Vientiane and was under the direction of Huu Tim Heng, who also built a Pepsi-Cola bottling plant on the outskirts of the city (McCoy, 1972). This plant, however, never bottled a single Pepsi but, rather, served as a front for the purchase of chemicals vital to the processing of heroin. Moreover, one Vang Pao, head of the Meo secret army, was extensively involved in heroin production, operating a heroin plant at Long Tieng, in Laos.

The CIA used the Meo tribespeople to combat leftist Pathet Lao forces in Laos. The only air transport in the area was the CIA's Air America. These planes ensured an adequate food supply to the Meo tribespeople through regular rice drops, thus allowing the Meo to "devote all their energies to opium production" (McCoy, 1972:283). The opium was purchased by Vang Pao's officers and flown to heroin plants in Long Tieng and Vientiane by Air America. Ultimately, the heroin was distributed to GIs in Vietnam and users in the United States. Indeed, syndicate

figures invaded Southeast Asia, helping create the then-major producer and exporter of heroin around the world—the Golden Triangle (Kruger, 1980) (see Figure 14.2). It is estimated that approximately 20 percent of U.S. troops were addicted to heroin during their tour of duty in Vietnam (Stanton, 1976). Moreover, as Bellis (1981) has argued:

> Between 1965 and 1970 the estimated number of active heroin addicts in the United States grew from about 68,000 to some 500,000. Extremely high and rapidly spreading incidence and prevalence were taken as indicators of "epidemic" heroin abuse, which grew to peak rates in American cities between 1969 and 1972. (p. 19)

It has been alleged further by Sheehan (1988) that much of the money generated by this drug trade was laundered through the Nugan Hand Bank. Nugan Hand operated a branch in Chiang Mai, Thailand (in the Golden Triangle), and several of the bank's officials—such as former CIA director William Colby—worked for the U.S. government at one time.

In 1968, "Operation Phoenix" (in Vietnam) was orchestrated by William Colby, who at the time was working for the CIA (Branfman, 1978). Although "Phoenix" was originally formed to incarcerate and assassinate members of the Vietcong—the National Liberation Front—it involved other state terrorist acts, such as the massive roundup, incarceration, murder, and torture of thousands of Vietnamese citizens. Colby, according to Branfman, established "quotas for the number of Vietnamese to be 'neutralized' each month" (p. 113). In the end, over 40,000 enemy civilians were murdered in a 3-year period, 1968–1971, and thousands more tortured (Chomsky and Herman, 1979). This, then, is a clear example of state-organized terror in violation of the U.N. Charter.

By 1972 the U.S. state had moved its covert operations to Chile, once again violating

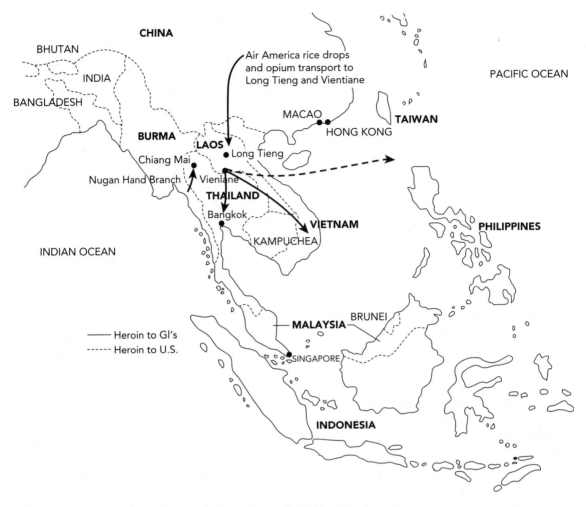

**FIGURE 14.2** CIA–Meo Tribe Rice–Heroin Connection in the Golden Triangle
*Source*: Adapted from McCoy (1972:249–281).

international law by overthrowing the democratically elected socialist, Salvador Allende. In the late 1960s the CIA had worked closely with International Telephone and Telegraph (ITT)—because of ITT's heavy investments in Chile—to prevent Salvador Allende from being elected president; if elected, Allende had pledged to nationalize ITT (Kornbluh, 2003). When this effort failed and Allende was elected in 1970, the CIA, working with the State Department, did all it could to destabilize the Chilean economy

through such practices as reducing U.S. aid to Chile (while increasing aid to the Chilean military); eliminating loans from U.S. banks and encouraging international financial institutions, such as the World Bank, to do the same; cutting supplies of and parts for U.S.-made machinery in Chile; and organizing a worldwide boycott of all Chilean products (Coleman, 2006). In addition to destabilizing its economy, the CIA worked with high officials in the Chilean military to overthrow Allende, which it did in 1973, resulting in the death of President Allende himself. A military dictatorship under the direction of Augusto Pinochet subsequently came to power. Immediately, the nationalization policies of Allende were overthrown, many democratic institutions were dismantled, and repression by the Pinochet regime grew rampant. Between 1973 and 1976, for example, over 100,000 people were detained for political reasons in Chile— over 20,000 of them were eventually killed during incarceration and an even larger number tortured (Herman, 1982). According to Amnesty International's *Report on Torture, 1975–1976,* in Chile under Pinochet:

> The most common forms of physical torture have been prolonged beating (with truncheons, fists, or bags of moist material), electricity to all parts of the body, and burning with cigarettes or acid. Such physical tortures have been accompanied by the deprivation of food, drink, and sleep. More primitive and brutal methods have continued to be used. On 19 December, one prisoner was found dead, his testicles burned off. He had also been subjected to intensive beating and electricity. One day later another prisoner who died from torture had the marks of severe burns on the genital organs. (1976:113)

During Pinochet's active and brutal repression of dissent in Chile, Congress approved George H. W. Bush, in 1976, to head the CIA (Maas, 1986). Under Bush's control, the agency continued its involvement in shady, covert operations, a few of which are as follows (Corn, 1988):

- The CIA secretly provided weapons and money to "our side of the Angolan war," much of the money never reaching the rebels but, rather, pocketed by President Mobutu Sese Seko of Zaire.
- The CIA secretly worked to destabilize the "democratic-socialist" Jamaican government of Michael Manly, spending an estimated

$10 million trying to overthrow the prime minister.

- Bush allegedly met, and kept on the CIA payroll, General Manuel Noriega of Panama, even though the United States had evidence linking Noriega to drug dealing and other criminal activities.

Perhaps most disturbing of all is the CIA's possible connection to "Operation Condor" while Bush was at its helm. In 1976, six Latin American states—Argentina, Bolivia, Brazil, Chile, Paraguay, and Uruguay—"entered into a system for the joint monitoring and assassinating of dissident refugees in member countries" (Herman, 1982:69). The program was encouraged by the CIA and sponsored and organized by Pinochet's secret police, DINA, which provided the initial funding and centralized coordination for the operation. Herman illustrates how Condor initially worked in Uruguay and Argentina:

> Under Operation Condor, political refugees who leave Uruguay and go to Argentina will be identified and kept under surveillance by Argentinean "security" forces, who will inform Uruguayan "security" forces of the presence of these individuals. If the Uruguayan security forces wish to murder these refugees in order to preserve Western values, Argentine forces will cooperate. They will keep the Uruguayans informed of the whereabouts of the refugees; they will allow them to enter and freely move around in Argentina and to take the refugees into custody, torture and murder them; and the Argentineans will then claim no knowledge of these events. (p. 70)

Approximately 30,000 Latin Americans were abducted and subsequently murdered under Operation Condor, a state terrorist transnational program in which the CIA acted as a link in the Condor terrorist chain (McSherry, 2001; Dinges, 2004).

**BOX 14.3** THE IRAN-CONTRA SCANDAL

In February 1979 the U.S. State Department, under President Jimmy Carter, recalled more than half its officials from Nicaragua and suspended all new economic and military aid to that country. In July of that year a revolution occurred in Nicaragua, whereby the dictator Anastasio Somoza was ousted and the Sandinista National Liberation Front (FSLN) assumed power (Black, 1981).

In early March 1981, President Ronald Reagan authorized covert CIA activities against Nicaragua (Oberdorfer and Tyler, 1983). The CIA worked with Argentineans and other governments in Central America to build a paramilitary force against Nicaragua, which became known as the Contras.

Toward the end of 1981, debate in Congress and throughout the country led to widespread criticism and increasing scrutiny of White House intentions in Central America, especially in Nicaragua. By December 21, 1982, Congress was so skeptical that it enacted the first Boland Amendment to the Defense Appropriations Act, terminating the use of any public money for the purpose of toppling or destabilizing the Nicaraguan government (Scheffer, 1987). Nevertheless, the Reagan administration chose to ignore the Boland Amendment by secretly seeking new ways to train and arm the Contras.

One such way was "Operation Elephant Herd" (Emerson, 1988), in which the CIA clandestinely obtained, on September 22, 1983, $12 million worth of military equipment (for deployment against Nicaragua) from the U.S. military. At least forty attacks using Elephant Herd equipment against Nicaraguan targets occurred in 1984, the most well known being on March 7 and consisting of speedboats armed with Bushmaster 25-millimeter cannon-guns firing on and destroying numerous oil facilities and storage tanks at various Nicaraguan ports. Moreover, during this time the CIA also engaged in the mining of Nicaraguan harbors, resulting in the destruction of small fishing boats as well as a Soviet oil tanker (Gutman, 1988:198–199).

In June 1986 the World Court (the United Nations International Court of Justice) ruled that these actions by the U.S. government violated the U.N. Charter. United States aid to the Contras, its support of attacks on Nicaraguan oil installations and ports, and the mining of Nicaragua's harbors constituted, according to the World Court, "force against another state." By organizing and supporting the Contras, the United States had violated Nicaraguan sovereignty, amounting "to an intervention of one state in the internal affairs of another." Finally, the World Court ordered the United States "to cease and to refrain" from violating international law and held further that the United States was obligated to pay reparations to Nicaragua. The United States simply ignored the rulings (Pfost, 1987).

Largely because of the foregoing crimes, in August 1984 Congress enacted a stronger Boland Amendment, which prohibited any administrative agency or entity involved in "intelligence activities" from "supporting, directly or indirectly, military or paramilitary operations in Nicaragua by any nation, group, organization, or individual" (cited in Scheffer, 1987:714). Congress also halted all military aid to the Contras (Gutman, 1988).

The Contras, however, obtained funds in two ways. First, considerable evidence suggests that the Contras were involved from the beginning in the illegal drug trade to support their cause (Marshall, Scott, and Hunter, 1987). In April 1988, for example, Senator John Kerry's Senate Subcommittee on Terrorism, Narcotics, and International Operations began exploring Contra drug ties throughout the 1980s. One year later, the subcommittee—in its report "Drugs, Law Enforcement, and Foreign Policy"—concluded the following: "It is clear that individuals who provided support for the Contras were involved in drug trafficking, the supply network of the Contras was used by drug trafficking organizations, and elements of the Contras themselves knowingly received financial and material assistance from drug traffickers" (U.S. Senate Subcommittee on Terrorism, Narcotics, and International Operations, 1989). Second, Oliver North (NSC liaison to the CIA) worked with others to build a private funding and supply network for the Contras (Ignatius, 1986:D1). One method they used was to sell arms secretly to Iran and then to divert the funds to the Contras.

Most distressing of all, of course, is the fact that as profits were secured in a variety of ways (such as illegally selling arms and drugs), the Contras conducted a campaign of terror. Certain organizations—from Witness for Peace (a religious group that maintained a permanent presence along the Nicaraguan border to monitor Contra-Nicaragua activity) to America's Watch and Amnesty International (two human rights organizations)—have documented atrocities committed by the Contras against Nicaraguan civilians. Moreover, former Assistant Attorney General of the State of New York Reed Brody (1985) headed a fact-finding mission to Nicaragua in 1984 and 1985, which obtained testimony from victims and eyewitnesses of Contra attacks against civilians.

United States foreign policy in Afghanistan during the 1980s contributed to the international terrorist acts of September 11, 2001. In 1979 the Soviet Union invaded Afghanistan to avoid having a fundamentalist Islamic state as its neighbor. The United States responded by covertly supporting the fundamentalist "jihad" against the Soviet occupation. Douglas Kellner (2003:32) summarizes this support:

> During this period, the CIA trained, armed, and financed precisely those Islamic fundamentalist groups who later became part of the Al Qaeda terror network that is now the nemesis of the West, the new "evil empire." In the battle to defeat Soviet Communism in the Cold War, the U.S. poured billions of dollars into Afghanistan to train "freedom fighters" that would overthrow the purportedly communist regime.... The military aid went into training and arming radical Islamic groups who would emerge with a desire to fight other wars for Islam in the countries that had earlier supported them in their jihad against the Soviet-backed regime in Afghanistan. Bin Laden and his Al Qaeda network thus emerge as a Frankenstein of U.S. policy. (p. 32)

Nevertheless, the "secret" support for the Afghan "jihad" against the Soviet occupation was also in part financed through the heroin trade. In the 1970s most of the heroin in the United States, as pointed out, came from the Golden Triangle geographical region. At that time, Afghanistan and northwestern Pakistan were virtually untapped opium areas, and heroin use was practically unknown in these countries (Lamour and Lamberti, 1974; Lifschultz, 1988). However, CIA support for Afghan rebels involved the Golden Crescent region (see Figure 14.3), which became one of the major heroin-producing areas of the world. The CIA arms pipeline from Karachi in the south through Pakistan to the Afghan mujahedeen in the north was "also one of the principal routes for the transport of heroin to Karachi for shipment to Europe and the United States" (Lifschultz, 1988:495). Moreover, a great deal of the poppy crop grew in areas controlled by Afghan rebels or in areas where they had influence (Sciolino, 1988). As Bellis (1981) reported,

> Not surprisingly, the unleashing of this opium flow from Afghanistan coincided perfectly with the arrival of the CIA on the Afghan–Pakistan border—to support and arm the tribes who were both producing opium and fighting the Russian invaders. (p. 86)

According to a General Accounting Office (1988) 1980s status report on drug abuse and drug trade, in the first six months of 1986, of the heroin in the United States, 19 percent came from the Golden Triangle and 40 percent from the Golden Crescent. In other words, as the CIA operations moved from Southeast Asia to Southwest Asia, so, it seems, did the heroin trade. Indeed, by 1995–96, production in Afghanistan had risen to 2,600 tons of raw opium, increasing to 2,800 tons in 1997 (Cooley, 2000).

The defeated Soviet troops left Afghanistan in 1989, and president George H. W. Bush immediately "decided to completely pull out of Afghanistan rather than build democracy and a viable government in that country" (Kellner, 2003:33). The result of that decision was a massive civil war that took place for years in Afghanistan, in which the notorious Taliban emerged as the victors in the mid-1990s. The Taliban, now in political control of Afghanistan, formed an alliance with bin Laden (who had also participated in the anti-Soviet "jihad") and his Al Qaeda group, who in turn "used Afghanistan to form networks that engaged in terrorism throughout the world" (p. 32). For example, in the late 1990s, Al Qaeda bombed two U.S. embassies in Africa—as we mentioned earlier in this chapter—and the Clinton administration responded by shooting missiles into a

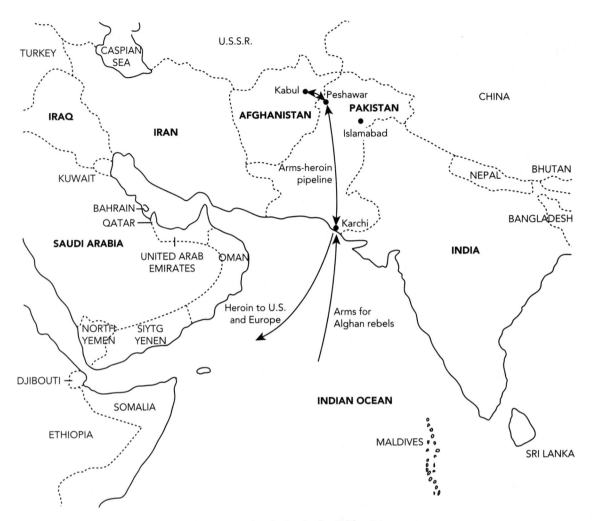

**FIGURE 14.3** Probable CIA-Supported Arms–Heroin Pipeline in the Golden Crescent
*Source*: Adapted from Bellis (1981:86); Lifshultz (1988:495–496); Sciolino (1988:110).

chemical weapons factory (allegedly owned by bin Laden) in the Sudan and Al Qaeda training camps in Afghanistan. However, it turned out that the camps had long ago been deserted and that the chemical factory was actually a legitimate pharmaceutical plant. Indeed, this pharmaceutical plant provided approximately 90 percent of Sudan's pharmaceutical products, resulting in literally "tens of thousands" of people—many of them children—suffering and dying from malaria, tuberculosis, and other treatable diseases (Chomsky, 2003).

Once it was determined that Osama bin Laden and Al Qaeda were behind the September 11, 2001, international terrorist attacks, on October 7, 2001, the U.S. state launched a ferocious air assault on an almost defenseless Afghanistan. Although the Taliban was an extremely repressive "government," especially toward women and girls, this state terrorist attack led to a "wholesale panic amongst residents of villages and cities" as well as the large-scale killing of civilians (Jones, 2004). It is estimated that as many as 3,600 civilian deaths occurred in the first two and a half months of the U.S. air campaign against Afghanistan, a figure higher than all the civilians killed in the September 11 attacks (Mahajan, 2002).

Moreover, a large number of Al Qaeda and Taliban fighters escaped capture, including Osama bin Laden, yet U.S. state officials decided to detain over 500 of those captured in a makeshift prison at the U.S. military base at Guantanamo Bay, Cuba. Labeled as "enemy combatants," those detained continue to be held without any formal charges filed against them, and they are being detained indefinitely without access to a lawyer. The detainees have also suffered torture and other cruel, inhuman, and degrading treatment, such as the use of painful stress positions, extended solitary confinement, use of military dogs as a threat, and prolonged exposure to extremes of heat, cold, and noise (Human Rights Watch, 2005a).

Although Afghans approved a new constitution in January 2004 and elected Hamid Karzai to a five-year term as president in October 2004 (Karzai was reelected in 2009), warlords and armed factions, including remaining Taliban forces, dominate most of the country and routinely abuse human rights (Human Rights Watch, 2005b). As Human Rights Watch points out in its report on Afghanistan:

> Political repression, human rights abuses, and criminal activity by warlords—the leaders of militias and remnants of past Afghan military forces, who were brought to power with the assistance of the United States after the Taliban's defeat—are consistently listed as the chief concerns of most Afghans....Local military and police forces, even in Kabul, have been involved in arbitrary arrests, kidnapping, extortion, torture, and extrajudi-

cial killings of criminal suspects. Outside Kabul, commanders and their troops in many areas have been implicated in widespread rape of women, girls, and boys, murder, illegal detention, forced displacement, and other specific abuses against women and children, including human trafficking and forced marriage....U.S. and coalition forces, active in Afghanistan under Operation Enduring Freedom since November 2001, continue to arbitrarily detain civilians, use excessive force during arrests of noncombatants, and mistreat detainees. (pp. 1, 3)

Moreover, in April 2009 a new law was established in Afghanistan that regulates marriage, divorce, and inheritance for the country's Shia population, requiring women to ask permission to leave the house except for urgent business, a duty to "make herself up" or "dress up" for her husband when demanded, and a duty not to refuse sex when her husband wants it, thereby legalizing wife rape (Human Rights Watch, 2009).

Finally, the Afghan drug economy continues to flourish. Afghanistan was the largest worldwide producer of opium in 2004, and opium cultivation in that year increased by two-thirds from the amount cultivated in 2003, resulting in an output of 4,200 tons (UNICEF, 2004). By 2008, Afghanistan remained the world leader in opium production, increasing its output to 7,700 tons (United Nations, 2008a).

In 1979 Saddam Hussein became president of Iraq and the Ayatollah Khomeini returned as the leader of Iran. Tensions arose between the Iranian Islamic republic and the secular nationalist Iraq. In mid-September 1980, Iraq attacked Iran, and the two countries remained at war until 1988. The U.S. state supported Iraq in its war efforts (although see Box 14.3) through loan programs with financing as well as intelligence information and military hardware. This support took place even though the U.S. state had solid evidence indicating Iraq was using chemical weapons "almost daily" against Iranian forces (Battle, 2003). In 1983 and 1984 Donald Rumsfeld headed a presidential envoy to the Middle East, meeting with Saddam Hussein on both occasions, yet during these meetings he never made any reference to Hussein about Iraq's chemical weapon use. Instead, military equipment was exported to Iraq, such as Bell helicopters (which subsequently were used to spray mustard gas on the Kurds), as well as dual-use equipment in the fabrication of missiles and enhancing Iraq's nuclear, bacteriological, and chemical war capabilities (Battle, 2003; Gareau, 2004).

Although publicly the U.S. state condemned Iraq's use of chemical weapons, it made no actual diplomatic attempt to stop that use, nor did it seem at all concerned about Iraq's repressive internal policies. Indeed, the U.S. state supported a regime in which terror was a systematic part of state policy. In its 1985 report on torture, for example, Amnesty International listed thirty types of torture used in Iraq, including beatings, burning, electric shock, and mutilation, and U.S.-based corporations sold Iraq chemicals used in producing mustard gas, Sarin, and other toxic chemical agents (Gareau, 2004). As Frederick Gareau (2004) describes Hussein's terror:

> His victims were tortured, killed, and their bodies were either returned to their families or put on public display. Either method of exposure was intended to strike terror in the target audience.... [T]he Iraq air force dropped 13,000 chemical bombs on its victims in the period from 1983 to 1988. (pp. 175, 177)

In addition, Hussein was ruthless toward the Shiites and the Kurds—a ruthlessness that escalated during U.S. state support for this terrorist regime. Some 300,000 Shiites were forced out of Iraq to become exiles in Iran and other countries, and approximately 250 Kurdish cities were gassed, killing approximately 7,000 and injuring as many as 20,000.

President George H. W. Bush signed National Security Directive 26 on October 26, 1989, affirming that the goal of U.S. foreign policy was to achieve normal relations with Iraq (Gareau, 2004). This relationship changed when on August 2, 1990, Iraq invaded and occupied Kuwait. Four days later the U.N. Security Council imposed comprehensive economic sanctions banning all trade with Iraq, and the U.N. eventually authorized the use of "all necessary means" to reverse the occupation. Subsequently, in January 1991, the U.S. state launched a bombing campaign against Iraq, targeting specifically civilian infrastructure, such as electrical plants, water treatment facilities, factories, roads, bridges, and telecommunications. The United States and its coalition forces dropped 84,200 tons of munitions on Iraq during 43 days of bombing, killing 110,000 civilians, including 70,000 children under the age of 5 and 7,000 elderly (Center for Economic and Social Rights, 2003). In addition, the comprehensive economic sanctions and embargo—sustained by a massive U.S. military presence in the Middle East—resulted in over 500,000 excess child deaths between 1991 and 1998 (UNICEF, 1999a; Halliday, 2004). Indeed, former U.N. Assistant Secretary General Denis Halliday (2004) stated that although the invasion and occupation of Kuwait by Iraq was illegal under the U.N. Charter, so too was the bombing of civilians and civilian infrastructure by the United States as well as the economic sanctions and embargo: "There is no possible justification for the murder of Iraqi children and adults, innocent of that invasion, by the United States, United Kingdom, and other powers simply because they cannot punish the leadership of Iraq. That is morally and legally unacceptable on all counts" (p. 268).

In April 1991 a cease-fire resolution included Iraq's complete withdrawal from Kuwait and an acknowledgment from Iraq that it would eliminate all weapons of mass destruction in its possession. From 1991 to 1998 and again in 2002, U.N. weapons inspection teams carefully monitored Iraq's elimination progress. Nevertheless, on March 19, 2003, the U.S. state once again invaded Iraq, allegedly because that country illegally continued to possess weapons of mass destruction and maintain a historical, and therefore dangerous, relationship with the terrorist organization Al Qaeda. These weapons, according to the U.S. state argument, could easily be made available by Saddam Hussein to Al Qaeda for use against the United States.

However, despite considerable effort by weapons inspectors prior to the invasion, no weapons of mass destruction were ever found in Iraq and no credible evidence existed indicating a link between Hussein and Al Qaeda (Clarke, 2004). Indeed, launching a massive invasion to overthrow a government and occupy its territory in response to an uncorroborated imminent threat—which also lacked U.N. Security Council authorization to invade—constitutes a serious violation of the U.N. Charter. In 1946 the International Tribunal at Nuremburg had concluded that Germany's invasion and occupation of Norway and Denmark—allegedly in self-defense to prevent future Allied invasions—actually violated international law and therefore constituted a war of aggression (Center for Economic and Social Rights, 2003). As the Tribunal stated in its decision:

> To initiate a war of aggression, therefore, is not only an international crime; it is *the supreme international crime*, differing only from other war crimes in that it contains within itself the accumulated evil of the whole. (p. 7)

The *invasion* of Iraq in 2003 was illegal under the U.N. Charter, and by 2009, it is estimated, 100,000 Iraqi civilians as well as over 4,000 U.S. soldiers, were the victims of the most recent *supreme international crime*. The *occupation* of Iraq by the U.S. military also violates international law. In addition to initiating a war of aggression, the Bush administration violated domestic and international law during this war through the torture of prisoners, summary execution and willful killing of civilians, and spying on U.S. citizens (Cohn, 2007). Moreover, according to the Geneva Conventions, an occupying power must quickly end its occupation (an occupation is always a temporary status), but in the interim it must (1) protect civilians and their property, (2) ensure the well-being of the occupied population, and (3) refrain from changing the country's legal and economic system. The U.S. state has systematically violated each of these. The following are a few examples (Center for Economic and Social Rights, 2004; Cohn, 2007).

- **Failure to provide public order and safety.** The United States allowed the wholesale looting of Iraq's public, religious, cultural, and civilian institutions and properties. The United States also created a climate of unbridled lawlessness by dismissing the entire army and security and law enforcement personnel without a backup plan to maintain public safety—predictably resulting in a sharp increase in violent crime, especially directed against women.
- **Unlawful attacks.** United States forces have routinely conducted indiscriminate attacks in populated areas of Iraq, causing widespread and unnecessary civilian casualties. Ambulances, medical staff, and facilities have been targeted by snipers and regular forces.
- **Unlawful detention and torture.** It is regular policy for U.S. forces indiscriminately to arrest and detain Iraqi civilians without charge or due process. Up to 90 percent of the Iraqis detained under the occupation are innocent bystanders swept up in illegal mass arrests. The much-publicized torture, rape, and murder of detainees—at Abu Ghraib prison, for example—is a systematic practice in U.S.

prisons throughout Iraq, the result of decisions made at the highest levels of the Bush administration.

- **Failure to protect the rights to health and life.** The United States is not ensuring access to health care and not preventing the spread of contagious disease. The health infrastructure is in disrepair, unsanitary conditions are widespread even in hospitals, drugs and medical supplies are in short supply, clean water

and sanitation are largely unavailable, and medical staff report disease outbreaks and increased mortality throughout the country.

- **Self-interested privatization.** The Coalitional Provisional Authority, under the direction of the United States, has issued a number of executive orders that aim to privatize Iraq's economy for the benefit of U.S. corporations, with little consideration for the welfare and rights of the Iraqi people.

---

**BOX 14.4   TORTURE, U.S. STYLE**

In 1948, the delegates to the United Nations, led by former first lady Eleanor Roosevelt, adopted the *Universal Declaration of Human Rights*, which specified that "no one shall be subjected to torture or to cruel, inhuman, or degrading treatment." This declaration became the foundation for the four antitorture Geneva Conventions, which the United States ratified in 1955. The first two conventions protect sick and wounded soldiers and sailors during war; the third defines who is a prisoner of war and establishes minimum standards for their treatment; the fourth protects civilians during time of war. Common Article 3 ("common" because it appears in all four conventions) describes minimal protections for noncombatants as well as for combatants who currently are "out of the fight" due to wounds, detention, etc. by proclaiming that such individuals "shall in all circumstances be treated humanly," including prohibitions of "cruel treatment and torture" and "outrages upon personal dignity, in particular, humiliating and degrading treatment." In essence, the Geneva Conventions outlawed torture as a violation of humanitarian international law.

Despite the foregoing conventions, in his important book *A Question of Torture*, Alfred McCoy (2006) documents how the CIA has been involved in torture since its inception in 1947. Initially, the CIA's torture programs were based on techniques developed during Hitler's rule in Germany and Stalin's rule in the Soviet Union. The CIA adopted from these regimes a variety of psychological torture methods, in which the MKUltra program of using LSD on unsuspecting individuals is the most notorious. McCoy goes on to document how the CIA additionally outsourced many torture methods to numerous Third World countries. From Uruguay to Vietnam to the Phil-

ippines, the CIA trained police forces and army personnel in a whole variety of psychological and physical torture methods. Such methods included abusing Filipino priests and "implanting tiny electrodes" in the brains of Vietcong prisoners (during the Vietnam War). In the latter, one purpose of the implants was for the CIA to use radio frequencies to cause the Vietcong prisoners to defecate or vomit suddenly. Yet, following a week of repeated failures in obtaining usable intelligence information, the "prisoners were shot by Green Beret troops and their bodies burned" (p. 66) (see Section 1.3 for information on the CIA's most recent form of outsourcing, "extraordinary rendition").

In addition to this long, 50-year history of CIA involvement in violations of the Geneva Conventions, the issue of torture became a public concern during President George W. Bush's alleged "global war on terror." The following is a "torture timeline" related to that administration's support for one technique that has long been regarded as a violation of international law as a form of torture, *waterboarding*, or immobilizing the detainee in an inclined position and then pouring water over the breathing passages so as to induce an experience of drowning through a gag reflex (Lowrey, 2009):

- **February 7, 2002:** President Bush issues an executive order denying Taliban and Al Qaeda detainees the protections afforded under the Geneva Conventions.
- **March 28, 2002:** The CIA and Pakistani intelligence service capture Abu Zubayda, a top Al Qaeda operative.
- **July 26, 2002:** Attorney General John Ashcroft concludes that waterboarding is lawful, allowing the CIA to use the technique on Zubayda.

- **August 1, 2002:** Jay Bybee, then head of the White House Office of Legal Council, sends a memo to the CIA stating that ten escalating techniques, leading to waterboarding, do not constitute torture and may be used. Bybee also concludes that acts that result in pain equivalent to "organ failure, impairment or bodily function, or even death," constitute torture; all lesser abuse is legal.
- **August, 2002:** During this month, Zubayda is waterboarded more than eighty times.
- **March 1, 2003:** United States and Pakistani forces capture Khalid Sheikh Mohammed, a top Al Qaeda operative.
- **March, 2003:** During this month, Mohammed is waterboarded 183 times.

The foregoing timeline is part of a long, worldwide history of government (including the United States) involvement in torture, in which five intertwined aspects of its perversity emerges (McCoy, 2006:13–14):

1. Torture releases a human capacity for cruelty as well as seductive illusions of omnipotence.
2. States that sanction torture often allow it to spread beyond a few selected targets to countless suspected enemies.
3. Torture offers an appearance of efficient information extraction so that perpetrators remain wedded to its use, refusing to acknowledge evidence of its limited utility and high political cost.
4. Torturers are rarely prosecuted for their crimes because they manipulate government structures with impunity.
5. States that sanction torture in defiance of their democratic principles pay a terrible price, by compromising their majesty and corrupting their integrity.

---

## THE STATE, TERRORISM, AND GLOBALIZATION

**Transnational political crimes** by the state must be understood in terms of their global context. Globalization is of course the process whereby individuals, peoples, economies, and states are increasingly interconnected and interdependent. One of the most important aspects of globalization, as we pointed out in Chapter 13, is the movement of capital that results from transnational corporations' search for profit in the expanding global economic market.

However, some scholars of globalization argue that transnational corporations are not simply an "important aspect" but actually have now supplanted the state as the major actor in the world. For example, Strange (1996) argues that "the impersonal forces of world markets" have now become "more powerful than the states to whom ultimate political authority over society and economy is supposed to belong" (p. 4). And Ohmae (1995) similarly put forth the position that we now live in a "borderless world" in which transnational capital is much more powerful than individual states. David Held and colleagues (1999) have described this conceptualization of globalization as "the hyperglobalist thesis" in which these scholars share the belief that:

[G]lobalization is primarily an economic phenomenon; that an increasingly integrated global economy exists today; that the needs of global capital impose a neoliberal economic discipline on all governments such that politics is no longer the "art of the possible" but rather the practice of "sound economic management." . . . [T]he authority and legitimacy of the nation-state are challenged: National governments become increasingly unable either to control what transpires within their borders or to fulfill by themselves the demands of their own citizens. (pp. 4–5)

In short, state managers around the globe are allegedly finding that their control and power have declined in significance and influence.

Although we recognize the increasing power of transnational corporations in fashioning the "global village," we believe that the U.S. state has not decreased—but, rather, has increased—its power on a global scale. In fact, one of the most significant driving forces of globalization has been the collapse of communism in the former Soviet Union (now Russia) and in countries previously under its sphere of influence (such as Poland, Hungary, and the Czech Republic). The result has been a lessening of East–West political and economic differences as well as a conceding of sole superpower status to the United States. To be sure, with this new global standing the door was opened wide for U.S. state managers to exercise dominance around the globe. Thus, Ronald Steel (2004) describes the contemporary U.S. state as one of the most powerful—if not the most powerful—empires the world has ever seen:

> A nation possessing this kind of power—the world's dominant economy, the currency with which the world reckons and pays its bills, the most powerful armed force with bases around the globe and a budget that nearly exceeds that of all other nations combined, and a messianic desire to spread its ideology and to mold the lives and minds of the rest of the world in its image—is by honest reckoning an imperial state. (p. 29)

This is "globalization from above" (Kellner, 2003) at its most powerful, in which the current U.S. state maintains worldwide hegemony and virtually no states have the ability to challenge that global domination. A defining feature of sole-superpower status is a unilateral militarism by which the U.S. state simply *shuns* international law and *overtly* engages in state terrorism. Kramer and Michalowski (2004) use the invasion and occupation of Iraq as an example of this unique historical phenomenon:

> The invasion and occupation of Iraq by the United States and its allies is a violation of international law, and as such constitutes state crime. It is a state crime, however, over which there is no effective social control, and for which there is no like-

lihood of formal sanction. As the most militarily and economically powerful nation in the world system, it appears that the United States and its leaders can, if they choose, violate international law with relative impunity. (p. 36)

But in addition to this negative aspect of "globalization from above" there is a negative aspect of "globalization from below." We noted one positive expression of "globalization from below" in our discussion of the antiglobalization movement and its struggle to minimize the devastating effects of globalization from above. However, not only has the antiglobalization movement emerged as a form of globalization from below, but international terrorist groups such as Al Qaeda have intensified their attacks and made use of globalization to do so (Kellner, 2003). Just as advanced forms of technology—such as airplanes—can be used to move people and goods quickly around the globe for transnational corporations, they can also be turned into weapons of mass terror and destruction. Indeed, globalization makes possible

> global terror networks as well as networks of commerce and communication. The circulation of commodities, technologies, ideas, money, and people can facilitate networks of terror, as well as trade and travel. The Internet makes possible the spreading of hate and fear, as well as knowledge and culture. Computers can be an integral part of a terror network just as they are part of businesses everywhere and many of our own everyday lives. And biotechnology, which promises such extravagant medical advances and miracles, can provide weapons of mass destruction as well. (p. 43)

Thus, the negative aspects of globalization from above has generated both types of globalization from below—antiglobalization movements and international terrorism—and both have made use of globalization to fashion their unique responses.

## REVIEW

This chapter examined the nature, extent, types, and costs of political crime in the United States in terms of (1) political crimes against the state (violations of the law for the purpose of modifying or changing social conditions), (2) domestic political crimes by the state (violations of the law by state officials and/or agencies whose victimization occurs *inside* the United States), and (3) transnational political crimes by the state (violations of domestic and international law by state officials and/or agencies whose victimization occurs *outside* the United States).

## POLITICAL CRIMES AGAINST THE STATE

1. Political crimes against the state involve intentional violations of criminal law for political purposes as well as various acts criminalized by the state for the purpose of curbing political dissent.
2. Political crimes against the state may be violent or nonviolent.
3. From the Revolutionary War onward, various groups in the United States have used violence in an attempt to modify or change the social order.
4. Historically, various groups in the United States also have been engaged in such nonviolent actions as civil disobedience and demonstrations, involvement that sometimes results in their criminalization.
5. Three types of terrorism have historically been directed at the state: political assassination, domestic terrorism, and international terrorism.

## DOMESTIC POLITICAL CRIMES BY THE STATE

1. Domestic political crimes by the state are violations of law by state officials and/or agencies whose victimization occurs inside the boundaries of the United States.
2. Two major types of domestic political crimes by the state are corruption (political bribery, election fraud, and corrupt campaign practices) and political repression (illegal repression of dissent).

## TRANSNATIONAL POLITICAL CRIMES BY THE STATE

1. Transnational political crimes by the state are violations of domestic and international law by state officials and/or agencies whose victimization occurs outside the boundaries of the United States.
2. Historically, both the CIA and the NSC have been involved in transnational political crimes—including sabotage, assassinations, and state terrorism (including torture).

## QUESTIONS FOR CLASS DISCUSSION

1. Should the concept of political crime encompass both crimes *against* the state and crimes *by* the state? Why?

2. Explain the difference between violent and nonviolent political crimes against the state. Discuss why you believe the state may be interested in criminalizing each.

3. Choose two examples from the category of domestic political crime by the state and explain why you think they occur in U.S. society.

4. Discuss some additional ways globalization may facilitate political crime.

5. Do you consider the wars against Afghanistan and Iraq as political crimes? Thoroughly explain your answer.

6. What is torture, and is it ever justified?

## FOR FURTHER STUDY

### READINGS

Cohn, Marjorie. 2007. *Cowboy Republic: Six Ways the Bush Gang Has Defied the Law.* Sausalito, CA: PoliPoint Press.

McCoy, Alfred. 2006. *A Question of Torture: CIA Interrogation, From the Cold War to the War on Terror.* New York: Metropolitan Books.

Miller, Mark Crispin, ed. 2008. *Loser Take All: Election Fraud and the Subversion of Democracy, 2000–2008.* Brooklyn, NY: IG Publishing.

Parenti, Michael. 2008. *Democracy for the Few.* Belmont, CA: Wadsworth.

Simon, David R. 2008. *Elite Deviance.* Boston: Allyn & Bacon.

### WEBSITES

1. <http://www.whoisleonardpeltier.info/>: This site updates readers on Leonard Peltier's case. It also offers links to e-mail discussion groups and to the FBI files on Peltier.

2. <http://www.actupny.org>: From ACT UP! AIDS Coalition to Unleash Power, this site provides some basic information regarding the tactics and philosophy of nonviolent civil disobedience. Readers can learn about the typical scenario after arrests have been made and the many ways to practice nonviolent protest.

3. <http://www.cesr.org>: This is the site of the Center for Economic and Social Rights, which was established to promote social justice through human rights. It has a wealth of information on violations of human rights around the world.

4. <http://www.oldamericancentury.org/bushco/bush_crime_family.htm>: This site for the Project for an Old American Century offers a history of possible crimes committed by the Bush family.

5. <http://ccrjustice.org>: This is the site for the Center for Constitutional Rights, an organization dedicated to advancing and protecting the rights guaranteed by the U.S. Constitution and the Universal Declaration of Human Rights.

# GLOSSARY

## A

**ABOLITIONISM** A movement and theory whose aim is the abolition of most coercive state institutions of social control (e.g., prisons, police, the death penalty) because they are inherently repressive and harmful.

**AGE** The length of time for which a human has existed. Economic benefits, social privileges, and political power are often based on age.

**AGGRAVATED ASSAULT** An unlawful attack by one person on another for the purpose of inflicting severe or aggravated bodily injury.

**AMERICAN EXCEPTIONALISM** A term that refers to the fact that among technologically developed societies the United States has by far the highest rates of homicide and incarceration.

**ANALOGOUS SOCIAL INJURIES** Legally permissible and preventable acts or conditions caused by individuals or social institutions where consequences are similar to those of illegal acts.

**ANARCHISM** A multifaceted social movement united on the need to abolish the state. Nowadays, anarchist theory is most likely to inspire leftist globalization protesters and environmentalists. Also an influence on cultural criminology.

**ANIMAL ABUSE** Any act that contributes to the physical, psychological, or emotional pain, suffering, or death of an animal or that otherwise threatens its welfare. The act may involve active maltreatment or passive neglect or omission, and it may be direct or indirect, intentional or unintentional.

**ANIMAL SEXUAL ASSAULT** Our preferred term for *bestiality*. Has various forms: zoophilia, adolescent sexual experimentation, aggravated assault, and commodification.

**ANOMIE** A condition of normlessness; a breakdown in the social order. A concept favored by Merton in his explanation of the high rate of crime and deviance in the United States.

**ARMED ROBBERY** The display of a deadly weapon to carry out a robbery.

**ARSON** The willful or malicious burning of a house, public building, motor vehicle, aircraft, or other property of another.

**AUTOMOBILE THEFT** The unlawful taking of, or the attempt to take, an automobile.

## B

**BATTERING** Slapping, shoving, pushing, and other violent acts that result in injury to the victim; it typically occurs for years.

**BORN CRIMINAL** Cesare Lombroso's theory that physical attributes are associated with, or even cause, criminal behavior.

**BRIBERY** The giving of money or property to state officials in return for favors.

**BURGLARY** The unlawful entry into a house, business, or other structure with the intent to commit a felony.

**C**

**CARJACKING**   The use of direct physical force to steal a motor vehicle from a driver.

**CHECK FRAUD**   Deliberate deception for personal gain by the use of a counterfeit or forged check.

**CHICAGO SCHOOL OF CRIMINOLOGY**   Part of the post-Progressive Era social science movement that evolved in Chicago between 1915 and the early 1940s.

**CHILD ABUSE**   Intentional acts of a parent, relative, or guardian that result, or are likely to result, in physical, mental, or emotional injury or impairment of a child. Child abuse has four forms: physical abuse, sexual abuse, emotional abuse, and child neglect.

**CIVIL DISOBEDIENCE**   A nonviolent action against the state or a refusal to obey certain laws considered unjust.

**CLASS STRUCTURE**   The more or less rigid social relationships that are associated with inequalities in wealth, income, occupation and other key economic aspects of life.

**CLASSICAL CRIMINOLOGY**   A criminology based on both free will and determinism and whose chief aim was to deter crime. It was part of the humanist reaction during the Enlightenment to the barbarities and inequities characteristic of feudal systems of justice. It was popularized by Cesare Beccaria and Jeremy Bentham.

**COLLECTIVE EMBEZZLEMENT**   Theft of funds from a savings and loan institution for personal gain, at the expense of the institution and with the approval of management.

**COMMUNISM**   A theory advocating the elimination of private property. Its proponents believe that with the abolition of private property and with the disappearance of the state, crime will almost disappear under communism.

**COMPARATIVE CRIMINOLOGY**   The systematic comparison of crime in two or more cultures.

**CONCEPTS**   Ideas that describe a property of an empirical datum or a relation among empirical data. They are usually a smaller part of a theory that is used to generate hypotheses.

**CONDUCT NORMS**   Rules of behavior that embody the values of some powerful group in society.

**CONFLICT THEORY**   An ancient theory that, when used in criminology, suggests that crime, criminalization, and criminal law must be seen in the overriding context of social, economic, and political inequality.

**CONFORMITY**   The most common (i.e., nondeviant and noncriminal) response in Robert Merton's typology of responses to frustrated opportunities.

**CONSENSUS THEORY**   Often juxtaposed with conflict theory to suggest that most people hold certain key values in common and that social structures are based on it.

**CONSTITUTIVE CRIMINOLOGY**   The most thoroughgoing postmodern perspective in criminology; a political perspective that seeks to lay bare the rhetoric and mystification that enters public discourse about crime.

**CONTAINMENT THEORY**   A theory suggesting that variation in the crime rates of different social groups is caused by variations in the ability to contain norm-violating behavior in the face of social change and cultural conflict.

**CONTROL BALANCE**   A theory claiming that the amount of control to which an individual is subject, relative to the amount of control he or she can exercise, determines the probability that deviance will occur as well as the likely type of deviance.

**CONTROL DEFICIT**   In Tittle's theory of control balance, if one is subject to control more than one controls, one has a control deficit.

**CONTROL SURPLUS**   In Tittle's theory of control balance, if one controls more than one is subject to control, one has a control surplus.

**CONTROL THEORY**   A theory arguing that to find the factors leading to delinquency one must look for the causes of conformity; delinquency turns out to be merely an absence of the causes of conformity.

**CONVICT CRIMINOLOGY**   A critical humanist theory advanced by ex-prisoners who claim that only they can fully understand the oppression and misery of prison life.

**CORPORATE CRIMES**   Illegal or socially injurious acts of intent or indifference that are committed in order to further corporate goals and that physically and/ or economically harm individuals in the United States and/or abroad.

**CORPORATE THEFT**   Type of theft, differing from other forms of theft in that it does not entail face-to-face confrontation, it is not always readily apparent that a theft has occurred, and it serves the interest of the corporation.

**CORPORATE VIOLENCE** Acts of violence committed by corporations against workers, consumers, or the public.

**CORRUPT CAMPAIGN PRACTICES** Various forms of illegal or unethical behaviors used to obtain political office, ultimately for the purpose of influencing state policy.

**CREDIT-CARD FRAUD** The use of stolen or fraudulent credit cards to purchase goods.

**CRIME** In criminal law, crime is an action or omission that is prohibited by law, that is voluntary, and that coincides with a defendant's mental state. This book uses an eclectic and more sociological approach to crime, however; we view crime as a dynamic outcome of the relationship between the state and the social relations embedded in gender, race, age, and class. Crime can be seen as a violation of conduct norms, as a social harm, as a violation of human and animal rights, and as a form of deviance.

**CRIME RATE** The prevalence of crime relative to the size of a population.

**CRIMINAL BIOGRAPHIES** Usually recorded by ethnographers, these are life-course data which document criminals' own personal accounts of their activities.

**CRIMINAL JUSTICE SYSTEM** The legally defined, authoritative system of surveillance, detection, policing, prosecution, and punishment of those who have committed crimes (and sometimes those who have not).

**CRIMINAL LAW** Rules enacted by legislatures or that result from judicial decisions that protect members of the public from state definitions of wrongdoing.

**CRIMINALIZATION** The process whereby criminal law is selectively applied to social behavior. It involves the enactment of legislation that outlaws certain types of behavior and provides for surveillance and policing of that behavior and, if the behavior is detected, for punishment.

**CULTURAL CRIMINOLOGY** Explores the political relationship between the constructions of meaning and the criminalization process, often with the aid of ethnographic material.

**CULTURAL RELATIVISM** The philosophical and sociological claim that beliefs and practices in one culture may translate only roughly or not at all, into those of another culture.

**D**

**DANGEROUS CLASSES** A derogatory nineteenth-century term applied by law-abiding citizens to describe those members of the working classes, the unemployed, and the unemployable who seemed to pose a threat to law and order.

**DECEPTIVE ADVERTISING** Applied to advertisements that are misleading in a material respect; advertisers can make false statements as long as they are not deceptive.

**DECRIMINALIZATION** The removal of criminal prohibitions for certain behaviors while still regulating them.

**DETERRENCE THEORY** Based on the image of criminals as rational, calculating actors, this theory looks for ways to persuade potential criminals to desist from their illegalities.

**DEVIANCE** Any social behavior or social characteristic that departs from the conventional norms and standards of a community or society and for which the deviant is sanctioned.

**DEVIANCE AMPLIFICATION** The process whereby agencies of social control (e.g., the police) and the mass media create deviance.

**DIFFERENTIAL ASSOCIATION** A theory that attempts to explain both the process by which a person learns to engage in crime and the content of what is learned.

**DRIFT** The lack of commitment to either the subculture of delinquency or conventional culture.

**DUMPING** A form of transnational corporate crime in which firms sell to other countries certain hazardous products banned or not approved for sale in the United States.

**E**

**ELDER ABUSE** Physical, sexual, and/or emotional abuse, as well as neglect, of elders. It is different from child abuse in that it also includes financial and/or material exploitation.

**ELECTION FRAUD** A form of state corruption that includes illegal voting, false voter registration, and stuffing ballot boxes.

**EMBEZZLEMENT** The taking of money from the workplace for one's personal use.

**EMPLOYEE THEFT** Stealing merchandise or job-related items from the workplace.

**ENLIGHTENMENT** A philosophical and humanist eighteenth-century movement professing that reason and experience, rather than faith and superstition, must replace the excesses and corruption of feudal societies. It opposed cruel and inhumane punishments and challenged the prevailing views of the time concerning the relation between crime and punishment.

**EPISTEMOLOGICAL RELATIVISM** The extraordinary claim that one can understand another culture only through the prism of one's own culturally determined system of values.

**ETHNOCENTRISM** The view that concepts and generalizations about one's own society necessarily apply to crime in other societies.

**EUGENICS** The "science" of good genes and the basis of the eugenics movement (c. 1870– 1930), which argued that the socially useful citizens should be encouraged to have children and that the socially and medically unfit should be isolated or forcibly prevented from breeding.

**F**

**FEAR OF CRIME** A type of fear that has numerous forms and originates in the complex relationships among the media, crime itself, various sociological and psychological dimensions of people's lives, and modern-day anxieties.

**FEMINISM** A critical perspective that maintains that women are discriminated against because of their gender and that seeks to use social change to end women's resulting subordination.

**FENCING** Buying, selling, or dealing in stolen goods.

**FINANCIAL FRAUD** A form of fraud that serves the interests of the corporation.

**G**

**GENDER** Historically and culturally developed patterns of behavior resulting from relationships between males/males, females/females, and males/females.

**GENERAL THEORY** A theory that is constructed according to the logic of the natural sciences and that seeks at once to be both as simple and as general as possible.

**GLOBAL CONDUCT NORMS** Rules of conduct, agreed on by the international community, that allow for prosecution of certain coercive relationships between a state and its citizenry and between one state and another.

**GLOBALIZATION** The worldwide process whereby individuals, peoples, economies, and states are becoming increasingly interconnected and interdependent.

**GREEN CRIMINOLOGY** The study of crimes, harms, and abuses committed by humans against the environment, against nature, and against nonhuman animals.

**H**

**HATE CRIMES** Violence committed against people because of their race, ethnicity, disability, religion, or sexual orientation.

**HISTORICAL DATA** Information about crime rates, criminals and control agencies, for example, which are derived from official statistics (on crime, prison populations, health, and so on), court records, books, newspapers, journals, pamphlets, plays, and oral histories.

**HUMAN RIGHTS** Natural and inalienable rights accorded to all human beings, such as the right to life, liberty, and happiness. They may also include rights essential to a dignified human existence, such as freedom of movement, free speech, a good education, employment, and so on.

**I, J**

**IDENTITY THEFT** Adopting another person's identity, usually to facilitate further crime.

**IDEOLOGY** Any set of structured beliefs, values, and ideas that can at once reflect social reality and distort it.

**IMITATION** Gabriel Tarde's idea that crime is influenced by the processes of imitation and that thereby people are socialized into criminality.

**INDIVIDUAL/GROUP TERRORISM** Terrorism that occurs when individuals or groups who are not necessarily supported by a state engage in political assassination and/or domestic and international terrorist acts.

**INCOME-TAX FRAUD** Cheating on one's income tax by, for example, underreporting wages.

**INNOVATION** One of the four deviant or criminal responses in Robert Merton's typology of responses to frustrated opportunities.

**INSIDER TRADING** Using information unavailable to the public to gain an advantage over others in the buying and selling of stock.

**INSTITUTIONAL ANOMIE THEORY** An extension of Mertonian anomie theory which applies it to the macro level of social organization.

**INSTITUTIONALIZED MEANS** Social regulations, controls, and procedures for moving toward and achieving goals and values.

**INTEGRATED THEORY** A theory that combines some of the assumptions and propositions of two or more other theories into an explanatory framework with a broader scope.

**INTERNATIONAL LAW** Various treaties, agreements, customary law principles, and general legal principles that serve to judge the actions and behavior of nation-states assenting to them.

**INTERPERSONAL COERCION** A woman's having sex with her husband or employer in the face of nonviolent threats.

**K, L**

**LABELING PERSPECTIVE** A perspective suggesting that crime and deviance exist in the eye of the beholder.

**LARCENY** The unlawful taking of property from the possession of someone other than one's employer.

**LEFT IDEALISM** A type of critical criminology that focuses almost exclusively on the harms of the ruling class and that ignores the development of a coherent program for curbing conventional crime.

**LEFT REALISM** The view that conventional crime is driven by relative deprivation and by reactionary and individualistic attitudes.

**LEGALIZATION** Complete removal of all criminal sanctions for certain behaviors, without subsequent regulation.

**LIBERAL FEMINISM** The view that women's subordinate status in society stems from socialization processes and from unequal opportunities and rights for women.

**LIFE-COURSE DATA** Data about patterns of crime collected and interpreted over the course of offenders' lives, including official crime data, self-reports, psychological evaluations, IQ tests, criminal histories, court records, incarceration records, and coroners' reports.

**LIFE-HISTORY DATA** Collection of information to craft a rich document of offenders' changing personal choices and life experiences over time.

**M**

**MANSLAUGHTER** The killing of another person through gross negligence or without specific intent.

**MARXIST FEMINISM** The view that class and gender divisions of labor together determine the social position of women and men in any society and that the gender division of labor derives from the class division of labor.

**MASS MURDER** This crime is committed when an individual kills two or more people at once rather than singly over time.

**METHODOLOGICAL RELATIVISM** A strategy that operates as a sensitizing device to variation in the definition and meaning of crime in other cultures.

**METHODOLOGY** Techniques of measurement used to collect and manipulate empirical data.

**MIDDLE-CLASS MEASURING ROD** Prevailing middle-class standards by which, in A. K. Cohen's theory of the origin of delinquent gangs, all adolescents are evaluated.

**MODE OF PRODUCTION** A Marxist concept denoting the means of production and the social relations of production.

**MODERNIZATION THESIS** The view that technological development produces common effects that tend to make all societies increasingly similar, irrespective of different or even antagonistic political systems.

**MOTOR VEHICLE THEFT** The unlawful taking of or the attempt to take a motor vehicle, such as an automobile, van, truck, or motorcycle.

**MURDER** The willful killing of one human being by another, usually with premeditation.

**N**

**NEOCLASSICAL CRIMINOLOGY**   The doctrinal and procedural compromise between classicism and positivism, devised roughly between 1890 and 1910, that has become the basis of criminal responsibility and punishment in most Western societies.

**NEWSMAKING CRIMINOLOGY**   The attempt to replace the mass media's biased view of what crimes are newsworthy with the broader context of the seriousness of all socially harmful activities.

**NORMS**   Social regulations, controls, and procedures for moving toward and achieving goals and values.

**O**

**OCCUPATIONAL CRIMES**   Crimes committed by individuals in the course of their occupations for direct personal gain.

**OCCUPATIONAL FRAUD**   A deliberate workplace deception practiced for personal financial gain.

**OCCUPATIONAL THEFT**   An offense that stems from an abuse of trust between employee and employer; it includes employee theft and embezzlement.

**OFFICIAL CRIME DATA**   Data collected by the government and its official agencies.

**P, Q**

**PANOPTICON**   Jeremy Bentham's "Inspection House" (c. 1780), which was designed as an institution of social control for prisoners, workers, the insane, schoolchildren, soldiers, etc.

**PARTICIPANT OBSERVATION**   Method whereby an observer more or less covertly takes part in the activities of a group s/he is studying.

**PATRIARCHY**   Male control of the labor power and sexuality of women.

**PEACEMAKING CRIMINOLOGY**   A critical perspective on the criminal justice system that emphasizes cooperation, compassion, and respect for all species.

**PHYSICIAN FRAUD**   A type of occupational fraud that involves writing pharmaceutical prescriptions, performing unnecessary surgical procedures, or overtreating Medicaid and Medicare patients.

**POLITICAL BRIBERY**   The accepting of money or property by state officials for political favors.

**POLITICAL CRIME**   Includes crimes against the state (violations of law for the purpose of modifying or changing social conditions) and crimes by the state, both domestic (violations of law and unethical acts by state officials and agencies where victimization occurs inside the United States) and transnational (violations of domestic and international law by state officials or agencies where victimization occurs outside the United States).

**POLITICAL REPRESSION**   Illegal or unethical conduct by state officials or agencies for purposes of repressing political dissent.

**PONZI SCHEME**   A form of fraud in which belief in the success of a nonexistent enterprise is fostered by the payment of quick returns to the first investors from money invested from later investors.

**POSITIVISM**   The belief that crime can be observed directly by using the procedures and explanatory logic of the natural sciences.

**POSITIVIST CRIMINOLOGY**   The second great theoretical movement in modern criminology, its method of analysis is based on the collection of observable scientific facts, and its aim is to uncover, to explain, and to predict the ways in which the observable facts of crime occur in uniform patterns.

**POSTMODERNISM**   This theoretical movement challenges all truth claims, emphasizing alternative discourses, meaning, and subjectivist accounts.

**PRICE-FIXING**   Violating antitrust laws through collusion to ensure profits above those that would be produced in a competitive industry.

**PRIMARY DEVIANCE**   An original act of crime or deviance that may derive from a wide variety of social, cultural, psychological, and physiological events.

**PROFESSIONAL MURDER**   Killing another individual for profit.

**PROHIBITION**   A period in the United States from 1920 to 1933 when the Volstead Act made it illegal to produce, distribute, or sell alcoholic beverages.

**PROPERTY CRIME**   The unlawful damage to or taking of the property of another.

**R**

**RACE**   Genetic differences in skin color, which only assume social significance when they are used to justify unequal treatment of one race by another.

**RADICAL CRIMINOLOGY** A criminological theory developed and practiced in the 1970s and 1980s that applied Marxist theory to the study of crime and social control.

**RADICAL FEMINISM** The viewpoint that masculine power and privilege are the root of all social relations in any society; all other relations (such as class) are secondary and derive from gender relations.

**RAPE** As traditionally defined in the criminal law, the carnal knowledge of a female forcibly and against her will, although an expanded definition is used in this book.

**RATIONAL CHOICE** Alleged basis of all calculated human action, including crime, that operates in some of the same ways as free will in theology.

**REACTION FORMATION** A process of adjustment whereby, for example, the academic success typically denied working-class boys is contemptuously redefined as sissy and whereby street knowledge is regarded as superior.

**REBELLION** One of four deviant or criminal responses in Robert Merton's typology of responses to frustrated opportunities.

**REINFORCEMENT** A key concept in social learning theory, which states that crime is largely a response to reinforcing stimuli. If individuals are rewarded for committing crimes, they are more likely to commit them again.

**REPRESSIVE LAW** In Durkheim's sociology, this type of law is religious in its origin and is associated chiefly with societies of mechanical solidarity. Its most common form is criminal law; its violation invites punishment.

**RESTITUTIVE LAW** In Durkheim's sociology, this type of law is associated chiefly with societies of organic solidarity. Its most common form is contract law; its violation invokes a demand to enforce the terms of a prior agreement.

**RESTORATIVE JUSTICE** A tactical movement based on reintegrative or constructive shaming and in which, through a respectful system of conferencing, both offenders and victims are treated with concern.

**RETREATISM** One of four deviant or criminal responses in Merton's typology of responses to frustrated opportunities.

**RITUALISM** One of four deviant or criminal responses in Merton's typology of responses to frustrated opportunities.

**ROBBERY** The unlawful taking of, or the attempt to take, something of value from another person or other persons by using violence or the threat of violence.

**ROUTINE ACTIVITIES THEORY** A theory claiming that patterns of crime and victimization are the result of the everyday interaction of likely offenders, suitable targets, and guardians.

**S**

**SECONDARY DEVIANCE** Society's reaction to some of those who engage in primary deviance, often causing them to accept their identity as a deviant.

**SELF-CONTROL THEORY** The idea that individual differences in criminal behavior derive from differences in self-control.

**SELF-REPORTS** Often generated through questionnaires, these are crime data based on their admissions of illegal or deviant activities by offenders themselves.

**SERIAL MURDER** Killing of two or more people over a period of time by the same individual.

**SEXUAL HARASSMENT** An offense that occurs when the submission to or rejection of sexual advances affects one's employment or when it affects one's work performance by creating an environment that is intimidating, hostile, and offensive.

**SHOPLIFTING** A type of larceny that entails the theft of property from a retail store by customers.

**SOCIAL CLASSES** Groups of people who share the same position in the same production system.

**SOCIAL COERCION** An offense that occurs when women feel that they should have sex with their husbands even if they do not want to because of social pressures—their wifely duty.

**SOCIAL CONSTRUCTIONISM** The view that nothing in society is objective or factual and that all aspects of society are to be understood as human creations.

**SOCIAL CONTRACT** A doctrine created by Enlightenment philosophers (1750–1800) that asserted that society is held together by a mutually beneficial agreement between citizens, property owners, and the state.

**SOCIAL CONTROL** Occurring in both public and private realms, control that has ideological and repressive forms, including primary socialization within the family and secondary socialization within peer groups, the educational system, and the media.

**SOCIAL DISORGANIZATION** A lack of fit between culturally prescribed aspirations and socially structured avenues for achieving them.

**SOCIAL ECOLOGY** A type of research that examines various geographical areas within cities, communities, and neighborhoods as well as the area concentrations, regularities, and patterns of social life in such fields as work/leisure, health/sickness, and conformity/deviance.

**SOCIAL HARM** According to Edwin Sutherland, any illegalities that cause social harm should be studied by criminologists, whether or not they are defined by criminal law as such.

**SOCIAL INEQUALITY** The fact that critical aspects of life such as economic benefits, life chances, social privileges, and political power are unequally distributed in society.

**SOCIAL LEARNING THEORY** The theory that holds that social behavior is a cognitive process in which personality and social environment are involved in a continuous process of reciprocal interaction.

**SOCIAL MECHANICS** A nineteenth-century discourse based on the belief that the same lawlike regularity existing in the heavens and in nature also exists in society.

**SOCIAL POSITION** One's individual location in society based on such social characteristics as class, gender, race, and age.

**SOCIAL PROBLEM** A social condition that is perceived as having harmful effects; opinions about whether a condition is a social problem vary among groups and depend on how and by whom the condition is defined and perceived in society.

**SOCIAL SOLIDARITY** Social order that is abstract and internal to consciousness and that is observable via other, more visible aspects of social life.

**SOCIALIST FEMINISM** The idea that the relationship of class and gender structures crime in society.

**SOCIETAL REACTION** Part of the process of deviance by which society labels primary deviants, thus giving them an identity that leads them to act in expected ways, causing secondary deviance.

**SOCIOLOGICAL PROBLEM** A sociological analysis of how patterns of crime arise from the interplay of political, economic, social, and ideological structures in society.

**SPECIESISM** The practices and ideologies that promote the satisfaction of human interests at the expense of animals.

**STALKING** One or more individuals repeatedly pursuing someone in a harassing and/or threatening manner; it can take place offline (physically) or online (through the Internet).

**THE STATE** The central political institution of a given society, whose major apparatuses are the government, the legal system, the military, and a variety of public bureaucracies.

**STATE-CORPORATE CRIME** Those illegal and harmful acts that occur at the intersection of state agencies and private corporations.

**STATE CORRUPTION** The illegal or unethical use of state authority for personal or political gain.

**STATE TERRORISM** Violations of international law that result in the use of force or violence to intimidate, coerce, or change a government or a civilian population for political reasons.

**STATISTICS** A set of techniques for the reduction of quantitative data to a limited number of more convenient and easily communicated descriptive terms.

**STATUS FRUSTRATION** The lack of status in middle-class life, which causes negative feelings and the search for status in delinquent subcultures.

**STIGMA** A sign of disgrace imposed on an individual.

**STRAIN** In Mertonian anomie theory, the many forms of response that arise from the lack of fit between socially acceptable means and socially desirable goals.

**STRONG-ARM ROBBERY** A robbery in which the offender does not use a weapon.

**SUBCULTURE** Applied to delinquency, a set of beliefs, values, codes, tastes, and prejudices that differ somehow from those of the main or dominant culture.

**T**

**TECHNIQUES OF NEUTRALIZATION** The process by which potential delinquents are freed from conventional social and moral controls and because of which they are then able to engage in delinquency.

**TERRORISM** The use of force or violence to intimidate, coerce, or change a government or a civilian population for political reasons.

**THEORIES** Sets of assumptions, mediated by concepts, that guide the interpretation of data and that try to explain both regularities and irregularities in data.

**TRANSNATIONAL CRIME** Crime committed across borders or across national boundaries.

**TRANSNATIONAL CORPORATE CRIME** Illegal behavior of transnational corporations that conduct business in more than one country and that harm members of other societies; such crime ranges from bribery to the export of hazardous products to dangerous working conditions.

**TRANSNATIONAL POLITICAL CRIMES** Violations of international law by a state in which the resulting victimization occurs outside that state's territory.

**U**

**UNOFFICIAL CRIME DATA** Nongovernmental data usually collected by private or independent agencies and researchers.

**UTILITARIANISM** The doctrine of free will that holds that all persons rationally and freely choose to engage in the social contract and that those who challenge this contract, break its rules, or pursue harmful pleasures or wickedness are liable to be punished.

**V**

**VICTIMIZATION SURVEYS** Surveys of representative samples of a general population that try to uncover what crimes have been experienced in a given period.

**VICTIMLESS CRIMES** Crimes created by the attempt to ban, through criminal legislation, the exchange of strongly desired goods and services between willing partners.

**VICTIM PRECIPITATION** Cited as a defense to a crime when the victim is said to be a direct, positive precipitator of the crime.

**WHITE-COLLAR CRIME** The term first coined by Edwin Sutherland to describe a crime committed by a person of respectability and high social status in the course of his or her occupation. It typically takes an economic form and is stimulated by economic cycles.

**W**

**WIFE RAPE** Differs from rape in that women are raped only by a husband or an ex-husband.

# REFERENCES

Abadinsky, Howard. 1989. *Drug Abuse: An Introduction.* Chicago: Nelson-Hall.

Adams, Carol. J. 1990. Deena—the World's Only Stripping Chimp. *Animals Voice Magazine* 3, no. 1.

Adams, Carol J., and Josephine Donovan, eds. 1995. Introduction. In *Animals and Women: Feminist Theoretical Explorations,* 1–8. Durham, NC: Duke University Press.

Adler, Freda. 1975. *Sisters in Crime: The Rise of the New Female Offender.* New York: McGraw-Hill.

———. 1983. *Nations Not Obsessed with Crime.* Littleton, CO: Fred B. Rothman.

Adler, Jeffrey S. 1989. A Historical Analysis of the Law of Vagrancy. *Criminology* 27 (2): 209–229.

Adler, Patricia A., and Peter Adler. 1998. Foreword to *Ethnography at the Edge,* edited by Jeff Ferrell and Mark S. Hamm, xii–xvi. Boston: Northeastern University Press.

Agnew, Robert. 1985. Social Control Theory and Delinquency: A Longitudinal Test. *Criminology* 23 (1): 47–61.

———. 1992. Foundation for a General Strain Theory of Crime and Delinquency. *Criminology* 30 (1): 47–87.

———. 1995. Strain and Subcultural Theories of Criminality. In *Criminology: A Contemporary Handbook,* edited by Joseph F. Sheley, 305–327. Belmont, CA: Wadsworth.

———. 1998. The Causes of Animal Abuse: A Social-Psychological Analysis. *Theoretical Criminology* 2 (2): 177–209.

———. 2005. *Pressured into Crime: An Overview of General Strain Theory.* New York: Oxford University Press.

Akers, Ronald L. 1973. *Deviant Behavior.* Belmont, CA: Wadsworth.

———. 1997. *Criminological Theories.* Los Angeles: Roxbury.

———. 1998. *Social Learning and Social Structure: A General Theory of Crime and Deviance.* Boston: Northeastern University Press.

———. 1999. Social Learning and Social Structure: Reply to Sampson, Morash, and Krohn. *Theoretical Criminology* 3 (4): 477–493.

———. 2008. Self-Control and Social Learning Theory. In *Out of Control: Assessing the General Theory of Crime,* edited by Erich Goode, 77–89. Stanford, CA: Stanford University Press.

Akers, Ronald L., and Gary F. Jensen, eds. 2007. *Social Learning Theory and the Explanation of Crime: A Guide for the New Century.* New Brunswick, NJ: Transaction Books.

Akers, Ronald L., Marvin D. Krohn, Lonn Lanza-Kaduce, and Marcia Radosevich. 1979. Social Learning and Deviant Behavior: A Specific Test of a General Theory. *American Sociological Review* 44 (4): 636–655.

Albanese, Jay. 2007. *Organized Crime in America.* Cincinnati: Anderson.

Altheide, David L. 2006. *Terrorism and the Politics of Fear.* Lanham, MD: Rowman & Littlefield.

Amnesty International. 1976. *Report on Torture, 1975–1976.* New York. Amnesty International.

——. 2004. *Clouds of Injustice: Bhopal Disaster 20 Years On.* London: Amnesty International Publications.

Anderson, David C. 1999. The Aggregate Burden of Crime. *Journal of Law and Economics* 42 (2): 611–642.

Anderson, Elijah. 1999. *Code of the Street.* New York: W.W. Norton.

Anderson, Margaret L. 1993. *Thinking About Women: Sociological Perspectives on Sex and Gender.* New York: Macmillan.

Anderson, Sarah, John Cavanagh, and Thea Lee. 2005. *Field Guide to the Global Economy.* New York: New Press.

Andrew, D. T. 1980. The Code of Honour and Its Critics: The Opposition to Dueling in England, 1700–1850. *Social History* 5 (3): 409–434.

Anetzberger, Georgia. 2008. Elder Abuse. In *Encyclopedia of Interpersonal Violence*, edited by Claire Renzetti and Jeffrey Edleson, 215–217. Thousand Oaks, CA: Sage.

Antonaccio, Olena, and Charles R. Tittle. 2007. A Cross-National Test of Bonger's Theory of Criminality and Economic Conditions. *Criminology* 45 (4): 925–958.

——. 2008. Morality, Self-Control, and Crime. *Criminology* 46 (2): 479–510.

Archer, Dane, and Rosemary Gartner. 1984. *Violence and Crime in Cross-National Perspective.* New Haven, CT: Yale University Press.

Archer, John E. 1985. "A Fiendish Outrage"? A Study of Animal Maiming in East Anglia: 1830–1870. *Agricultural History Review* 33 (Part II): 147–157.

——. 2006. Postmodern Theory and Criminology. In *The Essential Criminology Reader*, edited by Stuart Henry and Mark Lanier, 224–233. New York: Westview.

Asinoff, Robert. 1985. India Accident Raises Questions of Corporate Responsibility. *In These Times* December 19–January 8: 10.

Aulette, Judy Root, and Raymond Michalowski. 1993. Fire in Hamlet: A Case Study of State-Corporate Crime. In *Political Crime in Contemporary America: A Critical Approach*, edited by Kenneth Tunnell, 171–206. New York: Garland Press.

Bachman, Ronet. 1994. *Violence and Theft in the Workplace.* Washington, DC: Bureau of Justice Statistics.

——. 2001. Assault (Context of in the United States). In *Encyclopedia of Criminology and Deviant Behavior*, edited by Clifton D. Bryant, 37–40. New York: Brunner-Routledge.

Bailey, William C., and Ruth D. Peterson. 1995. Gender Inequality and Violence Against Women: The Case of Murder. In *Crime and Inequality*, edited by John Hagan and Ruth D. Peterson, 174–205. Stanford, CA: Stanford University Press.

Baker, Peter, and Scott Shane. 2009. Pressure Grows to Investigate Interrogations. *New York Times*, A1, A18.

Baldry, Anna C. 2003. Animal Abuse and Exposure to Interparental Violence in Italian Youth. *Journal of Interpersonal Violence* 18 (3): 258–281.

Balkan, Sheila, Ronald Berger, and Janet Schmidt. 1980. *Crime and Deviance in America: A Critical Approach.* Monterey, CA: Wadsworth.

Bandura, Albert. 1973. *Aggression: A Social Learning Analysis.* Englewood Cliffs, NJ: Prentice-Hall.

Barak, Azy. 2007. Sexual Harassment on the Internet. In *Gender Violence: Interdisciplinary Perspectives*, edited by Laura L. O'Toole, Jessica R. Schiffman, and Margie L. Kiter Edwards, 181–193. New York: New York University Press.

Barak, Gregg. 1996. Media, Discourse, and the O.J. Simpson Trial: An Ethnographic Portrait. In *Representing O.J. Murder, Criminal Justice, and Mass Culture*, edited by Gregg Barak, 104–122. Guilderland, NY: Harrow & Heston.

——. 1998. *Integrating Criminologies.* Boston: Allyn & Bacon.

——. 2007. Doing Newsmaking Criminology from Within the Academy. *Theoretical Criminology* 11 (2): 191–207.

Barlow, Melissa Hickman. 1998. Race and the Problem of Crime in Time and Newsweek Cover Stories, 1946 to 1995. *Social Justice* 25 (2): 149–183.

Bartol, Anne M. 2001. White-Collar Crime. In *Encyclopedia of Women and Crime*, edited by Nicole Hahn Rafter, 284–285. Phoenix, AZ: Oryx Press.

Basile, Kathleen C. 1999. Rape by Acquiescence: The Ways in Which Women "Give in" to Unwanted Sex with Their Husbands. *Violence Against Women* 5 (9): 1017–1035.

Battle, Joyce. 2003. *Shaking Hands with Saddam Hussein: The U.S. Tilts Toward Iraq, 1980–1984*. Washington, DC: National Security Archive.

Baumer, Eric P. 2007. Untangling Research Puzzles in Merton's Multilevel Anomie Theory. *Theoretical Criminology* 11 (1): 63–93.

Baumer, Eric P., and Regan Gustafson. 2007. Social Organization and Instrumental Crime: Assessing the Empirical validity of Classic and Contemporary Anomie Theories. *Criminology* 45 (3): 617–663.

Beccaria, Cesare. [1764] 1963. *Of Crimes and Punishments*. Translated by Henry Paolucci. Indianapolis, IN: Bobbs-Merrill.

Becker, Howard S. 1963. *Outsiders: Studies in the Sociology of Deviance*. New York: Free Press.

Beckett, Katherine, and Theodore Sasson. 2004. *The Politics of Injustice: Crime and Punishment in America*. 2nd edition. Thousand Oaks, CA: Sage.

Beirne, Piers, 1993. *Inventing Criminology: Essays on the Rise of* Homo criminalis. Albany: State University of New York Press.

———. 1994. The Law Is an Ass: Reading E. P. Evans, *The Medieval Prosecution and Capital Punishment of Animals*. *Society and Animals* 2 (1): 27–46.

———. 2006. Introduction (to the Chicago School). In Vol.1 of *The Chicago School of Criminology, 1915–1945*, vii–xxvii. Abingdon, Berkshire, UK: Routledge.

———. 2009. *Confronting Animal Abuse: Law, Criminology and Human–Animal Relationships*. Lanham, MD: Rowman & Littlefield.

Beirne, Piers, and David Nelken, eds. 1997. *Issues in Comparative Criminology. International Library of Criminology and Criminal Justice*. Aldershot, UK: Dartmouth.

Beirne, Piers, and Nigel South, eds. 2007. *Issues in Green Criminology: Confronting Harms Against Environments, Humanity, and Other Animals*. Cullompton, Devon, UK: Willan.

Belknap, Joanne. 2007. *The Invisible Woman: Gender, Crime, and Justice*. Belmont, CA: Wadsworth.

Bellis, David J. 1981. *Heroin and Politicians: The Failure of Public Policy to Control Addiction in America*. Westport, CT: Greenwood.

Benson, Donna J., and Gregg E. Thompson. 1982. Sexual Harassment on a University Campus: The Confluence of Authority Relation, Sexual Interest, and Gender Stratification. *Social Problems* 29 (3): 236–251.

Benson, Michael L., and Greer Litton Fox. 2004. *When Violence Hits Home: How Economics and Neighborhood Play a Role*. Washington, DC: National Institute of Justice.

Bentham, Jeremy. [1780] 1973. *An Introduction to the Principles of Morals and Legislation*. New York: Hafner Press.

Benton, Ted. 2007. Ecology, Community and Justice: The Meaning of Green. In *Issues in Green Criminology: Confronting Harms Against Environments, Humanity, and Other Animals*, edited by Piers Beirne and Nigel South, 3–31. Cullompton, Devon, UK: Willan.

Bergen, Raquel Kennedy, ed. 1998. *Issues in Intimate Violence*. Thousand Oaks, CA: Sage.

Bergen, Raquel Kennedy. 2008a. Marital Rape/Wife Rape, Marital Exemptions in Rape Statutes. In *Encyclopedia of Interpersonal Violence*, edited by Claire Renzetti and Jeffrey Edleson, 432–433. Thousand Oaks, CA: Sage.

———. 2008b. Marital Rape/Wife Rape. In *Encyclopedia of Interpersonal Violence*, edited by Claire Renzetti and Jeffrey Edleson, 431–432. Thousand Oaks, CA: Sage.

———. 1987. Structure and Control: Reconsidering Hirschi's Concept of Commitment. *Justice Quarterly* 4 (3): 409–424.

Bernard, Thomas J., and Jeffrey B. Snipes. 1996. Theoretical Integration in Criminology. In *Crime and Justice: A Review of Research*, edited by Michael Tonry, 20:301–348. Chicago: University of Chicago Press.

Bernard, Thomas J., Jeffrey B. Snipes, and Alexander L. Gerould. 2010. *Vold's Theoretical Criminology*. New York: Oxford University Press.

Bernburg, Jón Gunnar, Marvin D. Krohn, and Craig J. Rivera. 2006. Official Labeling, Criminal Embeddedness, and Subsequent Delinquency. *Journal of Research in Crime and Delinquency* 43 (1): 67–88.

Berry, Steve. 1998. Special Report: Time-Honored Oath to "Whole Truth" May Be Losing Aura. *Los Angeles Times*, August 9.

Bertelli, Anthony M., and Lilliard E. Richardson. 2008. The Behavioral Impact of Drinking and Driving Laws. *Policy Studies Journal* 36 (4): 545–569.

Best, Joel. 2004. *More Damned Lies and Statistics: How Numbers Confuse Public Issues*. Berkeley: University of California Press.

———. 2007. *Social Problems*. New York: W.W. Norton.

Black, Donald. 1970. Production of Crime Rates. *American Sociological Review* 35 (4): 733–748.

———. 1976. *The Behavior of Law*. New York: Academic Press.

———. 1989. *Sociological Justice*. New York: Oxford University Press.

Black, George. 1981. *Triumph of the People: The Sandinistas' Revolution in Nicaragua*. London: Zed Books

Blau, Judith R., and Peter M. Blau. 1982. The Cost of Inequality: Metropolitan Structure and Violent Crime. *American Sociological Review* 47 (1): 114–129.

Bloom, Sandra. 2008. Battered Women. In *Encyclopedia of Interpersonal Violence*, edited by Claire Renzetti and Jeffrey Edleson, 51–54. Thousand Oaks, CA: Sage.

Blumstein, Alfred. 2000. *Effects of NIBRS on Crime Statistics, NCJ–178890*. Washington, DC: U.S. Department of Justice.

Boeringer, S. D. 1996. Influences of Fraternity Membership, Athletics, and Male Living Arrangements on Sexual Aggression. *Violence Against Women* 2 (2): 134–147.

Bonger, Willem. 1905. *Criminality and Economic Conditions*. Bloomington, IN: Indiana University Press.

Booth, Jeb A., Amy Farrell, and Sean P. Varano. 2008. Social Control, Serious Delinquency, and Risky Behavior. *Crime & Delinquency* 54 (3): 423–456.

*Boston Herald*. 1988. 7 Cops Guilty in Racketeering Case. September 4, 10.

Bourgois, Philippe. 1996. In Search of Masculinity: Violence, Respect, and Sexuality Among Puerto Rican Crack Dealers in East Harlem. *British Journal of Criminology* 36 (3): 412–427.

Bourgois, Philippe. 2003. *In Search of Respect: Selling Crack in El Barrio*. New York: Cambridge University Press.

Bowcott, Owen. 2008. CCTV boom has failed to slash crime, say police. *The Guardian*, May 6, 1.

Bowker, Lee, ed. 1998. *Masculinities and Violence*. Thousand Oaks, CA: Sage.

Bowker, Michael. 2003. *Fatal Deception: The Untold Story of Asbestos*. New York: St. Martin's Press.

Box, Steven. 1983. *Power and Mystification*. New York: Tavistock.

———. 1987. *Recession, Crime, and Punishment*. London: Macmillan.

Brady, James P. 1983. Arson, Urban Economy, and Organized Crime: The Case of Boston. *Social Problems* 31 (1): 127.

Braithwaite, John. 1979a. Transnational Corporations and Corruption: Towards Some International Solutions. *International Journal of the Sociology of Law* 7 (2): 125–142.

———. 1979b. *Inequality, Crime, and Public Policy*. Boston: Routledge and Kegan Paul.

———. 1981. The Myth of Social Class and Criminality Reconsidered. *American Sociological Review* 46 (1): 36–57.

———. 1984. *Corporate Crime in the Pharmaceutical Industry*. Boston: Routledge and Kegan Paul.

———. 1989. *Crime, Shame, and Reintegration*. Cambridge: Cambridge University Press.

———. 1997. Charles Tittle's Control Balance and Criminological Theory. *Theoretical Criminology* 1 (1): 77–97.

———. 2002. Setting Standards for Restorative Justice. *British Journal of Criminology* 42 (3): 563–577.

Braithwaite, John, and Philip Pettit. 1990. *Not Just Deserts: A Republican Theory of Criminal Justice*. Oxford: Oxford University Press.

Branfman, Frank. 1978. South Vietnam's Police and Prison System: The U.S. Connection. In *Uncloaking the CIA*, edited by Howard Frazier, 110–127. New York: Free Press.

Bray, Howard. 1980. *Pillars of the Post*. New York: W.W. Norton.

Brecher, Jeremy. 1980. *Strike!* Boston: South End Press.

Brenner, M. Harvey. 1976. *Estimating the Social Costs of National Economic Policy. Joint Economic Committee of the U.S. Congress*. Washington, DC: U.S. Government Printing Office.

Britt, Chester L. 1997. Reconsidering the Unemployment and Crime Relationship: Variations by Age Group and Historical Period. *Journal of Quantitative Criminology* 13: 405–428.

Brody, Reed. 1985. *Contra Terror in Nicaragua: Report of a Fact-Finding Mission, September 1984–January 1985*. Boston: South End Press.

Brogden, Mike, and Preeti Nijhar. 2000. *Crime, Abuse, and the Elderly.* Portland, OR: Willan.

Broidy, Lisa, and Robert Agnew. 1997. Gender and Crime: A General Strain Theory Perspective. *Journal of Research in Crime and Delinquency* 34 (3): 275–306.

Brookman, F., Christopher Mullins, and T. Bennett. 2007. Gender, Motivation, and the Accomplishment of Street Robbery in the United Kingdom. *British Journal of Criminology* 47 (6): 861–884.

Brown, Alison P. 2007. Interpretation and the Case Study: The Challenge of a Relational Approach. *Theoretical Criminology* 11 (4): 485–500.

Brown, Julia S. 1952. A Comparative Study of Deviations from Sexual Mores. *American Sociological Review* 17 (2): 135–146.

Browne, Angela. 1995. Fear and Perception of Alternatives: Asking "Why Battered Women Don't Leave?" Is the Wrong Question. In *The Criminal Justice System and Women,* edited by Barbara Raffel Price and Natalie J. Sokoloff, 228–245. New York: McGraw-Hill.

Brownmiller, Susan. 1975. *Against Our Will: Men, Women, and Rape.* New York: Simon & Schuster.

Bruce, Marino, and V. Roscigno. 2003. "Race Effects" and Conceptual Ambiguity in Violence Research: Bringing Inequality Back In. In *Violent Crime: Assessing Race and Ethnic Differences,* edited by D. Hawkins, 238–254. New York: Cambridge University Press.

Bruce, Marino A., Vincent J. Roscigno, and Patricia L. McCall. 1998. Structure, Context, and Agency in the Reproduction of Black-on-Black Violence. *Theoretical Criminology* 2 (1): 29–55.

Buckler, Kevin, and James D. Unnever. 2008. Racial and Ethnic Perceptions of Injustice: Testing the Core Hypotheses of Comparative Conflict Theory. *Journal of Criminal Justice* 36: 270–278.

Buder, Leonard. 1986. In Partial Verdict, U.S. Jury Finds 6 Radicals Guilty of 2 Bombings. *New York Times,* March 5, B3.

Buergenthal, Thomas, and Sean D. Murphy. 2002. *Public International Law.* St. Paul, MN: West Publishing.

Buikhuisen, Wouter, and Fokke P. H. Dijksterhuis. 1971. Delinquency and Stigmatisation. *British Journal of Criminology* 11 (2): 185–187.

Buitrago, Ann Mari. 1988. *Report on CISPES Files Maintained by FBI Headquarters and Released Under the Freedom of Information Act.* New York: Fund for Open Information and Accountability.

Bulmer, Martin. 1984. *The Chicago School of Sociology: Institutionalization, Diversity, and the Rise of Sociological Research.* Chicago: University of Chicago Press.

Bureau of Justice Statistics. 2008. *Criminal Victimization, 2007.* Available at: http://www.ojp.usdoj.gov/bjs/cvict_v.htm.

Burgess, E. W. 1925. The Growth of the City: An Introduction to a Research Project. In *The City,* edited by Robert E. Park and E. W. Burgess, 47–62. Chicago: University of Chicago Press.

Burgess, Robert L., and Ronald L. Akers. 1966. A Differential Association-Reinforcement Theory of Criminal Behavior. *Social Problems* 14 (2): 128–147.

Burgoon, Brian. 1996. Job-Destroying Villain: Is It NAFTA or the Mexican Currency Crisis? In *Real World International,* edited by Marc Breslow, David Levy, and Abby Scher, 14–18. Somerville, MA: Dollars and Sense.

Bursik, Robert J. 1984. Urban Dynamics and Ecological Studies of Delinquency. *Social Forces* 63 (2): 393–413.

Cain, Maureen, and Alan Hunt. 1979. *Marx and Engels on Law.* London: Academic Press.

Calavita, Kitty, Henry N. Pontell, and Robert H. Tillman. 1997. *Big Money Crime: Fraud and Politics in the Savings and Loan Crisis.* Berkeley: University of California Press.

Calder, James. 2001. Robbery. In *Encyclopedia of Criminology and Deviant Behavior,* edited by Clifton D. Bryant, 452–456. New York: Brunner-Routledge.

Cameron, Mary Owen. 1964. *The Booster and the Snitch.* New York: Free Press.

Camic, Charles, and Yu Xie. 1994. The Statistical Turn in American Social Science: Columbia University, 1890 to 1915. *American Sociological Review* 59 (5): 773–805.

Cantor, David, and James P. Lynch. 2000. Self-Report Surveys as Measures of Crime and Criminal Victimization. *Criminal Justice* 4: 85–138.

Capaldi, Deborah M., Hyoun K. Kim, and Lee D. Owen. 2008. Romantic Partners' Influence on Men's Likelihood of Arrest in Early Adulthood. *Criminology* 46 (2): 267–299.

Caputo, Gail A. 2008. *Out in the Storm: Drug-Addicted Women Living as Shoplifters and Sex Workers.* Boston: Northeastern University Press.

Carlen, Pat, and Tony Jefferson, eds. 1996. Masculinities and Crime. Special Issue of the *British Journal of Criminology* 33 (6).

Carlson, Susan M., and Raymond J. Michalowski. 1997. Crime, Unemployment, and Social Structures of Accumulation: An Inquiry into Historical Contingency. *Justice Quarterly* 14: 101–133.

Carrabine, Eamonn, Pam Cox, Maggy Lee, Ken Plummer, and Nigel South. 2009. *Criminology: A Sociological Introduction*, London: Routledge.

Carson, Taj C. 2000. Organized Crime (The Mafia). In *Encyclopedia of Women and Crime*, edited by Nicole Hahn Rafter, 160. Phoenix, AZ: Oryx Press.

Caulfield, Susan L., and Angela R. Evans. 1997. Peacemaking Criminology: A Path to Understanding and a Model for Methodology. In *Thinking Critically About Crime*, edited by Brian D. MacLean and Dragan Milovanovic, 102–108. Vancouver, B.C.: Collective Press.

Cazaux, Geertrui and Piers Beirne. 2001. Animal Asure. pp. 8–10 in E. Mclaughlin and J. Muncie, eds. *Sage Dictionary of Criminology*. London: Sage.

Center for Constitutional Rights. 1988. Political Spying and the Central America Movement. *Movement Support Network News* 4: 13.

Center for Economic and Social Rights. 2003. *Tearing Up the Rules: The Illegality of Invading Iraq*. New York: Center for Economic and Social Rights.

———. 2004. *Beyond Torture: U.S. Violations of Occupation Law in Iraq*. New York: Center for Economic and Social Rights.

Centers for Disease Control and Prevention. 2008. Smoking and Tobacco Use Fact Sheet. Retrieved January 2, 2009, from: http://www.cdc.gov/tobacco/data_statistics/fact_sheet/Health_effects/health_rffects.htm.

Cernkovich, Stephen A., and Peggy C. Giordano. 1987. Family Relationships and Delinquency. *Sociological Quarterly* 20 (2): 131–145.

Chambliss, William J. 1964. A Sociological Analysis of the Law of Vagrancy. *Social Problems* 12 (1): 67–77.

———. 1975. Toward a Political Economy of Crime. *Theory and Society* 2 (Summer): 149–170.

———. 1988a. *Exploring Criminology*. New York: Macmillan.

Chambliss, William J., and Robert Seidman. 1982. *Law, Order, and Power*. Reading, MA: Addison-Wesley.

Chamlin, Mitchell B., and John K. Cochran. 2007. An Evaluation of the Assumptions That Underlie Institutional Anomie Theory. *Theoretical Criminology* 11 (1): 39–61.

Channel 4 (UK). 2009. Waterboarding, the coffin-and-insect box and "walling": The chilling details of how CIA tortured 28 terror suspects. Available at: http://www.google.com/imgres?imgurl=http://i.dailymail.co.uk/i/pix/2009/04/17.

Chang, Nancy. 2001. *The USA PATRIOT Act: What's So Patriotic About Trampling on the Bill of Rights?* New York: Center for Constitutional Rights.

Chapple, Constance L. 2005. Self-Control, Peer relations, and Delinquency. *Justice Quarterly* 22 (1): 89–106.

Chesney-Lind, Meda. 1995. Girls, Delinquency, and Juvenile Justice: Toward a Feminist Theory of Young Women's Crime. In *The Criminal Justice System and Women*, edited by Barbara Raffel Price and Natalie J. Sokoloff, 71–88. New York: McGraw-Hill.

Chesney-Lind, Meda, and Lisa Pasko. 2004. *The Female Offender*. Thousand Oaks, CA: Sage.

Chesney-Lind, Meda, and Randall G. Shelden. 2004. *Girls, Delinquency, and Juvenile Justice*. 3rd edition. Belmont, CA: Wadsworth/Thomson.

Chevalier, Louis. 1973. *Laboring Classes and Dangerous Classes in Paris During the First Half of the Nineteenth Century*. Translated by Frank Jellinek. Princeton, NJ: Princeton University Press.

Chiricos, Ted, Kele Barrick, William Bales, and Stephanie Bontrager. 2007. The Labeling of Convicted Felons and Its Consequences for Recidivism. *Criminology* 45 (3): 547–581.

Choe, Jongmook. 2008. Income Inequality and Crime in the United States. *Economic Letters* 101 (1): 31–53.

Chomsky, Noam. 2002. *9–11*. New York: Seven Stories Press.

———. 2003. *Hegemony or Survival: America's Quest for Global Dominance*. New York: Metropolitan Books.

Chomsky, Noam, and Edward S. Herman. 1977. The United States Versus Human Rights in the Third World. *Monthly Review* 29 (July–August): 22–45.

———. 1979. *The Washington Connection and Third World Fascism*. Boston: South End Press.

Church, Wesley T., Tracy Wharton, and Julie K. Taylor. 2009. An Examination of Differential Association and Social Control Theory. *Youth Violence and Juvenile Justice* 7 (1): 3–15.

Church Committee. 1976. Select Committee to Study Governmental Operations with Respect to Intelligence Activities. *Intelligence Activities and the Rights of Americans.* Washington, DC: U.S. Government Printing Office.

Churchill, Ward, and Jim Vander Wall. 1988. *Agents of Repression.* Boston: South End Press.

Clarke, Richard. 2004. *Against All Enemies: Inside America's War on Terror.* New York: Free Press.

Clarke, Ronald V., and Patricia M. Harris. 1992. Auto Theft and Its Prevention. In *Crime and Justice: A Review of Research,* edited by Michael Tonry, 16: 1–54. Chicago: University of Chicago Press.

Clinard, Marshall B., and Daniel J. Abbott. 1973. *Crime in Developing Countries: A Comparative Perspective.* New York: John Wiley.

Clinard, Marshall B., and Richard Quinney. 1973. *Criminal Behavior Systems.* New York: Holt, Rinehart & Winston.

Clinard, Marshall B., and Peter C. Yeager. 1980. *Corporate Crime.* New York: Free Press.

Cloward, Richard A., and Lloyd E. Ohlin. 1960. *Delinquency and Opportunity: A Theory of Delinquent Gangs.* New York: Free Press.

Cobbina, Jennifer E., Jody Miller, and Rod. K. Brunson. 2008. Gender Neighborhood Danger, and Risk-Avoidance Strategies Among Urban African-American Youths. *Criminology* 46 (3): 673–709.

Cohen, Albert K. 1955. *Delinquent Boys: The Culture of the Gang.* New York: Free Press.

Cohen, Jeffrey W., and Patrick J. Harvey 2006. Misconceptions of Gender: Sex, Masculinity, and the Measurement of Crime. *Journal of Men's Studies* 14 (2): 223–233.

Cohen, Stanley. [1972] 1980. *Folk Devils and Moral Panics: The Creation of the Mods and Rockers.* New York: St. Martin's Press.

Cohn, Marjorie. 2007. *Cowboy Republic: Six Ways the Bush Gang Has Defied the Law.* Sausalito, CA: PoliPoint Press.

Coleman, James. 2006. *The Criminal Elite: Understanding White-Collar Crime.* New York: Worth.

Collier, Richard. 1998. *Masculinities, Crime, and Criminology: Men, Heterosexuality, and the Criminal(ized) Other.* Thousand Oaks, CA: Sage.

Collins, Michael. 2008. Election 2004: The Urban Legend. In *Loser Take All: Election Fraud and the Subversion of Democracy, 2000–2008,* edited by Mark Crispin Miller, 97–115. Brooklyn, NY: IG Publishing.

Committee to Protect Journalists. 2009. *Annual Prison Census: Journalists in Prison as of December 1, 2008.* Available on March 9, 2009, at: http://www.cpj.org/.

Conklin, John. 1972. *Robbery and the Criminal Justice System.* New York: Lippincott.

Cook, Philip J., and Gary A. Zarkin. 1985. Crime and the Business Cycle. *Journal of Legal Studies* 14 (1): 115–128.

Cooley, John. 2000. *Unholy Wars: Afghanistan, America, and International Terrorism.* London: Pluto Press.

Cooney, Mark, and Callie Harbin. 2008. Less Crime, More Punishment. *American Journal of Sociology* 114 (2): 491–527.

Copes, Heith, and Michael Cherbonneau. 2006. The Key to Auto Theft: Emerging Methods of Auto Theft from the Offenders' Perspective. *British Journal of Criminology,* 46 (5): 917–2006.

Copes, Heith, and Samuel E. Wallace. 2001. Motor Vehicle Theft. In *Encyclopedia of Criminology and Deviant Behavior,* edited by Clifton D. Bryant, 393–396. New York: Brunner-Routledge.

Corbett, Claire. 2003. *Car Crime.* Portland, OR: Willan.

Corn, David. 1988. Bush's CIA: The Same Old Dirty Tricks. *The Nation* (August 27–September 3), 157–160.

———. 2003. *The Lies of George W. Bush: Mastering the Politics of Deception.* New York: Crown.

Costello, Barbara. 1997. On the Logical Adequacy of Cultural Deviance Theories. *Theoretical Criminology* 1 (4): 403–428.

Costelloe, Michael T., Ted Chiricos, and Marc Gertz, 2009. Punitive Attitudes Towards Criminals. *Punishment & Society* 11 (1): 25–49.

Cottle, Simon. 2006. Mediatizing the Global War on Terror: Television's Public Eye. In *Media, Terrorism, and Theory,* edited by Anandam P. Kavoori and Todd Fraley, 19–48. Lanham, MD: Rowman & Littlefield.

Coupe, Timothy, and Laurence Blake. 2006. Daylight and Darkness Targeting Strategies and the Risks of Being Seen at Residential Burglaries. *Criminology,* 44 (2): 431–464.

Courtois, Christine. 2008. Sexual Assault in the Military. In *Encyclopedia of Interpersonal Violence*, edited by Claire Renzetti and Jeffrey Edleson, 654–656. Thousand Oaks, CA: Sage.

Cowling, Mark. 2006. Postmodern Policies? The Erratic Interventions of Constitutive Criminology. *Internet Journal of Criminology*, downloaded on February 9, 2009, and available at: http://www.internetjournalofcriminology.com.

Cromwell, Paul F. 2002. Shoplifting. In *Encyclopedia of Crime and Punishment*, edited by David Levinson, 1508–1510. Thousand Oaks, CA: Sage.

Cromwell, Paul F., and Jason Jolicouer. 2001. Burglary. In *Encyclopedia of Criminology and Deviant Behavior*, edited by Clifton D. Bryant, 50–53. New York: Brunner-Routledge.

Cromwell, Paul F., James N. Olson, and D'Aunn Wester Avary. 1991. *Breaking and Entering: An Ethnographic Analysis of Burglary*. Newbury Park, CA: Sage.

Crosset, Todd, J. Ptacek, M. McDonald, and Jeffrey Benedict. 1996. Male Student Athletes and Violence Against Women: A Survey of Campus Judicial Affairs Offices. *Violence Against Women* 2 (2): 163–179.

Crosset, Todd, Jeffrey R. Benedict, and Mark McDonald. 1995. Male Student Athletes Reported for Sexual Assault: A Survey of Campus Police Departments and Judicial Affairs Offices. *Journal of Sport and Social Issues* 19 (2): 126–140.

Cruz, Michael. 2003. "Why Doesn't He Just Leave?" Gay Male Domestic Violence and Reasons Victims Stay. *Journal of Men's Studies*. 11 (3): 309–323.

Cullen, Francis T., and Steven F. Messner. 2007. The Making of Criminology Revisited. *Theoretical Criminology* 11 (1): 5–37.

Cullen, Francis, William J. Maakestad, and Gray Cavender. 1987. *Corporate Crime Under Attack*. Cincinnati, OH: Anderson.

Cullen, Francis, John Wozniak, and James Frank. 1985. The Rise of the Elderly Offender: Will a New Criminal Be Invented? *Crime and Social Justice* 23: 151–165.

Current Population Reports. 2009. *The Black Population in the United States*. Washington, DC: Census Bureau.

———. 2004. *Projections of the Population of the U.S. by Age, Sex, and Race: 2004 to 2080*. Washington, DC: U.S. Government Printing Office.

Currie, Elliott. 1998. *Crime and Punishment in America*. New York: Metropolitan.

———. 2007. Against Marginality: Arguments for a Public Criminology. *Theoretical Criminology* 11 (2): 175–190.

Curry, Timothy. 2000. Booze and Bar Fights: A Journey to the Dark Side of College Athletics. In *Masculinities, Gender Relations, and Sport*, edited by Jim McKay, Michael Messner, and Donald Sabo, 162–75. Thousand Oaks, CA: Sage.

Daly, Kathleen. 2002. Restorative Justice: the Real Story. *Punishment & Society* 4 (1): 55–79.

Daly, Kathleen, and Meda Chesney-Lind. 1988a. Battered Women: Implications for Social Control. *Contemporary Crises* 12 (4): 345–372.

———. 1988b. Feminism and Criminology. *Justice Quarterly* 5 (4): 101–143.

Daly, Kathleen, and Lisa Maher, eds. 1998. *Criminology at the Crossroads: Feminist Readings in Crime and Justice*. New York: Oxford University Press.

Daly, Kathleen, and Julie Stubbs, 2006. Feminist Engagement with Restorative Justice. *Theoretical Criminology* 10 (1): 9–28.

Davies, Pamela, Peter Francis, and Chris Greer, eds. 2007. *Victims, Crime and Society*. Thousand Oaks, CA: Sage.

Davis, Jason. 2005. Bribery. In *Encyclopedia of White-Collar & Corporate Crime*, edited by Lawrence Salinger, 110–112. Thousand Oaks, CA: Sage.

Debord, Guy. 1967. *The Society of the Spectacle*. Translated by Fredy Perlman and John Supak. Chicago: Black and Red.

DeFronzo, James. 1983. Economic Assistance to Impoverished Americans. *Criminology* 21 (1): 119–136.

de Haan, Willem. 1990. *The Politics of Redress: Crime, Punishment, and Penal Abolition*. Boston: Unwin Hyman.

de Haan, Willem, and Jaco Vos. 2003. A Crying Shame: The Over-Rationalized Conception of Man in the Rational Choice Perspective. *Theoretical Criminology* 7: 29–54.

DeHaven-Smith, Lance. 2008. Florida 2000: Beginnings of a Lawless Presidency. In *Loser Take All: Election Fraud and the Subversion Of Democracy, 2000–2008*, edited by Mark Crispin Miller, 45–57. Brooklyn, NY: IG Publishing.

DeKeseredy, Walter. 2008. "Separation/Divorce Sexual Assault." In *Encyclopedia of Interpersonal Violence*, edited by Claire Renzetti and Jeffrey Edleson, 637–638. Thousand Oaks, CA: Sage.

DeKeseredy, Walter. 2003. Left Realism on Inner-City Violence. In *Controversies in Critical Criminology*, edited by Martin D. Schwartz and Suzanne E. Hatty, 29–41. Cincinnati, OH: Anderson.

DeKeseredy, Walter S., and Barbara Perry. 2006. *Advancing Critical Criminology: Theory and Application*. Lanham, MD: Lexington Books.

Deo, Meera E., Christina Chin, Jenny J. Lee, Noriko Milman, and Nancy Wang Yuen. 2009. Missing in Action: Framing Race in Prime-Time Television. *Social Justice* 35 (2): 145–162.

Department of Justice. 2008. *Sourcebook of Criminal Justice Statistics*. Washington, DC: Department of Justice.

——. 2009. Stalking Victimization in the United States. Washington, DC: Bureau of Justice Statistics.

Department of Labor. 2009. *Labor Force Statistics Derived from the Current Population Survey, 1948–1987*. Washington, DC: U.S. Government Printing Office.

——. 2008. National Census of Fatal Occupational Injuries in 2007. Washington, DC: Bureau of Labor Statistics.

Desnoyers, Ronald C. Jr. 2005. Tax Evasion. In *Encyclopedia of White-Collar and Corporate Crime*, edited by Lawrence Salinger, 789–793. Thousand Oaks, CA: Sage.

Desroches, Frederick J. 2002. *Force and Fear: Robbery in Canada*. Toronto: Canadian Scholars' Press.

Diamond, Stanley. 1973. The Rule of Law Versus the Order of Custom. In *The Social Organization of Law*, edited by Donald Black and Maureen Mileski, 318–334. New York: Seminar Press.

DiCristina, Bruce. 2004. Durkheim's Theory of Homicide and the Confusion of the Empirical Literature. *Theoretical Criminology* 8 (1): 57–91.

Dinges, John. 2004. *The Condor Years: How Pinochet and His Allies Brought Terrorism to Three Continents*. New York: W.W. Norton.

Ditton, Jason. 1977a. *Part-Time Crime*. New York: Macmillan.

——. 1977b. Perks, Pilferage, and the Fiddle: The Historical Structure of Invisible Wages. *Theory and Society* 4 (1): 39–71.

——. 1979. *Controlology*. London: Macmillan.

——. 2000. Crime and the City: Public Attitudes Towards Open-Street CCTV in Glasgow. *British Journal of Criminology* 40 (4): 692–709.

Dixon, Keith. 1977. Is Cultural Relativism Self-Refuting? *British Journal of Sociology* 28 (1): 75–88.

Dobash, R. Emerson, and Russell P. Dobash. 1979. *Violence Against Wives*. New York: Free Press.

Dodge, Mary. 2009. *Women and White-Collar Crime*. Upper Saddle River, NJ: Prentice Hall.

Donaldson, Stephen. 2001. A Million Jockers, Punks, and Queens. In *Prison Masculinities*, edited by Don Sabo, Terry A. Kupers, and Willie London, 118–126. Philadelphia: Temple University Press.

Douglas, Jack D. 1977. Watergate: Harbinger of the American Prince. In *Official Deviance*, edited by Jack D. Douglas and John M. Johnson, 112–120. New York: Lippincott.

Douglas, Jack D., and Paul K. Rasmussen (with Carol Ann Flanagan). 1977. *The Nude Beach: Sociological Observations*. Beverly Hills, CA: Sage.

Dowie, Mark. 1979. The Corporate Crime of the Century. *Mother Jones* 4 (9): 23–25, 37.

Doyle, Jack. 2004. *Trespass Against Us: Dow Chemical and the Toxic Century*. Monroe, ME: Common Courage Press.

Duesterberg, Thomas J. 1979. Criminology and the Social Order in Nineteenth-Century France. Ph.D. diss., Indiana University.

Duhart, Detis T. 2001. *Violence in the Workplace, 1993–99*. Washington, DC: U.S. Department of Justice.

Durkheim, Émile. 1948. *The Elementary Forms of Religious Life*. 1912. Translated by Joseph W. Swain. Glencoe, IL: Free Press.

——. 1951. *Suicide: A Study in Sociology*. 1897. Translated by J. A. Spaulding and G. Simpson. New York: Free Press.

——. 1958. *Professional Ethics and Civil Morals*. 1900. Translated by Cornelia Brookfield. Glencoe, IL: Free Press.

——. 1982. *The Rules of Sociological Method*. 1894. Translated by W. D. Halls. London: Macmillan.

———. 1983 [1901]. Two Laws of Penal Evolution. In *Durkheim and the Law*, edited by Steven Lukes and Andrew Scull, 102–132. Translated by T. Anthony Jones and Andrew Scull. New York: St. Martin's Press.

———. 1984. *The Division of Labor in Society*. 1893. Translated by W. D. Halls. New York: Free Press.

Duster, Troy. 1987. Crime, Youth Unemployment, and the Black Underclass. *Crime and Delinquency* 33 (2): 300–316.

Dwyer, Lynn E. 1983. Structure and Strategy in the Antinuclear Movement. In *Social Movements of the Sixties and Seventies*, edited by Jo Freeman, 148–161. New York: Longman.

Egger, Steven A. 2001. Homicide, Serial. In *Encyclopedia of Criminology and Deviant Behavior*, edited by Clifton D. Bryant, 278–280. New York: Brunner-Routledge.

Einstadter, Werner, and Stuart Henry. 2006. *Criminological Theory*. 2nd edition. Lanham, MD: Rowman & Littlefield.

Eisnitz, Gail A. 1997. *Slaughterhouse*. New York: Prometheus Books.

Elias, Norbert. 1978. *The Civilizing Process*. Oxford: Oxford University Press.

Elliott, Caroline, and Dan Ellingsworth. 1997. Exploring the Relationship Between Unemployment and Property Crime. *Applied Economic Letters* 5: 527–530.

Elliott, Delbert S., and David Huizinga. 1983. Social Class and Delinquent Behavior in a National Youth Panel: 1976–1980. *Criminology* 21 (2): 149–177.

Emerson, Steven. 1988. *Secret Warriors: Inside the Covert Military Operations of the Reagan Era*. New York: G. P. Putnam.

Engels, Friedrich. 1845. 1970.*The Condition of the Working Class in England*. In *Karl Marx/Frederick Engels Collected Works*. Vol.4, 295–583. New York: International Publishers.

———. 1885. Anti-Dühring. London. Lawrence and Wishart.

———. [1888] 1970b. The Role of Force in History. In *Karl Marx and Frederick Engels: Selected Works*, 3: 377–428. Moscow: Progress Publishers.

———1893.1970 "Letter to F. Mehring in Berlin." In *Karl Marx and Frederick Engels Selected Works*. Vol 3, 495–499. Moscow: Progress Publishers.

Epstein, Samuel. 1978. *The Politics of Cancer*. San Francisco: Sierra Club Books. Ericson, Richard V., Patricia M. Baranek, and Janet B. L. Chan. 1980. *Visualizing Deviance*. Toronto, Ontario: University of Toronto Press.

Eschholz, Sarah. 2002. Racial Composition of Television Offenders and Viewers' Fear of Crime. *Critical Criminology* 11 (1): 41–60.

Eschholz, Sarah, Ted Chiricos, and Marc Gertz. 2003. Television and Fear of Crime: Program Types, Audience Traits, and the Mediating Effect of Perceived Neighborhood Racial Composition. *Social Problems* 50 (3): 395–415.

Evans, Ernest. 1983. The Use of Terrorism by American Social Movements. In *Social Movements of the Sixties and Seventies*, edited by Jo Freeman, 252–261. New York: Longman.

Eviatar, Daphne. 2005. A Big Win for Human Rights. *The Nation* (May 9): 20–22.

Exum, M. Lyn. 2002. The Application and Robustness of the Rational Choice Perspective in the Study of Intoxicated and Angry Intentions to Agress. *Criminology* 40 (4): 933–966.

Fagan, Abigail A., and John Western. 2005. Escalation of Deceleration of Offending Behaviors from Adolescence to Early Adulthood. *Australian and New Zealand Journal of Criminology*, 38 (1): 59–76.

Fagan, Jeffrey, Franklin Zimring, and Amanda Geller. 2006. Capital Punishment and Capital Murder: Market Share and the Deterrent Effects of the Death Penalty. *Texas Law Review* 84 (7): 1803–1867.

Faris, Robert E. L. [1967] 1970. *Chicago Sociology, 1920–1932*. Chicago: University of Chicago Press.

Farrell, G., and Ken Pease. 2001. *Repeat Victimization*. Monsey, NY: Criminal Justice Press.

Farrington, David P. 2002. In *The Oxford Handbook of Criminology*, 3rd edition, edited by M. Maguire, R. Morgan, and R. Reiner, 657–701. Oxford: Clarendon Press.

Fast, Jonathan. 2008. School Violence/School Shootings. In *Encyclopedia of Interpersonal Violence*, edited by Claire Renzetti and Jeffrey Edleson, 628–630. Thousand Oaks, CA: Sage.

Federal Bureau of Investigation. 2008. *Uniform Crime Reports, 2007*. Available at: http://www.fbi.gov/ucr/cius2007/index.html.

Federal Bureau of Investigation. 2009. *Uniform Crime Reports A Word about UCR Data.* Downloaded April 3, 2009, at: http://www.fbi.gov/ucr/word.htm.

Felson, Marcus. 1997. A "Routine Activity" Analysis of Recent Crime Reductions. *The Criminologist* 22 (6): 1–3.

———. 1998. *Crime and Everyday Life.* 2nd edition. Thousand Oaks, CA: Pine Forge Press.

———. 2006a. *Crime and Everyday Life.* Thousand Oaks, CA: Sage.

———. 2006b. *Crime and Nature.* Thousand Oaks, CA: Sage.

Felson, Richard B., and Steven Messner. 1998. Disentangling the Effects of Gender and Intimacy on Victim Precipitation in Homicide. *Criminology* 36 (2): 405–423.

———. 2008. Self-Control, Anomie, and Social Institutions. In *Out of Control: Assessing the General Theory of Crime,* edited by Erich Goode, 90–101. Stanford, CA: Stanford University Press.

Fenwick, Mark. 2003. Youth Crime and Crime Control in Contemporary Japan. In *The Blackwell Companion to Criminology,* edited by Colin Sumner, 125–142. New York: Wiley/Blackwell.

———. 2004. Crime Talk and Crime Control in Contemporary Japan. In *Cultural Criminology Unleashed,* edited by Jeff Ferrell, Keith Hayward, Wayne Morison, and Mike Presdee, 193–206 London: Routledge Cavendish.

Ferrell, Jeff. 1997. Against the Law: Anarchist Criminology. In *Thinking Critically About Crime,* edited by Brian D. MacLean and Dragan Milovanovic, 146–154. Vancouver, B.C.: Collective Press.

———. 2004. Boredom, Crime, and Criminology. *Theoretical Criminology* 8 (3): 287–302.

———. 2007. For a Ruthless Cultural Criticism of Everything Existing. *Crime, Media, Culture* 3 (1): 91–100.

Ferrell, Jeff, and Mark S. Hamm, eds. 1998. *Ethnography at the Edge: Crime, Deviance, and Field Research.* Boston: Northeastern University Press.

Ferrell, Jeff, Keith Hayward, Wayne Morrison, and Mike Presdee, eds. 2004. *Cultural Criminology Unleashed.* London: Glasshouse Press.

Ferrell, Jeff, Keith Hayward, and Jock Young. 2008. *Cultural Criminology: An Invitation.* Los Angeles: Sage.

Ferrell, Jeff, and Clinton R. Sanders, eds. 1995. *Cultural Criminology.* Boston: Northeastern University Press.

Ferrell, Jeff, and Neil Websdale, eds. 1999. *Making Trouble: Cultural Constructions of Crime, Deviance, and Control.* New York: Aldine de Gruyter.

Feyerabend, Paul. 1987. *Farewell to Reason.* London: Verso.

Figueira-McDonough, Josephina (with Elaine Selo). 1980. A Reformulation of the Equal Opportunity Explanation of Female Delinquency. *Crime and Delinquency* 26 (3): 333–343.

Finch, Emily. 2003. What a Tangled Web We Weave: Identity Theft and the Internet. In *Dot.cons: Crime, Deviance and Identity On the Internet,* edited by Y. Jewkes, 17–31. Portland, OR: Willan.

Finch, Emily, and Stefan Fafinski. 2009. *Identity Theft.* Portland, OR: Willan.

Findlay, Mark. 2008. *Governing Through Globalised Crime.* Cullompton, Devon, UK: Willan.

Finkelhor, David. 2008. *Childhood Victimization: Violence, Crime, and Abuse in the Lives of Young People.* New York: Oxford University Press.

Finkelhor, David, and Kersti Yllö. 1985. *License to Rape: Sexual Abuse of Wives.* New York: Holt, Rinehart & Winston.

Finn, Jerry. 2008. Cyberstalking. In *Encyclopedia of Interpersonal Violence,* edited by Claire Renzetti and Jeffrey Edleson, 163–165. Thousand Oaks, CA: Sage.

Fitzgerald, Amy J., Linda Kalof, and Thomas Dietz. 2009. Slaughterhouses and Increased Crime Rates: An Empirical Analysis of Spillover from "The Jungle" into the Surrounding Community. *Organization and Environment,* 22: 158–184.

Flavin, Jeanne. 2003. Feminism for the Mainstream Criminologist: An Invitation. In *The Criminal Justice System and Women.* 3rd edition, edited by Barbara Raffel Price and Natalie J. Sokoloff, 31–48. New York: McGraw-Hill.

Flavin, Jeanne, and Amy Desautels. 2006. Feminism and Crime. In *Rethinking Gender, Crime, and Justice: Feminist Readings,* edited by Claire Renzetti, Lynne Goodstein, and Susan Miller, 11–28. Los Angeles: Roxbury.

Flynn, Clifton P. 2008. A Sociological Analysis of Animal Abuse. In *The International Handbook of Animal*

*Abuse and Cruelty* edited by Frank R. Ascione, 155–174. West Lafayette, IN: Purdue University Press.

Forbes, G., L. Adams-Curtis, A. Pakalka, and K. White. 2006. Dating Aggression, Sexual Coercion, and Aggression-Supporting Attitudes Among College Men as a Function of Participation in Aggressive Sports. *Violence Against Women,* 12 (4): 441–455.

Forney, William Scott, Judith Cardona Forney, and Christy Crutsinger. 2005. Developmental Stages of Age and Moral Reasoning as Predictors of Juvenile Delinquents' Behavioral Intention to Steal Clothing. *Family and Consumer Sciences Research Journal,* 34 (2): 110–126.

Foucault, Michel, ed. 1975. *I, Pierre Rivière, having slaughtered my mother, my sister, and my brother.* Translated by Frank Jellinek. Lincoln: University of Nebraska Press.

———. 1979. *Discipline and Punish: The Birth of the Prison.* Translated by Alan Sheridan. New York: Vintage Books.

———. 1980. *Power/Knowledge: Selected Interviews and Other Writings, 1972–1977.* Translated by Colin Gordon et al. New York: Pantheon.

Frank, Nancy K., and Michael J. Lynch. 1992. *Corporate Crime, Corporate Violence.* Albany, NY: Harrow and Heston.

Frankenberg, Ruth. 1993. *White Women, Race Matters: The Construction of Whiteness.* Minneapolis: University of Minnesota Press.

Friedrichs, David O. 1996. *Trusted Criminals: White-Collar Crime in Contemporary America.* Belmont, CA: Wadsworth.

———. 2004. *Trusted Criminals: White-Collar Crime in Contemporary Society.* Belmont, CA: Wadsworth.

———. 2007. Transnational Crime and Global Criminology. *Social Justice* 34 (2): 4–18.

Friedrichs, David O., and Jessica Friedrichs. 2008. The World Bank and Crimes of Globalization: A Case Study. In *Global Criminology and Criminal Justice,* edited by Nick Larsen and Russell Smandych, 81–114. Peterborough, Ontario: Broadview Press.

Friedrichs, David O., and Martin D. Schwartz. 2008. Low Self-Control and High Organizational Control: The Paradoxes of White-Collar Crime. In *Out of Control: Assessing the General Theory of Crime,*

edited by Erich Goode, 145–159. Stanford, CA: Stanford University Press.

Fritner, M. P., and L. Rubinson. 1993. Acquaintance Rape: The Influence of Alcohol, Fraternity Membership, and Sports Team Membership. *Journal of Sex Education and Therapy* 19 (4): 272–284.

Fuller, John. 1998. *Criminal Justice: A Peacemaking Perspective.* Boston: Allyn & Bacon.

———. 2003. Peacemaking Criminology. In *Controversies in Critical Criminology,* edited by Martin D. Schwartz and Suzanne E. Hatty, 85–95. Cincinnati, OH: Anderson.

Fuller, Lon L. 1949. The Case of the Speluncean Explorers. *Harvard Law Review* 62 (4): 616–645.

Gabbidon, Shaun. 2010. *Criminological Perspectives on Race and Crime.* New York: Routledge.

Gabbidon, Shaun, and Helen Greene. 2008. *Race and Crime.* Thousand Oaks, CA: Sage.

Gadd, David, and Stephen Farrall. 2004. Criminal Careers: Interpreting Men's Narratives of Change. *Theoretical Criminology* 8 (2): 123–156.

Gadd, David, and Tony Jefferson. 2007a. On the Defensive: A Psychoanalytically Informed Psychosocial Reading of The Jack-Roller. *Theoretical Criminology* 11 (4): 443–467.

Gadd, David, and Tony Jefferson. 2007b. *Psychosocial Criminology: An Introduction.* Los Angeles: Sage.

Galliher, John F., and Allynn Walker. 1977. The Puzzle of the Social Origins of the Marihuana Tax Act of 1937. *Social Problems* 24 (3): 367–376.

Galton, Francis. 1869. *Hereditary Genius.* London: Macmillan.

Garda Research Unit. 2008. Garda Public Attitudes Survey, 2007. *Garda Research Reports* no. 1/08.

Gardiner, J. 1882. *The Politics of Corruption: Organized Crime in an American City.* New York: Russell Sage.

Gareau, Frederick. 2004. *State Terrorism and the United States: From Counterinsurgency to the War on Terror.* London: Zed Books.

Garitty, Michael. 1980. The U.S. Colonial Empire Is as Close as the Nearest Reservation. In *Trilateralism: The Trilateral Commission and Elite Planning for World Management,* edited by Holly Sklar, 238–688. Boston: South End Press.

Garland, David. 1985. *Punishment and Welfare: A History of Penal Strategies.* Aldershot, UK: Gower.

Garland, David. 1990. *Punishment and Modern Society.* Chicago: University of Chicago Press.

———. 1997. "Governmentality" and the Problem of Crime: Foucault, Criminology, Sociology. *Theoretical Criminology* 1 (2): 173–214.

Garrow, David. 1981. *The FBI and Martin Luther King, Jr.* New York: Penguin.

Garry, Eileen M. 1997. *Juvenile Firesetting and Arson.* Washington, DC: Office of Juvenile Justice and Delinquency Prevention.

Gasiorowski, Mark J., and Malcolm Byrne, eds. 2004. *Mohammad Mosaddeq and the 1953 Coup in Iran.* Syracuse, NY: Syracuse University Press.

Geis, Gilbert. 2000. On the Absence of Self-Control as the Basis for a General Theory of Crime. *Theoretical Criminology* 4 (1): 35–53.

General Accounting Office. 1988. *Controlling Drug Abuse: A Status Report.* Washington, DC:GAO/GGD.

Gibson, Mary. 2002. *Born to Crime: Cesare Lombroso and the Origins of Biological Criminology.* Westport, CT: Praeger.

Gibson, Mary, and Nicole Hahn Rafter. 2006. Editors' Introduction. In *Criminal Man,* by Cesare Lombroso, translated by Mary Gibson and Nicole Hahn Rafter, 1–36. Durham, NC: Duke University Press.

Gill, Martin. 2000. *Commercial Robbery.* London: Blackstone Press.

———. 2001. The Craft of Robbers of Cash-in-Transit Vans: Crime Facilitators and the Entrepreneurial Approach. *International Journal of the Sociology of Law,* 29 (3): 277–291.

Gill, M., J. Bryan and J. Allen. 2007. "Public Perceptions of CCTV in Residential Areas: 'It Is Not As Good As We Thought It Would Be'", *International Criminal Justice Review,* December 1, 2007; 17(4): 304–324.

Girshick, Lori. 2008a. Hate Crime (Bias Crime), Anti-Gay. In *Encyclopedia of Interpersonal Violence,* edited by Claire Renzetti and Jeffrey Edleson, 305–307. Thousand Oaks, CA: Sage.

———. 2008b. Same-Sex Intimate Partner Violence. In *Encyclopedia of Interpersonal Violence,* edited by Claire Renzetti and Jeffrey Edleson, 622–624. Thousand Oaks, CA: Sage.

Godfrey, Barry, Clive Emsley, and Graeme Dunstall. 2003. *Comparative Histories of Crime.* Portland, OR: Willan.

Goering, Laurie. 2008. Anti-terror Plans Raise "1984" Fears. *Chicago Tribune,* November 3.

Goetz, Barry. 2001. Arson. In *Encyclopedia of Criminology and Deviant Behavior,* edited by Clifton D. Bryant, 24–28. New York: Brunner-Routledge.

Goffman, Erving. 1961a. *Asylums.* New York: Anchor Books.

———. 1961b. *Encounters: Two Studies in the Sociology of Interaction.* New York: Bobbs-Merrill.

———. 1963. *Stigma.* Englewood Cliffs, NJ: Prentice-Hall.

Gonzalez, David. 2007. When American Dream Leads to Servitude. *New York Times,* April 24, available March 12, 2009 at: http://www.nytimes.com/2007/04/24/nyregion/24citywide.html.

Goode, Erich (ed.) (2009. *Out of Control: Assessing the General Theory of Crime.* Stanford, Ca.: Stanford University Press.

Gorgen, Thomas. 2006. "As If I Just Didn't Exist"—Elder Abuse and Neglect in Nursing Homes. In *Ageing, Crime and Society,* edited by Azrini Wahidin and Maureen Cain, 25–37. Portland, OR: Willan.

Goring, Charles. 1913. *The English Convict: A Statistical Study.* London: M.M.S.O.

Gottfredson, Michael R., and Travis Hirschi. 1990. *A General Theory of Crime.* Stanford, CA: Stanford University Press.

Gould, Eric D., Bruce A. Weinberg, and David B. Mustard. 2002. Crime Rates and Local Labor Market Opportunities in the United States: 1979–1997. *Review of Economics and Statistics.* 84 (1): 45–61.

Graber, Doris A. 1980. *Crime News and the Public.* New York: Praeger.

Grauerholz, Elizabeth, and Amy King. 1997. Prime-Time Sexual Harassment. *Violence Against Women* 3 (2): 129–148.

Gray, Emily, Jonathan Jackson, and Stephen Farrall. 2008. Reassessing the Fear of Crime. *European Journal of Criminology* 5 (3): 363–380.

Green, Mark, and John Francis Berry. 1985. *The Challenge of Hidden Profits.* New York: William Morrow.

Green, Mark, Beverly C. Moore, and Bruce Wasserstein. 1972. *The Closed Enterprise System.* New York: Bantam Books.

Greenberg, David F. 1977. Delinquency and the Age Structure of Society. *Contemporary Crises* 1 (2): 189–224.

———, ed. 1981. *Crime & Capitalism: Readings in Marxist Criminology.* Mountain View, CA: Mayfield.

———. 1983. Crime and Age. In *Encyclopedia of Crime and Justice,* edited by Sanford Kadish, 1: 30–35. New York: Macmillan.

———. 1985. Age, Crime, and Social Explanation. *American Journal of Sociology* 91 (1): 1–21.

———. 1988. *The Construction of Homosexuality.* Chicago: University of Chicago Press.

———, ed. 1993. *Crime and Capitalism: Readings in Marxist Criminology.* 2nd edition. Palo Alto, CA: Mayfield.

———. 2008. Age, Sex, and Racial Distributions of Crime. In *Out of Control: Assessing the General Theory of Crime,* edited by Erich Goode, 38–48. Stanford, CA: Stanford University Press.

Greenberg, Jerald. 1997. The STEAL Motive: Managing the Self-Determinants of Employee Theft. In *Antisocial Behavior in Organizations,* edited by Robert A. Giacalone and Jerald Greenberg, 85–108. Thousand Oaks, CA.

———. 2002. Who Stole the Money, and When? Individual and Situational Determinants of Employee Theft. *Organizational Behavior and Human Decision Processes* 89 (1): 985–1003.

Griscom, David L. 2008. How to Stuff the Electronic Ballot Box: "Hacking and Stacking" in Pima County, Arizona. In *Loser Take All: Election Fraud and the Subversion of Democracy, 2000–2008,* edited by Mark Crispin Miller, 116–130. Brooklyn, NY: IG Publishing.

Gros, Jean-Germain. 2008. Trouble in Paradise. In *Global Criminology and Criminal Justice,* edited by Nick Larsen and Russell Smandych, 67–86. Peterborough, Ontario: Broadview Press.

Grover, Chris. 2008. *Crime and Inequality.* Portland, OR: Willan.

Gurr, Ted Robert, Peter N. Grabosky, and Richard C. Hula. 1977. *The Politics of Crime and Conflict.* Beverly Hills: Sage.

Gutek, Barbara A. and Mary P. Koss. 2007. In *Gender Violence: Interdisciplinary Perspectives,* edited by Laura L. O'Toole, Jessica R. Schiffman, and Margie L. Kiter Edwards, 142–156. New York: New York University Press.

Gutierrez, Filomin C., and Donald J. Shoemaker. 2008. Self-reported Delinquency of High School Students in Metro-Manila: Gender and Social Class. *Youth and Society,* 40 (1): 55–85.

Gutman, Roy. 1988. *Banana Diplomacy: The Making of American Foreign Policy in Nicaragua, 1981–1987.* New York: Simon & Schuster.

Guttmacher, Manfred Schanfarber. 1951. *Sex Offenses.* New York: W.W. Norton.

Hagan, Frank E. 1997. *Political Crime: Ideology and Criminality.* Boston: Allyn & Bacon.

Hagan, John. 1989. *Structural Criminology.* New Brunswick, NJ: Rutgers University Press.

———. 1991. Destiny and Drift: Subcultural Preferences, Status Attainments, and the Risks and Rewards of Youth. *American Sociological Review* 56 (5): 567–582.

Hagan, John, and Bill McCarthy. 1997. *Mean Streets: Youth Crime and Homelessness.* New York: Cambridge University Press.

Hagan, John, Bill McCarthy, and Holly Foster. 2002. A Gendered Theory of Delinquency and Despair in the Life Course. *Acta Sociologica* 45: 37–46.

Hagan, John, and Ruth Peterson, eds. 1995. *Crime and Inequality.* Stanford, CA: Stanford University Press.

Hagan, John, Carla Shedd, and Monique R. Payne. 2005. Race, Ethnicity, and Youth Perceptions of Criminal Injustice. *American Sociological Review* 70 (3): 381–407.

Hall, Jerome. 1952. *Theft, Law, and Society.* New York: Bobbs-Merrill.

———. 1969. Theft, Law, and Society: The Carriers Case. In *Crime and the Legal Process,* edited by William J. Chambliss, 32–51. New York: McGraw-Hill.

Hall, Steve, Simon Winlow, and Craig Ancrum. 2008. *Criminal Identities and Consumer Culture.* Cullompton, Devon, UK: Willan.

Halliday, Denis. 2004. US Policy and Iraq: A Case of Genocide? In *Genocide, War Crimes, and the West,* edited by Adam Jones, 264–269. London: Zed Books.

Hamilton, Lee H. 1993. Case Closed. *New York Times* January 24, 17.

Hamlin, John E. 1988. The Misplaced Role of Rational Choice in Neutralization Theory. *Criminology* 26 (3): 425–438.

Hamm, Mark S. 1993. *American Skinheads: The Criminology and Control of Hate Crime.* Westport, CT: Praeger.

———. 2007. High Crimes and Misdemeanors: George W. Bush and the Sins of Abu Ghraib. *Crime, Media, Culture* 3 (3): 259–284.

Hattery, Angela J. 2009. *Intimate Partner Violence.* Lanham, MD: Rowman & Littlefield.

Hawkins, Darnell F. 2003. *Violent Crime: Assessing Race and Ethnic Differences.* New York: Cambridge University Press.

Hay, Carter, and Walter Forrest. 2008. Self-Control Theory and the Concept of Opportunity: The Case for a More Systematic Union. *Criminology* 46 (4): 1039–1071.

Hay, Douglas. 1975. Property, Authority, and the Criminal Law. In *Albion's Fatal Tree,* edited by Douglas Hay, Peter Linebaugh, John G. Rule, E. P. Thompson, and Cal Winslow, 17–63. New York: Pantheon.

Head, William B. 2001. Fences and Fencing. In *Encyclopedia of Criminology and Deviant Behavior,* edited by Clifton D. Bryant, 226–229. New York: Brunner-Routledge.

Hearn, Jeff, and Antony Whitehead. 2006. Collateral Damage: Men's "Domestic" Violence to Women Seen Through Men's Relation with Men. *Probation Journal* 53 (1): 38–56.

Heath, Linda, and Kevin Gilbert. 1996. Mass Media and Fear of Crime. *American Behavioral Scientist* 39 (4): 379–386.

Heidensohn, Frances. 1985. *Women and Crime: The Life of the Female Offender.* New York: New York University Press.

Held, David, Anthony McGrew, David Goldblatt, and Jonathan Perraton. 1999. *Global Transformations: Politics, Economics, and Culture.* Stanford, CA: Stanford University Press.

Henry, Stuart. 1976. The Other Side of the Fence. *Sociological Review* 24 (November): 793–806.

———. 1977. On the Fence. *British Journal of Law and Society* 4 (1): 124–133.

———. 1978. *The Hidden Economy.* London: Martin Robertson.

———. 1987. The Political Economy of Informal Economies. *Annals of the American Academy of Political and Social Science* 493 (September): 137–153.

Henry, Stuart, and Werner Einstadter, eds. 1998. *The Criminology Theory Reader.* New York: New York University Press.

Henry, Stuart, and Mark Lanier, eds. 2006. *The Essential Criminology Reader.* New York: Westview.

Henry, Stuart, and Scott A. Lukas. 2009. *Recent Developments in Criminological Theory.* Willington, VT: Ashgate.

Henry, Stuart, and Dragan Milovanovic. 1991. Constitutive Criminology: The Maturation of Critical Criminology. *Criminology* 29 (2): 293–315.

———. 1994. The Constitution of Constitutive Criminology: A Postmodern Approach to Criminological Theory. In *The Futures of Criminology,* edited by David Nelken. London: Sage.

———. 1996. *Constitutive Criminology: Beyond Postmodernism.* London: Sage.

Herek, Gregory M. 2009. Hate Crimes and Stigma-Related Experiences Among Sexual Minority Adults in the United States: Prevalence Estimates from a National Probability Sample. *Journal of Interpersonal Violence,* 24 (1): 54–74.

Herman, Edward. 1982. *The Real Terror Network.* Boston: South End Press.

Hewitt, Christopher. 2003. *Understanding Terrorism in America: From the Klan to Al Qaeda.* New York: Routledge.

Higgins, George E., Brian D. Fell, and Abby L. Wilson. 2007. Low Self-Control and Social Learning in Understanding Students' Intentions to Pirate Movies in the United States. *Social Science Computer Review* 25 (3): 339–357.

Hills, Stuart, ed. 1987. *Corporate Violence.* Totowa, NJ: Rowman & Littlefield.

Hills, Stuart L., and Ron Santiago. 1992. *Tragic Magic: The Life and Crimes of a Heroin Addict.* Chicago: Nelson-Hall.

Hinckle, Warren, and William Turner. 1981. *The Fish Is Red: The Story of the Secret War Against Castro.* New York: Harper & Row.

Hindelang, Michael J. 1970. The Commitment of Delinquents to Their Misdeeds: Do Delinquents Drift? *Social Problems* 17 (4): 502–509.

———. 1974. Moral Evaluations of Illegal Behaviors. *Social Problems* 21 (3): 370–385.

Hirschfield, Paul J. 2008. The Declining Significance of Delinquent Labels in Disadvantaged Urban Communities. *Sociological Forum* 23 (3): 575–601.

Hirschi, Travis. 1969. *Causes of Delinquency.* Berkeley: University of California Press.

———. 1983. Crime and the Family. In *Crime and Public Policy,* edited by James Q. Wilson, 53–68. San Francisco: Institute for Contemporary Studies.

Hirschi, Travis, and Michael Gottfredson. 1983. Age and the Explanation of Crime. *American Journal of Sociology* 89 (3): 552–584.

———. 1993. Commentary: Testing the General Theory of Crime. *Journal of Research in Crime and Delinquency* 30 (1): 47–54.

———. 2000. In Defense of Self-Control. *Theoretical Criminology* 4 (1): 55–69.

———. 2008. Critiquing the Critics: The Authors Respond. In *Out of Control: Assessing the General Theory of Crime*, edited by Erich Goode, 217–231. Stanford, CA: Stanford University Press.

Hirschi, Travis and Michael R. Gottfredson. 2008. "Critiquing the Critics: The Authors Respond." Pp.217=231 in Erich Goode (ed.) 2008. *Out of Control: Assessing the General Theory of Crime*. Stanford, CA.: Stanford University Press.

Hoffman, Abbie, and Jonathan Silvers. 1988. An Election Held Hostage. *Playboy* 35 (10): 73–74.

Hoffman-Bustamante, Dale. 1973. The Nature of Female Criminality. *Issues in Criminology* 8 (2): 117–132.

Hollinger, Richard C., and John P. Clark. 1983. *Theft by Employees*. Lexington, MA: Lexington Books.

Holmes, Ronald M., and James E. DeBurger. 1988. *Serial Murder*. Beverly Hills: Sage.

Holtfreter, Kristy. 2005. Employee Crimes. In *Encyclopedia of White-Collar & Corporate Crime*, edited by Lawrence Salinger, 284–288. Thousand Oaks, CA: Sage.

Holtfreter, Kristy, Michael Reisig, and Merry Morash. 2004. Poverty, State Capital, and Recidivism Among Women Offenders. *Criminology and Public Policy* 3: 185–208.

Honegger, Barbara. 1989. *October Surprise*. New York: Tudor.

Hopkins, Elaine. 1988. A Matter of Conscience for a G-Man. *The Progressive* 52 (3):14.

Horn, David G. 2003. *The Criminal Body: Lombroso and the Anatomy of Deviance*. New York: Routledge.

Human Rights Watch. 2005a. *Afghanistan*. New York: Human Rights Watch.

———. 2005b. *Guantanamo: Three Years of Lawlessness*. New York: Human Rights Watch.

———. 2008. *US/Jordan: Stop Renditions to Torture*. Available at: http://www.hrw.org/en/news/2008/04/07/usjordan-stop-renditions-torture.

———. 2009. *Afghanistan: New Law Threatens Women's Freedom*. Washington, DC: Human Rights Watch.

Humphreys, Laud. 1970. *Tearoom Trade: Impersonal Sex in Public Places*. Chicago: Aldine.

Hunter, Mic. 2000. Sexual Abuse of Children. In *Encyclopedia of Women and Crime*, edited by Nicole Hahn Rafter, 238–239. Phoenix, AZ: Oryx Press.

Huston, Aletha C., Halford H. Fairchild, and Edward Donnerstein. 1992. *Big World, Small Screen: The Role of Television in American Life*. Lincoln: University of Nebraska Press.

Iadicola, Peter, and Anson Shupe. 1998. *Violence, Inequality, and Human Freedom*. Dix Hills, NY: General Hall.

ICBS 2009. *International Crime Business Survey*. United Nations: Office on Drugs and Crime.

Ignatius, David. 1986. The Contrapreneurs: Skirting Congress and the Law for Years. *Washington Post*, December 7, D1, D2.

Intergovernmental Panel on Climate Change. 2008. *IPCC Fourth Assessment Report, 2007: Synthesis for Policymakers*. Available at: http://www.ipcc.ch/ipcc reports/ar4wg2.htm.

International Campaign for Justice in Bhopal. 2009. *25 Years of Courage in the Face of Corporate Crime*. Available April 6, 2009, at: http://www.bhopal.net/index1.html.

Internet Crime Complaint Center. 2009. *Internet Crime Report, 2008*. Available at: http://news.cnet.com/8301-1023_3-10208355-93.html.

Iovanni, LeeAnn, and Susan L. Miller. 2008. A Feminist Consideration of Gender and Crime. In *Out of Control: Assessing the General Theory of Crime*, edited by Erich Goode, 127–141. Stanford, CA: Stanford University Press.

IVAWS. 2009. *International Violence Against Women Survey*. Available on April 14, 2009, at: http://www.heuni.fi/12859.htm.

Jacobs, Bruce A., and Richard Wright. 2008. Researching Drug Robbery. *Crime & Delinquency* 54 (4): 511–531.

Jacobs, David. 1981. Inequality and Economic Crime. *Sociology and Social Research* 66 (1): 12–28.

Jaggar, Alison M. 1983. *Feminist Politics and Human Nature*. Totowa, NJ: Rowman & Allanheld.

Jaggar, Alison M., and Paula Rothenberg, eds. 1984. *Feminist Frameworks*. New York: McGraw-Hill.

Jamieson, Dale. 2003. *Morality's Progress: Essays on Humans, Other Animals, and the Rest of Nature.* Oxford: Oxford University Press.

Jefferson, Tony. 1996. From "Little Fairy Boy" to the "Compleat Destroyer": Subjectivity and Transformation in the Biography of Mike Tyson. In *Understanding Masculinities: Social Relations and Cultural Arenas,* edited by M. Mac an Ghail, 153–167. Buckingham, UK: Open University Press.

Jeffery, Clarence Ray. 1965. Criminal Behavior and Learning Theory. *Journal of Criminal Law, Criminology, and Police Science* 56 (3): 294–300.

Jenkins, Philip. 1984. Varieties of Enlightenment Criminology. *British Journal of Criminology* 24 (2): 112–130.

———. 1988. Myth and Murder: The Serial Killer Panic of 1983–1985. *Criminal Justice Research Bulletin* 3 (11): 1–7.

———. 1994. *Using Murder: The Social Construction of Serial Homicide.* New York: Aldine de Gruyter.

———. 2003. *Images of Terror: What We Can and Can't Know About Terrorism.* New York: Walter De Gruyter.

———. 2009. Failure to Launch: Why Do Some Social Issues Fail to Detonate Moral Panics? *British Journal of Criminology* 49 (1): 35–47.

Jesilow, Paul D., Henry N. Pontell, and Gilbert Geis. 1993. *Prescription for Profit: How Doctors Defraud Medicaid.* Berkeley: University of California Press.

Jewkes, Yvonne, and Majid Yar, eds. 2009. *Handbook of Internet Crime.* Portland, OR: Willan.

Joe, Karen A., and Meda Chesney-Lind. 1998. "Just Every Mother's Angel": An Analysis of Gender and Ethnic Variations in Youth Gang Membership. In *Criminology at the Crossroads: Feminist Readings in Crime and Justice,* edited by Kathleen Daly and Lisa Maher, 87–109. New York: Oxford University Press.

Johansen, Bruce, and Roberto Maestas. 1979. *Wasicbu: The Continuing Indian Wars.* New York: Monthly Review Press.

Johnson, David T. 2008. The Homicide Drop in Postwar Japan. *Homicide Studies* 12 (1): 146–16.

Johnson, Devon. 2009. Anger About Crime and Support for Punitive Criminal Justice Policies. *Punishment & Society* 11 (1): 51–66.

Johnson, Michael P. 2001. Conflict and Control: Symmetry and Asymmetry in Domestic Violence. In *Couples in Conflict,* edited by Alan Booth, Ann C. Crouter, and Mari Clements, 95–104. Mahwah, NJ: Lawrence Erlbaum Associates.

———. 2007. Domestic Violence: The Intersection of Gender and Control. In *Gender Violence: Interdisciplinary Perspectives,* edited by Laura L. O'Toole, Jessica R. Schiffman, and Margie L. Kiter Edwards, 257–268. New York: New York University Press.

Johnson, Michael P., and Kathleen J. Ferraro. 2000. Research on Domestic Violence in the 1990s: Making Distinctions. *Journal of Marriage and the Family* 62 (November): 948–963.

Johnstone, John W. C., Darnell F. Hawkins, and Arthur Michener. 1994. Homicide Reporting in Chicago Dailies. *Journalism Quarterly* 71 (4): 860–872.

Jones, Adam, ed.. 2004. *Genocide, War Crimes, and the West: History and Complicity.* London: Zed Books.

Jones, Nikki. 2008. Working the Code: On Girls, Gender, and Inner-City Violence. *Australian and New Zealand Journal of Criminology* 41 (1): 63–83.

Joseph, Janice. 2003. Cyberstalking: An International Perspective. In *Dot.cons: Crime, Deviance, and Identity on the Internet,* edited by Yvonne Jewkes, 105–125. Portland, OR: Willan.

Junger-Tas, Josine. 1994. Delinquency in Thirteen Western Countries: Some Preliminary Conclusions. In *Delinquent Behavior Among Young People in the Western World: First Results of the International Self-Report Delinquency Study,* edited by Josine Junger-Tas, GertJan Terlouw, and Malcolm W. Klein, 370–385. Amsterdam: Kugler Publications.

Jurik, Nancy, and Peter Gregware. 1992. A Method for Murder: The Study of Homicides by Women. *Perspectives on Social Problems* 4 (2): 179–201.

Katz, Jack. 1988. *The Seductions of Crime.* New York: Basic Books.

Kaufman, Joanne M., Cesar J. Rebellon, Sherod Thaxton, and Robert Agnew. 2008. A General Strain Theory of Racial Differences in Criminal Offending. *Australian and New Zealand Journal of Criminology,* 41 (3): 421–437.

Kellner, Douglas. 2003. *From 9/11 to Terror War: The Dangers of the Bush Legacy.* New York: Rowman & Littlefield.

——. 1901. *Experimental Sociology: Delinquents.* New York: Macmillan.

Kelly, Orr, and Ted Gest. 1982. Reagan Revolution Takes Firm Hold at Justice. *U.S. News and World Report,* April 26, 24–26.

Kendall-Tackett, Kathleen. 2000. Incest Victims. In *Encyclopedia of Women and Crime,* edited by Nicole Hahn Rafter, 114. Phoenix, AZ: Oryx Press.

——. 2008. Incest. In *Encyclopedia of Interpersonal Violence,* edited by Claire Renzetti and Jeffrey Edleson, 350–351. Thousand Oaks, CA: Sage.

Kendall-Tackett, Kathleen, and Roberta Marshall. 1998. Abuse. In *Issues in Intimate Violence,* edited by Raquel Kennedy Bergen, 47–63. Thousand Oaks, CA: Sage.

Kerbo, Harold, and Mariko Inoue. 1990. Japanese Social Structure and White-Collar Crime. *Deviant Behavior* 11 (2): 139–154.

Kernsmith, Poco. 2008. Stalking. In *Encyclopedia of Interpersonal Violence,* edited by Claire Renzetti and Jeffrey Edleson, 687–688. Thousand Oaks, CA: Sage.

Kilday, Anne-Marie. 2007. *Women and Violent Crime in Enlightenment Scotland.* London: Boydell and Brewer.

Kimmel, Michael S., and Matthew Mahler. 2003. Adolescent Masculinity, Homophobia, and Violence: Random School Shootings, 1982–2001. *American Behavioral Scientist* 46 (10): 1439–1458.

King, Harry, and William J. Chambliss. 1984. *Box-Man: A Professional Thief's Journey.* New York: John Wiley.

Kitsuse, John I., and Aaron V. Cicourel. 1963. A Note on the Uses of Official Statistics. *Social Problems* 11 (2): 131–139.

Kitsuse, John I., and David C. Dietrick. 1959. Delinquent Boys: A Critique. *American Sociological Review* 24 (2): 208–215.

Kleck, Gary, and Ted Chiricos. 2002. Unemployment and Property Crime: A Target-Specific Assessment of Opportunity and Motivation as Mediating Factors. *Criminology* 40: 649–680.

Klein, Jessie. 2006. Cultural Capital and High School Bullies: How Social Inequality Impacts School Violence. *Men and Masculinities,* 9 (1): 53–75.

Klemke, Lloyd W. 1992. *The Sociology of Shoplifting: Boosters and Snitches Today.* Westport, CT: Praeger.

——. 2001. Shoplifting. In *Encyclopedia of Criminology and Deviant Behavior,* edited by Clifton D. Bryant, 469–472. New York: Brunner-Routledge.

Klockars, Carl B. 1974. *The Professional Fence.* New York: Free Press.

Komiya, Nobuo. 1999. A Cultural Study of the Low Crime Rate in Japan. *British Journal of Criminology* 30 (3): 369–390.

Kornbluh, Peter. 2003. *The Pinochet File: A Declassified Dossier on Atrocity and Accountability.* New York: W.W. Norton.

Koss, Mary P., and J. Gaines. 1993. The Prediction of Sexual Aggression by Alcohol Use, Athletic Participation, and Fraternity Affiliation. *Journal of Interpersonal Violence* 8 (1): 94–108.

Kramer, Ronald C. 1992. The Space Shuttle Challenger Explosion: A Case Study of State-Corporate Crime. In *White-Collar Crime Reconsidered,* edited by Kip Schlegel and David Weisburd, 214–243. Boston: Northeastern University Press.

Kramer, Ronald C., and Raymond J. Michalowski. 1990. *Toward an Integrated Theory of State-Corporate Crime.* Unpublished manuscript.

——. 2004. *War, Aggression, and State Crime: A Criminological Analysis of the Invasion and Occupation of Iraq.* Unpublished manuscript.

Kramer, Ron, Raymond Michalowski, and Dawn Rothe. 2005. "The Supreme International Crime": How the U.S. War in Iraq Threatens the Rule of Law. *Social Justice* 32 (2): 52–81.

Krohn, Marvin D. 1999. Social Learning Theory: The Continuing Development of a Perspective. *Theoretical Criminology* 3 (4): 462–476.

Kruger, Henrik. 1980. *The Great Heroin Coup.* Boston: South End Press.

Kubrin, Charles E., and Eric A. Stewart. 2006. Predicting Who Reoffends: The Neglected Role of Neighborhood Context in Recidivism Studies. *Criminology* 44: 165–198.

Kunstler, William. 1978. FBI Letters: Writers of the Purple Rage. *The Nation,* December 30, 721–722.

Kupers, Terry A. 2001. Rape and the Prison Code. In *Prison Masculinities,* edited by Don Sabo, Terry A.

Kupers, and Willie London, 111–117. Philadelphia: Temple University Press.

Kurtz, Howard. 1988. E. F. Hutton to Plead Guilty. *Washington Post*, April 2, A3.

LaFree, Gary. 1999. Declining Violent Crime Rates in the 1990s: Predicting Crime Booms and Busts. *Annual Review of Sociology* 25: 145–169.

LaFree, Gary, and Kriss A. Drass. 2002. Counting Crime Booms Among Nations: Evidence for Homicide Victimization Rates, 1956 to 1998. *Criminology* 40 (4): 769–800.

LaFree, Gary, and Michelle Hussong. 2001. Race and Crime. In *Encyclopedia of Criminology and Deviant Behavior*, edited by Clifton D. Bryant, 441–448. New York: Brunner-Routledge.

Lamour, Catherine, and Michael R. Lamberti. 1974. *The International Connection: Opium from Growers to Pushers*. New York: Pantheon Books.

Lane, David. 1996. *The Rise and Fall of State Socialism*. Cambridge: Polity Press.

———. 2007. Post State Socialism: A Diversity of Capitalisms? In *Varieties of Capitalism in Post-Communist Countries*, edited by David Lane and Martin Myant, 13–39. London: Palgrave.

Lane, Jodi, and James W. Meeker. 2003a. Ethnicity, Information Sources, and Fear of Crime. *Deviant Behavior* 24 (1): 1–26.

———. 2003b. Women's and Men's Fear of Gang Crimes: Sexual and Nonsexual Assault as Perceptually Contemporaneous Offenses. *Justice Quarterly* 20 (2): 337–371.

Langton, Lynn, and Nicole Leeper Piquero. 2007. Can General Strain Theory Explain White-Collar Crime? *Journal of Criminal Justice* 35 (1): 1–15.

Larsen, Nick, and Russell Smandych, eds. 2008a. *Global Criminology and Criminal Justice*. Peterborough, Ontario: Broadview Press.

———. 2008b. Introduction: Foundations for a Global Criminology and Criminal Justice. In *Global Criminology and Criminal Justice*, edited by Nick Larsen and Russell Smandych, 1–21. Peterborough, Ontario: Broadview Press.

Laub, John H. 1983. *Criminology in the Making: An Oral History* Boston: Northeastern University Press.

———. 2004. The Life Course of Criminology in the United States: The American Society of Criminology 2003 Presidential Address. *Criminology* 42 (1): 1–26.

Laub, John H., and Robert J. Sampson. 1988. Unraveling Families and Delinquency: A Reanalysis of the Gluecks Data. *Criminology* 26 (3): 355–380.

Lea, John, and Jock Young. 1984. *What Is to Be Done About Law and Order?* New York: Penguin.

———. 1986. A Realistic Approach to Law and Order. In *The Political Economy of Crime: Readings for a Critical Criminology*, edited by Brian MacLean, 358–364. Englewood Cliffs, NJ: Prentice-Hall.

Lee, Chul-joo, and Oscar Gandy, 2006. A Case Study of Why Local Reporting Matters: Photojournalism Framing of the Response to Hurricane Katrina. *Rethinking the Discourse on Race*. St. John's University School of Law, April 28.

Lee, Matthew R., and William B. Bankston. 1999. Political Structure, Economic Inequality, and Homicide: A Cross-National Comparison. *Deviant Behavior* 19: 27–55.

Lee, Matthew R., and Graham C. Ousey. 2007. Counterbalancing Disadvantage? Residential Integration and Urban Black Homicide. *Social Problems* 54 (2): 240–262.

Lee, Murray. 2007. *Inventing Fear of Crime: Criminology and the Politics of Anxiety*. Cullompton, Devon, UK: Willan.

Lefkowitz, Bernard. 1997. *Our Guys: The Glen Ridge Rape and the Secret Life of the Perfect Suburb*. New York: Vintage.

Lemert, Edwin M. 1951. *Social Pathology: A Systematic Approach to the Theory of Sociopathic Behavior*. New York: McGraw-Hill.

———. 1967. *Human Deviance, Social Problems, and Social Control*. Englewood Cliffs, NJ: Prentice-Hall.

Lens, Sidney. 1973. *The Labor Wars: From the Molly Maguires to the Sitdowns*. New York: Doubleday.

Leonardsen, Dag. 2004. *Japan as a Low-Crime Nation*. New York: Palgrave MacMillan.

———. 2006. Crime in Japan: Paradise Lost? *Journal of Scandinavian Studies in Criminology and Crime Prevention* 7: 185–210.

Levin, Jack, and Jack McDevitt. 1993. *Hate Crimes: The Rising Tide of Bigotry and Bloodshed*. New York: Plenum Press.

Liebert, Robert M., and Joyce Sprafkin. 1988. *The Early Window: Effects of Television on Children and Youth.* New York: Pergamon Press.

Lifschultz, Lawrence. 1988. Inside the Kingdom of Heroin. *The Nation* (November 14): 477, 492–496.

Link, Bruce G., Francis T. Cullen, James Frank, and John F. Wozniak. 1987. The Social Rejection of Former Mental Patients: Understanding Why Labels Matter. *American Journal of Sociology* 92 (6): 1461–1500.

Liska, Allen E. 1981. *Perspectives on Deviance.* Englewood Cliffs, NJ: Prentice Hall.

Loader, Ian, and Richard Sparks. 2002. Contemporary Landscapes of Crime, Order, and Control: Governance, Risk, and Globalization. In *The Oxford Handbook of Criminology,* 3rd edition, edited by Mike Maguire, Rod Morgan, and Robert Reiner. Oxford: Oxford University Press.

Loeber, Rolf, N. Wim Slot, and Magda Stouthamer-Loeber. 2006. A Three-Dimensional, Cumulative Developmental Model of Serious Delinquency. In *The Explanation of Crime: Context, Mechanisms and Development,* edited by Per-Olof Wikström and Robert J. Sampson, 153–194. Cambridge: Cambridge University Press.

Lombroso, Cesare. 1876. *L'uomo delinquente (Criminal Man).* Milan: Hoepli.

Lombroso, Cesare, and William Ferrero. 1895 [1972]. *The Female Offender.* 1893. Reprint, London: T. Fisher Unwin.

Lowrey, Annie. 2009. The Torture Timeline. *Foreign Policy.* Available at www.foreignpolicy.com.

Luckenbill, David F. 1977. Criminal Homicide as a Situated Transaction. *Social Problems* 25 (2): 176–186.

———. 1981. Generating Compliance: The Case of Robbery. *Urban Life* 10 (1): 25–46.

Lynch, James P., and Lynn A. Addington. 2007. *Understanding Crime Statistics: Revisiting the Divergence of the NCVS and UCR.* Cambridge: Cambridge University Press.

Lynch, Michael J. 1990. The Greening of Criminology: A Perspective on the 1990s. *The Critical Criminologist* 2 (3): 1–4, 11–12.

Lynch, Michael J., and Raymond J. Michalowski. 2006. *Primer in Radical Criminology: Critical Perspectives on Power, Crime and Identity.* Monsey, NY: Criminal Justice Press.

Lynch, Michael J., and Paul Stretesky. 2003. The Meaning of Green: Contrasting Criminological Perspectives. *Theoretical Criminology* 7 (2): 217–239.

———. 2007. Green Criminology in the United States. In *Issues in Green Criminology: Confronting Harms Against Environments, Humanity, and Other Animals,* edited by Piers Beirne and Nigel South, 248–269. Cullompton, Devon, UK: Willan Press.

Lynch, Michael J., Paul Stretesky, and Paul Hammond. 2000. Media Coverage of Chemical Crimes, Hillsborough County, Florida, 1987–97. *British Journal of Criminology* 40 (1): 112–126.

Lynd, Robert S. 1939. *Knowledge for What?* Princeton, NJ: Princeton University Press.

Lyng, Stephen. 2005. *Edgework: The Sociology of Risk Taking.* New York: Routledge.

Maas, Peter. 1986. *Manhunt.* New York: Random House.

MacKinnon, Catharine A. 1984. Not a Moral Issue. *Yale Law and Policy Review* 2 (2): 32–145.

MacLean, Brian D., and Dragan Milovanovic, eds. 1998. *Thinking Critically About Crime.* Vancouver, B.C.: Collective Press.

Mahajan, Rahul. 2002. *Full-Spectrum Dominance: U.S. Power in Iraq and Beyond.* New York: Seven Stories Press.

Mahoney, Patricia, Linda M. Williams, and Carolyn M. West. 2001. Violence Against Women by Intimate Relationship Partners. In *Sourcebook on Violence Against Women,* edited by Claire M. Renzetti, Jeffrey L. Edleson, and Raquel Kennedy Bergen, 143–178. Thousand Oaks, CA: Sage.

Maier, Mark, and James W. Messerschmidt. 1998. Commonalities, Conflicts, and Contradictions in Organizational Masculinities: Exploring the Gendered Genesis of the Challenger Disaster. *Canadian Review of Sociology and Anthropology* 35 (3): 325–344.

Mandino, Carole. 2000. Old Enough to Know Better? Aging and Criminal Justice. In *Investigating Difference: Human and Cultural Relations in Criminal Justice,* edited by Criminal Justice Collective, 161–170. Boston: Allyn & Bacon.

Marcuse, Herbert. 1964. *One-Dimensional Man.* Boston: Beacon Press.

Markowitz, Gerald, and David Rosner. 2002. *Deceit and Denial: The Deadly Politics of Industrial Pollution.* Berkeley, CA: University of California Press.

Mars, Gerald. 1983. *Cheats at Work*. Boston: Unwin.

Marshall, Ineke Haen. 2008. The Criminological Enterprise in Europe and the United States: A Contextual Exploration. In *Global Criminology and Criminal Justice*, edited by Nick Larsen and Russell Smandych, 47–66. Peterborough, Ontario: Broadview Press.

Marshall, Johnathan, Peter Dale Scott, and Jane Hunter. 1987. *The Iran-Contra Connection*. Boston: South End Press.

Martin, Susan E. 2001. Hate Crimes. In *Encyclopedia of Criminology and Deviant Behavior*, edited by Clifton D. Bryant, 254–257. New York: Brunner-Routledge.

Marx, Gary T. 1981. Ironies of Social Control: Authorities as Contributors to Deviance Through Escalation, Non-Enforcement, and Covert Facilitation. *Social Problems* 28 (3): 221–246.

Marx, Karl. [1842a] 1975. Comments on the Latest Prussian Censorship Instruction. In *Karl Marx/Frederick Engels Collected Works*, 1: 109–131. London: Lawrence and Wishart.

———. [1842b] 1975b. Proceedings of the Sixth Rhine Province Assembly. Debates on the Law on Thefts of Wood. In *Karl Marx/Frederick Engels: Collected Works*, 1: 224–263. London: Lawrence and Wishart.

———. [1852] 1969b. The Eighteenth Brumaire of Louis Bonaparte. In *Karl Marx and Frederick Engels: Selected Works*, 1: 398–487. Moscow: Progress Publishers.

———. [1853] 1956. Capital Punishment. In *Karl Marx: Selected Writings in Sociology and Social Philosophy*, edited by T. B. Bottomore and Maximilian Rubel, 228–230. New York: McGraw-Hill.

———. [1857–1858] 1973. *Grundrisse: Introduction to the Critique of Political Economy*. Translated and introduced by Martin Nicolaus. New York: Vintage.

———. 1859. Population, Crime, and Pauperism. *New York Daily Tribune*, September 16.

———. [1859] 1969c. Preface to A Contribution to the Critique of Political Economy. In *Karl Marx and Frederick Engels: Selected Works*, 1: 502–506. Moscow: Progress Publishers.

———. [1868] 1967. *Capital*. 3 vols. New York: International Publishers.

———. [1871] 1969d. The Civil War in France. In *Karl Marx and Frederick Engels: Selected Works*, 2: 190–244. Moscow: Progress Publishers.

Marx, Karl, and Friedrich Engels. [1845] 1976. *The German Ideology*. Moscow: Progress Publishers.

———. [1848] 1969a. The Communist Manifesto. In *Karl Marx and Frederick Engels: Selected Works*, 1: 108–137. Moscow: Progress Publishers.

Mathews, Roger. 2002. *Armed Robbery*. Portland, OR: Willan.

Matsueda, Ross L. 1997. "Cultural Deviance Theory": The Remarkable Persistence of a Flawed Term. *Theoretical Criminology* 1 (4): 429–452.

———. 2008. On the Compatibility of Self-Control and Social Disorganization. In *Out of Control: Assessing the General Theory of Crime*, edited by Erich Goode, 102–126. Stanford, CA: Stanford University Press.

Mattera, Philip. 1985. *Off the Books*. New York: St. Martin's Press.

Matthews, Roger. 1987. Taking Realist Criminology Seriously. *Contemporary Crises* 11 (4): 371–401.

Matza, David. 1964. *Delinquency and Drift*. New York: John Wiley.

———. 1969. *Becoming Deviant*. Englewood Cliffs, NJ: Prentice-Hall.

Matza, David, and Gresham M. Sykes. 1961. Juvenile Delinquency and Subterranean Values. *American Sociological Review* 26 (5): 712–719.

Mawby, Rob. 2001. *Burglary*. Portland, OR: Willan.

Mawby, Rob C., and William Gisby. 2009. Crime, Media and Moral Panic in an Expanding European Union. *Howard Journal* 48 (1): 37–51.

Mayer, P. 1953. Gusii Initiation Ceremonies. *Journal of the Royal Anthropological Institute* 83:9–36.

McCaghy, Charles H., Peggy C. Giordano, and Trudy Knicely Henson. 1977. Auto Theft: Offender and Offense Characteristics. *Criminology* 15 (3): 367–385.

McClennen, Joan C. 2005. Domestic Violence Between Same-Gender Partners: Recent Findings and Future Research. *Journal of Interpersonal Violence* 20 (2): 149–154.

McClintock, Michael. 1985. *The American Connection: State Terror and Popular Resistance in Guatemala*. London: Zed Books.

McCorkle, Jill. 2003. Embodied Surveillance and the Gendering of Punishment. *Journal of Contemporary Ethnography* 32 (1): 41–76.

McCorkle, Richard C., and Terance D. Miethe. 2003. Robbery. In *Encyclopedia of Murder and Violent*

*Crime,* edited by Eric Hickey, 394–400. Thousand Oaks, CA: Sage.

McCoy, Alfred. 1972. *The Politics of Heroin Southeast Asia.* New York: Harper & Row.

———. 2006. *A Question of Torture: CIA Interrogation, From the Cold War to the War on Terror.* New York: Metropolitan Books.

McCullagh, Ciaran. 1996. *Crime in Ireland: A Sociological Introduction.* Cork, Ireland: Cork University Press.

McFarlane, Judith M., Jacquelyn C. Campbell, Susan Wilt, Carolyn J. Sachs, Yvonne Ulrich, and Xiao Xu. 1999. Stalking and Intimate Partner Femicide. *Homicide Studies* 3 (4): 300–316.

McGarrell, Edmund F., and Thomas C. Castellano. 1991. An Integrative Conflict Model of the Criminal Law Formation Process. *Journal of Research in Crime and Delinquency* 28 (2): 174–196.

McNulty, Thomas, and Paul Bellair. 2003. Explaining Racial and Ethnic Differences in Serious Adolescent Violent Behavior. *Criminology* 41: 709–749.

McSherry, J. Patrice. 2001. *Operation Condor: Deciphering the U.S. Role.* Crimes of War Project. Available at: http://www.crimesofwar.org.

Mead, Margaret. 1928. *Coming of Age in Samoa.* New York: Blue Ribbon Books.

Merton, Robert K. [1938] 1969. Social Structure and Anomie. In *Delinquency, Crime, and Social Process,* edited by Donald R. Cressey and David A. Ward, 254–284. New York: Harper & Row.

Messerschmidt, James W. 1986a. *The Trial of Leonard Peltier.* Boston: South End Press.

———. 1986b. *Capitalism, Patriarchy, and Crime: Toward a Socialist Feminist Criminology.* Totowa, NJ: Rowman & Littlefield.

———. 1987. Feminism, Criminology, and the Rise of the Female Sex Delinquent, 1880–1930. *Contemporary Crises* 11 (3): 243–263.

———. 1993. *Masculinities and Crime: Critique and Reconceptualization of Theory.* Lanham, MD: Rowman & Littlefield.

———. 1997. *Crime as Structured Action: Gender, Race, Class, and Crime in the Making.* Thousand Oaks, CA: Sage.

———. 2000. *Nine Lives: Adolescent Masculinities, the Body, and Violence.* Boulder, CO: Westview.

———. 2004. *Flesh & Blood: Adolescent Gender Diversity and Violence.* Lanham, MD: Rowman & Littlefield.

———. 2007. "We Must Protect Our Southern Women": On Whiteness, Masculinities, and Lynching. In *Race, Gender, and Punishment: From Colonialism to the War on Terror,* edited by Mary Bosworth and Jeanne Flavin, 77–94. New Brunswick, NJ: Rutgers University Press.

Messner, Michael A. 2002. *Taking the Field: Women, Men, and Sports.* Minneapolis: University of Minnesota Press.

———. 2005. Still a Man's World? Studying Masculinities and Sport. In *Handbook of Studies on Men & Masculinities,* edited by Michael S. Kimmel, Jeff Hearn, and Raewyn Connell, 313–325. Thousand Oaks, CA: Sage.

Messner, Michael A., and Mark Stevens. 2002. Scoring Without Consent: Confronting Male Athletes' Sexual Violence Against Women. In *Paradoxes of Youth and Sport,* edited by Margaret Gatz, Sandra Ball Rokeach, and Michael A. Messner, 225–240. Albany: State University of New York Press.

Messner, Steven F., and Richard Rosenfeld. 2007. *Crime and the American Dream.* 4th edition. Belmont, CA: Wadsworth/Thomson Learning.

Messner, Steven F., Helmut Thome, and Richard Rosenfeld. 2008. Institutions, Anomie, and Violent Crime: Clarifying and Elaborating Institutional-Anomie Theory. *International Journal of Conflict and Violence* 2 (2): 164–181.

Michael, Jerome, and Mortimer J. Adler. [1933] 1971. *Crime, Law, and Social Science.* Montclair, NJ: Patterson Smith.

Michalowski, Raymond J. 1985. *Order, Law, and Crime.* New York: Random House.

———. 2007. Border Militarization and Migrant Suffering: A Case of Transnational Social Injury. *Social Justice* 34 (2): 62–76.

Michalowski, Raymond J., and Ed Bolander. 1976. Repression and Criminal Justice in Capitalist America. *Sociological Inquiry* 46 (2): 99–110.

Michalowski, Raymond J., and Ronald C. Kramer. 1987. The Space Between Laws: The Problem of Corporate Crime in a Transnational Context. *Social Problems* 34 (1): 34–53.

Miethe, Terance D., and Richard C. McCorkle. 1997. Gang Membership and Criminal Processing: A Test of the "Master Status" Concept. *Justice Quarterly* 14 (3): 407–427.

Mill, John Stuart. [1851] 1970. *The Subjection of Women.* New York: Source Book Press.

Miller, Jody. 1998. "Up It Up": Gender and the Accomplishment of Robbery. *Criminology* 36 (1): 37–66.

———. 2001. *One of the Guys: Girls, Gangs, and Gender.* New York: Oxford University Press.

———. 2002. The Strength and Limits of "Doing Gender" for Understanding Street Crime. *Theoretical Criminology* 6 (4): 433–60.

———. 2008. *Getting Played: African American Girls, Urban Inequality, and Gendered Violence.* New York: New York University Press.

Miller, Jody, and Christopher Mullins. 2006. Stuck Up, Telling Lies, and Talking Too Much: The Gendered Context of Women's Violence. In *Gender and Crime: Patterns of Victimization and Offending,* edited by Karen Heimer and Candace Kruttschmidt, 44–66. New York: Routledge.

Miller, Mark Crispin, ed. 2008. *Loser Take All: Election Fraud and the Subversion of Democracy, 2000–2008.* Brooklyn, NY: IG Publishing.

Miller, Walter B. 1958. Lower-Class Culture as a Generating Milieu of Gang Delinquency. *Journal of Social Issues* 14 (3): 5–19.

Milovanovic, Dragan. 2006. Edgework: Negotiating Boundaries. In *The Essential Criminology Reader,* edited by Stuart Henry and Mark Lanier, 234–246. New York: Westview.

Mintz, Morton. 1986. A Crime Against Women: A. H. Robbins and the Dalkon Shield. *Multinational Monitor,* January 15, 17.

Miyazawa, Setsuo. 1993. The Enigma of Japan as a Testing Ground for Cross-Cultural Criminological Studies. *Annales Internationales de Criminologie* 32: 81–102.

———. 2008. The Politics of Increasing Punitiveness and the Rising Populism in Japanese Criminal Justice Policy. *Punishment & Society* 10 (1): 47–77.

Mokhiber, Russell. 1999. *Corporate Predators: The Hunt for Mega-Profits and the Attack on Democracy.* Monroe, ME.: Common Courage Press.

Mokhiber, Russell, and Robert Weissman. 2004. The Ten Worst Corporations of 2004. *Multinational Monitor* 25 (12): 1–26.

Moore, Sally Falk. 1978. *Law as Process.* London: Routledge and Kegan Paul.

Morash, Merry. 1999. A Consideration of Gender in Relation to Social Learning and Social Structure: A General Theory of Crime and Deviance. *Theoretical Criminology* 3 (4): 451–462.

Morgan, Phoebe. 2008. Sexual Harassment. In *Encyclopedia of Interpersonal Violence,* edited by Claire Renzetti and Jeffrey Edleson, 661–662. Thousand Oaks, CA: Sage.

Morgan, Robin. 1980. Theory and Practice: Pornography and Rape. In *Take Back the Night: Women on Pornography,* edited by Laura Lederer, 134–147. New York: William Morrow.

Morrison, Toni. 1992. *Playing in the Dark: Whiteness and the Literary Imagination.* New York: Vintage.

Moyers, Bill. 1988. *The Secret Government: The Constitution in Crisis.* Washington, DC: Seven Locks Press.

Mullins, Christopher W. 2006. *Holding Your Square: Masculinities, Streetlife, and Violence.* Portland, OR: Willan.

Mullins, Christopher, and Jody Miller. 2008. Temporal, Situational, and Interactional Features of Women's Violent Conflicts. *Australian and New Zealand Journal of Criminology* 41 (1): 36–62.

Mullins, Christopher, and Richard Wright. 2003. Gender, Social Networks, and Residential Burglary. *Criminology* 41: 813–839.

Mydans, Seth. 2009. First on Cambodia's Docket: A Man Whose Jail Sent 14,000 to a Killing Field. *New York Times,* February 17, A5.

Nash, Nathaniel. 1985. Capitalist Punishment. *The New Republic* (May 27): 56.

National Center on Elder Abuse. 2005. *Elder Abuse Statistics.* Washington, DC: National Center on Elder Abuse.

National Church Arson Task Force. 1997. *First-Year Report for the President.* Washington, DC: U.S. Government Printing Office.

National Coalition of Anti-Violence Programs. 2008. *Anti-Lesbian, Gay, Bisexual, and Transgendered Violence in 2007.* New York: NCAVP.

National Commission on the Causes and Prevention of Violence. 1970. *Final Report: To Establish Justice, To Insure Domestic Tranquility.* New York: Bantam Books.

Nee, Claire and Amy Meenagan. 2006. "Expert Decision Making in Burglars." *British Journal of Criminology* 46 (5): 935–949.

Nerenberg, Lisa. 2002. *Abuse in Nursing Homes.* National Center on Elder Abuse. Washington, DC: National Center on Elder Abuse.

Newburn, Tim, and Elizabeth A. Stanko. 1994. *Just Boys Doing Business? Men, Masculinities, and Crime.* New York: Routledge.

Newman, Oscar. 1973. *Defensible Space: Crime Prevention Through Urban Design.* London: Macmillan.

Nixon, Howard L. 1997. Gender, Sport, and Aggressive Behavior Outside Sport. *Journal of Sport and Social Issues* 21 (4): 379–391.

O'Donnell, Ian. 2008. The Fall and Rise of Homicide in Ireland. In *Violence in Europe: Historical and Contemporary Perspectives,* edited by Sophie Body-Gendrot and Pieter Spierenburg, 79–92. New York: Springer.

O'Donnell, Ian, and Eooin O'Sullivan. 2003. The Politics of Intolerance—Irish Style. *British Journal of Criminology* 43 (1): 41–62.

O'Neil, William L. 1969. *The Woman Movement: Feminism in the United States.* New York: Barnes and Noble.

O'Toole, Laura. 2007. Subcultural Theory of Rape Revisited. In *Gender Violence: Interdisciplinary Perspectives,* edited by Laura L. O'Toole, Jessica R. Schiffman, and Margie L. Kiter Edwards, 214–222. New York: New York University Press.

O'Toole, Laura L., Jessica R. Schiffman. And Margie L. Kiter eds. 2007. *Gender Violence: Interdisciplinary Perspectives.* New York: New York University Press.

Oakley, Ann. 1972. *Sex, Gender, and Society.* New York: Harper & Row.

Oberdorfer, Don, and Patrick E. Tyler. 1983. U.S.-Backed Nicaraguan Rebel Army Swells to 7,000 Men. *Washington Post* (May 8): A1, A10, A11.

Ohmae, K. 1995. *The End of the Nation State.* New York: Free Press.

Ortiz, Roxanne Dunbar. 1977. *The Great Sioux Nation.* Berkeley, CA: Moon Books.

Oster, Anna, and Jonal Agell. 2007. Crime and Unemployment in Turbulent Times. *Journal of European Economic Association* 5 (4): 752–775.

Paolucci, Henry. [1764] 1963. Translator's introduction to *On Crime and Punishments,* by Cesare Beccaria, ix–xxiii. Indianapolis, IN: Bobbs-Merrill.

Parenti, Michael. 2008. *Democracy for the Few.* New York: Wadsworth.

Parker, Donn B. 1976. *Crime by Computer.* New York: Charles Scribner.

Paternoster, Raymond, and Robert Brame. 1997. Multiple Routes to Delinquency? A Test of Developmental and General Theories of Crime. *Criminology* 35 (1): 49–80.

Patterson, E. Britt. 2006. Poverty, Income Inequality, and Community Crime Rates. *Criminology* 29 (4): 755–776.

Paulsen, Derek J. 2003. Murder in Black and White: The Newspaper Coverage of Homicide in Houston. *Homicide Studies* 7 (3): 289–317.

Payne, Allison Ann, and Steven Salotti. 2008. A Comparative Analysis of Social Learning and Social Control Theories in the Prediction of College Crime. *Deviant Behavior* 28: 553–573.

Payne, Brian. 2005. Workplace Deaths and Violence. In *Encyclopedia of White-Collar & Corporate Crime,* edited by Lawrence Salinger, 864–868. Thousand Oaks, CA: Sage.

Payne, Brian K., Jonathan Appel, and DoHee Kim-Appel. 2008. Elder-Abuse Coverage in Newspapers: Regional Differences and Its Comparison to Child-Abuse Coverage. *Journal of Elder Abuse & Neglect* 20 (3): 265–275.

Peacock, Patricia. 1998. Marital Rape. In *Issues in Intimate Violence,* edited by Raquel Kennedy Bergen, 225–235. Thousand Oaks, CA: Sage.

Pearce, Frank, and Steve Tombs. 1999. *Toxic Capitalism: Corporate Crime and the Chemical Industry.* Toronto: Canadian Scholars' Press.

Peelo, Moiro, Brian Francis, Keith Soothill, Jayn Pearson, and Elizabeth Ackerley. 2004. Newspaper Reporting and the Public Construction of Homicide. *British Journal of Criminology* 44 (2): 256–275.

Pepinsky, Hal. 2006. *Peacemaking: Reflections of a Radical Criminologist.* Ottawa: University of Ottawa Press.

Pepinsky, Harold E., and Richard Quinney, eds. 1991. *Criminology as Peacemaking.* Bloomington: Indiana University Press.

Peralta, Robert, and Michael Cruz. 2006. Conferring Meaning onto Alcohol-Related Violence: An Analysis of Alcohol Use and Gender in a Sample of College Youth. *Journal of Men's Studies* 14 (1): 109–125.

Pereetti-Watel, Patrick. 2003. Neutralization Theory and the Denial of Risk: Some Evidence from Cannabis Use Among French Adolescents. *British Journal of Sociology* 54 (1): 21–42.

Pérez, Deanne M., Wesley G. Jennings, and Angela R. Gover. 2008. Specifying General Strain Theory: An Ethnically Relevant Approach. *Deviant Behavior* 29: 544–578.

Perry, Barbara J. 1998. Defenders of the Faith: Hate Groups and Ideologies of Power in the United States. *Patterns of Prejudice* 32 (3): 32–54.

———. 2008a. Hate Crimes (Bias Crimes), Racially Motivated. In *Encyclopedia of Interpersonal Violence*, edited by Claire Renzetti and Jeffrey Edleson, 310–312. Thousand Oaks, CA: Sage.

———. 2008b. *Silent Victims: Hate crimes Against Native Americans*. Tucson, AZ: University of Arizona Press.

Peterson, Ruth D., Lauren J. Krivo, and John Hagan, eds. 2006. *The Many Colors of Crime: Inequalities of Race, Ethnicity and Crime in America*. New York: New York University Press.

Petit, Jacques G. 1984. The Birth and Reform of Prisons in France. In *The Emergence of Carceral Institutions: Prisons, Galleys, and Lunatic Asylums, 1550–1900*, edited by Pieter Spierenburg, 125–147. Rotterdam: Erasmus University.

Pew Hispanic Center. 2009. A Rising Share: Hispanics and Federal Crime. Available on February 21, 2009, at: http://pewhispanic.org/reports/report.php.

Pfohl, Stephen. 1984. The Discovery of Child Abuse. In *Deviant Behavior*, edited by Delos Kelly, 45–65. New York: St. Martin's Press.

Pfost, Donald. 1987. Reagan's Nicaraguan Policy: A Case Study of Political Deviance and Crime. *Crime and Social Justice* 27/28: 66–87.

Phillipson, Coleman. [1923] 1975. *Three Criminal Law Reformers: Beccaria, Bentham, Romilly*. Montclair, NJ: Patterson Smith.

Piquero, Alex, and Matthew Hickman. 1999. An Empirical Test of Tittle's Control Balance Theory. *Criminology* 37 (2): 319–341.

Piquero, Alex R., David P. Farrington, and Alfred Blumstein. 2007. *Key Issues in Criminal Career Research*. Cambridge: Cambridge University Press.

Piquero, Nicole Leeper, and Alex R. Piquero. 2006. Control Balance and Exploitative Corporate Crime. *Criminology* 44 (2): 397–430.

Platt, Tony. 1974. Prospects for a Radical Criminology in the United States. *Crime and Social Justice* 1 (Spring/Summer): 2–10.

Platt, Tony, and Cecilia O'Leary. 2003. Patriot Acts. *Social Justice* 30 (1): 5–22.

Pogrebin, Mark, ed. 2004. *About Criminals: A View of the Offender's World*. Thousand Oaks, CA: Sage.

Polk, Kenneth. 1994. *When Men Kill: Scenarios of Masculine Violence*. New York: Cambridge University Press.

Porter, Louise E., and Alison J. Laurence. 2006. Behavioral Coherence in Group Robbery: A Circumplex Model of Offender and Victim Interactions. *Aggressive Behavior* 32 (4): 330–342.

Porterfield, Austin L. 1946. Delinquency and Its Outcome in Court and College. *American Journal of Sociology* 49 (3): 199–208.

Prados, John. 1986. *President's Secret Wars*. New York: William Morrow.

Pratt, Travis C., and Francis T. Cullen. 2000. The Empirical Status of Gottfredson and Hirschi's General Theory of Crime: A Meta-analysis. *Criminology* 38 (3): 931–964.

Presdee, Mike, 2000. *Cultural Criminology and the Carnival of Crime*. London: Routledge.

President's Commission on Law Enforcement and the Administration of Justice. 1967. *The Challenge of Crime in a Free Society*. Washington, D.C.: U.S. Government Printing Office.

Presidential Commission. 1986. *Report on the Space Shuttle Challenger Accident*. Washington, DC: U.S. Government Printing Office.

Project for Excellence in Journalism. 2008. Story Topics on Local TV News, 2005. Available at: http://www.journalism.org/.

Ptacek, James. 1998. Why Do Men Batter Their Wives? In *Issues in Intimate Violence*, edited by Raquel Kennedy Bergen, 181–195. Thousand Oaks, CA: Sage.

Public Citizen. 2004. *The Ten-Year Track Record of NAFTA: The Mexican Economy, Agriculture, and Environment*. Washington, DC: Public Citizen Global Trade Watch.

Purdy, Elizabeth. 2005. Medical Malpractice. In *Encyclopedia of White-Collar & Corporate Crime*, edited by Lawrence Salinger, 519–521. Thousand Oaks, CA: Sage..

Quetelet, Adolphe. [1831] 1984. *Research on the Propensity for Crime at Different Ages*. Translated by Sawyer Sylvester. Cincinnati, OH: Anderson.

———. 1842. *A Treatise on Man*. Translated by R. Knox and T. Smibert. Edinburgh: Chambers.

———. 1848. *Du systéme social et des lois qui le régissent*. Paris: Guillaumin.

Quinney, Richard. 1970. *The Social Reality of Crime*. Boston: Little, Brown.

———. 1973. There's a Lot of Us Folks Grateful to the Lone Ranger: Some Notes on the Rise and Fall of American Criminology. *Insurgent Sociologist* 4 (Fall): 56–64.

———. 1977a. *Class, State, and Crime*. New York: Longman.

———. 1997. Socialist Humanism and Critical/Peacemaking Criminology: The Continuing Project. In *Thinking Critically About Crime*, edited by Brian D. MacLean and Dragan Milovanovic, 114–117. Vancouver, B.C.: Collective press.

Quinney, Richard, and John Wildeman. 1977. *The Problem of Crime*. New York: Harper & Row.

Rafter, Nicole Hahn, ed. 1992. Criminal Anthropology in the United States. *Criminology* 30 (4): 525–545.

———. 2000. *Shots in the Mirror: Crime Films and Society*. New York: Oxford University Press.

Rafter, Nicole Hahn, and Mary Gibson. 2004. Editors' Introduction. In *Criminal Woman, the Prostitute, and the Normal Woman*, by Cesare Lombroso and Guglielmo Ferro, translated by Nicole Hahn Rafter and Mary Gibson, 3–33. Durham, NC: Duke University Press.

Ranelagh, John. 1987. *The Agency: The Rise and Decline of the CIA*. New York: Simon & Schuster.

Regan, Tom. 1983. *The Case for Animal Rights*. Berkeley: University of California Press.

Reichel, Philip, ed. 2005. *Handbook of Transnational Crime & Justice*. Thousand Oaks, CA: Sage.

Reiman, Jeffrey. 2006. *The Rich Get Richer and the Poor Get Prison: Ideology, Class, and Criminal Justice*. Boston: Allyn & Bacon.

Reisner, Marc. 1991. *Game Wars: The Undercover Pursuit of Wildlife Poachers*. New York: Viking.

Reiter, Rayna. 1975. *Toward an Anthropology of Women*. New York: Monthly Review Press.

Renzetti, Claire M. 2000. Lesbian Partner Battering. In *Encyclopedia of Women and Crime*, edited by Nicole Hahn Rafter, 148–149. Phoenix: Oryx Press.

———. 2008. Serial Murder/Serial Killers. In *Encyclopedia of Interpersonal Violence*, edited by Claire Renzetti and Jeffrey Edleson, 638–640. Thousand Oaks, CA: Sage.

———. 2009. *Feminist Criminology*. New York: Routledge.

Revkin, Andrew C. 2009. Environment Issues Slide in Poll of Public Concerns. *New York Times*, 13.

Richards, Stephen C. 2008a. USP Marion: The First Federal Supermax. *Prison Journal* 88 (1): 6–22.

Richards, Stephen C. 2008b. Convict Criminology: Voices from Prison. *Race/Ethnicity: Multidisciplinary Global Contexts* 2 (1): 121–136.

Richardson, Michael, and Brad Friedman. 2008. The Selling of the Touch Screen "Paper Trail": From Nevada to the EAC. In *Loser Take All: Election Fraud and the Subversion Of Democracy, 2000–2008*, edited by Mark Crispin Miller, 131–146. Brooklyn, NY: IG Publishing.

Riedel, Marc. 2008. Workplace Violence. In *Encyclopedia of Interpersonal Violence*, edited by Claire Renzetti and Jeffrey Edleson, 762–765. Thousand Oaks, CA: Sage.

Ritchie, Robert C. 1986. *Captain Kidd and the War Against the Pirates*. Cambridge, MA: Harvard University Press.

Roberto, Karen. 2008. Sexual Abuse of the Elderly. In *Encyclopedia of Interpersonal Violence*, edited by Claire Renzetti and Jeffrey Edleson, 653–654. Thousand Oaks, CA: Sage.

Roberts, Aki, and Gary LaFree. 2004. Explaining Japan's Postwar Violent Crime Trends. *Criminology* 42 (1): 179–209.

Roediger, David R. 1991. *The Wages of Whiteness: Race and the Making of the American Working Class*. New York: Verso.

Rosenblum, Karen. 1975. Female Deviance and the Female Sex Role: A Preliminary Investigation. *British Journal of Sociology* 25 (2): 169–185.

Rosenburg. Micah. 2009. Exotic Animals Trapped in Net of Drug Trade. *Thomson Reuters*, February 6.

Rosenfeld, Richard, and Steven F. Messner. 1991. The Social Sources of Homicide in Different Types of Societies. *Sociological Forum* 6 (1): 51–70.

Rosoff, Stephen M., Henry N. Pontell, and Robert Tillman. 2007. *Profit Without Honor: White-Collar Crime and the Looting of America*. Upper Saddle River, NJ: Prentice Hall.

Ross, Debra E. 2005a. Credit Card Fraud. In *Encyclopedia of White-Collar & Corporate Crime*, edited by Lawrence Salinger, 227–229. Thousand Oaks, CA: Sage.

———. 2005b. Film Recovery Systems. In *Encyclopedia of White-Collar & Corporate Crime*, edited by Lawrence Salinger, 319–320. Thousand Oaks, CA: Sage.

Ross, Dorothy. 1991. *The Origins of American Social Science*. Cambridge: Cambridge University Press.

Rottman, David. 1980. *Crime in the Republic of Ireland*. Paper no. 102. Dublin: Economic and Social Research Institute.

Roversi, Antonio. 2008. *Hate on the Net: Extremist Sites, Neo-Fascism On-Line, Electronic Jihad*. Williston, VT: Ashgate.

Ruggiero, Vincent. 2002. "Attac": A Global Social Movement? *Social Justice* 29 (1/2): 48–61.

Ruschke, Georg, and Otto Kircheimer. 1939. *Punishment and Social Structure*. New York: Russell and Russell.

Russell, Diana E. H. 1986. *The Secret Trauma: Incest in the Lives of Girls and Women*. New York: Basic Books.

———. 1990. *Sexual Exploitation*. Beverly Hills, CA: Sage.

Russell, Dick. 1988. Welcome to Dioxinville, Arkansas. *In These Times*, March 9–15, 8–13.

Russell, Stuart. 2006. The Failure of Postmodern Criminology. *Critical Criminology* 8 (2): 61–90.

Sampson, Robert J. 1999. Techniques of Research Neutralization. *Theoretical Criminology* 3 (4): 438–451.

Sampson, Robert J., and John H. Laub. 1993. *Crime in the Making: Pathways and Turning Points Through Life*. Cambridge, MA.: Harvard University Press.

———. 2003. Life-Course Desisters? Trajectories of Crime Among Delinquent Boys Followed to Age 70. *Criminology* 41 (3): 555–592.

Sampson, Robert J., and William Julius Wilson. 1995. Toward a Theory of Race, Crime, and Urban Inequality. In *Crime and Inequality*, edited by John Hagan and Ruth D. Peterson, 110–125. Stanford, CA: Stanford University Press.

Sands, Philippe. 2008. *Torture Team: Rumsfeld's Memo and the Betrayal of American Values*. London: Palgrave Macmillan.

Sanday, Peggy. 1981. The Socio-Cultural Context of Rape: A Cross-Cultural Study. *Journal of Social Issues* 37 (1): 5–27.

———. 1996. *A Woman Scorned: Acquaintance Rape on Trial*. New York: Doubleday.

Sasson, Theodore. 1995. *Crime Talk: How Citizens Construct a Social Problem*. New York: Aldine de Gruyter.

Sawyer, R. G., E. E. Thompson, and A. M. Chicorelli. 2002. Rape Myth Acceptance Among Intercollegiate Student Athletes. *American Journal of Health Studies* 18 (1): 19–25.

Scarpitti, Frank R., and Carol Calwin Lenhart. 2001. Credit Card Fraud. In *Encyclopedia of Criminology and Deviant Behavior*, edited by Clifton D. Bryant, 106–109. New York: Brunner-Routledge.

Scheffer, David J. 1987. U.S. Law and the Iran-Contra Affair. *American Journal of International Law* 81 (3): 696–723.

Schneider, Jacqueline L. 2005. The Link between Shoplifting and Burglary: The Booster Burglar. *British Journal of Criminology* 45 (3): 395–401.

Schrag, Clarence. 1962. Delinquency and Opportunity: Analysis of a Theory. *Sociology and Social Research* 46 (2): 167–175.

Schur, Edwin M. 1968. *Law and Society: A Sociological View*. New York: Random House.

Schwartz, Martin D., and Carol A. Nogrady. 1996. Fraternity Membership, Rape Myths, and Sexual Aggression on a College Campus. *Violence Against Women* 2 (2): 148–163.

Schwartz, Richard D., and Jerome C. Miller. 1964. Legal Evolution and Societal Complexity. *American Journal of Sociology* 70 (2): 159–169.

Schwartz, Richard D., and Jerome H. Skolnick. 1964. Two Studies of Legal Stigma. In *The Other Side*, edited by Howard S. Becker, 103–117. New York: Free Press.

Schwendinger, Julia, and Herman Schwendinger. 1974. *The Sociologists of the Chair: A Radical Analy-*

*sis of the Formative Years of North American Sociology (1883–1922)*. New York: Basic Books.

———. 1975. Defenders of Order or Guardians of Human Rights? In *Critical Criminology*, edited by Ian Taylor, Paul Walton, and Jock Young, 113–146. London: Routledge and Kegan Paul.

———. 1977. Social Class and the Definition of Crime. *Crime and Social Justice* 7 (Spring/Summer): 4–13.

———. 1983. *Rape and Inequality*. Beverly Hills, CA: Sage.

Sciolino, Elaine. 1988. Fighting Narcotics: U.S. Is Urged to Shift Tactics. *New York Times* (April 10): A1, A10.

Seager, Jodi. 1993. *Earth Follies: Coming to Feminist Terms with the Global Environmental Crisis*. New York: Routledge.

Sebastian, Tim. 1999. Scenes from Hell. *BBC News*. Available at: http://news.bbc.co.uk/1/hi/world/258903.stm.

Sellin, Thorsten. 1938. *Culture Conflict and Crime*. New York: Social Science Research Council.

Shaw, Clifford R. 1930. *The Jack-Roller: A Delinquent Boy's Own Story*. Chicago: University of Chicago Press.

———. 1939. *The Natural History of a Delinquent Career*. Chicago: University of Chicago Press.

Shaw, Clifford R., and Henry D. McKay. [1942] 1969. *Juvenile Delinquency and Urban Areas*. Chicago: University of Chicago Press.

Shaw, Clifford R., et al. 1929. *Delinquency Areas: A Study of the Geographic Distribution of School Truants, Juvenile Delinquents, and Adult Offenders in Chicago*. Chicago: University of Chicago Press.

Sheehan, Daniel. 1988. *Inside the Shadow Government*. Washington, DC: Christic Institute.

Shenon, Philip. 1988. Enemy Within: Drug Money Is Corrupting Enforcers. *New York Times* (April 11): A1, A2.

Shenoy, Chaitra. 2008. Hate Crimes (Bias Crimes), Religiously Motivated. In *Encyclopedia of Interpersonal Violence*, edited by Claire Renzetti and Jeffrey Edleson, 313–314. Thousand Oaks, CA: Sage.

Sheptycki, James. 2003. Against Transnational Organized Crime. In *Critical Reflections on Transnational Organized Crime, Money Laundering and Corruption*,

edited by Margaret E. Beare, 120–144. Toronto: University of Toronto Press.

Sheptycki, James. 2005. Relativism, Transnationalization and Comparative Criminology. In *Transnational and Comparative Criminology*, edited by J. Sheptycki and A. Wardak, 69–90. London: Glasshouse Press.

———. 2008. The Accountability of Transnational Policing Institutions. In *Global Criminology and Criminal Justice*, edited by Nick Larsen and Russell Smandych, 247–273. Peterborough, Ontario: Broadview Press.

Sheptycki, James, and Ali Wardak, eds. 2005. *Transnational and Comparative Criminology*. London: Glasshouse Press.

Shihadeh, Edward S., and Graham C. Ousey. 1998. Industrial Restructuring and Violence: The Link Between Entry-Level Jobs, Economic Deprivation, and Black and White Homicide. *Social Forces* 77: 185–206.

Short, James F., Jr., Joachim J. Savelsberg, Gary F. Jensen, and Charles R. Tittle. 1999. Symposium on Control Balance: Toward a General Theory of Deviance. *Theoretical Criminology* 3 (3): 327–352.

Shostak, Marjorie. 1983. *Nisa: The Life and Words of a !Kung Woman*. New York: Vintage Books.

Shover, Neal. 1996. *Great Pretenders: Pursuits and Careers of Persistent Thieves*. Boulder, CO: Westview Press.

Shover, Neal, and Carol Y. Thompson. 2006. Age, Differential Expectations, and Crime Desistance. *Criminology* 30 (1): 89–104.

Sick, Gary. 1991. *October Surprise: Americas Hostages in Iran and the Election of Ronald Reagan*. New York: Times Books.

Sidel, Ruth. 2006. *Unsung Heroes: Single Mothers and the American Dream*. Berkeley: University of California Press.

Simon, David R. 2008. *Elite Deviance*. Boston: Allyn & Bacon.

Simon, David R., and D. Stanley Eitzen. 1986. *Elite Deviance*. Boston: Allyn & Bacon.

Simon, Jonathan. 2007. *Governing Through Crime: How the War on Crime Transformed American Democracy and Created a Culture of Fear*. New York: Oxford University Press.

Simon, Rita. 1975. *Women and Crime*. Lexington, MA: DC Heath.

Simon, Thomas, and James Mercy. 2001. *Injuries From Violent Crime, 1992–1998*. Bureau of Justice Statistics, NCJ-168633.

Simons, Marlisle. 2009. 5 Top Serbs Found Guilty of War Crimes in Kosovo. *New York Times* (February 27): A11.

Simons, Marlisle, and Neil MacFarquhar. 2009. Warrant Is Approved for Leader of Sudan. *New York Times* (February 12): A6.

Simpson, Sally S., and Gilbert Geis. 2008. The Undeveloped Concept of Opportunity. In *Out of Control: Assessing the General Theory of Crime*, edited by Erich Goode, 49–60. Stanford, CA: Stanford University Press.

Singer, Peter. 1975. *Animal Liberation*. New York: Avon.

Skinner, B. F. 1953. *Science and Human Behavior*. New York: Macmillan.

Smart, Carol. 1976. *Women, Crime, and Criminology: A Feminist Critique*. Boston: Routledge and Kegan Paul.

———. 1998. The Woman of Legal Discourse. In *Criminology at the Crossroads: Feminist Readings in Crime and Justice*, edited by Kathleen Daly and Lisa Maher, 21–36. New York: Oxford University Press.

Smith, Cary Stacy, and Li-Ching Hung. 2008. Robbery. In *Encyclopedia of Interpersonal Violence*, edited by Claire Renzetti and Jeffrey Edleson, 611–613. Thousand Oaks, CA: Sage.

Smith, Douglas, and Christy A. Visher. 1980. Sex and Involvement in Deviance/Crime: A Quantitative Review of the Empirical Literature. *American Sociological Review* 45 (4): 691–701.

South, Nigel, and Piers Beirne, eds. 2006. *Green Criminology*. Aldershot, Hants, UK: Ashgate.

Southern Poverty Law Center. 2009. *The Year in Hate: Number of Hate Groups Tops 900*. Montgomery, AL: Southern Poverty Law Center.

Southworth, Cindy, Sarah Tucker, Cynthia Fraser, and Toby Shulruff. 2008. High-Tech Violence Against Women. In *Encyclopedia of Interpersonal Violence*, edited by Claire Renzetti and Jeffrey Edleson, 329–331. Thousand Oaks, CA: Sage.

Sparks, Richard F. 1981. Surveys of Victimization: An Optimistic Assessment. *Crime and Justice: An Annual Review of Research* 3: 1–60.

Spitzer, Steven. 1975. Toward a Marxian Theory of Deviance. *Social Problems* 22 (5): 638–651.

Spunt, Barry. 2002. Self-Report Surveys. In *Encyclopedia of Crime and Punishment*, edited by David Levinson, 1465–1467. Thousand Oaks, CA: Sage.

Srebnick, Amy Gilman, and René Lévy, eds. 2005. *Crime and Culture: A Historical Perspective*. Aldershot, UK: Gower.

Stack, Steven, and Mary Jeanne Kanavy. 1983. The Effect of Religion on Forcible Rape: A Structural Analysis. *Journal for the Scientific Study of Religion* 22 (1): 67–74.

Stanko, Betsy. 2007. From Academia to Policy Making: Changing Police Responses to Violence Against Women. *Theoretical Criminology* 11 (2): 209–219.

Stanko, Elizabeth. 1985. *Intimate Intrusions: Women's Experiences of Male Violence*. Boston: Routledge and Kegan Paul.

———. 2000. Victims R Us: The Life History of "Fear of Crime" and the Politicization of Violence. In *Crime, Risk and Insecurity*, edited by Tim Hope and Richard Sparks, 13–29. London: Routledge.

Stanton, Duncan. 1976. Drugs, Vietnam, and the Vietnam Veteran: An Overview. American *Journal of Drugs and Alcohol Abuse* 3: 557–570.

*Statistical Abstract of the United States*. 2009. Washington, DC: U.S. Government Printing Office.

Steel, Ronald. 2004. Totem and Taboo. *The Nation* 279 (8): 29–35.

Steffensmeier, Darrell J. 1983. Organization Properties and Sex Segregation in the Underworld: Building a Sociological Theory of Sex Differences in Crime. *Social Forces* 61 (4): 1010–1032.

———. 1986. *The Fence: In the Shadow of Two Worlds*. Totowa, NJ: Rowman & Littlefield.

Steffensmeier, Darrell, and Emilie Anderson Allan. 1995a. Criminal Behavior: Gender and Age. In *Criminology: A Contemporary Handbook*, edited by Joseph Sheley, 83–114. Belmont, CA: Wadsworth.

———. 1995b. Age Inequality and Property Crime: The Effects of Age-Linked Stratification and Status-Attainment Processes on Patterns of Criminality Across the Life Course. In *Crime and Inequality*, edited by

John Hagan and Ruth D. Peterson, 95–115. Stanford, CA: Stanford University Press.

Steffensmeier, Darrell J., and Jeffrey T. Ulmer. 2004. *Confessions of a Dying Thief.* Hawthorne, NY: Aldine de Gruyter.

Stolzenberg, Lisa, Stewart J. D'Alessio, and David Eitle. 2004. A Multilevel Test of Racial Threat Theory. *Criminology* 42 (3): 673–698.

Strange, S. 1996. *The Retreat of the State: The Diffusion of Power in the World Economy.* Cambridge: Cambridge University Press.

Sullivan, Dennis. 2008. Facing Into the Teeth: Hal Pepinsky Brings Peacemaking to Fields of War. *Contemporary Justice Review* 11 (3): 299–317.

Sumner, Colin. 1994. *The Sociology of Deviance: An Obituary.* New York: Continuum.

Surette, Ray. 2007. *Media, Crime, and Criminal Justice: Images, Realities, and Policies.* Belmont, CA: Thomson Wadsworth.

Sutherland, Edwin H. 1937. *The Professional Thief: By a Professional Thief.* Chicago: University of Chicago Press.

———. [1924] 1947. *Criminology.* Philadelphia: J. B. Lippincott.

———. [1942] 1956. Development of the Theory. In *The Sutherland Papers*, edited by Albert Cohen, Alfred Lindesmith, and Karl Schuessler, 13–29. Bloomington: Indiana University Press.

———. [1949] 1983. *White Collar Crime.* New Haven, CT: Yale University Press.

Sykes, Gresham M., and David Matza. 1957. Techniques of Neutralization: A Theory of Delinquency. *American Sociological Review* 22 (6): 664–670.

Tallmer, Matt. 1987. Chemical Dumping as a Corporate Way of Life. In *Corporate Violence*, edited by Stuart Hills, 111–120. Totowa, NJ: Rowman & Littlefield.

Tannenbaum, Frank. 1938. *Crime and the Community.* Boston: Ginn.

Tappan, Paul W. 1947. Who Is the Criminal? *American Sociological Review* 12 (1): 96–102.

Tarde, Gabriel. [1890] 1903. *The Laws of Imitation.* Translated by F. Parsons. New York: Henry Holt.

Taylor, Ian, Paul Walton, and Jock Young. 1973. *The New Criminology.* London: Routledge and Kegan Paul.

Thacher, David. 2004. The Rich Get Richer and the Poor Get Robbed: Inequality in US Criminal Victimization, 1974–2000. *Journal of Quantitative Criminology* 20 (2): 89–116.

Thomas, William I. 1923. *The Unadjusted Girl: With Cases and Standpoints for Behavior Analysis.* Boston: Little, Brown.

Thomas, William I., and Florian Znaniecki. 1918–1920. *The Polish Peasant in Europe and America.* Chicago: University of Chicago Press.

Thornberry, Terence, and R. L. Christenson. 1984. Unemployment and Criminal Involvement: An Investigation of Reciprocal Causal Structures. *American Sociological Review* 49 (3): 398–411.

Thrasher, Frederic Milton. 1927. *The Gang: A Study of 1,313 Gangs in Chicago.* Chicago: University of Chicago Press.

Thurman, Quint, and Brenda Vose. 2001. Tax Fraud. In *Encyclopedia of Criminology and Deviant Behavior*, edited by Clifton D. Bryant, 490–493. New York: Brunner-Routledge.

Tifft, Larry L., and Dennis C. Sullivan. 2001. A Needs-Based, Social Harms Definition of Crime. In *What Is Crime?*, edited by Stuart Henry and Mark M. Lanier, 179–203. Lanham, MD: Rowman & Littlefield.

———. 2006. Needs-Based Anarchist Criminology. In *The Essential Criminology Reader*, edited by Stuart Henry and Mark Lanier, 259–277. New York: Westview.

*Time.* 1983. *Wife Beating: The Silent Crime.* September 5, 23.

Tittle, Charles R. 1995. *Control Balance: Toward a General Theory of Deviance.* Boulder, CO: Westview.

———. 1997. Thoughts Stimulated by Braithwaite's Analysis of Control Balance Theory. *Theoretical Criminology* 1 (1): 99–110.

———. 1999. Continuing the Discussion of Control Balance. *Theoretical Criminology* 3 (3): 344–352.

Tittle, Charles R., Lisa M. Broidy, and Marc G. Gertz. 2008. Strain, Crime, and Contingencies. *Justice Quarterly* 25 (2): 283–312.

Tjaden, Patricia, and Nancy Thoennes. 1998. *Prevalence, Incidence, and Consequences of Violence Against Women.* Washington, DC: U.S. Department of Justice.

Tombs, Robert. 1980. Crime and the Security of the State: The Dangerous Classes and Insurrection in Nineteenth-Century Paris. In *Crime and the Law: The Social History of Crime in Western Europe Since 1500,* edited by V. A. C. Gatrell, Bruce Lenman, and Geoffrey Parker, 214–237. London: Europa.

Tomlinson, Edward C., and Jerald Greenberg. 2009. Understanding and Deterring Employee Theft with Organizational Justice. In *Research Companion to the Dysfunctional Workplace,* edited by Janice Langlan-Fox, Gary L. Cooper, and Richard J. Klimoski, 148–166. Boston: Edward Elgar Publishers.

Tomsen, Stephen. 2002. *Hatred, Murder and Male Honour: Anti-Homosexual Homicides in New South Wales, 1980–2000.* Canberra: Australian Institute of Criminology.

Tomsen, Stephen, ed. 2008. *Crime, Criminal Justice, and Masculinities.* Burlington, VT: Ashgate.

———. 2009. *Violence, Prejudice and Sexuality.* New York: Routledge.

Tseloni, Andromachi, and Ken Pease. 2003. Repeat Personal Victimization: "Boosts" or "Flags"? *British Journal of Criminology* 43 (1): 196–212.

Tunnell, Kenneth D. 1992. *Choosing Crime: The Criminal Calculus of Property Offenders.* Chicago: Nelson-Hall.

———. 2006. *Living Off Crime.* Lanham, MD: Rowman & Littlefield.

Turk, Austin. 1969. *Criminality and Legal Order.* Chicago: Rand McNally.

———. 1979. Analyzing Official Deviance: For a Non-partisan Conflict Analysis in Criminology. *Criminology* 16 (3): 459–476.

———. 2000. Political Offenders. In *Encyclopedia of Women and Crime,* edited by Nicole Hahn Rafter, 87–88. Phoenix, AZ: Oryx Press.

Tushnet, Mark. 1988. *Central America and the Law: The Constitution, Civil Liberties, and the Courts.* Boston: South End Press.

Uggen, Christopher, and Michael Massoglia. 2003. Desistance from Crime and Deviance as a Turning Point in the Life Course. In *Handbook of the Life Course,* edited by Jeylan T. Mortimer and Michael J. Shanahan, 311–329. New York: Springer.

Ullman, Sarah. 2008. Gang Rape. n In *Encyclopedia of Interpersonal Violence,* edited by Claire Renzetti and Jeffrey Edleson, 287–288. Thousand Oaks, CA: Sage.

UNICEF. 1986. *Demographic Yearbook, 1984.* New York: United Nations, Department of International Economic and Social Affairs, Statistical Office.

———. 1999a. *Child and Maternal Mortality Survey.* New York: United Nations.

———. 1999b. *Global Report on Crime and Justice,* edited by Graeme Newman. New York: Oxford University Press.

———. 2004. *Afghanistan: Opium Survey 2004.* New York: United Nations.

United Nations. 1983. *Human Rights: A Compilation of International Instruments.* Publication E.83.XIV.1. New York: United Nations.

———. 2008a. *Afghanistan: Opium Survey 2008.* New York: United Nations.

———. 2008b. *Total Recorded Intentional Homicides, 2004.* United Nations: Office on Drugs and Crime.

Unnever, James D. 2008. Two Worlds Far Apart. *Criminology* 46(2):511–538.

Unnithan, N. Prabha, Mark Pogrebin, and Paul B. Stretesky. 2008. Gun Felons and Gun Regulation: Offenders' Views About and Reactions to "Shall-Issue" Policies for Carrying Concealed Weapons. *Criminal Justice Policy Review* 19 (2): 196–214.

U.S. Department of Health and Human Services. 2008. *Child Maltreatment.* Washington, DC: U.S. Government Printing Office.

U.S. Department of Homeland Security. 2009. *Right-wing Extremism: Current Economic and Political Climate Fueling Resurgence in Radicalization and Recruitment.* Washington, DC: Department of Homeland Security.

U.S. Department of Labor. 2004. *Bureau of Labor Statistics: Injuries, Illnesses, Fatalities, 2002,* available at http://stats.bls.gov/iif/oshsum.htm#02Summary% 20News%20Release.

U.S. Department of Labor Statistics. 2008. *National Census of Fatal Occupational Injuries in 2007.* Available at: http://www.bls.gov/news.release/pdf/.

U.S. House Subcommittee on Crime. 1980. *Increasing Violence Against Minorities.* Washington, DC: U.S. Government Printing Office.

U.S. Senate Subcommittee on Terrorism, Narcotics, and International Operations. 1989. *Drugs, Law*

*Enforcement, and Foreign Policy.* Washington, DC: U.S. Government Printing Office.

Useem, Bert, and Anne Morrison Piehl. 2008. *Prison State: The Challenge of Mass Incarceration.* Cambridge: Cambridge University Press.

Valier, Claire. 2002. *Theories of Crime and Punishment.* New York: Longman.

Valukas, Anton R., and Ira Raphaelson. 1988. Judicial Corruption. In *Prosecution of Public Corruption Cases,* edited by U.S. Department of Justice, 1–15. Washington, DC: Department of Justice.

van Dijk, Jan. 2000. Implications of the International Crime Victims Survey for a Victim Perspective. In *Integrating a Victim Perspective Within Criminal Justice,* edited by Adam Crawford and Jo Goodey, 97–121. Aldershot, UK: Ashgate.

———. 2008. *The World of Crime.* London: Sage.

van Dijk, Jan, John van Kesteren, and Paul Smit. 2007. *Criminal Victimization in International Perspective.* United Nations: Office on Drugs and Crime.

Vaughn, Michael G., Matt DeLisi, Kevin M. Beaver, and John Paul Wright. 2009. Identifying Latent Classes of Behavioral Risk Based on Early Childhood: Manifestations of Self-Control. *Youth Violence and Juvenile Justice* 7 (1): 16–3.

Vayrynen, Raimo. 2004. *Anti-Globalization Movements at the Crossroads.* University of Notre Dame: Kroc Institute for International Peace Studies.

Verrill, Stephen. 2004. The Age–Crime Relationship: A Function of Differential Association, Variable-Interval Reinforcement, and Extinction. Paper presented at the Annual Meeting of the American Society of Criminology.

Vinton, Linda. 2001. Violence Against Older Women. In *Sourcebook on Violence Against Women,* edited by Claire M. Renzetti, Jeffrey L. Edleson, and Raquel Kennedy Bergen, 179–192. Thousand Oaks, CA: Sage.

Vold, George B. 1958. *Theoretical Criminology.* New York: Oxford University Press.

Wachholz, Sandra. 2005. Hate Crimes Against the Homeless: Warning-Out New England Style. *Journal of Sociology and Social Welfare* 32 (4): 141–163.

———. 2007. At Risk: Climate Change and Its Bearing on Women's Vulnerability to Male Violence. In *Issues in Green Criminology: Confronting Harms*

*Against Environments, Humanity and Other Animals,* edited by Piers Beirne and Nigel South, 161–185. Cullompton, Devon: Willan.

Wadsworth, Tim, and John M. Roberts. 2008. When Missing Data Are Not Missing: A New Approach to Evaluating Supplemental Homicide Report Imputation Strategies. *Criminology* 46 (4): 841–869.

Wahidin, Azrini, and Maureen Cain, eds. 2006. *Aging, Crime, and Society.* Portland, OR: Willan.

Walklate, Sandra. 2004. *Gender, Crime, and Criminal Justice.* Portland, OR: Willan.

Walmsley, Roy. 2007. World Prison Population List, International Centre for Prison Studies (King's College London). Available March 9, 2009, at: http://www.kcl.ac.uk/depsta/law/research/icps/downloads/world-prison-pop-seventh.

Walsh, Dermot. 1986. *Heavy Business: Commercial Burglary and Robbery.* Boston: Routledge & Kegan Paul.

Walsh, Jeffrey A., and Ralph B Taylor. 2007. Community Structural Predictors of Spatially Aggregated Motor Vehicle Theft Rates: Do They Replicate? *Journal of Criminal Justice* 35 (3): 297–311.

Walsh, Marilyn E. 1977. *The Fence.* Westport, CT: Greenwood Press.

Walsh, Patrick D. 2005. Check Kiting. In *Encyclopedia of White-Collar & Corporate Crime,* edited by Lawrence Salinger, 158. Thousand Oaks, CA: Sage.

Ward, Lester. 1883. *Dynamic Sociology.* New York: Appleton.

Warr, Mark. 2001. Age and Crime. In *Encyclopedia of Criminology and Deviant Behavior,* edited by Clifton D. Bryant, 4–6. New York: Brunner-Routledge.

———. 2002. *Companions in Crime.* New York: Cambridge University Press.

Washington, James Melvin, ed. 1986. *A Testament of Hope: The Essential Writings of Martin Luther King, Jr.* New York: Harper & Row.

Weber, Leane, and Benjamin Bowling. 2008. Policing Migration: A Framework for Investigating the Regulation of Global Mobility. In *Global Criminology and Criminal Justice,* edited by Nick Larsen and Russell Smandych, 209–226 Peterborough, Ontario: Broadview Press.

Webster, Colin. 2007. *Understanding Race and Crime.* New York: Open University Press.

Webster, Colin. 2008. Marginalized White Ethnicity, Race, and Crime. *Theoretical Criminology* 12 (3): 293–312.

Weis, Joseph G. 1976. Liberation and Crime: The Invention of the New Female Criminal. *Crime and Social Justice* 6 (Fall): 17–27.

Weld, William F. 1988. Introduction: Why Public Corruption Is Not a Victimless Crime. *Prosecution of Public Corruption Cases*, edited by U.S. Department of Justice, i–v. Washington, DC: Department of Justice.

Weldon, W. F. R. 1894–1895. An Attempt to Measure the Death Rate Due to the Selective Destruction of *Carcinus moenas* with Respect to a Particular Dimension. *Proceedings of the Royal Society of London* 57: 360–382.

Weyler, Rex. 1982. *Blood of the Land.* New York: Everest House.

White, Rob. 2008. *Crimes Against Nature: Environmental Criminology and Ecological Justice.* Cullompton, Devon, UK: Willan.

Whitehead, Antony. 2005. Man-to-Man Violence: How Masculinity May Work as a Dynamic Risk Factor. *Howard Journal of Criminal Justice* 44 (4): 411–422.

Wiesner, Margit, Deborah M. Capaldi, and Hyoun K. Kim. 2007. Arrest Trajectories Across a 17-Year Span for Young Men: Relation to Dual Taxonomies and Self-Reported Offenses Trajectories. *Criminology* 45 (4): 835–863.

Wikström, Per-Olof H. 2007. Individuals, Settings, and Acts of Crime: Situational Mechanisms and the Explanation of Crime. In *The Explanation of Crime: Context, Mechanisms, and Development*, edited by Per-Olof H. Wikström and Robert J. Sampson, 61–107. Cambridge: Cambridge University Press.

Wilcox, Pamela, Tamara D. Madensen, and Marie Skubak Tillyer. 2007. Guardianship in Context. *Criminology* 45 (4) :771–803.

Williams, Christopher R. 2007. Potential Spaces of Crime: The Playful, the Destructive, and the Distinctively Human. *Crime, Media, Culture* 3 (1): 49–66.

Williams, James W. 2008. The Lessons of Enron: Media Accounts, Corporate Crimes, and Financial Markets. *Theoretical Criminology* 12 (4): 471–499.

Williams, Katherine S. 2008. Using Tittle's Control Balance Theory to Understand Computer Crime and Deviance. *International Review of Law, Computers and Technology* 22 (1–2): 145–155.

Willis, Kate. 2006. Armed Robbery: Who Commits It, and Why? Washington, DC: National Criminal Justice Reference Service.

Wilson, James Q. 1985. *Thinking About Crime.* New York: Vintage.

Wines, Michael. 2009. China Says U.S. Distorts Facts in Report on Rights. *New York Times*, (February XX): A8.

Winlow, Simon. 2001. *Badfellas: Crime, Tradition and New Masculinities.* New York: Berg.

Wise, David. 1976. *The American Police State.* New York: Random House.

Wolak, Janis, David Finkelhor, and Kimberly Mitchell. 2004. Internet-Initiated Sex Crimes Against Minors: Implications for Prevention Based on Findings from a National Study. *Journal of Adolescent Health* 35 (5): 424–433.

Wolfe, David A. 1985. Child-Abusive Parents: An Empirical Review and Analysis. *Psychological Bulletin* 97 (3): 462–482.

Wolfgang, Marvin E. 1958. *Patterns in Criminal Homicide.* Philadelphia: University of Pennsylvania Press.

———. 1967. International Criminal Statistics: A Proposal. *Journal of Criminal Law, Criminology, and Police Science* 58 (1): 65–69.

Wolfgang, Marvin E., and Franco Ferracuti. 1967. *The Subculture of Violence.* London: Tavistock.

Wollstonecraft, Mary. [1792] 1975. *A Vindication of the Rights of Women.* New York: W. W. Norton.

Wonders, Nancy (2007). Globalization, Border Reconstruction Projects, and Transnational Crime. *Social Justice* 34 (2): 33–46.

Wooden, Wayne S. and Randy Blazak. 2001. *Renegade Kids, Surburban Outlaws: From Youth Culture to Deliquency.* Belmont, CA.: Wadsworth.

Wotipka, Christine Min, and Kiyoteru Tsutsui. 2008. Global Human Rights and State Sovereignty: State Ratification of International Human Rights Treaties, 1965–2001. *Sociological Forum* 23 (4): 724–754.

Wozniak, John F. 2008. Poverty and Peacemaking Criminology: Beyond Mainstream Criminology. *Critical Criminology*, 16 (3): 209–223.

Wright, Gordon. 1983. *Between the Guillotine and Liberty: Two Centuries of the Crime Problem in France.* New York: Oxford University Press.

Wright, Richard T., and Scott H. Decker. 1994. *Burglars on the Job: Streetlife and Residential Break-ins.* Boston: Northeastern University Press.

———. 1997. *Armed Robbers in Action: Stickups and Street Culture.* Boston: Northeastern University Press.

Wyden, Peter. 1979. *Bay of Pigs: The Untold Story.* New York: Simon & Schuster.

Yablonsky, Lewis. 1962. *The Violent Gang.* New York: Macmillan.

Yin, Peter. 1985. *Victimization and the Aged.* Springfield, IL: Charles C. Thomas.

Young, Jock. 1971. The Role of the Police as Amplifiers of Deviancy, Negotiators of Reality, and Translators of Fantasy. In *Images of Deviance,* edited by Stanley Cohen, 27–61. Harmondsworth, UK: Penguin.

Young, Jock. 2007. *The Vertigo of Late Modernity.* Los Angeles: Sage.

———. 2007. *The Vertigo of Late Modernity.* London: Sage.

Zimring, Franklin E., and Gordon Hawkins. 1997. *Crime Is Not the Problem: Lethal Violence in America.* New York: Oxford University Press.

# AUTHOR INDEX

# SUBJECT INDEX